G. C. Gilbert   in the   2019
To our
family.

ISBN 978-0-282-72166-4
PIBN 10264678

HANDBOOK FOR TRAVELLERS

IN

ERKS, BUCKS, AND OXFORDSHIRE.

INCLUDING A PARTICULAR DESCRIPTION OF

THE UNIVERSITY AND CITY OF OXFORD,

AND THE DESCENT OF THE THAMES TO MAIDENHEAD AND WINDSOR.

THIRD EDITION, REVISED.

WITH A TRAVELLING MAP AND PLANS.

LONDON:

JOHN MURRAY, ALBEMARLE STREET.

1882.

The Third Edition of the Handbook for Berkshire, Buckinghamshire and Oxfordshire has been revised and corrected, as far as possible, up the time of its publication. But in a work of this kind the utmost ca may fail to secure perfect accuracy, and the Editor will thankful receive notices of any faults or omissions, if directed to the care Mr. Murray, 50, Albemarle Street.

LONDON: PRINTED BY WILLIAM CLOWES AND SONS. STAMFORD STREET,
AND CHARING CROSS.

CONTENTS.

SECTION I.—BERKSHIRE.

SECTION II.—BUCKINGHAMSHIRE—continued.

SECTION III.—OXFORDSHIRE.

MAPS AND PLANS.

HANDBOOK

FOR

BERKS, BUCKS, AND OXFORDSHIRE.

SECTION I.

BERKSHIRE.

INTRODUCTION.

Boundaries and Divisions.—Berkshire, written Barkshire by Leland, and so pronounced in the locality, is styled by the Saxon Chroniclers Bearrucscire, and by mediæval writers Bercheira. The real meaning of the name is doubtful. Asser fancifully derives it from "the wood of Berroc, where the box-tree grows most abundantly" (*Life of Alfred*); others from some great "bare oak" ("such is the meaning of Berroc"), under which public assemblies were held. The name given by Cæsar (*Bell. Gall.*) to the people of the western part of the district is Bibroci, which does not assist in the solution. Berkshire is bounded on the N. by Gloucestershire, Oxfordshire, and Bucks, from all of which it is separated by the Thames; on the W. by Wilts; on the S.W. by Hants; on the S.E. by Surrey. The extreme length of the county (from Shrivenham to Old Windsor) is 50 m., and its extreme breadth (from the Thames N.W. of Oxford to the border of Hants below Newbury) 31 m. Its area is 752 sq. m. Population in 1861, 176,256; in 1871, 196,475, and in 1881, 218,382. The county, with its included boroughs, returns 8 members to Parliament.

"Berkshire naturally divides itself into 4 districts. Of these the

[*Berks, &c.*]   B northern district is the Vale of White Horse, and the southern the Vale of the Kennet. Each of these vales runs E. and W., and between them the hill district, a high chalk range, the continuation of the Wiltshire downs, runs right across the county, from Lambourne and Ashdown in the W. to Streatley in the E. At Streatley the Thames passes through this range of hills, which, after the temporary interruption, march away N.E. through Oxfordshire and Bucks; but, as though unwilling to let the queen of English rivers slip entirely away from them, the hills recross the stream into Berks at Wargrave, and from that point to Maidenhead, confine the Thames again in a chalky embrace. This small outlying district of chalk forms the N. part of the fourth or forest district of Berks. The remainder of the forest district, comprising the towns of Windsor and Wokingham, Windsor Forest, Ascot Heath, and the neighbouring villages, is separated from the Vale of Kennet by the river Loddon.

" Each of these four districts has its distinct characteristics, and each has minor divisions of its own. Thus, the Vale of the White Horse comprises on its N. side a low range of secondary hills, which run along the bank of the Thames from Faringdon to Radley, and include Cumnor and Bagley Wood. These are sand-hills, while the soil of the vale proper is for the most part a strong grey loam, mixed with large quantities of vegetable mould.

" The hill district includes the high chalk range, of which the White Horse Hill and Cuckamsley Hill (or Scuchamore Knob) are the highest points. Towards the N. the range is bold, and the descent into the vale steep, and the hills are indented with a number of little 'cooms' or meadows clothed with copse, while towards the S. it melts gradually away into the Vale of the Kennet. There is very little soil over the chalk on the higher part of the range, which is still used chiefly for sheep-walks.

" The Vale of the Kennet comprises the low lands which lie along its banks, and include clays, gravels, and a large and deep bed of peat; and the strip of wild and high sandy common land which runs along the extreme S. boundary of the county.

" The Forest district comprises the small outlying piece of the chalk range which has strayed back over the Thames at Wargrave, and leaves it at Maidenhead, and the forest proper, which, however, includes towns and flourishing hamlets, and many hundred acres of good enclosed land, from Windsor to the Loddon. Formerly the forest stretched right away up the Vale of Kennet to Hungerford, some 40 miles as the crow flies." —*Quarterly Review*, No. 211. Leland speaks of a " great warfeage of timbre and fier wood at the W. ende of the (Maidenhead) bridge; and this wood," he adds, " cummith out of Barkshir, and the great woddis of the forest of Windelesore and the greate Frithe." Windsor Castle stands on a solitary mass of chalk, surrounded by stiff clay.

Geology.—The geology of Berkshire is interesting, and it has been studied by Prestwich, Rupert Jones, Whitaker, and others. The oldest rocks belong to the Oolite, and are found in the N.W. of the county, in the form of Coral Rag, Oxford Clay, Kimmeridge Clay, and Portland Sand. The Cretaceous system is well represented, and constitutes the central portion of the county. The Eocene is represented by the Reading Beds, and the London Clay near Newbury. There are also deposits of alluvium, and many remains of prehistoric man have been found in the barrows of the Berkshire Downs.

Rivers, Canals, and Railways.—The Thames, which becomes the boundary of the county near Lechlade, in a circuitous course of 110 m., divides it from Gloucestershire, Oxfordshire, and Bucks. The lower part of its course is extremely beautiful, and the river itself—

> " Though deep, yet clear; though gentle, yet not dull;
> Strong without rage ; without o'erflowing, full."—*Denham.*

At Abingdon it receives the *Ock,* which rises near Shrivenham, and during its course of 20 m. has several small tributaries; the pike in this river are esteemed remarkably fine. In the parish of Sonning the Thames is joined by

> " The Kennet swift, for silver eels renown'd " (*Pope*),

which, rising in Wilts, enters Berkshire near Hungerford, and, flowing E. for 30 m., receives—1, near Newbury, the *Lamborne,* which rises in the chalk-hills above the town of that name, and has a course of 15 m.; 2, near Aldermaston, the *Enburn,* which rises near Inkpen, and flows E. for 17 m. Both the Kennet and the Lamborne are good fishing-streams, and produce trout, eels, crayfish, roach, and dace. The trout of the Kennet are of great size ; those of the Lamborne are of paler colour and not so much esteemed. The Kennet has been made navigable from Newbury to the Thames, a distance by the stream of 20 m. Between Shiplake and Wargrave

> " The Loddon slow, with verdant alders crown'd " (*Pope*),

falls into the Thames at Reading. The Blackwater rises near Aldershot, in Hampshire, and forms the boundary between Surrey and Hampshire for 7 m.; then for 8 m. or 9 m. it forms the boundary between Berkshire and Hampshire, till it joins the Whitewater near Swallowfield, at Thatchers Ford, for which for 7 m. it forms a boundary, and afterwards flows for 12 m. within the county, passing through Hurst Park, and receiving the Emme brook on the way. The small river *Cole* rises near Shrivenham, divides Berks from Wilts, and falls into the Thames near Lechlade.

Berkshire has two canals: 1, *the Wilts and Berks Canal,* which leaving the Thames just below Abingdon, is carried through the Vale of White Horse, past Wantage, into Wiltshire; 2, *the Kennet and Avon Canal,* which commences at Newbury, forming a continuation of the river Kennet navigation, and passes up the Vale of Kennet by Hungerford into Wiltshire.

B 2

The Great Western Railway traverses Berkshire from Maidenhead to Shrivenham, with branch lines from Didcot to Oxford, from Maidenhead to High Wycombe, and from Reading to Hungerford. There are also lines from Reading to Basingstoke, and from Didcot to Newbury. The South-Eastern and South-Western Companies have some mileage in the county; their lines unite at Wokingham, and have a common stat. at Reading.

Climate, Agriculture, Manufactures. — The climate of Berks is esteemed one of the healthiest in England. The chalk-hills in the W. are remarkable for their invigorating air, and the vales, having pure streams running through them, are considered no less healthy. Agriculture has attained only a moderate degree of perfection in Berks. In the rich soil of the vales great crops of corn are obtained with slight trouble; and the county abounds in yeomen, who cultivate small farms of 40, 50, or 80 acres, and are slow to adopt modern improvements. Jethro Tull, the famous agriculturist (d. 1740, æt. 60), introduced the practice of drilling at Prosperous Farm near Shalbourn, and professional drillmen now obtain a livelihood by going from place to place and letting out a drilling-machine to farmers who cannot afford one of their own. A valuable manure for clover is obtained by converting into ashes a substratum of a species of peat, of compact vegetable matter, by which the meadows on the Kennet, near Newbury, are underlaid. The country near Reading abounds in market-gardens; water-cresses are cultivated at Letcombe and elsewhere for the London market on a very large scale; and the banks and low islands of the Thames are frequently cultivated as osier-beds, and are found exceedingly profitable.

Berkshire is celebrated for its pigs. The true breed is black with white spots, but some are nearly white; their snouts are short, jowls thick, and their ears stand up. The Berkshire·sheep, called the *Not*, is now almost superseded. The clothing trade was very early established in Berkshire, and many places that are now mere villages were once market towns. The chief manufactures now are of paper, on a limited scale, rope, twine, and sacking, and—which is of recent introduction—of agricultural implements, and coarse pottery. Brewers, maltsters, and millers carry on business on a large scale in many of the towns, and the breeding and training of race-horses employs many hands about the Ilsleys and other places on the downs. As purely local, but yet from their extent important branches of business, may be mentioned Huntley and Palmer's biscuit factories, and Suttons' flower-farm, both at Reading, and Hyde and Clark's clothing factory at Abingdon.

History.—The earliest inhabitants of Berkshire are supposed to have been the Attrebates in the N., the Bibroces in the S.E., and the Segontiaci in the S.W. Berkshire was included in the Roman province of Britannia Prima, and the station of Spinæ occupied the site of Speenhamland near Newbury. Other Roman stations are said, but with less certainty, to have existed in the county: Bibracte is fixed by Whittaker at Bray; Pontes, by Horsley ('Britannia Romana'), at Datchet, though it was more probably at Staines; and Camden thought that Calleva was identical with Wallingford; later research has placed it at Silchester (see *Handbook for Hants*).

Under the Heptarchy, Berkshire belonged to Wessex; but Offa of Mercia conquered a large part of it from Cynewulf. Wantage was a royal seat in the time of Ethelwulf, and there his son Alfred the Great was born. Berkshire was the scene of many conflicts with the Danes, and the figure of the White Horse near Uffington (Rte. 5) has been till of late regarded as the memorial of a victory gained over them by Alfred and his brother Ethelred; but this idea is now given up by antiquaries in general. We know from the 'Saxon Chronicle' that in the year 871 the Danes took Reading, and shortly after fought three battles, in two of which they were defeated, the last time at Æscesdun (the hill of the Ash-tree), the precise locality of which seems not ascertainable, farther than that it was not near Uffington. Turner ('History of the Anglo-Saxons') thinks that Merantune, where the Saxons were soon afterwards defeated, and where Ethelred was mortally wounded, was Moreton, near Wallingford; and Lysons identifies the Ethandane, where Alfred gained the victory which restored him to his throne, with Eddington, near Hungerford; but these identifications are now believed to be erroneous. Berkshire was repeatedly ravaged by the Danes, and both Reading and Wallingford were burnt by them in 1006.

At Wallingford the Conqueror received the submission of Archbp. Stigand and the principal Saxon nobles, before marching to London. There a castle was built by his chief captain in these parts, Robert D'Oiley, where the fugitive Matilda found a secure refuge in 1141, and there, in 1153, the convention of Wallingford declared that Stephen was to reign for life, but that Henry II. was to be his successor. No great events occurred in the county in connection with the Wars of the Roses, but this was amply atoned for in the Civil War. Then Reading, Abingdon, Wallingford, and Faringdon all sustained sieges, and the two sanguinary battles of Newbury were fought. The army of the Prince of Orange occupied the county, and it was at Hungerford that he came to an agreement with King James's commissioners.

Windsor, from which Berks has received the name of "the Royal County," was a residence of the sovereigns before the existing Castle was built: William the Conqueror, William Rufus, and Henry I. kept their Christmas at Windsor. Henry I. was married there to his second queen, Adeliza of Louvaine. In 1263 it was seized by Simon de Montfort. Iu 1349 Edward III. founded the Order of the Garter, and about the same time he began the enlargement of the Castle. From the time of Edward IV. to the death of William IV. the Castle chapel was the frequent burial-place of royalty. George III. and George IV. were frequent residents at Windsor, and, from his great love of the county, and his frequently hunting over it, George III. was especially considered "a Berkshire gentleman," and in this capacity presented the organ of Salisbury Cathedral, as the inscription on its front testifies.

Reading Abbey was founded by Henry I., who was buried within its walls, with his queen Adeliza, his daughter Matilda, and Prince William, son of Henry II. There in 1359 John of Gaunt was married to Blanche of Lancaster; and there also, in 1464, the marriage of Edward IV. to Elizabeth Woodville was first made public. In the town of Reading Archbp. Laud was born, 1578.

Faringdon Castle, defended by Robert Earl of Gloucester against Stephen, was totally destroyed by him when taken. Wallingford Castle defied all his efforts, and remained to stand a siege in the Civil War. Radcot Bridge was the scene of the defeat of Vere Earl of Oxford (1389) in the reign of Richard II. Bisham contained the graves of Richard Neville the Kingmaker, and his brother, Lord Montague (1470), and of Edward Plantagenet, the Nevilles' grandson. Cumnor was rendered famous by the death of Amy Robsart. Ruscombe was the residence of the Quaker Penn; and Besilsleigh the home of the Speaker Lenthall. Caversham Bridge was the scene of a skirmish (1643), and Newbury of two great battles (1643–44), during the civil wars, when Donnington Castle became illustrious by its brave defence against the Parliamentarians, having been before renowned for its supposed connection with Chaucer. Lady Place at Hurley was the spot where the coming of William of Orange was arranged, and the skirmish at Reading was the first sign of opposition to his mounting the throne.

Antiquities.—Several Roman roads, in all probability only adaptations of British ones, crossed the county; that from Glevum (Gloucester) to Londinium entered Berks near Lamborne, and is still traceable as far as Spinæ (Speenhamland). The Icknield Street crossed the county in two lines, one represented by "the Ridge Way," which runs along the edge of the chalk range, over E. and W. Ilsley Downs, Cuckamsley Hill, &c., and the other by the road beneath the same hills which is known as the Ickleton Way; the two unite again, when once clear of its hills. Part of the road from Silchester to London is traceable on Bagshot Heath, and is known as "the Devil's Highway." The site of the Roman station of Spinæ is unquestionable; and the vallum which surrounded Wallingford is still to be traced.

The Berkshire hills are in very numerous instances crowned by *Camps*, about which antiquaries were formerly divided, some considering them Roman, others Danish. It is now ascertained that, in the majority of instances, they are British. Among the most noted may be mentioned, Uffington Castle, on White Horse Hill; Hardwell Castle, and Alfred's Castle, all in the W. part of the county; Letcombe or Sagsbury, Cherbury Camp, near Pusey; Badbury Camp, near Faringdon; and Sinodun Hill, near Wittenham. Coles Pits, at Little Coxwell, are probably the remains of a British town.

The chalk downs which stretch across the N. of the county are literally studded with *Barrows*, of which that on Cuckamsley Hill, the group called the Seven Barrows, near Lamborne, and Churn Knob, near Blewbury, are perhaps the most remarkable. Equally noticeable are the "dykes" which traverse the hills, and have hitherto been considered merely as roads; now it is thought probable that they were lines of defence, or at least of boundary between the British tribes. Warton, in his 'History of Kiddington,' makes some interesting remarks on the subject. "These ramparts," he says, "seem intended to have had some effect even on the eye. Being dug out of a bed of chalk, and belting the hills far and wide with white, more especially if we suppose some assistance from an artificial facing, they must have been visible at a vast distance; and this whiteness they might have retained for much more than a century, till the putrescence of their surfaces at length created a coat of mould and turf. In the same manner, barrows dispersed over a boundless length of verdant plains were at first conspicuous and striking studs of white for many miles. Here was a savage idea of sepulchral pomp; and these open monuments of Saxon or Danish chieftains by no means exhibited their present figure of common and obscure hillocks, in their early construction. They must have had even a picturesque appearance in the landscape. With the same notions the Saxons conceived and fabricated their famous military trophy, the White Horse." This last is the great antiquity of the county, probably older than is generally supposed; Wayland Smith's Cave and the Blowing Stone are also both of much interest. They all stand in a district where the sports of the field are actively pursued, and often serve as places for meets of hounds; so, are little likely to be interfered with. One great sport pursued there is coursing, so vividly described by Sylvester, the Lamborne poet:—

> " So have I seen on Lamborne's pleasant downs,
> When yelping beagles, or some deeper hounds,
> Have start a hare, how milk-white Minks and Lun
> (Grey bitches both, the best that ever run)
> Held in one leash, have leapt, and strained, and whined,
> To be restrained, till, to their master's mind,
> They might be slipt to purpose; that, for sport,
> Watt might have law neither too long nor short."

Of ancient *Castles* there are scarcely any *remains* except at Windsor. A fragment of a tower and an oriel window is left of Wallingford; at Donnington there is a picturesque gateway; at Shillingford some chimneys; of Aldworth only the foundations remain. Reading, Newbury, Faringdon, and Brightwell castles have entirely disappeared.

The oldest *Manor-house* in Berks is that of Appleton near Abingdon, supposed to be temp. Henry II. East Hendred retains its ancient domestic chapel of the 13th centy. The manor-house of Cumnor is destroyed. Fyfield has the solar in a very perfect state; the hall has Dec. doorways. There are remains of Tudor houses at Wytham, Sutton Courtenay near Abingdon, and Little Shefford near Newbury. The beautiful old timber mansion of the Norreys family at Ockwells, and Ufton Court, the home of Pope's Arabella Fermor, are now only farmhouses. Shaw House, near Newbury, is a good specimen of the Elizabethan period.

The principal *Monastic Remains* are those of Abingdon, where the

gatehouse and some portions of the abbot's house are still standing; and
of Reading, where the abbey mills, and shapeless fragments of the
church and other parts remain; the gatehouse, which stood till 1861,
has been rebuilt. The ancient doorway of Bisham is built into the
beautiful but later manor-house. Some small traces are left of the
Benedictine Monastery at Hurley; and the church of the Grey Friars at
Reading has been restored.

Among the *Churches* of the county, Avington deserves the first place,
as an interesting and perfect specimen of very early Norman. The
little church of Padworth, though much injured, presents some good
Norm. details. Uffington is a remarkable and perfect E. E. church.
Shottesbrooke is a fine specimen of Dec.; and St. George's Chapel at
Windsor of Perp. The churches of St. Helen Abingdon, Wantage,
Faringdon, Bisham, and Sonning are all of much interest. Welford
and Great Shefford have ancient round towers, and Tidmarsh and
Remenham semicircular apses. To the antiquary and ecclesiologist
the following church details will be interesting.

Fonts.—Many of early character, and good. *Norm.* Appleford,
Eaton Hastings, Finchampstead, Purley, Sulhamstead, Great Shefford,
Welford. *E. E.* Englefield, Hatford, Wantage; Childrey, Long Wit-
tenham, and Woolhampton, of lead, as is also Clewer (Norm.) *Dec.*
Ardington, Buckland. *Perp.* Chieveley, Compton Beauchamp, Dench-
worth, Hagbourn, Hurley, St. Lawrence and St. Mary Reading,
Steventon.

Glass.—14*th cent.* Basildon, Brightwell, Hagbourne, Long Wittenham, North Moreton. 15*th cent.* Letcombe Regis, Shillingford,
Sutton Courtenay, St. George's Chapel, Windsor, Little Shefford.

Tombs.—13*th cent.* Cumnor, Didcot. 14*th cent.* Aldworth (very
remarkable), Hatford, Sparsholt (wooden effigies), Sonning, Wantage.
15*th cent.* Englefield, Fyfield, St. George's Chapel, Windsor, Little
Shefford.

Brasses.—Blewbury, Bray, Childrey, Denchworth, West Hanney, East
Hendred, Lamborne, Shottesbrooke, Wantage, Windsor, Little
Wittenham.*

The *Views* from White Horse Hill, from Faringdon Clump, from
Sinodun Hill near Wittenham, and from Cumnor Hurst, command a
wide extent of country. That of Oxford from Bagley Wood is of great
beauty, as is that of the course of the Thames, from the hills above
Bisham, and above Medmenham.

Of *Country Seats* the most remarkable are Ashdown, high up among
the downs; Coleshill, a good and perfect specimen of the architecture
of Inigo Jones; Pusey, from having been given to the family of that
name in the time of Canute; Wytham Abbey, with its beautiful woods;

* In the dearth of topographical works on Berkshire our readers will thank us for
mentioning the 'Address on the Archæology of Berkshire,' by the *Earl of Carnarvon.*
Murray, 1859. This little brochure is equally attractive for the elegance of the style in
which it is written and the extreme interest of the facts selected.

and the modern houses of Bearwood, Beckett, and Aldermaston, the latter of which is also remarkable for its wild park and "snakery," and its fine old timber.

The best collection of *Pictures*, after Windsor, are the galleries of Bearwood, and Basildon; Coleshill, Buckland, and Beckett also contain a few good pictures.

The *Angler* will find abundant employment on the banks of the Thames and of the Kennet, especially near Hungerford, mentioned by Evelyn as "celebrated for its troutes." The *Artist* will be chiefly interested in the distant views of Windsor, in the older parts of the Forest, and in the scenery on the banks of the Thames, especially near Pangbourne, Bisham, and Maidenhead. Picturesque bits may also be found at Abingdon, Donnington Castle, Little Shefford, and among the hills near Aldermaston; and the villages on the downs, often almost hidden in trees, have a character of their own, that will repay the sketcher.

The Berkshire *Dialect*, once very strongly marked, is giving way before the progress of education, but *him* and *her*, *he* and *she*, *us* and *we*, are still constantly misapplied; *a* and *o* are interchanged, *z* takes the place of *s*, and *v* of *f*, and *thik* and *thak* stand for *this* and *that*. A girl, complaining of her stepmother, said, "Whaat's her to do wi' we? uz doan't balong to zhee." A slight specimen of this dialect may be given, which fairly represents the pronunciation of the villagers on the downs; it is from the ballad of 'The Scouring of the White Horse' (Rte. 5):—

> " Tha owld Wheete Haarse waants zetten a reets,
>   Aan' tha Squyeer haa praamized gud chaar;
> Zo waa'll gee un aa scraap tu kape un in zhaap,
>   Aan' a'll laazt vor maany aa yaar.
>
> " A wus maad aa laang laang teem agwo,
>   Wi' aa gurt daal o' laabour aan' paains,
> Bey Keng Aalfard tha Graat, whan a spwiled thaar consate,
>   Aan' caadled thay wosherds tha Daans.
>
> " Tha Bleaawun Stwun en daays gwoon bey
>   Wur Keng Aalfard's boogle haarn;
> Aan' tha thaarnin' tree yu med plaanly zee,
>   Aaz be caall'd Keng Aalfard's thaarn.
>
> " Thaar 'll bey baakzwaard plaay, aan' clrmmin' tha powl,
>   Aan' aa ruace vur aa peg aan' a chaaze,
> Aan' uz thenks aaz hizn's aa dummell zowl
>   Aaz dwoant caare vur zich spwoorts aaz thaaze."

SKELETON TOUR.

The following week's tour comprises all the chief objects of interest in the county:—

Days.

1. *Windsor*, by the Forest, Binfield, and Bearwood, to Reading. (Rtes. 1, 2, 3.)

Days.

2. *Reading*, Abbey Ruins and Churches By rail to Aldermaston (and Ufton Court), thence to Newbury. Shaw House and Donnington Castle. (Rte. 6.)

3. By Avington, Wickham, Welford, and the Sheffords, to Lamborne. (Rte. 7.)

4. By the Seven Barrows, Wayland Smith's Cave, the White Horse, Uffington, and Sparsholt, to Wantage. (Rte. 5.)

5. Faringdon, Pusey, Fyfield, Besilsleigh, Appleton, Cumnor, to Abingdon (Rtes. 8, 9.)

6. Sutton Courtenay, Wittenham, Wallingford, Cholsey, Aldworth, Basildon, Pangbourne. (Rtes. 4, 5.)

7. Rail to Twyford—Sonning, Wargrave, Hurley, Bisham (or by water down the Thames, *a most delightful excursion*, see Rte. 10) to Maidenhead, whence see Bray, Ockwells, Shottesbrooke. (Rte. 4.)

ROUTES.

₊ The names of places are printed in *italics* only in those routes where the *places* are described.

ROUTE 1.

WINDSOR: THE CASTLE AND THE GREAT PARK.

Great Western or South-Western Rlys.

INDEX.

Windsor may be reached from almost any part of London in little more than an hour, by proceeding on the Metropolitan or Metropolitan District lines to Paddington (or on the West London line to Southall), and joining the G. W. Rly., on which we travel to Slough (Rte. 11), and thence pass on a branch to Windsor. Or it may be reached, in just as little time, from Cannon-street, Ludgate-hill or Waterloo, proceeding by the S.-W. Rly. through Richmond, Staines, and Datchet; this line, in the latter part of its course, skirts the Thames, and affords very fine views of the Castle and Home Park. Carriages and flys are to be had at each terminus. The G. W. stat. is in George-street, very near Castle-hill ; the S.-W. is in Datchet-road, and is built in imitation of the Perp. style of architecture. Almost contiguous to it, facing Thames-street, is an approach to the Castle, called the Hundred Steps, by which access is gained to the Lower Ward. They are somewhat fatiguing to ascend.

The town of Windsor (*Inns:* White Hart, Castle) stands on the right bank of the Thames, opposite Eton, and has for ages been famous, not only for its fine situation, but for its Castle having been, at least from the early part of the 12th centy., a customary residence of the Sovereign (*post*). It is an ancient borough, now returning 1 M.P. (Pop. 12,273), is connected with Eton and Datchet by handsome iron *Bridges*, and is placed mainly to the S. and W. of the Castle, the mound of which occupies the E. side of the High-street. The *Church*, a modern E. E. structure (rebuilt 1822), has pre-served a few monuments from the old ch., and has also an altar-piece of the Lord's Supper, of early execu-tion, which was discovered in 1707 hidden behind wainscoting in St. George's Chapel, and was in use there till 1788, when it was displaced, and was presented to the parish by George III. A district church, Trinity, erected in 1843, has a hand-some carved stone pulpit, a memo-rial of Col. Stephenson, Coldstream Guards. There are two chapels of ease: the second erected in 1876. The *Town Hall*, built by Sir C. Wren, has on the exterior statues of Queen Anne and Prince George of Den-mark, and in the hall portraits of

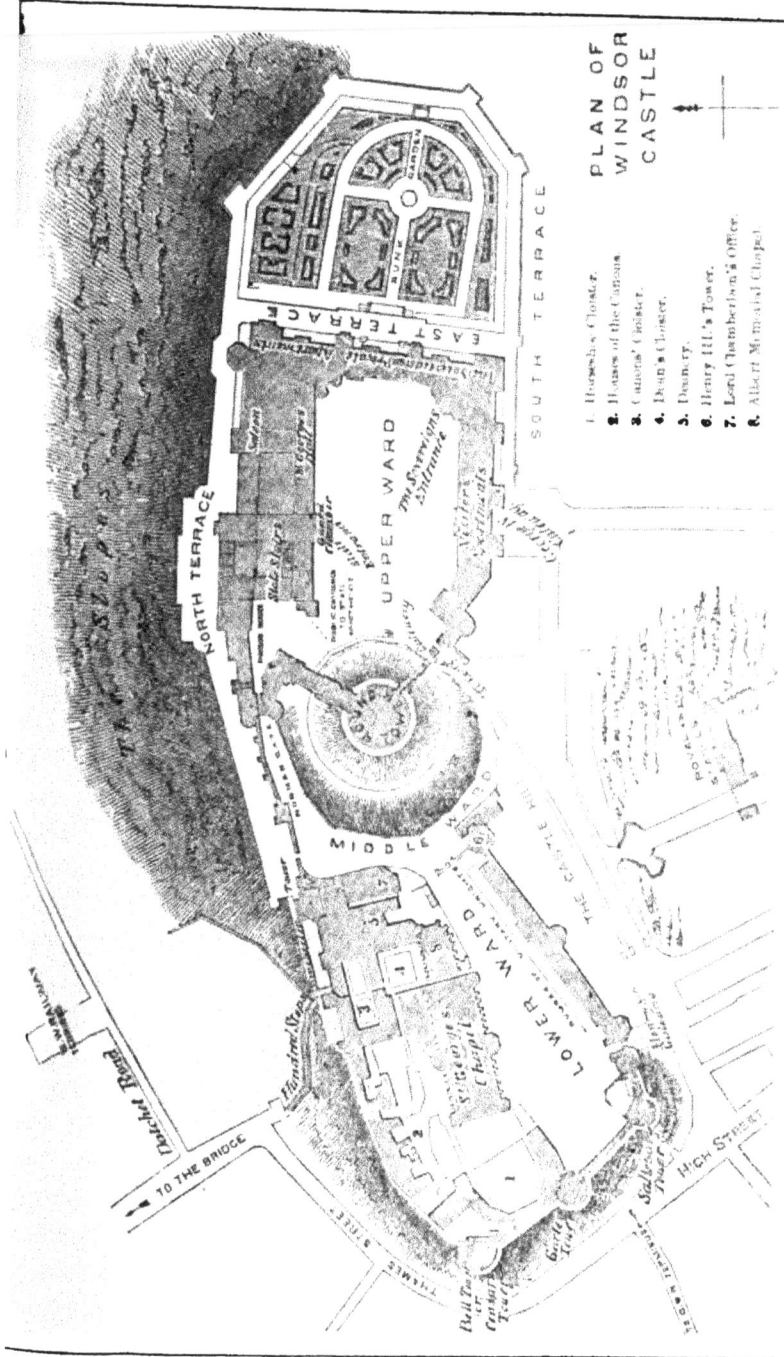

PLAN OF
WINDSOR
CASTLE

1. Horseshoe Cloister.
2. Houses of the Canons.
3. Canons' Cloister.
4. Dean's House.
5. Deanery.
6. Henry III.'s Tower.
7. Lord Chamberlain's Office.
8. Albert Memorial Chapel.

Sovereigns and others, some being the gift of George IV. The *Barracks*, which accommodate both horse and foot, are near the Great Park. The Cavalry Barracks are at Spittal. The Infantry (Victoria) Barracks are in Sheet Street.

Near the river, at the foot of the Hundred Steps, on the rt., was a house, destroyed 1860, supposed, with much reason, to have been that which Shakespeare had in his mind, as the *House of Mrs. Page*, in the 'Merry Wives of Windsor.' This part of the town, then called "Windsor Underowre," was formerly the property of the Abbot of Reading. The only memorial of this possession is in the Abbot's Pile, a name still retained for a wooden pile on the Eton bank of the Thames, near Tangier Mill (*Annals of Windsor*). The bridge connecting Windsor with Eton (Rte. 11), commands a fine view of the Castle.

A public-house in Peascod-street, called the *Duke's Head*, derives its name from having been the house of Villiers, Duke of Buckingham. Thither Charles II. used to come from the Castle, and thence they used to walk together to Filberts, the house of Nell Gwynne.

Hints for Visitors.—The State Apartments at Windsor Castle are open gratuitously to the public, during the absence of the Court, on Mondays, Tuesdays, Thursdays, and Fridays, between 11 and 4 from April 1 to Oct. 31; and between 11 and 3 from Nov. 1 to March 31. Visitors or residents in Windsor may obtain tickets at the Lord Chamberlain's Office, near the Winchester Tower, at the head of the Lower Ward of the Castle, the tickets being available for the day of issue only.

The Royal Stables and Riding-School may be seen between 1 and 3 by an order from the Clerk of the Stables. The Round Tower is open

on the same days as the Castle, and needs no ticket of admission, but a guide is required. 2 hrs. are hardly enough to see well Castle, Terrace, and Chapel.

The *Albert Memorial Chapel* can be visited every day, except Mondays and Tuesdays, between 12 and 3. *St. George's Chapel* may be viewed daily (excepting Wednesdays) between 12½ a.m. and 4 p.m. Divine service on Sundays at 11 a.m. and 5 p.m.; on week days at 10.30 a.m. and 5 p.m.

The *North Terrace* is open all day long, and should be visited for the sake of its splendid prospect; some visitors will also find an attraction in a monster gun from China placed there. The circuit of the three terraces, which gives a view of the beautiful sunk garden in front of the Private Apartments, can be made only on Saturdays and Sundays, in the absence of the Court.

WINDSOR CASTLE occupies a commanding and isolated eminence of chalk, the only one within a circuit of many miles. On all sides it is a most picturesque object, but the best views are those from the South-Western Rly. near Datchet; from the curve of the Great Western Rly. before reaching the Stat., where the broad river, overhung by the old houses of the town, is seen washing the base of the Castle-hill; and from the hill at the end of the Long Avenue, whence the "proud keep of Windsor," as it is described by Burke, is seen rising above a forest of oaks and beeches.

Windsor, then called Windlesore, from the winding river, was the property of Edward the Confessor, who, "for the hope of eternal reward, for the remission of all his sins, the sins of his father, mother, and ancestors, and to the praise of God," gave it to the Abbey of Westminster; but William the Conqueror, "being enamoured of the pleasant situation of the place, first built several little lodges in the forest for the convenience of hunting;" and finally, justly estimating the commanding situation of the hill, obtained it in exchange for some lands in Essex, and built a Norm. castle on the height, which Henry I. added to. From his reign to the present time, Windsor Castle has been the frequent residence of the Sovereign; and many great councils of the realm have been held within its walls. Henry I. married here in 1122 his 2nd wife Adeliza, when the Archbishop of Canterbury was so furious at the Bishop of Salisbury putting on the crown of the new Queen, "that he could hardly be entreated by the lords to refrain from striking off that of the King." Here Henry II., as Fabyan narrates, caused an old eagle to be painted on the walls, with four smaller birds, of which three tore its body, and the fourth pecked out its eyes; and when asked its meaning, he said, "These betoken my four sons, which cease not to pursue my death, especially my youngest son John." John frequently resided here, and hence his grant of Magna Charta at Runnymede (see *Handbook for Surrey*). Here many children were born to the royal Henrys and Edwards, the greatest of whom, afterwards Edward III. (born Nov. 13, 1312), hence derived his appellation of Edward of Windsor." In this castle he founded the Order of the Garter in 1349, with the motto, "Honi soit. qui mal y pense" (literally, " Shame be to him who thinks evil of it"); and, converting the old fortress into a residence for its officers, and for the dean and canons of the Church, he built a new palace higher up the hill to the E., for his own use, under the superintendence of William of Wykeham. Edward the Black Prince married the Fair Maid of Kent in the Castle Chapel. Here, also, the aged King sorrowed over the deathbed of Philippa, the

" good Queen of England," a sce touchingly described by Fro' At Windsor was born Henry contrary to the wishes of his fathe who is said to have prophesied,—

" I, Henry, born at Monmouth,
Shall small time reign, and much get,
But Henry of Windsor shall reign long and
lose all."

The Castle was much altered and modernised by George IV. under Wyatt, who was knighted and changed his name to Wyattville. Wyatt professed to preserve the general features of the ancient fortress, and yet to adapt it to the requirements of modern comfort; but the lover of history must regret that the Castle, added to by so many kings, and presenting memorials of so many ages, should be reduced to a state of uniformity. It is at its W. extremity only that the Castle of the 13th centy. has in any degree maintained its original aspect to the present day. The N.-W. tower (Clewer tower, corrupted into Cæsar's) has been used as a belfry and clockhouse, probably from the time of Edward III. Norden's view (temp. James I.) represents it with its cupola very nearly in the same state as it appeared until the commencement of the alterations made in 1872. The lower or prison story has remained intact from its foundation. It consists of a chamber 22 ft. in diameter, vaulted on plain massive stone ribs; the walls 12½ ft. thick, with arched recesses terminating in loop-holes. The whole is constructed of chalk, faced and arched with freestone, and is an interesting and perfect specimen of the period.

It may be useful, before entering upon a general description, to note the age of the separate buildings yet remaining, constructed under the different Sovereigns, viz.:—

HENRY II. — Foundations and lower storey of S. side of upper ward from Devil Tower to Victoria Towers.

HENRY III.—The outer walls of the lower ward, including the Salisbury and Garter towers (restored) and the Clewer Tower. The wall of the S. ambulatory of the Dean's Cloister, with its E. E. arcade. The door behind the altar in St. George's Chapel, which is the W. door of the chapel of Henry III.'s palace. The remains of the Domus Regis on the N. of the chapel, included in the house of one of the canons, and the King's Hall, now the Chapter Library.

EDWARD III.—The Gate-house an old Norman Gate, rebuilt by Henry III. and afterwards by Edward III., N. of the Keep or Round Tower. The Round Tower, in which the wood-work of his time remains supporting the existing principal floor. The groining of the Devil's Tower, and the Rose Tower. The Dean's Cloister. The Servants'. Halls under the State Apartments; these retain their groined vaults.

EDWARD IV.—St. George's Chapel; the arcade in the aisles, with their groined vaults, and the Horseshoe Cloisters, or Fellerlock.

HENRY VII. — The splendid groined vault of the nave of St. George's. The Tudor buildings on N. side, now a portion of the Royal Library, and the S. and E. walls of the Tomb-house.

HENRY VIII.—The groined vault of the choir of St. George's. The casing of the W. or outer Gateway.

ELIZABETH.—The Royal Library, and buildings on the W. part of the N. terrace.

The Castle consists of 2 great divisions, the Lower and the Upper Ward, separated by the Round Tower, or Keep. Proceeding up Castle-hill, the iron gates at the top form the *Queen's Entrance*, leading to the George IV. Gateway, which fronts the Long Walk (*post*). The *Public Entrance* is by an archway called, from its builder, Henry VIII.'s

Gateway, flanked by two octagonal towers, and approached by a bridge. It leads into the *Lower Ward*, where, on the rt. is the long low line of houses appropriated to the Military Knights, with the tower of their governor (Garter Hall) in the centre, beyond which is Henry III.'s Tower, covered with ivy; opposite to it is the Winchester Tower, so called from its builder, William of Wykeham, Bishop of Winchester. On the l. is the Salisbury Tower, for the knights on the later foundation; the Garter Tower; and the gateway leading to the Horseshoe Cloister, and the houses of the minor canons and lay clerks of the chapel, beyond which is the ancient belfry tower.

Opposite the gateway is *St. George's Chapel*, one of the finest existing examples of Perp. Slightly to the E. of its site a chapel was built by Henry I., and dedicated to Edward the Confessor; it was rebuilt by Edward III., and dedicated to St. George, the patron of his newly-founded Order of the Garter.

The building is 232 ft. long by 66 ft. broad; transept, 104 ft. The nave is of 7 bays, the choir of 6, with an E. ambulatory and N. and S. aisles. There are 6 chapels, thus arranged :—S.-W., Lady Chapel or Beaufort Chapel. N.-W., Urswick Chapel. N., Rutland Chapel, also the Hastings chantry. S.-E., Lincoln Chapel. S., King's (or Aldworth) Chapel, Bray's Chapel, and the Oxenbridge chantry.

The mass of the existing chapel was built in the reign of Edward IV., the stone roof of the nave, which was of wood before, being added by Henry VII., and that of the choir by Henry VIII. In the interior no portion is left unornamented, the walls being covered with a delicate panelling of Gothic work, and the ribs of the columns spreading over the roof in rich tracery, adorned with painted coats-of-arms of the knights of the Garter, and with the

"Rose en soleil," the well-known cognizance of Edward IV. The usual entrance is by the S. porch, beside which notice a small *Brass* let into the wall, in honour of George Brooke, yeoman of the guard to four of the Tudors, with the inscription—

> " He lyved content with meane estate,
> And long ago prepared to dye ;
> The idle parson he did hate ;
> Poor people's wants he did supply."

The great W. window occupies the whole end of the nave, and contains some ancient stained glass collected from various parts of the chapel, supplemented by bad modern work. The side windows, by *West*, are very inferior. On the l. is the richly-painted *Lady Chapel* or *Beaufort Chapel*, containing two monuments of that family : one, an altar-tomb, to the founder, Charles Somerset, Earl of Worcester(d. 1526); the other, supported by Corinthian pillars, to Henry 1st Duke of Beaufort (d. 1699). The Marquis of Worcester (d. 1646), author of the 'Century of Inventions,' and the faithful friend of Charles I., for whom he defended Raglan Castle, is buried here without a monument. Opposite, on the rt., is the *Urswick Chapel*, so called from Dean Christopher Urswick (d. 1505). Here, in a golden light, is the monument of the Princess Charlotte, executed by Mr. *C. Wyatt*, from public subscription, her beatified spirit is represented rising from the couch upon which her corpse is lying. To make room for this, a fine stone screen was removed to the S. aisle.

Nearly opposite the Beaufort Chapel, and between two of the pillars of the nave, is a monument erected by the Queen to the memory of the *Duke of Kent*. It consists of a white marble recumbent figure of the Duke, by *Boehm*, resting on an alabaster sarcophagus, designed by *Scott*. In the S.-E. corner of the nave there is a splendid statue by

Boehm of Leopold I., *King of Belgians*, Her Majesty's uncle ; near to this a brass tablet rec the untimely death of Prince Al ayou, the son of Theodore, King Abyssinia. Between the Ursw and the Rutland Chapel a ma mural tablet, by Count Glei has been erected to the memory *King George V.* of Hanover, who buried in the Royal Vault.

Beneath the modern organ-scr the visitor enters the *Choir*, wh the richness of the architecture splendour of the dark carved o of the time of Henry VII., is creased by the effect of the swo helmets, banners, and mantles of knights of the Garter, suspend over the stalls. Here the installati ceremonies of the Order have be performed ever since their first ce bration on St. George's Day, 134 The stalls of the Sovereign a princes of the blood are under th organ ; next come those of foreig Sovereigns. The brass-plates at th back of the stalls bear the name arms, and dates of former knight among which are those of the Er perors Sigismund and Charles V Francis I. of France, and Casimir IV of Poland, who all belonged to th Order, which Denham declares,—

> " Foreign kings and emperors esteem
> The second honour to their diadem."

Lord Burleigh and the Earl of Surre are also among the illustrious mem bers commemorated here.

In the centre of the choir is stone bearing the names of thos who are interred in the *Royal Vaul* beneath. Here Queen Jane Seymou was buried, 1537, with the epitapl by Bishop Godwin,—

> " Phœnix fana jacet nato Phœnice, dolendum
> Secula Phœnices nulla tulisse duas."

Which has been translated by his son Morgan Godwin :—

> " Here a Phœnix lieth, whose death
> To another Phœnix gave breath ;
> It is to be lamented much,
> The world at once ne'er knew two such."

Here, in 1547, Henry VIII. was
'ed by his own desire, " by his
and loving wife Queen Jane."
tomb which he ordered for him-
, and wh:ch is minutely described
Speed, with its 634 statues and 44
tories, was never put up. Charles
was also buried here " in silence
1 sorrow, his pall white with the
,w which fell upon it in its pas-
to the chapel, Feb. 8, 1649,
out any service, as the governor
ld not allow Bishop Juxon to
the king after the service of
Church of England ; neither
uld the lords allow of his way.
ere was therefore nothing read
the grave, though the bishop's lips
re observed to move." Charles II.,
m motives that are variously stated
y Clarendon and others, professed
difficulty in finding the place of
urial ; but in 1813 the coffin was
scovered and opened. Sir H. Hal-
rd, who was present, describes the
mplexion of the face as dark and
iscoloured. " The forehead and
emples had little or nothing of their
muscular substance; the cartilage
of the nose was gone; but the left
ye, in the moment of first exposure,
was open and full, though it vanished
almost immediately. The shape of
the face was a long oval. The hair
was thick at the back of the head,
and nearly black; that of his beard
was of a reddish brown. On holding
up the head, the muscles of the neck
had evidently contracted consider-
bly ; and the fourth cervical verte-
bra was cut through transversely,
leaving the substance of the divided
portions smooth and even—an appearance which could only have
been produced by a heavy blow from
a very sharp instrument, and which
urnished the last proof wanting to
dentify Charles I." The tomb of
Henry VIII. was opened at the same
time, when, as a bitter epigram
declared, he looked—

' Much like a butcher, only somewhat paler."

[*Berks, &c.*]

A few steps further E., below the
first step leading to the altar, is the
entrance to a second Royal Vault
(constructed beneath Wolsey's Tomb-
house by George III.), where are
buried,—

Prince Octavius and Prince Alfred,
children of George III., removed
from Westminster Abbey.

Augusta, Duchess of Brunswick,
sister of George III.

Princess Charlotte and Princess
Elizabeth, children of the Duke of
Clarence (afterwards William IV.).

Died.

Princess Amelia ..	Nov. 2, 1810
Princess Charlotte ..	Nov. 6, 1817
Queen Charlotte ..	Nov. 17, 1818
Duke of Kent	Jan. 23, 1820
George III.	Jan. 29, 1820
Duke of York	Jan. 5, 1827
George IV.	June 26, 1830
William IV.	June 20, 1837
Princess Augusta ..	Sept. 22, 1840
Queen Adelaide ..	Dec. 2, 1849
George V., King of Hanover	June, 12, 1878

The funeral of the Duchess of
Kent, mother of the Queen, took
place in St. George's Chapel, March
25, 1861; but in fulfilment of her own
request, her body was afterwards
removed to Frogmore. The late
Prince Consort was also buried here
Dec. 23, 1861, but his remains also
have been removed (*post*). No person is allowed to enter the royal
vault without the permission of the
Lord Chamberlain. The coffins of
the kings are covered with crimson,
the others with purple velvet. The
vault is surrounded by recesses,
formed by Gothic octagonal columns,
each with a range of 4 shelves, for
the reception of the coffins.

The E. window of the chapel was
filled till lately by a semi-opaque
picture of the Resurrection by West.
to admit which much of the ancient
tracery was removed. This has
now been restored, and the aper-

c

tures filled with stained glass by the
Dean and Chapter, as a memorial of
the Prince Consort. The lower compartments represent "the acts of a
good Prince." The reredos, by
Philip, was designed by *Scott*.

On the l. of the altar is the *Gothic
iron screen* for the tomb of King
Edward IV., supposed to be the work
of *Quentin Matsys*. Its elaborate
tracery is one of the finest products
of the hammer existing, and merits
minute inspection. Here hung the
king's coat-of-mail, and his surcoat
of crimson velvet, embroidered with
pearls, rubies, and gold, which were
carried off by the Parliamentarian
soldiers when the chapel was defaced
in 1643. Above the screen two oriel
windows give light to the *Royal
Closet* or pew occupied by the Queen
when she attends divine service in
this chapel. The view on looking
back from this point is especially
rich in colour.

On March 10, 1863, the marriage
of the Prince of Wales, with the
Princess Alexandra of Denmark was
celebrated in this chapel; as was
that of the Princess Louise to the
Marquis of Lorne, March 22, 1871,
the Duke of Connaught to Princess
Louise Margaret of Prussia, March
13, 1879, and of the Duke of Albany
with Princess Helen of Waldeck in
April, 1882.

In making the circuit of the
chapels, the first in the N. aisle is
the *Rutland Chapel*, with a fine
altar-tomb for Sir George Manners
(d. 1513), ancestor of the Rutland
family, and his wife Anne (d. 1528),
niece of Edward IV.; the chapel
was founded by her father, Sir
Thomas St. Leger, in memory of his
wife Anne, Duchess of Exeter (d.
1476); he was beheaded in 1483 for
conspiring against his brother-in-law
Richard III., but was allowed to be
buried here, and the effigies of himself and his wife appear on a brass

on the wall in heraldic dresses. Proceeding E. notice on l. a number of
stained windows, which surround the
choir, and are filled with portraits of
royal personages, commencing with
Edward III. and ending with William
IV. and Queen Adelaide. Rt. is the
Hastings Chantry, built by his widow
to contain the tomb of William Lord
Hastings, the chamberlain of Edward IV., beheaded by Richard III.,
1483, but afterwards allowed to be
buried, "his body with his head,"
beside the tomb of his master, while
the priest appointed to pray for his
soul had a special house close to the
N. door of the chapel. This chantry
is dedicated to St. Stephen, whose
life is represented in painting on the
wall. Rt. near this, is the statue of
Field-Marshal William Earl Harcourt (1830), by *Sevier*. Further rt.
is the tomb of Edward IV., who was
interred here April 19, 1483, "with
great funeral honour and heaviness
of his people."

On a stone near are inscribed the
names of two of his children (George,
Duke of Bedford, and Mary), who
died before him. His queen, Elizabeth Woodville, was buried (1492)
by her children near the king, but
with scant ceremony; her grave is
within the choir. Beyond, on rt. is
the monument of the Princess Louisa
of Saxe Weimar, niece of Queen Adelaide, who died at Windsor.

At the E. end of the N. aisle is
the entrance to the *Chapter-house*,
in which the sword of Edward III.
is preserved, and where there is a
full-length portrait of that monarch
in his robes of state.

Opposite the E. end of the choir is
the entrance to the *Ruyal Tomb-house*,
formerly known as the *Wolsey
Chapel*, now as the *Albert Chapel*,
built by Henry VII., who intended
it for the burial-place of the Tudors
before building his chapel in Westminster Abbey. It was granted by

Henry VIII. to Wolsey, who there began a splendid monument for himself, composed of black and white marble, with brazen columns, candlesticks, &c. It is said Benedetti received 4250 ducats for the portion which he finished, and that the expenses of the gilding had already exceeded 380*l.* The unfinished tomb was seized by the Parliament in 1646, and the ornaments were sold by Col. Venn, governor of Windsor Castle, as "old brass," for 600*l.* The black marble sarcophagus was allowed to lie neglected till used for its present purpose as the covering of Nelson's tomb in St. Paul's Cathedral. In the reign of James II. Verrio was employed to paint the ceiling of the Tomb-house, and mass was performed there, which led to its being defaced by the populace, after which it remained untouched till its partial restoration (by Wyatt) in 1800 by George III., who constructed the vault beneath it, in which he and his family are buried. On the death of the Prince Consort Her Majesty caused the chapel to be converted into a splendid memorial under the direction of Sir G. G. Scott. Accordingly the walls were panelled with "marble pictures" by Baron Triqueti; Medallion portraits of the Royal Family were executed by Miss Durant, the windows were filled with stained glass by Clayton and Bell, the roof was covered with mosaic by Salviati, and the floor inlaid with rare marbles. The altar is a slab of Levanto marble, and the reredos is inlaid with lapis lazuli, malachite, alabaster, and porphyry. In the nave in front of the altar is a magnificent cenotaph by Baron Triqueti, upon which reposes a figure of the Prince Consort in white marble. The body of the altar-tomb rests upon a great slab of black and gold Tuscan marble ; the corners are supported by angels, and statuettes in niches adorn the sides. In removing a portion of the wall on either

side of the doorway leading to the cloisters, several fragments were discovered, supposed to be remains of the chapel of Henry III. These relics form portions of the jamb of a door with ogee mouldings, pillars, &c. On one of the stones is an angel's wing, while the mouldings and surfaces still bear the crimson, green red, and black colours with which they were decorated in curved and zigzag lines. The whole of the stones seem to have belonged to the Early English or Norman periods. The Albert Memorial chapel was finished in November 1875.

Turning into the S. aisle from E. to W., the 1st chapel on the l. is the *Lincoln Chapel*, with a magnificent altar-tomb to the Earl of Lincoln (d. 1584), an eminent statesman in the time of Henry VIII., Edward VI., and Elizabeth, in the last of which reigns he became Lord High Admiral. He is represented, with his countess, lying upon a mat, with their 8 children beneath. The shrine of Sir John Shorne was removed hither from North Marston (Rte. 15), and the stained windows which once existed exhibited his extraordinary history. Near this is the memorial niche of Richard Beauchamp Bishop of Salisbury (d. 1481). In the centre of the arch above he is represented kneeling with Edward IV., before a cross. Opposite is a niche where he ordered a Breviary to be placed, as the inscription tells, "to this intent, that priests and ministers of God's Church may here have the occupation thereof, saying therein their divine service, and for all other that listen to say thereby their devotion." The Breviary was replaced by a black-letter Bible secured by a chain at the Dissolution, but the niche is now empty.

A short distance W., notice a black marble slab in the pavement ; it marks the grave of Henry VI., whose body was removed hither from Chertsey by Richard III.—

" Here o'er the martyr-king the marble weeps;
While fast beside him once-fear'd Edward sleeps . . . . . .
The grave unites, where e'en the great find rest,
And blended lie th' oppressor and th' opprest."—*Pope.*

Stowe writes that after his removal here "the meek usurper" was worshipped by the name of the Holy King Henry, and his hat of red velvet was thought to heal the headache of such as put it on. Prayers to him were inserted in service-books of the early part of the 16th centy. Reformed opinions spread early among the canons and singing men of the chapel, and the fact was a grief to them, against which one at least ventured to remonstrate. Fox says that " As [Canon] Testwood chanced to walke in the church in the afternoone, and beheld the pilgrims, especially of Devon and Cornwall, how they came in by plumps with candles and images of wax in their hands, it pitied his heart to see such great idolatrie committed, and how easily the people spent their goods in coming so farre to kiss a spur and have an old hat set on their heads; insomuch that hee could not refraine, but went up to them, and with all gentleness began to exhort them to leave such false worshipping of dumbe creatures." Lambarde also tells how " Windsore was polluted with the evil worship of Holy King Henry (as they called him). The seely bewitched people gadded hither on pilgrimage, being persuaded that a small chippe of his bedstead (which was kept here) was a precious relique, and to put upon a man's heade an olde red velvet hatte of his (that lay theare) was a sovereign medecine against the headache." Proceeding W., on rt. is a black marble stone, with a ducal coronet and the name " Charles Brandon;"

it covers the grave of the Duke of Suffolk (d. 1545), who married Mary, sister of Henry VIII. and widow of Louis XII. of France. Further W. is the *Oxenbridge Chapel*, founded (1522) by a canon of that name. It is dedicated to St. John Baptist, and contains some pictures of the events of his life, with figures in the costume of Henry VIII. Near this is the screen removed from the Urswick Chapel, containing the monument of its founder, with a touching Latin epitaph.

Opposite is the beautiful little *King's*, or *Aldworth Chapel*, so called from the monuments of that family which it contains. It is supposed to have been built by Oliver King, Bishop of Exeter, 1492, and afterwards (1495) translated to Bath and Wells, when he built the Abbey Church at Bath. Here are the tombs of two children of his family:—" Dorothy King (1630), lent to her parents, but speedilie required againe;" and " William King (1633), being soon wearie of his abode on earth, left his parents to preserve a memorial of him, after 10 weeks' pilgrimage." The stained windows above this part of the aisle represent the coronation of William III., and Queen Anne presenting her bounty to the bishops. On rt. are portraits on panels of Edward IV., Edward V., and Henry VII., with an inscription beseeching prayers for the soul of their secretary, Bishop Oliver King.

Beyond is the beautiful monument by *Sir G. G. Scott*, which, as the inscription tells, " was erected by Queen Victoria as a tribute of respect and affection to her beloved aunt Mary Duchess of Gloucester, A.D. 1859." The top of the tomb is composed of serpentine marble, in which is inserted the figure of the cross, with the rose, thistle, and shamrock enamelled. The front and ends of the tomb are of white marble, and the inscriptions are enclosed in panels of serpentine

with mosaic borders, each panel diapered with the arms of England.
Immediately above are 4 bas-reliefs
by _Theed_, which represent " Clothing
the naked," " Giving bread to the
hungry," " Receiving the weary."
"Visiting the sick." On the same
tomb are commemorated other members of the royal house of Gloucester,
viz. William Henry Duke of Gloucester, 1805; Maria Duchess of
Gloucester, 1807; Princess Maria
Matilda of Gloucester, 1775; William Frederick Duke of Gloucester,
1834; Princess Sophia Matilda of
Gloucester, 1844. [A monument to
the memory of Leopold, King of
the Belgians, also erected by the
Queen, was once placed at the S.-W.
angle of the nave, closely adjoining
the Beaufort Chapel. It was removed to Esher in 1874. It consists
of a recumbent figure of the king,
guarded by the Belgic lion, and was
executed by Miss Durant.]
1. near the S. door is the _Bray
Chapel_, founded (temp. Henry VII.)
by Sir Reginald Bray (d. 1502), who
built the beautiful roof of the nave,
and is buried here without a tomb. It
contains the font, and monuments to
Thomson Bishop of Gloucester, 1612;
Brideoake Bishop of Chichester,
1678 (both had been Deans of Windsor); the learned Dr. Waterland,
1740; and Canon Hallam (father of
the historian), 1824. A monument to
the memory of the Prince Imperial,
who was killed in South Africa
during the Zulu war, was placed in
this chapel by permission of the
Queen in May, 1881. It consists of
a recumbent figure of the Prince in
white marble, by Boehm.

The number of relics of English
saints which enriched St. George's
Chapel before the Reformation is
worthy of notice. It contained bones
of SS. Osyth, Richard, David, Margaret of Scotland, Thomas of Hereford, William of England, William
of York, and Thomas of Canterbury,
and the offerings at their altars gave

it great wealth of jewels, chalices, &c.
Much of this, of course, was lost at
the Reformation; and the building
itself suffered terrible maltreatment
at the hands of the Parliamentarians.
Christopher Wren, the father of the
architect, was then dean, but he was
driven out, and died in comparative
penury. Clarendon, almost incident-
ally, gives us an idea of the havoc
made, when speaking of the funeral
of Charles I. The Duke of Richmond and others, he says, by permission, " went into the ch., to make
choice of a place for burial. But
when they entered into it, which
they had been so well acquainted
with, they found it so altered and
transformed, all tombs, inscriptions,
and those landmarks pulled down,
by which all men knew every particular place in that ch., and such a
dismal mutation over the whole, that
they knew not where they were."
After the funeral, the governor,
Colonel Whichcot, " took the keys
of the ch., which was seldom put
to any use." Bruno Ryves, the first
dean after the Restoration, laboured
zealously to repair the damage done;
but, as Rickman remarks, all the
modern work is merely a slavish
copy of certain detached parts, and so
contrasts unfavourably with the compositions of the ancient architects.

Behind the Albert Chapel are the
beautiful _Dean's Cloisters_, built by
Edward III., of which the S. wall is
most interesting, as being a fragment of the ancient chapel of Henry
III., preserved, and adapted to its
present purpose, when the rest of
the chapel, which occupied part of
the site now filled by the cloisters,
was destroyed. The details of the
carving on the ancient capitals are
very curious; and within the 1st
arch is a relic of the ancient mural
painting, for the promotion of which
Henry III. was so remarkable, being
a crowned portrait of that monarch
himself, discovered behind the plaster in 1859. Part of the picture

was destroyed, but the head remains intact. A deed of 1248 is still extant, for payment to be made to William the monk of Westminster for the execution of this very painting. The projecting window on the opposite side of the cloister is interesting as being that of the room once occupied by Anne Boleyn.

Behind the Dean's, we come to the *Canons' Cloister.* Here is the entrance to the *Hundred Steps;* whence a flight of 122 steps, issuing from an ancient sallyport, open from sunrise to sunset, communicates with the lower part of the town. A passage on the l. leads, by the beautiful E. E doorway of Henry III., to the N. side of the chapel, where several of the canons' houses are situated. In one of these Henry Hallam was born in 1777. In the outer wall of a neighbouring house the *Domus Regis of Henry III.* is still to be traced. Orders still extant given to Walter de Burgh, 24th Henry III., for constructing rooms for the King and Queen's use, exactly tally with the traces of those apartments still existing. In pulling down the other walls of this building, many fragments of an earlier construction were discovered, which perhaps belonged to the original castle of the Conqueror, but had been inclosed and lost sight of in the building of Henry III.

Retracing our steps, and passing the Albert Chapel, we come to the *Deanery,* built by Dean Christopher Urswick, 1500, and bearing his arms and name. It superseded the old Deanery, at which occurred the sad leave-taking between Richard II. and his Queen Isabella, then only 11 years old, described by Froissart: —" After the canons had chanted very sweetly [in the chapel], and the King himself had chaunted a collect and made his offerings, he took the Queen in his arms and kissed her 12 or 13 times, saying sorrowfully, ' Adieu, madame, until we meet

again.' And the Queen began to weep, saying, ' Alas! my lord, will you leave me here?' Upon which the King's eyes filled with tears, and he said, ' By no means, mamye; but I will go first, and you, ma chère, shall come there afterwards.' Then the King and Queen partook of wine and comfits at the Deanery, and all who chose did the same. Afterwards the King stooped down and took and lifted the Queen from the ground, and held her a long while in his arms, and kissed her at least 10 times, saying over, ' Adieu, ma chère, until we meet again ;' and then placed her on the ground and kissed her at least twice more; and, by our Lady, I never saw so great a lord make so much of, or show such affection to a lady, as did King Richard to his Queen. Great pity it was that they separated, for they never saw each other more."

l. Behind the Deanery is the *Winchester Tower,* once the residence of the great prelate and architect William of Wykeham, who built it, as announced by the inscription " Hoc fecit Wykeham," and afterwards the abode of Sir J. Wyattville, the modern architect of the Castle.

Just beyond the Deanery, on the l. is the Lord Chamberlain's office, where tickets to view the State Apartments can be obtained.

Between the Upper and Lower Wards stands the *Round Tower,* or Keep of the Castle, formerly called " La Rose," planted by Edward III. on the summit of a lofty artificial mound, and surmounted, when the Sovereign resides here, by the royal standard of England. This was the residence of the Governor or Castellan, to whose care distinguished state prisoners were intrusted. John King of France, taken at Crecy, was confined in King John's tower ; and David King of Scotland, taken at Neville'sCross, in the tower connected with it by the wall at the S.W. of the

Upper Ward, which wall is said to have been built in order to enable the royal prisoners to communicate more easily. Here also James I. of Scotland was long detained by Henry IV. and Henry V.; and hence, in the time of Henry VIII., the gallant Earl of Surrey gazed down from the grated windows upon his fair Geraldine, and composed sonnets to her in his cell. Under the Commonwealth, too, it had many unwilling inmates. The last prisoner of state was the Maréchal de Belleisle, captured while crossing the territory of Hanover in the reign of George II. The most distinguished Governor of this tower was Prince Rupert, who filled the office after the Restoration. Evelyn describes how he " trimmed up the keep and handsomely adorned his hall with furniture of arms," and how " the huge steep stairs were invested with this martial furniture, so disposed as to represent festoons, without any confusion, trophy-like; while his bedchamber and ample rooms, hung with tapestry, curious and effeminate pictures, were extremely different from the other, which presented nothing but war and horror." All is now modernised. A flight of 150 stone steps leads into the interior. It is worth ascending them in clear weather, to enjoy the view, which is said to extend over 12 counties. The tower was raised 39 ft., and the flag-turret added, by *Wyattville*.

The *Garden* at the foot of the keep is gay with flowers disposed in various fanciful devices, as the Star of the Garter, &c. It was whilst walking in this " pleasaunce " that James I. of Scotland, so long a captive here (1405–1424), wooed successfully Lady Jane Beaufort, niece of the Cardinal and daughter of the deceased Earl of Somerset, whom he took back with him as his wife on his return to Scotland. His poem, called the ' King's Quhair ' (or Book), describes the garden :—

" Now there was made, fast by the tower's wall.
A garden faire, and in the corners set
An arbour green, with wandes long and small
Rail'd about; and so with leaves beset
Was all the place, and hawthorn hedges knet,
That lyf (person) was none, walking there forebye,
That might within scarce any wight espye."

Those proceeding to see the interior of the Castle must turn to the l. of the Round Tower, under the second gateway, which bears the name of the *Norman Gate*, after passing which they enter the Upper Ward. On their rt. is the entrance to the Round Tower; on their l. a flight of steps leads through the wing of the Castle built by Elizabeth, down to the magnificent North Terrace (*post*).

The *Upper Ward* occupies the site of the Castle built originally by Henry II., and altered and enlarged by Edward III., which was built by the French king's ransom, according to Stow, who also says that the Scotch king's ransom was used in the remodelling of the Lower Ward; and that these alterations were suggested by the captive monarchs themselves while walking with Edward III. At present it forms an extensive quadrangle, surrounded on three sides by buildings containing the State and private apartments, while on the fourth rises the Keep, between the Upper and Lower Wards. The centre of the quadrangle was formerly occupied by the magnificent dragon-fountain of Queen Mary, now destroyed. At its S.W. angle stands an equestrian *Statue of Charles II.*, erected to that " best of kings," as the inscription styles him, by Tobias Rustat, housekeeper at Hampton Court, who is mentioned by Evelyn as "Toby Rustate, page of the backstairs, a very simple, ignorant, but honest and loyal creature." The carvings on the pedestal are by *Gibbons,* "The fruit, fish, and implements," observes Walpole, "are all exquisite; while the man and horse may serve for a sign to draw the passenger's eye to the pedestal." There are 2 carriage-entrances to this quadrangle; one of St. George, adjoining the Devil's Tower, the other, called George IV.'s Gateway, between the York and Lancaster Towers, opening upon the Long Walk, and commanding a full view of it from end to end.

The *State Apartments,* situated in the Star Building of Charles II., are entered by a Gothic porch on the l., adjoining King John's Tower (or Rose Tower). Their ceilings were decorated with mythological subjects by *Antonio Verrio,* who was appointed chief painter by Charles II., but who has since fallen into general disrepute, partly through the satire of Pope—

" On painted ceilings we devoutly stare,
   Where sprawl the saints of Verrio and
   Laguerre"—

and Walpole. The apartments are approached by a narrow staircase, decorated with a portrait of Sir J. Wyattville. On the staircase and anteroom are fine old German pictures. The rooms are shown in the following order :—

1. The *Queen's Audience Chamber.* —The ceiling, by *Verrio,* represents Queen Catherine of Braganza as Britannia, attended by the goddesses to the temple of Virtue. The Gobelins tapestry represents events in the history of Esther and Mordecai. The portraits are William II. and Frederick, Princes of Orange, father and grandfather of our William III., by *Honthorst,* and a very interesting picture of Mary Queen of Scots by *Janet,* with her execution at Fotheringay represented in the background, and a curious inscription.

The frames of these portraits are all exquisitely carved by *Gibbons.*

2. The *Queen's Presence Chamber,* with a ceiling by *Verrio,* has fine Gobelins tapestry, with the sequel of the history of Esther of the tapestries in the Queen's audience-chamber, and portraits of the Duchess of ·Orleans, youngest daughter of Charles I., by *Mignard,* and of the Princesses Elizabeth and Dorothea of Brunswick, by *Mytens.*

3. The *Guard Chamber,* fitted up with armour. Over the fireplace is the famous shield of *Benvenuto Cellini,* given by Francis I. to Henry VIII., on the Field of the Cloth of Gold. At the end of the room, on a portion of the mast of the Victory, perforated by a ball at the battle of Trafalgar, is a bust of Nelson, by *Chantrey,* with Marlborough on the rt. and Wellington on the l., having over their heads the banners of Blenheim and Waterloo, by the annual presentation of which, on the anniversaries of those victories, the domains of Blenheim and Strathfieldsaye are held.

The armour in this room is very interesting. It includes that of the Duke of Brunswick, 1530 ; Lord Howard of Effingham, the Admiral against the Armada, 1588 ; the Earl of Essex, Elizabeth's favourite, 1596 ; Henry Prince of Wales, eldest son of James I., 1612 ; his brother, Prince Charles; Prince Rupert of the Rhine, 1630. The two cannons were taken in the Punjab in the Sikh war. Two chairs, made from the wood of " Alloway's auld haunted kirk " and from an elm-tree from Waterloo, may be noticed.

4. *St. George's Hall,* in which all the festivities of the Order of the Garter are held, appropriately fitted up by Wyatt, with the coats of arms of all the Knights since the foundation of the Order ; the numbers on each referring to the names painted on the panels below. The banners of the original Knights of the Order

have recently been hung along the top of the walls, immediately beneath the richly decorated ceiling, and their names have been inscribed upon the oak panels in the recesses of the windows. Here are full-length portraits of the following Sovereigns:—

James I., *Vandyke.*
Charles I., *Vandyke.*
Charles II., *Lely.*
James II., *Lely.*
Mary II., *Kneller.*
William III., *Kneller.*
Anne, *Kneller.*
George I., *Kneller.*
George II., *Zeman.*
George III., *Gainsborough.*
George IV., *Lawrence.*

5. The *Grand Reception Room*, a magnificent chamber, ornamented in the style of Louis XIV., and hung with six fine specimens of Gobelin's tapestry, representing the story of the Golden Fleece. It also contains a large malachite vase, presented by the Emperor of Russia.

6. The *Waterloo Chamber* is decorated with portraits of all the chief persons who bore a prominent part in the Congress of Vienna. They are almost all by *Sir Thomas Lawrence*, and were painted for George IV.

Sovereigns are:—Francis I. of Austria, Alexander of Russia, Frederick William of Prussia, Pope Pius VII. (the Pope sate 9 times for this portrait, which is the finest Lawrence ever painted), Charles X., George III. (*Beechey*), George IV. and William IV.—with the royal Dukes of York and Cambridge, Duc d'Angoulême, and Prince Leopold.

Generals: — Wellington, Hill, (*Pickersgill*), Anglesea, Picton, Kempt, Blucher, Platoff, Czernitshoff, Archduke Charles, William Prince of Orange, Prince Schwartzenburg, Duke of Brunswick, Overoff.

Ministers: — Alten, Castlereagh, Liverpool, Canning, Gonsalvi, Metternich, Hardenberg, Nesselrode,

W. von Humboldt, Capo d'Istrias, Bathurst, Munster, Duc de Richelieu.

7. The *Grand Vestibule* contains armour of the time of Elizabeth and Charles I.; a large cannon, sent by Rajah Brooke from Borneo, and a smaller one taken from Tippoo Saib at Seringapatam. At the N. end there is a fine statue of Her Majesty with her favourite dog, Sharp, by Boehm.

8. The *State Ante-room* has a painted ceiling by Verrio, representing a Banquet of the Gods, carvings by Gibbons, and a copy in glass of Reynolds' portrait of George III. in his coronation robes.

9. The *Zuccarelli Room* contains a number of sacred pictures and landscapes by *Zuccarelli*. Over the entrance is Henry Duke of Gloucester, son of Charles I.; on the l. George I. (*Fountaine*) and II.; on the rt. Frederick Prince of Wales, and George III.

10. The *Vandyke Room.*—No gallery in the world can display so many fine portraits by this great master. They are 22 in number :—

1. Portrait erroneously supposed to be Jan Snellincs, the friend of Vandyke.
2. Charles I. on a grey horse, with M. de St. Antoine, his equerry, on foot. This picture formed part of the private collection of Charles I., was sold by the rebels for 200*l.* to Remé van Lemput, a Dutch painter, and recovered by Charles II. through a lawsuit.
3. Mary Countess of Dorset, as St. Agnes, probably only a copy.
4. Prince Charles, aged 9, with Princess Mary and the Duke of York.
5. Henrietta Maria, full length.
6. Portrait of Vandyke himself.
7. Sir Kenelm Digby.
8. Charles II., aged 11, in armour.
9. Lucy Countess of Carlisle.
10 Henrietta Maria, full front.
11. The children of Charles I. In the centre Prince Charles, 7 years of age, with a dog; on his rt. Princesses Elizabeth and Mary; on his l. Princess Anne with Prince James sitting nearly un-

dressed on a stool. 1637. This picture hung in Charles I.'s breakfast-room at Whitehall.

12. Head of Charles I. 3 times on one canvas, painted for Bernini, who executed from it a bust for Whitehall.

13. Madame de St. Croix.

14. Henrietta Maria, in profile, half-length, painted by Vandyke for Bernini to model from.

15. George and Francis Villiers, sons of the 1st Duke of Buckingham. 1635. Belonged to James II.

16. Thomas Prince of Carignan, in armour, with the commander's bâton. A duplicate of this is at Munich.

17. Venetia, wife of Sir Kenelm Digby; a male figure and 2 children bound at her feet, symbolical of Calumny.

| 18. Queen Henrietta Maria, in white silk her hair adorned with pearls and a red band, taking some roses from a table, on which lies the crown. This picture hung in Charles I.'s bedroom.

19. Duchess of Richmond, only daughter of George Villiers 1st Duke of Buckingham, painted as St. Agnes, with the symbols of the Lamb and Palm-branch, with which the silk-dress and expression ill correspond.

20. Thomas Killigrew and Thomas Carew, poets. Dated 1638.

21. Charles I., in royal robes, seated; next him his son Prince Charles; on the l. Henrietta Maria, also seated, little Prince James on her arm. Beyond the pillar the Tower of London in the distance. 1632.

22. Henry, Comte de Berg.

This concludes the series of rooms now shown to the public. Among those formerly exhibited were the following:—

(a.) The *Queen's Closet*, which contained a number of pictures, including portraits of Erasmus, a copy of Holbein (*Pens*); Henry VIII. Edward VI., Sir H. Guildford, and a magnificent portrait of Thomas Howard, Duke of Norfolk, father of the unfortunate Earl of Surrey (*Holbein*); and the celebrated picture of The Misers, said to be the picture whereby *Quentin Matsys*, the smith of Antwerp, is believed to have obtained his wife, an artist's daughter, in marriage, having proved by its execution that he also was an artist. Hence also his epitaph at Antwerp, "Connubialis amor de Mul-

cibre fecit Apellem." "The strength of this picture," says *Kugler*, "lies essentially in the effort at character in the painter's conception of the subject. Two men sit at table; one, who counts his gold, and notes down the sum in his account-book, appears to be a merchant; the other, who familiarly lays his hand on his shoulder, and looks with malicious pleasure towards the spectator, seems to have just succeeded in outwitting him. There are several repetitions and copies of this picture in existence, besides free imitations by later artists."

(b.) The *King's Closet.*—The Emperor Charles V., and the Duke of Alva, *Sir Antony More*; portraits of the painter and his wife, *Van Cleeve*; the Woman of Samaria, *Guercino*; St. Catherine, *Domenichino*; an officer in the Papal Guard, "probably the portrait of Lorenzo Cibo, praised by Vasari," *Parmegiano*; Gardener of the Duke of Florence, with a knife in his hand, *Andrea del Sarto.*

(c.) The *King's Drawing Room*, or the *Rubens Room*, entirely filled with portraits by that master:—

1. His 1st wife, Elizabeth Brandt, one of his finest portraits.
2. St. Martin and the Beggar. The composition probably alone by Rubens, the execution by Vandyke.
3. The Virgin and Infant Saviour, with St. John, St. Francis, St. Elizabeth, and St. Joseph.
4. Philip IV. of Spain, on horseback.
5. The painter himself. This belonged to Charles I.
6. Winter. "The uncomfortable feeling of winter is admirably expressed. Rubens, who painted all and everything, has here even put in the single flecks of snow." (*W.*)
7. Archduke Albert of Austria.
8. Summer. This and its companion-picture belonged to Villiers Duke of Buckingham.
9. Sir Balthazar Gerbier and his family. Supposed with much reason to be by *Vandyke*.
10. Male portrait in ruff.

(d.) The *Council Chamber.*—A female head, *Annibale Caracci*; St.

John, in a landscape, from the collection of Charles I., *Correggio;* the Countess of Desmond, at the age of 120, *Rembrandt ;* Silence; The Virgin and Sleeping Jesus, with St. John approaching, *Annibale Caracci;* Martin Luther; Stallhof; a German merchant reading a note; Head of a young German, *Holbein ;* 2 interiors of churches, the dark effect remarkably good, *Peter Neefs ;* John Duke of Marlborough, *Kneller ;* William Duke of Cumberland, *Sir J. Reynolds.*

The *Private Apartments of the Queen* are handsome, and the views from the windows are magnificent. A *Corridor,* 520 ft. long, by *Sir J. Wyattville,* gives access to the entire suite of apartments, and runs round the S. and E. sides of the quadrangle. It is filled with choice works of art, and the walls are decorated with pictures, including, Maria Theresa at Presburg on the day of her coronation; all the state events in the reign of the present Queen, her coronation, her marriage, the baptism and the marriage of the Prince of Wales, &c. ; *Canaletti's* views of Venice and Rome, among the best that he ever painted : the Grand Canal, St. Mark's and the procession of the Bucentaur, the Giant's Stairs, and the Arch of Titus and Temple of Jupiter Stator at Rome are the most remarkable. Other landscapes, in which some of the chief buildings in London are introduced, are by *Zuccarelli.*

Among the portraits are those of Pitt, Thurlow, Eldon, Canning, Sir W. Scott, Sir W. Curtis, and of the Princess Charlotte when a child, by *Lawrence.* There are busts of Her Majesty when a child, of her royal uncles, of Pitt, Fox, Sheridan, Lord Grey, Canning, Wellesley, the authors of Great Britain, and many military heroes. including Wellington, Blucher, Platoff, &c.

Among the many beautiful cabinets is one which belonged to Car-

dinal Wolsey. The Queen's private staircase is prettily conceived, and, being triangular in its plan, shows a difficulty ingeniously overcome by the architect.

Between the Long Corridor and St. George's Hall, is a small *Passage,* panelled with interesting pictures of the Tudor family, and of the leading characters of the time of the Reformation, including Luther as "Junker Georg," and Linacre the physician.

The *King's Room,* with a large window, looking on the private garden, is that in which George IV. and William IV. died. Hither the Prince Consort was removed the week before his death, and here he died, Dec. 14, 1861.

The *Great Drawing Room* is noticeable for its magnificent furniture of red silk; the *Dining Room* for its rich mirrors and gilded Gothic tracery, and for its solid silver-gilt wine-cooler by *Flaxman,* decorated with vine tendrils, foliage, and grapes, among which little cupids are sporting. The *Armoury,* composed of objects presented to the different kings on various occasions, and arranged under the superintendence of the late Prince Consort, may now be considered one of the finest collections of the kind in the kingdom. The *Plate Room* contains, among its curiosities, the St. George candelabra of silver, 4 ft. high; a wine-fountain taken in the Spanish Armada : a Mexican bread-basket of gold; Nell Gwynn's gold bellows; *Flaxman's* Shield of Achilles; a nautilus shell set in gold, by *Benvenuto Cellini;* a jug which belonged to Charles XII. of Sweden, taken at Pultawa; the footstool of Tippoo Saib, a tiger-head of gold, with teeth of crystal, and a jewelled bird, which crowned the canopy of his throne.

The *Royal Private Library* contains a magnificent collection of *Drawings by the Old Masters ;* those of *Leonardo da Vinci* are contained in 3 vols., a collection unrivalled, and approached only by those of the ex-Grand Duke of Tuscany, and that in the Ambrosian Library at Milan. The drawings by *Michael Angelo* are numerous, comprising several studies for the frescoes in the Sistine Chapel, and others mentioned by Vasari. 53 drawings are attributed to *Rafaelle*, from which Passavant has selected 18 as genuine, comprising studies for the cartoon of 'Feeding Sheep' at Hampton Court, for the figure of Poetry in the Camera della Segnatura, for the Expulsion of Adam and Eve in the Loggie of the Vatican, and for the figure of Jonah in Sta. Maria del Popolo. There are also drawings by *Luca Signorelli* (a study for Orvieto); *Fra Bartolomeo*; *Andrea del Sarto*; *Filippo Lippi*; *Correggio*; *Parmegianino.* Several volumes contain drawings of *Guido Reni*; 2 those of Rafaelle's pupils, especially *Giulio Romano* and *Caravaggio*; 11 the *Caracci*; 16 *Guercino*; 24 *Domenichino*; beside several of *Claude*, *Poussin*, and *Albert Dürer.* But the gems of the collection are 2 vols., containing 87 portraits, by *Holbein*, of the court of Henry VIII., comprising those of Jane Seymour, Prince Edward as a child, Dean Colet, and More. Another collection, of *English Historical Prints*, perhaps the most valuable in England, was made for Windsor by the Queen and the Prince Consort, and was alphabetically arranged by the latter with his well-known taste and judgment. There is also a valuable collection of miniatures of the Royal family from the time of Henry VII. The windows of the library overlook the beautiful Eton playing-fields. One is in a recess, which formed the boudoir of Queen Anne, in which the scene of Mrs. Masham and the cup of tea is said to have taken place. The *Terrace*, more than 2900 ft. long, which surrounds the Upper

Ward of the Castle on 3 sides should on no account remain unvisited. It is the finest walk of the kind in existence. Evelyn says of it, "The Terrace towards Eton, with the Park, the meandering Thames, and sweet meadows, yields one of most delightful prospects in the world." At the E. end a projection has been thrown out, which encircles the Queen's *Private Flower Garden.* From the W. end of the Terrace may be seen the huge inscription on the Winchester Tower, "Hoc fecit Wykeham." Abp. Parker relates that these words were originally placed here by William of Wykeham himself while building the Castle, and that the King would have been seriously offended at his thus arrogating to himself the credit of the building, if the prelate had not adroitly explained the inscription to mean that the Castle made *him.* Wyattville perpetuated the inscription by affixing these letters to the ashlar work of the Tower. On this Terrace Elizabeth walked for an hour every day, attended by her court; it was also the favourite walk of both the Charleses, and Charles I. constructed an ornamental gate at its E. extremity, the very gate beneath whose pediment afterwards paced the guard who held him in captivity. The family processions here, in the time of George III., are described by Mad. D'Arblay:—"The King and Queen, the Prince of Mecklenburgh, and Her Majesty's mother, walked together; next them, the princesses and their ladies, and the young princes, making a very gay and pleasing procession of one of the finest families in the world. Every way they moved, the crowd retired to stand up against the wall as they passed, and then closed in to follow." The whole length of the Terrace is thrown open on Saturday and Sunday, and is enlivened on Sunday evenings by a band of music.

Below the Terrace are the *Slopes*, planted with a variety of trees and shrubs, intersected by shady walks, but to which the public are not admitted. At the foot of the Slopes was the Tournament-ground, where Edward III. used to take part in the jousts, with his shield bearing a white swan, and the motto:—

"Hay, hay, the white swan,
By God's soul, I am thy man."

The *Home Park*, immediately adjoins the Castle, and incloses 500 acres: it was walled by William III. In this Park, and the fields near Frogmore, Shakespeare laid many scenes of the 'Merry Wives of Windsor.' It was here particularly that Falstaff, disguised as "a Windsor Stag," was tormented by the fairies. A withered and barkless oak, enclosed by a railing, long stood in the line of the avenue of elms, and bore the name of *Herne's Oak* (according to tradition, Herne was a woodman who had in some way incurred the displeasure of Queen Elizabeth, and hung himself on a tree that she would have to pass), though it is more probable that the real tree was accidentally cut down by George III. in 1796. It was blown down in Aug. 1863, but a young oak has been planted in its place.

"There is an old tale goes that Herne the hunter,
Sometime a keeper here in Windsor Forest,
Doth all the winter time, at still midnight,
Walk round about an oak, with great ragged horns,
And there he blasts the tree and takes the cattle,
And makes milch kine yield blood, and shakes a chain
In a most hideous and dreadful manner.
. . . . . Marry, this is our device,
That Falstaff at that oak shall meet with us,
Disguised like Herne, with huge horns on his head."—*Shakespeare.*

Not far off is *Adelaide Lodge*, a cottage of the late Queen Adelaide, consisting of 2 unpretending rooms, with a garden laid out by her.

Frogmore House, near the road leading to Runnymede and Egham, was formerly the residence of Queen Charlotte, and of the Princess Augusta, who died here, Sept. 22, 1840. Here also Her Majesty's mother, the Duchess of Kent, died, March 16, 1860, after a lingering illness. Her remains are interred in a *Mausoleum* in the grounds, which was begun by her order during her lifetime, but was not completed till after her death. It is a small circular structure consisting of two chambers surmounted by a dome, supported by 16 Ionic columns. The lower chamber contains the remains of Her Royal Highness, in a sarcophagus of grey granite, while in the upper one there is a very beautiful marble statue of the Duchess by Theed. In front of the Mausoleum there is a monumental cross of Cairngall granite, erected by the Queen to the memory of Lady Augusta Stanley (d. March 1st, 1876), the wife of Dean Stanley, and for 30 years in the service of Her Majesty and the Duchess of Kent. In the same grounds, and within sight of this, is the *Mausoleum* of the Prince Consort; a magnificent memorial, erected by Her Majesty from designs by Professor Grüner and Mr. Humbert. The first stone was laid in March 1862. The body is interred under the dome, and covered by a recumbent marble effigy, by Baron Marochetti. The walls of the interior of the building are panelled with rich marbles, and are further decorated by bas-reliefs, urns and statues in niches, and frescoes. The floor is inlaid with polished marbles, the ceiling with Venetian mosaics, and the windows are filled with stained glass. In 1881 a memorial cenotaph to the Princess Alice was placed within the Mausoleum by Her Majesty. It is surmounted by an exquisitely sculptured effigy of the Princess in white marble by Boehm. The Mausoleums are never shown to the public.

2 m. E. of the town, on the right bank of the Thames, is the village of *Old Windsor*, where, on a site probably to the W. of the ch., near the river, was the palace of Edward the Confessor, which was the predecessor of the Castle. Here, according to Fabyan, the great Earl Godwin died :— "Sitting at the King's board, with the other lords, he perceived that the King suspected him of his brother Alfred's death, and said, ' So may I safely swallow this morsel of bread, that I hold in my hand, as I am guiltless of the deed.' But as soon as he had received the bread, forthwith he was choked. And the King commanded that he should be drawn from the table, and so conveyed to Winchester, and there buried." Here William of Malmesbury narrates that Wulwin, a blind wood-cutter, besought the King to restore his sight, when the King, mildly answering, " By our Lady, I shall be grateful if God, through my means, shall choose to take pity upon a wretched creature," laid his hands on the blind man, when the blood dripped from his eyes, and he saw, exclaiming with rapture. " I see you, O King! I see you, O King !" Here also Roger of Wendover tells that Earl Tosti seized his brother Harold by the hair when about to pledge the King in a cup of wine at the banquet; Harold caught him in his arms, and dashed him violently against the ground, till they were parted by the soldiers.

Windsor Great Park is separated from the Castle by part of the town, and by the high road. Besides large portions used as farms, it contains about 1800 acres, which abound in delightful drives and walks, through forest-scenery, and are occupied by herds of deer. Here Henry VIII. rode forth hawking, and held his great archery meetings, at one of which Barlow, a Londoner, so out-shot the rest that the King dubbed

him Duke of Shoreditch : and here also Elizabeth used to hunt in the early morning, and, as a special compliment, would cut the throat of the deer with her own hand.

The Park is traversed for 3 m. by the great avenue known as the *Long Walk* (begun by Charles II., and completed by William III.), which passes the site of the Upper Lodge, the residence of the Princess Anne, when under the displeasure of William III., and afterwards inhabited for many years by George III. and his family. Hither the materials of Holbein's Gate at Whitehall, removed 1759, were brought by the Duke of Cumberland, who intended to have erected it as a termination to the avenue, but his death prevented the execution of the design. The carriage-road down this avenue was constructed in 1710. Parallel to this, on W., runs the Queen's Walk, an avenue planted under Queen Anne, 1707.

At the extremity of the Long Walk is *Snow Hill*, where, raised on a block of granite, stands a colossal equestrian leaden statue of George III. in a Roman toga, by *Westmacott*. The view of the Castle from hence, with groups of beech-trees in the foreground, is exceedingly fine. ½ m. S.E. from the extremity of the Long Walk is *Cumberland Lodge*, the residence of the Duke who conquered at Culloden. Not far from it stood the *Royal Lodge*, a cottage in the Gothic style, built by George IV., and forming his favourite retreat, in which he spent the last years of his life, secluded as much as possible from public view. After his death it was all pulled down, except the Dining-room and Conservatory. Near it stands a tasteless modern *Gothic Chapel*. Close to *Sandpit Gate* is the *Heronry*, celebrated for its beech-trees.

1 m. l. of Snow Hill is *Cranbourne Lodge*. (Rte. 2.)

A delightful drive of 3 m. leads

from Snow Hill to *Virginia Water* (*Inn*: Wheatsheaf), the largest artificial lake in the kingdom, formed at great expense, and fed by a running stream, which escapes from it in an artificial cascade by the side of the Bagshot road. The banks are wooded, but flat and uninteresting: they are adorned on one side by a Swiss Cottage, which has replaced the *Chinese fishing-temple*, from the gallery in front of which George IV. used almost daily to enjoy the amusement of angling; and on the other, by fragments of a picturesque *Colonnade* of porphyry, granite, and marble, brought from the ruins of Leptis Magna, near Tripoli. Upon the lake used to float a miniature frigate. Other objects in this part of the grounds are the *Hermitage*, on a height overlooking the water; the *Belvedere*, a turreted triangular building, with a battery of 21 guns, used by the Duke of Cumberland in the campaign of 1745; and the *Cascade*, near the Bagshot road, adjoining which is a sort of grotto, formed of stones dug up on Bagshot Heath, and supposed to have been a cromlech.

At Virginia Water is a Stat. on the branch of the South-Western Railway from London to Reading. (Rte. 3.)

The return to Windsor by road may be varied by taking the road by Englefield green, Coopers hill, and Old Windsor.

Windsor Forest, which once measured 120 m. in circumference, is now almost entirely enclosed, and converted into arable land, but here and there a wild bit of wood and common remains, which, with patches of heath in the sandy soil, still give the country something of a forest-like character.

To Dropmore, Cliefden, and Burnham Beeches, a drive of 17 m., is a pleasant day's *Excursion*. (Rte. 10.)

ROUTE 2.

WINDSOR TO READING, BY CLEWER, WINKFIELD, AND BINFIELD.

By Road. 18 m.

The village of *Clewer* lies 1 m. W. of the direct road, and is well worth a visit. The *Church* of St. Andrew, originally Norm., was restored in 1855. It contains a leaden font of great antiquity; also a tablet to Field Marshal Earl Harcourt, the confidential attendant for many years of George III. and his family (d. 1830), and a brass plate commemorating the prowess of a Berkshire bowman :—

" He that lyeth under this stone
Shot with 100 men, himself alone.
This is true that I doe say,
The match was shot at Oldfield, at Bray;
I will tell you before you goe hence,
That his name was Martyne Expence."

St. Stephen's Church, erected in 1872, is a brick building in the E. E. style. Attached to it are middle-class and national schools, and a college for ladies.

At Clewer is a large establishment, the *House of Mercy*, or Church Penitentiary, founded in 1849, a red-brick building of ornamental aspect, by *Woodyer*. About 80 female penitents are maintained in it, under the direction of a Warden and several Sisters, who wear a peculiar dress. The chapel, fitted up with stalls for the Sisters and chairs for the penitents, is simple, but very beautiful, adorned with coloured brick-work in the interior, with a high timber-roof and richly-stained windows; the altarpiece is exquisitely carved. An inner court has a large stone cross. The establishment has been greatly enlarged of late, and now comprises also an *Orphanage* for 40 children, a convalescent hospital, and a cottage hospital for ladies of limited means. The whole is well worth inspection.

Clewer Park (Sir D. Gooch, Bart., M.P.) contains three or four good pictures, including — *Murillo*, the Assumption of the Virgin, with the Apostles surrounding the empty tomb; The Virgin seated, showing the sleeping Infant to St. Joseph, the infant St. John in adoration. *J. Ruysdael*, Sea View in Holland; *Weenix*, Dead Game. The rest of the pictures were sold in June 1876.

Passing Clewer-green and *St. Leonard's Hill* (Sir T. H. L. Brinckman, Bart.), we have at 3 m., on l., *Cranbourne*, on the outskirts of Windsor Great Park. Some huge oaks still remain; one, 36 ft. in circumference, is called William the Norman. Only a fragment now exists of *Cranbourne Lodge*, a hunting-seat, built by Lord Ranelagh in the reign of Charles II., and successively inhabited by Charles Duke of St. Alban's, William Duke of Cumberland, the Duke of York, the Duke of Gloucester, and the Princess Charlotte.

6 m. *Winkfield*. The Perp. *Church* has been almost rebuilt, but retains its 17th-centy. brick tower. Among other monuments it contains one to Lord Metcalfe (d. 1846), of Indian celebrity, with epitaph by Lord Macaulay. There is also a curious mural *Brass*, which represents Thos. Montagu, in his dress as yeoman of the guard, holding his halberd in one hand, and with the other distributing loaves to the poor (d. 1630). The village contains a group of model cottages similar to those that were erected on the ground adjoining the Exhibition of 1851. N. of the village is *Winkfield Park* (Gilbert Blane, Esq.), and beyond that, *New Lodge*, a very beautiful modern house (Madame Van de Weyer).

7 m. *Warfield*. Here is a very handsome Dec. and Perp. *Church*, with a fine E. window of 5 lights, 3 sedilia and a piscina, 2 stone screens, a *Brass* (Humphrey Staverton, 1592), and several monuments of the Walsh family, now ennobled as Lords Ormathwaite. The Church was completely restored in 1876 by G. E. Street, at a cost of £3000. *Warfield Park* (Lord Ormathwaite).

10 m. N. 1 m. is *Binfield*. The *Church*, originally E. E., has been almost rebuilt, and added to, in 1848 and 1859. It retains a handsomely carved oak pulpit, with the hour-glass stand bearing the arms of the Smiths' and Farriers' Company of London (1628). There is also a small *Brass*, with French inscription, for Walter de Annesfordhe, a priest (1361), and several modern memorial windows. Here also is the grave of Catherine Macaulay, the female historian of the last century; her principal work was the 'History of England from the Accession of James I. to the Revolution.' She died at Binfield, June 23, 1791. Binfield was the early home of Pope, who speaks of his father's house here as—

" My paternal cell,
A little house, with trees a-row,
And, like its master, very low."

1½ m. from the ch., in the woods of *Binfield Park House* formerly the seat of Mrs. Young, but sold in 1877 to Lord Arthur Hill, is a grove of beech-trees, which was a favourite resort of the poet, who is said to have composed many of his earlier pieces beneath a tree which formerly existed here, with the inscription " Here Pope sung," but which is now destroyed. W. of Binfield is *Billingbear Park* (Lord Braybrooke).

12 m. 2 m. N. is *Hurst*, with a ch. of little interest externally, but containing some fine monuments, especially that of Lady Margaret Savile, the widow of Sir H. Savile, the Provost of Eton, and founder of

the Savilian Professorships in Oxford; and others for the Harrisons of Hurst Place, an Elizabethan mansion, where the Queen of Bohemia once resided. Sir Richard Harrison raised two troops of horse for the service of Charles I. : he and his lady have a splendid monument of white marble. Secretary Windebank, the friend of Laud, was a native of Hurst, and was visited there by him when Bishop of St. David's, on which occasion, as he records in his Diary, he preached several times in the ch. (once on the occasion of a public fast, July 20, 1625), and also visited Hurst Place.

We rejoin the Reading road at 13½ m.; and at 18 m. reach Reading, the road and the rly. detailed in Rte. 3 being nearly parallel.

ROUTE 3.

STAINES TO READING, BY SUNNING-DALE, ASCOT, AND WOKINGHAM.

South-Western Railway. 25 m.

For the route to Staines and thence to Egham see Handbook for Surrey. The first stat. in Berkshire is

24 m. Virginia Water (Stat.); 2 m. E. of the large artificial lake from which it has its name (Rte. 1).

At Virginia Water, there is a branch through Chertsey and Addlestone to the main line at Weybridge.

28 m. Sunningdale (Stat.). This is a newly settled district on the border of the forest, and abounds in beautiful scenery. The ch. is a brick and stone edifice in the Lombardic style. 1 m. W. is Sunninghill, where
[Berks, &c.]

there is a small inn called the Wells Hotel, once very celebrated for the 2 chalybeate springs which still remain in its old-fashioned garden, and which were a great object of resort from Windsor. The ch. was rebuilt in 1828, and has lately been restored. The churchyard has a fine old yew-tree. In the Vicarage garden are 3 trees, planted by Burke, Chesterfield, and Bolingbroke respectively. The country here is entirely occupied by a succession of parks and gentlemen's seats, the largest of which is Silwood Park (C. P. Stewart, Esq.).

At Sunninghill Walter Scott visited Canning's friend George Ellis, and "Mr. and Mrs. Ellis heard the first two or three cantos of the unpublished 'Lay of the Last Minstrel' under an old oak in Windsor Forest."—See Lockhart's Life of Scott.

30 m. Ascot (Stat.). The Racecourse, with its handsome Grand Stand, is very near the stat., and occupies an elevated situation, which commands fine views over the surrounding country, consisting of heathery downs, interspersed with woods of fir and birch. The course is circular, and is only short of 2 m. by 66 yds. The first half is on the descent, and the last half, called the Old Mile, is up-hill the greater part of the way. The last 1½ m. of the above is called the Swinley Course. When the rest of Windsor Forest was enclosed, the racecourse and the avenues thereto were directed by Act of Parliament to be "kept and continued as a racecourse for the public use at all times." The races, which take place early in June, were founded by the Duke of Cumberland (the hero of Culloden), one of the most conspicuous characters on the English turf of past days, and the breeder of the famous horse Eclipse. "From the death of Charles II., till the period of the
D

Duke's coming upon the turf, racing had languished, perhaps from want of more support from the Crown and the higher aristocracy, and H. R. H. was the man to revive it. This was not effected without difficulty. Having, however, the military maxim of ' Persevere and conquer,' he was not deterred from the object of his pursuit, till he became possessed of the best stock, best blood, and most numerous stud in the kingdom." (*Quart. Rev. XLIX., Darvill's English Race-horse*). The Races are held in June, and are very popular, the presence of Royalty adding interest to them. A cup was given to Ascot Races by the Emperor Nicholas of Russia after his visit to England; this being refused at the time of the Crimean war, the gift was continued by the Emperor of the French.

Ascot Heath (*Inn* : Ascot H.) now contains many handsome modern residences, a brick ch. in E. E. style, the Royal kennels, for H. M.'s Buckhounds, some training establishments, and the extensive *Nursery* of Messrs. Standish. To the S.W. extend the *Swinley Woods*, a large tract of still unenclosed forest-land, containing many picturesque ferny glades, and fine old oaks. *Swinley Paddocks* are a preserve of deer for the Great Park.

" Here waving groves a chequer'd scene display,
And part admit, and part exclude the day ;
There, interspers'd in lawns and opening glades,
Thin trees arise that shun each other's shades.
Here in full light the russet plains extend ;
There wrapt in clouds the blueish hills ascend."
          Pope's ' Windsor Forest.'

33 m. *Bracknell* (Stat.). The village consists mainly of one long street, with a handsome modern E. E. church of chalk and flint, the chancel of which was restored in 1874. 2 m. W. is the mother parish of *Easthamp-*

stead, which had a royal residence, in occasional use as late as the time of James I. The *Church*, rebuilt in 1867, is in a mixed Byzantine and E. E. style, and retains the pulpit of the old ch., dated 1631, as well as the monuments of Sir William Trumbull (d. 1716), Secretary of State in the reign of William III., and his lady, the friends and correspondents of Pope, who wrote the epitaph of Sir William, which is extant in his works, but is not inscribed upon the monument. Here is the monument of the poet Fenton, also a friend of Pope, with an epitaph by him, 1732. He had long resided in the Trumbull family as tutor, and he died here, " of indolence and inactivity," as Pope declares in one of his letters. Notice in the churchyard a noble yew-tree, 63 ft. in circumference.

4 m. N.W. of Bracknell Stat., and about equidistant from Ascot Stat. is Bracknell Road, a larger village, with several gentlemen's houses in and about it.

Easthampstead Park (Marquis of Downshire) is a modern building in the Elizabethan style, and occupies the site of the old hunting-seat.

1 m. S. of Easthampstead Park is an irregular fortification, on an eminence, with a double ditch, known as *Cæsar's Camp*, S. of which, running across Bagshot Heath, are traces of a Roman road, known as the *Devil's Highway*. From the camp the handsome buildings of *Wellington College* (*post*) are very conspicuous.

38 m. *Wokingham Stat.* The line from Staines here joins the Reading branch of the S. E. Rly. (*Inn* : Rose). The town (Pop. 3100) stands on high ground on the verge of the old royal Forest, and gave the title of Baron to Prince George of Denmark, the husband of Queen Anne. Before

the opening of the rly. it was in a somewhat secluded position, and the sport of bull-baiting is said to have been carried on in it later than at any other place in England. The Dec. and Perp. *Church* has a grave-slab for Godwin, Bp. of Bath and Wells, who was a native, and died here, 1590; as also some 16th-centy. brasses. It was restored in 1864, when also a district ch. was erected, the pop. having greatly increased. In the centre of the town is a showy pile of buildings by *Poulton* and *Woodman* of Reading, replacing the ancient Town-hall. Among various charities is one founded by Abp. Laud, and at Luckley Green is *Lucas Hospital*, for 16 poor men, the gift of Henry Lucas, 1665. The Rose Inn gave rise to the song of 'Molly Mog;' the story being, that Gay, Swift, Pope, and Arbuthnot amused themselves, when detained here by the wet weather, in the composition of a song, to which each contributed a verse in turn, taking the fair maid of the inn as their subject. "John Mog was then landlord of the Rose, and had two daughters, Molly and Sally, of whom Sally was in fact the cruel beauty and the subject of the song. But each with was too far gone to distinguish—

"His senses all lost in a fog;
And nothing could give satisfaction
But thinking of sweet Molly Mog."

So the honour, if honour there be, has clung to Molly, who, after all, died a spinster in 1766, at the age of 67." The lover, who is represented as pining for her, is said to have been the last heir male of the Standens of Arborfield (*post*).

1 m. W. of Wokingham is the fine estate of *Bearwood* (J. Walter, Esq., M.P.) a large and beautiful park, retaining much of its wild forest character, interspersed with masses of rhododendrons, which render it a blaze of colour in spring, and con-

taining a large artificial lake. The *House*, rebuilt in 1869 by *Kerr*, is a stately edifice of red brick with stone facings. It has a gallery, 70 ft. by 24 ft., which contains a fine collection of pictures, chiefly of the Dutch school of the 17th centy. The most remarkable are—

Drawing Room.—Paul Potter, a cattle-piece, painted on wood, signed and dated 1647. "At a certain distance the effect of the animals is that of life itself, and the carefulness of execution is such—for instance in the ear of the light-coloured cow—that the delusion of reality is increased on the closest inspection." (*W.*) *Berghem*, 2 landscapes with figures and cattle. *Karel Dujardin*. Peter de Hoghe, a Dutch garden with figures. *Sasso Ferrato*, Virgin and Child. *Gonzales Cocques*, a family group in a landscape: "one of the finest works of this rare and charming master." (*W.*) *Isaac and Adrian von Ostade.*

Dining Room.—Jacob Ruysdael, view of the castle of the Counts of Bentheim on the Lower Rhine. There are repetitions of this subject at Dresden and Amsterdam, which are far surpassed by this, which was probably painted as a commission for Count Bentheim himself. *Adrian von Ostade*, Adoration of the Shepherds: "tone golden and clear, execution spirited and careful." (*W.*) *Isaac von Ostade*, peasants passing a ford: "remarkable for clear and glowing colouring and spirited execution." (*W.*)

Middle Drawing Room.—Francesco Albano, Christ appearing to the Magdalen. *Jan van der Heyden*, a landscape, with figures by *A. van de Velde*. *Frans Mieris*, portrait of a young painter holding a palette, signed 1667. *Nicholas Maas*, portrait of an old woman seated.

Hall.—J. Baptista Weenix, a seaport: "a rich picture, clear in colour, and careful in execution." (*W.*) *Abraham Mignon*, a fruit-piece. *Jo-*

hann George Plazer, " 2 pictures, richly finished, but crude and un-mannered."

The village of Bearwood, a district detached from Hurst in 1845, has a very pretty small *Church* built by the late Mr. Walter, who is buried in the ch.-yard. Within the ch. is a monumental effigy by Noble, erected by the Humane Society, to J. Balston Walter, who lost his life in rescuing his younger brother from the frozen lake of Bearwood. There is a fine view from the hill on which the ch. stands, and on the slope are *Alms-houses* for aged servants of 'The Times.'

3 m. W. of Wokingham is *Arbor-field*, formerly the property of the Bullocks, one of whom was known as " Hugh of the Brazen Hand." *Arbor-field Hall* (Mrs. Hargreaves). In the old manor-house, described in 'Our Village' under the name of " The Old House at Aberleigh," Mr. Standen, the unlucky suitor of Molly Mog, died at the age of 27.

2 m. W., in the parish of Shin-field, is the site of *Beaumys Castle*, built by Nicholas Lord de la Beche, 1338, which underwent "an out-rageous assault in 1352, when John de Dalton, coming with an armed force, killed Michael de Poynings, uncle to Lord Poynings, Thomas le Clerk, and others; frightened the chaplain to death; and carried off several prisoners, among whom was Margaret Lady de la Beche."— *Lysons.*

3. m. S.W. of Arborfield is *Swal-lowfield*, where Clarendon had a house, at which Lysons and others, without much foundation, assert that he wrote his celebrated History. Miss Mitford died at Swallowfield in Jan. 1855, and is buried under a lofty cross in the churchyard. *Swal-lowfield Park* (Col. Sir Chas. Rus-sell, Bt., V.C.).

[From Wokingham, *Wellington College* and the *Royal Military College, Sandhurst*, may be readily visited by rail, there being stat. for each on the Reading and Reigate line.

Wellington College (Stat.). *Inn :* Wellington Hotel, comfortable. *Wel-lington College*, founded in memory of the Great Duke, for the educa-tion of sons of officers of the army, the first stone was laid by the Queen, June 2, 1856. It occupies a wild and elevated situation on an open sandy height, and has a fine view over the country. The build-ings are of brick, in the Louis XV. style, with high pitched roofs, from designs by *Shaw;* to which *Sir G. G. Scott* has since added a *Chapel* and *Library*, in Italian Gothic. The chapel, erected at a cost of 8000*l*., is of 6 bays with apsidal ending, and surmounted by a graceful spire rising to the height of 120 ft.; the screen and stalls are of carved oak, erected in memory of the Prince Consort, one of whose latest public acts was the laying of the foundation-stone. The entrance-gateway in the centre is surmounted by the arms of the great Duke; and statues and busts of military men adorn the front and the cloister. The plan of the college consists of two quadrangles, surrounded by arcades of commu-nication; the first being the school quadrangle, the second the hall quadrangle. In the former, on the N., is the entrance-gateway, with the porter's lodge and office on each side of it; also the head-master's residence on one side, and the steward's on the other. On the S. side is the school, in the centre of the building, and on the E. and W. sides the class-room and boys' library. In the second quadrangle on the S. side is the hall, on the E. side the kitchen and domestic offices, and on the W. the under-masters' rooms and their library.

In the kitchen-court is a large plunging-bath for the boys. The upper stories comprehend the dormitories, divided into separate rooms, and extending from N. to S. on the E. and W. sides of the two quadrangles; the hall and school running transversely, and being only one story in height.

The great *Broadmoor Prison* for criminal lunatics at Crowthorne, is about 1½ m. from Wellington College Stat.

Blackwater (Stat.). *Sandhurst College* is near the stat., but 2 m. from the village. It is encircled by fir plantations, and has a rather extensive lake, which is made use of for instruction in pontooning, &c. The College is a plain Doric edifice, with a handsome portico, and was calculated to contain 400 cadets and 30 senior students, besides masters and officers, but the number has not been kept up. A chapel, riding-school, gymnasium, and observatory, are attached to the College; and in the grounds are a cemetery, and a rifle range. The first branches of this institution were temporarily placed at High Wycombe in 1799, and were removed to Great Marlow in 1802, by their founder H. R. H. the late Duke of York, whence they came here on the erection of the present building in 1812. The affairs of the college are under the control of a board of commissioners, under the presidency of the Commander in Chief, and the post of Governor is usually filled by a General. The course of study has of late been considerably modified, and now gives especial prominence to modern languages. The cadets reside in the college, but the officers and tutors have separate houses, which form a terrace and a square. Along the Bagshot and Frimley roads extend some clusters of houses, termed *York Town* and *Cambridge Town*, which present nothing remarkable. The *Church* of Sandhurst is modern E.E., but preserves the Norm.

font, and a brass, 1608. At Blackwater, the 3 counties join. The S.E. rly. continues by Aldershot, Guildford, and Reigate, to London.]

43 m. *Earley* (Stat.) Earley may almost be considered a suburb of Reading, and has only sprung up since 1867. It includes the site of the once famous seat of *White Knights*, now divided into a number of residences with spacious pleasure-grounds. Sir H. Englefield built the house on the site of a hospital for lepers, and it afterwards became the property of the 4th Duke of Marlborough, who rendered its gardens celebrated by their valuable collection of foreign trees. *Earley Court* (Captain J. F. Hall) and *Bulmershe Court* (J. J. Wheble, Esq.) lie N. of White Knights. At Early Court, Scott, Lord Stowell, died in 1836; and Bulmershe Court was the residence of Mr. Addington (afterwards Viscount Sidmouth), who here often entertained Pitt, Windham and others of his eminent colleagues.

45 m. Reading (Stat.) (Rte. 4.)

ROUTE 4.

MAIDENHEAD TO DIDCOT, BY TWYFORD, READING, PANGBOURNE [WALLINGFORD].

Great Western Rly. 30¾ m.

½ m. after leaving Taplow Stat. (Rte. 11) the Rly. crosses the Thames by a very fine bridge with elliptical arches, and enters Berks. Immediately N. is the town of *Maiden-*

head, with a Stat. on the Thame and Oxford line (Rte. 12.)

Maidenhead (*Inns:* Orkney Arms, beyond the Bridge; Bear, in the town), a market town on the rt. bank of the Thames, and on the old Bath road (Pop. 8219); the main street was formerly filled with inns and posting-houses. The beauty of the surrounding scenery makes the place the residence of many opulent families. The chief attractions are the Banks of the Thames, Dropmore, Cliefden, and Burnham Beeches. The name is by Leland said to refer to the head of a certain British virgin presented here; but it is properly Maidenbythe, a wharf for timber having existed at this spot from very early times. The town is singularly devoid of objects of interest, though Mr. Gorham, afterwards of Brampton-Speke, once a curate here, has filled a volume with its history, the most important event of which is, the incorporation by Edward III. in 1352 of a guild to keep the wooden bridge in repair. This bridge was the scene of a fierce skirmish Jan. 5, 1400, between the new made King Henry IV. and the partisans of Richard II.; the Duke of Surrey (Richard's brother) held the bridge till night, so as to allow his friends to make good their retreat, "and then," says the chronicler, "stole away quietly, taking away with him all of the town horse and foot, to serve King Richard." (*Chron. de la Traison et Mort de Rich. II*). The bridge was superseded in 1772 by the present structure, a good work by Sir R. Taylor, well seen from the railway. The ch. ˙was replaced in 1826 by a structure of very small architectural pretensions, but which perpetuates the legendary origin of the name of the town by a painted window. The ch. of St. Luke was erected in 1867, and is of freestone in the E.E. style. The modern ch. of *Boyne Hill* (in the

parish of Bray) is a handsome structure of red and white brick, with lofty spire, and deserving a visit for the sake of its glass, its carvings, and its reminiscences of religious controversies.

At Maidenhead, in July, 1647, Charles I., after several years' separation, was allowed to meet his three children at the Greyhound Inn. The town was strewn with flowers and decked with green boughs. They dined, and drove to Caversham, where apartments were prepared in which they passed 2 days together.

Maidenhead Thicket, which lies to the W. of the town, had formerly so bad a repute, that, in the reign of Elizabeth, the Vicar of Hurley, who served the cure of Maidenhead, was allowed an extra salary as amends for the danger of passing it.

1½ m. S. of Maidenhead, on the rt. bank of the river, is the *Church* of *Bray,* a large building of E. E. and Dec. style, with a Perp. tower of stone and flint; restored in 1859. It contains some good *Brasses,* from 1378 to 1594, particularly one for Sir John Foxle and his 2 wives, which is a fine example engraved by Waller; but its chief celebrity in common estimation arises from its versatile vicar, Simon Aleyn (d. 1588), who is described by Fuller as living under Henry VIII., Edward VI., Mary, and Elizabeth, and being "first a Papist, then a Protestant, then a Papist, then a Protestant again. He had seen some martyrs burnt at Windsor, and found this fire too hot for his tender temper. This vicar being taxed by one with being a turncoat and an unconstant changeling, 'Not so,' said he, 'for I have always kept my principle, which is this, to live and die the vicar of Bray.'" Hence his declaration in the well known ballad:—

" To teach my flock I never miss'd,
  Kings were by God appointed;
And they are damn'd who dare resist
  Or touch the Lord's anointed.
And this is law, I will maintain
  Unto my dying day, sir,
That, whatsoever king shall reign,
  I 'll be the vicar of Bray, sir."

In connexion with another vicar, the story is told that James I., when hunting one day, rode on before his hounds to search for luncheon, and came to the inn at Maidenhead, when the landlord lamented that he had nothing left in his house, for the Vicar of Bray and his curate were upstairs, and had ordered all that there was, but perhaps they would allow him to join them. The king went upstairs and asked permission, which was glumly given by the vicar, but cordially by the curate. All dinner time the king told so many stories that he made them roar with laughter. At last came the bill, when the king, searching his empty pockets, protested that he had left his purse behind him, and could not pay: upon which the vicar angrily protested that he would not pay for him, but the curate expressed his pleasure in being able to make some return for the amusement he had given them. The bill paid, they all went out upon the balcony, when the huntsmen, riding into the town and seeing the king, went down upon one knee in the street, as was then the custom. The vicar, overwhelmed with confusion, flung himself at the king's feet and implored forgiveness ; to which James replied, " I shall not turn you out of your living, and you shall always remain Vicar of Bray, but I shall make your curate a Canon of Windsor, whence he will be able to look down both upon you and your vicarage."

Jesus Hospital, founded by William Goddard, 1627, for 40 poor persons, is a very picturesque quadrangle of brick almshouses, enclosing a garden-plot planted with flowers.

There is an old chapel, and the statue of the founder remains over the entrance.

1 m. further down the river is *Monkey Island*, so called from a pavilion built there by the 3rd Duke of Marlborough, covered in the inside with paintings of monkeys, by Clermont, in various ludicrous attitudes. Another building on the island, used as a billiard-room, has a fine carved ceiling.

2 m. W. of Bray are the remains of the picturesque manor-house of Ockwells, or Ockholt (now a farmhouse), which much resembles the timber halls of Cheshire. It is of the time of Henry VII., but is usually placed earlier, from the fact of antelopes appearing as supporters of the royal arms in one of the hall-windows, which would seem to give the date of Henry VI. The manor was originally granted to Richard de Norreys, the cook of Queen Eleanor, wife of Henry III., in 1267, whose descendants remained there till 1786. The old hall formerly contained a series of stained windows in which the Norreys arms were frequently repeated, with their motto, " Feythfully serve."

26 m. On l. 2 m. *White Waltham*, with a ch. rebuilt in 1868 with the addition of a lofty stone tower. Hearne, the antiquary, was a native of the village, his father being the parish clerk. The moated manorhouse (now a farm) was once the residence of Prince Arthur, son of Henry VII. Hearne relates a story of a Mr. John Bower, who held the living for 67 years, dying in 1644. Preaching before Queen Elizabeth, he addressed her as "my royal queen," which a little while after he changed to " my noble queen." " What," said her majesty, " am I ten groats worse than I was?" which pun so overwhelmed the preacher

that he never ventured on a sermon again, but always read a homily.

1 m. W. further, 6 m. from Maidenhead, is *Shottesbrooke* (Cap. Robson), a manor formerly held by providing charcoal to make the crown and regalia at a coronation, a tenure explained by its owner in the reign of William Rufus being Alward the goldsmith. The park contains the most beautiful Gothic *Church* in the county; it is pure Dec., elegant in proportions and complete in plans, cruciform, surmounted by a spire. The fine tracery of the E. window deserves especial notice, as also the external masonry of square close-jointed flint. The ch. was built 1337, by Sir William Trussel, who also founded a college here. He lies in the N. transept, beneath a richly wrought canopy of Gothic arches, and, according to Hearne, is " wrapt up in lead, with his wife in leather at his feet." His daughter Margaret, Lady Pembrugge, is buried near him, under a slab, with a fine brass (1401). There is likewise a brass of a priest and a franklin (c. 1370), engraved by Waller. Here also is the tomb of of Sir R. Powle, 1678, and of Sir T. Noke, "who for his great age and virtuous life was reverenced by all men, and commonly called Father Noke." His Latin epitaph is by Lady Hoby of Bisham, the learned sister of Lady Bacon and Lady Burleigh. In the churchyard is buried Dr. Dodwell, who here wrote his ' De Cyclis Veterum,' and his learned friend Dr. Francis Cherry, the patron of Hearne, with the epitaph, " Hic jacet peccatorum maximus, 1713." When the ch. was restored (1852), traces of its Norm. predecessor were found.

" A little body of nonjuring friends were settled at Shottesbrooke; at their head was Francis Cherry of Shottesbrooke House, whose worth and hospitality, combined with genteel accomplishments and a hand-

some person, rendered him the idol of Berkshire. His house, in which he was able to make up 70 beds for the officers and soldiery who were quartered upon him in the Revolution, was always open to the deprived clergy, and became a complete hotel for friendship, learning, and distress. Bp. Ken divided his time between Shottesbrooke and Longleat House. Bowdler and his family were frequent guests, and Robert Nelson would frequently ride over from Lord Berkeley's at Cranford. Dr. Grabe always found a welcome there. Charles Leslie, disguised in regimentals, was concealed by Mr. Cherry for 6 months at a house belonging to him at White Waltham. The display of his horsemanship in the hunting-field would sometimes pique the emulation of King William ; and Mr. Cherry, observing one day that he was closely pressed by the king, risked his life for the sake of breaking the usurper's neck, and plunged into a frightfully deep and broad part of the Thames, in the hope that William might be induced to follow. To the Princess Anne he would always pay the most particular attention, riding up to her calash ; but when she assumed her father's crown the queen missed Mr. Cherry from her side, and pointed him out in the distance to her attendants, saying, ' There goes one of the honestest gentlemen in my dominions.' "—*Memoirs of the pious Robert Nelson.*

Local tradition tells, that when the architect of Shottesbrooke Ch. was placing the last stone on the top of the spire, he called for wine to drink the king's health ; after drinking it, he immediately fell to the ground, was dashed to pieces, and buried on the spot ; also that a coffin-shaped stone was placed over his remains, the interjection "O! O!" which he uttered when dying, being the only thing engraven upon it.

31 m. *Twyford Junction Stat.* On N. a *Branch Line* to Henley (Rte. 10).

Twyford, takes its name from the two fords over the river Loddon, which falls into the Thames 3 m. N. There is a *Charity* at Twyford consisting of a chapel, schoolhouse, and house for the chaplain and master, due to the gratitude of Mr. Polehampton, a merchant (1721), who, having been found as an infant on a cold night in December, half-famished and frozen, at a door (of the house opposite the school) in the village, was taken in, cared for, and instructed in those rudiments of learning which laid the foundation of his future prosperity.

1 m. E. is *Ruscombe*, with a restored ch. (Trans.-Norm.). William Penn died, July 30, 1718, in a large house near the ch., pulled down about 1840.

33 m. 1 m. N. is *Sonning* (Rte. 10). The line here runs for about 2 m. in a cutting, in some parts 60 ft. deep, and 200 ft. wide at top.

On leaving the Sonning cutting, on rt. 1 m. is *Holme Park* (which recently belonged to R. Palmer, Esq., long M.P. for Berks). The rly. again enters the valley of the Thames at the point where

" Clear Kennet overtakes
His lord, the stately Thames,"

and traverses the rich alluvial meads to Reading.

On S., near the line, is *Earley Court* (Captain J. F. Hall), where Scott, Lord Stowell, died (see Rte. 3). Soon after, the Kennet is crossed near its junction with the Thames. Next the huge *County Gaol* is seen, a red-brick building with white stone facings. Close adjoining are the remains of Reading Abbey, amid which is a Roman Catholic chapel, by *Pugin*, in which several

carved stones from the ruins are preserved. Across the river rises the wooded hill of Caversham (Rte. 10).

36 m. READING JUNCTION STAT. Here the lines of the South-Western and South-Eastern Companies fall in, furnishing communication with Guildford, Reigate, Dover, &c. (see *Handbooks for Kent and Surrey*); and lines are given off to Basingstoke, Newbury, Hungerford, Devizes, &c.

READING (*Inns*: Great Western Hotel, Queen's Hotel), Pop. 42,050, is situated on the Kennet, 1½ m. above its junction with the Thames. It is a very flourishing town, which has more than quadrupled its pop. within the present centy. (pop. in 1801, 9742). It possesses few objects of antiquarian interest, being now chiefly remarkable for its great Rly. Stat., its Gaol, and for Huntley and Palmer's manufacture of biscuits.

The earliest mention of Reading is in 868, when Ivor the Dane fixed his head-quarters there. Of the Norm. castle, which was held for Stephen, not a trace remains, except in the name of *Castle-street*. Reading was visited by several kings, and by Queen Elizabeth no less than six times. Parliaments were held here, and in 1625 the law courts were transferred from London during Michaelmas Term, on account of the outbreak of the plague. In 1643 the town endured a siege from the Parliamentary army under Essex; the mound in the Forbury is a part of the intrenchments then thrown up. The town was again occupied by the royalists after the first battle of Newbury, but soon abandoned. In December, 1688, there was a sharp encounter at Reading between the forces of King James and those of the Prince of Orange. The former, though the more numerous, being also fired on from the houses, were driven out. Shortly after, a rumour that the disbanded Ir:sh soldiers were ravaging and murdering wherever they went, raised such a panic, that it received the name of "the Irish Cry." This anniversary, and the belief that the Irish soldiers intended to massacre the inhabitants during divine service, were long commemorated by the ringing of bells and the ballad of the 'Reading Skirmish,' which told how—

" Five hundred Papishes came there
    To make a final end
Of all the town in time of prayer,
    But God did them defend."

The *Townhall*, a building in the French Gothic or Renaissance style, augmented 1882 by additions which cost £60,000, contains a large *Concert Hall, Public Library, and Museum.*

In a house in Broad-st., now destroyed (engraved in Man's 'Hist. of Reading'), Abp. Laud was born, the son of a clothier : in his prosperity he founded charities for his native town, which still remain. Sir Thomas White, the founder of St. John's College at Oxford, was also a native of Reading, and established 2 scholarships in his new foundation for his native place. "John Bunyan was well known at Reading, where he sometimes went through the streets dressed like a carter, with a long whip in his hand, to avoid detection. In a visit to that place he contracted the disease which brought him to the grave." John Blagrave the mathematician, Joseph Blagrave the astrologer, Merrick the poet, and Judge Talfourd, were also natives of Reading.

The primary cause of the prosperity of this borough was the wealth of its abbey ; but as early as the time of Edward I. it was famous for its cloth manufacture, which has now disappeared ; but it still remains a great mart for corn and agricultural produce. There are also iron foundries, engine works, malt houses and breweries. *Huntley and Palmer's*

biscuit manufactory employs 3000 hands, and the Reading iron works 400. Messrs. Sutton's seed establishment extends over more than 3000 acres of land, and is well worth a visit.

St. Lawrence Church, erected in 1434, near the market place, has a tall flint tower with detached tourelles, good Perp. windows, and a restored E. E. chancel. It once possessed a silver gridiron, containing a relic of St. Lawrence. There are some 15th-centy. *Brasses ;* and one of 1584 for Edward Butler, five times mayor, but it has lost the inscription recorded by Ashmole :—

" Christ is to me as life on earth, and death
    to me is gain,
Because I trust through Him alone salvation
    to obtain.
So brittle is the state of man, so soon it doth
    decay,
So all the glory of the world must pass and
    fade away."

The N. aisle contains the monument of John Blagrave, having the effigy in a cloak and ruff, holding a globe and a quadrant, with the epitaph—

" Johannes Blagravus
    Totus mathematicus
    Cum matre sepultus."

He left a legacy for the encouragement of Reading maidservants :— The churchwardens of each of the 3 parishes were to choose maidservants of 5 years' standing, who were to meet and throw dice for a purse of 10*l.* on Good Friday. "This is lucky money," says Ashmole ; "for I never yet heard of a maid who got the 10*l.*, but soon after found a good husband."

St. Mary's, founded on the site of a nunnery built by Elfrida, to expiate the murder of her stepson, was formerly called the Minster, which name still remains as that of the adjoining street. The ch. is said to have been rebuilt (1551) with the materials of the abbey and friary, "and the singular mixture of good and bad Gothic seems to verify this account" (*J. H. P.*). The nave has a good roof of early character, older than the corbels on which it rests. There is a memorial window to the late Bishop Wilberforce, erected in 1873. The chequered tower of flint and ashlar, the monument of William Kendrick and his wife, and the old poorbox (date 1627) merit notice. Near this ch. was the *Oracle*, of Jacobean architecture, the ancient Woolmerchants' and Dyers' Hall, founded by John Kendrick in 1626, but pulled down about 1863. It derived its name from Orchil (*Rocella tinctoria*), a lichen brought from the Canary Isles, and used in dyeing. *St. Giles's Church* was much damaged during the siege of 1643: the tower has been rebuilt, and is surmounted by a slender spire. At the N.W. extremity of the town is the *Greyfriars' Church*, a fragment of the old monastic ch., which long served as the borough gaol, but was in 1864 again adapted to religious use. Notice the beautiful Dec. W. window; also the side windows of the aisles. There are several modern churches, and numerous chapels, but none of any architectural merit.

The chief object of interest in Reading is its Benedictine Abbey, now a mere shell, but formerly the third in size and wealth of all English abbeys. Founded by Henry I., 1121, it was endowed by him with the privilege of coining, and he further secured its fortunes by presenting it with the hand of St. James the Apostle, which had been given to him by his daughter Maud. When he died at Rouen of eating stewed lampreys, his heart, tongue, brains, and bowels were buried there and the rest of his body was sent to Reading Abbey. His daughter, who was the wife of the Emperor Henry IV. and mother of Henry II., was likewise interred here. Her epitaph is recorded by Camden:—

" Magna ortu, majorque viro, sed maxima partu :
Hic jacet Henrici filia, sponsa, parens."

Here also was buried William the eldest son of Henry II. (d. 1156). Some of these royal tombs were destroyed and the bones "thrown out" at the dissolution in 1539, when Hugh Faringdon the abbot was hung, drawn, and quartered, for denying the royal supremacy. The magnificent monument of Henry I. was destroyed temp. Edward VI.

Many parliaments have been held at Reading. Here Henry II. held one in 1184, and here he, in 1185, received Heraclius, patriarch of Jerusalem, who presented him with the keys of the Holy Sepulchre and the royal banners of the city. Here met the convocation for the trial of Longchamp Bishop of Ely, regent during the absence of Richard I.; and two ecclesiastical councils—one under the legate Pandulph in the reign of John, the other under Archbishop Peckham in 1270. Here also Richard II. was reconciled to his nobles in 1389, through the intervention of John of Gaunt. Henry VIII. converted the abbey into a palace, occasionally residing there himself. It was afterwards frequently occupied by the sovereign till its destruction in the great rebellion. "The ruins, though stripped, by destroyers of more than ordinary patience and industry, of almost every stone which cased the walls, still, though built only of small flints, defy the injuries of time and weather, and have more the appearance of rocks than of the work of human hands "—*Englefield.* Huge masses of the stone were used in building the hospital of the Poor Knights of Windsor ; others by Gen. Conway for a bridge across the Wargrave-road. Among the remains still standing are a portion of the great hall in which the parliaments were held, and where the marriage of Edward IV. with Elizabeth Woodville was first made public ; and of the ch., dedicated to St. Thomas à Becket, which once contained the royal monuments, and in which John of Gaunt was married to Blanche of Lancaster in 1359. The foundation of a Norm. apsidal chapel may still be seen at the E. end of the Roman Catholic chapel, into the walls of which many Norm. fragments have been built. The site is now laid out and planted as a pleasure-ground.

In the *Forbury* (suburb, *Vor-burg*) now an open green, is the *Abbey Gateway*, visible from the Rly. It was rebuilt by *Scott*, the old gateway having fallen down in 1861. An Assize Court-house, of very incongruous appearance, adjoins it. Within the brick shell of the *Abbey Mill*, on a branch of the Kennet, just behind this gate, are several Trans.-Norm. arches—one with the zigzag. In the Forbury, close to St. Lawrence's Ch., was the *Grammar-School* (forming part of the Town-hall), at which Archbishop Laud was educated, and of which the Marian martyr, Julins [Jocelyn] Palmer, was master. This school, which greatly flourished under the well-known Dr. Valpy, head-master, was removed to a new site on the London road in 1871. The various *Almshouses* of the town form a handsome group of buildings in Castle-street, erected 1865.

The *County Hospital*, on the London road, has a fine Ionic portico.

Fuller tells the story of Henry VIII. and the Abbot of Reading, how, "As the King was hunting in Windsor Forest, having lost his way, he was invited to the Abbot's table, where he passed for one of the royal guard. A sirloin of beef was placed before him, on which the King laid on so lustily as not disgracing one of that place for which he had been mistaken. 'Well fare thy heart,' quoth the Abbot, 'for here, in a cup of sack, I remember the health of his Grace your master. I would give 100 pounds on condition that I could feed so lustily on beef as you do. Alas! my weak and squeezie stomach will hardly digest the wing of a small rabbit or chicken.' The King pleasantly pledged him, and departed undiscovered. Some weeks after, the Abbot was sent for, clapt into the Tower, kept close prisoner, and fed for a short time on bread and water; yet not so empty was his body of food as his mind was filled with fears, making many suspicions to himself when and how he had incurred the King's displeasure. At last a sirloin of beef was set before him, when he verified the proverb that two hungry meals make a glutton. In springs King Henry, out of a private lobby where he had placed himself. 'My lord,' quoth the King, 'deposit presently your 100 pounds in gold, or else no going hence all the days of your life. I have been your physician to cure you of your squeezie stomach, and here, as I deserve, I demand my fee for the same.' The Abbot down with his dust, and, glad he escaped so, returned to Reading, as somewhat lighter in purse, so much more merry in heart, than when he came thence."

Reading was formerly connected with Caversham by a picturesque old bridge, with a chapel of the Virgin, covered by a rude fisherman's hut. A handsome iron bridge has succeeded it, the road to which is raised considerably above the old level. " On an island below it, now a verdant meadow, was fought a wager of battle between Robert de Montfort and Henry de Essex, in the presence of King Henry II." Essex, who was accused of cowardice or treachery in throwing away the royal standard at Consillt (see *Handbook for North Wales*), was defeated, but he was allowed to save his life by becoming a monk in Reading Abbey.

The environs of Reading are exceedingly pleasant, though the low meadows near the Thames often suffer from winter floods.

Three-Mile Cross, 3 m. on the Basingstoke road, was the residence of Miss Mitford, who has described it in 'Our Village.' Her 'Recollections of a Literary Life' is also full of local descriptions. She afterwards lived at *Swallowfield*, and died there (Rte. 3).

Leaving Reading the rly. keeps very near the river, and being carried at some height above, affords fine views of the valley, and the opposite (Oxfordshire) bank, as described in Rte. 10. The line passes through the grounds of *Purley Hall* (F. Wilder, Esq.), and reaches at

41½ m. *Pangbourne* (Stat.). *Inns:* Elephant, George, both much resorted to by anglers. The view across the river to *Whitchurch* is very fine (Rte. 10). 2 m. S. are the almost adjoining villages of *Sulham* and *Tidmarsh*, both pleasantly placed. The ch. of Sulham is modern, in a very neatly-kept ch.-yard.; but that of Tidmarsh is E. E., with a semi-octagonal apse (engraved in 'Gloss. of Architecture'). The doorway is rich Norm., and there are 2 good 15th-centy. *Brasses*. *Tidmarsh House* (J. Hopkins, Esq.).

43 m. On W. the handsome lodge-gates of *Basildon Park* (C. Morrison, Esq.). Basildon *Church* lies on the other side of the line, which almost immediately after crosses the Thames into Oxfordshire by a fine 4-arched bridge. The ch., in front of which a Roman pavement was discovered in making the rly., has a good Dec. chancel, and an E. E. South doorway.

Basildon Park, a handsome white stone building, with Corinthian portico, was in the 18th centy. the seat

of the Fanes (Viscount Fane of Ireland). It is remarkable for the works of art which it contains, of which the following are worth notice:—

Hall.—A quadrangular Roman altar from the Strawberry Hill collection, ornamented with a bas-relief of the death of Opheltes; a landscape by *Turner*, in the style of Claude, "a chef-d'œuvre of this great master."

Octagon.—*Wm. Hilton*, scene from Milton's 'Comus'; *Sir Chas. Eastlake*, Flight of Francesco Carrara, Duke of Padua, and his Duchess, from Giov. Galeazzo Visconti; *Turner*, a landscape; *Collins*, the Fisherman's Farewell; *Webster*, the Sick Girl; *Hogarth*, the Punch Club, a well-known picture, showing the various effects of the beverage; *Pickersgill*, portrait of Alex. von Humboldt; *Wilkie*, a young girl confessing (Rome, 1827); *Stanfield*, Italian sea-coast; *Hilton*, Penelope recognising Ulysses.

Library.—*N. Poussin*, Bacchanalian scene, "one of the finest specimens of the master;" *Rembrandt*, a portrait, supposed to be his daughter; *Rubens*, the Virgin and Child, with St. Joseph, "in a powerful transparent golden tone"; *Parmigianino*, Cupid, formerly in the Pal. Barberini at Rome; a fine bronze statue of a Mænad.

Pink Drawing-Room.—*Leonardo da Vinci*, half-length female figure; over mantelpiece, a bas-relief in ivory by *François du Quesnoy.*

Oak Room. — *Teniers*, an old woman of Antwerp with a doctor; interior of a stable; *Guercino*, St. Sebastian pierced with arrows; *Vandyke*, portrait of Charles I.; portraits of two ladies seated, Dorothy Percy, and Lucy Percy, countesses of Leicester and Carlisle (Waller's heroines), from Strawberry Hill; *Sir Joshua Reynolds*, his own portrait;

Poussin, two landscapes; *Watteau*, a group of ladies and gentlemen listening to the guitar of Pierrot; *Hobbema*, a cottage and trees—"its effect is equally powerful and transparent"; *Dujardin*, the Farrier's Shop; *Gyssels*, dead game; *Backhuysen*, a sea-piece; *A. von Ostade*, room in a tavern after dinner; *Van de Velde*, *Paul Potter*, *Both*, landscapes. *School-Room.*—*Harlow*, the Trial of Catherine of Aragon; *Greuze*, study for a picture in the Louvre.

44¾ m. *Goring* (Stat.) This, and the opposite village of *Streatley*, will be found described in Rte. 10.

[A most interesting visit may be made from Goring to *Aldworth*, a village 4 m. W., lying at the foot of the Berkshire downs. The small *Church* is a good Dec. edifice, with E. E. tower, and has been well restored by *St. Aubyn.* It is remarkable for 9 fine *Monumental Effigies*, which represent 6 knights in armour (5 with legs crossed, and 6 or 7 ft. in stature), 1 civilian and 2 females; 6 of these figures are under enriched Dec. canopies; 2 are on altar-tombs; 1 is in the ch.-yard. They represent members of the family of De la Beche (Flemings, who came over with the Conqueror), lords of this manor temp. Edward II. and III.; the last of them, Sir Nicholas, was tutor to the Black Prince (d. 1347). Queen Elizabeth is said to have ridden on a pillion behind the Earl of Leicester, all the way from Ewelme, to inspect these celebrated tombs. " In the E. ende of ye yle did hang a Table fairly written in Parchment, of all ye names of ye family of De la Beche: but ye Earle of Leicester, coming with ye Queen Elizabeth in progresse, tooke it down to show it her, and it was never brought againe."—*Symonds' Diary.*
" The common people call the statue under the outside of the ch., *John Everafraid*; and say further

that he gave his soul to the Devil, if ever he was buried either in churche or churchyard, so he was buried under the churche wall, under an arche." The story—a similar tale is current elsewhere (see Rte. 26)—is still current among the villagers, who call 3 of the other statues, John Long, John Strong, and John Neverafraid. " The 5 cross-legged effigies were probably Sir Robert de la Beche, Sir John and William his sons, and Thomas and William his grandsons, who all died before 1310, and may all have been personally engaged in the Holy Wars. Sir Robert was probably the founder of the ch., and his statue would be that under the S. wall. Philip de la Beche, his grandson, founded the chancel and S. aisle, and he doubtless erected the 5 cross-legged effigies to his ancestors. The 2 tombs on the S. side may be presumed to be Sir Philip, that in the centre of the ch. to be his son Sir John. The other effigies on the same tomb are doubtless Sir Nicholas and his wife Margaret, the last of the family."—*Hewitt's* 'Hundred of Compton.'
In the churchyard is an old *yew* whose trunk measures 9 yards in circumference. Nothing remains of the Castle de la Beche but the name in the " Beche Farm," where many encaustic tiles have been found.]

47¼ m. *Moulsford Junction Stat.* Hence a *Branch Line* of 3¼ m. runs off on rt. to Wallingford (*post*). The small Dec. ch. of Moulsford has been restored by *Sir G. G. Scott.* The river scenery here is very beautiful.

1¼ m. N. is *Cholsey* (the " Island of Ceol "), where was formerly an expiatory monastery, founded 986, by Ethelred for the murder of Edward the Martyr. It was granted by Henry I. as a country retreat to the Abbots of Reading. There remained until the beginning of this century a very ancient stone barn, 51 ft. high, 54 ft. wide, and 303 long. A tablet on the wall of its successor records the fact that "In this barn John Lanesley threshed, for Mr. Joseph Hopkins, 5 quarters 7 bushels and a half of wheat in 13 hours, on March 15, 1747." The ch. of Cholsey was founded about the same time as Reading Abbey, the lower part of the tower is of early Norm. character. The ch. is cruciform, with very massive Norm. walls and later windows inserted. At the W. end an addition has been made in the 13th centy., of one bay with lancet windows of fine E. E. work. The ch. is much in want of a judicious restoration; it has been greatly neglected.

2 m. N.W. of Cholsey is the interesting Church of North Moreton. The chancel is early Dec., and has on the S. side a chapel which preserves some good early glass, and several monuments with floriated crosses. The tower is Perp. with a bold open parapet. The curious angle piscina is engraved in Rickman. The mutilated Church of South Moreton has a buttress with a niche in which is sculptured a shield of arms; it also is figured by Rickman. 1 m. W. is Hagbourn, with a fine Church mainly E. E., but with late Perp. clerestory. The village cross remains almost perfect, and is made to support a sundial. Harwell, 2 m. further W., has a fine cruciform Church, the nave Trans.-Norm., the transepts E. E., and the chancel Dec., with some original painted glass. The ch. contains a memorial of the singular legacy of Christ. Elderfield, 1652, who left lands for the purpose of purchasing "2 milch cows every spring to be given to the 2 poorest men in the parish, for their sustenance." As it was found impossible for the poor men to get pasture for their cows, the trustees of this legacy give it away in meat at Christmas instead.

[51 m. Wallingford Stat. (Inn: Lamb). A bridge of many arches over the Thames and adjoining marsh, leads into this dull old borough town of 2803 inhab. (1 M.P.) It is nearly enclosed on three sides by remarkable earthen Ramparts, of unknown age, forming a parallelogram. Within this it is probable the Romans made a settlement, which is confirmed by the ground plan, two main streets crossing in the centre, and by the quantity of Roman coins found here. Within the rampart in the N.E. corner stood The Castle, of which there are only scant remains, including three moated earthworks and a huge mound now grown over with trees. In the grounds of the modern mansion, called The Castle (residence of Kirby Hedges, Esq., the latest historian of Wallingford), as well as in the Croft and "Kine Croft," these high banks may be seen. Adjoining it are the ruins of St. Nicholas Chapel, an ivy covered tower, door way, and windows. From the earliest times the "ford" over the Thames here was a frequented pass, and the Castle, which commanded it, was an important fortress.

The town at the time of the Conquest was in the possession of Wygod, a Saxon Thane, who received William and the Normans in a friendly manner. His daughter and his lands were given to Robert d'Oiley, who, beside building a castle at Oxford, greatly strengthened that of Wallingford. This castle was of great importance as a fortress during the stormy times which followed. Hither the Empress Maud, mother of Henry II., fled through the snow, after her escape from Oxford Castle, to Brian Fitzcount, its owner by his marriage with the heiress of Robert d'Oiley. She was pursued by Stephen, who built a castle at Crowmarsh, on the opposite side of the river, in order to blockade her more easily, but she again escaped to Gloucester. Brian, however, held out for several years against all the power of Stephen, and when he was apparently reduced to extremity. in 1153, Prince Henry came to his rescue. A treaty was in consequence made at Wallingford, which secured the young prince's eventual succession to the throne, and Brian then did homage to Stephen. Henry II. seized on the castle and town, soon after his accession, and granted a charter to the burgesses; he also held a council here in 1155. In 1231 Henry III. granted the castle to his brother Richard Earl of Cornwall, who transmitted it to his son Edmund, upon whose death it again fell to the crown, and so remained for many years. Edward II. in 1317 bestowed the castle on his queen, and from that time forth it was often used as a royal residence, and sometimes as a state prison. Joan of Kent, the widow of the Black Prince, died here in 1385, and it was the residence of the young queen Isabel during the absence of Richard II. in Ireland. It was afterwards granted to Queen Catherine, the widow of Henry V.

Leland, in the 16th centy., describes the Castle as "sore yn ruine;" but Camden, writing somewhat later, says that its size and magnificence were still such as to amaze him, coming there, as a lad, from Oxford. Wallingford was the last place in Berkshire which held out for Charles, and was taken by Fairfax, July 27, 1646, after a 65 days' siege bravely sustained by Governor Blagge. In 1652 it was slighted and destroyed by order of the Council of State.

Of the 14 churches mentioned by Leland, 3 only remain. *St. Mary's* (restored) is late Perp.; on its tower (date 1653), surmounted by 4 pinnacles, is a mounted figure said to represent King Stephen. *St. Leo-*

nard's (rebuilt 1849, by *Hakewell*, except the N. wall) has a Norm. doorway and two N. arches in the chancel. *St. Peter's*, near the bridge, contains the grave of Sir William Blackstone, to whom a modern Gothic monument has been erected on its S. wall.

On the opposite bank, in Oxfordshire, is the small plain Norm. *Church* of *Crowmarsh* (restored) ending in an apse, probably the work of D'Oiley.]

———

Leaving Moulsford, the line crosses an open plain, known as *Hagbourne Marsh*. On N.E. appear the Dyke Hills, near Dorchester, and on W. the high ground and conical hills that form the Berkshire downs.

53¼ m. *Didcot Junction Stat.* Hence the line runs W. to Swindon (Rte. 5) and the West; N. to Oxford, Banbury, &c. (Rtes. 19, 24), and S. to Newbury. The village of Didcot is very small, but the *Church* (E. E., Dec. and Perp.) has some fragments of good early painted glass, and an effigy, supposed to be that of the first mitred abbot of Abingdon (c. 1270). There is a restored cross in the ch.-yard, and a very fine yew-tree.

2 m. N. E. of Didcot are the 2 villages of *Little Wittenham* and *Long Wittenham*. The *Church* of the first has been rebuilt; it contains the tomb of Sir Henry Dunch and his wife, who was the aunt of Oliver Cromwell. Long Wittenham *Church* (restored) is mainly Dec., and of much interest. It retains some original glass, has a remarkable leaden font, of Trans.-Norm date, numerous encaustic tiles, and a very singular piscina, a small cross-legged effigy in armour lying on the edge; it is engraved in 'Glossary of Architecture.' Six large iron spear-

heads, found in the Thames near this place in 1843, are preserved in Ashmolean Museum, Oxford.

ROUTE 5.

DIDCOT TO SWINDON, BY WANTAGE, UFFINGTON, FARINGDON.

Great Western Rly. 24 m.

Leaving Didcot (Rte. 4), we have at 2 m. *Sutton Courtenay*, 1½ m. N. The manor, which was an early possession of the abbots of Abingdon, was exchanged by the Abbot Rethunus with Kinwulf, King of the Mercians, for the ancient royal palace in the Isle of Andersey, close to the monastery, where the King had kept his hounds and hawks to the great annoyance of the monks. Henry II. gave it to Reginald Courtenay, ancestor of the Earls of Devon, by whom it was twice forfeited: first by Thos. Courtenay, who fought against Edward IV. at Towton; and afterwards, when it had been restored to the family, by the attainder of Henry Marquis of Exeter, 1539.

The *Church* was given by the Conqueror to the Abbey of Abingdon. It still retains some Norm. work, and a Trans.-Norm. font, but is chiefly Dec. and Perp. One of its Trans.-Norm. windows is engraved in ' Glossary of Architecture.' Here is a monument to Sir R. Hyde, of

[*Berks, &c.*]

Blaygrave, 1615, a descendant of the Hydes of Denchworth, stating the tradition that Canute gave the Manor of Denchworth to the Hydes in the year 1017. Not far from the ch. is the *Manor-house*, of the time of Edward III., which was used by the abbots as a place of country retirement. The interior is in parts very perfect, its hall retaining its ancient roof and pointed windows filled with Dec. tracery, and one of the chambers at the end of the hall its open roof.

1 m. E. is *Appleford*, where the small Norm. and E. E. ch. has a singular Trans.-Norm. font, round below and octagonal at top.

3 m. *Steventon* (Stat.). The village lying low, and so subject to floods, has a raised causeway through its entire length, pleasantly planted with trees. The *Church*, Dec. and Perp., has some rich moulded imposts to the tower arches, ornamented on the one side with the ball-flower and on the other with stalked roses—"a curious and rich specimen." (*J. H. P.*) There is a good *Brass* for Richard Do and his 2 wives (1476).

6¾ m. *Wantage Road Stat.* is in the hamlet of *Grove*, which has a small modern ch. A tramway connects the station with the town of Wantage, and cars meet every train. Steam power was used here for the first time in England for tramway purposes.

1 m. N.W. is *West Hanney*, with a fine cruciform *Church*. The chancel is late and poor Perp., but the rest is well worth examination. The nave has Norm. pillars, some of them altered into Dec.; the transepts are E. E.; the S. aisle is Dec., with square-headed windows and a rich panelled parapet; the N. doorway is good Norm.; the S. doorway equally good Dec. There are *Brasses*, ranging from 1370 to 1611, one being that of Sir Christopher Lytcot, 1599,

E

"who was knighted in the camp before Rouen by the French king Henry IV.;" he is represented in a highly ornamented suit of armour. The town of *Wantage* (*Inn* : Bear), is 2½ m. S. of the stat. (Pop. 3488). It is celebrated as the *birthplace of King Alfred*, and appears to have been his own patrimony, as he left it by will to his wife. The site of the Saxon palace in which Alfred was born is supposed to be an enclosure called the *High Garden*, on the S. side of the brook (a branch of the Ock) which runs through the town. The adjoining orchard is still called *Court Close*.

Wantage was at the Conquest retained by the crown, but passed afterwards through a series of noble hands, among which were Baldwin de Bethune, William de Valence, Hugh Bigod, Fulk Fitzwarren, and the Bourchiers Earls of Bath. The Fitzwarrens obtained a grant of a market from Henry III., but this was allowed to fall into disuse, and has only been revived since the opening of the rly.

The cruciform *Church of SS. Peter and Paul* is large and handsome, with a central tower, open below, and resting upon 4 magnificent Dec. piers. The nave is E. E., with Perp. clerestory and aisles. The transepts are Dec.; the chancel Perp., with a restored Dec. E. window; the font large, E. E. There is a fine alabaster monument of Sir William Fitzwarren, a Knight of the Garter, and his lady, of the 14th centy.; a large brass of Sir Ivo Fitzwarren, 1414, and several smaller ones, including an early brass (1320) of a priest. The ch. has been recently restored by Street.

Wantage, though in a purely agricultural district, is remarkable for its schools. The *National School*, by Woodyer, is worth visiting from the drawings on its walls. The *Grammar-School*, built by a subscription raised at the jubilee in

honour of Alfred, in 1849, has a fine Norm. doorway, a relic of the former ch., and the oldest object in the town. There is also *St. Michael's Home* for training girls for service; and *St. Mary's Home* for penitents, under the superintendence of the Sisters of Mercy.

A fine *statue of King Alfred*, by Count Gleichen, presented to the town by Col. Loyd Lindsay, was unveiled in 1877 by the Prince of Wales. It stands in the centre of the market-place.

The *Town Hall* was erected in 1877.

Bishop Butler, the author of the 'Analogy,' was born at Wantage, son of a Dissenter, 1692, in a house called the Priory, adjoining the churchyard, and was educated at the grammar-school.

¼ m. W. of the town, at the Mead, are *King Alfred's Bath* and *Well;* the latter a basin of clear water, in a pretty dingle, formed by a number of small petrifying springs.

1 m. E. of Wantage is the hamlet of *Charlton*, in the manor-house of which, then the property of the Wilmots, Charles I. occasionally resided in 1643 and 1644.

2¼ m. N.-W. of Wantage is *Denchworth*. The *Church*, a conspicuous object from the rly., has an early Norm. doorway. The N. transept, or Lady-Chapel, with its squint, is E. E., the chancel and S. transept are Dec., and the font is good Perp. The low Perp. tower contains 4 bells. In the chancel are a brass of Will. Say, 1493; and several good brasses, with effigies of the Hyde family (1516–1567). One of these is a *rescript*, of very early date (1333), probably brought from Bisham Abbey, where it was originally placed to record its foundation by Sir W. de Montagu, and the laying of the first stone by King Edw. III. There are some curious *graffiti* on it, and it bears the following inscription :—

"Edward Roy danglete qe fist le siege deuant la cite de Berewyk et coquyst la bataille illeoqs et la dite cite la veille seinte Margarete lan de gae mccccxxxiii mist ceste pere a la requeste Sire William de Montagu foundour de ceste mesoun."

In the S. transept are the monuments of the Geering family, who succeeded the Hydes in the Manor. At the *Vicarage* are preserved, as heirlooms, a "mermaid's rib," presented to the Vicar in 1693, and a library of 150 volumes, formerly chained in the church, and some of which are of the 15th centy. Near the church is the moated *Manor House*, where Amy Robsart lived with the Hydes for some time previous to her fatal residence at Cumnor (1558–9). Here she was often visited by her husband, Lord Rob. Dudley; and here also Sir Thomas Pope, founder of Trin. Coll. Oxford, was a frequent visitor.

[From Wantage several places of interest in early English history may be visited, the chalk ridge to the S. being the "Ashdown," where the Danes were defeated by Alfred. Almost every eminence is crowned by earthworks, on the date of which various opinions may be entertained; the White Horse, Wayland Smith's Cave, the Blowing Stone, are all within a moderate distance; and several picturesquely placed villages are to be met with, that would supply abundant employment to the artist. "They are queer, straggling, old-fashioned places, the houses being dropped down without the least regularity, in nooks and out-of-the-way corners, by the sides of shadowy lanes and footpaths, each with its patch of garden. They are built chiefly of good grey stone, and thatched; though since 1850, red brick cottages have multiplied, for the vale is beginning to manufacture largely both brick and tiles. There are lots of waste ground by the side of the road in every village, amounting often to

village greens, where feed the pigs and ganders of the people; and these roads are old-fashioned, homely roads, very dirty and badly made, and hardly endurable in winter, but still pleasant jog-trot roads running through the great pasture-lands, dotted here and there with little clumps of thorns, where the sleek kine are feeding, with no fence on either side of them, and a gate at the end of the field, which makes you get out of your gig (if you keep one), and gives you a chance of looking about you at every quarter of a mile."—*Tom Brown's Schooldays.*

2 m. S. W. is *Letcombe Regis*, where was a hunting seat of King John; a moated farmhouse is believed to occupy the site. The (restored) *Church*, mainly Dec. and Perp., has a good E. window of old stained glass, some Trans.-Norm. and E. E. portions, and a round Norm. font with the scallop ornament.

1 m. S. is the village of *Letcombe Basset*, with a small and admirably restored church, the transept of which is Norm. and E. E., and the font E. E. To this place Dean Swift retired in April, 1718; and during his residence there wrote his pamphlet, 'Free Thoughts on the Present State of Affairs.'

"By faction tired, with grief he waits awhile,
His great contending friends to reconcile,
Performs what friendship, justice, truth require;
What could he more, but decently retire?"

The Letcombes are celebrated for watercresses, which are sent up in large quantities to the London markets; the training of racehorses is also a source of occupation.

On the hill above is the earthwork called *Letcombe Castle*. It is supposed to have been a British town, and contains an area of 26 acres; the form is nearly circular, and it was protected by a double vallum, but the outer one has been almost entirely destroyed. A remarkable cist, containing a human skeleton, with flint implements and early pottery was found in 1871 in this inclosure, under a wedge-shaped stone protruding from the earth.

4 m. W. of Wantage is *Sparsholt*, where there is a very fine Dec. ch. The N. doorway of the nave is rich and peculiar Norm., and the iron-work of the door seems to be original. The chancel is chiefly Dec., with a mailed effigy in a highly-finished Dec. recess. There is also another early effigy, of wood; and in the S. transept 2 other wooden effigies on altar-tombs, ornamented at the sides with 9 figures of knights in different attitudes. All these effigies are of the 14th centy., and were painted and gilt. They are sup-posed to be memorials of the Achard family. The roof, and a Dec. screen in the transept, are engraved in the 'Gloss. of Architecture.'

1 m. W. from Sparsholt is the small Norm. ch. of *Kingston Lisle*. *Kingston Lisle House* (Victor W. B. Van de Weyer, Esq.) has a pretty glen in the park, and some fine old trees. A short distance S., on the road to Lamborne, under the shade of a tree, guarded by a padlock which requires a silver key, and in front of a public-house which bears its name, is the *Blowing Stone*, sometimes called King Alfred's Trumpet, considered one of the great natural curiosities of the county. It is of the species of red sandstone called Sarsen stone, and is about 3 ft. high, 3 ft. 6 in. broad, and 2 ft. thick. It is pierced with holes on each side, of which 7 are in the front, 3 at the top, and several behind; at the N. end is also an irregular hollow place. The sound produced by a person blowing into any of these holes resembles the bellowing of a calf, and, it is said, can be heard in fine weather at Faringdon Clump, 6 m. distant (*post*). If a small stick be pushed in at the hole at the top, it will come ⸲ut at one at the back of the stone.

The stone is said to have been found on White Horse Hill, and, as a local poet sings,

" Atkins has preserved with care
This mystic remnant of the day
When Alfred ruled with regal sway:
And when the wise decrees of Fate
Made friend and foe confess him Great,
This trumpet loudly did-proclaim
His wars, his wisdom, and his fame."

White Horse Hill and Uffington Camp lie about 2 m. W. of Kingston Lisle, but are more readily reached from the Uffington Stat. (*post*)]

10¾ m. *Challow* (Stat.) The 2 villages *East* and *West Challow* lie S. of the stat. near the Berks and Wilts Canal. The *Churches* of both are of interest. That of E. Challow, though partly rebuilt, has Trans.-Norm. W. and S. doorways, an E. E. stoup, and a good Dec. E. window; that of W. Challow has a Trans.-Norm. W. doorway, and Perp. chancel with screen of the same date. There is a large agricultural imple-ment factory at East Challow.

Half a mile S. of W. Challow is *Childrey*. The ch. contains a curious font, some ancient stained glass win-dows, and some very interesting monuments. The nave was restored in 1878. In this parish there is a house built in the 15th centy., in which Charles I. slept on the night of his march from Oxford to Marl-borough.

1½ m. N. is *Stanford-in-the-Vale*, with a fine *Church*, mostly Dec. The very curious piscina, with reliquary on top, is figured in 'Gloss. of Architecture.' Notice in the chancel the large *Brass* of Roger Campdene (1398); also the Elizabethan pulpit. 1 m. N. is *Hatford*, a small E.E. ch., consecrated in 1874, with Norm. door, and the Dec. canopied tomb of a priest. 1 m. S.E. is the small E.E. chapel of *Goosey*, the door key of which is original. 2 m. E. is *Charney Basset*, with a ch. originally Norm., but greatly altered. Close to it is a 13th-centy. building, supposed to have been a grange of the abbey of

Abingdon. The chapel is now a granary; other portions, used as a farmhouse, retain their original windows and open timber roof. 1 m. further E. is *Lyford*, with a small E.E. chapel, having low side-windows. 13 m. *Uffington Junction Stat.* On N. a *Branch line* of 3½ m. goes off to Faringdon (*post*).

Uffington is a pleasant village under the White Horse Hill. The name is taken to mean Offa's town; Offa, King of Mercia, having gained it, 780, by the conquest of Kinewulf, King of Wessex. The place is minutely described in the opening chapter of 'Tom Brown's School-days.'

The noble *Church* (founded by Faritius, abbot of Abingdon, 1105) is mostly of E. E. character, and has a very fine central octagonal lantern-tower, once surmounted by a spire, destroyed by lightning in 1720, with plain windows in four of the faces, and without buttresses. "The chancel has 3 lancet windows with detached shafts, having bands and foliated caps; under these are 3 small circular openings with good mouldings: the side-windows are also lancets with detached shafts, except one which is a Dec. insertion; the sedilia and piscina are fine examples of E. E.; the tower arches are fine and lofty E. E. On the E. side of the N. transept are 2 very remarkable recesses for altars, with high-pitched gable-roofs and 3 windows in each of a peculiar form, as if the heads of the windows were cut off by the slope of the roof, but evidently all original work: this example is believed to be unique. The S. transept is nearly the same as the N., but has only one altar-recess. The nave is plain, with N. and S. doorways, and the doors have good E. E. iron work upon them. The S. doorway has a fine E. E. porch, with a groined vault and room over it, in which is an original fireplace and chimney."—*J. H. P.*

The E. window is filled with good stained glass; but the only monument of interest is an Elizabethan one to John Saunders, who founded a free school in the village. Several of the details of this beautiful ch. are figured in Rickman, and in the 'Gloss. of Architecture.'

1 m. S. of the village rises the *White Horse Hill*, so named from a rude figure of a galloping steed cut in the turf near its summit, and which has "given its name to the vale upon which it has looked down these thousand years or more." The figure, which is exceedingly rude, and which certainly is not much like an actual horse, still bears a kind of resemblance to the horse stamped on many British coins. It is cut on the N.W. face of the hill, and, being 374 ft. in length, and stretching over an acre of ground, is visible from a distance of 20 m. when the afternoon sun is shining upon it. It is formed by trenches 2 or 3 ft. deep, and about 10 ft. broad; the head, neck, body, and tail are represented by one continuous line, varying very little in width, and the legs are each formed by a single line. According to the local tradition of centuries, which was accepted by Wise and by more modern Berkshire antiquaries, but is now called in question, the horse is a memorial of the battle of Æscesdun (A.D. 871), when Ethelred and Alfred gained a great victory over the Danes, in which their King Bagsæc was slain; and the annual custom of Scouring the White Horse was from early times the occasion of a rustic festival, attended by athletic games. This custom had died out in 1780, but was revived in 1828, 1838, and 1843. In 1858 an unusually brilliant festival took place under the auspices of the late E. Atkins, Esq., of Kingston Lisle, which gave rise to Mr. T. Hughes' story of the 'Scour-

ing of the White Horse.' The
ballad of the Scouring is a curious
specimen of the Berkshire dialect.
Mr. Hughes, in a communication
to the Newbury District Field Club
(June, 1871), says : " I am not
sure that our White Horse was cut
out on the hill after the battle of
Ashendon. Indeed, I incline to
believe that it was there long before,
and that Ethelred and Alfred could
not have spent an hour on such a
work in the crisis of 871." It has
been remarked, that any trophy cut
by such pious kings would probably
be in the form of a Christian cross,
as at Whiteleaf and Bledlow (Rte.
12), and not the horse of their
idolatrous ancestors. And objec-
tors of another class have remarked
that the horse is represented galloping with the wrong leg foremost,
whence they conclude it to be only
the work of idle shepherds. For instances of horses cut out on chalk
cliffs in modern times, see *Handbook
for Wilts, &c.*, under the heads of
" Calne," " Chippenham," " Marlborough," " Weymouth."

" Below the White Horse is a
curious deep and broad gully called
' the Manger,' into one side of which
the hills fall with a series of sweeping curves, known as ' the Giants'
Stairs.' They are not a bit like
stairs, but covered with short green
turf and tender bluebells, and gos-
samer and thistle-down gleaming
in the sun, and the sheep-walks
running along their sides like ruled
lines."—*Tom Brown.* The other
side of the Manger is known as
" the Dragon's Hill," where, according to local folk-lore, St. George
killed the dragon, " whose blood
made a pool on the top, and ran
down the steps on the other side,
where the grass has never grown
since." The story is told by Job
Cork, the Uffington shepherd-poet:

" Ah, sur, I can remember well
The stories the old volk do tell—
Upon this hill which here is zeen,
Many a battle there have been.

" If it is true as I heerd zay,
King Gaarge did here the dragon slay,
And down below on yonder hill,
They buried he, as I've heerd tell."

At the summit of the hill, which
is 893 ft. above the level of the sea,
is the large oval camp known as
Uffington Castle, 700 ft. in diameter
from E. to W., and 500 ft. from N. to
S. It is surrounded by a high inner
vallum, with a slighter one on the
outside, which have been considered
by Camden and other authorities to
be Danish. The views from it are
very extensive, embracing parts of
eight counties. ¼ m. N.W. is another
camp, called *Hardwell Castle*, nearly
of a square form, and surrounded also
by a double vallum : its dimensions
140 by 180 ft. About 1 m. S.W. is
Alfred's Camp, a smaller circular
encampment, with a single vallum.
The traditionary account is, that at
the battle of Ashdown the Danes
occupied Uffington, Ethelred Hardwell, and Alfred the other camp ;
but modern investigation makes it
highly probable that the battle was
fought considerably more to the
eastward, possibly in the vicinity of
Cwichelm's law (Rte. 8).

Following the hill westward for
¼ m., close to the ancient Ridgeway,
the cromlech known as *Wayland
Smith's Cave* is reached, marked by
a spot of ground slightly raised,
and a circle of trees. It consists
of three large stones, with a
fourth laid upon them, and many
others scattered around. In plan
it is a Latin cross, and the remaining capstone, 10 ft. × 9 ft., covers
the E. transeptal cells. Its origin
is wrapped in mystery. Wise and
Gough suppose it to be Danish, the
burial-place of King Bagsæc, slain
at Ashdown ; Lysons believes it to
be British. The local tradition that
an invisible smith called Wayland
had his abode on this spot, who
would shoe a traveller's horse if left
here for a short time, with a piece of
money for payment, gave rise to one

of the most striking scenes in Sir W. Scott's novel of 'Kenilworth.' It is believed that Wayland Smith's fee was sixpence, and that, unlike other workmen, he was offended if more was offered.

At the foot of the hill on which stands Hardwell Castle is the village of *Compton Beauchamp.* It has a Dec. and Perp. cruciform *Church*, the Dec. E. window containing some original painted glass; there is a pillar piscina, a good Perp. octagonal font, and some ancient encaustic tiles. The moated *Manor-house* (Sir Jas. Bacon), has a quaint old terraced garden, with a fine dark yew-avenue, known as "The Cloister Walk."

[16½ m. *Faringdon* (Stat.). (*Inn:* Crown. Pop. 3525.) Faringdon, under the name of *Fearndune*, was a residence of the Saxon kings, at which Edward the Elder died in 925. The castle was held against Stephen by Robert Earl of Gloucester, and when taken was demolished; on its site King John built a Cistercian cell, as an appendage to Beaulieu. In the Civil War, Faringdon was held for the king during a considerable period, and its Manor-house was one of the last places that surrendered to the Parliament. The town stands on the side of a hill, in a sheltered situation, and commands fine views of the Berkshire downs on the one hand, and the valley of the Thames on the other. Brewing, malting, and bacon curing are the chief occupations.

The large cruciform *Church* (restored) is now mainly E.E., but with a low Norm. tower, once surmounted by a spire. The chancel is very fine E. E., as is the S. porch, which has a door of the same date, with ancient iron work. On the N. side of the nave is a small Norm. doorway, with embattled and zigzag mouldings. The Pye chapel and the Unton chapel each contain some

fine alabaster monuments: among them notice that of Sir Alexander Unton and two wives, in tabard and heraldic mantles (1547), and of Sir Edward Unton, who, when ambassador for Elizabeth in France, sent a challenge to the Duke of Guise, who, as he affirmed, in speaking evil of his mistress, "had most shamefully and wickedly lied." In the nave is the tomb of Sir Marmaduke Rawdon, who successfully defended the town against the Parliamentary forces. There are also several *Brasses*, from 1471 to 1547.

Faringdon House (Daniel Bennett, Esq.), near the ch., and approached through a noble avenue of elms, was built by Pye, the poet laureate, on the site of the ancient mansion which was garrisoned for Charles I. It was captured June 24, 1646, after a spirited defence of 55 days, and the loss of 40 of its garrison. It was during this siege that the ch. spire was beaten down, together with the whole of the S. aisle and transept. The latter have, however, been rebuilt in the same style, but may easily be distinguished from the original work.

Faringdon Clump, a grove of Scotch firs, planted by Pye, on an eminence of iron-sand just outside the town, is the chief landmark in the Vale of White Horse, and commands an extensive view over the plain—

" Whence White Horse
Sends presents to the Thame by Ock, her only flood."

This is the scene of Pye's poem of 'Faringdon Hill.' It is open to the pedestrian, and seats placed here and there allow the prospect to be contemplated at leisure. A road called Church Path, leading N. towards Littleworth, where there is a small modern ch., commands a noble prospect of the valley of the Thames for many miles.

2½ m. N. is *Radcot Bridge*, where Vere Duke of Ireland was defeated by the insurgent nobles of 1387, but escaped by swimming his horse across the river.

" Here Oxford's hero, famous for his boar,
    While clashing swords upon his target
    sound,
And show'rs of arrows from his breast
    rebound,
Prepared for worst of fates, undaunted
    stood,
And urged his beast into the rapid flood ;
The waves in triumph bore him, and were
    proud
To sink beneath their honourable load."
                            Thame and Isis.

This bridge and Newbridge, are the oldest on the Thames, both having been built in the 13th centy. Notice the E.E. ribbed arches, and the socket still remaining on the crown of the centre arch.

The bridge was fortified for the king during the Civil War as an outwork to Faringdon, but was surrendered, after a 15 days' siege, in May, 1646. The village of Radcot is in Oxfordshire (Rte. 25).

2¼ m. N.W. of Faringdon is *Eaton Hastings*, with a small E. E. *Church*, worth a visit. There are good Dec. E. and W. windows, a Trans.-Norm. chancel-arch with star moulding, a massive Norm. font, and very elegant E. E. sedilia ; also some blue and yellow encaustic tiles in the chancel. The chancel was restored in 1872, and the nave in 1874. 1½ m. W. is *Buscot*, where also is a good E.E. *Church*, with Perp. tower. "There are two piscinas on the S. side, both E.E., one on each side of the window, the sill of which serves for the sedilia."—(*J. H. P.*) *Buscot House* (R. Campbell, Esq.) is a handsome stone mansion, built 1780, standing in an extensive deer park. In this neighbourhood beetroot is extensively cultivated for distillery purposes.]

18¼ m. *Shrivenham* (Stat.). The village, 1 m. N. (locally called " *Shrinham* "), is a very clean, pleasant-looking place, which has much benefited by the liberality of the Bar-

rington family. The *Church* retains its central tower and supporting arches, which are good Perp. ; the rest of the structure has been rebuilt at various times, in very bad taste, some parts affecting Norm., but the windows all of 4 lights, and square headed. The ch. contains two monuments, of interest to admirers of the Commonwealth. One is to John Wildman, the Anabaptist (afterwards Sir John Wildman, of Becket, d. 1693), who directed by his will " that, if his executors should think fit, there should be some stone of small price set near his ashes, to signify, without foolish flattery, to his posterity, that in that age lived a man who spent the best part of his days in prisons, without crimes, being conscious of no offence towards man, for that he so loved his God that he could serve no man's will, and wished the liberty and happiness of his country, and of all mankind." The other is to John Wildman, his son (d. 1710), who " preferred confinement for many years with his father, who was a prisoner in the Isle of Scilly, in the reign of Charles II., to the full enjoyment of his liberty." There is also a monument to John's adopted son, John Shute, afterwards the first Viscount Barrington (d. 1793), for 39 years a distinguished member of the House of Commons ; and one to Samuel Barrington, Admiral of the White, 1800, who was distinguished in the wars of 1741–56, especially by the capture of the French ship 'Count St. Florentine;' the admiral's epitaph is by Mrs. Hannah More. Near the ch. are 6 *alms-houses*, founded and endowed by Henry Marten the regicide.

Beckett (Viscount Barrington) is a fine mansion in the Tudor style, built by the sixth Viscount, 1831–4, from the designs of his brother-in-law, the Hon. Thomas Liddell, a large old manor-house, part of which had been burnt in the Civil Wars, being pulled down to make room for it. It contains some good family portraits by *Sir J. Reynolds* and *Sir T. Lawrence*, some fine landscapes by *Both*, and some interesting French miniatures, including two of Louis XIV., when young and old, by *Petitôt*. Among the curiosities are the chessboard and men of Charles I., in the original velvet bag in which they were sold by the Parliament. The grounds are adorned by a large sheet of artificial water, overhung at one corner by a curious stone summer-house, built by Inigo Jones, which enjoys the reputation of being the oldest in England. It contains some handsome Delft dishes from Queen Mary's dairy.

Beckett, formerly called Becote, belonged to the Earls of Evreux, who gave it to the Priory of Norion in Normandy. It was seized in 1204 by King John, who probably occasionally resided here, as a mandate of his to the Sheriff of Oxfordshire is dated from Beckett. The manor was afterwards held by a family who derived their name (De Beckote) from the place, and who held it by tenure of meeting the King whenever he should pass Fowyeare's Mill Bridge in Shrivenham, with two white capons in their hands, and saying, "Ecce Domine istos duos capones quos alias habebitis sed non nunc."

19¼ m. The line enters Wiltshire, and reaches at

24 m. *Swindon Junct. Stat.* (See *Handbook for Wilts.*)

ROUTE 6.

READING TO NEWBURY`AND HUNGERFORD.

Branch of G. W. Rly. 25½ m.

This raily. goes off on l. immediately from the main line at Reading Stat. (Rte. 4.) At 1 m. on l. is *Coley Park* (J. B. Monck, Esq.), the old seat of the Vachells, whose ancient mansion, Coley House, was the residence of Charles I. for several days during the Civil Wars. At Coley Cross Edward VI. was met by the mayor and aldermen of Reading on his visit to their town, and presented with two yokes of oxen. [Just beyond Coley Park the *Basingstoke Branch* runs off on l. The only stat. in Berkshire is 7½ m. *Mortimer*, or *Stratfield Mortimer*, as it is more proporly called. Here is a handsome ch. with lofty spire, built 1869 in lieu of a decayed structure originally Norm., and preserving some ancient monuments. This stat. give the readiest approach to the Roman city of *Silchester*, for which, with the remainder of the route to Basingstoke, see *Handbook for Hants.*]

3 m. On N. 1½ m. *Tilehurst*. The Church, originally Perp. of very poor character, was rebuilt, with the exception of the N. aisle, in 1856. It is Dec., with painted glass windows, an alabaster reredos, and carved oak stalls; and preserves the monument of Sir Peter Vanlore, a rich merchant, 1627, and his lady. Lloyd, Bishop of Worcester, 1717, was a native of this place. Tilehurst Stat. on the Reading and Swindon main line was opened in April, 1882. It

is 2 m. from Reading and 3 m. from Pangbourne. *Calcot House* (J. H. Blagrave, Esq.), "a large square brick house with wings, backed by splendid timber, and looking out due S. over the pleasantest of parks, full of dappled fallow-deer, was the seat of 'the Berkshire lady,' whose story, which 'lives both in prose and verse,' is briefly this :— The John Kendrick who bequeathed 7500*l.* to build the Oracle at Reading, for the maintenance of the cloth trade (*ante*, Rte. 4), left a noble fortune, part of which descended to a beautiful Miss Kendrick, who is described as refusing numberless offers of marriage, till at length—

> Being at a noble wedding
> In the famous town of Reading,
> A young gentleman she saw,
> Who belonged to the law.

This is Benjamin Child, a barrister, to whom, on her return home, she writes a challenge to mortal combat in Calcot Park. Going thither, he finds a masked lady, who informs him that she is the challenger.

> 'So now take your choice,' says she,
> ' Either fight or marry me.'
> Said he, ' Madam, pray what mean ye?
> In my life I ne'er have seen ye ;
> Pray unmask, your visage show,
> Then I'll tell you, ay or no.'
>
> *Lady.*—' I will not my face uncover
> Till the marriage rites are over ;
> Therefore take you which you will—
> Wed me, Sir, or try your skill.'

He consents to marry the masked swordswoman ; they drive to church in her coach, which is in waiting, and the wedding takes place. Then they proceed to Calcot House where he is left alone for 2 hours in ' a beautiful and fair parlour,' when the steward comes to question him, as though he had an eye to the spoons. At length the mistress herself entering, says,

> *Lady.* ' Sir, my servants have related
> That some hours you have waited
> In my parlour ; tell me who'
> In this house you ever knew ?'

> *Gent.* ' Madam, if I have offended,
> It is more than I intended ;
> A young lady brought me here.'
> ' That is true,' said she, ' my dear.'

Then Benjamin Child finds himself happily married to the mistress of Calcot.

> Now he's clothed in rich attire
> Not inferior to a squire—
> Beauty, honour, riches, store !
> What can man desire more?

In the parish register is recorded the birth of the two daughters of the Berkshire lady and Benjamin Child, in Sept. 1712 and Sept. 1713. It is but a century and a half ago that these events happened, in times more prosaic than our own."

5¼ m. *Theale* (Stat.). The *Church* is a modern edifice (Theale being a newly-formed parish) in the E. E. style, built in a very costly manner by the late Mrs. Shepherd and her brother Dr. Routh, the President of Magdalen Coll., Oxford.

2¼ m. S.E. is *Burghfield.* The *Church*, rebuilt in 1843, is a large Romanesque cruciform structure, with apse. In the porches are preserved three effigies from the old ch. ; one is of wood, of 14th centy. date. It was this living which Bolingbroke wished Swift to take in exchange for his deanery.

1 m. N.W. is *Englefield*, where, in the Park or Chase, Ethelwulf, alderman of Berks, fought with the Danes in 871, just before the battle of Æscesdun. Simeon narrates that he urged on his soldiers, saying, " Though they attack us with the advantage of more men, we may despise them, for our commander Christ is braver than they." At any rate the Pagans were discomfited, and two of their great sea-Earls, unaccustomed to the saddle, were unhorsed and slain. This ancient manor of the Englefields was forfeited to the Crown by the attainder of Sir J. Englefield, on the charge of plotting to rescue Mary Queen of Scots. It was granted to Sir F.

Walsingham, from whose family it passed to John Pawlet, the famous Marquis of Winchester, who ended his days here after the demolition of Basing (1674). The story of the Englefields is charmingly narrated by Lord Carnarvon in his 'Archæology of Berks,' 1859. The modern Tudor mansion, built by its present possessor, Richard Benyon, Esq., consists of a series of projecting bays, having a tower in the centre, and fine stone terraces beneath.

In the park, which abounds in deer, is the little E. E. *Church,* restored by *Scott.* Here is the monument of the Marquis of Winchester, inscribed with verses by Dryden, and an epitaph which tells how he was "a man of exemplary piety towards God, and of inviolable fidelity towards his sovereign, in whose cause he fortified his house at Basing, and defended it against the rebels to the last extremity." In the S. aisle, in niches under the wall, are effigies of a cross-legged knight in mail, temp. Edw. II. (?), and a lady of the 14th centy. in wood. Near the altar, and separating it from the Englefield aisle, is a fine grey canopied tomb, from which the brasses have been removed. Several other monuments are curious, especially that of J. Englefield and all his family, 1605, and a bas-relief representing the death of Mrs. Mary Benyon, 1777. E. E. piers and arches support the roof, and in the N. aisle is a fine E. E. window, with detached shafts.

1 m. N. is *Bradfield,* remarkable for *St. Andrew's College,* founded by the munificence of the Vicar, the Rev. T. Stevens, opened as a grammar-school 1850, and enrolled as a foundation-school 1859, for 16 founder's boys and 153 commoners. In 1862 it was incorporated by Royal Charter; and the Warden is now authorised to admit 300 commoners. It is a picturesque building, and contains a good dining-hall, with stained-glass windows. The *Church,* which has been beautifully restored by *Sir G. G. Scott,* and preserves some Trans.-Norm. and Dec. features, as well as the Jacobean tower of flint and brick, has a fine chancel in the E.E. style, and some good stained glass. There is a way hence to Aldworth (Rte. 4) through winding lanes, frequently bordered by old yews and hollies, and across the picturesque wooded common of *Ashhampstead,* where the manor of Hartridge was held by keeping a goshawk for the King.

7 m. On S. 1 m. *Ufton Nervet,* a village with a Perp. ch., rebuilt in 1862. At a short distance, on a thickly-wooded eminence, approached by a picturesque lane, is *Ufton Court* (the property of R Benyon, Esq), described by Pope in his letters, and the home of Arabella Fermor, celebrated by him in his 'Rape of the Lock,' under the name of Belinda. The house has been much injured, and is now divided into several habitations; but the variety of its gables and the dark projecting porch of carved oak render it still very picturesque. Behind the house is a raised terrace where Arabella must often have walked, with steps leading down into a flower-garden, which still retains its original form. Below the terrace is a subterranean passage communicating with the dining-room. The hall retains its beautiful ceiling with pendants, and its black and white chequered pavement; there is "a haunted staircase," and upstairs in the long passages are a number of trap-doors and secret chambers in the depth of the wall, which afforded protection to priests during the prevalence of the penal laws Rooms called "the Chapel" and "the Priest's Vestry" are shown in the top of the house. The old *Barn* should be observed —its fine timber roof, and the peculiar ornament in the win-

dows. Near it is a magnificent old oak-tree.

8¾ m. *Aldermaston* (Stat.). The village lies more than 1 m. S., on the bank of a branch of the river Kennet, on which it has a wharf. 1 m. further S., at the top of the hill, are the lodges of *Aldermaston Court* (Higford Burr, Esq.), a modern Elizabethan mansion, built by *Hardwick*, 1851, which contains a great deal of very fine old tapestry and curious carved furniture collected at Venice. The windows of the Library preserve some of the stained glass from the old Hall, with the arms of its former possessors, the Forsters, and their alliances with the families of Delamare, Sandes, Hungerford, Barrett, Kingsmill, Harpsden, Milborne, Achard, and Popham. The clocktower is very conspicuous from the railway.

The *Park*, which is one of the wildest and most varied in this part of England, is 5 m. in extent, and contains 1000 acres. There is a broad lake, and the fern-clad deer paddocks are studded with old thorn-trees, yews, and gigantic oaks, whilst several portions of the old lime avenues remain. The common snake abounds, being protected by Mr. Burr, who says, "I never hear of any ladies being frightened by them, so shy and retiring are they in their habits."—*Reading Mercury*, Aug. 12, 1871. The original house, mentioned by Evelyn as built "à la moderne," was partly burnt down, and partly destroyed at the erection of the present building; the inscription which adorned it,

Hump. ⎱ Forster ⎰ Vivimus et ædificamus
Anna ⎰   ⎱ uno animo,
                 Utunque Deo et Fato
                 consecravimus, 1636—

and some of the old buildings, remain behind the present conservatory. The fine old staircase, engraved by Nash, which has a balustrade ornamented with figures, is preserved in the present house.

The manor was granted to Robert Achard by Henry I. (Queen Matilda being witness). The last of the Achards died in 1353, leaving a daughter, who brought the estate by marriage to Sir Thomas Delamare. His granddaughter and heiress married Sir George Forster, whose family lived here till 1711. The last female of the family married Lord Stawell, whose only daughter married Ralph Congreve, Esq. "A memorial of this Lord Stawell exists in the coronet inwoven in the ornaments of the beautiful iron gates; almost the only memorial he has left, except the tradition of his insatiable love of gambling, which reduced his estate to an inalienable residence, and gave rise to the local proverb, 'When clubs are trumps, Aldermaston House shakes.'"

In the park, very near to the house, is the *Church*, E. E. and Dec.; the Dec. tower has a late Norm. doorway, built in at the W. end. The ch. contains the large and beautiful alabaster monument of Sir George Forster, 1526, and his lady, with 11 sons in armour, and 8 daughters in the angular headdresses of that period, under Gothic canopies round the side; the knight's feet rest upon a hind, his crest (a Hind's Head) is still the sign of the village Inn; and a tiny dog bites the gown of the lady. Behind this tomb is a chapel, in which the position of the ancient altar is occupied by the tomb of Mr. Ralph Congreve.

1¼ m. S.E. of Aldermaston is the Roman amphitheatre of *Silchester*, the largest in Britain except that of Dorchester, measuring 50 yards by 40. It is just within the boundary of Berks, but is, for completeness, described with Silchester in *Handbook for Hants*.

1½ m. E. *Padworth*. This manor was held, from an early period, by the Cowdrays, on the tenure of providing a sailor to manage the ropes of the Queen's ship whenever she went to Normandy. The little ch., formerly a very interesting specimen of enriched Norm. architecture, has been injudiciously treated. Close by is *Padworth House* (C. D. Griffith, Esq.).

2 m. N. of Aldermaston Stat is *Beenham Vallence*, with a ch. rebuilt in 1859. It contains a monument to the Rev. Thomas Stackhouse, author of the 'History of the Bible,' many years vicar (d. 1752, aged 72). He was a remarkable man, but his life presented a sad picture of the consequences of intemperance. " He would often stray down to a public-house called Jack's Booth, on the Bath road, and stay there for 2 or 3 days at a time; it is even said that a great part of his History was written in an arbour at the bottom of the garden. He would come up from hence on a Sunday morning, and ask pardon of God in the pulpit for his folly and wickedness, and warn his congregation against the vice of drunkenness, yet he would probably in a week or two again yield to the same temptation."

2¼ m. N.W. of Beenham is *Bucklebury*, with a *Church* originally Trans.-Norm., but now greatly altered. It, however, has still a good Norm. S. doorway; and it contains several monuments of the Winchcombes. There is a very fine yew-tree in the ch.-yard. The register contains a list of the rectors from 1303.
The manor of Bucklebury was purchased at the Dissolution by John Winchcombe, a son of the rich clothier called Jack of Newbury. He built himself a fine Tudor manor-house, now destroyed. Lord Bolingbroke married a descendant of his, and resided at Bucklebury, where he received a visit from Swift in 1711, which the latter thus describes in a letter to Stella:—" Mr. Secretary was a perfect country-gentleman at Bucklebury: he

smoked tobacco with one or two neighbours; he inquired after the wheat in such a field; he went to visit his hounds, and knew all their names; he and his lady saw me up to my chamber just in the country-fashion. His house is just in the midst of 3000l. a year he had by his lady, who is descended from Jack of Newbury, of whom books and ballads are written; and there is an old picture of him in the room."

2 m. N.E. is *Stanford Dingley*, a Trans.-Norm. *Church*, restored in 1870, with a curious wooden bell-tower built up within the walls of the nave. " The S. doorway is very uncommon, the inner head trefoiled, with a circular ornament introduced at the point; over this is a well-moulded pointed arch, partly concealed by the plaster ceiling of the porch; the door has E. E. iron work " (*J. H. P.*). There are 3 *Brasses*, one of Margaret Dyneley, " wife of William, esquire to the King," 1444, and 2 small ones, temp. James I.

' 10¾ m. *Midgham* (Stat.). Wool-hampton ch. 1¼ m. N.E., was rebuilt in 1861, and is a handsome edifice, with stained glass windows. The old Norm. font, of stone, with an arcade and figures in lead, has been preserved.

13½ m. *Thatcham* (Stat.). The ch., Trans.-Norm. and Dec., with Perp. N. door, has been restored; it contains the monument of W. Danvers, Judge of Common Pleas, temp. Henry VII. (d. 1504).

17 m. *Newbury* (Stat.). The town of Newbury (*Inns:* The Chequers, moderate; in Speenhamland, White Hart), Pop. 7939, stands on the river Kennet, and is also intersected by the Kennet and Avon Canal. It is supposed to have originated in the Roman Spinæ, of which the name still remains in *Speen*, and *Speenhamland*, as the part of

the town N. of the river is called. The earliest mention of this name is in a charter obtained by the Saxon Abbot Bethmee from King Kenwulf, in 821, fronting " all the wood which is called Spene " to Abingdon Abbey. At the time of the Domesday-Book, two villages, Spone and Bagnor, occupied this site, and Ulmiton, or Ulward's Town, had sprung up in the neighbourhood, then nearly twice the size of Reading. The manor was granted by William to Ernulf of Hesdin, the 1st Earl of Perche, but was forfeited by his descendant in the time of Stephen and annexed to the crown. King John lived much at his huntinglodge of Kingsclere, and often visited Newbury. According to an old legendary ballad he was concealed in the house of an old spinning woman at Newbury when he fled from his insurgent barons, and built the almshouses now called St. Bartholomew's Hospital, in token of his gratitude. The manor of Newbury afterwards came into the possession of the earls of Pembroke, and has since been given as a jointure to Queen Jane Seymour and to Queen Anne of Denmark.

The town was one of the most flourishing seats of the cloth trade, which here produced its hero towards the end of the 15th centy. John Winchcombe, better known as *Jack of Newbury*, was a clothier, who had raised himself to great local eminence, and kept 100 looms at work. When, in Henry VIII.'s absence, the Scotch invaded England, he was ordered to send out four men armed with pikes and two horsemen for the king's service, and answered the call by marching N. at the head of 50 tall men well mounted, and 50 footmen with bow and pike, " as well armed and better clothed than any." Whether he reached Flodden is doubtful, though the ballad of the ' Newberrie Archers ' gives the particulars of the exploits of his men.

On Henry's return from France, Jack had the honour of entertaining him at Newbury, which he did in splendid fashion, and declined the honour of knighthood. But Jack's crowning work was his carrying to a successful issue the clothiers' petition, when, " by reason of the wars, many merchant strangers were prohibited from coming to England, and also our merchants, in like sort, were forbidden to have dealings with France and the Low Countries," so that the cloth trade had fallen very low. Wolsey, to whom the deputation was first referred, put the matter off from time to time, being of opinion that "Jack of Newbury, if well examined, would be found to be infected with Luther's spirit." Jack, in his turn, exasperated the Cardinal by saying, "If my Lord Chancellor's father had been no hastier in killing calves than he in despatching of poor men's suits, I think he would never have worn a mitre." But the King took the matter up, and the clothiers got their order, "that merchants should freely traffic one with another, and the proclamation thereof should be made as well on the other side of the sea as the land." A portrait said to be his, but really representing his son John (d. 1557), was long preserved in the old market-house.

Newbury, though its clothing trade has disappeared, is a thriving town, with many large maltsters and millers. It rests on a stratum of peat, not more than ½ m. wide, but many miles in length, which is cut for fuel or manure, and abounds in curious geological remains. In consequence of this foundation, the houses shake perceptibly when any heavy waggon passes through the streets. The Kennet, which divides the town, is more famed for eels than for trout.

The *Church of St. Nicholas* is a large Perp. structure, with W. tower, which has octagonal turrets. It is believed to have been built, in part at least, by the great clothier, as the initials "J. S." (John Smallwood, *alias* Winchcombe) occur on the bosses of the roof of the nave. There is also a brass to his memory (d. 1520). The ch. was restored in 1868. Dr. Twiss, a noted Puritan, and Thos. Penrose, one of the minor poets (d. 1769), have been among the rectors of Newbury. The ch. of St. Nicholas and the churchyard are kept in beautiful order, and are well worth a visit. St. John's ch. is modern.

Newbury has long been noted for its corn-market, and one for wool has of late been added. A handsome *Corn Exchange* was built in 1862. The old custom here, that everything must be paid for on delivery, gave rise to the local proverb—

> " The farmer doth take back
> His money in his sack."

There is a *Literary Institute* at Newbury, in the museum of which a good collection of local geological specimens is to be seen.

The Martyrs of Newbury.

As in other towns that "stood by clothing," reformed opinions early prevailed at Newbury, and Christopher Shoemaker was in 1518 burnt there for reading the Gospels to another person. But a more noted sufferer was Julins [Jocelyn] Palmer, who had been master of the Reading grammar school. He was a fellow of Magdalen College, Oxford, and a Romanist, but he was so struck by the constancy exhibited by the bishops there (at whose burning he was present), that he became a Protestant, and suffered death, with two others, at a place called the Sandpits at Newbury, July 16, 1556. "When they were come to the place where they should suffer, they all three fell to the ground, and Palmer with an audible voice pronounced the 31st Psalm, but the other two made their prayers secretly to God .... and so forthwith they put off their raiment, and went to the stake and kissed it. And when they were bound to the post Palmer said, ' Good people, pray for us, that we may persevere to the end; and for Christ's sake beware of Popish teachers, for they deceive you.' As he spake this, a servant of one of the bailiffs threw a faggot at his face, that the blood gushed out in divers places. For the which fact the sheriff reviled him, calling him cruel tormentor, and with his walking staff brake his head, that the blood likewise ran about his ears. When the fire was kindled and began to take hold upon their bodies, then lift up their hands towards heaven, and quietly and cheerily, as though they had felt no smart, they cried, ' Lord Jesu strengthen us, Lord Jesu assist us, Lord Jesu receive our souls.' And so they continued, without any struggling, holding up their hands, and knocking their hearts, and calling upon Jesu, until they had ended their mortal lives."— *Foxe.*

The Battles of Newbury.

During the Civil War the townsmen of Newbury were vehemently Parliamentarian, and loud complaints of their "seditious demeanour," even after the Restoration, occur in the State Papers preserved in the Public Record Office. The immediate neighbourhood of the town was the scene of two indecisive battles, commonly known as the first and the second battle of Newbury.

The *First Battle* occurred in 1643, when the town was held by the royalists. On Sept. 16, Essex, who commanded the Parliamentarian army that had relieved Gloucester, attempted to reach Newbury by a forced march over Enborne Chase, intending to proceed thence to London, but was driven to Hungerford, in consequence of an attack made by the royalists under Prince Rupert, in the middle of the chase, when "the dragoons in both sides gave fire in full bodies on one another on the side of the hill, so that the woods above and the valleys below did echo with the thunder of the charge." During this conflict many of the queen's life-guard were cut to pieces, and the Marquis de Vieuville was taken mortally wounded, making known his rank in his last words, "Vous voyez un grand Marquis mourant." On Sept. 18 Essex was encamped "in the fields," between Enborne and the present road to Newbury, and in order to force his way, drew out his men in battle array on "Biggs' Hill," which name still remains applied to a cottage, on the borders of what till lately was Enborne Common. The king's lines, which commanded the London road, and which were defended in the rear by the river Lamborne and the guns of Donnington, must have extended from Newbury along "the hill" to Newbury Wash, where his main force was drawn up, and whither Essex, "finding his soldiers full of mettle," advanced by a narrow lane up Speen Hill, in which but 6 men could march abreast, seizing upon the table-land at the top, which he continued to occupy throughout the day. The king was unwilling to risk an engagement, but was forcibly led into it by the rashness of his officers, whose eagerness was such, that, leaving their doublets behind, they led out their men to battle in their shirts. The artillery were at first unavailable, but the royal cavalry, headed by the Earl of Carnarvon, charged with wonderful boldness, so that they routed the horse of the enemy in most places, though the leader himself fell in the midst of his triumph. The Parlia-

mentarian foot however behaved well, and the London trained bands stood firm, and kept their ground steadily at Newbury Marsh, though Prince Rupert charged them in person with the cry "Queen Mary in the field!" Essex, in a white hat, which he refused to change, was among them, and eventually, rallying his men, with undaunted courage led them up the hill, driving the infantry of the king "from hedge to hedge," and gained possession of "the hill, the hedges, and the river" Kennet.

Meantime the royalists, observing that Essex's men for distinction's sake wore branches of fern and broom in their hats, adopted the same badge, and, shouting "Friends!" fell stealthily upon the Parliamentarian rear, but after a sharp conflict were put to flight. After 6 hours' fight, "the cannon did still dispute with one another, as if the battle was but new begun;" and when at length night drew on, it left neither side to claim a victory, though it was a hard hand-to-hand fight to the last, and darkness sank over 6000 men dead upon the field. On the following morning Essex carried out his design of retiring to Reading, Prince Rupert suffering him to proceed, with his whole army, till they were engulfed in the narrow lane near Theale, now called "Dead Man's Lane," when he fell upon their rear with fearful execution.

Among the 60 cartloads of slain carried into the town, were the Earl of Carnarvon, who in the morning had been seen measuring a gateway with his sword, amid a crowd of laughing Cavaliers, to see how Essex's horns could pass through when they should lead him in as prisoner, and whose dead body came into Newbury the same evening, stretched across a horse "like that of a calf"; the Earl of Sunderland, only 23 yrs. old; and the blameless

Lord Falkland, who had received the Sacrament that morning, and had gone out to battle, saying, " I am weary of the times, and foresee much misery to my country, but I believe I shall be out of it ere night." Clarendon describes him in a beautiful memoir, and says that, " If there were no other brand upon this odious and accursed war than that single loss, it must be most infamous, and execrable to all posterity." He is commemorated by Pope in the line—

" See Falkland dies, the virtuous and the just ;"

and by Southey, who wrote an inscription for a column at Newbury, commencing—

" On this field
Did Falkland fall, the blameless and the brave."

A solitary poplar long marked the spot where he fell, but it was cut down several years ago. A monument, 33 ft. in height, and containing about 40 tons of granite, terminated by a monolith 17 ft. in height, has been erected to his memory, by those " to whom the Majesty of the Crown and the Liberties of their country are dear." Chain-shot, cannon-balls, and other relics, are constantly found on the battle-field ; and 3 tumuli still exist where the slain were interred, 2 on the Wash, and 1 on Enborne Common.

The *Second Battle of Newbury* took place on Sunday, Oct. 27, 1644, Charles having come thither to relieve Donnington Castle, which was besieged by the Earl of Manchester, and being himself quartered in Newbury, at a house on the W. of Cheap Street. The suburban villages Speen and Shaw were both in possession of the royalists ; Shaw House, or Dolman's as it was then called, being occupied by Col. Page, and every hedge and hollow in its neighbour-

[*Berks, &c.*]

hood lined with ambushed skirmishers and marksmen.

Hostilities were commenced early on Sunday morning by a sudden attack of 1000 men of Manchester's force, who descended the hill undiscovered upon Shaw House, but being routed by Sir J. Astley, they were driven back upon their own men, who were coming to assist them. A succession of warm skirmishes continued till the afternoon, when, by a sudden movement, Waller led his men across the Lamborne, and seized Speen, a feat commemorated in the popular stanza :

" My friend Billy Waller, in doublet white,
    And without any arms, either rusty or bright,
Charged through them twice like a little sprite,
        Which nobody can deny."

Hence he immediately proceeded to attack the king's horse " in the open fields under the hill of Speen," where the king himself then was with the Prince of Wales, but here he was repulsed by Col. Campfield, while the Earl of Cleveland charged the l. wing of the Parliamentarians, and succeeded in driving them back, but was himself taken prisoner. Meantime the troops under Manchester advanced upon " Dolemans," "singing of psalms as they went," but were repulsed by Sir J. Brown and Lieut.-Col. Page, who " pursued them from the house with notable execution ;" and by Col. Lisle, unarmed and clad in " a good Holland shirt," who charged them 3 times, shouting " For the crown !" " For Pr. Charles !" " For the Duke of York !" while a storm of musket-bullets hailed upon them from every window and parapet of the old manor-house. At length night approached, " for which neither party were sorry," when all the royal forces drew up about Donnington, and, leaving their wounded and ordnance there, abandoned Newbury, which thencefor-

F

ward remained in the hands of the Parliament, and retired to Oxford, unmolested by the enemy, who, "it being a fine moonlight night, were not ignorant of their retreat."

Speenhamland is a kind of suburb of Newbury, connecting it with the old Bath road, which passed N. of the town, and had at Speen and Speenhamland large *Inns*, the heavy charges at which provoked many a complaint. One, the *Pelican*, was thus commemorated by Quin:

> " The famous Inn at Speenhamland,
> That stands below the hill,
> May well be called the Pelican, ·
> From its enormous bill."

This, however, is a joke of the past; the Inn is now excellent, reasonable, and much resorted to during the fishing-season.

1 m. N. W. is the village of *Speen*, or *Church Speen.* The *Church* is a large edifice, rebuilt 1860, except the brick tower, in the E. E. style. It contains an altar-tomb, with the effigy of John Baptiste de Castilion (d. 1598), to whom a manor in this parish was granted in 1565. An effigy of his son's wife, 1603, is habited in a farthingale and flowered gown, with a veil nearly to the feet. There are also monuments to the Craven family; among others to Elizabeth, Lady Craven, who married the Margrave of Anspach, and resided at *Benham Park* (R. Sutton, Esq.), a handsome classic edifice near the river.

1 m. N. E. is *Shaw House* (Mrs. Eyre), still, in spite of injuries received in the Civil Wars (it was the centre of conflict in the second battle of Newbury), the most stately Elizabethan mansion in Berks. It is built of rich red brick, with stone dressings, and is surrounded by old-fashioned shrubberies. The garden still shows some of the earthworks thrown up during the war, and a large collection of cannon - balls, picked up on the spot, is preserved

in the hall. On the night before the battle, Charles was the guest of Sir John Dolman : and in the oak wainscot of the drawing-room is a hole, made, according to tradition, by a bullet fired at the king, while he was dressing in the bow window. It bears the inscription, " Hanc juxta fenestram, rex Carolus primus, instante obsidione schoppopetrae ictu tantum non trajectus fuit, die Octob. xxvii. MDCXLIV."

The house was built in 1581 by Thomas Dolman, a member of an old Yorkshire family who had settled in Newbury as a clothier, and having made a fortune, retired here to live as a country gentleman. The proceeding was distasteful to the townsmen, and they expressed their feelings in the lines—

> " Lord have mercy upon us, miserable sinners;
> Thomas Dolman has built a new house,
> And has turned away all his spinners."

To which he retorted in the haughty lines still remaining over the gateway—

> " Edentulus vescentium dentibus invidet,
> Et oculos caprearum talpa contemuit."

The ch. of Shaw, rebuilt in 1840, in the Norman style, has several monuments of the Dolmans, who retained possession of the manor until the 18th cent. Col. Dolman, a noted member of the old Commonwealth party after the Restoration, was the brother of Sir John, the host of the king. A chancel was added in 1877 to the memory of H. R. Eyre, Esq.

1 m. N. of Newbury, crowning a hill to the l. of the Oxford road, and shrouded by ancient trees, are the picturesque remains of *Donnington Castle*, now limited to an ivy-mantled gateway, with a tall tower on either side and a piece of wall adjoining, much of the material having been used in building a modern mansion, *Castle House* (Stephen Matthews, Esq.), at the foot of the hill. The place

has always been associated with the poet Chaucer, and local tradition, backed by the writings of Camden, Sylvester, Godwin, and others, asserts that he lived in the castle, which Grose declares to have been presented to him by John of Gaunt. Speight speaks of the "elde oak" at Donnington, called Chaucer's oke;" and Evelyn declares that "among the trees in Donnington Park were three which were remarkable from the ingenious planter and dedicator (if tradition hold), the famous English bard Geoffrey Chaucer: of which one was called the king's, another the queen's, and a third Chaucer's, oak;" while Ashmole further asserts that Chaucer "composed many of his celebrated pieces under an oak in Donnington Park." It is, however, unfortunately the fact, that Donnington did not come into the Chaucer family till 1418, 18 yrs. after the poet's death (John of Gaunt never having been the possessor of this place at all, but of Donnington in Leicestershire, see *Handbook for Leicester*), when it passed from the Abberburys (one of whom had bought it for 100s. from Edward II.) to the poet's grand daughter Alice, whose tomb is at Ewelme (Rte. 20), and who married—1st. Sir John Phelipp; 2nd. Thos., Earl of Salisbury; and 3rd. Wm. de la Pole, Duke of Suffolk, who resided with her at Donnington. Here she may have been visited by her father, Thos. Chaucer, the poet's only son, by whom the trees were probably planted.

During the Civil Wars Donnington Castle was the centre of conflict. It was first attacked by Gen. Middleton in Aug. 1644, when its governor, Col. Boys, in answer to a summons to surrender, first declared his resolution of maintaining his trust, and then repulsed his assailants, after an assault of 6 hrs., with a loss of 100 men. On Sept. 19 Col. Horton succeeded in beating down 3 of the

towers, and, relying on this success, declared that, unless the castle was surrendered, he would spare no life within it: to which Boys replied, that he "would keep the place, and would neither give or take quarter;" and that night, again making a sally, repulsed his besiegers with loss. Threats that his enemies would not leave one stone upon another were only met by the response that he was not bound to repair the castle, but, by God's help, he would keep the ground; and he did so, until in April, 1646 he received the King's order to surrender. Round the Castle are still to be seen traces of the outworks thrown up during the siege, the strength of which explains its successful defence.

Half-way up the Castle Hill is *Donnington Priory*, built on the site of a small priory of Trinitarians, which was founded by Sir Richard Abberbury, guardian of Richard II., in 1394, at the same time with *Donnington Hospital.*

At the foot of the hill flows the Lamborne, a celebrated trout-stream, which the inhabitants, "in spite of the evidence of their eyes," still believe to answer to the account of the local poet Sylvester:

"Little Lambs-Bourne . . . .
All summer long (while all thy sisters shrink)
Men of thy team a million daily drink;
Beside thy waste, which then in haste doth run,
To wash the feet of Chaucer's Donnington:
But (while the rest are full unto the top)
All winter long thou never showst a drop,
Nor sendst a doit of needless subsidy
To cram the Kennet's wantless treasury,
Before her stores be spent and springs be stayed—
Then, then alone, thou lendst a liberal aid."

2 m. S. of Newbury is *Sandleford*, where a priory was founded c. 1200 by Geoffrey, Earl of Perche. On its site is a modern house called *Sandleford Priory* (W. P. B. Chatteris, Esq.) where lived Mrs. Montagu, celebrated for the literary society of which she was the centre. Johnson,

Goldsmith, Burke, Reynolds, Beattie, and Mrs. E. Carter were among her constant visitors. "Dr. Stillingfleet was in the habit of attending her literary parties in a full suit of cloth, with blue worsted stockings, and rendered himself so entertaining that the ladies used to delay their discussions until his arrival, declaring, 'Wo can do nothing without our blue stockings'—whence the *bas bleu*. Mrs. Montagu converted the old chapel of the Priory—which contained an interesting tomb of a Crusader, supposed to be the Earl of Perche—into a dining-room, connecting it with the house by a beautiful octagon drawing-room, a fact noticed by Mrs. H. More in one of her letters. Madame D'Arblay mentions a visit here, and Cowper has immortalized the feather hangings in the lines—

> ' The birds put off their feathery hue
> To dress a room for Montagu.'

Mrs. Montagu died in 1800."—*Godwin*.

19 m. On S. is *Enborne*, with a Norm. and E. E. ch., having a debased Perp. E. window; there is a good Norm. font, circular, with arcade. The parish contains two ancient manors, in which a custom prevailed, that, if a widow of a copyholder was guilty of incontinency, she forfeited her life-interest in her husband's copyhold, which could only be recovered by her riding into court on a black ram, repeating a ludicrous petition in rhyme. (See Addison in the 'Spectator,' No. 623.)

8 m. S. of Newbury is *Highclere*, the beautiful park and mansion (Sir C. Barry, architect) of the Earl of Carnarvon.

Adjoining Enborne on W. is *Hampstead Marshall*, a small parish, with a red-brick ch. of the time of James I. In it is buried Sir Balthazar Gerbier (d. 1667).

The manor of Hampstead Marshall

was bestowed by Henry I. on one Gilbert, who took the name of Marshal, from his office in the royal household. His grandson was John the Marshal, whose controversy with Becket about the manor of Pagham, in Sussex, gave occasion for the proceedings against the archbishop. His son was William, created Earl of Pembroke, who became the Protector of the kingdom on the death of King John. His five sons, who all became earls of Pembroke, all died without issue, and this extinction of the male line of John the Marshal was popularly looked on as a proof of the abiding anger of St. Thomas of Canterbury. The earldom of Pembroke was bestowed by Henry III on his half-brother, William de Valence, but the marshalship and the manor were conveyed by Maude, the Protector's daughter, to her husband, Hugh Bigod Earl of Norfolk. From him they passed to his son and his nephew, both named Roger; but the latter, after a fierce contest with Edward I., had to surrender both (1302), when they were regranted to him for life only. On his death the office and the manor were separated, and whilst the former was granted to succeeding earls or dukes of Norfolk, the latter passed through various hands. In the time of Elizabeth it belonged to Sir Thomas Parry, the treasurer of the royal household, who built himself a stately mansion. In 1620 this was purchased by Sir William Craven, afterwards Lord Craven, and the faithful friend of Elizabeth of Bohemia. He pulled down the house, and, under the guidance of Sir B. Gerbier, replaced it by a stately pile, in imitation of the Castle of Heidelberg. This house was accidentally burnt in 1718, and was succeeded by the present edifice, which stands in a fine deer-park, and is occupied by the Marquis of Donegal.

22 m. *Kintbury* (Stat.). Kintbury, or Kenetbury, was given by Elfrida to the nunnery founded by her at Amesbury, and remained in their possession until the Dissolution, when it was purchased by John Cheyney, after which it was long the property of the Darrells of Littlecote, several of whom are buried in the ch. This, a Trans.-Norm. and Dec. structure, with E. E. tower, contains several other monuments; among them, one for Charles Dundas, M.P. for Berks for more than 50 years. He was created Baron Amesbury, July 16, 1832, and died on the 7th June following, when his title became extinct. There is also a *Brass* for John Gunter (1524), and his wife, though she is buried elsewhere. *Christ Church* is a modern edifice, by *Bury*, of red brick with stone dressings, and has a very effective tower and spire.

Barton Court, formerly the seat of Lord Amesbury, is now occupied by Sir R. Sutton.

1 m. N.W. is *Avington,* a village possessing one of the most interesting churches in the county, a very small edifice (75 ft. by 14 ft. 7 in.), which has been judiciously restored. " This," says Rickman, " is a very curious and fine Norm. ch., with a rich arch between nave and chancel, which seems to have failed at an early period, and been lately drawn, too much depressed, and looking like 2 arches, which appearance it has not really. This arch and that of the S. door are very fine ones; there is a curious division in the chancel (which is nearly as long as the nave), with different groinings, but no appearance of this division outside." The chancel seems to have had a groined roof in two bays. The E. E. windows and turret, mentioned by Rickman, are now gone, and a small chancel or vestry on the N. was built in 1877. There is a rude Norm. font. It is circular, and is adorned with 11 figures in ecclesiastical vestments, among whom the foul fiend is seen with horns and hoofs. The ch. is covered with ivy, and close to it is the picturesque old vicarage. The manor of Avington belonged in the time of Edward the Confessor to the family of Gounere; after the Conquest to Richard Puingeant, who probably built the ch. It also once belonged to William Longespée Earl of Salisbury, son of Fair Rosamond, and afterwards to Francis Choke, who is buried in Shalbourn ch. (*post*).

3 m. S. is *West Woodhay*, picturesquely situated at the foot of the downs, with a handsome manorhouse by Inigo Jones (Rev. J. Sloper). The old ch., now replaced by a plain brick structure, contained the tomb of Sir Benjamin Rudyerd, a poet and eminent politician of the Commonwealth, who is spoken of by Southey as " one of the most upright and able statesmen of his time, and one of the most eloquent men in that age of English eloquence." After his desire for peace had led to his expulsion from the House he retired to West Woodhay, where he died, May 31, 1658.

1¼ m. W. of West Woodhay is *Inkpen*, with a small *Church* mostly modern, but possessing a Trans-Norm. doorway and some E. E. windows, and a tomb with cross-legged effigy.

Inkpen Beacon is 1011 feet above the level of the sea, and is the highest point of the chalk in the S. of England.

25¼ m. *Hungerford Stat.* This is a considerable market-town (*Inn:* a good country inn, Three Swans P.H.), partly in Wiltshire. (Pop. 2965). It is watered by the Kennet and the Kennet and Avon Canal, and has long been a favourite resort for the angler, being mentioned by Evelyn as " a toune famous for its troutes." It was anciently called *Ingleford Charman* or *Charman Street*, which Gough thinks may be a corruption of the Ford of the

Angles, on Herman Street, the ancient Roman roa l. The name Charnham Street is preserved in one of the avenues to the town, which consists chiefly of two good streets, with a new town-hall, in which is carefully preserved an ancient horn given to the townsmen by John of Gaunt along with the fishery in the Kennet, which is a considerable source of revenue to the corporation. An imitation of this horn, which is blown as a summons to the election of constable, &c., and to call tenants to the manor-court, bears the date 1634, and the inscription, "John a Gaun did giue and grant the riall [royalty] of fishing to Hungerford toune, from Eldren Stub to Irish Stil, excepting som seueral mil pound. Jehosphat Lucas was cunstabl." The ch., which was rebuilt in 1814, contains a good Perp. font from the old edifice. In 1880 the nave was reseated; and other improvements were effected at a cost of 8000*l*. The effigy of Sir Robert de Hungerford, temp. Edw. III., which was formerly placed in a chantry on the S. side of the ch., was for many years banished to the ch.-yd. It has just been placed in the N. aisle, and the curious and well-preserved 14th-centy. inscription from the chantry has been let into the wall above it. It was at Hungerford that the Prince of Orange met the commissioners of King James in Dec. 1688, when an agreement was come to, which eventually placed the Prince on the English throne.

Hungerford Park (Geo. S. Willes, Esq.) was the residence of the Barons Hungerford down to the 16th centy. Being then in the hands of the crown, Elizabeth bestowed it on the Earl of Essex. The present house is a modern structure,

Littlecote Hall (the seat of the Pophams), 2 m̃., in Wilts, is a very interesting house (see Notes in Scott's 'Rokeby'); but it is not sh)wn to strangers.

8 m. S. is *Shalbourn*, partly Wiltshire. The Dec and Perp. c contains the monument of Fran Choke, bearing his effigy in armo a id the inscription "Praye ye al f the sole of frances Choke desessed the yere of oure Lord Ã. 1562." The c was restored in 1872–73 by Bodley, a cost of 2800*l*, when a new aisle w added. and the tower rebuilt. Tl ceiling of the ch. and the screen a verv effective. There is a fine Nor arch.

Jethro Tull, who considerabl improved agriculture by the introdu tion of drill machinery, and othe. wise, resided at Prosperous Farm i this parish in 1730, and introduce here his new methods of farming.

There is a bleak road of 14 m. over the hills from Hungerford by Great Shefford to Wantage. (Rtes. 5, 7.)

Marlborough Stat. (*Inn:* Castle and Bull.) See *Hdbk. for Wilts.*

ROUTE 7.

NEWBURY TO SHRIVENHAM.

By Road. 19 m.

This route is exceedingly interesting to the architect, almost every place passed through having a ch. well worth notice. Or a portion of it may be made to furnish an agreeable excursion, by proceeding from the Newbury Stat. to Donnington, Wickham, Welford, and the Shef-

part rds, rejoining the rly. at Hunger-
l Pen rd; the round will be about 15 m.
of Fr y road, and 9 by rly.
in an Quitting Speenhamland by the
e re Oxford road, we soon turn off on l.,
l se and proceed towards Lamborne, hav-
l." Tu ing the pretty "troutful stream" of
Bo it the same name almost constantly
aisle in view on r.
ilt.   4 m. *Boxford*, with a poor Perp.
tree. ch.; the low square tower dates only
le \ from 1841.
6 m. *Welford*. The *Church*, in a
ident pretty situation, has a most pic-
ntrol turesque round tower, and in the
oth churchyard the shaft of a cross.
'are. "The lower part of the tower and a
odt portion of the wall, a N. door, and
inc some windows now stopped, are all
H i Norm. The ch. and chancel are
ni E. E., with a modern E. window,
(bra and a very good Perp. S. aisle and
porch. The upper part of the tower
'as and sp're are late E. E., and almost
t. Dec. The tower becomes octagon
above, and the spire ribbed, with 8
good double windows. This is one of
the largest of the round towers, and
constructed, as to the early part of it,
of small stones. There is a very fine
round font, curious from its Norm.
forms and E. E. details: it has 16
intersecting arches round it."—*Rickman.* The ch. has been well restored.

Welford House (C. Eyre, Esq.), a
very handsome modern house, in
general effect resembling one of the
old Flemish town-halls, has a deer-
park.

1½ m. S.W. is *Wickham*, a chapelry
of Welford. "The tower has a ba-
lustre belfry window, and quoins
which look very much like Saxon
long and short work. The walls of
the tower are very thick, the masonry
consisting of flint and mortar in alternate layers of about 3 inches. The
windows are small, round-headed,
splayed both inside and out. The
body of the ch., with its aisles and
chancel, was rebuilt from a design
of *Mr. B. Ferrey*, in the Dec. style,

in 1846-9, at the expense of the
Rev. W. Nicholson, rector of Welford. The work is done in the most
sumptuous manner, and the sculpture
of the foliage on the capitals and
bosses is equal to the best ancient
work."—(*J. H. P.*) The manor of
Benham Level, in Welford parish,
was held by the service of keeping a
pack of dogs, at the King's expense,
for h's use.

8 m. A short distance E., across
the stream, and shaded by flourishing trees, is the pretty village of
Little or *East Shefford*. The *Church*
is small, and of debased Perp. architecture, but it contains a fine monument of Sir Thomas Fettyplace and
his wife, with alabaster effigies. He
is habited in armour; his head reclining on a helmet much ornamented, but the crest (an eagle's
head) is broken off; it stood on a
wreath of flowers. His sword and
dagger are gone. Round the tomb are
angels supporting shields. Against
the N. wall of the chancel is the
tomb, in grey marble, of John Fettyplace, 1524, and his wife and children; under an arch their effigies in
brass plates, kneeling. The arms,
both on window-glass and tomb, are
Fettyplace, quartering Besils, im-
paled with Legh. Shefford was deserted by the Fettyplaces for Besilsleigh near Cumnor. Of their *Manor-
house*, only the great hall and one
other apartment remain, now turned
into a barn. Some of the windows
are perfect; the gables are supported
by corbels; on a projecting stone is
a shield of the arms of Besils quartering Legh. Within is some magnificent timber-work. The fireplace
is very large; near it is a recess,
formerly a bay window.

9 m. *Great* or *West Shefford*. The
E. E. *Church*, restored in 1871, has
a Norm. circular tower at the W.
end, to which a Perp. octangular
story has been added, and a Trans.-
Norm. doorway. The font is Norm.,
enriched with scrolls of foliage.

Charles I. passed the night at Shefford Nov. 19, 1644. Here the Hungerford and Wantage road is crossed.

10 m. East Garston, called commonly "Argason," has a cruciform Church, originally Norm., but much altered by the insertion of Dec. or Perp. windows, and the nave has modern wooden arches on the S. side. "There is a pillar piscina, with a sculptured cap beneath a trefoiled recess, with a good bold moulding; it is Trans.-Norm. work, an example rarely met with." (*J. H. P.*) The chancel was rebuilt in 1875 by Sir Robert Burdett, and the Seymour chapel by the vicar and his friends. This manor was held by the terms of finding a knight to serve the King for 40 days, whenever he should be at Kidwelly, in South Wales; and the neighbouring manor of Bockhampton by keeping a pack of harriers for the King's use; but the knight was to be paid, and the dogs fed, at the royal charge. ½ m. beyond Garston is the hamlet of *Eastbury*, with a market-cross, indicating that it was once of more importance than it is at present.

12 m. *Lamborne*, a primitive-looking little place, with a scattered population of 2379 (*Inn:* Red Lion, very comfortable: filled at times of coursing matches). This is a good centre for exploring the antiquities of the Downs. The *Church* is a large and fine cruciform structure, chiefly Dec., but with Perp. E. window, a Perp. N. aisle, and Norm. tower, with 4 octagonal turrets, and 8 bells upon which chimes are played every hour. There are 2 chantry chapels for John Estbury, 1372, and John Estbury, 1485; the latter founded some alms-houses, arid until of late the almoners used to meet twice daily for prayer in rude stalls surrounding his tomb; they now attend the ordinary service in the body of the ch. There are some well-preserved

brasses to the memory of members of the Garrard family, upon one of which we read: "Here lyeth Roger Garrard Gent. and Elizabeth his wife, whose bodyes rest in the earth their mother, and whose soules doe live with God their Father, 1631." Under a Garrard monument of carved stone on the left of the altar, dated 1608, occurs the following lines:—

"Three children more at one birth Agnes had,
We are all baptisde, hir in one grave laid."

In the N. transept is the tomb of Sir Thomas Essex and his wife Margaret, 1558, with their effigies in alabaster. In 1876 an east window, representing the last judgment, was erected to the memory of Bishop Milman of Calcutta, who was vicar of Lamborne.

Lamborne was a possession of King Alfred, who left it by will to his queen. After the Conquest it was granted to the Fitzwarrens. It was divided into several manors, one of which was held, temp. Henry III., by the great justiciary, Henry de Bath, passed from him to the Bohuns, and was by Henry VIII. sold to Sir William Essex, under-treasurer of the Exchequer, whose son Sir Thomas is buried in the ch. Charles I. was at Lamborne soon after the battle of Newbury.

Lamborne Place (H. Hippisley, Esq.) is a modern Elizabethan house, built 1843, in succession to Sir W. Essex's house, on a site traditionally said to be that of Alfred's palace. It contains, beside other pictures, a portrait of Charles I., said to have been painted during his stay at Lamborne, and an extensive collection of ancient armour and old china. Joshua Sylvester, the poet, and translator of 'Du Bartas,' long resided in the old house in the service of the Essex family. Though now little read, he is justly termed by Southey "the silver-tongued Sylvester," and his poems·abound in pleasing local allusions.

* Let me, good Lord, among the great unkenn'd,
My rest of days in the calm country end:
Let me deserve of my dear eagle brood
For Windsor Forest walks in Alme's wood:
Be Hadley pond my sea; Lamb's-bourn
my Thames;
Lamborne my London; Kennet's silver
streams
My fruitful Nile; my singers and musicians
The pleasant birds with warbling repetitions;
My company, pure thoughts, to work Thy
will;
My court a cottage on a lowly hill,
Where, without let, I may so sing Thy
name,
That times to come may wonder at the
same."
Sylvester's 'Du Bartas,' p. 30.

The poet's wish to end his days at Lamborne was not fulfilled; he became secretary to a company of London traders, and died in their service at Middleburg, in Holland, Sept. 28th, 1618, aged 55.

The Lamborne river rises in the plantations of Lamborne Place. It abounds with trout, which are of a paler colour than those taken in the Kennet.

N. of Lamborne stretch wide open downs, on which the business of *Horse-Training* and the sport of Coursing are carried on; the hills that bound the view overlook the Vale of White Horse (Rte. 5).

2 m. N. is what are called the *Seven Barrows*, from the fact that, of the numerous tumuli scattered about, 7 are in closer proximity than the rest. They were opened in 1850, and proved to be British (*Journ. Arch. Inst.* vol. viii.), thus showing the fallacy of the supposition of Gough, Wise, and others, that they mark the burial-places of the Danish leaders slain at Ashdown. This, and other considerations, have led antiquaries in general to remove the site of that battle further eastward (Rte. 8). Passing near Wayland Smith's Cave (Rte. 5), we arrive, at 16 m., at *Ashbury*, where the fine

Dec. and Perp. *Church* will repay an attentive examination. Notice the rich Norm. S. doorway, and the squint filled with Dec. tracery between the S. aisle and transept. There are *Brasses* for John de Walden, c. 1360, W. Skelton, 1448, both priests, good examples of academic and processional costume. The interior of the church was completely restored in 1872. The Sunday-school system is said to have been originated at Ashbury by the Rev. J. Stock, the curate, in 1777. He collected the children of the poor in the ch. and gave them instruction between the services. Being removed in the following year to Gloucester, he there became acquainted with Mr. Raikes, who at once saw the value of the "innovation," as it was deemed, and gave it such hearty support as to be usually considered its founder. The manor of Ashbury, which had been given to Glastonbury Abbey by Edred, was purchased at the Dissolution by Sir W. Essex. The *Manor-house* (now a farm) is moated, and has some fragments of stained glass; it is of 15th cent. date.

At a considerable distance S. of the ch., and high up on the downs, is *Ashdown Park* (Earl Craven). The situation is so remarkable, that tradition is called on to account for it. Accordingly we are told that a Craven, who was Lord Mayor of London [Sir W. Craven was Lord Mayor in 1610], fleeing from the plague in the metropolis, rode on and on, till on these downs he spied a solitary farmhouse. There, for the first time, he felt he should be secure, and there he built a house, with 4 avenues leading to the 4 cardinal points, and with windows on each side of all the rooms, in order that, if the plague came in on one side, it might go out on the other. The existing house was built in the style of Coleshill, by *Webb*, the nephew of Inigo Jones, who inherited his plans.

All the chimneys unite in two massive quadrangular piles on either side, while between them is a belvedere, having a cupola in the centre, containing a lantern, which is occasionally lighted as a beacon to guide travellers among these hills. On the oak staircase are some of the stags' horns brought by Elizabeth of Bohemia from Germany ; and there are portraits of her, of William Lord Craven, the devoted friend whom she is said to have married near the end of her life, of Prince Rupert, Prince Maurice, and the four Princesses, by *Honthorst.*

Lying on the turf, stretching in long array both within and without the park wall, in front of Ashdown House, are the extraordinary stones known as the *Sarsen* (Saracen?) *Stones,* looking like a flock of sheep scattered under the trees, whence probably their name of *Grey Wethers.* They are remains of a tertiary stratum of Bagshot sand, indurated, with which the chalk was once overlaid. The larger stones of Stonehenge and Avebury are probably of the same formation (see *Handbook for Wilts*). It is remarkable that the sides of the Downs, which are elsewhere clothed with short turf, are here covered with long grass. E. of the house is the small circular camp known as *Alfred's Castle* (Rte. 5), which Aubrey says "was almost quite defaced" in his time, "by digging for the Sarsen stones to build my Lord Craven's house."

19 m. *Shrivenham* (Stat) (Rte. 5).

ROUTE 8.

NEWBURY TO OXFORD, BY EAST ILSLEY AND ABINGDON.

By Road. 27 m.

Leaving Newbury (Rte. 6), the road runs at the foot of the hill (on the l.), which is crowned by the ruins of Donnington Castle. Rt. 1 m. is Shaw House. (See Rte. 6.) Passing over Snelsmore Heath —

4 m. *Chieveley,* a village lying off the high road, was occupied by the Parliamentary troops on the night before the second battle of Newbury. The *Church* has a good E. E. chancel ; the nave was of the same date, but it was rebuilt in the same style in 1873. The tower also is E. E., but with Perp. doorway inserted, and Dec. battlements.

6 m. A road branches off on l., 2 m., to *Peasemore,* of which the manor belonged to Thos. Chaucer, the son of the poet. The ch., rebuilt in the Dec. style, with tower and lofty spire, contains the monument of Mr. Wm. Coward, 1739, who, "out of an income of 110*l.*, maintained a most hospitable table, rebuilt the church tower, and gave the great bell and the communion plate."

1 m. S. W. is the small new ch. of *Leckhampstead,* which has replaced a Trans.-Norm. edifice. The manor was one of those bestowed by Edward II. on Piers Gaveston. On the border of the parish towards Welford (Rte. 7) is a boundary-stone, called *Hang Man Stone,* from a grim legend, which relates that a man there came to an untimely end.

He had stolen a sheep, and was carrying it away, with its hind-legs
tied together round his neck; he
sat down to rest on the stone, but
the struggling sheep pulled him
over, and he was found next day
strangled. *Chaddleworth,* 2 m. N. W.,
has a ch., originally Norm., but
altered in the E. E. style. The
manor (which was given by the Conqueror to Robert d'Oiley, and afterwards belonged to the mother of
Edward I., who bought it for the support of her granddaughter Eleanor of
Britanny, then a nun at Ambresbury)
shared in the singular custom which
prevailed concerning widows at Enborne (Rte. 6). In this parish, in
a retired situation among woods, is
the farmhouse of *Ellensfordsmere,*
which marks the site of the Abbey
of *Poghley,* built for Augustine
canons by Ralph of Chaddleworth
in 1161, destroyed in 1532. *Woolley
Park* (P. Wroughton, Esq.) is a
handsome mansion, in a well-wooded
deer-park. 2 m. N.E. is *Bright
Waltham* ("Brickleton" in the ver-
nacular), the ch. of which belonged
to Battle Abbey. It is Norm. and
E. E , and has been restored b *Street.*
It contains a Norm. font., and a small
Brass for John Newman, wife, and
son, 1517.

[On E. are several interesting
churches. *Hampstead Norris,* 3 m.,
is an extensive parish, in which a
Roman villa was discovered in 1833,
and which also contains a British
earthwork called *Grimsbury Castle.*
This is of circular form, and incloses
a copious spring, which is never
known to fail, even in the driest
seasons. The *Church* is mainly E. E.;
"at the E. end are 2 lancet windows
externally, but splayed internally,
so as to terminate in a single round
moulding, very simple, but good"
(*J. H. P.*). There is also a trefoiled
piscina, supported on a shaft; but
the Norm. font has been removed,
and is now at Stone (Rte. 14).
The tower is Perp., with very thick

walls of flint, and a Perp. porch to
the Norm. N. door, which has the
billet moulding.
2 m. S., and near Grimsbury
Castle, is the Norm. ch. of *Frilsham.*
The chancel has a Perp. E. window,
and the tower is a modern imitation
of E. E., badly executed in brick.
1¼ m. N.E. is *Yattendon,* once,
like many other Berkshire villages,
a market-town. Sir John Norreys,
Master of the Wardrobe to Henry
VI., had licence to embattle a manor-
house here (now destroyed) in 1447.
The ch. was also probably built by
him. It contains the tomb of another
Sir John Norreys, who served in the
Netherland wars, and died in 1597,
furious at not having been more
amply rewarded for his services,
which are detailed in an immense
epitaph. Carte, who wrote a great
part of his 'History of England' in
the village, died here 1754, and is
also buried in the ch.
2 m. N. is *Ashhampstead,* with a
Trans.-Norm. ch., to which a wooden
bell-tower was added in the 15th
cent.; the timbers have curious
Perp. mouldings.

3 m. N. from Ashhampstead is *Aldworth* (described in Rte. 4), 2 m. W.
of which is *Compton Parva,* generally
supposed to occupy the site of a
Roman town. The ch. is a mere
fragment of a Trans.-Norm. edifice,
the N. aisle of which has been destroyed. On an eminence known as
Cow Down, following the shape of
the hill, is an entrenchment called
Perborough Castle, evidently British,
but also occupied by the Romans,
numerous relics of that people having been found there. Near this is
one of the many large farms bearing
the name of *Cold Harbour* often met
with in the vicinity of a Roman
road. To the N. stretch *Compton
Downs,* now used for horse-training,
and on which some antiquaries consider the battle of Ashdown to have
been fought. It seems probable that

the term "Æscesdun" really applies to the whole tract of elevated land between Streatley and Ashbury (Rte. 7), and thus the exact site of the conflict can never be determined; still, the weight of probability is in favour of the eastern, rather than the western district.

This famous battle took place early in the year 871, when, after a contest at Reading, in which the Pagans "had possession of the place of carnage," i. e. the victory. "King Ethelred and his brother Alfred fought the whole army of Pagans on Ashdown. The Danish army was in two bodies; in the one were Bagsæc and Halfdene, the heathen kings; in the other were the earls. The Christian army was also divided into two bodies. Things being so settled, the King remained a long time in prayer, hearing the mass, and said he would not leave it till the priest had done, or abandon the protection of God for that of men. And so he did, which afterwards availed him much with the Almighty, as we shall see in the sequel. But the Pagans came up quickly to the fight. Then Alfred, although holding a lower authority, could no longer support the troops of the enemy, unless he retreated or charged upon them without waiting for his brother; so he marched out promptly with his men in a close column, and gave them battle." Alfred fought with the troops of the earls, and King Ethelred with the troops of the Kings, the Christians coming up from below, and the Pagans occupying the higher ground, where was a single stunted thorn-tree, "around which the opposing hosts came together, with loud shouts from all sides, the one to pursue their wicked course, the other to fight for their lives, their dearest ties, and their country. And when both hosts had fought long and bravely, at last the

Pagans by God's judgment, could no longer bear the attack of the Christians, and, having lost great part of their men, took to a disgraceful flight, and all the Pagan host pursued its flight, not only until night, but 'the next day, even until they reached the stronghold from which they had come out. The Christians followed, slaying all they could reach, until it became dark." "And the flower of the Pagan youth was there slain, so that neither before nor since was ever such destruction known since the Saxons first gained Britain by their arms." "There fell in that battle King Bagsæc ('slain by the spear of King Ethelred,' Brompton), and these earls with him; that old Earl Sidroc, to whom may be applied that saying, 'the ancient of evil days,' and Earls Sidroc the younger, Osberne, Frene, and Harold."— Saxon Chronicles.]

Returning to the main road we reach at

9 m. East Ilsley, formerly called Hildesley or Huldesley, a small market-town on a hill-side. Gough and others consider the name a corruption of "Hildelæg," or "Battle-field," and have placed the battle of Ashdown here. Another opinion is, that it represents the Saxon town of Nachesledorne, or the Solitary Thorn Tree, so named from an ancient tree held sacred by the Druids, and the "single thorn-tree of stunted growth," around which, according to Asser, the conflict was the fiercest. The small ch. is mainly E. E., but with low Dec. tower; and the N. aisle is a modern addition.

The Hildesleys were long lords of the manor, and have their monuments in the ch. John Hilsey, who succeeded Bishop Fisher at Rochester (1535-38), was one of this family. Rich. Wightwick, the benefactor of Pembroke College, Oxford, of which he may be considered the co-founder with Tesdale, was rector of this parish, and gave the great bell in the tower.

Ilsley is now chiefly remarkable for its sheep-market, which existed as early as the reign of Henry III., and which is the largest in this part of England. It is held on every alternate Wednesday, from the Wednesday fortnight before Easter to the first Wednesday in July. There are also fairs almost monthly, for the sale of sheep, lambs, and wool; that of August 26 is the largest, 50,000 sheep and lambs often being sold at it. The qualities of the place are summed up in the rhyme:

" Ilsley, remote amidst the Berkshire downs,
Claims these distinctions o'er her sister
   towns:
Far famed for sheep and wool, though not
   for spinners,
For sportsmen, doctors, publicans, and sin-
   ners."

The turf of the downs is particularly light and springy, well adapted not only for horse-training, but fox-hunting and coursing.

1½ m. N.W., almost hidden in a pleasant valley, is *West Ilsley*, with a poor Perp. ch., to which a Jacobean porch has been added. A north aisle was erected in 1876. The remote village has acquired a certain celebrity from two versatile men who were once its rectors. The learned Antonio de Dominis, Archbishop of Spalatro, who was converted to Protestantism and fled to England, was presented to this living by James I., in 1616. He wrote 'De Republica Ecclesiastica,' and preached constantly against the Papal power; but having been made Dean of Windsor, and being angry at obtaining no higher preferment, he re-entered the Romish Church, on promise of pardon from Gregory XV. He returned to Rome, hoping to be made a cardinal, but was, instead, imprisoned in the castle of St. Angelo, and died there, probably by poison in 1624, or

1625. He was succeeded by Goodman, Bishop of Gloucester, who was visited here by Charles I. (in the old rectory-house, now destroyed), on his way to Donnington Castle in 1644. He had been driven from his see, but was for some years allowed to hold this living. Refusing, at length, to sign certain canons of doctrine and discipline, he was, says Walker, "spoiled, plundered, and utterly undone"; and he died, Jan. 1656, in the Romish faith. Fuller says that "he was the single bishop of 200 who had lived since the Reformation, whom the vile and detestable practice of those who engross to themselves the name of Protestants had scandalized into Popery." He always professed the most devoted loyalty, but, with the inconsistency that marked his character, he dedicated his 'Discourse on the Trinity' to Cromwell.

On the downs W. of the Ilsleys are the small Norm. churches of *Catmore* and *Farnborough*. The manor of Catmore has been in the hands of the Eystons of East Hendred (*post*) for more than 5 cents., and the ch. has been restored by them.

11 m. The *Ridgeway* is crossed by a British road which traverses the county from E. to W. The Berkshire downs here reach nearly their greatest elevation, the *Cuckamsley Hills* being 800 ft. high. The name, as well as *Scutchamfly* or *Scutchamore*, is a corruption of Cwichelm's law, or hill, the spot being said to be the burial-place of Cwichelm, who reigned conjointly with Cynegils over the W. Saxons, and was killed on these downs in 626 fighting against Edwin of Northumbria, who came hither to avenge an attempt to murder him. A tumulus on the top of the hill, called *Scutchamore Knob*, 21 ft. high and 140 yds. in circumference, is supposed to mark his resting-place. The Saxon Chronicle, describing the battle of Æscesdun, narrate-

how the ·Danes " turned along Æsceadun to Cwicchelmeslawe, and there awaited better cheer," — an account versified by Robert of Gloucester,—

" Much sorrow they deede in Berkschire about Asshedoune,
And about Quicholmes destroyed many a towne."

Cwichelm's law is believed to have been a common place of assembly for the people of Wessex; and, as it is remote from the sea, it was, in the time of Ethelred II., considered safe from the inroads of the Danes. But we read in the 'Anglo-Sax. Chron.,' under the year 1006, that this was mistaken confidence. " They [the Danes] went to Wallingford, and burned it all down; and were then one night at Cholsey, and then went along Ashdown to Cwichelm's law, and there tarried out of threatening vaunt, because it had often been said, if they came to Cwichelm's law, they would never go to the sea. They then went home by another way."

These hil's were formerly the scene of a celebrated fair, which was abolished by James I., 1620, in order to promote the welfare of the market at East Ilsley. From one point the straight green road of *Golden Mile* leads down towards East Hendred.

12 m. *Cuts Gore,* properly Keats Gore, from the family who formerly owned it. Here were once the great stables built by the Duke of Cumberland for his racehorses, in which the celebrated " Eclipse " was born and bred.

13 m. *Chilton,* a village with a Norm. ch. altered to Dec. The manor-house. called *Latton's Place* (now a farmhouse), retains the armorial bearings of its former owners the Lattons. Eastward spreads *Chilton Plain,* on which an eminence, called *Churn Knob,* is traditionally said to be the spot where Birinus commenced the conversion of the people of Wessex (635) by preaching

before King Cynegils. It overlooks the Grym s dyke, a British line of fortification.   2 m. E. is *Blewbury,* with a Trans.-Norm. ch.. altered in part by the insertion of Dec. windows, and the destruction of a central tower; the existing tower is Perp. and at the W. end. There are several good *Brasses,* 1496–1548 ; among them one for John Latton of Chiltⁿn (d. 1548), in tabard The N. and S. porches are of good carved timber work, but are in a decaying state, as are some stone effigies in the ch.-yd. The church has recently been re stored. Numerous tumuli are found on the surrounding downs, and Blew burton hill is cut into a series of terraces, evidently for defensive purposes. A number of coins have been dug up in the immediate neighbourhood.

15 m. 1½ m. W. is *East Hendred,* a very picturesque and interesting village. At its entrance are the remains of a monastery called " Jesus of Bethlehem," which was an offshoot of that at Sheen, near Richmond, consisting of a stone chapel with some fine Perp. windows. now converted into a granary. Beyond this are the gates of *Hendred House* (Charles John Eyston, Esq.), which is adorned with ancient monograms, and which has remained in the hands of the family of Eyston from the 13th centy. Attached to it is the E. E. and Dec. chapel of St. Amen or Amand, remarkable as one of the only three, the others being Stonor (Rte. 20) and Hazlewood, in Yorkshire, *Handbook for Yorks.*), that are believed to have never ceased to celebrate the service of the Roman Catholic Church. Its existence is known as early as 1291; and it was open to all comers till the arrival of the Prince of Orange. when, while his army was passing over Golden Mile (*ante*), some of the soldiers defaced and plundered the chapel; and, " taking some of the church stuffe

with them to Oxford, dressed up a mannekin in it, and set it up on the top of a bonfire." Though the chapel was despoiled of its revenues at the dissolution, its ancient glebe is still called "the Church Furlough," and the abode of its priest, now a farm-house, is still St. Amand's. In one of the windows is the cipher of Hugh Faringdon, last Abbot of Reading. In the old library adjoining is preserved the tomb of Robert first Abbot of Poghley (*ante*). Coins of "Ædelred, rex Anglorum," have been picked up near the chapel. The Eystons are the descendants of Sir Thomas More, through the marriage of his son "Jack More" with Anne Crisaker, the heiress of Barnborough in Yorkshire, which remained till lately in the hands of the family. Among the relics of Sir Thomas preserved at East Hendred are his drinking-cup, a very fine original portrait of him by *Holbein*, and two curious portraits on wood, of Sir T. More and Cardinal Pole. Here also is one of the huge and curious pictures of the More family, of which there are four others in existence, viz. those at Basle in Switzerland. Nostell (*Handbook for Yorks.*), Cokethorpe (Rte. 25), and that belonging to Lord Petre. Among the figures seen here, but not always included, are those of Pattison the fool, and Heresius the servant of Sir Thomas. The figure of Mrs. More was unfortunately cut off while the picture was at Barnborough. Another relic preserved here is the ebony staff of Bishop Fisher, which supported him on the scaffold.

The *Church*, of which Chicheley was once the rector, is, as to the nave, Trans.-Norm.; the chancel is of the transition period from Dec. to Perp. It was enlarged and restored in 1861, and "it is remarkable in having an arcade, dividing the two southern aisles, of slender piers without arches, of which the most eastern pier is original." It also contains a lec-

tern of the 13th centy.. and some ancient brasses. The N. chantry is the burial-place of the Eystons, and is filled with their monuments. Several brasses to "merchants in cloth and wool" (Henry and Roger Eldysley, 1439; W. Whitwey, 1479) bear witness to the ancient mercantile importance of East Hendred. The picturesque field beyond the ch., where terraces still remain in the turf, was probably the drying-ground of the cloth which was sold at the fairs on Cuckamsley Hill. East Hendred gave two abbots to Abingdon—Rob. de Hendred, 1284; and Rich. de Hendred, 1289.

John Paternoster held land here temp. Edward I., by tenure of saying a paternoster every day for the King's soul.

West Hendred, 1 m. distant, has a Dec. and Perp. ch.; notice the chancel, which has remained almost unaltered, and has a good piscina and low side-window.

2 m. S. is *East Lockinge*, a good Dec. ch., with fine ancient iron work on the doors; the tower is late Perp. and bears the date 1504. *Lockinge House* (Col. Loyd Lindsay) is a fine mansion. A dell in the grounds has a very copious spring, which gushes from the chalk marl

1 m. W. from West Hendred is *Ardington*, a fine ch., mainly E. E.; the N. doorway is particularly good; the S. door is Dec., with the ball-flower and foliage on the mouldings. The Manor-house, the home of Clarke the antiquary, belonged to Mr. Vernon, who here collected the pictures which he in 1847 bequeathed to the nation.

17 m. On E. 1 m. is *Milton*, with a small Dec. and Perp. ch. (restored) *Milton House* (J. B. Barrett, Esq.), built by Inigo Jones, has a Roman Catholic chapel, with ancient stained glass windows. 2 m. N.E. is *Sutton Courtenay* (Rte. 5).

19 m. *Drayton*. The *Church* is

principally E.E , with a good E. window, but the N. aisle and the tower are Perp. A chancel was erected in 1872, and an ancient cross in the ch.-yd. has lately been restored. The rood-loft remains, converted into a gallery; there is an ambry, with the original door and iron work remaining, which is unusual, and a curious Elizabethan poor-box. In the ch. is preserved the remains of a beautiful alabaster reredos, with the painting and gilding nearly perfect, which was dug up in the chancel in making a vault. The old Manor-house, now a farm, has a 15th-centy. chapel, used as a lumber-room.

21 m. *Abingdon* (*Inns*: Queen's Hotel, Crown and Thistle, Lion). This town (pop. 5662) communicates with the Great Western Rly, by a branch line of 2 m. (Rte. 19). It lies in a rich plain at the junction of the Ock with the Thames, and has had a British origin ascribed to it; but this is a mere legend. It really sprang up around a great abbey founded in the 7th centy., remained during the middle ages a dependency thereon, though occasionally a troublesome one, and only became of consequence after the 14th cent., when the cloth trade was introduced to it, as well as many other Berkshire towns. Leland, writing about 1534, says: " The town stondith by clothing;" but it received a fatal blow by the suppression of the monasteries. Sir John Mason, a native, procured a charter from Queen Mary, on a representation of its poverty, and it then acquired the right of sending two members (now reduced to one) to Parliament. Its cloth trade, however, has forsaken it, and its main business now is in brewing, malting, and rope-making; but a large factory for ready-made clothing employs 2000 persons (principally women) in the town and the adjacent villages.

According to a Cottonian MS. there was here a town called *Seovechesham* or *Seusham*, which was a wealthy city, a royal residence, and a place of religious worship, even in early British times. It was not, however, occupied by the Saxon kings, until the Mercian Offa, paying an accidental visit to the place, became enamoured of the Isle of Andersey, which was situated in the river opposite the abbey. This was at that time occupied by rich lay monks, but the King persuaded them to give it up in exchange for the manor of Goosey (Rte. 5), and built a palace there, where he resided, and where his son and successor King Egfrid, died. Cynulf, the next king, gave up the palace to his huntsmen and falconers, who made themselves so disagreeable to the monks, that Abbot Rethunus persuaded the King to restore Andersey to them in exchange for the manor of Sutton Courtenay and 120l. of silver. The site of Andersey is supposed to be a tract of land encircled by the Thames and a small stream that falls into the main river at Culham Bridge. Leland mentions the site of the palace as occupied by a barn, and the foundations of buildings may still be traced in the first meadow out of the town, on the E. side of the bridge.

The story told in the 'Chronicle of Abingdon' (Master of the Rolls' Collection) is, that the site originally chosen for the monastery was a hill called Aben-dun, at Bayworth, in the neighbouring parish of Sunningwell, probably in Bagley Wood; and this is said to have derived its name from a certain holy Aben, who " stole away from the massacre at Stonehenge, and lived here in retirement, where the inhabitants, flocking to him to hear the word of God, built him a dwelling-house and a chapel in honour of the Holy Virgin, after which, he, disliking their resort, stole away to Ireland." It is, however, more probable that the name simply had its origin from the direct connection of the abbey with the place. The abbey was founded on the hill, about 680, by Cissa, viceroy of Centwin, King of the W. Saxons, in honour of the Virgin, to contain 12 Benedictine monks, over whom his nephew Heane was appointed abbot. The foundation of Cissa was confirmed by Ceadwall, the successor of Centwin, who also gave him the town of Seovechesham, commanding that it should henceforward be called Abbendon from the abbey-hill.

"The Abingdon Chronicle gives 500 years of history, more or less trustworthy and complete, from a charter of Ina, King of the West Saxons, to Abbot Heane in 687, down to the accession of Richard I. The town and monastery were founded and endowed, then ravaged by the Danes in Alfred's reign, restored, and again fleeced by some king unknown." It was refounded and endowed by Edred, who induced St. Ethelwold, then a monk at Glastonbury, afterwards Bp. of Winchester, to become its abbot, when the building, removed to its present situation, was consecrated in great pomp by St. Dunstan, and each saint presented it with two bells of his own workmanship. "This was the second Benedictine house established in England. No exertion of its new superior was wanting to render it the parent of many others. Aware that continental monasteries excelled in reading and singing, he procured masters from Corby, to instruct his own society in these attractive arts. He seems to have doubted whether, even under Dunstan, there had been opportunities for a thorough acquaintance with monastic discipline : he sent, accordingly, Osgar, one of his monks, to Fleury, for farther instruction. Thus he laid a secure foundation of popularity for his favourite sys-

[*Berks, &c.*]

tem by the attractions of public worship, and well-defined, rigid austerity of discipline. Rightly, therefore, was he termed, in after ages, 'the father of monks.' "— (*Soames,* 'Angl.-Sax. Church.') The abbey was completed in 963 by the Abbot Ordgar, and it continued to grow in wealth and influence down to the very period of its dissolution. Its abbots had a seat in Parliament, and their power and pride were such as to draw from the author of 'Piers Plowman,' in the middle of the 14th centy., a direct prophecy of their downfall :

" Ac [eke] ther shal come a kyng,
And confesse yow religiouses,
And bete you as the Bible telleth
For brekynge of your rule;
. . . .
And thanne shall the abbot of Abyngdune,
And al his issue for evere,
Hav a knok of a kyng,
And incurable the wounde."
Vision, vv. 6239–63.

At the time of the Domesday survey, the abbey possessed no less than 30 manors in Berkshire, beside lands in the counties of Oxford, Warwick, and Gloucester, some of which it had then recently purchased. Among its abbots were Siward, the coadjutor of Abp. Edsige ; Spearhafoc, elected Bp. of London, but displaced by Norman influence at the court of Edward the Confessor. The first abbot in Norman times was Ethelhelm, who is denounced as a most merciless plunderer by the Chronicler. After him came Faritius, the builder of Uffington ch. (Rte. 5), a man greatly lauded; as is Ingulf, who had been Prior of Winchester. He gave to th · abbey a great bell, called "Hildelhubel."

William I. favoured the monks of Abingdon, and on a visit to them in 1080 he left with them his son Henry for his education, who thus gained his appellation of Beauclerk. "The 'Chronicle,' however, tells much of discord and disorder within, just such as would

G

be bred by prosperity, and were likely to invite sooner or later royal interference. After the close of the 'Chronicle' we read a second dark period in the abbey story. We hear of fights with the town, generally caused by 'the unreasonable dealings of the abbot and convent' in the matter of a market. In 1327, the town, aided by the Mayor of Oxford, 'accompanied, 'tis said, with some scholars of a desperate condition, and glad of any diversion rather than to study,' attacked the abbey, burnt part of it, drove out the monks, and destroyed their muniments. Twelve of the ring-leaders were afterwards hung. The abbey was dissolved in 1538, its yearly revenues amounting then to 1876l. (about 20,000l. of present value). The last abbot (Rowland, *alias* Pentecost) was rewarded for his ready surrender with the manor of Cumnor" (Rte. 9.)—(*C. D C.*, in 'Oxford Proceedings.')

Leland speaks warmly of the extent and magnificence of the conventual buildings, but very little indeed is now left of them. The Perp. gatehouse, converted into a police-station, gives access to the premises of a brewer, among which fragments of 13th-centy. domestic architecture may be seen. They consist of a fire-place, temp. Hen. III., with elegant slender pillars, and a remarkable chimney, both probably belonging to the abbot's house; all traces of the great ch. have disappeared.

Adjoining the gateway is the *Church of St. Nicholas*, mostly Perp., but with a good doorway of late Norm. character. "Attached to the N. side of the tower is a singular square stair-turret, of larger dimensions than usual, with a gabled roof, and a small triangular window in the gable" (*J. H. P.*); this window is figured in 'Gloss. of Architecture.'

Opposite the ch. formerly stood

the *Grammar School*, founded by John Royse, 1563; now removed to a more open situation near the Recreation Ground (or Albert Park, as it is termed). The new building is a showy structure of red brick, with white stone facings. One of the earliest pupils of the old school was Thomas Tesdale, who afterwards founded Pembroke College, Oxford, mainly for youths from Abingdon. Thomas Godwin, author of 'Roman and Jewish Antiquities,' Lord Chief Justice Holt, and Newcome, Archbishop of Armagh (born in the town 1729), were educated here. Other eminent natives of Abingdon have been—St. Edmund, Archbishop of Canterbury, 1234–40; his brother Robert Rich, and his two sainted sisters, Margaret and Alice, successively prioresses of Catesby (see *Handbook for North Hants*), on whose birthplace Rich. Earl of Cornwall built a chapel in 1288; Sir John Maon, whose father was a cowherd, and mother the sister of one of the abbey monks, from whom he received his education, and by whom he was sent to Oxford, where he so pleased Henry VIII. by a graceful compliment paid on his visit in 1523, that he took him with him to court and sent him to Paris to complete his education after which he rose in that and the three succeeding reigns to be Privy Councillor, Ambassador to France, and Chancellor of the University of Oxford. Abbot, Speaker of the House of Commons, and Moore, author of 'The Gamester,' have been among the celebrities of Abingdon in later years.

Next to its abbey, Abingdon owed a large portion of its prosperity to its *Bridge*, built by John Huchyns in 1416, with stone given by Sir Peter Besils, of Besilsleigh, "a knight courteous and kind, for his father's soul and his friends," and the men's wages, to the amount of

1000 marks, supplied by the rich Geoffrey Barber. A very early copy of some contemporary verses, and a picture representing the building of the bridge, are preserved in the hall of Christ's Hospital (*post*). These verses show that it was regarded as a religious duty to build bridges :

" Another blissed besines is brigges to make
That there the pepul may not passe
[away] after greet showres.
Dole it is to drawe a deed body oute of a lake,
That was fulled in a fount stoon [washed in the font], and a felow of oures."

The bridge was taken charge of by a guild of the Holy Cross, a fraternity which existed here at least as early as the year 1389, when they are mentioned as maintaining a priest, and being governed by two proctors chosen annually. They were incorporated in 1442, and endowed with lands worth 40l. per annum, to enable them to keep the road between Abingdon and Dorchester in repair, to maintain 13 poor men and women, and to provide a chaplain for St. Helen's, Sir John Golafre (buried at Fyfield, Rte. 9), and Thomas Chaucer, son of the poet, being trustees. This guild was dissolved with the other religious foundations by Henry VIII. In 1553 it was refounded, at the request of Sir John Mason, and received a charter from Edward VI. under the name of *Christ's Hospital*, which it still bears.

St. Helen's, near the river, is a very fine ch. in dimensions, having a nave and chancel of equal breadth and three aisles, forming a spacious rectangle, at the N.E. angle of which rises the tower, surmounted by the lofty octagonal spire, with its flying buttresses, which is so conspicuous an object in all distant views of the town, and in Turner's picture of Abingdon. Cissa, the sister of Heane, the first abbot, founded a nunnery here in 690, of which she became the first prioress. Her foundation was afterwards removed to Wytham (Rte. 9), but the site of her nunnery was always called the Manor of St. Helen, and is believed to be that of the present ch. The greater part of the building is Perp., of various dates (the N. aisle temp. Henry VI., S. aisle 1539), but the tower is E.E., with a good doorway. The N. aisle has a rich timber ceiling, painted with figures of kings, prophets, and saints, under carved canopies, and was, according to local tradition, saved from the abbey at the dissolution. In the S. aisle is the *Brass* of Geoffrey Barber (d. 1417), once bailiff of Bristol, but at his death a merchant of Abingdon, and a great benefactor to the town : his body was removed from the abbey church, and re-interred here with great ceremony. In the N. aisle is the tomb of John Royse, the founder of the Grammar School. The ch., which has hitherto been much blocked with high pews and galleries, was completely restored in 1873; a carved oak rood-screen was placed between the chancel and the nave, and several stained glass windows were inserted. A modern ch. (St. Michael) is a small edifice, in the Dec. style, by *Sir G. G. Scott*.

Christ's Hospital adjoins St. Helen's ch.-yd., and is a picturesque structure of brick and timber, surmounted by a cupola ; along the front runs a low cloister, decorated on the interior with texts, and on the exterior with paintings representing the virtue of almsgiving, with figures supposed to include portraits of Geoffrey Barber, King Edward VI., and Sir John Mason. In the old oak hall are their arms in stained glass, and their portraits, with those of many other benefactors, including Sir Peter Besils, Lionel Bostock, and Thomas Tesdale, the founder of Pembroke College, and his wife. The picture of

. G 2

the rich Geoffrey Barber giving John Huchyns money to build the bridge, with the building going on in the background, is very curious; as are the verses already referred to: part run as follows:

" Kyng Herry the fyft, in his fourthe yere,
He hath i-founde for his folke a brige in Berkschire,
For cartis with carlage may goo and come clere,
That many wynters afore were mareed in the myre."
. . . .

" Now is Culham hithe (ferry) i-come to an ende,
And al the contre the beter and no man the worse."
. . . .

" Culham hithe hath caused many a curse.
I-blyssed be our helpers we have a better waye,
Withoute any peny for cart and for horse."

In one of the windows of St. Helen's Ch. also long remained the distich:

" Henricus Quartus quarto fundaverat anno
Rex pontem Burford super undas atque Culhamford."

On the outer wall of the E. end of the wooden cloister is a representation of the celebrated stone *Cross* which was erected by the brotherhood in the market-place, and from which the cross at Coventry is supposed to have been copied. It was totally destroyed by Waller, May 31, 1644. to revenge a repulse which his army had received at New Bridge (Rte. 9). Richard Symonds, who saw it a few weeks before its destruction, describes it (in a MS. in the British Museum) as octangular, having 3 rows of statues—the first of 6 grave kings; the second of the Virgin, 4 female saints, and a mitred prelate; the third, of small figures of apostles and prophets: the whole orna-mented with coats of arms painted and carved. At this cross, as Aubrey narrates, Richard Corbet, Bp. of Norwich and Dean of Christchurch, sang ballads after he was made a

doctor of divinity; for, "the Dean being one market-day with some of his companions at the taverne by the Crosse, a ballad-singer com-playned that he had no custom, and could not put off his ballads; where-upon the jolly Doctor puts off his gowne, and puts on the ballad-singer's leathern jacket, and being a handsome man, and having a rare full voice, he presently vended a great many, and had a great au-dience."

The site of the Cross is now occu-pied by the *Market-house*, a hand-some modern Romanesque structure, designed by Inigo Jones. Above is the *County Hall*, which has several good portraits, and is surmounted by a tower, from which a very agreeable view is commanded.

Abingdon was garrisoned for the king at the early part of the Civil War, and it was for a considerable time the head-quarters of his horse. He paid it a visit, with his queen and family, April 17, 1644. In May of the same year a council of war was held here, soon after which the garrison quitted the place on the approach of the Earl of Essex, who plundered the town, and fortified it for the Parliament. Various at-tempts which the Royalists after-wards made to recover it were all unsuccessful, though Prince Rupert contrived at one time to regain pos-session of the abbey and to place 500 men there. The Parliamentary garrison practised the plan of hang-ing all Irish prisoners without a trial to such extent as made "Abing-don law" proverbial.

23 m. On r. 2 m., *Radley* (stat.), once a manor of the Abbey of Abing-don, from which it was purchased by George Stonehouse, Clerk of the Board of Green Cloth to Queen Elizabeth. The red-brick mansion has the reputation of being the best-built house in the county. It is

now incorporated with *St. Peter's College*, opened June 9th, 1847, of whose Warden it is the residence. Near it are the red-brick buildings containing the dormitories, school-rooms, and studies of the boys, and a *Chapel*, fitted up with fine stained glass and rich carving, ancient and modern. There is also an extensive gymnasium. The object of this institution is to give boys the advantage of a public-school education, based on strictly ecclesiastical principles; the Rev. W. Sewell was the first Warden, and the system pursued is fully explained in a volume of Sermons by him. Beyond the Park is the village *Church*, Perp., with a modern chancel; it contains a fine tomb of Sir Wm. Stonehouse, 1632, and his eldest son Sir John. The chancel has some good Perp. painted glass, and rich old woodwork, collected from various sources.

23 m. On l. a lane turns off to the pretty village of *Sunningwell*, so called from the stream which runs through it, where " a gospel used to be read to bless the springs on procession days as late as 1688."— *Aubrey.* The *Church*, partly E. E. and Dec., is entered by a very curious W. porch (octangular, and of Elizabethan architecture, with Gothic doors and windows, and Ionic columns); it is supposed to have been in great measure rebuilt by Bp. Jewell, who was once curate here. The interior has open Dec. seats and a late Elizabethan altar-rail. It was restored in 1877. Before the altar is the grave, inscribed S. F., of Samuel Fell, Dean of Christ Church and Rector of this place, who died of grief on hearing of the execution of Charles I., Feb. 2, 1649. A second stone, close beside him, commemorates his wife and children. From the tower of this ch. it is said Roger Bacon used to make his astronomical observations. Hearne mentions that on Shrove Tuesday children used to go round this village in the dusk, singing—

" Beef and bacon's
Out of season,
I want a pan
To parch my peas on."

after which they threw stones at all people's doors, which made people shut their doors on that evening. This custom still partially exists, but the verses are altered.

The road enters *Bagley Wood* at the spot mentioned by Hearne. " One Blake hung upon an oak in the way to Abingdon, beyond the half-way gate. This traitor betrayed 3 Christian kings, and would have betrayed the 4th, upon which he was hanged, within 2 days after his design was discovered, upon the said oak, which is still called ' Blake's Oak.' " The wood was formerly a haunt of robbers, and here St. Edward of Abingdon was once attacked by them, but his protestations of poverty being found to be true, he was allowed to proceed unharmed. An unlucky Franciscan, Brother Walter, who there fell among thieves, hardly escaped with his life, his captors pretending to disbelieve that he could belong to the order, as he wore shoes, which the rule did not allow him to do. Bagley Wood, which belongs to St. John's College, was once a favourite walk with the students, but it is now strictly shut up, and only mere glimpses of its pleasant flower-clad glades can be had from the dusty road. One who used to delight to roam at liberty in it (Dr. Arnold), says, " Some of my most delightful remembrances of Oxford and its neighbourhood are connected with the scenery of the late autumn: Bagley Wood in its golden decline, and the green of the meadows reviving for awhile under the influence of a Martinmas summer, and then fading finally off into its winter brown." From the top of the hill at the end of the wood is a splendid view of Oxford,—its spires, towers, and groves rising in the midst of the green valley. Hence, there is a rapid descent into the fertile plain. Spence's 'Anecdotes' describe Pope stopping on his journey to Oxford, and giving up his carriage to a lady who was overturned on this hill. The Great Western Rly. is crossed, and then the Thames, before reaching

27 m. OXFORD, which is entered by Folly Bridge, leading to St. Aldate's Street. (Rte. 19.)

ROUTE 9.

OXFORD TO HIGHWORTH.
CUMNOR.

By Road. 22 m.

The road leaves Oxford by the station, and is called the Seven Bridge Road, from the number of bridges by which it crosses the many branches of the river which here intersect the low meadows. Crossing the main stream of the Thames at the suburb of *Osney Town,* the site of *Osney Abbey* is passed on l., and Berkshire is entered. 1 m. *Botley,* a hamlet of Hinksey (Rte. 19, Exc. (*h*). On rt., a pleasant lane winding through meadows leads to Wytham, or Witham (1½ m.), a collection of very neat cottages, known in Oxford as " the Strawberry village." There is a fine view of

Oxford the whole way, which will remind the Italian traveller of the distant views of Bologna.

Wytham Abbey (Earl of Abingdon) is a 16th-centy. stone building, with a fine embattled gate-tower surmounted by 2 octangular turrets. It was built by one of the Harcourts, whose arms are to be seen upon a ceiling, and has been enriched with much of the spoil of Rycote (Rte. 22).

Close to the Abbey is the *Church,* rebuilt in 1814, mainly with old materials from Cumnor Hall; some of the windows have Trans.-Dec., and others Perp. tracery. The churchyard gate, inscribed "Janua vitæ verbum Domini," is also from Cumnor, but the name and date, " Antonius Forster, 1571," have been effaced. There is a *Brass* of a man in armour, and wife, supposed to be Richard and Alice de Wygtham, 1455.

The *Wytham Woods,* stretching over the hill behind the Abbey, are intersected by rides and drives of great beauty, chiefly through grass lanes. Admittance is only granted by a special order from Lord Abingdon. At the furthest point of the woods is a wild open space covered with thyme and cistus, whence there is a fine view over the Vale of Ensham. Here was situated the Castle of Cynewulf, King of the W. Saxons, which was besieged and taken by Offa, King of Mercia, who made it his palace. Near the same place was a nunnery, founded by the sister of Ceadwalla in the 7th cent., but deserted by the nuns when Cynewulf built his castle.

The manor of Wytham was early the property of the Wyghtams, who became extinct temp. Edw. IV. The manor afterwards passed to the Harcourts, and from them to the Crown. In 1589 it was granted to Sir John, afterwards Lord Williams of Thame, whose daughter and heiress brought it by marriage to Henry Lord Norris, son of the Sir Henry Norris executed as the lover of Anne Boleyn. It came to the Berties by the marriage of Montagu Bertie, Earl of Lindsey, with the daughter of Edward Wray, groom of the chamber to James I., whose wife Elizabeth was the daughter and heiress of Francis Lord Norris.

1½ m. The road turns off on rt. to Ensham, Burford, and Cheltenham.

3 m. *Cumnor*, on the brow of the hill. This was formerly a seat of the abbots of Abingdon, was used by them as a place of retirement in case of sickness, and was given by Henry VIII. to the last abbot, Rowland, as a reward for his ready compliance in the surrender of the monastery. In 1560 the estate was bought by Anthony Forster, Esq., almost immediately after which occurred the tragedy which has made the name of Cumnor familiar to the world.

Anne or Amy was daughter of Sir John Robsart, a man of high family and large property in Norfolk. She married Lord Robert Dudley at Sheen June 4, 1550, in the presence of Edward VI., as is stated in that king's journal. Her husband was raised to the peerage, as Lord Denbigh one day, and Earl of Leicester the next (Sept. 28, 29, 1563); but some years before this he had been treated with such marked favour by Elizabeth, that it was rumoured she would have married him, had he not had a wife already. The sudden death of the lady, on Sept. 8, 1560, at the age of 28, whilst residing far from the court, in the house of her husband's especial friend, Anthony Forster, almost inevitably gave rise to the idea that she had been murdered. Sir Walter Scott has adopted this view in his novel of 'Kenilworth,' and it is likely ever to be the prevalent one, although some later writers have attempted to prove it to

be unjust. According to the story as found in Ashmole, who faithfully reproduced whatever traditions he heard, Forster and an associate named Varney, first attempted to destroy the lady by poison, and, failing in this, forcibly sent her servants away to Abingdon-market, and then, "whether first stifling her or else strangling her, afterwards flung her down a pair of stairs and broke her neck, using much violence upon her." He adds that "Sir R. Varney, afterwards dying in London, cried miserably, and blasphemed God, saying that all the devils in hell did tear him in pieces; and that Forster, being formerly a man addicted to hospitality, company, mirth, and music, was afterwards observed to forsake all this, and, being affected with much melancholy (some say madness), pined and drooped away." Scott, as a novelist, took liberties with situation, as well as with history; and as he gave Amy the title of Countess, which her husband had not the power of bestowing till 3 yrs. after her death, and represented her as an inmate of Kenilworth, during the Queen's visit there 15 yrs. later, so he decked the unpretending monastic residence with lofty towers and spacious apartments; his first acquaintance with the story having been formed through Mickle's ballad of 'Cumnor':

> " Full many a traveller had sigh'd
> And pensive wept the Countess' fall,
> As wandering onward he espied
> The haunted towers of Cumnor Hall."

The mansion was really a low quadrangular edifice surrounding a small court, in a close immediately adjoining the ch. on the W.

In Pettigrew's 'Inquiry into the Death of Amy Robsart,' some original letters between Dudley and a friend named Blount (preserved in the Pepysian Library, Cambridge), are relied on as proving the innocence of both Dudley and Forster. The same writer also states that Ashmole's account of the subsequent life of the latter is incorrect: he lived for 12 years after the death of Amy Robsart, loving music to the last, building a new house, and only 2 yrs. before his death entered public life as member for Abingdon. Motley (*United Netherlands*, i. 368) also writes, "Leicester's participation in the death of his first wife was a matter of current belief among his contemporaries. 'He is infamed by the death of his wife,' said Burghley, and the tale has since become so interwoven with classic and legendary fiction, that the phantom of the murdered Amy Robsart is sure to arise at every mention of the earl's name. Yet a coroner's inquest—as appears from his own secret correspondence with his relative and agent at Cumnor—was immediately and persistently demanded by Dudley. A jury was impannelled —every man of them a stranger to him, and some of them enemies— Anthony Forster, Appleyard and Arthur Robsart, brother-in-law and brother of the lady, were present, according to Dudley's special request; 'and, if more of her friends could have been sent,' said he, 'I would have sent them;' but with all their minuteness of inquiry, 'they could find,' wrote Blount, 'no presumption of evil,' although he expressed a suspicion that 'some of the jurymen were sorry they could not.' That the unfortunate lady was killed by a fall downstairs was all that could be made of it by a coroner's inquest, rather hostile than otherwise, and urged to rigorous investigation by the supposed culprit himself. Nevertheless, the calumny has endured for three centuries, and is likely to survive as many more." The Dudley chamber, the supposed scene of the murder, was long shown, and the house was not entirely pulled down till 1811, when the windows and doorways were removed by Lord

Abingdon to be used in his new ch. at Wytham. 3 solitary arches long remained, but nothing is now left of the house, except the low wall adjoining the churchyard. The ch., mainly Trans.-Norm. and E. E., has a good Dec. piscina (engraved in 'Gloss. of Arch.'), and 2 tombs with crosses fleurée, in recesses, supposed to be for abbots of Abingdon; there is also a fine Elizabethan monument for Anthony Forster, his wife, and 3 sons. He is represented in armour, and an elegiac inscription of 32 lines describes him as amiable and learned, a great musician, builder, and planter. He was probably a connexion of Lord Leicester, to whom he left Cumnor by will. There are also some *Brasses* of the Stavertons.

In the village is an Inn with the sign of the "Bear and Ragged Staff;" but it has sprung up since the date of Scott's novel.

On the E. of the road rises the wooded hill called *Cumnor Hurst.* It affords, among other plants, Ornithogalum luteum, *yellow star of Bethlehem;* Lathræa squamaria, *toothwort;* Listera nidus avis, *bird's-nest orchis.*

[W. 1 m. *Bablockhythe Ferry.* Rte. 19, Exc. (*i.*).]

5 m. *Besilsleigh* (E. Kyffin Lenthall, Esq.), which derived its name from the ancient family of Besils, who obtained the estate by marriage in 1350. "At this Legh," writes Leland, "be very fayre pastures and woodes; the Blessells hathe been lords of it syns the time of Edward the First. The Blessells cam out of Provence in Fraunce, and were men of activitye in feates of armes, as it appearith in monuments at Legh; how he faught in listes with a strange knyghte that challengyd hym, at the whiche deade the kynge and quene at that tyme of England were present. The Blessells were countyed to have pocessyons of 400 marks by the yere."

From the Besils the estate passed to the Fettyplaces, by whom it was sold in 1634 to William Lenthall (the Speaker of the Long Parliament), from whom it descended to its present proprietor. The old manor-house is destroyed, except a picturesque fragment of the offices, now used as a farm-house, and the massive stone pillars of the gateway, which stand isolated among the trees in the field. The old mansion surrounded a quadrangular court, and was very magnificent: Cromwell and other leading men of his day are said to have been frequent guests there. Here was once preserved the famous picture of Sir Thomas More's family now at Cokethorpe (Rte. 25). On pulling down the building, a large room, or rather cell, was discovered, which had evidently been used as a place of concealment: it was in the lower part of the building, and the only access to it was by a chair lowered by pulleys from the top of the house. It was probably a "priest's hole," but the tradition of the neighbourhood makes Cromwell to have been once concealed in it: a new "fact" for his biographers. The small *Church* has early Dec. windows, a Norm. piscina, and a timber porch of fair Jacobean character. It contains a handsome monument to Sir John Lenthall, the father of the Speaker.

1 m. N.W. is *Appleton*, with a Trans.-Norm. *Church*; one of the sculptured capitals is engraved in the 'Gloss. of Architecture.' There is a *Brass*, with skeleton in shroud, for John Goodryngton (d. 1518), and a fine Elizabethan tomb for Sir John Fettyplace (d. 1593), lord of one of the three manors into which the parish is divided. The moats alone remain of two manor-houses, inclosing modern farms; but what is now called the *Manor-house* (Rev. J. C. Coen) has very considerable remains of the original Trans.-

Norm. edifice; the doorway of the hall is engraved in Parker's 'Domestic Architecture,' vol. i.

8 m. *Tubney*, with a very elegant small ch., built by *Pugin* in 1848, in place of one long fallen to decay.

9 m. *Fyfield*. The *Church* is Dec., with W. door E. E., and a Perp. aisle added on N. This aisle is divided by a screen, forming the E. part into a chantry chapel, in which is the tomb of Sir John Golafre (d. 1442), with his effigy in armour above, and a cadaver below. In the chancel is a tomb without effigy or inscription, traditionally said to be that of Lady Katherine Gordon, the widow of Perkin Warbeck, but at her death the wife of Christopher Ashfield of this place. Adjoining the ch. is the ancient *Manor-house* of the Golafres, a Dec. structure, built c. 1350, by Sir John Golafre, who had married the heiress of John of Fyfield; the knight buried in the ch. was their grandson. The house has been well restored by the present occupant (Jas. Parker, Esq.) This is one of the manors purchased by Sir Thomas White, and bestowed by him on his college (St. John's) at Oxford. In this parish is a magnificent *elm* 36 ft. in circumference, popularly believed to be the resort of witches, who dance here at midnight; also of—

" Maidens, who from the distant hamlets come,
To dance round Fyfield elm in May."
M. Arnold.

10 m. *Kingston Bagpuze*. The ch. is a small plain building, erected 1799; it has an apsidal chancel. In this parish is *New Bridge*, a 13th-centy. structure, similar to Radcot Bridge, still in use. It is mentioned by Leland, as the oldest of all the bridges on the Thames, "lying in low meadows, often overflowed with rage of rain." A Parliamentary party received a severe defeat here, May 27, 1644; in re-

venge for this they, 4 days after, hewed down the market-cross at Abingdon. *Kingston House* (J. B. Jenkins, Esq.) 1½ m. N. W. is *Longworth*, once the property of 'Sir H. Marten, father of the regicide. The *Church* is chiefly E. E. and Dec.; but "the nave has on N. 3 Trans.-Norm. arches, springing from corbels on massive square piers, having hood-moulds of early character, with singular terminations; on S. are 3 E. E. arches on plain round pillars, the hood-moulds similar to those on N., but terminated by heads; the clerestory and roofs are late and bad Perp." (*J. H. P.*) Dr. Fell, bishop of Oxford, was born at Long-worth in 1625. *Cherbury Camp*, probably a British earthwork, in which there is said to have been a palace of Canute, is near.

13 m. On N. 1 m. *Hinton Wal-drist*, once a market-town, has an interesting small cruciform ch.; it is E.E. and Dec., and the battlements of the tower have small heads on the merlons.

14 m. On S. 1 m. *Pusey*, with a small cruciform ch. r. built about 130 years ago, in better taste than might be expected. It contains some hand-some marble monuments for mem-bers of the family of Allan-Pusey, an ancestor of whom is said to have received the manor from Canute, to be held by tenure of a horn, which is still preserved in Pusey House. It bears the following legend up·n a silver-gilt band of the 15th centy., elegantly wrought: — "I. Kyng Knowde [Canute] geue Wyllyam Pecote thys horne to holde by thy lond." It is not known by the family whether the horn was really and truly the original horn given to their ancestor by King Canute. Camden said:— "The family of Pusey held the village of Pusey, in Berkshire, in fee, by a horn which was first given to William Pecote by King Canute. Dr. Hickes, in

1681, states that in his time both the horn and manor were possessed by Charles Pusey, who had had recovered the manor in the Court of Chancery, before Lord Chancellor Jefferies: the horn itself being produced in Court, and with universal admiration received, admitted, and proved to be the identical horn by which, as by a charter, Canute had conveyed the manor of Pusey 700 years befor. The horn is that of an ox of middling size, mounted in silver-gilt, in work-manship of the latter part of the 15th centy. The colour of the horn is dark brown, which proves it to be a real ox-horn, and not, as was some-times the case, made of ivory. It is 2 ft. 6 in. long, and 9¼ in. high from its feet; the circumference at the largest end is 1 ft.; in the middle, 9¼ in.; and at the small end, 2¼ in. The dog's head at the orifice was formerly moveable, turning upon a joint, so as to make it either a hunt-ing or a drinking horn." The earliest historical mention of the family was in 1155, when Henry de Pesie held the manor. The present family (of French Protestant origin) changed their name of Bouverie for that of Pusey on succeeding to the property by marriage.

Pusey House (S. E. B. Pusey, Esq.) contains a fine picture by *Gaspar Poussin*.

In the reign of Edward I. Alice Paternoster held lands here by ser-vice of saying a paternoster 5 times a-day, for the souls of the King's ancestors; and Richard Paternoster succeeding to an estate in this parish said the Lord's Prayer thrice before the barons of the exchequer, as John, his brother, had done previously, instead of paying a relief.

14½ m. On N. 1 m. *Buckland*, with a very fine cruciform *Church*, restored 1870, mostly E. E.; the N. transept, is the burial-place of the Throckmorton family: in it is also a fine *Brass*, for John Yate, and family, 1578.

Buckland House (Sir N. W. G. Throckmorton, Bart.). built 1757, from designs of Wood of Bath, has some fine pictures, and a ceiling by *Cipriani.* Here are also valuable MSS., including many original letters of Cowper the poet.

A gallery leading to the dining-room contains some curious relics, among them a chemise of Mary Queen of Scots, and a gold medal of Charles I., taken from the body of Sir Baynham Throckmorton (the last of the Gloucestershire branch of the family). Here also is preserved a coat, the wonder of 1811, in which year it was made. In one day 2 sheep belonging to Sir John Throckmorton were shorn, the wool spun, spooled, warped, loomed, and woven; the cloth burred, milled, dyed, dried, sheared, and pressed; after which the coat was made up by White, a New-bury tailor, and worn by Sir John at an agricultural dinner, at the Pelican, in Speenhamland, in presence of 5000 spectators, within 13 hrs. 20 min. from the time the sheepshearing commenced. The scene is represented in a picture which still remains in the old adjoining ivy-grown house of the Yates family, from whom the estate came to the Throckmortons by marriage. The lower story is now occupied by the stables. At the back is a fine oriel window.

17 m. *Faringdon* (Stat.) Rte. 5.

19 m. *Coxwell.* The ch. is a plain structure, E. E. with Perp. tower, and some Dec. windows. There are 2 *Brasses*, for William Morys, "sütym fermer of Cokyswell," and wife, c. 1500. The manor was given to Beaulieu Abbey by John, and the abbey barn, doubtless occupied by Morys, still remains. It is 140 ft. by 40 ft., with walls 4 ft. thick, and has mouldings that show it to belong to the Dec. period, and crosses on the gables. The original

roof remains, plain open timber, carried partly on two rows of wooden pillars resting on stone plinths (*J. H. P.*). On Badbury Hill is a circular camp, 600 ft. in diameter, with fosse 30 ft. wide. At Little Coxwell are the *Coles Pits*, a series of 273 excavations, from 7 to 22 ft. in depth, extending over a space of 14 acres; nothing is known of their history.

20 m. *Coleshill* is a model village, in which no public-house or inn is allowed, mostly consisting of neat stone cottages built on a uniform plan, and with pleasant gardens, by the 2nd Earl of Radnor. The *Church*, originally Trans.-Norm. and E. E., has a good Perp. tower, and a modern Dec. chancel; it contains the monument of Sir Henry Pratt, 1647; a quatrefoil window with the arms of Sir R. Mark Stuart and his wife; and a marble cenotaph, by *Ryshraoh*, to their daughter, afterwards Countess of Radnor. The E. window, representing the Nativity, was brought from Angers 1787. Near the ch. are the steps and shaft of the village cross. *Coleshill House* (Earl of Radnor), erected by *Inigo Jones* in 1650, stands in a fine park. It is of a perfect quadrangular shape, and a fine specimen of its period, resembling a French château, its tall stone chimneys having the appearance of turrets at a distance. It contains a fine hall and many good family portraits, among which are several by *Sir J. Reynolds*, but the principal pictures of the Bouveries are at Longford in Wilts. On the estate is an extensive Model Farm. The small river *Cole* skirts the village, and falls into the Thames near Lechlade. Crossing the stream we enter Wiltshire, and reach at 22 m. *Highworth.* (See *Handbook for Wilts.*)

Shrivenham Stat. is 4 m. S. E. (Rte. 5).

ROUTE 10.

THE THAMES,

FROM GORING TO MAIDENHEAD, BY PANGBOURNE, MAPLEDURHAM, CAVERSHAM, SONNING, SHIPLAKE, WARGRAVE, HENLEY, MEDMENHAM, HURLEY, BISHAM, MARLOW, HEDSOR, COOKHAM, [DROPMORE], AND CLIEFDEN.

87 m.

The descent of this portion of the Thames is one of the most delightful expeditions which can be made in the S. of England, and takes the tourist through the most beautiful scenery of the 3 counties of Berks, Oxford, and Bucks, along a river which fully justifies the description of Denham:

" Though deep, yet clear; though gentle, yet
     not dull;
Strong without rage, without o'erflowing
     full."

Goring — 85 m. from London Bridge by the stream, and which has a stat. on the Great Western Rly. (Rte. 4)—is perhaps the best point for commencing the excursion, as Nuneham, the only point of much beauty higher up the river, is easily accessible by rail. Boats may be obtained either here or at Streatley on the opposite bank. As the river during the whole excursion forms the boundary between Berks

and Oxfordshire and Bucks, it has been thought better to describe both banks equally, instead of maintaining the distinction usually observed between counties in the Handbooks.

1. *Goring* (Oxon), (*Inns:* The Miller of Mansfield, and the Queen's Arms), formerly *Little Nottingham.* The small *Church of St. Thomas à Beckett*, close to the river, is worth visiting. Part of it is Norm. and very curious; at the N. W. corner of its embattled tower (Norm. and Perp.) is a small round tourelle, with a conical top. The ch. contains some good brasses. Adjoining the ch. was once an Augustinian nunnery, founded temp. Henry II., and afterwards granted to Sir T. Pope, the founder of Trinity College, Oxford. On the rt. bank is *Streatley* (Berks), (*Inn:* Swan on the River, Bull in the Village), united to Goring village by a wooden bridge over the Thames, but 2 m. from Goring stat. It is an exceedingly pretty village, and is situated on a platform between the river and the steep escarpment of the hills; in summer it is a favourite resort of artists. The ch., mostly Trans.-Norm. has a late Perp. tower; there are some 16th-centy. *Brasses.* Sir Samuel Shepherd, the eminent Attorney-General and Scotch judge, was a native of this place; he died here, and is buried in the churchyard. Streatley is supposed to have its name from its situation on the ancient Icknield St., which here descended the hill and crossed the Thames by a ford to Goring. Some imagine this to have been the ancient Calleva, an opinion which is supported by its position on the Thames, by the 3 Roman roads, the Icknield St. and those from Winchester and Dorchester, which pass through it, and by the number of Roman remains which have been found in its vicinity.

Goring Lock. Fall 5 ft.

The river here is wide and beautiful; a large island is covered with fine trees. A melancholy accident occurred here in 1674, when 60 persons were drowned in the lock in returning from Goring Feast. The accident is described in a rare tract, called 'Sad and deplorable News from Oxfordsheir and Barksheir,' proving that this was one of the signs of the Day of Judgment.

The Berkshire downs, sprinkled with juniper, and here and there a remarkable yew-tree, rise abruptly behind Streatley, and stretch far away westward; the views are extensive, commanding the windings of the river for many miles. *Unwell Wood*, 3 m. N. W., on a spur of the hills, is celebrated for its orchises, as the down is for its coursing matches. In these woods also is found the Convallaria multiflora, or *Solomon's seal*.

2½ m. S.W. is *Aldworth*, with the remarkable tombs described in Rte. ·4. The hilly road from Streatley to ·Pangbourne affords some picturesque views.

Descending the stream we have at 2 m. rt. the *Grotto* (Arthur Smith, Esq.); and at 2½ m. *Basildon.* The river, which is here crossed by the Rly., makes a sudden bend amidst beautiful woods. *Basildon Park* (C. Morrison, Esq.) contains a fine collection of pictures, described Rte. 4.

l. *Whitchurch Park*.

rt. 4 m. *Pangbourne* (Berks). *Inns*: Swan by the river, George, and Elephant and ˙ Castle in the village. This village, which derives its name from the *Pang*, a famous trout-stream, is a great resort of anglers and artists, has a stat. on the Great Western Rly., and is one of the most picturesque villages upon the river. In this parish is *Bere Court*, described by Leland as the "fair manor-place of brick" of the abbots of Reading, the last of whom, Hugh Faringdon, constantly resided here. His portrait in stained glass adorned the E. window of the chapel, habited in

his robes, and kneeling before a crucifix, with a scroll proceeding out of his mouth, inscribed "In te Domine speravi." It was afterwards the abode of Sir J. Davis, a famous sea-captain, in the reign of Elizabeth, who was involved in the fall of his patron Essex, and sentenced to death, but was afterwards reprieved, and is buried in Pangbourne ch. His monument represents a recumbent figure of the knight with his two wives, surmounted by a canopy.

l. *Whitchurch* (Oxon), a large village, is united to Pangbourne by a bridge, rebuilt 1853. The *Church*, originally Norm., has been almost rebuilt, but has a good S. doorway; the Perp. porch now serves as the vestry. Notice the *Brasses* of Thomas Walysch (1420), and of Roger Gery (c. 1450) in the chancel, and that of Peter Winder, in ecclesiastical vestments (1620), outside. Sir John Soane, founder of the Soane Museum, and architect˙ of the Bank of England, the son of a bricklayer at Reading (d. 1837), was born at Whitchurch.

Whitchurch Lock. Fall 3 ft.

l. *Combe ˙Lodge.* ·

l. *Hardwick House*(P. L. P. Lybbe, Esq.), a fine red-brick Tudor manor-house, on a site occupied by the Hardwicks, temp. Richard II. The S. front was erected by Anthony Lybbe, after the restoration of Charles II. The banks of the river are here exceedingly beautiful; green lawns studded with noble trees slope down from the hills.

A short distance N. of Hardwick House is the scattered hamlet of *Collen's End.* Here, it is said, Charles I. came to play at bowls whilst residing at Caversham; and the rustic *Inn* has as its sign a portrait of the King, apparently copied from Vandyke. Though much faded from exposure to the weather, the work is evidently superior to that of a common sign-painter. Beneath it are the lines—

" Stop, Traveller, stop; in yonder peaceful glade,
His favourite game the royal Martyr play'd;
Here, stripp'd of honours, children, freedom, rank,
Drank from the bowl, and bowled for what he drank;
Sought in a cheerful glass his cares to drown,
And changed his guinea ere he lost his crown."

6 m. l. *Mapledurham House* (Oxon), (M. C. Blount, Esq.). celebrated by Pope as the place whither his love, Martha Blount, retired from London, when

" She went to plain-work, and to purling brooks,
Old-fashion'd halls, dull aunts, and croaking rooks."

The house is a venerable Elizabethan mansion, which was garrisoned by Sir Charles Blount for the king in the civil wars. A fine oak staircase, with carved vases of flowers upon the landings, leads to the upper story. The rooms are full of pictures, chiefly family portraits, including Sir M. Blount, 1530, and his two sons, Thos. and Chas.; Lord Mountjoy, to whom the portrait of Elizabeth was probably a present; Martha Blount as a child and grown up, and again with her sister Theresa, in a beautiful picture by *Jervas* (they both died here); Pope, *Jervas.* The ch., which stands embowered in trees near the river, was restored in 1864. It has a S. aisle, which is the ancestral burial-place of the Blounts, containing a fine tomb of Sir Rich. Blount and his wife Elizabeth; although it still belongs to them, no service but that of the Church of England is ever performed in it.

Mapledurham Lock. Fall 5 feet. A mile below the lock there is a ferry, and on the Berkshire bank the Roebuck Inn.

6 m. rt. *Purley*, with a small Perp. ch., rebuilt 1870-1877, which contains a monument by *Nollekens* to

Anthony Storer. *Purley Hall* was the residence of Warren Hastings whilst his trial was pending.

11 m. l. *Caversham Church* (Oxon). *Inns:* Crown, White Hart. Pop. 2500. The ch., which is partly Norm., was partially restored in 1857, and more fully in 1880. It suffered much during the operations about Reading in the civil war. Here was formerly a priory of black canons, a cell of Nutley Abbey, which was said to contain the spear that pierced our Saviour, "brought hither by an angel with one wing; a piece of the holy halter Judas hanged withall; the holy dagger of King Henry VI.: and the holy knife that killed Sainte Edward; with many other." Hence a handsome iron bridge crosses the river to Reading, below which on an island was fought the wager of battle between Rob. de Montfort and Henry de Essex, in the presence of Henry II. At Caversham died the great William Marshall, Earl of Pembroke, the guardian of Henry III. The place was fortified during the civil wars by the King's forces, who were, however, driven from their post by the Earl of Essex. He planted his ordnance on the height, by which he was able so to injure the town of Reading, that, after many houses were destroyed, the governor, who was himself wounded, offered to surrender, if his soldiers might depart with all the honours of war, which at first was refused. Charles and Prince Rupert, in spite of a partial defeat at Dor-chester, advanced to the rescue as far as Caversham Bridge, where a fierce fight ensued, in which they were completely repulsed; after this the garrison surrendered, but were allowed to march out with their arms, ammunition, and colours. Here

" Old South, a witty preacher reckon'd,"

lived while preparing his celebrated sermons for the press.

1. on the hill is *Caversham Park* (Mrs. Crawshay), a very conspicuous object from the river. In the original mansion Queen Anne of Denmark was splendidly entertained by Lord Knollys in 1613. There also, in July, 1647, the children of Charles I. were allowed to meet him, when they spent two days together, "which was the greatest satisfaction the king could have, and the receiving whereof he imputed to the civility of General Fairfax and the good disposition of the army."—*Clarendon.* Evelyn, coming here a few years later, saw "my Lord Craven's house at Causham all in ruins, his goodly woods felling by the rebels." General Cadogan, who was one of Marlborough's veterans, and succeeded him as commander-in-chief, was created Viscount Caversham, and resided here (d. 1726). Caversham Park was destroyed for the second time by fire in 1850, after which the present house was built.

In *Caversham Warren* is found the Orchis aranifera, or *spider orchis.*

Caversham Lock. Fall 3 ft. 6 in.

rt. READING, the county town of Berks, described Rte. 4.

12 m. rt., just below Reading, the Thames is joined by

" The Kennet swift, for silver eels renown'd."
Pope.

rt. *Earley Court* (Captain G. F. Hall), where Scott Lord Stowell died, is seen across the rich flat meadows.

rt. The woody heights are those of *Holme Park* (Miss Palmer), which commands a lovely view over the river.

Sonning Lock. Fall 4 ft. 6 in.

14 m. rt. *Sonning* (Berks) (*Inn:* White Hart, close to the river, a pleasant country inn, resorted to by anglers, and on the Oxfordshire side the French Horn), with hanging woods, in a lovely situation, sloping to the river, which is here crossed by a bridge whose records are older than those of any other on the Thames. In the 10th and 11th cents. this place was the seat of a bishop for Berks and Wilts, and the names of 9 of its holders have been preserved, viz., Athelstan, Odo, Osulf, Alfstan, Alfgar, Sigeric, Alfric, Brightwold, and Heremann (who united the bishopric of Sherborne to his own, and, " in the reign of Edward the Elder, transferred his see to Sherborne, by synodal authority and that king's munificence"). After the deposition of Richard II., his child-wife, Isabella of Valois, fled hither to the Bishop of Salisbury, who still resided at Sonning, which remained in the diocese of Salisbury. The bishops retained their palace here till the reign of Elizabeth, when it was exchanged with the Crown; the site of the palace is now marked by an aged ash-tree on a rising ground above the river.

Before the Reformation there existed here a chapel of St. Sarac, which was a celebrated place of pilgrimage for the cure of madness. The oldest portion of the present beautiful *Church (of St. Andrew,* whose image is over the N. porch) dates from 1200. The S. aisle is Dec. in the best style, and there is a good chequered Perp. tower. The most remarkable feature is a sculptured arch in the N. chancel aisle, the keystone of which bears the arms of the see of Salisbury, while on one side is a representation of Christ blessing the 12 Apostles, and on the other kings and queens crowned. The *Brass* of Lawrence Fytton, bailiff of Sonning, is dated 1434, and there are other brasses, of the Barker family (1549–89). Lord Stowell (d. 1836) is buried here; his monument has a long inscription by H. Addington, Lord Sidmouth. The ch. was restored in 1853, under the care of the upright and amiable vicar, Hugh Pearson (d. 1882), to whom a monumental effigy will be set up. The bells are celebrated.

In a house in the upper part of the village Sydney Smith wrote 'Peter Plymley's Letters.' At a house called the Grove (H. A. Knox, Esq.) Miss Rich was in the habit of receiving Pitt, Wyndham, Addington, Adm. Villeneuve (who lost the battle of Trafalgar), and many distinguished French émigrés.

17 m. l. *Shiplake* (Oxon). The *Church*, situated on a chalk cliff, picturesquely overhanging one of the finest bends on the river, is mostly Dec.; it contains an E. E. piscina, and some ancient wood-carving and 7 rich stained windows from the ruined ch. of St. Bertin at St. Omer, sacked during the 1st French Revolution. It was rebuilt in 1869 by G. E. Street. The embattled tower is profusely covered with ivy; the S. aisle, the oldest part of the edifice, was probably the original ch. Here James Granger, author of the 'Biographical History of England,' died at the altar whilst administering the Holy Communion, April 14, 1776.

" Such privilege what saint e'er knew?
    To whom such honour shown?
His Saviour's death in rapturous view,
    And unperceived his own."

Here Alfred Tennyson was married. In the vestry is preserved the first model for the W. end of St. Paul's, used in making the original model of the whole, which was the favourite of the great author.

Shiplake Lock   Fall 5 ft. 6 in.

17¾ m. rt. The Thames receives the river *Loddon*, here divided into several distinct channels—

" The Loddon slow, with silver alders
    crown'd,"

of Pope, who also celebrates it as the nymph Lodona in his 'Windsor Forest,' in an imitation of the story of Alpheus and Arethusa.

18 m. rt. *Wargrave* (Berks). *Inn:* George and Dragon. Pop. 1785. Here is a ferry across the river. Near this the river is crossed by the Henley branch of the Great Western Rly. carried on a rough timber viaduct. The ch., which is cruciform, is of various dates, and has a very clumsy-looking 17th-centy. tower. It contains the monument of Mr. Day, author of 'Sandford and Merton,' who was killed here by a fall from his horse.

Wargrave Hill (E. Jekyll, Esq.) was the residence of Joseph Hill, Cowper's friend, the "Septus Hill" to whom so many of his letters are addressed.

1 m. l. *Harpsden* (Oxon), whose Dec. and Perp. ch., restored, contains a cross-legged effigy and some good *Brasses*, one to Walter Elmes, rector 1511.

Harpsden Court (J. B. Carbonell, Esq.), an ancient house near the ch., formerly contained 7 halls, of which one was called the "Beggars' Hall."

20 m. *Marsh Lock*. Fall 4 ft. 6 in.

21 m. l. HENLEY. *Inn:* Red Lion, close to the bridge; an excellent, old-fashioned country inn, with very reasonable charges. On a pane of glass in a parlour window of the Red Lion, Shenstone wrote the lines—

" Whoe'er has travell'd life's dull round,
    Where'er his stages may have been,
May sigh to think that he has found
    His warmest welcome at an inn."

Henley (from *Hen*, old, and *Lye*, place —traditionally the "oldest place in all Oxfordshire," (Pop. 4604), stands on one of the most beautiful spots in the whole course of the Thames, the broad and full river being here flanked by gentle hills, covered with hanging woods, occasionally varied by scarps of chalk. The town is readily reached by rail from Twyford (Rte. 4), and is much resorted to in summer.

Henley is the last place in Oxfordshire. There is a beautiful road eastward hence along the Buckinghamshire bank of the river, by which all the places on that side may be visited. At Danesfield it passes through the beautiful *Bassla Woods*, whence it descends *Red-Pits Hill* to Marlow (*post*). After passing Cookham, the road ascends the hills and passes between the beautiful parks of Hedsor, Dropmore, and Cliefden, descending upon Maidenhead by Taplow Court.

The road on the Berkshire side of the river ascends the hill by Park Place to the pretty village of Hurley, whence pleasant by-roads and lanes may be followed through Bisham and Cookham to Maidenhead (Rte. 4).

The river is crossed at Henley by a handsome *Bridge* of Headington stone, built 1786, and adorned with sculptured masks of the Thames and the Isis, by the Hon. *Mrs. Damer*, daughter of General Conway, of Park Place. Passing the bridge, the beautiful reach of the river is entered, lined by tall poplars, and backed by the luxuriant woods of Park Place, where the celebrated Henley Regatta is held. This, which may be considered as the parent of all amateur regattas. had its origin in a contest between the two Universities on this reach in 1829, which excited so much interest as to suggest the idea of its becoming annual. This was first actually carried out in the regatta, June 24, 1839, since which it has obtained a universal popularity. "We have seen on the Oxford water, during the season, eighteen or nineteen boats in daily competition; at Cambridge a yet greater number have been found similarly struggling for that superiority which has usually decided the question, 'Who shall row at Henley?'"—*Bell's Life*.

The Dec. and Perp. *Church*, near the bridge (restd.) is conspicuous from its square Perp. tower, with six-sided turrets, said to have been built by Wolsey; its windows are filled with modern painted glass. At the W. end is the effigy, wrapped up in a [*Berks, &c.*]

cloak, of Lady Elizabeth Periam, sister of Lord Bacon, and benefactress of Balliol College, at Oxford (d. 1621). Sir Godfrey Kneller's widow was Susannah Cawley, daughter of the vicar of Henley: she is buried here with her father and mother; there are monuments to the parents. The famous "Jack Ogle," of temp. Charles II. and James II., is also buried in this church; he was notorious for his humorous frolics, for one of which see 'Tatler,' No. 132; his sister was one of the Duke of York's many mistresses:—

"But Death at length did Ogle take at Henley upon Thames,
Where he was buried decently in the third year of King James."

A slab near the S. door of the ch., with the inscription, "Ici repose le Général Dumouriez," marks the grave of that officer, who died at Turville Park, 1823, aged 83. In the vestry is a library left by Dean Aldrich (1729), rector of Henley, as the foundation of a parochial library, but never added to. In the ch.-yd. is buried Rich. Jennings, the master-builder of St. Paul's Cathedral.

1½ m. N.W. of Henley is *Rotherfield Greys*, with the interesting old Greys Court and a magnificent tomb of Lord Knollys in the ch. (See Rte. 20.) At *Greys*, the parish adjoining Henley, are a Gothic ch. and schools by Ferrey, 1849.

2½ m. rt. 1 m. *Park Place* has beautiful hanging woods upon the chalk cliff, which rises nearly 300 ft. above the river. In the grounds is a Druidical temple, presented to General Conway (the friend of Horace Walpole) by the inhabitants of Jersey, and removed from a hill near St. Helier's in that island in 1785. It consists of 45 stones of granite, and is 60 ft. in circumference. A tunnel in the cliff leads to a miniature (so called) amphitheatre. The house commands lovely views. A cedar in the grounds is said to have

H

been planted by George III. when a boy. The arch over which the Twyford road passes is built of pudding-stone and grey wethers.

23 m. l. *Fawley Court* (Bucks), a handsome edifice, with four regular fronts, by *Wren*, 1684. The old manor-house, which belonged to Bulstrode Whitelock, son of Judge Whitelock, and author of the 'Memorials,' (d. 1688), was terribly injured by the Royalist soldiery under Sir John Byron, quartered here in 1642.

" Sir John Biron and his brother," he says, " commanded those horse, and gave order that they should commit no insolence at my house, nor plunder my goods ; but soldiers are not easily governed against their plunder, or persuaded to restrain it ; for there being about 1000 of the king's horse quartered in and about the house, and none but servants there, there was no insolence or outrage usually committed by common soldiers on a reputed enemy which was omitted by these brutish fellows at my house. . . . . . They spent and consumed 100 load of corn and hay, littered their horses with sheaves of good wheat, and gave them all sorts of corn in the straw ; divers writings of consequence, and books which were left in my study, some of them they tore in pieces, others they burnt to light their tobacco, and some they carried away with them, to my extreme great loss and prejudice in wanting the writings of my estate, and losing very many excellent manuscripts of my father's and others, and some of my own labours.

" They broke down my park pales, killed most of my deer, though rascal and carrion, and let out all the rest, only a tame young stag they carried away and presented to Prince Rupert, and my hounds, which were extraordinary good. They ate and drank up all that the

house could afford ; broke up all my trunks, chests, and places ; and where they found linen, or any household stuff, they took it away with them, and cutting the beds let out the feathers, and took away the ticks. They likewise carried away my coach, and four good horses, and all my saddle-horses, and did all the mischief and spoil that malice and enmity could provoke barbarous mercenaries to commit, and so they parted.

" This," he concludes, " is remembered only to raise a constant hatred of anything that may in the least tend to the fomenting of such unhappiness and misery."

The *Church*, which has a plain E.E. tower, is fitted up with relics brought in 1748 from Cannons, the seat of the Duke of Chandos, near Edgeware ; the carving of the pulpit and altar is by *Gibbons*. In the S. chapel is a large monument, with effigies of Sir James and Lady Whitelock, 1632. The ch.-yd. contains a fine yew-tree.

Just below Fawley Court is the *Island*, with a small Grecian temple, whence the boats start for Henley Bridge in the regatta. The river below this is frequently studded with islands of this kind, which are often planted with large trees, such as ash and abeles. The smaller islands are called *Eyots* or *Aits* ; " these occur everywhere, sometimes singly and far apart, and sometimes in clusters, and are almost as various and beautiful as they are numerous. They are generally planted with osiers ; and as they occur in the shallows, are frequently surrounded by rushes, while the willow-herb, loosestrife, and similar flowers, encompass them with a belt of brilliant colours."— *Thorne.*

Opposite Fawley Court is the pretty village of *Remenham* (Berks), backed by high wooded hills. The small Norm. ch., restored in 1870, has a semicircular apse, and a good N. porch of wood, with fine Perp. carving.

23½ m. l. *Greenland House* (Rt.Hon. W. H. Smith, M.P.). The old house underwent a siege of six months by the Parliamentary forces (1644) in the time of Sir John d'Oyley, when the garrison was forced to capitulate and the building almost destroyed. The fortifications raised during the siege are still visible, and a great number of cannon-balls were dug up in the park in 1850 when the house was enlarged.

24 m. l. 1½ m. up the valley of the Hamble is *Hambleden* (Bucks). Pop. 1550. *Inns*: Flower Pot, and Aston. A very pretty village, once possessed by Earl Algar, and after him by the De Clares and the Scropes. The *Church* in Rickman's time had been, he says, "much patched and modernized. It is a large cross ch. of flint, with a modern W. tower (1721); there seems to have been originally a Norm. tower at the intersection, and there are portions of the 3 later styles. There is a good Norm. font, a S. door with good plain mouldings, and 3 stalls, and a water-drain in the chancel, with ogee heads and good crocketed canopies." It has since been restored (1860), but it is much to be regretted that all the monuments except two have been removed from the chancel, and that the reredos, being alabaster, and devoid of colour, should be of feeble and poor design. The priest's door has been not only blocked up, but wholly obliterated. In the transept are some *Brasses* of the Sheepwash family, with the singular bearing, sheep in a wash-brook; many of the Scrope family are buried in the chancel. In the N. aisle is a fine alabaster monument of Sir Cope d'Oyley, his wife and 10 children, with a quaint epitaph by Quarles: he was the brother of Lady d'Oyley, who, he tells us,

"Was in spirit a Jael, Rebecca in grace, in heart an Abigail; In works a Dorcas, to the Church a Hannah, And to her spouse Susannah. Prudently simple, providently wary. To the world a Martha, and to heaven a Mary."

Here also is buried Thomas, 2nd Lord Sandys of the Vine, without an inscription (c. 1560). Hambleden was the birthplace of St. Thomas (Cantilupe) of Hereford, who was baptised in the ch., in the Norm. font which still exists. In consequence of the property which he possessed at Hambleden, Edmund Earl of Cornwall founded a magnificent shrine at Ashridge in honour of this saint.

The *Manor-house* was built by Scrope, Earl of Sunderland, 1624. Charles I. took refuge here with Mr. Ashburnham and Mr. Hudson, April 28, 1646, on his way to St. Albans, and escaped by the connivance of Whitelock.

2½ m. higher up, at the head of the Hambleden valley, is *Fingest*, where the Bishops of Lincoln had a palace. One of these, Bishop Burghersh (d. 1340), according to tradition, could not rest in his grave until the encroachments he had made on the common to enlarge his park had been restored—his ghost appearing "in a keeper's dress," and begging that the portions illegally taken might be disparked.

In the neighbourhood is *Turville Park* (C. Scholefield, Esq.), once the residence of Gen. Dumouriez.

24½ m. rt. *Culham Court.*

l. *Yewden* (Hon. Admiral George Grey), remarkable for a fine old hedge of clipped yew.

25 m. l., in a lovely and secluded situation, close to the river, by a little inn and ferry-house, are the small remains of *Medmenham Abbey*, which, though so much patched up and added to (the tower and cloister being modern) that it is difficult to distinguish which are the really old parts, is still very

picturesque. The greater part of the existing building is not monastic but the remains of a manor-house of the Duffields, who possessed the estate from a short time after the dissolution till ,1779. The abbey, an offshoot from the Cistercian monastery at Woburn, gradually fell into decay through the poverty of its inhabitants, so that at the dissolution there were only two monks, and its revenues were reduced to 1*l*. 3*s*. 6*d*. Its foundation charter is dated Jan. 3, 1201, but the monks did not take up their abode here till 1212. The abbot was Epistolar of the Order of the Garter at Windsor, his office being to read the Epistle at the feast of St. George. Over the door in the ivy-covered gable at the side of the present building is the inscription "*Fay ce que voudras*," a memorial of another order, who took this sentence as their motto, and lived here in the middle of the last century, calling themselves Franciscans, from their founder Francis Dashwood, afterwards Lord le Despencer. All that took place at Medmenham was then wrapped in mystery : the workmen who furnished and adorned the abbey were never allowed to pass the doors, and were hurried back to London as soon as their work was finished ; and the servants were prohibited all intercourse with the neighbourhood. Some of the scenes enacted here are described in ' Chrysall or the Adventures of a Guinea,' in which the mysterious rites appear to have been Bacchic festivals, Devil-worship, and a mockery of all the rites of religion, combined with the worst forms of debauchery ; and Churchill gives the same impression :

" Whilst Paul the aged chalks behind a door,
Comp~ll'd to hire a foe to cast it up ;
Dashwood shall pour, from a communion cup,
Libations to the goddess without eyes,
And bob and nob in cyder and excise."
        Churchill's ' Candidate.'

But Langley, in his ' Hundred of

Desborough,' maintains that the common account of the doings of the Medmenham " monks " is a gross exaggeration. One night, in the midst of their orgies, the profligate party, it is said, were overwhelmed with terror at the apparition of a huge ape, hideously attired, which had been lowered down the chimney ; they for a long time believed that the fiend himself had appeared among them, and their meetings were then finally broken up. The Franciscans always slept in cradles, and a fragment of the cradle of Wilkes, who was one of the members, is still shown as a relic. All other traces of the society are now swept away, except the motto, but some of the pictures from Medmenham, representing the mysteries, are preserved at the Thatched House Tavern in London. The Swan-uppers (*post*) used to have a great annual dinner at Medmenham.

A short distance N. of the ruins is the E. E. parish ch., restored more then forty years ago by Mr. Scott Murray, of Danesfield ; there is a good E. window of modern stained glass ; and a brass dated 1415. On a slight eminence immediately above the ch. there is a 17th centy. house, from which a fine view of the river and its valley may be obtained.

26 m. l. *Danesfield* (C. R. S. Scott Murray, Esq.), so called from an ancient horseshoe entrenchment of great extent near the house, supposed to be of Danish origin. The beautiful woods which clothe the steep escarpment of the hills towards the river abound in holly, yew, and box, which is here considered to be indigenous, and, like those of Clief-den, but on a smaller scale, they are intersected by winding walks, with lovely views over the valley. The house is large and handsome. Attached to it is a Roman Catholic chapel commenced by *Pugin*, and completed by his son, which contains

a rich altarpiece representing scenes in the history of St. Carlo Borromeo, a beautiful crucifix by *Seitz*, and some curious old pictures of the history of the Virgin. The room leading to the chapel contains a fine picture of Pope Pius IX., by *Seitz*. In the house is preserved a withered hand, which is, with some reason, supposed to be that presented by Henry I. to Reading Abbey, and reverenced there as the hand of St. James the Apostle. It answers exactly to "the incorrupt hand" described by Hoveden, and was found among the ruins of the abbey, where it is supposed to have been secreted at the dissolution.

Below Danesfield, just above New Lock, the river is bounded on the l. by high chalk-cliffs, which abound in fossils.

l. *Harleyford* (Sir Wm. R. Clayton, Bt.), designed by Sir Robert Taylor, is beautifully situated, and contains some fine pictures. The road between Danesfield and Harleyford winds through beautiful pine and beech woods of forest-like character, called *Bassla*.

No one who sees this part of the river can avoid being struck by the beautiful swans which are here so common. "The Thames swans are property; the principal owners being the Dyers' and Vintners' Companies. The nests of the swans are built on the aits, or in the osier-beds beside the river. They are compact structures formed of twigs and osiers, or reeds, and are so built as to be out of the reach of the water, every pair of swans having its 'walk' or proper district within which others do not build.

"A great deal of pains is taken to preserve the swans, and a waterman, or some person living near the swans'-walk, generally has charge of each pair, and receives a small sum for every cygnet that is reared. It is his duty to see that the nests are not disturbed, and to prevent as much as possible the eggs from being stolen; he also, within the influence of the tide at least, builds the foundation of the nest. The mark of the Vintners' Company is *two nicks*, from which came the well-known sign of the Swan with two nicks, or, as corrupted *necks*."—*Thorne*.

The City authorities, whilst they remained sole conservators of the Thames, used to go up the river every year in August, in gaily-decorated barges, to mark and count their swans—an expedition called "*Swan-upping*," from the duty of the official visitors to take *up* the swans and mark them. The Upping-days began on the Monday after St Peter's day. The "Uppers" had a difficult task, as, the swans being very strong, scuffling with them in the tangles of the river is exceedingly dangerous, and recourse was had to strong crooks called "Swan-hooks." Though there is now no ceremonial, the swans are still looked after by fishermen, who are paid by public subscription, especially on the occasion of the Henley regatta.

27 m. rt. *Hurley* (Berks.) a picturesque village with old timber houses. In a park-like meadow, with cedars, surrounded by the original walls, at the end of a secluded lane, are the remains of the famous *Lady Place*, once the residence of Richard Lord Lovelace, so celebrated in the Revolution of 1688. "This mansion, built by his ancestors out of the spoils of Spanish galleons from the Indies, rose on the ruins of a house of our Lady in this beautiful valley, through which the Thames, not yet defiled by the precincts of a great capital, rolls under woods of beech, and round the gentle hills of Berks. Beneath the stately saloon, adorned by Italian pencils, was a subterranean vault, in which the bones of ancient monks had sometimes been found. In this dark chamber some

zealous and daring opponents of the government held many midnight conferences during that anxious time when England was impatiently expecting the Protestant wind."— *Macaulay*, vol. ii. It is said that these vaults were made subservient to the Meal Tub Plot by Dangerfield, and the spot where the meal tub stood, in which the papers implicating several Roman Catholics were found, is still pointed out. The house itself, which was "a perplexing labyrinth of panelled rooms," some of the paintings on which were attributed to Salvator Rosa, was entirely destroyed in 1837, and portions of the vaults are now all that remain. The last inhabitant of Lady Place was the brother of Admiral Kempenfelt, and here he and the Admiral planted two thorn-trees which he took a great pride in. One day on coming home he found that the tree planted by the Admiral had withered away, and said, "I feel sure that this is an omen that my brother is dead"; that evening came the news of the loss of the 'Royal George.'

The *Church*, f. 1086, by Geoffrey de Mandeville, a soldier in the battle of Hastings, was consecrated by St. Osmund, Bp. of Salisbury, and annexed to Westminster Abbey. It is a long narrow ch. retaining its Norm. W. end. It contains a monument by *Flaxman*—2 kneeling boys with reversed torches. In the vestry is a monument—two stone figures, with scutcheons above them, of the Lovelaces, under one of which is the date 1601. Some fragments of the priory are to be traced in the different farm-buildings, and on the N. side of the ch. portions of the quadrangle of the monastery and of the refectory may be seen. Several engraved slabs are let into one of the walls of the quadrangle, on one of which we read, "The priory of St. Mary Hurley, founded in the reign of William the Conqueror by Geoffrey de Mandeville and his wife

Lecelina in 1086." Hurley is well known to geologists as furnishing fossils of the Tertiary formation, including fine specimens of the elephant, rhinoceros, tiger, &c.

Hurley Lock. Fall 3 ft. 4 in.

On the Backwater on the Bucks side is Harleyford House (Sir W. Clayton).

Temple Lock. Fall 4 ft 6 in. On rt. bank Temple House (Col. Owen Williams), then Bisham Grange.

rt. 28 m., shrouded in fine trees, *Bisham Abbey* (G. H. Vansittart, Esq.). The scenery of this beautiful spot is well known from the pictures of De Wint and other water-colour artists, who have portrayed the broad sweep of the transparent river, the gigantic trees, the ch., and the abbey with its mossy roof, projecting oriels, and tall tower, in every effect of cloud or sunshine.

Bisham, or Bustleham, as it was then called, was, in the reign of Stephen, given by Robert de Ferrers to the Templars. Prior to their dissolution they had granted it to Hugh Despenser, and from him it came to the Montacutes. In 1338 it was turned into a priory (the chief of 5 monasteries) by William, the first Montacute Earl of Salisbury. The brass erected by King Edward to commemorate the foundation, is now in Denchworth ch. The last Prior, Barlow, was made Bishop of St. David's, and, afterwards marrying, had 5 daughters, who each married a bishop.

Among the noble persons interred in the conventual ch. were Montacute Earl of Salisbury, the patron, moved here from Cirencester; William Earl of Salisbury, his son, who fought at Poictiers; his son John Earl of Salisbury, beheaded and attainted 1400; his son Thomas Earl of Salisbury, who died at the siege of Orleans in 1428; his son-in-law Richard Neville Earl of Salisbury, beheaded at York in 1460 for his attachment to the Yorkist cause; his 2 sons, Richard Neville, the King-maker, and John Marquis of Montague, who fell in the battle of Barnet, 1471; and his great-grandson Edward Plantagenet Earl of Warwick (son of George Duke of Clarence, by Richard Neville's daughter Isabel), beheaded in 1499 on a charge of attempting to escape from the Tower. None of these monuments exist now, though they were not destroyed at the dissolution, but were standing in the hall within the last century. Tradition relates that William, Earl of Salisbury, going to the Holy Land, came to Bisham Abbey to take leave of his friends, when his daughter, a nun at the Convent, *De Fontibus*, at Little Marlow, met him. A squire, who had been in love with her before, persuaded her to elope with him, and they escaped in a boat, but were taken at Marlow. She was sent back to her convent, and he was shut up in the abbey tower, whence he tried to escape by means of a rope made from his clothes torn into shreds; the rope broke, and he, dreadfully injured, was taken into the abbey, where he afterwards became a monk.

Bisham was granted by Henry VIII. to his repudiated wife Anne of Cleves, but, owing to his dying soon after the grant was made, the privy-seal was not affixed to the deed till the reign of Mary. Of her time a letter remains in the British Museum from Anne of Cleves, entreating the Queen for the sake of their dear father and brother to allow her to exchange Bisham with Sir Philip Hoby for his house in Kent. The Hobys were friends of Cecil, and some curious letters to him from Philip Hoby remain in the Public Record Office. In one of them Hoby humorously threatens him with all sorts of ills if he continues to decline his invitation to pass his Christmas at Bisham.

Sir Philip Hoby was the last English papal legate at Rome, where he died, and his brother Sir Thomas was ambassador in France, and died in Paris, 1566. The widow of the latter had both their bodies brought back to Bisham, and erected for them a magnificent monument still to be seen in the ch., on which, being the most learned lady of the period, she wrote 3 epitaphs in Greek, Latin, and English, one of them ending in the lines,

"Give me, O God! a husband like unto
　Thomas,
Or else restore me to my husband Thomas;"

the first part of the prayer was fulfilled in her marriage to Lord John Russell in 1574. She died 1609.

The two sisters of Lady Hoby (daughters of Sir Antony Cooke) were Lady Bacon and Lady Cecil, and to them was given theycare of the Princess Elizabeth, but they, not liking the office, were allowed partially to transfer their trust to their brother-in-law, Sir Thomas Hoby, who succeeded Sir Philip at Bisham. In this way Elizabeth came to spend part of 3 yrs. here, when the bow-window in the great chamber was thrown out for her and the daïs erected 16 in. above the floor. That her residence at Bisham was not disagreeable is seen from her speech to Sir Thomas when he first went to court after she became Queen: "If I had a prisoner whom I wanted to be most carefully watched, I should intrust him to your *charge*; if I had a prisoner I wished to be most tenderly treated, I should intrust him to your *care*."

The hall and the pointed doorway are part of the foundation of Montacute; the rest of the building was built by the Hobys.

The hall, 60 ft. long, beautifully restored 1859, has a fine ancient lancet window of 3 lights at one end, with buttery hatch, and a dark oak gallery at the other. In the dining-room is a picture of Lady Hoby, with a very white face and hands, dressed in the coif, weeds, and wimple, then allowed to a knight's widow. In this dress she is still supposed to haunt a bed-room, where she appears with a self-supported basin moving before her, in which she is perpetually trying to wash her hands; but it is remarkable that the apparition is always in the negative, the black part white, the white black. The legend is that, because her child William Hoby could not write without making blots, she beat him to death. It is remarkable that about 1840 in altering the window-shutter a quantity of children's copy-books of the time of Elizabeth were discovered, pushed into the rubble between the joists of the floor, and that one of these was a copy-book which answered exactly to the story, as if the child could not write a single line without a blot.

Behind the tapestry in one of the bed-rooms (representing the history of Tobit) a secret room was discovered with a fireplace, the chimney of which is curiously connected with that of the hall for the sake of concealing the smoke.

The *Bath* of Princess Elizabeth no longer remains in the grounds at Bisham; the spring which supplied it is still left.

The *Conventual Barn* of Spanish chestnut still remains, and the original moat round the garden.

rt. the *Church*, beautifully situated on the river-bank. The whole was modernised in execrable taste about the beginning of this centy., but was restored by Terrey, 1849, in the early Dec. style. Many improvements have since been effected; the latest the erection of a N. aisle in 1878, the gift of Col. Owen Williams of

Temple House. It contains two very beautiful stained glass windows. In the S. aisle there is a fine monument to Lady Russell. The *Hoby Window* is remarkable as a good specimen of the decadence of the art; it contains a shield said to be the richest in England. There are some queer but costly marble Jacobean monuments of the Hobys, two effigies of knights in armour, their heads raised on their elbows, and a pyramid with 4 swans to Margaret Hoby, daughter of Sir H. Hunsdon and niece of Anne Boleyn.

1. 29 m. GREAT MARLOW (Bucks) (Stat.), is connected with the Wycombe and Thame line by a branch 4½ m. long (Rte. 12), a large market-town, returning one M.P. (*Inn:* Crown, in the town; on the riverside near the bridge the "Complete Angler," best.) Pop. 5518. The handsome suspension-bridge was erected in 1835 at a cost of 20,000*l.* rt. of the bridge is a curious old building, a monastic barn of Bisham Abbey, in which French prisoners were kept during the war. The query, "Who ate puppy-pie under Marlow Bridge?" the ordinary "chaff" for every bargee down the river, had its origin in the story of the landlord of the inn at Medmenham who, having notice that the bargemen intended to plunder his larder, baked a pie of young puppies, which they took and ate under Marlow Bridge, believing them to be rabbits.

Marlow belonged to Algar of Mercia, and was granted to Queen Matilda. It was early made a parliamentary borough, but voluntarily dropped the expensive honour. By the exertions of John Hampden and others, it regained the franchise in the time of Charles I. The Royal Military College was established at Marlow in 1799 under Colonel Le Marchant, who was killed at Salamanca (July 24, 1812).

The *Church of All Saints,* an ugly

modern Gothic edifice, with a spire, of stone and brick, was erected 1835 in the place of a beautiful old ch. in which the Parliamentary soldiers were quartered in 1642.

The present ch. has been re-modelled. The new chancel, completed in 1876, contains a memorial window to Bp. Milman, of Calcutta, formerly vicar of Marlow. In the churchyard is the grave of Langley, who wrote the 'History of the Hundred of Desborough and Deanery of Wycombe.' On the staircase of the gallery is the monument of Sir Myles Hobart, Kt., of Harleyford (d. July 4, 1652), a member for Marlow of the parliament of March, 1627-8, who especially distinguished himself in opposing the designs of the Court—himself locking the door of the house, during the reading of a protest against tonnage and poundage, &c. For this act he was imprisoned till 1631, but the Long Parliament voted a grant of 5000l. to his children, as a testimonial to his meritorious sufferings. The monument is of historical value as the first erected in England at the expense of the country. Its inscription is quaint. He died by the upsetting of his carriage on Holborn Hill, and a bas-relief (like that on the monument of Mr. Thynne in Westminster Abbey) represents the 4 horses running away with the coach down the hill. Another quaint monument, with a bewildering epitaph, represents Katherine Willoughby, 1597. At the entrance of the gallery is a picture of the Spotted Negro Boy, painted from life by Coventry, 1811, an extraordinary *lusus naturæ*, who died here, and is buried in the ch.-yd. Notice the lofty cross to the memory of Major Hugh O'Donel Clayton, and the monument, with long inscription, to Archibald Douglas, 7th Marquis of Queensberry (d. 1858), who, however, does not sleep beneath it.

The district ch. of Holy Trinity, by Scott, was erected in 1852 at a cost

of 3000l. in Dec. style. It contains several good stained glass windows, reredos and mural paintings. On S. wall of nave is a marble tablet to Col. A. Higginson, who laid the first stone of this ch. There is also a chapel of ease at Handy Cross about 3 m. from the town.

The pretty modern *Rom. Cath. Church* by *Pugin*, is considered one of the best of his small churches: a convent is attached to it. The Town-hall was erected by *Wyatt*. The house known as the *Old Deanery* has an ancient kitchen and 2 fine Gothic windows, with Dec. tracery.

Shelley lived at Marlow in 1817, and wrote his 'Revolt of Islam' "in his boat as it floated under the groves of Bisham, or during wanderings in the neighbouring country, which is distinguished for its beauty." The house in which he lived, and where he was visited by Byron is in West Street at the commencement of the Henley Road. Francis Edward Smedley (d. 1864), novelist, also resided here.

Seymour Court, on the hill above Marlow (T. O. Wethered, Esq., M.P.), is traditionally said to be the birthplace of Queen Jane Seymour. There is a fine view thence over the town and valley, which embraces some of the most beautiful scenery to be found along the whole course of the Thames. A pleasant walk leads over the hills to Cookham.

The manor of Marlow belonged to the Nevilles (whence they came to be buried at Bisham), and thus fell to Lady Anne (the widow of Warwick), to whom, after she had been disseised of this and others, they were restored (3 Henry VII.) for life only. The manor was part of Queen Mary's maintenance when princess. On coming to the throne she granted it to Lord Paget, the ancestor of the Anglesey family.

Marlow Lock. Fall 5 ft. 6 in.

31 m. l. *Little Marlow*, a posses-

sion of Queen Edith, granted to Odo of Bayeux. Here was a small Benedictine nunnery, founded by Geoffrey Despenser, temp. Henry II. In the E.E. and Perp. ch. is the tomb of the builder of the chancel, Nicholas de Ledwyck, 1430. Restored in 1866 by R. P. Pope.

Before reaching Cookham, the river is crossed by the Rly. to High Wycombe. (Rte. 12.)

32 m. rt. *Cookham* (Berks) Stat. *Inns:* Bel and the Dragon; by the river-side, near the bridge, the Ferry Hotel (Llewellen's). very good, much resorted to by anglers. The *Church* is the E. E., with a good tower of flint at the W. end. It contains the tomb of Norreys, cook to Eleanor, Queen of Henry III., and several good *Brasses*, 1458–1557. In the N. wall of the chancel is the canopied altar-tomb of Robert Pecke, " Master-clerk of the Spycery under K. Harry the Sixt" (d. 1510). A marble monument by *Flaxman* represents the death of Sir Isaac Pocock, 1810, while in a boat upon the Thames. A meeting of the Witanagemote was held at Cookham during the Saxon period.

The Thames is here crossed by a wooden bridge. Cookham is a Stat. on the branch from Maidenhead to Thame. (Rte. 12.)

In making the " New Cut," for the convenience of navigation at *Sashes*, below Cookham, about 1830, a number of Roman swords and javelin-heads were found mingled with skeletons.

A pleasant by-road leads hence to Maidenhead, crossing Battle Mead, so called from a skirmish in the Civil Wars.

Cookham Lock. Fall 4 ft.

32 m. l. *Hedsor* (Lady Boston), a fine undulating park, with grassy oak-crowned knolls (on one of which is a sham castle), beautiful views, and woods sloping down to the river. The house was built, 1778, by Wil-

liam 1st Lord Boston, formerly equerry to Frederick Prince of Wales, from a plan inflicted on him by George III. It was a homely brown brick building, but has lately been rebuilt. The ch., beautifully situated on the ridge of the hill within the park, contains monu- ments of the Hyndes and Parkers : and the churchyard that of Nath. Hooke, author of the ' Roman His- tory.' Very near the ch., in the park, through which the public have a right of way, are 2 magni- ficent old yew-trees. Hedsor, though beautiful, is the least interesting of the three places which meet at the cross-roads called *Nobleman's Corner.*

Behind Hedsor Park, by which it is separated from the river, and beyond the Maidenhead road, is the beautiful park of *Dropmore* (Hon. G. M. Fortescue), part of a wild common enclosed by Lord Grenville, and richly diversified with heather and rhododendrons. The house was built and the grounds laid out and planted (1801-5) by Lord Grenville, Prime Minister of George III., who lowered a hill in front of it consider- ably, so as to let in a view of Windsor Castle. It contains a fine library. Near the house is a beautiful Ita- lian garden, with straight walks and flowers. The collection of pines is perhaps unequalled in beauty and growth, being among the earliest plantations of rare foreign conifers in this country. Deodars are seen in avenues as well as single, 60 and 70 feet high. Notice P. insignis, which stands the winter well, 50 ft., also P. Douglasii 65 ft. and 85 ft., P. nobilis 43 ft., P. excelsior 60 ft., and an Araucaria imbricata 80 ft. high, the largest and finest not only in England but in Europe. Among the curiosities of Dropmore are—an oak said to have been planted by Eliza- beth as princess; an oak from the celebrated tree at Boscobel, with an inscription to proclaim that it was not preserved in honour of the escape of King Charles, but of the restoration of the monarchy; and an arbour formed by one of the stone alcoves of old London Bridge. *The pleasure grounds are 600 acres in extent, and are shown on application at the lodge every day except Sunday.*

In July, 1831, Rogers wrote the following lines at Dropmore:—

" Grenville, to thee my gratitude is due
For many an hour of studious musing here.
Search where we would, no fairer bowers than these.
Thine own creation; where, called forth by thee,
' Flowers worthy of Paradise, with rich inlay,
Broider the ground,' and every mountain pine,
Elsewhere unseen (his birthplace in the clouds,
His kindred sweeping with majestic march
From cliff to cliff along the snowy ridge
Of Caucasus, or nearer yet the moon)."

Close adjoining Dropmore grounds are those of Cliefden (see below).

34 m. rt. *Formosa* (Mr. Sloane Stanley) a very charming seat of the Young family. The island has an area of 50 acres, and is the largest island on the upper Thames, opposite which is

34 m. l. *Cliefden* (Duke of Westminster), to which " the river here owes its chief loveliness; and whether we view the valley of the Thames from it, or float leisurely along the stream and regard it as the principal object, we shall alike find enough to delight the eye and kindle the imagination. The towing - path lies along the Berkshire side of the river, and Cliefden, which is on the opposite side, is a magnificent object from it. The rambler who approaches by land should by all means hire a boat at Maidenhead Bridge, and row gently along, if he would see this part in all its varied beauty. Cliefden runs along the summit of a lofty slope which overhangs the river. The steep bank is clothed with luxuriant

foliage, forming a hanging wood of great beauty, with open glades intervening so as to increase the gracefulness of the foliage by the contrast; and a few islands deck this part of the river, and occasionally little tongues of land run out into it, or a tree overhangs it, helping to give vigour to the foreground of the rich land scape."

These exquisite woods abound in magnificent yews, pines and cypresses, which hang from the chalk cliffs, their twisted roots exposed to the air, and cling and cluster round the winding walks and steep narrow staircases which lead in every direction to the heights above. The wild clematis hangs in luxuriant wreaths from the tops of the highest trees, and in their shade the Atropa Belladonna and other flowering plants grow luxuriantly. In the cliff are many small caves, once inhabited by robbers. Near the waterside a spring rises in a rocky basin and falls into the river, near which the Duke of Buckingham built a picturesque cottage for the benefit of visitors. The views from the summit are beautiful, " unequalled along the Thames, except by that from the north terrace of Windsor."

Evelyn speaks of Cliefden as " the stupendous natural rock, wood, and prospect, of the Duke of Buckingham." This was George Villiers, the favourite of Charles II., who commenced the original house. When he had killed the Earl of Shrewsbury in a duel, the Countess holding his horse disguised as a page, he fled with her to—

" Cliefden's proud alcove,
The Bower of wanton Shrewsbury and of love."

Horace Walpole says of him, " When this extraordinary man, with the figure and genius of Alcibiades, could equally charm the Presbyterian Fairfax and the dissolute

Charles; when he alike ridiculed that witty king and his solemn chancellor; when he plotted the ruin of his country with a cabal of bad ministers, or, equally unprincipled, supported its cause with bad patriots, one laments that such a man should have been devoid of every virtue." The portrait of the Duke has been drawn by four masterly hands; Burnet has hewn it with a rough chisel: Count Hamilton touched it with a delicacy that finishes while it seems to sketch; Dryden caught the living likeness; Pope completed the historical resemblance. His house, designed by *Archer* (Walpole's 'Groomporter of Architecture'), was much improved and adorned by the Earl of Orkney. It was of red brick, with stone dressings, and had sweeping colonnades and square wings, with a noble terrace 433 ft. long.

Frederick Prince of Wales, father of George III., resided here for a short time, during which the first performance of Thomson's masque of 'Alfred' took place in his presence; and the famous national air of 'Rule Britannia,' composed by Dr. Arne, was played here for the first time on August 1st, 1740.

This house was burnt, May 20, 1795, through the carelessness of a maid reading a novel and letting her candle catch the curtains, and then falling down in a fit till the fire had gained head. In 1830 it was rebuilt by Sir G. Warrender of Lochend, after which it was purchased by the Duke of Sutherland, and again rebuilt by him, after a second conflagration, from a design by *Barry.*

The present magnificent house rises from a wide lawn on the heights, raised on a broad terrace. Though very simple, it is exceedingly imposing. The centre is a revival of Inigo Jones's design for old Somerset House. A huge inscription commemorates its second resurrection from the flames, in 1849.

Visitors may gain admittance to the grounds and gardens of Cliefden, when the family are away, on application to the head gardener; the house is not shown.

In the meadow opposite Cliefden is *White Place* (E. M. Leycester, Esq.) It formerly belonged to Villiers Duke of Buckingham; and the fine elm avenue is believed to be haunted by a certain "White Lady without a head," one of his victims.

36 m. l. *Taplow Court* (Mrs. Grenfell), a picturesque modern turreted house, in beautiful grounds, overhanging the river. This was the seat of the Earl of Orkney, distinguished in the wars of the Duke of Marlborough. The saloon was built in imitation of the Norm. cathedral of Kirkwall!

36 m. *Boulter's Lock.* Fall 6 ft. The weir diverts water to turn the Corn Mills. Between this and Maidenhead Bridge on the island to the l. the handsome house of Sir Roger Palmer: on rt. Raymead and Thames Hotels, and close to the bridge the Guard's Club House, Orkney Cottage, and Skindles Orkney Arms Hotel.

37 m. MAIDENHEAD. Stat. on Gt. Western Ry. (Rte. 4).

SECTION II.

BUCKINGHAMSHIRE.

INTRODUCTION.

BUCKINGHAMSHIRE is said by Camden to derive its name from the Saxon "buchen," beech-trees, which, more than any other, clothe the sides of its chalk hills; and this derivation is sometimes accepted, but it is more probably derived from the *Bocingas*, an ancient Anglo-Saxon family whose marc or settlement was at Buckingham, from which the county was named upon the division of Mercia in 806. The extreme length of the county is 53 m., and its extreme breadth 27 m. It is bounded on the N. and N.W. by Northamptonshire; on the W. by Oxfordshire; on the S. by Berkshire; and on the E. by Bedfordshire, Herts, and Middlesex. Its area is 738 sq. m., and at the census of 1871 it had 175,879 inhabitants, and in 1881, 176,277. It, including 4 boroughs, returns 8 M.P.s.

The principal rivers are :—1. The Thames, which divides Bucks from Berks during a course of 28 m., from Henley to Eton and Datchet; 2. the Colne, which divides Bucks from Middlesex; 3. the Ouse, which first touches the county at Turweston, near Brackley, and, dividing it for some miles from Northamptonshire, afterwards flows, first E. and then N.E., past Buckingham and Newport Pagnell to Olney, a few miles below which it quits the county, after a sinuous course of 43 m.; 4. the Thame, which rises near Stewkley, and flows S.W., a course of 28 m., to Thame. Beside these, are the Ousel—remarkable for its fine pike, perch, and bream—which unites several small streams on the N. of the Chilterns, and flows N. 25 m. to join the Ouse at Newport Pagnell; the Towe, which forms a boundary between Bucks and Northampton from Grafton Regis to its junction with the Ouse near Stony Stratford;

the Mease, or Misbourn, which rises at Missenden, and, passing through the Chalfonts to Denham, falls into the Colne; and the Wye, which rises at West Wycombe and joins the Thames near Hedsor. The latter is noted for its fine trout, and the large number of flour and paper mills to which it supplies motive power. The Chess, which rises at Chesham, and flows into the Colne, and the Ray, an affluent of the Cherwell, have their upper courses in this county.

Bucks is intersected by the Chiltern Hills, which enter the county from Oxfordshire, and, crossing it to the N.E., run into Bedfordshire near Dunstable. Their highest point, Combe Hill, near Wendover, is 905 ft., and the Ivinghoe hills have nearly as great elevation. The name is said by Camden to be derived from the Saxon word "cylt," or "chilt," signifying chalk. They were once all so covered with beech-woods as to be almost impassable, till Leofstan, Abbot of St. Alban's, cut some of them down because of the shelter they afforded to thieves—whence the proverb, "Here if you beat a bush, it's odds you'd start a thief." It was to put down the banditti who abounded in these hills, and to protect the inhabitants, that the "Steward of the Chiltern Hundreds" was first appointed. The duties have long since ceased, but the nominal office is retained in the gift of the Chancellor of the Exchequer, and is given to members of the House of Commons who wish to resign their seats, as they are not permitted to do so except by the acceptance of an office, which, being held as one of honour and profit under the Crown, vacates the seat. The W. part of the Chilterns was occupied by the forest of Bernwood, which was disforested by James I. Muswell Hill, near Brill, is 744 ft., and Bow Brickhill, near Fenny Stratford, 683 ft.

The *Grand Junction Canal* traverses the county from N. to S., keeping on the E. border, but having branches to Aylesbury, Buckingham, and Wendover. The *London and N.-W. Railway* pursues a nearly parallel course, and has branches from Cheddington to Aylesbury, from Bletchley to Winslow and Buckingham, and from Wolverton to Newport Pagnell. The *Great Western Railway* main line traverses the county from near West Drayton to Maidenhead, and thence a new line runs to Thame and Oxford, with branches from Prince's Risborough to Aylesbury and Watlington. From Aylesbury a line runs to join the Oxford and Cambridge line at Verney Junction. The *South-Western Railway* runs by Datchet to Windsor.

Geology.—Five different geological formations traverse the county from N.E. to S.W. 1. The S.E., between the Thames and Colne, is occupied by plastic clay. 2. Succeeding to this is the chalk, forming the range of the Chiltern Hills. 3. The Tetsworth (or Kimmeridge) clay, forming the fertile soil of the Vale of Aylesbury. 4. The limestone, known as Aylesbury stone. 5. The oolitic formations, which occupy the N. of the county.

Bucks is chiefly occupied by pasture-lands. It contains 150,000 acres of meadows and pastures, and is said to feed 20,000 milch-cows; the

'airy produce is valued at 500,000*l.* yearly; Aylesbury ducks fetch
high price in the market. Fuller mentions that the "biggest-bodied
ep in England" were bred in his time in the Vale of Aylesbury,
ere a single field at Quarrendon let for 800*l.* (at least 8000*l.* of our
oney). This is still the most fertile part of the county. "Bucking-
mshire bread and beef" has long been a proverb.
. The chief manufactures of Bucks are now paper, silk, coarse pottery,
1 particularly wooden chairs, which are produced in large numbers;
eech being employed for the low-priced articles, and walnut and cherry
or the better kinds; many women and children earn a living by trim-
ming the small shoots of the trees for skewers for the London butchers.
These industries, with agricultural-implement making, have almost
entirely taken the place of the lace manufacture, which formerly was
all-important, but has now been removed to Nottingham and other
towns where machinery is employed.

History.—The Romans included Bucks in their province of Flavia
Cæsariensis, and under the Saxons it formed at first part of Wessex,
but was subsequently included in Mercia. Legendary history makes
the range of the Chilterns the scene of many important events,
as the battle of Great Kimble, in which the two sons of Cymbeline
were killed; and the battle of Chearsley, in which Cerdic and
Cynric fought against the Britons; there is better warrant for a battle
of Bledlow ("the bloody hill"), in the time of Edward the Elder,
when the great Whiteleaf Cross is supposed to have been cut upon
the side of the chalk hill to commemorate the Saxon victory over
the Danes. The Mercian kings had a palace at Winslow, and
Offa II. is especially mentioned as holding his court there. Edward
the Elder built a fortress at Buckingham, and Edward the Confessor
had a palace at Brill, where Henry I. and Henry II. afterwards
held courts, and which, still later, belonged to Richard Earl of Cornwall. Edward the Black Prince is said to have given a name to
Prince's Risborough, and to have built a palace there. The shrine of
Sir John Shorne at North Marston was long celebrated as an object
of pilgrimage. At Fenny Stratford Richard Duke of Gloucester took
his nephew Edward V. out of the hands of the Woodvilles. The
Marian persecution was severely felt among the Buckinghamshire towns,
and Amersham witnessed the death of several Protestants. From the
palace of Edmund Earl of Cornwall, at Ashridge, the Princess Elizabeth
was carried to the Tower. She established the Creslow Pastures as the
royal feeding-grounds, from which time to that of Charles II. the Christ
Meadow and the Heaven Meadow, which had belonged to the Knights
of St. John of Jerusalem, fatted cattle for the royal table. The
old manor-house at Chequers was the prison of Lady Mary Grey.
At Drayton Beauchamp Hooker lived as rector, "possessing his soul
in patience and peace." Gayhurst was remarkable as the home of
Sir Everard Digby, one of the Gunpowder Plotters, and afterwards
of his more illustrious son Sir Kenelm. At Horton, Milton passed five of

his early years, and wrote the 'Allegro' and 'Penseroso,' 'Comus,' 'Lycidas,' and 'The Arcades ;' and to Chalfont St. Giles he retired during the plague of London, and there he completed his 'Paradise Lost' and commenced his 'Paradise Regained.' At Great Hampden lived John Hampden; and there he is buried. Boarstall Tower was taken and retaken in the civil wars; and Aylesbury, Newport Pagnell, and other Buckinghamshire towns, had to stand sieges : they were all in the Parliamentary interest. Dinton was the home and hiding-place of Simon Mayne the regicide ; and there, in a cave, dwelt John Bigg, the mysterious Dinton Hermit, who was believed to have been the executioner of the king. Penn is buried in the humble Quakers' burial-ground at Jordans. Edmund Waller lived at Hall Barns, near Beaconsfield, where he is buried in the churchyard; a spot that witnessed John Hampden's Sunday muster of the trainbands. Lady Rachel Russell rests in the church of Chenies, amid the marble monuments of a long line of her husband's house. Edmund Burke lived at Gregories, and is buried in Beaconsfield church. Stoke Poges was the home of Gray ; and its churchyard, the presumed scene of his most beautiful poem, contains his grave. Cowper lived and wrote at Olney, which he has immortalized in his poems. Medmenham was rendered notorious by the vices of the last century ; Hartwell illustrious as the home of the exiled royal family of France ; and Stowe, once the resort of authors, poets, and statesmen, is now little more than a witness to the fall of a great family.

Antiquities.—Several ancient British and Roman roads crossed the county; of these, the Watling Street coincides with the road between Brickhill and Stony Stratford; the Ikenield Street ran along the edge of the Chiltern range; and the Akeman Street, the turnpike road from Aylesbury to Bicester, is supposed to be on the site of the road from Alchester to Londinium. There are several tumuli in the county; some have not been opened, but of those which have been searched, some have been rich in relics. An ancient camp, called Kimble Castle (Cunobeline's), remains near Ellesborough, and the foss and bank of a British camp are still in good preservation at Cholesbury; but the most remarkable early memorial is the Whiteleaf Cross, cut in the hill above Prince's Risborough, of which the perpendicular part is 100 ft. high, the transverse 70 long, supported on a triangle. There is a similar, but smaller, cross at Bledlow. Nothing beyond earthworks exist of the once strong *Castles* of Hanslope, Lavendon, Prince's Risborough, Weston Turville, and Whitchurch. The site of the castle of Buckingham is now occupied by the church.

The *Monastic Remains* are very small. Nutley, turned into a farmhouse, is still exceedingly picturesque. The remnant of Medmenham, in a lovely situation close to the Thames, has been much added to in modern times. Part of the domestic buildings of Burnham Abbey remain, now used as a barn. Of Bradwell and Missenden only the most insignificant fragments are left.

Several ancient *Mansions* still exist: Liscombe House, with its chapel of the 14th centy.; Dinton Hall, built by Archbishop Warham; the Elizabethan manor-house at Gayhurst; Chequers, rich in old pictures and historic relics; the picturesque gatehouse at Boarstall; and Creslow, with its desecrated chapel.

Of the Buckinghamshire *Churches*, the most remarkable is *Stewkley*, a rich Norm. structure; Upton and Wing also are Norm., and there are Norm. doorways at Dinton and Water Stratford; Stantonbury has a Norm. chancel arch. To the E. E. period belong Chetwode, Aylesbury, Lillingstone Dayrell; and Newport Pagnell has an E. E. arcade, though mainly Perp. Hanslope is E. E., Dec. and Perp. Chesham, Clifton Reynes, Emberton, Great Horwood, and Olney are all excellent specimens of Dec. Maidsmorton, Hillesdon, and Eton College Chapel are Perp., and all deserve close examination.

"Buckinghamshire is one of the very few counties in England, which contains no great representative church, and not one monastic church, nor does it contain any very important parochial churches. . . . I think I am quite justified in saying that it is by no means a rich county for the ecclesiologist." There are about sixty desecrated churches in this county.

There is a very large number of ancient circular *Fonts* in Bucks, among the finest of which may be mentioned those at Aylesbury, Maidsmorton, Hughenden, and Leckhamstead. There are Dec. fonts at Astwood, Chilton, Drayton Parslow, and North Marston; and Perp. at Ditton and Wing. In North Crawley Church is a fine Dec. *Roodloft*. Of ancient *Tombs*, those at Ashendon, Clifton Reynes, and Hughenden have cross-legged effigies; those of the Montforts and Wellesburnes at the latter place are especially interesting. At Ivinghoe is the curious effigy known as Grandfather Greybeard, believed to be Peter de Chaceport, 1254; at Haversham is the fine tomb of Lady Clinton, 1422; at Thornton that of the founder, John Barton, 1443. Chenies is remarkable for containing a complete series of the tombs of the house of Russell, while the numerous monuments of the Dormers scattered over the county present another curious family portrait-gallery. The county is rich in *Brasses*; of which the most notable are at Drayton-Beauchamp, 2 of the Cheyne family, 1368, 1375; at Denham that of Agnes Jordan, last abbess of Syon, c. 1540; at Thornton, Robert Ingleton and his 3 wives, 1472; at Clifton Reynes, Sir John Reynes, 1428; at Stoke Poges, Sir William Molyns, 1425.

The most extensive *Views* in the county are obtained from the hills E. of Prince's Risborough; from Ellesborough churchyard; from Penn Beacon, near Amersham; and from Brill, in Bernwood Forest. The Glen of the Lyde at Bledlow is a remarkable natural chasm, of very picturesque character originally, but not improved by its present occupation as a watercress-bed.

The *Country Seats* along the Buckinghamshire bank of the Thames
[*Berks, &c.*]   I

are celebrated for their beauty; especially Cliefden, for its hanging-woods and extensive views, and Hedsor, for its wild undulating park. Equally beautiful is the park of Ashridge, on the high eastern boundary of the county overhanging Herts. Other country-houses of interest are Chequers and Hampden, nestling among the beechwoods of the Chilterns; Hartwell, Winchendon, Lodge Hill, Waddesden, Mentmore, both creations of the Rothschilds, and Doddershall Hall, near Aylesbury; and the new mansion of Bulstrode near Beaconsfield. The *Gardens* of Dropmore are justly celebrated for their *Pinetum*, one of the finest in England; those at Stowe are remarkable for their temples and statues. There are some good *Pictures* at Langley Park and Ashridge; Liscombe House contains interesting portraits; Chequers a matchless collection of the family and friends of Oliver Cromwell; and Claydon many family portraits of historic interest.

The *Artist* will find the best subjects for his pencil along the banks of the Thames, or among the wooded valleys of the Chilterns. The old house at Chenies, Boarstall Tower, Creslow Manor-house, and the ruins of Nutley Abbey, are picturesque.

The only rare plant indigenous in Bucks is *Dentaria bulbifera*, or " Bulb-bearing Coralwort."

SKELETON TOUR.

Days.
1. Rly. to Windsor : by Eton, Upton, Slough, Stoke Poges, and Burnham to Maidenhead. (Rte. 11.)

2. By road to Cliefden, Dropmore, and Hedsor to Great Marlow. Excursion to Medmenham and Hambleden Ch. (Rte. 10.)

3. Rly. to High and West Wycombe. Road to Beaconsfield. (Rte. 13.)

4. Road to Amersham, Chenies, and Chesham. (Rte. 14.)

5. Road by Missenden and Hampden to Wendover and Aylesbury. (Rte. 14.)

6. Rly. to and from Buckingham. (Rte. 15.)

7. Excursion from Aylesbury to (1) Hartwell, Dinton, Winchendon, Nutley Abbey, Brill, and Boarstall; or (2) to Creslow Pastures, North Marston, and Doddershall House. (Rte. 16.)

8. Road to Prince's Risborough and Bledlow. (Rte. 12.)

9. Rail from Prince's Risborough to Leighton Buzzard Stat. Excursion to Stewkley and Liscombe. Rail to Wolverton. (Rte. 18.)

10. Rail and road to and from Newport Pagnell and Olney. See Gayhurst, Weston Underwood, and Clifton Reynes. (Rte. 18A.)

ROUTES.

. The names of places are printed in *italics* only in those routes where the *places* are described.

ROUTE 11.

LONDON TO TAPLOW AND MAIDENHEAD, BY SLOUGH [ETON].

Great Western Rly. 22¼ m.

For the country from London to West Drayton, see *Handbook for Middlesex.* 1 m. beyond, at 14 m. from Paddington, we cross the river Colne, and enter Bucks.

14¼ m. ¼ m. N. is the pleasant village of *Iver.* The ch. (Norm. and Perp.) has been restored by *Scott.* It contains the monuments of Sir George and Sir Edward Salter, carvers to Charles I., with the effigy of Lady Mary, wife to the latter, rising from her coffin in her shroud. On Iver Heath is a modern ch. of no particular merit.

Ritchings Park (Mrs. Meeking), S. of the line, was the residence of Lord Bathurst, who here collected all the clever men of his time. From him it passed, in 1739, to the Earl of Hertford, to whom Pope dedicated his 'Epistle on the Use and Abuse of Riches.' Lady Hertford, the Eusebia of Dr. Watts, and the Cleora of Mrs. Rowe, was in the habit of assembling the poets of the day at her house. Shenstone flattered her in his poem on 'Rural Elegance,' and Thomson dedicated to her his poem of 'Spring,' but afterwards offended her by preferring a carouse with Lord Hertford to listening to her poems. She gives an exaggerated description of the place in a letter to Lady Pomfret : "'We have just taken a house by Colnbrook. It belongs to my Lord Bathurst, and is what Mr. Pope calls in his letters ' extravagante bergerie.' The environs perfectly answer that title, and come nearer to my idea of a scene in

I 2

Arcadia than any place I ever saw. The house is old, but convenient; and when you are got within the little paddock it stands in, you would believe yourself 100 miles from London. This paddock is a mile and a half round, which is laid out in the manner of a French park, interspersed with woods and lawns. There is a canal in it about 1200 yds. long and proportionably broad, which has a stream constantly running through it, and is deep enough to carry a pleasure-boat. It is well stocked with carp and tench, and at its upper end is a greenhouse containing a good collection of orange, myrtle, geranium, and oleander trees. "In one of the woods there is a cave, which, though little more than a rude heap of stones, has charms for me. A spring gushes out at the back of it, which, falling into a basin, whose brim it overflows, passes along a channel in the pavement, where it loses itself. The entrance to this recess is overhung with periwinkle, and its top shaded with beeches, large elms, and birch. "On the spot where the greenhouse stands there was formerly a chapel dedicated to St. Leonard, who was certainly esteemed a tutelar saint of Windsor Forest and its purlieus. We have no relics of the saint but an old covered bench, with many remains of the wit of Lord Bathurst's visitors, who inscribed verses upon it. Here is the writing of Addison, Pope, Prior, Congreve, Gay, and, what he esteemed no less, of several fine ladies. [These have now disappeared, but one avenue is known as Pope's Walk.] "There is one walk which I am extremely partial to, and which is rightly called the Abbey Walk, since it is composed of prodigiously high beech-trees that form an arch through the whole length, exactly resembling a cloister."

2 m. S. of Ritchings is *Colnbrook,*

supposed to be the Ad Pontes of Antoninus. It is separated from Middlesex by the Colne, whence its name, though, according to the ballad 'Thomas of Reading,' it derives its name from Thomas Cole the Reading clothier, who was murdered by the landlord at the inn here, on his way to London. Both town and river probably derive their name from the Roman *Colonia* established there. It is a decayed market town (Pop. 1153), and has a modern ch., completely restored in 1877, which has replaced a structure of the time of Edward III. The only interest of the place is the connection of Milton with its vicinity.

"Part of the town of Colnbrook is in the parish of *Horton,* which extends in the opposite direction to the vicinity of Windsor. The village of Horton is 1 m. distant, between it and the Wraysbury Stat., on the London and South-Western Rly. It has no appearance of a continuous street; but a great tree in the centre of the space where 3 roads meet suggests that there may be more habitations about the spot than are at first visible; and, on looking down one of the roads, the suggestion is confirmed by the sight of a church-tower, a few paces to the left, all but hidden by the intervening foliage. On making towards this church one finds it to be a small but very ancient edifice, probably of the 13th or 14th centy., standing back from the road in a cemetery, in the front of which, and close to the road, are two extremely old yew-trees. The tower, which is square, is picturesquely covered with ivy; the walls are strong, and chequered with flints and brickwork; and the entrance from the cemetery is by a low porch. The stranger would see no old inscriptions or tombstones in the cemetery—nothing old in it but the yew-trees; but within the ch. he would find both ·stone and woodwork of sufficient antiquity. There is an old Norm. arch within the main porch; there is a nave with 2 aisles and a chancel; between the nave and the aisles are short circular columns supporting arches; the pulpit and the pews look as if they had served already for a centy. or two of rural English Sundays. In one of these pews, or on the spot occupied by one of them, Milton had worshipped regularly with others of his family, while resident in the adjoining village, from the 24th to the 30th yr. of his age. Milton's mother, whose maiden name was Bradshaw, is buried here, and a plain blue stone on the chancel floor has the record: 'Heare lyeth the body of Sara Milton, the wife of John Milton, who died the 3rd of April, 1637.'

"With the exception of the ch., the chancel of which has been restored, Horton, as it was known to Milton, is to be found in the roads, the paths, and the general aspect of the fields and vegetation, rather than in the actual houses now remaining. Around the village is a rich, teeming, verdurous flat, charming by its appearance of plenty, and by the goodly show of food along the fields and pastures, and in the nooks where the houses nestle. There are elms, alders, poplars, and cedars; there is no lack of shrubbery and hedging · and in spring the orchards are all abloom with pink and white for miles round. What strikes one most in walking about the neighbourhood is the canal-like abundance and distribution of water. There are rivulets brimming through the meadows among rushes and water-plants; and by the very sides of the ways, in lieu of ditches, there are slow runnels, in which one can see the minnows swimming. On the whole, without taking into account the vicinity of other scenes of beauty and interest,—including nothing less than royal Windsor itself, the towers and battlements of which govern the whole landscape—Horton was, and might still be, a most pleasant place of rural retirement, either after London or Cambridge.

"There was a tradition that Milton's house was one which stood on the site of a new mansion, called Berkin Manor-house, near the ch., but on the opposite side of the road, with streams of water running through and along the grounds; and in the garden of this house there was shown, till the other day, the remnant of an apple-tree, under which, according to the innocent style of local legend about such things, Milton 'used to compose his poetry.' 90 yrs. ago a portion of Milton's house was still standing, and was known as the '*Poet's House.*' Its pigeon-house existed till within the last 50 yrs." —*Masson's Life of Milton.*

Hence he wrote to his friend Diodati, "You ask me of what I am thinking: as God shall help me, of immortality! But how shall I attain it? My wings are fledging, and I meditate a flight."

Here he wrote 'Comus' (1634); 'Lycidas' (1637); and the 'Arcades,' which made part of a dramatic entertainment at Harefield, the seat of the Countess of Derby (*Handbook for Middlesex*); 'the Sonnet to the Nightingale;' and probably the 'Allegro' and 'Penseroso.'

"The nightingale, which abounds at Horton to a remarkable degree, occurs both in 'Comus' and the 'Allegro;' and in the morning scene in the 'Allegro' are some details which might be claimed by Horton, as not so common in other localities; 'the towers and battlements,

　　　Bosom'd high in tufted trees,'

are almost evidently Windsor Castle; and a characteristic morning sound at Horton to this day, we are told, is that of 'the hounds and horn' from Windsor Park when the royal huntsmen are out."—*Ibid.*

16 m. *Langley Marsh* (Stat.), properly *Langley St. Mary's.* The ch., S. of the line, is mainly Dec. and Perp., with a low square tower and small spire. The arms of Sir John Kidderminster, who built the tower 1649, are emblazoned on the manor-pew; he also founded a Divinity Library, which, possibly hidden during the civil wars, was discovered accidentally behind the wainscoting about the year 1830. The *Alms-houses* built by him are picturesque. From this part of the line is a fine view of Windsor Castle.

1 m. N. is *Langley Park* (Sir R. B. Harvey, Bart.), once a royal manor, but granted by Charles I. to Sir J. Kidderminster. In the 18th centy. it became the property of the 2nd Duke of Marlborough, who built the present house, a noble mansion which contains a fine collection of pictures, including St. Michael and Satan, *Luca Giordano;* Holy Family, *Carlo Maratti;* Holy Family with 4 saints, a very beautiful specimen of *Sebastian del Piombo;* a woman putting on her stocking, *Mieris;* views of Venice, *Canaletti;* landscape, *Wilson;* a lovely head of a child, and the celebrated full-length portrait of Mrs. Siddons as the Tragic Muse, *Sir Joshua Reynolds.* The property was sold to Sir R. B. Harvey, grandfather of the present proprietor, in 1788. The house stands in a finely timbered park of oaks and cedars, and at a short distance N. on a hill is the *Black Park,* consisting of fir-plantations, surrounding a sombre-looking lake, approached by rude winding paths.

18 m. *Slough Junction Stat.,* one for the main line, and one for the West London traffic. Hence there is a branch line 2½ m. into Windsor, which runs till within 1¼ m.

of the terminus on an embankment whence a viaduct nearly 6000 ft. long carries it into the middle of the town. The Thames is crossed by an arch of 187 ft. span, so as to allow vessels to pass in sail. Carriages and post-horses are always ready at Slough Stat.; but there is no omnibus to Eton or Windsor. *Slough,* which before the opening of the rly. consisted only of a few inns and other accommodation for the traffic on the Bath road, better known as *Salt Hill,* is now a well-built town of some 5080 inhab. (*Inns:* Royal Hotel, adjoining stat.; this consists merely of the offices of a vast establishment, called the *Queen's Hotel,* now converted into an orphan asylum.) The church of St. Mary (now the Par. Ch.) was built in 1837 at a cost of 3200*l.*; it is a very plain structure of brick, but a handsome Gothic chancel has recently been added, at Chalvey there is a district church erected in 1860-1 at a cost of 2000*l.*

Near *Salt Hill,* on the Bath road, is the tumulus, celebrated as the scene of the *Eton Montem* (*post*).

½ m. S. is the mother *Church of Upton-cum-Chalvey,* a small Norm., edifice, long abandoned to ruin. but well restored by *Ferrey;* it has a fine Norm. N. door, with good carvings, some plain Norm. and some E. E. windows; the E. and W. windows are Perp. insertions. The parish has increased so much that it was found necessary to enlarge the church, and considerable additions were made to it in 1876-7, by which 380 new seats were provided. There are several *Brasses* for members of the Bulstrode family (1472-1599), one being remarkable as having an inscription in Hebrew. Here Sir W. Herschel is buried. The " ivy-mantled tower " has been thought to be that alluded to in Gray's ' Elegy.' On the l. of the road to Windsor is the red-brick house where Sir William Herschel lived, and in the garden of which his great telescope was set up; here most of his discoveries were made, including that of the planet Uranus. It bears the name of Herschel House.

1½ m. from Slough we reach ETON (*Inn:* the Christopher), of which the beautiful chapel is conspicuous from far and near rising above its elm-trees, and calling to mind Gray's verses:

" Ye distant spires, ye antique towers,
    That crown the wat'ry glade,
  Where grateful Science still adores
    Her Henry's holy shade;
And ye, that from the stately brow
Of Windsor heights, th' expanse below,
  Of grove, of lawn, of mead survey;
Whose turf, whose shade, whose flowers
    among,
Wanders the hoary Thames along
  His silver winding way."

Eton College, ever since its foundation, has held the first position among the public schools of England, and "an Eton man" is still always an honourable appellation; while those who visit this beautiful spot can understand the affection with which the place itself inspires those who are educated there.

One mile from Slough we come to the *Playing Fields,* broad green meadows, extending along the banks of the river and shaded by noble elm-trees. A small stream known as Chalvey Brook intersects them, whose water, considered beneficial to the eyes, has its source in Queen Anne's well, situated in a pretty grove of trees near the village of Chalvey, whence Queen Anne and afterwards Queen Charlotte had the water carried up to Windsor Castle in buckets. The view of the Castle from the meadows is magnificent. Opposite the Playing Fields is a field called the Timbralls or Timber Halls, devoted to cricket and football. On the W. side there is a double row of Fives Courts. A little further on, on the rt., are the new schools, there is a

large block of schoolrooms, surrounding two quadrangles. In the outer quadrangle a Russian gun, taken at Sebastopol. Next, on the left, a gateway leading into Weston's Yard, a quadrangle, having on the E. side the school library, and buildings occupied by the boys on the foundation or " King's Scholars."

The College of the Blessed Mary of Eton beside Windsor was founded Oct. 11, 1440, by Henry VI., " when," says Fuller, " it was high time some school should be founded, considering how low grammar-learning then ran in the land." It had originally endowments for a provost, 10 " sad " priests, 4 lay clerks, 6 choristers, 25 poor grammar-scholars, and 25 poor men whose duty it was to pray for the king. It had in 1872 on the foundation a provost, vice-provost, 6 fellows, 3 conducts, 70 king's scholars, and 10 clerks and 12 choristers. Beside there are above 800 scholars (Oppidans) not on the foundation. Great changes were introduced in 1872 by the Public Schools Parliamentary Commission. The distinction between the school and the college was abolished, and a governing body was appointed, consisting of the Provosts of Eton, and of King's College, Cambridge, the President of the Royal Society, the Lord Chief Justice, and the masters of the school, respectively; and four members co-opted by the rest of the governing body. An entirely new set of statutes and regulations were made by this governing body, containing precise provisions for entrance examinations, payments for board and education, succession to boarding houses, &c. Attached to the foundation are several scholarships at King's College, Cambridge (4 given annually); 2 scholarships at Merton College, Oxford; and 47 livings. Among distinguished provosts who have presided over Eton, have been William of Waynflete (d. 1486), the founder of Magdalen Coll., Oxford, afterwards Bishop of Winchester and Lord Chancellor, its second provost and first head master (who probably drew up the statutes, which are in imitation of those of William of Wykeham at Winchester, of which school he was head master before he came to Eton); Roger Lupton, who built the great tower and gateway to the cloisters, 1503–35; Sir Thos. Smith, Secretary-of-State, and a well-known diplomatist of the reigns of Henry VIII., Edward VI., Mary, and Elizabeth (1512–77); Sir H. Savile (1549–1622), reader to Queen Elizabeth, and one of the greatest scholars of her time, who published St. Chrysostom while at Eton, and founded professorships of astronomy and geometry at Oxford; Thomas Murray, tutor and secretary to Prince Charles; Sir H. Wotton (1568–1639), the eminent statesman and ambassador of James I., beloved and praised by Isaak Walton, with whom he used to fish; Dr. Steward, Clerk of the Closet to Charles I., turned out by the Parliament; Francis Rous (1658), Speaker of the Barebones Parliament, who saved Eton from confiscation, and founded 3 scholarships; Nicholas Monk, brother of the Duke of Albemarle, and afterwards Bp. of Hereford; Rd. Allestree, Canon of Christ Ch., who built the Upper School; and Dr. Hawtrey, famed for his success as head master, and esteemed for his elegant scholarship.

Among boys on the foundation, afterwards illustrious, were John Hales (1584–1656), called the "ever-memorable," a somewhat free-thinking writer; Bp. Pearson, Bp. Fleetwood, Earl Camden, Dean Stanhope, Sir Robert Walpole, Sir William Draper, and Longley, Archbishop of Canterbury.

Among those not on the foundation were Edmund Waller, Harley Earl of Oxford, Lord Bolingbroke, the great Earl of Chatham, Lord Lyttelton, Gray, Horace Walpole, West, Wyndham, Fox, Canning, Fielding, Praed, Adml. Lord Howe, Lord Wellesley, Duke of Wellington, and Hallam.

The old part of the College, begun 1441, finished 1523, is built principally of red brick with stone dressings, and chimneys elaborately ornamented, and consists of 2 quadrangles. The first of these contains on the E. the picturesque clock-tower, which resembles those of St. James's and Hampton Court; on the N. the *Lower School*, on the walls of which, as well as on those of the *Upper School*, the names of many celebrated members may be seen, with the old dormitory known as the "*Long Chamber*" above it, now for the most part divided into separate compartments; on the W. the *Upper School*, supported on an arcade, by *Sir Christopher Wren*; on the S. the *Chapel*. In the centre is a bronze statue by *Bird*, placed by Provost Godolphin (1719) to the "never-fading memory" of Henry VI. The second and smaller quadrangle, called the *Green Yard*, which is surrounded by a cloister, contains the entrance to the hall and the lodgings of the provost and fellows.

The *Hall* (for the scholars on the foundation) is a curious apartment, with a daïs for the dignitaries, and 3 fireplaces, discovered behind the panelling at its restoration; that at the end is unique, as being behind the daïs, and is coeval with the foundation. The stained window above, by *Hardman*, represents scenes in the life of Henry VI. The panelling is richly decorated with the arms of the provosts and benefactors. Among the portraits is a fine one of Sir R. Walpole. S. of this is the *Library*, containing a large number of Oriental MSS., collected by Mr. Pote at Putna; a prayer-book of Queen Mary; the Mazarin Bible, the first book ever printed—1448; and a copy of the 'Nibelungenlied,' one of the only two of the kind ever printed, presented by the King of Prussia. The *Provost's Lodgings* contain portraits of Queen Elizabeth, Sir T. Smith, Sir H. Savile by *Corn. Jansen*, Sir H. Wotton, and an original portrait of Jane Shore in a necklace (and nothing else), said to have been given by her to Provost Post, who was her confessor. The *Election Hall* has some curious stained windows, representing different forms of torture, including the pressing to death, practised as a punishment for refusing to plead. The *Election Chamber* contains portraits of Henry V., VI., VII., commonly believed to be originals, and the portraits presented to Dr. Keate by his scholars, and given by his widow to the College. In other rooms are other portraits of scholars presented to Drs. Bernard, Foster, Davis, Heath, and Goodall.

An account of the erection of Eton College, from original documents, some of them bearing the signature of Henry VI., is given in 'Records of Bucks,' vol. iv., No. 3.

The *New Buildings*, in the Tudor style, include dormitories and the *School Library*, which contains nearly 6000 volumes, and a large collection of stuffed birds presented by Dr. Thackeray, late Provost of King's; also portraits of Henry VI., an early copy; Henry VII., an original; Porson, by *Newenham*; a cast of the Dying Gladiator; and a copy, in marble, of the Apollo Belvidere.

The *Chapel*, 175 ft. in length, in outline much resembles King's College Chapel at Cambridge, and is a very fine specimen of late Perp. The interior was restored, 1848–60, and fitted up with dark oak stalls and seats. The E. window—a present from the boys—is filled with stained glass by *Willement*, and there are 2 memorial windows to Etonians who fell in the Crimea. The remaining windows in the chapel were fitted with stained glass by the munificence of Rev. J. Wilder, one

of the Fellows. A new carved stone organ screen, intended as a memorial of Etonian officers killed during the Afghan and South African campaigns, was erected in 1882. There are also many *Brasses*, but most of them have been removed from their original places, and are fixed on the walls of the antechapel; they range in date from 1489 to 1657.

On the l. is the little chantry of Provost Lupton (temp. Henry VII.), containing his tomb. His rebus, a tun with the word " Lup " above it, is carved over the door. Many curious mural paintings, in oil, on the legends of the Virgin, were discovered upon the walls in restoring the chapel. They were in a very high style of art, probably the work of one of the many Flemish painters in England during the reign of Henry VII., VIII.

Among the celebrated persons buried in the chapel are Ld. Grey de Wilton, henchman to Henry VIII.; Longland, Bp. of Lincoln, his confessor; Provost Francis Rous, 1658; Dr. Allestree, who built the Upper School and cloisters, 1680; Nathaniel Ingelo, author of 'Bentivoglio and Urania;' and Sir H. Wotton, with the extraordinary epitaph—

" Hic jacet hujus sententiæ primus auctor,
' Disputandi pruritus, Ecclesiarum scabies ;'
" Nomen alias quære."

There is also a fine tomb of Dr. Murray, 14th provost, with his effigy coloured after life. The most recent tomb (1879) is that of Provost Hawtrey. In the ante-chapel is a statue of the founder, by *Bacon*, 1786, placed there by the Rev. E. Bentham, one of the fellows, at a cost of 700*l.* and *Chantrey's* monument to Provost Goodall.

The *Graveyard* contains the tomb of the Ever-Memorable Hales, restored by Provost Hawtrey. Close by is *Baldwin's* or *Barne's Pool Bridge*, connecting the town with the precincts of the College—a relic of the

13th centy., when it marked the limits of the town in that direction. Opposite to the W. door of the chapel, on the rt. of the road from Slough, is Keate's Lane, leading to Dorney and the Maidenhead road. A little way down this, on the l., is an octagonal brick building formerly a mathematical schoolroom, now a museum of geology and zoology. On the opposite side of the road is a chemical laboratory, built in 1870. The next building on the same side is the racquet-court, and adjoining this a set of lecture-rooms for scientific teaching. Beyond these the road opens out into South Meadow, from which the banks of the river can be easily reached. Above the N. wing of the new schools there is an astronomical observatory containing a good telescope, presented by one of the masters.

From the head-mastership of Dr. Bernard (before which the procession was not military and took place annually on Feb. 2) to the abolition of the custom in 1846, Whit-Tuesday was triennially celebrated here by the *Eton Montem*, when the scholars, attired in a variety of fancy costumes, marched to Salt Hill (a slight elevation beside the Bath road, supposed to be a tumulus), where contributions of "salt" were levied on each of the numerous spectators and visitors, who received in return a pass ticket, inscribed "Mos pro lege" or "Pro More et Monte." The so-called "salt" often amounted to more than 1000l. and once to 1300l., so that, after the expenses of the day were paid, a large sum remained, which was given to the captain of the school.

The river is constantly covered with boats, and its vicinity to the College has given Etonians that excellence in swimming and rowing of which they are justly proud. Prizes are given for swimming races, distance diving, and "headers."

On June 4th, King George III.'s birthday, now the school "Speech-day," a procession of boats takes place in the afternoon from the *Brocas*, a large meadow above the bridge, to *Surley Hall*, 3 m. up the river, and the evening closes with a display of fireworks.

The town of Eton, which is connected with Windsor by an iron bridge, contains nothing to detain the tourist, its church being modern.

[From Eton some places of interest in the S.E. corner of Bucks may be visited; they lie in the vicinity of the Thames, amid pleasant scenery.

2 m. S.E. is *Datchet*, the scene of Falstaff's miseries in the 'Merry Wives of Windsor.' "The muddy ditch at Datchet Mead, close by the Thames' side," into which he was thrown "glowing hot, like a horse-shoe, hissing hot," and, "having a kind of alacrity in sinking, had been drowned, but that the shore was shelving and shallow," existed until the time of Queen Anne, when it was converted into a covered drain, now known as *Hoghole*. Datchet *Church* is a small E. E. and Dec. edifice, in which Christopher Barker, Queen Elizabeth's printer, is buried, as also Lady Katherine Berkeley, daughter of Lord Mountjoy, 1559. The village, which has a *Stat.* on the South-Western line, is connected with Windsor by the Victoria bridge, and with Old Windsor by the Albert bridge, both handsome iron structures, which command very beautiful views, the prospect of Windsor Castle from the former being particularly striking.

1 m. above Datchet, Isaak Walton used to fish "for a little samlet or skegger trout, and catch 20 or 40 of them at a standing." With him fished "that undervaluer of money, the late Provost of Eton College, Sir H. Wotton, a most dear lover and frequent practiser of the art of

angling," who styled it "his idle time, not idly spent," and found it, "after tedious study, a rest to his mind, a cheerer of his spirits, a diverter of sadness, a calmer of unquiet thoughts, a moderator of passions, a procurer of contentedness, and that it begat habits of peace and patience in those that professed and practised it." Wotton built a fishing-house here, where Walton spent some days with him every year. The painter Verrio afterwards built a summer-house on the site, and here Charles II. came to fish.

> " Methinks I see our mighty monarch stand,
> The pliant rod now trembling in his hand :
> . . . .
> And see, he now doth up from Datchet come,
> Laden with spoils of slaughter'd gudgeons,
> home." *Pope.*

Both houses are now destroyed, but the place is still well known to anglers from its fishing-house of *Black Pots.*

Near Datchet is *Ditton Park* (Duke of Buccleuch). The manor once belonged to the Moleyns and Hungerfords, and a house was built on it by Sir Ralph Winwood, author of 'Memorials of Affairs of State,' temp. James I. His daughter and heiress carried it into the Montagu family, and the daughter of the last Duke of Montagu conveyed it to the Duke of Buccleuch, the friend of Sir Walter Scott, who was a frequent visitor. The Jacobean house, which had long been a resort of the *bels esprits* of society, was burnt in 1812.

"On the right of the road from Datchet to Wraysbury, at about 1 m., is a farm-house called *King John's Hunting Lodge* (though really built some centuries later). It has a rude porch, primitive windows, and curious gables, all betokening the architecture of bygone times. In the inside are huge oaken timbers, low roofs, and grotesque carvings. 2 of the windows of the bed-rooms contain some stained glass of the arms of a king of England at an early period. 2 enormous walnut-trees at the back of the house measure at 3 ft. from the ground 24 ft. in circumference.

4 m. *Wraysbury* (anciently Wyrardisbury), a pleasant village, on a branch of the Colne, over which is a suspension-bridge; there is also a Stat. on the South-Western line to Windsor. The E. E. and Dec. *Church* has been well restored : in it notice the brass of John Stonor (1512) in the dress of an Eton scholar. A footpath by the ch. leads to a ferry for *Magna Charta Island,* opposite which is Runnymede (See *Handbook for Surrey*). On the river's bank, embosomed in trees, is *Ankerwyke House* (J. Anderson, Esq.), which occupies the site of a Priory of Benedictine nuns, founded in honour of St. Mary Magdalen, by Sir Gilbert Montfichet, temp. Henry II. The Priory was afterwards given by Edward VI. to Sir Thomas Smith, Provost of Eton, who resided here. Of the monastic buildings only the *Hall* remains. There is an immense yew-tree measuring 28 ft. in girth at 3 ft. from the ground, beneath which, according to local tradition, Henry VIII. used to meet Anne Boleyn.]

[A delightful excursion may be made from Slough to Wexham, Stoke, Farnham, Burnham Beeches, Dropmore, and Cliefden, rejoining the rail at Maidenhead. The distance is about 14 m., making ample allowance for occasional *détours.*

1 m. N.E. of Slough Stat. is the small but interesting ch. of *Wexham.* Almost every window is of different style, from Norm. to Perp.; and the encaustic tiles of the altar platform are in excellent preservation. 1½ m. further W. is

Stoke Poges, the *Church* standing

on a rising ground, and its white spire very conspicuous. The ivy-clad tower is E. E., and stands at the E. end of the N. aisle; the chancel arch is Norm., and the E. window Perp. In the chancel is the Dec. canopy of a tomb, believed to be that of Sir John Moleyns, treasurer to Edward III., and there are *Brasses* for several members of that family, as Sir John (1425), and Eleanor Moleyns, Lady Hungerford (1476). On the S. side is the *Hastings Chapel*, with the coronet and heraldic maunch outside; it is of late Perp. character. The W. front has been injudiciously restored,—a window being substituted for the door, although there was already a large window above.

Near the E. end of the ch. is a plain tomb with an epitaph by Gray to Mary Antrobus and " Dorothy Gray, the careful, tender mother of many children, of whom one alone had the misfortune to survive her."

The poet was afterwards, according to his own wish, buried in the same vault,—a fact recorded by an inscription placed on the sill of the window of the Hastings Chapel.

Though other places have their advocates (as Thanington, see *Handbook for Kent*), *Stoke Churchyard* is usually regarded as the scene of Gray's 'Elegy': the different points in the description—"the ivy-mantled tower," " the rugged elms," " the yew-trees' shade," " yon wood," " the heath,"—perhaps applying more exactly here than elsewhere. Gray was accustomed to spend his college vacations at Stoke, at the house of his aunt, Mrs. Rogers; and in 1741 his mother and his aunt Antrobus came to live here, in a house described by him as " a compact box of red brick, with sash windows," when Stoke became his home. It was called West-end Cottage, and is still standing (with the name of Stoke Court), though much enlarged, altered, and beautified. His room is known, and

a walnut-tree, alluded to in one of his letters, is still existing. Just outside the ch.-yd. is a monument in shape of a sarcophagus or large tea caddy, containing on each face a few lines from Gray's ' Elegy,' or other poems, erected by Mr. John Penn.

Close to the churchyard and, within the grounds of *Stoke Park*, is the only remaining wing of the *Old Manor-house*, described by Gray in his ' Long Story ' :—

" In Britain's Isle, no matter where,
    An ancient pile of building stands,
The Huntingdons and Hattons there
    Employ'd the power of fairy hands
To raise the ceiling's fretted height.
    Each panel in achievements clothing,
Rich windows that exclude the light,
    And passages that lead to nothing "

Amicia de Stoke brought the estate to Robert Poges, whose granddaughter married Sir John Moleyns, from whom it descended to Hastings Earl of Huntingdon, who rebuilt the house in the reign of Elizabeth, when, according to tradition, Sir Christopher Hatton lived here.

" Full oft within the spacious walls,
    When he had fifty winters o'er him,
The grave Lord Keeper led the brawls,
 . The seals and maces danced before him."

The fragment of the old house contains some portraits, china, and other curiosities, and is worth a visit. The estate was afterwards seized for a Crown debt, when James I. gave it to Chief Justice Coke, who lived in retirement here for some years until his death (1629–34), just before which his papers were seized on suspicion that he had given dangerous advice to the members of the Parliament of 1629. His daughter married John Villiers, elder brother of the Duke of Buckingham, who was created Baron Villiers of Stoke Poges and Viscount Purbeck; she became unhappily conspicuous in the time of Abp. Laud, being sentenced to a public penance for adultery, and forcibly rescued from prison by her paramour, Sir Robert Howard. The estate was purchased by Thomas Penn, 2nd son of Penn of Pennsylvania, and the modern house was built by *Wyatt.* in 1789, for John, his son, who erected the memorial to Gray. It contains some choice paintings.

In the conservatory is a bas-relief representing the repulse of Cæsar on an occasion when he attempted to land upon the coast of England. Underneath is an inscription taken from Cæsar's Commentaries,—"Hoc usum ad pristinam fortunam Cæsari defuit." This bas-relief, which was executed in 1706, deserves especial notice as a most remarkable work of that period. Its artist, *Deare*, was an Englishman of the greatest promise, who died young at Rome. (For an account of him see 'Smith's Life of Nollekens.') He was much patronized by Mr. Penn, for whom he made this. The Gardens, originally laid out by *Repton* and *Browne*, are very pleasant; and in the park, which has a fine sheet of water, is a column surmounted by a statue of Coke.

Baylis House, once the residence of Lord Chesterfield, and afterwards of Lord Chancellor Loughborough (who died there 1805) is now a R. C. school with chapel; it is a fine brick mansion, built in 1695 by Dr. Godolphin, Provost of Eton, and has a noble avenue of trees. *Stoke Place* is the seat of Col. R. Howard Vyse.

2 m. W. of Stoke is *Farnham Royal*, an old manor of the Verdons, Furnivals, and Talbots, held by service of finding a glove for the king's right hand, and supporting it at his coronation. The ch. (restored 1868) contains a *Brass* for Eustace Mascall, described as "pistile reader" in Windsor Castle (d. 1567), who is said to have been the superintendent of Wolsey's buildings at Oxford.

Bp. Chandler of Durham (d. 1750) is also buried here.

1 m. further W. are the *Burnham Beeches* — an unequalled fragment of forest scenery, delineated by numberless artists. Gray, writing to Horace Walpole, Sept. 1737, says, "I have at the distance of half a mile, through a green lane, a forest (the vulgar call it a common), all my own, at least as good as so, for I spy no human thing in it but myself. It is a little chaos of mountains and precipices: mountains it is true that do not ascend much above the clouds, nor are the declivities quite so amazing as Dover Cliff, but just such hills as people who love their necks as well as I may venture to climb, and crags that give the eye as much pleasure as if they were more dangerous; both vale and hill are covered with most venerable beeches and other reverend vegetables, that, like most other ancient people, are always dreaming out their old stories to the winds:

" And as they bow their hoary tops relate,
  In murm'ring sounds, the dark decrees of
  fate;
  While visions, as poetic eyes avow,
  Cling to each leaf and swarm on every
  bough."

The beeches are all pollarded. According to tradition, this was done by Cromwell's soldiers, who converted the loppings into gunstocks.

In 1879 there was a likelihood of Burnham Beeches being enclosed and converted to other purposes. This induced the Corporation of London to purchase the site with the object of preserving the land as an open space for the public. 874 acres were thus purchased for 6000*l.* exclusive of the timber.

Burnham *Church*, restored in 1862, is E. E. and Dec., the E. window very fine. There are several *Brasses*, one of which has an acrostic inscription for "Thomas Eyer" (d. 1581). About 1 m. S. of the ch. is the moated site of *Burnham Abbey*, founded in 1265, by Richard, King of the Romans "There are considerable remains of E. E. domestic work, built of flint in a very substantial manner, with stone dressings; the windows are all lancet-shaped, though generally small, the chapel and refectory being entirely destroyed; there are some good E. E. doorways and other details" (*J. H. P.*) "Collected in ye p'ish of Burnham towards ye rebuilding of the Church of St. Paul in Lond.' £1 . 4 . 3 " (Par. Reg. Oct. 16. 1678).

At Britwell in this parish there is a remarkable library collected by the late Mr. Miller, M.P., now the property of S. Christie Miller, Esq. It contains the first book printed by Caxton in this country. The library is not shown nor used, as the tenure of the property is connected with the preservation of the books and MSS.

For *Dropmore* and *Cliefden* see Rte. 10.]

Leaving Slough, the traveller will notice on N. the spire of Stoke Poges and the tower of Burnham, whilst S. Windsor Castle and the valley of the Thames are seen to great advantage.

22¼ m. *Taplow and Maidenhead Junction Stat.*

Taplow is a village, with a modern ch. on the site of a 13th-cent. building. Some remarkable *Brasses* have been preserved. Among them notice that of Nicholas de Aumberdene (c. 1350), a very early example of civil costume on such memorials.

The Gt. Westn. Railway crosses between Taplow and the Thames.

Maidenhead, separate *Stat.* (Rte.

4), lies 1 m. W. beyond the river, on the Wycombe and Thame line to Oxford (Rte. 22), which here diverges rt.

1 m. N.E. is *Hitcham*, where the small Dec. *Church* has a very fine E. window of 4 lights. At Hitcham Sir William Clerke (lord of the manor) was visited by Queen Elizabeth in 1602, upon which occasion "he so behaved himself, that he pleased nobody, but gave occasion to have his vanity and misery spread far and wide." Here lived Dr. Friend, who was famous for his long epitaphs, which led Pope to write the epigram—

"Friend! for your epitaphs I'm grieved,
    Where still so much is said:
One half will never be believed,
    The other never read."

ROUTE 12.

MAIDENHEAD TO THAME, BY HIGH WYCOMBE, HUGHENDEN, PRINCE'S RISBOROUGH,

25¾ m.

The Thame Branch of G. W. Rly. diverges from the main line after it crosses *Maidenhead Bridge*, see Rte. 4.

27¼ m. (from Paddington) *Cookham* (Stat.) The village (*Inn* : Llewellyn's Ferry Hotel; best, and very good) lies some distance E. on the bank of the river, and is described in Rte. 10.

28¾ m. *Bourne End* (Stat.). Ere reaching this the Rly. crosses the Thames, giving a beautiful view of Cliefden woods and Hedsor, crowned by its sham Castle, and enters the valley of the Wye, a small stream, which drives a number of paper-mills. Marlow Stat. (Rte. 10) lies 4½ m. to the W., and is connected with it by a branch line. In 1871 an ancient British boat was found in the Thames at Bourne End. It is 25¼ ft. long by 3¾ wide, and cut out of a solid oak tree, with two seats near the stern.

30 m. *Wooburn Green* (Stat.). This is a scattered village, the inhabitants of which are mostly employed in the numerous paper-mills.

The *Church*, which has recently been restored—the interior in 1857 and the exterior, 1868—is Trans.-Norm., with a singular E. window, exhibiting a mixture of Dec. and Perp. styles, and a square Perp. tower at W. end, contains some monuments of the Whartons, and some *Brasses*—among them, John Goodwin and Pernell his wife, "first founders of the stepull of Oburne Deyncourt," 1488; Thomas Swayn, Prebendary of Aylesbury, Bp. Atwater's chaplain, 1519; and Arthur, son of Philip, Lord Wharton, 1642. There are several good stained glass windows—The E. window was inserted in 1881 as a memorial to the late Alfred Gilbey, Esq. Another one commemorates W. King, who was parish clerk about 50 years. In the N. chancel aisle there is a monument to perpetuate the "virtues and manly sense of Elizabeth Bertie." The Bishops of Lincoln formerly had a palace here. Adjoining their chapel was a small room called Little-Ease (which existed as a coal-hole within the last 60 yrs.), for the confinement of heretics, where, according to Foxe, Thomas Chase, of Amersham, 1506, was "barbarously butchered" by strangling, and was afterwards buried in Norland Wood, between

this and Little Marlow. The manor having been alienated by Bishop Holbeach, the Goodwin family removed hither, of whom Sir Francis Goodwin, the friend of Hampden, was several times knight of the shire. "The dispute concerning the legality of his election, 1604, proved the cause of establishing the great constitutional doctrine that the House of Commons have the sole right of judging and deciding on the validity of their own elections and returns."—*Lysons*. His granddaughter married Philip, "the good Lord Wharton,"—"an old Roundhead, who commanded a regiment against Charles I. at Edgehill" (*Macaulay*). He was one of Cromwell's House of Peers, and a great friend of Puritan teachers, who, when exiled, found an asylum and a home at Wooburn, where he received William III. soon after his accession. On his death he left a charge on his estates to supply a certain number of Bibles annually to every parish where he had property, which are still furnished by his representatives, 20 falling to the share of Wooburn. He died in 1695, and was succeeded by his son Thomas, who also had taken an active part during the civil war; he was appointed to many honourable and lucrative posts by William III., and created by George I. Earl of Rathfarnham and Marquis of Catherlough in Ireland, Marquis of Wharton and Malmesbury in England. He was a man of considerable abilities but gay, magnificent, and licentious in practice. He took great pains with the education of his son Philip, by whom he was succeeded upon his death in 1715. Philip was created Duke of Wharton in 1718, and was the notorious Duke commemorated in the verses of Pope. He died, aged 32, in the Monastery of Poblet in Catalonia, where he was buried, without a friend or servant to attend him. He had for a while resided at Wooburn, in almost royal state, and was believed to have spent 100,000*l.* on the gardens alone   Nothing is now left of the buildings but part of the stables and a dovecote.   The old mansion was taken down in 1750. The moat and fish-pond still exist, with a stately row of poplars, and an Oriental plane 18 ft. in girth; traces of the terraces may still be seen cut in the hill, where the gardens were laid out.   The present mansion of *Wooburn House* (Alfred Gilbey, Esq.) is built on the site of the old stables.   The ancient and picturesque cottages to the west of the church contain remains of the Deyncourt mansion, belonging to which was a cruciform chapel, 36 ft. long by 24 ft wide.   Notice two old carved figures on exterior of public-house to S. of church.   They are said to represent the founders.   Lace-making was formerly carried on here to a great extent, and the lace for Princess Charlotte's wedding-dress was made by a woman in the village.

31¼ m. *Loudwater* (Stat.)   This is a hamlet of High Wycombe, with several large paper-mills.

34¼ m. *High* (or *Chipping*) *Wycombe* (Stat) (*Inns*:   Red Lion, Falcon), an ancient borough now returning one M P. Pop. 4011). The principal manor belonged to Edith, the Queen of Edward the Confessor, was at the Conquest bestowed on Robert d'Oiley, and by Edward IV. granted to the chapter of St. George, Windsor. It is a clean, pleasant-looking town, in a valley through which the little river Wye runs, and surrounded by beech-clad hills.   The great trade is chair-making: beech wood being employed for ordinary work, and walnut, birch, cherry, &c., for the better kinds.

The *Church of All Saints* is large

and handsome, and the interior was restored by *G. E. Street*, 1875, at a cost of 10,000*l.*   The early Norman ch. was consecrated by S. Wulston, Bp. of Worcester, 1076; the present building erected in 1273 by the Abbess of Godstow; the tower (which formerly stood in the centre) by Sir Roland Messenger in 1522, the battlements and pinnacles being added by Lord Shelburne in 1755.   The handsome wooden screens mentioned by Rickman were destroyed in 1863 during a so-called "restoration."   The ch. is 200 ft. in length, and is the largest in the county; it was formerly very rich in sepulchral brasses, but most of them were destroyed at the Rebellion. The former altarpiece, "S. Paul preaching to the Druids," by *Mortimer*, is now in the Council Chamber at the Guildhall.   In the N. aisle of the chancel is the huge monument, by *Scheemaker*, of Henry Petty, Earl of Shelburne, who bequeathed 2000*l.* for the purpose of its erection; he is represented in marble, reclining on a sarcophagus ornamented with a medallion of his father, Sir Wm. Petty: Religion opens a book to him; Virtue, Learning, Charity, and a Roman warrior stand to the rt. and l.   There is also a monument, in the Bower Chapel, by *Carlini*, to Sophia Lady Shelburne, died 1771. In the church-yard observe the curious epitaph of Thomas Aldridge, 1783.   A house called the *Priory*, near the ch., is worth notice.

The *Grammar School*, founded by Sir E. Peckham, in 1548, occupies the site of an *hospital of St. John Baptist* (1190), and some arches, piers, &c. of its Norm. chapel remain.   They were opened out and repaired (1882) and deserve the attention of the architect.   A new school was erected 1881, but as much of the ancient edifice is preserved as the plans permitted.

Edmund Waller, the poet, was member for Wycombe in 1625; also Sir E. Verney, Charles I.'s standard-bearer, who fell at Edgehill, 1639-40; and Thomas Scott, the regicide, during the Protectorate. John Archdale, a Quaker, was chosen to represent High Wycombe in 1698, but as he declined to take the oaths his election was set aside.

A little S. of Wycombe, on the Marlow road, is the *Abbey* (Lord Carington), formerly the seat of the Petty family, rebuilt by *J. Wyatt.* It stands beside a broad sheet of water, in a finely timbered park, and near the site of the ancient hospital of S. Margaret. Park open week-days. House not shown.

Both British and Roman remains have been found in the neighbourhood of Wycombe, particularly tesselated pavements, some of which have been laid open at the expense of Lord Carington.

King John visited this town three times, viz.. Oct. 27, 1204; May 10, 1207; May 2, 1208. John Munday, Lord Mayor of London in 1522, and William Alley, Bp. of Exeter, 1560, were natives of Wycombe.

Just after leaving High Wycombe Stat. is a beautiful view up the valley to the rt.; the white front of Hughenden House can be seen very plainly.

Hughenden, 2 m. N. of High Wycombe, in a beautiful wooded district. The *Church* was thoroughly restored in 1874-5, at a cost of 6300*l.*, from designs by A. W. Blomfield, and the nave was rebuilt. Of the six bells, two date from the time of Edward III., and have Latin inscriptions upon them, and two were added in 1875. The ch. contains some finely-embroidered silk, velvet and linen. The altar frontal was worked by Mrs. Blagden, the wife of the vicar, and is a magnificent example of modern embroidery. In the centre is a white floriated Latin cross, upon which

[*Berks, &c.*]

are fourteen roses, the eyes of which are crystals; while in the centre of the arms of the cross there is a large crystal surrounded by a ring of pearls. The chalice veil of Buckinghamshire lace is extremely beautiful. In the Montfort chapel are some curious effigies attributed to the De Montfort family. The cross-legged knight, in military costume of the end of the 13th centy., is supposed to be Richard, youngest son of Simon de Montfort, and grandson of King John, who returned to England after the banishment of his family, when he assumed the name of Wellesbourne, and resided at Rockhols in this parish. On the shield are the arms of Montfort, Earl of Leicester, viz., a lion rampant with double tail, devouring a male child. On the right breast of the surcoat are the arms of Wellesbourne, viz., a griffin segreant holding a child in its paw. In Meyrick's 'Ancient Armour' this figure is quoted as the earliest example of the dagger and sword being worn together, and he gives 1286 as the date of the tomb. The next figure in a niche in the N. wall has a plain round helmet on the head, a collar of roundlets and a gamboised coat with roundlets at the bottom of the skirt. No. 3 is a striking monument upon the window ledge, and represents a knight in pointed helmet and mixed plate and chain armour of the time of Edward III. No. 4 stands against the east wall of the chapel on N. side of the window, and is very rudely sculptured. No. 5, on the other side of the window wears a close helmet, and holds a mace or masuel in his right hand; and is probably the only instance in England of such a weapon occurring upon a monumental effigy. Near this effigy observe a small brass of Rob. Thursby, 1493, a former vicar of Hughenden. In S.W. corner of the chapel is an emaciated figure in a shroud; on its breast is a little figure

K

with outstretched hands, symbolical of the departing spirit. In the Montfort chapel is a memorial window to John Norris, Esq., of Hughenden Manor, and near the piscina a curious monument to Thomas Lane, 1621. On the S. side of chancel there are windows to the memory of Jane, first wife of T. J. Reynolds, Esq., of Totteridge, and Sir W. N. Young and Sir G. J. Young, who died in the Crimea, 1854. The central window on S. of nave was inserted in 1882 by the undergraduates of Oxford, and depicts Angels ministering to our Lord. Lord Beaconsfield's vault is under the window of the Montfort chapel; it was constructed for the reception of the remains of Mrs. Willyams of Carnanton, Cornwall (d. 1863), who was buried here at her express desire. She bequeathed to the late Earl the whole of her property, amounting, it is said, to 40,000*l.* Here are also commemorated the Viscountess Beaconsfield (d. 1872) and James Disraeli, brother of the late Lord Beaconsfield (d. 1868). The monument consists of three arches, the centre a trefoil, the side ones lancet shaped, enclosing three recessed slabs of red Scotch granite, upon which the inscriptions are cut. The cornice is sculptured to represent lilies, roses, etc. Lord Beaconsfield died on April 19, 1881, and was buried here on the 26th, and on the following Saturday, the Queen, accompanied by Princess Beatrice, visited the tomb, and placed upon the coffin a wreath and cross of flowers. The mural paintings in the sanctuary of Hughenden ch. form part of the memorial to the late Earl of Beaconsfield. The various memorials in the order of their erection are as follow:— 1. Two bells, completing the peal, presented by Mr. Robert Warner, dedicated August 20, 1881. 2. The E. window, erected by his devoted friends, Lord Rowton, Sir Nathaniel de Rothschild, Bart., and Sir Philip

Rose, Bart., dedicated September 4, 1881. 4. The W. window erected by the subscribers to the Hughenden Memorial Fund, dedicated October 23, 1881. 4. The fresco paintings of the sanctuary, from the same fund, dedicated on Christmas Day, 1881. 5. A pair of brass candelabra, presented by two members of Lord Beaconsfield's household. The monument which her Majesty commissioned Mr. R. Belt to prepare as a memorial of the late Lord Beaconsfield is erected immediately above the seat habitually occupied by the late statesman. The spot was selected by her Majesty that her gift might be at once a testimony of his humility and greatness, as well as a touching record of that friendship which can so rarely exist between Sovereign and subject. The centre of the memorial is occupied by a striking profile portrait, carved in low relief in marble, placed within a quatrefoil cartouch, which is flanked by buttresses and crowned by a carved and crested canopy, in which figures an heraldic hatchment of the late Earl's arms and supporters. Beneath this is a tablet bearing the following graceful dedication penned by her Majesty herself:—" To the dear and honoured memory of Benjamin, Earl of Beaconsfield, this memorial is placed by his grateful and affectionate Sovereign and friend Victoria R.I. 'Kings love him that speaketh right.'—Proverbs xvi. 13. February 27, 1882."

Hughenden Manor House, now occupied by Sir Samuel Wilson, is a handsome mansion on a hill to the W. of the ch. " The most effective trees and shrubs have been distributed with skill and judgment in the grounds and park around the mansion, which occupies a commanding site, overlooking the valley of the Wye, and a wide stretch of finely timbered country." On a hill in the park there is a monument erected by Lady Beaconsfield to the memory of Isaac D'Israeli, the author of 'The Curiosities of Literature.' The park is enlivened by a small stream called by Leland the Higdenbrook; but which the late Earl designated " that ancient river, the river Kishon."

To the l. of the road leading from High Wycombe to West Wycombe is a large circular earthwork, Desborough Castle, from which the Hundred is named: in the field below Roman coins and other remains have been found. The Camp, locally the "Roundabout," is 140 yds. in diameter: height of bank from bottom of ditch 22 ft., from the interior 10 ft. Whilst felling trees here in 1743, the framework of a Gothic window was found. It is said to have been erected by Ina, K. of Wessex, and named after his Queen, Desburga; but its origin and use are disputed points among antiquaries.

36½ m. *West Wycombe* (Stat.) Near the stat. is seen a steep grass-covered hill on the top of which is a building with a huge ball on top, which might be supposed to be a summerhouse, but which is really a church. The village stretches along the main road towards Stokenchurch, having on S. *West Wycombe House* (Dowager Lady Dashwood), and on N. the new ch. of St. Paul, and the high hill on which the old ch. stands. In the centre of the village is an old house, the lower part now divided into labourers' cottages, but the large upper room, from which a clock projects over the street, is styled the *Church loft*, and is used for parish purposes. In one of the wooden posts supporting the building is the impress of an ancient crucifix. Under it, an uninviting entry, called Church Lane, leads to the hill (the keys of the ch. are kept at the parish clerk's); half-way up, beneath an artificial ruin, is the entrance to the *Caves*, excavated by Lord le Despencer, and penetrating

for ¼ m. into the hill; they were dug merely for the purpose of getting the chalk, but the character of their maker was so strange, that to this day he is credited in the neighbourhood with all sorts of sinister designs in forming them. The path, which is very slippery, sometimes divides and leaves a huge pillar of chalk to support the roof. A copious spring rises in one part. The guide who shows the ch. will, if desired, provide candles for the caves: but it must be remarked, that they are very cold and uninviting. Lord le Despencer was Francis Dashwood, notorious for his vices, but especially as the founder of the Franciscans at Medmenham (Rte. 10), who were the disgrace of the last century. In 1763 he rebuilt the ch. in the extraordinary fashion in which it now appears, and commemorated the exploit by an inscription outside, " Hanc Ædem condidit Franciscus Baro le Despencer, anno Christi MDCCLXIII," under which is a fresco exhibiting the tortures of St. Lawrence, to whom the ch. is dedicated. This is now almost obliterated. A mortuary chapel has been erected for the Dashwood family, though the last bart. is buried in the ch.-yard. In other respects, the ch. remains as originally erected, and its internal fittings are most extraordinary: the pulpit and reading-desk are mahogany arm-chairs, apparently raised upon chests of drawers, of which the drawers, when pulled out, form steps; the font is a bronze tripod, supporting a basin surrounded by doves, in pursuit of which a serpent is climbing. The ceiling of the chancel has a painting of the Last Supper (observe the eye of Judas, which seems to follow you); a *Brass*, for R. East and his wife (1683), and some painted glass saved from the old ch. remain; the floor is of marble. In the chancel is some wood carving by *Grinling Gibbons*. There are six bells; the

K 2

oldest dated 1581. The top of the ball is 646 ft. above the sea-level. The view from the tower is extensive; the ch. of High Wycombe rises finely at the end of the valley, through which the rivulet of the Wye winds. The huge ball at the top contains a room with seats for half-a-dozen persons.

Abutting against the E. wall of the ch.-yd. is the extraordinary hypæthral *Mausoleum*, built in 1763 from funds bequeathed by George Bubb Dodington, as an inscription records. It is hexagonal in form, has a number of openings of various shapes and sizes, and at the E. end a lofty arch closed by an iron gate. It has a cornice supported by Tuscan columns both inside and out, and in the recesses are several monuments, some kneeling figures in white marble, some busts, others urns of classic form. In the centre is a small Ionic temple, under which is an urn for Sarah, Baroness le Despencer (d. 1769), having the inscription "Mors solamen miseris."

Here is also a monument for Paul Whitehead (b. 1710, d. 1774) with the inscription by Garrick,—

" Here lies a man misfortune could not bend,
Praised as a poet, honour'd as a friend!
Though his youth kindled with the love of fame,
Within his bosom glow'd a brighter flame!
Whene'er his friends with sharp afflictions bled,
And from the wounded deer the herd was fled,
Whitehead stood forth, the healing balm applied,
Nor quitted their distresses—till he died."

This was Paul Whitehead, a satirist, and one of the Medmenham Franciscans. He bequeathed his heart to Lord le Despencer, his patron, and it was deposited in an urn here, Aug. 16, 1775, with a kind of mock funeral service, attended by the regiment of Bucks militia (of which his lordship was colonel), with the accompaniment of an in-

cantation set to music by Dr. Arnold. The urn is inscribed—

" Unhallow'd hands this urn forbear;
No gems nor orient spoil
Lie here conceal'd; but, what's more rare,
A heart that knew no guile."

But the heart, which was enclosed in lead, was constantly taken out to be shown to visitors, and in 1839, it disappeared; it is supposed that one of them carried it off in his pocket.

The Mausoleum was restored by Lady Dashwood in 1880.

A church was erected in the village in 1875 by Lady Dashwood, and there is another district ch. at Downley.

West Wycombe House (Dowager Lady Dashwood), is a large classic building erected by Sir Francis Dashwood, but greatly added to in the way of ornament by his son of the same name, who became Lord le Despencer. The S. front has a colonnade and loggia filled with busts and statuary; the W. or grand front has an Ionic portico. The ceilings of the principal rooms are painted with mythological subjects. The house contains a number of family portraits; also John Milton; a Holy Family, *Rubens*; the Raising of Lazarus, *P. Veronese.* The grounds and park partly laid out by *Repton*, abound in statuary, and are enlivened by a lake and the rivulet winding through them. The house is shown on Wednesdays from May to September, inclusive.

39 m. On E. is *Bradenham*, with a small Dec. and Perp. *Church*, the best feature being a chantry built by William Lord Windsor in 1542, and restored by *Street.* It contains a handsome monument to the Hon. Charles West, eldest son of Lord Delawarr, 1684, and his wife, daughter of Sir E. Pye, who purchased the estate of the Windsors; and one to Isaac D'Israeli, author of the 'Curiosities of Literature,' erected by his daughter-in-law, the Vis-

countess Beaconsfield. He long resided at *Bradenham House*, built by William, Lord Windsor, and visited by Queen Elizabeth in her return from Oxford in 1566.

42¼ m. *Prince's Risborough Junc.* (Stat.). Here a branch (7¼ m. long, with *Stat.* at *Little Kimble*) runs N. to Aylesbury (Rte. 14). The town (Pop. 2549) derives its name from Edward the Black Prince, who is said to have built a palace in it. A moated spot near the ch., called the Mount, is supposed to mark its site, but some writers consider this to be an ancient encampment. The *Church*, a spacious structure, originally E. E. has been restored by *Blomfield;* in the S. aisle is a beautiful E. E. window, with detached shafts, and a row of long low Dec. niches.

[Prince's Risborough (*Inn:* George) is a convenient spot for exploring the Chiltern hills, which offer much beautiful woodland scenery, as well as fine churches, ancient encampments, mediæval mansions, and a remarkable monument of Saxon times.

(*a.*) The *Whiteleaf Cross* lies about 1 m. E. of the town. It is cut out on the W. side of a hill on the Hampden estate, called Green Holly, and consists of a Latin cross rising from a triangular base 340 ft. wide. The vertical stem of the cross is about 100 ft. long, 50 ft. broad; the arms measure 70 ft., and are about 12 ft. broad; the trench is cut 2 or 3 ft. deep in the chalk. It is believed to commemorate a victory of Edward the Elder over the Danes in 910. The view from the top of the hill is very extensive. A care has been taken of this cross, which might well be extended to similar objects of interest. By an Inclosure Act (9 George IV.) it is styled " the ancient memorial or land mark," and is directed to be kept in proper order by the lord of the manor, the owner of the Hampden estates. A number of Roman coins have been found on Soldiers' Mount near the cross.

(*b.*) *Wendover* is 6 m. N. E. by the road from Prince's Risborough, or a mile less by a footpath E. of Chequers (*post*). Pursuing the high road, the first object, at 1 m., but slightly to the W., is the beautiful restored *Church* of *Monks' Risborough.* The tower is E. E., but the body is Dec. and Perp.; there is a good 14th century. rood-screen, a Norm. font, and *Brasses,* 1431, 1460, 1520; the oldest is for Robert Blundell, rector. Near the ch. are traces of monastic fishponds, and a stone pigeon-house. Into a house near the ch. are built fragments from *Old Place,* an abbey grange, destroyed 1859. There will be a station at Wendover on the projected Rickmansworth and Aylesbury line. The ch. of Wendover was restored in 1870 by *G. E. Street.*

2¼ m. *Great Kimble.* The Dec. *Church,* restored in 1876, stands on a mound, probably sepulchral: it has a piscina, and a font somewhat resembling the ornamented one at Aylesbury (Rte. 14). There are also some encaustic tiles, of good design, remaining. " Worth noting and curious to think of, since it is indisputable, on this very day, two obscure individuals, Peter Aldridge and Thomas Lane, assessors of ship money over in Buckinghamshire, had assembled a parish meeting in the Church of Great Kimble, to assess and rate the ship money of the said parish. There in the cold weather, at the foot of the Chiltern Hills, 11th January, 1635, the parish did attend, John Hampden, Esq., at the head of them, and by a return still extant, refused to pay the same, or any portion thereof, witness the above Assessors, witness also two parish Constables, whom we remit from such unexpected celebrity. John Hampden's share for this parish is 31s. 6d.; for another parish it is 20s.; on which latter sum, not on the former, John Hampden, was tried."— *Carlyle.*

On a hill S. of the ch. is an earthwork known as *Cunobeline's Camp.*

Less than a mile N. is *Little Kimble* (Stat.). The Dec. *Church* was restored by Lady Frankland Russell, in 1875, the late owner of Chequers (see (c.)). It once belonged to St. Alban's Abbey. The space between the two Kimbles is styled the Happy Valley, and it certainly is a most picturesque spot.

4 m. *Ellesborough Church*, standing on a hill 449 ft. high from which there is a noble view in every direction. S. lie the yew- and box-clad hills of Chequers, E. the romantic valley that leads to Wendover, and N. and W. the fertile Vale extending from Aylesbury to Thame. The ch. is mainly Perp.; but the font is rich Dec. work. It was restored in 1852 and 1871. There are some 16th-centy. brasses of the Hawtreys of Chequers, and a Jacobean monument for one of them (Brigetta) who brought that estate into the Croke family. The tomb is black, with a very fine effigy of the lady in white marble; her epitaph describes her as "Foeminæ nihil habens nisi sexum" (d. 1638). There are several other Croke memorials, and in the ch.-yard is the tomb of Thos. Edwards (d. 1757), author of the 'Canons of Criticism:' he had been an officer in the army, but was so ready a Greek scholar as to be a formidable opponent of Bishop Warburton.

½ m. beyond Ellesborough Ch. is *Butler's Cross*, where a by-road from Great Hampden to Stoke Mandeville crosses the Icknield Way. A very neat small country inn (the Russell Arms) will afford any needful refreshment before entering the gorge of the hills that leads to Wendover (Rte. 14), and concludes a most picturesque journey of about 6 m.

(c.) 3 m. N. E., and closely adjoining the Kimbles, as the villages are called, is *Chequers Court* (Mrs. Frankland Russell Astley), one of the most beautiful estates in the county, and of interest to many from its collection of relics of the Cromwell family. The house is no longer shown, owing to the misconduct of former visitors, to any but those furnished with an introduction to the owner. The name is believed to be derived from its having been the property of John de Scaccariis, an officer of the Exchequer in the time of John. This house was replaced by another built c. 1326, as that gave way in 1566 to the present most picturesque edifice. The S. front has been altered, but the rest remains very much as it was when the unhappy Lady Mary Grey was a prisoner in it, in 1566–67, under the care of William Hawtrey, whose initials, W. H., still remain on the N. front, with a haw-tree between them, and chequers on either side. She had given offence to her jealous cousin Elizabeth, by venturing to marry Thomas Keys, a military man, and both were imprisoned for the rest of their lives. Keys died in 1570: his wife survived him eight years, during which she was shifted from one keeper to another, Sir Thomas Gresham being one of the number.

The house is placed in a valley, and therefore commands but a very limited view. Notice the noble elm (not a very common tree here) at the S.W. angle.

In the drawing-room is a fine portrait of Sir Wm. Hawtrey, son of Lady Mary's keeper, and his wife Winifred Dormer. The library, 81 ft. long, is a very beautiful room, hung with portraits and adorned with stained glass.

The chief interest of the house rests, however, in the collection of relics of Oliver Cromwell and his family, which is unrivalled, and which exists here in consequence of the marriage, 1664, of Sir John Russell of Chequers with Frances, youngest daughter of the Protector and widow of Robert Rich, the grandson of the Earl of Warwick. Cromwell was in consequence a frequent visitor at this house.

Among the portraits are Oliver Cromwell at 3 yrs. old; Oliver Cromwell in armour, with a page tying his sash; Oliver Cromwell on horseback, painted on copper; Oliver Cromwell, half-length, by *Walker;* his mother, in a close black cap (very like him); his 2 sons, Richard, afterwards Lord Protector, by *Walker;* Henry, Lord Deputy of Ireland, and also as a boy;—his 4 daughters, Bridget, wife of Henry Ireton, afterwards of Charles Fleetwood; Mary, Lady Falconberg; Frances, Lady Russell; Elizabeth, Mrs. Claypole; John Claypole and Ireton, his sons-in-law; Thurloe, his Secretary of State; Jeremy White, his chaplain; Lambert, his President of the Council; Col. Sandys; and Cornet Joyce, who took Charles I. prisoner from Holmby House to Newmarket, and had charge of him in the Isle of Wight. Among the relics are—the mask of Cromwell's face taken after death; his clothes, and jack boots; his miniature, set in a ring, which belonged to one of his daughters; his sword; his watch; and an impression of the Great Seal of the Commonwealth.

Among other valuable pictures in the house are—Charles II., after the battle of Worcester, with Col. Lindsay, meeting Lord Wilmot and Col. Gunter, preparatory to Charles's escape into France: a curious unknown portrait (in the ante-room), the facsimile of one at Dinton, inscribed

" Away I passe from that I was,
 What I gave I have, that I kep I lose;"

Mrs. Ellis, *Sir P. Lely;* the Countess of Richmond, mother of Henry VII., believed to be an original; the Fable of the Lion and the Mouse, a masterpiece of *Snyders,* the background by *Rubens.*

N. W. of the house rises a grassy point in the Chiltern range, known as the *Beacon Hill,* a spot of exquisite beauty unrivalled in the neigh-

bourhood, whence it is believed that even the Malvern Hills can occasionally be distinguished. The view extends over an immense plain, sprinkled with numerous churches, mansions, and villages, among which the town of Aylesbury with its quaint spire, and the towers of the great house of Mentmore, are conspicuous. The undulating downs on the E. extend to Edlesborough (Rte. 18) and on the W. is the conical hill known as *Piccadilly,* above which, in a wood, is a camp supposed to be Danish: while S. the eye rests on the beech-woods of Hampden. Immediately beneath, three beautiful box-fringed valleys debouch upon the plain, of which that on the N. is *Velvet Lawn,* a well-known spot even for London picnics, admission being liberally granted. It is bounded on E. by the Castle Hill or *Cymbeline's* (Cunobeline's) *Mount,* whence, according to tradition, that king, as the British generalissimo, went to oppose Julius Cæsar, and where there are traces of an ancient entrenchment: while at its foot, itself rising on a lofty mound, is the Ch. of Ellesborough (*ante*). The valley in the centre, " Silver Spring," ends with the picturesque Ch. of Little Kimble; while that on the S., the " Happy Valley," is closed by the Ch. of Great Kimble. A sunset view of this scene will not readily be forgotten. The visitor should descend by some of the many winding paths into the woods, in order to appreciate the immense size and beauty of the box-trees. In Gerard's ' Herbal,' published 1599, box is mentioned as " growing in many waste and barren hills in England," but there are now only two other places where it can be really recognised as indigenous.

(*d.*) 3 m. E. is *Great Hampden,* the road lying across the high ground called Risborough hillock, and by the ancient farm of Parsloes. *Hampden House* was the paternal seat of John Hampden, and is still possessed by his descendants in the female line, the Hobarts (Earl of Buckinghamshire). It is a gloomy mansion approached by a fine avenue of beech-trees, and is of interest from its historical recollections, though its exterior is little like what it was in the days of the great opponent of ship-money. A house is traditionally said to have existed here in the time of John, and an apartment in the N. W. front bears the name of "King John's room;" the whole N. front, however was altered in the classic style in 1754, and the S. front is a modern imitation of Tudor architecture.

John Hampden, whose father died when he was 3 yrs. old, was brought up here. Hither he returned after the dissolution of the Parliament of 1628; here he lost and mourned over his first wife, and spent the years that intervened between the 3rd and 4th Parliaments of Charles . in study (his favourite author eing, it is said, Davila, the historian f the Civil Wars in France), in eld-sports and in active opposition) the measures of the government. e thus gained such popularity that when, in 1642, it was intended to arrest him, a large body of Buckinghamshire freeholders repaired to London and followed the king to Hampton Court, expressing their determination to protect him. At the breaking out of the civil war, he was very active in getting the militia of his county into the field; and after his death as many soldiers as could be spared from the adjacent quarters of the army brought his body to be buried in his own church, marching with arms reversed, muffled drums, and their heads uncovered, chanting the 90th Psalm as they came, and the 43rd as they departed, and, says a writer of the day, "Never were heard such piteous cries at the death of one man as at Master Hampden's."

Sir John Birkenhead, the royalist writer of the 'Mercurius Aulicus,' speaks of him very differently, under the date of Saturday, June 24, 1643 : " This day we were advertised that Master John Hampden (the principal member of the Five) was dead of those wounds he received on Sunday last. If so, the reader may remember that in the 15th week of this Mercurius we told the world what fair warnings Master Hampden had received since the beginning of this rebellion, whereof he was a chief incendiary : how he has buried his son and heir and his two daughters; two only sons surviving, whereof one was a cripple and the other a lunatic; which, though this desperate man was unwilling to make use of, yet sure it may startle the rest of his faction ; especially if they consider that Chalgrove Field, where he received this mortal wound, was the self-same place where he first mustered and drew up men in arms to rebel against the king. But whether the death of the Lord Brooke or Master Hampden be the better lesson against treason and rebellion, let posterity judge."

The house, which is entered by a fine old hall with open gallery, and windows filled with painted glass of Scriptural subjects, brought from Italy, contains some historical relics. Among them are a small bust and 2 portraits of John Hampden, one of them by *Jansen*, brought from Strawberry Hill, both of doubtful authenticity; a full-length portrait of Henrietta Maria; also Sir Kenelm Digby, *Vandyck* (?); Ralph, Earl of Lindsay; Bishop Bonner; Oliver Cromwell in armour; Richard Hampden, Chancellor of the Exchequer, in his robes; and Mr. Child, who died in the house on the eve of his intended marriage with the daughter of Robert 1st Viscount Hampden. There is a full length of Elizabeth in the room occupied by her when she visited Griffith Hampden (John Hampden's grandfather, by whom the house was almost rebuilt in preparation for her), but that which is shown as her bed, with chintz hangings lined with satin, is evidently of much later date. A long room at the top of the house called John Hampden's Library, is filled with old books; and in a small library below, is a Bible that belonged to Philip Cromwell, the uncle of the Protector, in which are entries of Oliver's birth and those of his brothers and sisters. In the Park, which is diversified with oak-covered knolls, is the avenue, still called the Queen's Gap, which was cut to make an entrance for Elizabeth on her visit.

In the park and almost adjoining the house, is the picturesque *Church*, where, on the S. wall of the chancel, is the plain, dark-grey tablet erected by Hampden to his first wife Elizabeth Simeon (d. 1634), with his beautiful epitaph upon her. Close beside it is the grave of John Hampden, without any memorial. It was opened by his historian Lord Nugent, when his body was found in such a perfect state, that the picture on the staircase of the house was known to be his from the likeness. Close by are brasses of John Hampden, 1446, and of Sir J. Hampden and his 2 wives, 1553. Opposite, bedecked with Cupids, is the monument of another John Hampden, the last heir male (d. 1754), who left the estate to the Trevors, from whom it passed to the Hobarts. It is adorned with a tree hung with shields bearing the arms and alliances of the Hampdens, at the foot of which is a representation of the battle of Chalgrove Field. The parcel of land, belonging to Hampden, in Great Kimble parish, upon which he refused to pay the sum of 31s. 6d. assessed for ship-money, 's still pointed out on the S. side of the avenue.]

44¼ m. *Bledlow* (Stat.) (Rte. 4.) A station on the Wycombe, Thame, and Oxford branch of the G. W. R.

The village is called Bledelaw in Domesday, and the name is supposed to mean "Bloody Hill," referring to some defeat inflicted on the Danes, which is commemorated by a Gieek cross cut on the side of Winhill, much smaller than the one at Whiteleaf (*ante*). The manor was given by the Conqueror to his half-brother, the Earl of Moretaine. The *Church*, restored in 1876, was originally E. E., but has been much altered. It still retains some sculptured capitals, a Dec. niche in the N. aisle, a good lancet-window in the chancel, some fragments of old glass, a very fine cup-shaped font, and a brass for W. Heron, vicar, 1525. The arrangement of the seats is peculiar, the pews only surrounding the ch. in a single row, the remainder being filled by low benches. The register contains a curious entry relating to the fire of London, headed "A Lamentation." Part of it runs thus: "St. Paul's, all that could be burnt, excepting some timber and lead which covered the high altar, which to some is *malum bonum omen*."

Adjoining the ch. on the N. is a deep ravine called the Glen of the Lyde, where a number of springs burst out of the chalk, and form a large pool, in which water-cresses are cultivated. The sides are clothed with ancient trees, and the scene is very picturesque. The ch. stands so near the edge that it seems in imminent danger, and accordingly a popular rhyme foretells that

" They that live, and do abide,
Shall see the church fall in the Lyde."

1 m. S., on the high ground called Bledlow Ridge, a small district ch. was built in 1868.

1 m. beyond Bledlow the rly. enters Oxfordshire.

48¼ m. *Thame* (Stat.). Rte. 22.

ROUTE 13.

LONDON TO HIGH WYCOMBE, DEN-
HAM, GREGORIES, BULSTRODE,
BY BEACONSFIELD,

By Road.   29 m.

For the country to Uxbridge (15 m.)
see *Handbook for Middlesex.* Crossing the Colne, we enter Bucks at
15½ m.

17 m. *Denham Place* (B. H. Way,
Esq.), built by Sir Roger Hill, 1667,
on the site of an old manor-house of
the Peckhams, came to the present
owner through the marriage of Louis
Way (d. 1771) with Abigail Locke,
Sir Roger's granddaughter. The
house, a large red brick edifice, with
a bold projecting cornice, has a beautiful old chapel, which retains its
ancient gilded seats, decorated with
the dove bearing the olive-branch,
the crest of Sir Roger Hill, and a
stained window richly emblazoned
with coats-of-arms. The rooms contain many quaint old pictures, and
some fine tapestry of Jason and the
Golden Fleece; many have elaborate cornices, some of which are
coloured; that of the drawing-
room represents hawking, fishing,
stag-hunting, and fox-hunting, on
its 4 sides. In a secret room, now
destroyed, Sir Roger Hill was supposed, by local tradition, to have
secreted the body of a footman whom
he is said to have murdered. Denham Place was frequently visited
by Captain Cook, who was a friend
of Mr. Way, and it was the beloved
"pastoral retreat" of Sir Humphrey
Davy, who used to repair hither for
fishing, as is mentioned in his 'Last
Days of a Philosopher.' More recently it has been the occasional
residence of some of the Buonaparte
family.

Denham *Church* is Perp., and has
been restored. It contains the hand-

some altar-tomb, with effigies, of
Sir Edmund Peckham and his lady
(1564, 1570), and the monument of
their son Sir Robert Peckham, who
died at Rome 1569, and is buried
there in the ch. of St. Gregory, but
whose heart is deposited here. Sir
Roger Hill, the builder of Denham
Place, has a bust. There are several
Brasses, from 1494 to 1612, the most
remarkable of which is that of Agnes
Jordan, Abbess of Syon (d. 1544),
one of the only 2 brasses of the kind
known; the other is at Elstow, Beds.
(See *Handbook for Beds.*); there is
also a remarkable incised slab for
Philip Edelen, preacher, 1656.

The railway connecting Uxbridge
with Rickmansworth passes through
Denham.

1 m. N. of the village, and approached by a magnificent lime
avenue more than ½ m. long, is *Denham Court* (N. G. Lambert, Esq.),
once the seat of the Bowyers, where
Charles II. was for a while concealed
by the lady of the house. Four
curious panel-pictures commemorate
the affair. The 1st represents the
young king dressed as a scullion in
the kitchen; the 2nd shews him
among the rushes of the moat; the
3rd shews the turkey, bleeding at
the head, which his hostess hung
over the panel behind which he was
concealed, to keep off the blood-
hound which was tracking him; the
4th is a fine portrait of Lady Bowyer
herself. Dryden was a friend of Sir
William Bowyer, and it was at Denham that he translated the 1st
Georgic and part of the last Æneid.
Hence he wrote, " Nature has con-
spired with art to make the garden
one of the most delicious spots in
England. It contains not above 5
acres, just the compass of Alcinous'
garden, but Virgil says, Laudato
ingentia rura exiguum colito." The
house has been much modernised,
but retains its ancient moat.

18 m. A road goes off on rt. to
Aylesbury (Rte. 14).

19 m. 1¼ S. is *Fulmer*, where the small plain brick ch., rebuilt in 1610 by Sir Marmaduke Dayrell, has a very splendid marble monument for him (d. 1630) and his lady. He is represented in gilt armour, and the inscription states that he was servant to Queen Elizabeth in her wars by sea and land, and cofferer to King James I. and King Charles I. Opposite the tomb hangs his helmet.

In 1877, Mrs. Dent, of Fernacres, obtained a faculty to build a new chancel and organ-chamber, as a memorial to her son, Lancelot Wm. Dent.

20 m. *Gerard's* or *Jarrett's Cross.* (*Inn*: Bull, small but clean). Here, on a wide common, is a memorial *Church*, erected, 1859, by the Misses Reid, to their brother Major-Gen. Reid, long M.P. for Windsor; it is of coloured brick, and presents a curious modern adaptation of Lombard architecture by *Sir W. Tite.*

On l. are the gates of *Bulstrode Park* (Duke of Somerset). A legendary explanation of the name states that, when William the Conqueror subdued this kingdom, he gave the estate of the Shobbington family, who lived here, to one of his followers, and sent 1000 men to assist him in taking possession. But the Saxon owner, calling in the aid of his neighbours, gallantly resisted the invader, entrenching himself within an earthwork in the park, which is still shown as evidence of the story, and, as his party wanted horses, mounted them upon bulls, when, sallying out of their camp, their strange equipment so confounded the Normans that many of them were slain. The king, hearing of the affair, sent for the valiant Saxon, with a promise of safe-conduct to and from his court. The Saxon paid the Conqueror a visit riding upon a bull, accompanied by

his 7 sons similarly mounted, and the result of the interview was that he was allowed to retain his estate. In commemoration of these events he assumed a bull's head as his crest, together with the name of Bulstrode. There is a distich preserved in the neighbourhood, that—

"When William conquer'd English ground,
Bulstrode had per annum three hundred
pound."

Bulstrode Whitelock, the author of 'Memorials of English Affairs,' was maternally descended from this family. Bulstrode was the property of Judge Jeffreys, and after his death came into the possession of King William's Earl of Portland, who greatly improved the house, and died there in 1709. H. Walpole describes Bulstrode as "a melancholy monument of Dutch magnificence, having a brave gallery of old pictures, and a chapel with two fine windows of modern painted glass; and a ceiling formerly adorned with the assumption, or rather the *presumption*, of Chancellor Jeffreys, to whom it belonged; but a very judicious fire hurried him somewhere else." Bulstrode continued a chief seat of that family for more than a century, and the letters of Mrs. Montagu give a lively account of the society that assembled there in the time of Margaret, Duchess of Portland, the owner of the Barberini or Portland vase. In 1809 her son, the 3rd duke, died; when, in pursuance of the directions in his will, all the deer on the estate were killed and buried in the park, and the property was soon after purchased by the Duke of Somerset. After a few years the house was pulled down, but a new mansion was built by *Ferrey* in 1862. The gardens contain some fine cedars, tulip-trees, and deciduous cypresses. The large circular entrenchment in the park, enclosing an area of 21 acres, is worthy of notice.

¼ m. S. is *Hedgerley*, a small village, with a *Church* rebuilt by *Ferrey*, 1852. In it is a singular *Brass* for Margaret Bulstrode (d. 1540), which is entirely made up of fragments of earlier date. " On the reverse of the effigy is part of an epitaph in English verse, on that of some children, the lower portion of a figure of a bishop or abbot, c. 1530, showing the chasuble, pastoral staff, and dalmatic. At the back of the shield is a representation of our Saviour's Resurrection, and behind the inscription a memorial of Thos. de Totyngton, abbot of St. Edmund's Bury, who died 1312. This inscription (whose date is not before the 16th cent.) runs thus :

" Totyngton Thomas Edmundi qui fuit abbas,
Hic jacet, esto pia albi Ductrix virgo Maria. "

The verses behind the figure are only partially legible" (Haines, ' Mon. Brasses '). *Hedgerley Park* (Rice R. Clayton, Esq.), has some Doric pillars from Lady Place (Rte. 10).

23 m. *Beaconsfield* (*Inns*: Manor, Saracen's Head) (Pop. 1635), consists mainly of one long wide street and two shorter ones. The *Church*, restored 1869, has a good flint and stone tower, and contains, beside some brasses, a curious incised slab to Thomas Waller and wife (1626, 1627), displaying 2 flaming hearts conjoined. Until 1863 a simple tablet only commemorated Edmund Burke, his son Richard, his brother, and his widow, he having forbidden any other memorial in his will, but a *Brass* has since been placed on his grave. " There is a circumstance connected with his burial that ought not to pass into oblivion. He was so imbued with a dread of revolution and revolutionists, that he entertained a fear his bones should be taken up by some of them ; he refused to be buried in a leaden coffin, and the

rector, on examining the locality lately, found the ground broken up, and the bones scattered about the grave " (*G. C. Du Pré*, ' Gent. Mag.' Oct. 1860). Burke was member for the adjacent borough of Wendover, and the peerage which George III. had designed for him was to have taken its designation from Beaconsfield. Mr. Disraeli, when called upon to select a title for his wife, chose at the same time to indicate his admiration for Burke, and to emphasise his connection with the county by adopting the title ; and of course the Viscountess Beaconsfield settled the style of the earldom. Mrs. Disraeli received the title in Nov. 1868 ; her husband in Aug. 1876 ; he died April 19th, 1881.

In the churchyard, beneath an old walnut-tree, is a tomb surmounted by an obelisk, which marks the grave of · Edmund Waller, the poet-lover of Sacharissa, who died 1687. Having fallen into decay, it was restored in 1862. It was in Beaconsfield churchyard that John Hampden exercised the trained bands on a Sunday in the year 1633, for which he was summoned before the council, and had to make his submission. The old *Rectory-house* contains some interesting remains of a cell of Burnham Abbey, of 13th-centy. date.

¼ m. S. of Beaconsfield is *Hall Barns* (Edw. L. Lawson, Esq.), the home of Edmund Waller, who was lord of the manor, and built a house here for himself. The existing mansion is not that which he built, but was erected, 1712, from designs of Thomas Milner. It is dismantled of all memorials connected with the poet, except his portrait in the entrance hall, his books and pictures having been long since dispersed by auction. " It is a square brick house, with pilasters, and stone dressings to the windows. The gardens retain much of their original character—broad terrace walks, sheltered by lofty screens of laurel and yew."—(_Jesse._) Obs. the carved oak gable-end of the entrance Lodge. " The _Garden House_ was built by Colin Campbell for the poet's grandson, to contain busts of poets."— (_Vitruv. Britan._, iii. 49, 50.) Two large reception-rooms were built by Sir Gore Ousely, a former owner, for the express purpose of entertaining King William IV. and Queen Adelaide.

Gregories, the home of Burke, who changed its name to Butler's Court, stands a short distance N.W. of the town. The house was burned down in 1813, but the shrubberies remain, and bear the name of " Burke's Grove." Burke purchased the estate —600 acres—for 22,000_l._ Hence he wrote his letters to Barry, who was supported by his generosity in Italy, and to whom he describes his house as " hung from top to bottom with pictures ; " and here he received the forlorn poet Crabbe, whom he so nobly took by the hand, raising him from destitution to independence, and for some time receiving him into his family circle. He was visited here by Dr. Johnson, who, " after wandering about the grounds in admiration, succeeded by a reverie, exclaimed, ' Non equidem invideo, miror magis.' "—(_Boswell._) While dwelling here, Burke lost his son Richard, after whose death he never could bear to look towards Beaconsfield Ch., the place of his interment. " One day, while he was walking in his park, the feeble old horse of his son came close up to him and laid its head upon his bosom, which so affected him that his firmness was totally overpowered, and, throwing his arms over its neck, he wept long and loudly. In 1797 he returned from Bath, to die at Beaconsfield, saying, as he set out, " It is so far, at least, on my way to the tomb, and I may as well travel it

alive as dead."—_Prior's Life of Burke._

The dagger which Burke threw down in the heat of debate in the House of Commons was long preserved in the house of his bailiff's son near Beaconsfield. The original of Sir Joshua Reynolds's ' Infant Hercules ' was still living there, a portly farmer, down to 1850.

1 m. N. is _Wilton Park_ (J. Du Pré, Esq.), a good Palladian house, standing in very extensive and well-wooded grounds.

1 m. E., on the road leading to Chalfont St. Giles, at the back of the Friends' Meeting-house, is a small rough enclosure called _Jourdan's Burial-ground_, appropriated to the sepulture of Quakers, but no longer used. Within it, well known, though unmarked by any stone, is the grave of William Penn, the founder of Pennsylvania, who was buried here, August 5, 1718, amid a large gathering of his followers and friends, who followed his remains from Rushcombe near Twyford, where he died. His 2 wives, and several of his children, lie beside him. Thomas Elwood, the friend of Milton, is also buried here. For Chalfont St. Giles see Rte. 14.

25 m. 2 m. N. is _Penn_, remarkable for its wide views, especially that from _Penn Beacon_, and its beechwood glades, in one of which is _Penn House_ (Viscount Curzon). The ch., originally E. E., has been greatly injured by injudicious modern alterations, but contains several monuments and brasses of the Rook, Penn, and Curzon families. At _Penn Street_, considerably to the N., is a beautiful cruciform ch. with lofty spire, by _Ferrey._

There has been erected by Sir Philip Rose, Bart., in the grounds of _Rayners_, Penn, an interesting memorial of the visit of the Queen to Hughenden ch.-yard on the Saturday after Lord Beaconsfield's funeral. It consists of an obelisk of polished red granite, on a pedestal of the same material, resting on a base of Portland stone. The inscription on the obelisk is—" The Right Hon. Benjamin Disraeli, Earl of Beaconsfield, K.G., ever to be remembered as author, orator, statesman, patriot, and friend. Born Dec. 21, 1804; died April 19, 1881." An inscription on the pedestal records the fact that the Queen passed the spot on her journey, when she designedly followed the route taken by Lord Beaconsfield on his return from his last visit to Windsor Castle.

26 m. On S. *Loudwater* (Rte. 12.)
29 m. *High Wycombe.* (Rte. 12.)

ROUTE 14.

LONDON TO AYLESBURY.

By Road. 39 m.

The journey from London for the first 18 m. is the same as in Route 13. We then turn N.-ward, and at 20 m. we have on r. *Chalfont House* (J. N. Hibbert, Esq.), once the ancient manor of *Brudenels*, in a beautifully wooded undulating park, watered by the Misbourne, and containing perhaps the largest ash-tree in England. 25 ft. in circumference. The house was built by General Churchill, and bears evidence to the taste of his brother-in-law, Horace Walpole, in its Strawberry-hill Gothic, though now further improved

and altered. Walpole frequently visited here, and speaks of Mr. Chute having made "the sweetest plan imaginable" for the remodelling of the house. Here is a fine portrait by *Gainsborough.*

21 m. *Chalfont St. Peter's* (formerly Chalfhunt, locally pronounced Charffunt), a large village, intersected by the Misbourne without a bridge, where there is an admirable adaptation of a red brick ch. of the last centy. by *Street,* 1854. Here are good *Brasses* of William Whappelode, 1398; William Whappelode, steward of Cardinal Beaufort, 1446; and Robert Hanson, priest, 1545; this last is a palimpsest, a figure a centy. earlier having been altered to suit the change of costume (Haines, 'Mon. Brasses'). A house on rt., called *The Grange* (Thos. Wright, Esq.) was once the residence of Judge Jeffreys. At the cross-roads is an obelisk to commemorate George III. being in at the killing of a stag, on that spot, while hunting.

23 m. *Chalfont St. Giles,* a secluded village, W. of the high road, is interesting as the place of refuge chosen by John Milton during the plague of London (1665). The house in which he lived, "a pretty box," as he called it, hired for him by his friend Elwood the Quaker, and in which he (already blind) concluded his 'Paradise Lost,' and drew out his first design of 'Paradise Regained,' still exists a humble, half-timbered cottage, and bears the name of Milton on its front. Chalfont is, little changed, and quite as quiet as in Milton's days.

The *Church,* principally Dec. and Perp., has a fine E. window, and was restored by *Street* in 1863; some frescoes were then discovered over the chancel arch and in the S. aisle, and have been preserved. It contains several *Brasses,* one of them for Thos. Fleetwood, "Lord of the Vache," d. 1570. The ch. also contains the mausoleum of Francis Hare, Bishop of Chichester, once chaplain to the great Duke of Marlborough, whom he accompanied on the fields of Blenheim and Ramillies. He acquired the *Vache* by marriage with the heiress of the Alstons, and died there, 1740. The Vache is said to have been a royal dairy farm in the time of John, and was once a moated residence, with chapel. It belonged to the Fleetwoods in the 16th and 17th cents., but was forfeited by the attainder of the regicide; in it, James Fleetwood, Bishop of Worcester (1675-83), was born in 1602. The house is now modernized (T. N. Allen, Esq). It long remained the property of the Hare family, but in the latter part of the last centy. was occupied by Sir Hugh Palliser, Bart., the rival of Keppel. He died there, March 19, 1796, after great suffering from wounds received in a naval action in 1747.

26 m. *Amersham* (anciently Agmondesham, called Elmodesham in Domesday) (*Inns:* Crown, Griffin), is very pleasantly placed in a wooded valley, and is a chief seat of the beechwood chair making, an industry rather largely carried on in the Chiltern district. (Pop. 3000). At the Conquest it was granted to Geoffrey de Mandeville, having previously belonged to Edith, the queen of Edward the Confessor. From his descendants it passed to the Bohuns, with whom it continued until the attainder of the Duke of Buckingham in the reign of Richard III. Henry VIII. parted with it in 1526 to Sir John Russell, afterwards ennobled as Lord Russell of Chenies, and subsequently Earl of Bedford. Amersham became a borough at an early date, but ceased to send representatives to parliament after the reign of Edward II. Its privilege

was recovered in 1624, mainly by the exertions of John Hampden. Waller the poet, his son Edmund (who became a Quaker), Algernon Sydney, and other men of eminence, have sat for it, but it was disfranchised by the first Reform Bill (1832). Among eminent natives may be mentioned, —beside Waller, born at Coleshill, 1 m. off,—Walter de Agmondesham, Chancellor of England in 1291, John Amersham, monk of St. Albans, c. 1450, who wrote in defence of his bosom friend the Abbot John Wheathamsted; Thomas Dorman, a Romanist, who wrote 'Against Alexander Nowel, the English Calvinist;' and John Gregory, described by Anthony Wood as "the miracle of his age for critical and curious learning," who, persecuted for his loyalty, died in misery at Kidlington, in 1646. (Rte. 24.)

The *Church* is mainly Perp., though there are traces of Dec. work : "the best thing is the groining of the S. porch, which has some rich bosses at the intersection of the ribs" (*W. C.*). It has a fine E. window brought from a private chapel at Lamer, near Hatfield, a seat of the Drake family who have a chantry filled with their monuments, they having long been resident at *Shardeloes*, near the town (*post*). There are several *Brasses* (1430-1623) of the Brudenells, Carbonells, and Drakes; one is to a child, John Drake, aged 4, which has under his kneeling figure the verses—

" Had he lived to be a man,
This inch had grown but to a span;
Now he is past all fear of pain,
'Twere sin to wish him here again.
View but the way by which we come,
Thou'lt say he's best that's first at home."

One of the Drake monuments is by *Scheemaker*, and a modern one, by *Weekes*, to T. T. Drake (1852) is very chaste and beautiful. Two early incumbents of this ch. became prelates: William de Marchia, Bp. of Bath and Wells (1293-1302), whose election is the subject of a remarkable letter preserved among the Public Records (Hardy's 'Le Neve,' vol. i. p. 135); and William Grey, Bp. of Ely (1454–1478), and Lord Treasurer. The register contains the entry of the baptism of Edmund Waller, son of Robert Waller of Coleshill, March 9, 1605–6. A fly-leaf contains a mem. that on Oct. 20, 1656, Paul Ford was elected registrar according to the Parliamentary ordinance of 1653, and was sworn in by Francis Russell, Esq., J.P. To this Benj. Robertshaw, rector in 1731, has appended some uncomplimentary remarks on the Parliamentary party, which was very strong in Buckinghamshire. "This Francis Russell lived at Chalfont St. Giles, on the confines of this parish : he was one of Oliver's justices, and a fit man for ye times. I knew his son, a kind of Non. Con., who came to poverty and sold ye farm. General Fleetwood lived at ye Vache, and Russell on ye opposite hill, and Mrs. Cromwell, Oliver's wife, and her daughters, at Woodrow High House, where afterwards lived Captain James Thomson; so ye whole country was kept in awe, and became exceedingly zealous and very fanatical, nor is ye poison yet eradicated. But ye Whartons are gone, and ye Hampdens agoing." The Duke of Wharton had died abroad in poverty in this very year, and the male line of the Hampdens became extinct in 1754. John Knox preached in this ch. on the 10th July, 1553—during the nominal reign of Lady Jane Grey—and in his sermon he "warned the faithful in England against the approaching retribution for the giddy ways of the past years." Here also Richard Baxter maintained a controversy for a whole day with "certain giddy minds from Chesham," at which several troopers "assisted" — "but whether they took part in the discussion, or were present merely to keep the peace between the bellige-

rent parties, does not very clearly appear" ('Bucks Records,' vol. ii.). In 1413 several Lollards suffered death at Amersham, and in the next century several burnings took place there. "William Tylesworth was burnt at Amersham (1506) (the rendezvous of God's children in those days), and Joan, his only daughter, and a faithful woman, was compelled with her own hands to set fire to her dear father;" and John Scrivener, in 1521, "his own children being forced to set the first fire upon him" (*Fuller*). The scene of these and other martyrdoms was a close near the ch.-yard, called Stanleys, which, according to local tradition, has remained barren ever since, in spite of all attempts to fertilize it ('Gent. Mag.,' Oct., 1811). "On investigation of late years, it was found to be full of flints, which being partially removed, the ground has since become better than heretofore; still, however, in a dry season showing a difference from the surrounding land. Granting the tradition to be true, this spot may have been originally selected for the purpose, as being a piece of waste land, and, from its situation on the hill, visible to the whole town" ('Bucks Records,' vol. ii.).

The woody hamlet of *Coleshill*, 1 m. S., was the birthplace of Waller the poet, who, tradition says, there composed some of his verses under a tree. still known as Waller's Oak. "Towards the decline of life he bought a small house, with a little land, at Coleshill, and said 'he should be glad to die, like the stag, where he was roused.' This, however, did not happen" (*Johnson*). He died and was buried at Beaconsfield, (Rte. 13.)

27 m. on l. *Shardeloes* (T. T. Drake, Esq.), a handsome modern mansion on a hill in a beautiful park. The place is first mentioned, temp. Edward III., as forfeited by Simon de Bereford, an adherent of Queen

Isabella and Mortimer. In the reign of Elizabeth it belonged to William Tothill, who here received Queen Elizabeth, and was presented by her with portraits of herself and her chancellor Sir Christopher Hatton, which are still preserved; there are also some fine landscapes by *Vernet*, &c. This William Tothill had no less than 33 children, through one of whom (the mother of John Drake, *ante*) the estate passed to a gentleman of Surrey, Francis Drake, of Esher, whose descendants still hold it.

[4 m. E. of Amersham (and 4 m. from Rickmansworth Stat.) is *Chenies*, formerly *Isenhampstead*, which obtained its present name from its former possessors, the ancient family of Cheyne. It is one of the prettiest villages in the county, both in itself and its situation on the *Chess*, and shows the influence of a great and wealthy family in its neat cottages, picturesquely grouped around the village green, which has a fountain shaded by elm-trees. The living and much of the adjoining land are the property of the Russells, to whom they came by the marriage of the 1st Earl of Bedford with the heiress of Sapcote. The beautifully restored parish *Church* (Dec. and Perp., with Norm. font) contains 2 remarkable *Brasses*—1. Lady Cheyne (widow of Sir John Cheyne of Drayton Beauchamp), and her second husband, Edmund Molyneux, 1494; 2. her niece and heiress, Anne Phelyp, 1510. The N. chapel has been the burial-place of the Russells since 1556; it is hung with banners, and contains a series of regal-looking tombs, which are like a family portrait-gallery, and are described by H. Walpole as "the house of Russell robed in alabaster and painted." There are 7 monuments in all; one is immense in marble, cherubimed and seraphimed, crusted with bas-reliefs and titles (coats-of-arms) for the 1st Duke of Bedford and his

[*Berks, &c.*]

Duchess." These are seated with looks averted from a medallion of their son Lord Wm. Russell (beheaded in Lincoln's Inn Fields 1683), raised on a pillar between them, and covered by a canopy. On either side between the pillars are medallions of their other children. Among the other monuments are those of John 1st Earl and his Countess Anne Sapcote, through whom he obtained the property; of Francis Earl of Bedford and his Countess, 1585; of their daughter Anne Countess of Warwick and their granddaughter Lady F. Bouchier, erected "by Anne Countess of Dorset, her deare cosen, at her own costes and charges, 1612;" and a white marble monument by Wilton and Chambers to Wriothesley, 2nd Duke of Bedford, and his Duchess, 1711. In the vault beneath are interred more than 50 of the house of Russell; with them lies Rachel, widow of Lord William Russell and author of the Letters, who is buried without a monument.

In this ch. the famous Anne Countess of Dorset was married to Philip Earl of Pembroke in 1630.

Close to the ch. is a most picturesque fragment of the *Manor-house* of the Sapcotes, almost rebuilt by the 1st Lord Russell in the time of Henry VIII. Leland (about 1538) says, "The olde house of the Cheyneis is so translated by Lord Russell, that hath this house on the right of his wife, that little or nothing of it in a manner remaineth untranslated; and a great deal of the house is even newly set up, made of brick and timber, and fair lodgings be new erected in the garden. The house is in divers places richly painted with antique works of white and black" (*Itin.* vol. i.). Here Queen Elizabeth was entertained 1570. Since the migration to Woburn this has been a farm-house, and only one wing of the original quadrangle remains.

The *Monk's Walk*, along the brow

L

of the hill, shaded by elm-trees, is remarkable.

Just across the county border is *Chorleywood*, a village that owes much to the enlightened exertions of the late Mr. Wm. Longman, the publisher (see *Handbook for Herts*).

1½ m. N.W. of Chenies is the hamlet of *Latimer*, with a Perp. ch. rebuilt by *Blore*. *Latimer House*, the seat of Lord Chesham, is, as described by H. Walpole, "finely situated on a hill in a beech wood, with a river at the bottom, and a range of hills and woods at the opposite side." The house, which he laments over as having undergone "Batty-Langley discipline," an Elizabethan red-brick mansion, has been almost entirely rebuilt from designs of *Blore*. The drawing-room is an enlargement of the chamber in which Charles II. slept when he was entertained here by the Countess of Devonshire and her son (then a minor), before his flight to the continent. The house contains some fine family portraits, and a good collection of the old masters, removed hither from Burlington House. Here was born the Hester Sandys mentioned by Fuller as living to see 700 persons descended from herself.

3 m. N. of Amersham is *Chesham*, a rather considerable market town (Pop. 2200), where shoe-making, lace-making, but especially work in beech wood, is largely carried on. (*Inns*: Crown, George.) The country around is very picturesque, and the little river Chess is a famous trout stream. The cruciform ch. is mainly Perp., with central tower and spire; it was restored by *Scott* in 1869, when frescoes of the Last Judgment were discovered. 1 m. S. is *Chesham Bois*, so named from a family of De Bois, settled there in the 13th cent. The ch. is E. E. and Dec., with some modern additions, and some good 14th-centy. glass. There are monuments of the Cheyne family, among

them, John Cheyne, the patron of Hooker, and a curious *Brass* for Benedict Lee, son of Roger Lee, c. 1520, a chrysome child, represented in "the white vesture, commonly called the chrysome," a proof that it died within a month of baptism.]

There will be a station at Chesham on the Rickmansworth and Aylesbury Line.

28¾ m. *Little Missenden*, with a small ch., originally E. E. and Dec., with a lofty square tower.

31 m. *Great Missenden*, a large village in a beautifully wooded valley. The cruciform ch. is Dec. and Perp., and has several brasses.

Great Missenden Abbey (Mrs. Carrington) retains in its cloisters some scanty remains of the flint walls of a religious house founded for Black Canons in 1133.

Just beyond the village a road turns off l. to Hampden and Chequers; but as these places are more easily reached from Prince's Risborough, they are described in Rte. 12.

About 1 m. S.W. of the Abbey is *Honour End Farm*, where a monument, erected 1863, has an inscription, stating that for those lands " John Hampden was assessed 20s. shipmoney, levied by command of the King, without authority of law, 4th August, 1635," &c.

33 m. 1 m. E. is *Lee*, where a small E. E. ch. with several good features has been replaced by a modern brick edifice; a noble yewtree, probably older than the ancient ch., remains.

36 m. *Wendover* (*Inn*: Red Lion) stands in a very picturesque situation, surrounded by hills, from one of which (Combe Hill) St. Paul's, London, can be seen. It forms a capital centre of a very pretty district, and a coach runs every day in summer to London and back through interesting scenery. It was a

royal manor, and was granted by Edward III. to Alice Perrers. The town belonged to the Hampden family, and John Hampden was its representative in Parliament, as was, afterwards, Edmund Burke; it was disfranchised by the Reform Act of 1832. The *Church of St. Mary* is ¼ m. distant from the town, and is reached by a pretty walk along the banks of a stream. " It was to have been placed on a field adjoining the town, and there the building of it was begun; but the materials were all carried away in the night by witches, or, as some relate the tradition, by fairies, and deposited where the ch. now stands. The field where it was to have been built is still called Witchall Meadow." — *Notes and Queries.* It is mainly Dec., and has been restored by *Street.* There is a curious *Brass* for William Bradshawe and wife (1537), with effigies of their 9 children, and the names of 23 grandchildren. Wendover is distant 3 m. from the nearest rly. stat. (Little Kimble), but by means of a navigable cut it is in communication with the Grand Junction Canal; the reservoir is a fine sheet of water. Barkham Down, a little above Wendover, commands an admirable view. *Chequers Park* is 3 m. distant. There will be a station at Wendover on the Rickmansworth and Aylesbury line. Dean Colet, the founder of St. Paul's School, was the son of Sir Henry Colet, Lord Mayor of London, and owner of the *Hall*, near the town, which is now the residence of a gentleman farmer of the same name.

37 m. 1 m. W. *Stoke Mandeville,* with a modern E. E. ch.; the ancient edifice, ¼ m. off still stands, but is disused. Some lands for which John Hampden refused to pay shipmoney were then part of this parish; but of late years they, with portions of other parishes, have been formed

into a new district called *Prestwood,* which has a very pretty small Dec. ch. 1 m. E. is *Weston Turville,* with a handsome Dec. and Perp. ch., restored by *Brandon,* and a rectory house designed by *Scott.* Most of the so-called Aylesbury ducks are reared in this parish.

39 m. AYLESBURY.   (Pop. 7795) *Inns:* George; Crown. The site of the White Hart, formerly the principal inn, is now occupied by a handsome Corn Exchange. Railways to London, by Cheddington (L. & N. W. Rly., Rte. 18) and by Prince's Risborough (G. W. Rly., Rte. 12), and to the N. viâ Verney Junction (Rte. 17). The assizes and quarter sessions are held here now, instead of at Buckingham, and Aylesbury is usually considered the county town. It stands on high ground, an outlying mass of oolite, whilst the *Vale of Aylesbury* owes its fertility to the Kimmeridge clay. This high ground was once occupied by a British stronghold, captured by Cuthwulf of Wessex in 571; here a ch. was afterwards founded, from which the place obtained the name of Aeglesberge, or Church town. The manor of Aylesbury was granted by John to Geoffrey Fitz Piers, Earl of Essex, came afterwards to the Botelers, one of whom founded the Greyfriars monastery (c. 1386), next to Sir W. Boleyn, the grandfather of Queen Anne, and after her to John Pakington. He came to court in the time of Elizabeth, was knighted by her, and greatly favoured; he, however, injured his fortune by his expenses, and suddenly retired, being, as he said, " resolved to feed upon bread and verjuice until he had made up for his extravagance." The queen hearing of this, granted him a forfeited estate in Suffolk of 800*l.* a year; but when he went to take possession, he was so affected by the misery of the dispossessed family, that he refused to accept the gift, and kept to his reso-

L 2

lution of retiring to his own impoverished home. Lloyd ('Worthies,' ii. 504) says of him, "This new star was a nine days' wonder [no doubt for his disinterestedness], engaging all eyes until it set, satisfied with its own glory. He came to court, he said, as Solomon did, to see its vanity; and retired also, as he did, to repent it." He retrieved his fortunes; but his grandson, Sir John, suffered most severely in the Royal cause, being obliged to convey away the manor to Col. Scott, the regicide. This was set aside at the Restoration, and the manor belonged to his descendants until 1802, when it was sold to the Temple family; it is now the property of Acton Tindal, Esq., but most of the old manorial rights have long been parted with. The County Hall and New Corn Exchange form one side of the Market square, which is a fine open space, the old market house, which was built in imitation of the Temple of the Winds at Athens, having been taken down. The White Hart, though externally modernized, had a timber balcony round the courtyard, ornamented with ancient wood carvings brought from Salden House, an old seat of the Fortescues, near Winslow. Straw-plaiting is now carried on rather extensively, but lace-making, once the chief trade, has almost disappeared. A large business is done in agricultural produce, among which Aylesbury ducks, of large size, form an important item.

The *Church of St. Mary* is a fine E. E. cruciform structure (about 1250), with numerous alterations and additions down to the latest Perp. The large W. window is an example of debased Perp., but the doorway leading into the S. transept is a fine specimen of that style. The ch. consists of a nave with N. and S. aisles (to which chapels have been added at a later period); a low tower with fine E. E. triforium,

surmounted by a campanile or clocktower of the age of Charles II.; transepts; and a noble chancel, beautifully restored and filled with stained glass, after designs by *Willement* and *Oliphant.* On the N. of the chancel is the organ chamber, with a sacristy beyond, and a sleeping chamber over it with an ancient fire-place. The sacristy is a very curious chamber, lighted by 2 small lancet-windows; it is fitted up with an oak quadrant wardrobe of 15th centy., with a swinging horse for the vestments, and an aumbry; the door is fastened by an ancient bar-lock, turned by a winch-key from without. On the S. of the chancel are an inner and an outer vestry: the latter of Dec. architecture. Adjoining are 2 Dec. tombs with canopies. The circular Trans.-Norm. *Font* is richly ornamented with sculptured foliage. In the N. transept is a fine monument for Lady Lee, wife of Sir Henry Lee, and daughter of Sir William Paget, first Lord Paget. The figures of the lady and her daughter kneel, and below them are two infants in swaddling clothes: part of the inscription runs thus:

"A knight her freere, Sir Harry Lee behight,
 To whom she bare three impes, which had
   to name,
 John, Henry, Mary, slayn by fortune's
   spight;
 First two being young, which caused their
   parents' moan,
 The third in flower and prime of slender
   yeares:
 All three do rest within this marble stone,
 By which the fickl'ess of worldly joyes
   appears."

In the same transept is the effigy of a knight in armour, of the 14th centy.; it was dug up on the site of the Greyfriars monastery, and is supposed to commemorate James Boteler, Earl of Ormond, who founded that house. The ch. was restored 1848–69 by *Sir G. G. Scott.* During the restoration an ancient Saxon crypt was discovered. It is supposed to form part of the old church in which St. Osyth was buried in the 9th centy.

The *Prebendal House*, adjoining the ch.-yard, is now the private property of the vicar. Being formerly leased for lives, it came by marriage into the possession of John Wilkes, M.P. for Aylesbury, and he often resided there. During his contests with the Government, he had warm supporters and also bitter opponents in the town. He was an *ex officio* trustee of the Grammar School, and one of the latter composed a song, accusing him of peculation in office, and comparing him to the Dragon of Wantley:

"But the Aylesbury men, like fools,
  Thought John Wilkes a greater rarity;
They made him Trustee of the Schools,
  And he swallow'd up the charity."

A short 2 m. from Aylesbury, on the Thame road, is *Hartwell House* (E. D. Lee, Esq.), in the grounds of which stands the parish ch., built in 1756, after the model of the York chapter-house, but with the addition of E. and W. towers, one forming the chancel, the other the vestibule. The house, which has been in the possession of the Lee family since the time of James I., is of great interest, from the museum collected by the late owner (Dr. Lee, d. 1866), as well as from having been the abode (1810–14) of the exiled Louis XVIII. and the Duchess d'Angoulême, the "Child of the Temple," but it is not now shown. The N. or principal front is Jacobean, and there is furniture of the same date. From this front a fine double avenue of trees extends across the park. The grounds have been greatly improved since the late owner's death; but the chief apartments occupied by the Bourbons are kept as they were in his time.

"Hartwell," says Dr. Doran, "is hidden from passers by on the highway by a screen of superb trees, and it was nearly 2 centies. old when the king took possession. If it wanted dignit of elevation, it possessed dignity of breadth. There was an agreeable variety in its several aspects. Of its four faces, directed towards the cardinal points of the compass, one had an ancient and melancholy aspect: the second had a grave Elizabethan [Jacobean] cheerfulness; the third was light, airy, and smiling; and the fourth had a trimmed polished air of modernly invented comfort. The house was strong enough to resist a siege. It had, and has, its porticoes, its porches and its quaint seats. . . . The drawing-room was of royal dimensions and beauty: staircases quaintly noble, with oaken rails and statues; carved ceilings; marble mantelpieces, perplexing those who gazed on them by their abundant allegorical difficulties; and panelled walls whereon the representatives of old valour and ancient loveliness kept their silent state, added to the general effect: altogether, Hartwell was a house wherein misery might be tolerably comfortable upon 24,000*l.* a year. In this and in the out-buildings 140 persons were quartered; the number, including visitors, often exceeding 200." "So numerous a party required such extensive accommodations, that the halls, gallery and the larger apartments were often divided and subdivided into suites of rooms and closets, in some instances to the great disorder and confusion of the mansion. Every out-house, and each of the ornamental buildings in the park, that could be rendered capable of decent shelter, were densely occupied: and it was curious to see how the second and third class stowed themselves away in the attics of the house, converting one room into several by the adaptation of light partitions. On the ledges, and in the bows of the roof,

they formed gardens, which were stocked with plants, shrubs, and flowers."—*Smyth's* '*Ædes* Hartwellianæ.'
Louis XVIII. led a very retired life at Hartwell, but won a large amount of popularity. He was as affable as he was unostentatious: and would enter into conversation even with strangers whom he casually encountered in his rare and brief walks. The library was converted into a court reception-room, the drawing-room being surrendered to the Prince and Princess de Condé, to whom it served both as saloon and dormitory. In the library the King's couch was raised on a daïs. The rooms ordinarily inhabited by him were the study and a small room adjoining. The apartment above the library was that in which the Queen died, and where she lay in state. The dethroned king of Sweden afterwards occupied this room. The apartments of the Duke and Duchess d'Angoulême were at the S.E. angle of the building. It was while seated in the middle window, overlooking the approach to the house (March 25, 1814), that Madame Gonet, one of the court ladies, first caught sight of the carriages which dashed in bearing the joyful news from Bordeaux, and uttered exclamations which disturbed the royal family at their prayers. On leaving England the King made a gift of 100*l.* to the poor of the parish; and, by his especial command, each new French ambassador paid a complimentary visit to Hartwell, and made a formal report of the fact; but the practice was not observed after his decease.

In the room where the queen died are the pictures of Louis XVIII. and the Prince de Condé, sent over by them after the restoration; in the adjoining room of the Archbishop of Toulouse remain his lectern and missal; in the room of Louis XVIII.

is his Prie-Dieu; and in their temporary chapel, the confessional of the royal family. The very bells retain their old names—the King's Room, the Queen's, Archbishop's, Duc de Berry's, d'Angoulême's, Damas', d'Avaray's, &c. Independently of its reminiscences, the chief object of interest in the house itself is the staircase, which is adorned with 24 figures of kings and warriors in oak, standing on the balustrade. A large room in the upper floor is used as a museum, and contains a fine collection of the fossils found in the neighbourhood arranged by Prof. Morris; there are also some Egyptian antiquities, and a good number of MSS. including 13th-centy. Bible and 14th-centy. Missal, both exquisitely written. Among the pictures are two fine portraits, Sir J. Suckling and Wm. Marquis of Newcastle, *Vandyke*; Frederick Prince of Wales, Lady Charlotte Lee, Lady Elizabeth Lee, *Reynolds*; Sir Thomas Lee, *Kneller*; 2 portraits, by *Rembrandt*, of an aged man and woman.

The neighbourhood of Hartwell is very interesting in a geological point of view; it abounds in fossils, especially in ammonites. The fine white sand is remarkably pure and transparent, and is much used for glass for optical purposes.

1 m. beyond Hartwell is *Stone*, where is the Bucks Lunatic Asylum, in digging the foundations for which many Roman remains were discovered. The cruciform *Church* is mainly E. E., but with some remains of Norm. work; the chancel was rebuilt in 1844. A "double-faced" brass in this ch. has been described by Admiral W. H. Smyth (' Records of Bucks,' vol. ii. 173). The font is circular, with rude figures of dragons, and is believed to have belonged to the ch. of Hampstead Norris, Berks (Rte. 8).

1½ m. W. is *Dinton*, with a plain E. E. *Church;* the S. doorway of a

Norm. edifice remains, with a curious sculpture in the tympanum. Two dragons are seen devouring fruit from a tree, and St. Michael appears thrusting the cross down the throat of one of them. According to the Swedish annals, this ch. of Dinton served as the model of the Cathedral of Lund, which an Anglo-Saxon architect, named Donatus, built, c. 1072, for Bishop Egino. Marryat, in his ' One Year in Sweden,' speaks of the close resemblance of the two. In the ch. is buried Simon Mayne, the regicide, who resided in the adjoining Manor-house.

Dinton Hall (Rev. J. J. Goodall) contains some Norm. portions, but was chiefly built temp. Hen. VII. by Archbishop Warham, who resided here. His arms, with those of the king, are to be seen in the stained glass of the Hall window; and the initial W. is frequently repeated in other parts of the house. The stained glass on the staircase is interesting. Among the pictures is a very fine portrait of Oliver Cromwell, who slept at the Hall occasionally during the siege of Oxford. Two of his swords are preserved here, one used at the siege of Drogheda, and the other at Naseby. There existed, till a few years ago, the secret chamber in the roof in which Mayne was concealed for some time, until obliged to surrender from famine. It was under a staircase, and could only be discovered when three of the steps were lifted up, disclosing a trough lined with cloth, up which he could crawl. Mayne had a clerk, named John Bigg, who became celebrated as the *Dinton Hermit*, and who, according to the local tradition, was the person who cut off King Charles's head. He lived in a neighbouring cave, where he died, aged 67, in 1696, by which time his garments had become extraordinary as pieces of patchwork, and his shoes made up of 1000 pieces of leather from con-

stant mending. One of them is still preserved at the Manor-house, the other is in the Ashmolean Museum at Oxford. Other curiosities are—a beautiful Anglo-Saxon glass dug up at Dinton Castle, and a jug with a portrait of Edward IV. upon it. On the same spot some ancient spears were found, one still remaining through the neck of a skeleton.

2 m. beyond Dinton is *Haddenham*, with a fine *Church*, mainly E. E., but with Trans.-Norm. chancel arch, and Perp. E. window. The tower has an arcade figured in the ' Gloss. Architecture,' and there are 2 brasses of priests, 1420, 1428. Edmund of Haddenham, a mediæval chronicler, was a native.

2 m. W of Dinton, on the bank of the Thame, are the remains of *Notley Abbey* (or St. Mary de Parco), founded by William Giffard, Earl of Buckingham, 1162, for Augustine monks from Arras. The remains are now incorporated into a picturesque farm-house, which has a turret at one angle, and some fine Gothic windows. Within, the original broad stone staircase remains, and some of the monastic rooms, with the words "En lui plesa'c" (plesance) constantly repeated in red and black letters upon the cornices. The roof of the hall was removed by the Berties to Chesterton, near Bicester (Rte. 28). The fine cruciform E. E. *Church of Long Crendon*, 1 m. W., has one of the bells from Notley, inscribed "In multis annis resonat campana Johannis." The Perp. font rests upon lions. There is a very fine monument of Sir John and Lady Dormer, 1605 (kept in repair by a charity founded by him), and *Brasses* of John and Agnes Canon, 1460, 68.

3 m. W. is *Worminghall*, with a small plain *Church*, partly rebuilt in 1847. It contains a curious *Brass* of Philip King and his family, 1592. "Wormenhall gave the Church 2

Bishops (John King Bp. of London, and Henry King Bp. of Chichester), who were born in the same house and in the same room."—*Fuller.* Dr. Rob. King, another member of this family, was the last Abbot of Oseney and first Bp. of Oxford.

ROUTE 15.

AYLESBURY TO BUCKINGHAM.

L. and N.-W. Rly.   16½ m.

Leaving Aylesbury by the G. W. stat., the line traverses rich pastures, agreeing with the description in Drayton's 'Polyolbion':

"Aylesbury's vale that walloweth in her wealth,
And (by her wholesome air continually in health)
Is lusty, firm, and fat; and holds her youthful strength."

Fuller speaks of one pasture called Berryfield, in the manor of Quarrendon, which let yearly for 800*l.*—equal to 8000*l.* at present.

2 m. E. 1 m., in a marshy meadow, is the ruin of *Quarrendon Chapel,* now reduced to a few roofless arches, and the remains of a beautiful Dec. E. window : it contained the fine monuments of the Lee family, including that of Sir Henry Lee and his mistress Ann Vavasour, whose tomb bore the inscription—

" Underneath this stone entombed lies a fair and worthy dame,
Daughter to Henry Vavasour, Ann Vavasour her name.
She living with Sir Henry Lee, for love long time did dwell;
Death could not part them, but here they rest within one cell."

She shared the fate of Fair Rosamond at Godstow, and was disentombed and turned out by the bishop of the diocese. This was the Sir Henry Lee of Elizabeth's time, who lived in the great mansion of the Lees at Quarrendon (now entirely destroyed); but was confounded by Sir W. Scott with a 2nd Sir H. Lee of Charles I., and introduced by him into the novel of 'Woodstock.' He received a visit of 2 days from Elizabeth at Quarrendon, and afterwards lived to a great age, in retirement, at Lee's Rest, but was at length so pleased by a visit from James I., who presented a ring to Mrs. Vavasour, that he was induced to go again to court, and died from the exertion. At Quarrendon were born the Saxon saints Edburg and Eaditha, daughters of Frewald, lord of the country. Edburg gave her name to Adderbury, Ellesborough, and to the Burg, afterwards Burgfield, at Quarrendon. They were first buried at Aylesbury, but Edburg was afterwards removed to Edburgton in Suffolk. Cressy's 'Church History' mentions 7 English saints of this name. St. Osyth was her niece, and was abbess of Chich in Essex, but was beheaded here by Inguar and Hubba, 2 Danish pirates, and was buried at Aylesbury. She was familiarly called St. Sythe, and was much revered. "In those dayes when they went to bed they did rake up the fire and make a + in the ashes, and pray to God and St. Sythe to deliver them from fire and from water and from all misadventure." —*Aubrey,* 113.

6 m. *Quainton-road* (Stat.). The restored Dec. and Perp. ch. of *Quainton,* 1 m. N.E., has a screen with 8 coloured figures of saints, and several good *Brasses*— Joan Plessi, 1360, John Lewys, 1422, and John Spence, 1485, both priests, and Lady Verney, 1509. In the chancel are the monuments of the Dormers; a

fine one of Judge Dormer, who died of grief 1726, for the death of his only son. The death-bed of the son, Fleetwood Dormer, is represented on the tomb, with the parents in agonies of grief. The Winwood aisle contains the altar-tomb of Richard Winwood, son of Sir Ralph, Charles I.'s secretary (who founded the almshouses close by). On the Green are the remains of an ancient stone cross.

In this parish is *Doddershall Hall* (Mrs. Pigott), an interesting house, built 1639, containing much old furniture and carving. The stone hall and the library have curious oak cornices decorated with monsters. "The Brown Hall" is oak, and has a remarkable recess for the fireplace. Among the portraits is one believed to be Christobella, Lady Saye and Sele, who lived here, and founded a school. She boasted that she had married her first husband for love, her second for riches, and her third for honour. Some verses written in her praise with a diamond, by Pope, long remained on one of the windows of the house.

Almost adjoining Whitchurch, E., are *Creslow Pastures*, from the time of Elizabeth to Charles II. feeding-grounds for cattle destined for the royal tables. They are still of extra-ordinary fertility; and one of them, "the great pasture," contains 327 acres. The original name was Christ Low or Christ's Meadow; one of the largest pastures is still called Heaven's Low.

The *Manor-house* (now a farm-house) is a very picturesque and remarkable building; "the original parts, Edward III., including the crypt and tower; alterations 15th centy., of which period a pointed doorway remains: great alterations temp. Charles I., of which plaster ceilings and square windows remain." In 1120 the manor was given to the Knights Templars, from whom it passed to the Knights of St. John, who had the privilege of giving rites of sepulture when the rest of the kingdom was under interdict, so that many illustrious persons were probably buried in the chapel. After their dissolution it remained among the crown demesnes till 1673. In 1653 it was granted to Cornelius Holland the regicide, called by Browne Willis "a miscreant upstart," and said by him to have been born in a neighbouring cottage. At the Restoration, when he was attainted for high treason, it reverted to the Crown, and in 1662 was leased to Sir T. Clifford, to whose successor, Lord Clifford, it was conveyed in 1673.

At the W. corner of the house is an octagonal turret with walls 6 ft. thick. Beneath is a crypt with a beautifully groined ceiling cut in the solid rock. Near it is another called "the Dungeon," without windows, and with a massive stone roof. From these crypts a subterranean passage is reported to lead to the great pasture. Several of the rooms have beautiful Gothic details. In the hall are stucco ornaments (including the Tudor rose and fleur-de-lis), said to have been placed there by order of Elizabeth when the house was preparing for one of her progresses. One of the rooms has its ghost, in a silk dress, supposed to be that of Rosamond Clifford.

Close to the house are the picturesque remains of the chapel desecrated by Cornelius Holland, and now used as stables. The N. wall retains its beautiful Trans.-Norm. doorway.

3 m. E. is *Hardwick*, with a good E. E. ch., restored by *Street* in 1872-73. In the churchyard is a monument recording the burial of 247 men killed in the battle of Aylesbury, March 21, 1643. Many fossil remains of saurians have been found

in this parish. In the adjoining hamlet of Weedon is *Lilies* (Henry Cazenove, Esq.), a house standing in a very sequestered spot amid thick woods. It is built on the site of an ancient nunnery, whose ch. occupied the position of the present kitchen garden. This was the property of the late Lord Nugent, who wrote the 'Legends of Lilies.'

1 m. N. is *Whitchurch*. The fine E. E. ch. has a lofty embattled tower and Dec. chancel, with sedilia and piscina, and rich screen-work. There are some slight traces of the castle of the Bolebecs.

Passing the restored E. E. ch. of *Oving*, we reach, at 2 m. N. W. of Whitchurch, *North Marston*, where the very fine *Church* is E. E. and Dec.; the chancel, however, is rich Perp., with oak stalls and panelling. The S. aisle is Dec., and contains a piscina, a window with a niche on each side, and a squint, all profusely decorated with the four-leaved flower. The E. window and reredos were erected by the Queen to the memory of John Camden Neild, Esq., who died 1852, leaving his immense fortune, about 250,000l., to her. Near them are the *Brasses* of R. Sanders, 1602, and Elizabeth Sanders, 1613, with quaint inscriptions.

Tradition tells that the chancel was built out of offerings at the tomb of a devout rector (in 1290), Sir John Shorne, who was revered as a saint after his death, and the place became populous in consequence of pilgrimages to a well which was blessed by him. Browne Willis mentions people who remembered a sign which pointed the way "to Sir John Shorne's shrine." *Bp. Latimer*, in one of his sermons, says, " I have to tell you of the Christian man's pilgrimage, but ye shall not think that I will speak of the Popish pilgrimage, in running hither and thither, to Mr. John Shorne, or to our Lady of Walsingham." *Foxe*, in speaking of the

punishments of Protestants in Bucks, says that " some were compelled to make pilgrimages to Sir John Shorne;" also, that some were forced by the officials to bear witness against the Vicar of Wycombe, because, when he met " certain coming from Sir J. Shorne, he said they were fools, and called it idolatrous." This sainted person was especially invoked for the ague. " If we were sycke of the pestilence we ran to Sainte Rooke; if of the ague, to Sainte Pernel or Master John Shorne."—*Michael Wood*. Many miracles were attributed to him, but his chief feat was long commemorated in the E. window of the ch. and on the wall of the Holy Well, which showed how—

" Master John Shorne,
   Gentleman born,
   Conjured the Devil into a boot."

It is also alluded to in the 'Fantaisie of Idolatrie,' quoted by Foxe:—

" To Maister John Shorne,
   That blessed man born,
      For the ague to him we apply,
   Which he jugeleth with a bote;
   I beshrowe his herte rote
      That will trust him, and it be L."

An upper chamber still remains attached to the ch., with a fire-place, and aperture into the chancel, supposed to have been for the priest watching at the shrine. In 1478 Richard Beauchamp, Dean of Windsor, obtained licence from Pope Sixtus IV. to remove the shrine to Windsor, where he placed it in the Lincoln Chapel, whose windows long portrayed the history of the saint and of his squeezing the Devil into the boot. Sir John is represented on the roodscreens of Cawston, Gateley and Suffield (Norfolk), and Sudbury (Suffolk), crowned with a nimbus. He probably had his name from the village of Shorne near Rochester. There was also an image of him at Canterbury, alluded to in a poem of the 16th centy., by John Heywood.

> " I am a palmer, as you see,
> Which of my life I much have spent
>
> . . . . . .
> At Saint Davies, and at Saint Denice,
> At Saint Matthew, and at Saint Mark in Venice,
> At Maister John Shorne in Canterbury."

At the bottom of the village is " Sir John Shorne's Well," which never fails all the year round. Like the well at Otford (*Handbook for Kent*) it is said to have been supplied by the sainted rector, who struck his staff into the ground on that spot, in answer to the prayers of his congregation in a time of drought.

9½ m. *Granborough - road* (Stat.). Granborough Ch. is good Perp., with square tower. 2 m. E. is *Hogston,* where the E. E. and Dec. ch. has some good windows, but the chancel is modern and bad, and the small square tower is of wood. There are some memorials of the family of Mayne, and a mutilated 14th-centy. effigy, which holds a ch. in its hand; it is supposed to represent William de Bermingham, the founder of a chantry here, 1342.

10½ m. *Winslow-road Stat.* Winslow has also a stat. on the Bletchley and Oxford line, where it will be found described (Rte. 17).

11½ m. *Verney Junction Stat.* (Rte. 17).

13 m. 1 m. E. is *Adstock,* where the Dec. and Perp. ch., dedicated to St. Cecilia, has a very early Norm. doorway; and a good E. E. chancel-arch, supported on corbel heads. It was restored in 1875.

15 m. *Padbury* (stat.). The village, a short distance E. of the line, has a Dec. and Perp. ch., with modern tower and porch. This place was, in July 1643, the scene of "a handsome smart conflict between a party of 500 horse and dragoons, commanded by Colonel Middleton, on the Parliament party, and a regiment of horse, commanded by Sir

Charles Lucas, on the King's; where, after a very soldierly contest, and more blood drawn than was usual upon such actions, the king's party prevailed, returning with some prisoners of name, and the slaughter of 100 of their enemy, not without some loss of their own " (*Clarendon*). The Earl of Essex on this retired as far as Uxbridge, " giving over any thought of fighting with the king, till he should be recruited with horse, men, and money; and suffering in the talk of the people " (*Ibid*).

16½ m. Buckingham. (*Inn:* White Hart). Rly. to Banbury, but the road is 6 m. shorter. The town (Pop. 3585) stands on rather high ground almost encircled by the river Ouse, which is crossed by 3 bridges. Though a very ancient place it has few remains of antiquity, having suffered greatly from a fire in 1724. It was fortified by Edward the Elder in 918, and soon after the Conquest had a strong castle built by Walter Giffard, the first Norman Earl of Buckingham. In the time of Edward III. it was one of the staples for wool, and it is still considered the county town, though the assizes have been removed, and it is inferior in population and trade to Aylesbury. The old ch., having been greatly damaged by the fall of its lofty spire, was pulled down in 1777, and a new ch. built at a short distance on the old castle mound. This *Church,* which has been justly esteemed one of the most unsightly in England, although expensively decorated in its Grecian interior, has been almost rebuilt by *Sir G. G. Scott,* a native of Gawcott, a hamlet of this town. The greater part is now pure E. E., with a fine E. window of 5 lights, and a rich S. porch; but much of the N. side and the W. front remain in their original ugliness. No burials have ever been allowed in the churchyard, which is surrounded by a broad shady walk, and from its elevated position commands extensive views. The original churchyard also is ornamentally planted, and in it is preserved the stump of the old market cross. It is of Dec. architecture, and serves to mark the site of the W. door of the ch. In this ch. when it was pulled down was discovered the coffin of St. Rumbald, of whom the legend is, that he lived only 3 days, during which time he discoursed largely, says Fuller, "of all the commonplaces of popery;" was baptised and bequeathed his body to King's Sutton, his birthplace, for 1 year; to Brackley for 2 years; and then to Buckingham for ever. He was also much reverenced in Kent, his chief shrine being at Boxley, where there was an image of St. Rumbald, which was pretended to be "a touchstone of chastity," only to be lifted by those who had never sinned in thought or deed (*Handbook for Kent*). The few public buildings of Buckingham are not remarkable for beauty. The Town-hall is of brick, with the crest of the Temples (a swan ducally gorged) for a vane, and in the market-place is the borough gaol, built by Lord Cobham in 1748, in imitation of a Norman castle. In the butcher market is the *Grammar School*, endowed by Edward VI. with the revenues of a chantry founded by Matthew de Stratton, Archdeacon of Bucks, t. Henry III.; some portions remain, with Dec. and Perp. windows, and the entrance to the inclosure is by a Norm. door, the relic of some still earlier foundation. A good house, called *Lamberts*, built 1611, occupies the site of a mansion in which Katharine of Aragon once sojourned. During the civil war Lamberts was occupied by Prince Rupert, and here also Charles I. was entertained in 1644. The old Vicarage-house, with its remarkable twisted chimneys (1611), is the successor to the mansion in which Queen Elizabeth

dined in August, 1568, when on her way to Bicester.

At a very short distance from Buckingham, on the Brackley road, is the commencement of the noble avenue of elms leading to *Stowe*, the princely seat of the Duke of Buckingham. The avenue, which is nearly 2 miles in length, affords a most agreeable ride or walk, a well-kept footpath running along its E. side. Passing over 3 or 4 gentle swelling hills, you reach the simple, but stately *Corinthian Arch*, 60 ft. high, designed by Thos. Pitt, Lord Camelford. From this point the house is well seen, consisting of a centre faced with a portico, flanked by 2 wings, the total length of the façade being 916 ft.

The art treasures that made Stowe so famous have long been dispersed, but the house is again occupied. Neither the house nor pleasure-grounds, however, are shown to the public.

The *Gardens* of Stowe were perhaps the finest example of landscape gardening in this country. They were originally laid out by Sir Rich. Temple, Viscount Cobham, the friend of Pope, who thus alludes to them in the Moral Essays:

"Still follow sense, of every part the soul;
Parts, answering parts, shall slide into a
  whole;

Spontaneous beauties all around advance:
Start even from difficulty, strike from
  chance;
Nature shall join you, Time shall make it
  grow
A work to wonder at—perhaps a Stowe."

" In the grounds of Stowe, Thomson drew fresh inspiration for his amended ' Seasons' :

"O lead me to the wide-extended walks
And fair majestic paradise of Stowe!
Not Persian Cyrus on Ionia's shores
E'er saw such sylvan scenes; such various
  art
By genius fired, such ard· nt genius tamed
By cool, judicious art; that in the strife
All-beauteous Nature fears to be outdone."

"In these 'Elysian Vales' the great Lord Chatham when a young man acquired his early love of liberty; here Capability Brown filled the office of kitchen-gardener, and caught that taste for landscape-gardening of which he has left so many memorable examples; here Congreve and Vanbrugh were frequent visitors; here Pope delighted to think down hours to moments; and here Horace Walpole occasionally stayed on state occasions."

These pleasure-grounds have an extent of not less than 700 acres. On entering you are first struck by the broad expanse of a lake—

" The vast parterres a thousand hands shall make—
Lo! Cobham comes, and floats them with a lake!'"

beyond which appears the house: while amidst the graceful foliage of trees of noble growth, and many varieties of species, peer forth various ornamental buildings and temples. The most remarkable of these are the Temple of Ancient Virtue, surrounded by a circular colonnade, containing statues by *Scheemaker* of Socrates, Homer, Lycurgus, and Epaminondas, with Latin inscriptions by George Lord Lyttelton. Near it rises a cedar-tree, 22 ft. in girth; the rostral column to Capt. Grenville, who fell in a sea-fight against the French, under Lord Anson, 1747.

The monument to Capt. Cook is in the Temple of British Worthies, situated at a point surnamed the Elysian Fields, watered by a dark pool called the river Styx. "The *Temple of Venus* at Stowe," says Walpole, "has simplicity and merit." It is by *Kent.* The *Queen's Temple,* in honour of Queen Charlotte, 1789, contains a Roman tesselated pavement, found at Foxcote near Buckingham in 1844. The Gothic temples command a fine view. There are also a column, 115 ft.

high, surmounted by a statue of Lord Cobham; a grotto; and one or two small cascades. The *Palladian Bridge,* resembling that at Wilton, is a fine architectural structure, with a roof supported by a colonnade. The *Temple of Friendship* was erected by Lord Cobham to receive the busts of his political friends (all sold in 1849). Before the temple was finished the party was entirely broken up. H. Walpole says, "In the Temple of Friendship, among 20 memorandums of quarrels, is the bust of Mr. Pitt. Mr. James Greville is now in the House, whom his uncle disinherited for attachment to that very Pylades. He broke with Mr. Pope, who is deified in the Elysian Fields, before the inscription for his head was finished. That of Sir John Barnard, which was bespoke by the name of a bust of my Lord Mayor, was, by a mistake of the sculptor, done from Alderman Perry. I have no patience at building and planting a satire."—(1753.)

The *Gothic Temple* is somewhat of carpenter's Gothic, though be-praised by Horace Walpole. "In the heretical corner of my heart I adore the Gothic building, which by some unusual inspiration Gibbs has made pure, beautiful and venerable. The style has a propensity to the Venetian or Mosque Gothic, and the great column near makes the whole put one in mind of St. Mark's at Venice! The windows are throughout consecrated with painted glass, most of it from the Priory at Warwick."

The *Bourbon Tower* is surrounded by trees planted by Louis XVIII. and the exiled French princes on a visit to Stowe 1808. In front of the *Temple of Concord and Victory* (erected to record the glories of the Seven Years' War, by Lord Cobham) young oaks were planted by Queen Victoria, during her visit to Stowe, January, 1845, and 2 cedars by Prince Albert. "There is a charm-

ing flower - garden, thickly surrounded by high trees, firs, cedars,
evergreens, and flowering shrubs."
  "At Stowe," it has been remarked,
"every acre brings to one's mind
some instances of the parts or, pe-
dantry, of the taste or want of taste,
of the ambition or love of fame, of
greatness or miscarriage, of those
who have inhabited, decorated,
planned or visited the place—Pope,
Congreve, Vanbrugh, Kent, Gibbs,
Lord Cobham, Lord Chesterfield,
the mob of nephews, the Lytteltons,
Grenvilles, Wests, Leonidas Glover,
Wilkes, the late Prince of Wales,
the King of Denmark, Princess
Amelia ; and the profound monuments of Lord Chatham's services,
now enshrined there, then anathe-
matized there, and now again commanding there ; with the Temple
of Friendship like the Temple of
Janus, sometimes open to war and
sometimes shut up in factious cabals ;
all these images crowd upon one's
memory, and add visionary personages to the charming scenes, that
are so enriched with fanes and temples that the real prospects are little
less than visions themselves."
  Horace Walpole gives an amusing
account of the visit of the Princess
Amelia to Stowe :—" We all of us,
giddy young creatures of near three-
score, supped in a grotto in the
Elysian Fields, and were refreshed
with rivers of dew and gentle
showers that dripped from all the
trees, and put us in mind of the
heroic ages when kings and queens
were shepherds and shepherdesses,
and lived in caves, and were wet to
the skin two or three times a day."
Again, " On Wednesday night a
small Vauxhall was acted for us in
the grotto in the Elysian Fields,
which was illuminated, as were the
thickets and two little barks on the
lake. The idea was pretty ; but as
my feelings have lost something of
their romantic sensibility, I did not
quite enjoy such an entertainment

al fresco as I should have done 20
years ago. The evening was more
than cool, and the destined spot
anything but dry. There were not
half lamps enough, and no music ·
but an old militia-man who played
cruelly on a kind of tabor and pipe.
As our procession descended the
vast flight of steps into the garden
in which was assembled a crowd of
people from Buckingham and the
neighbouring villages to see the
Princess and the show, the moon
shining very bright, I could not
help laughing as I surveyed the
troop, which, instead of tripping
lightly to such an Arcadian entertainment, were hobbling down by the
balustrade, wrapped up in greatcoats
and cloaks for fear of catching cold."
—*W. to G. Montagu,* July 7, 1770.
  The famous sale of the Art-
Treasures at Stowe (Aug. 1848), by
Messrs. Christie and Manson, which
occupied above 30 days, was perhaps
the most remarkable sale of a private collection ever known, far superior even to those of Fonthill and
Strawberry Hill ; things having retained a fanciful value ever since
merely from the fact of having been
bought here. It was especially rich
in magnificent Sèvres and Majolica
ware. Among the most interesting
objects sold, were the inkstand of
Sixtus V. ; the travelling organ of
James II., which had afterwards
belonged to the Duke of Wharton ;
a table given by Villiers Duke of
Buckingham to the Countess of
Shrewsbury ; the famous Chandos
portrait of Shakspeare ; a celebrated
miniature of Charles II., by *Cooper ;*
Queen Anne's toilette glass ; ivory
chairs of Tippoo Saib, given by
Warren Hastings to Queen Charlotte ; and the statue of the marine
Venus from the baths of Agrippa.
  At *Luffield,* on the N. of Stowe
Park, were the ruins of a Benedic-
tine Abbey, founded 1124, now
destroyed.
  Within the distance of 5 miles

from Buckingham, the tourist will find several interesting *Churches*. On the S. are—

(a) 1 m. W. *Tingewick*, E. E. and Perp. Notice on the chancel wall a very curious *Brass* of Erasmus Williams, rector, 1608. He is surrounded by his musical, astronomical and geometrical instruments, with a facetious epitaph. Roman foundations and other antiquities were discovered here in 1860–62.

(b) 2 m. S. of Tingewick, *Chetwode*, the ch. of an Augustinian priory founded here 1244; chancel very fine E.E., with some old stainedglass, the E. window composed of 5 lancets.

(c) 1 m. E. of Chetwode, *Preston Bisset*, a fine Dec. ch. with very excellent 2 and 3 light windows, doorways with fine mouldings and corbel heads, and good Dec. sedilia.

(d) 2 m. E. of Preston Bisset, *Hillesden*, very fine Perp. though late (c. 1493); the S. porch particularly good, with panelling on the side walls and groined ceiling. From an attentive study of this ch. Sir. G. Scott, who was born at Gawcott, a neighbouring village, derived some of his knowledge of Gothic architecture. " It is to myself peculiarly dear," he writes, " as having been the delight of my youth, and its study led me to devote my life to the art of which it is so charming an example." The church was very carefully réstored by Sir G. Scott shortly before his death. Close to the E. end of the ch. stood the manor-house of the Denton family, purchased and pulled down by the late Duke of Buckingham.

(e) 1¼ m. S. of Hillesden is *Twyford*, which though rebuilt, is of interest for its *Brasses* (John Everdon, rector, 1413; Thos. Giffard, 1550): there is also a cross-legged effigy in armour, supposed to be Sir John Giffard, t. Henry III. The ch. was thoroughly restored by *Scott* in 1875 at a cost of 2200*l*. The E. window illustrates the legend of S. Nicholas, and is one of the best of

its kind in the country. It contains 45 figures in the eight compartments of which it is composed. On the N. are—

(f) 2 m. E. *Maidsmorton Church*, a very beautiful specimen of Perp., founded, according to a tablet in the interior, by "sisters and maids, daughters to Lord Pruet," 1450. Hence the name. The tower windows are enriched with arrow-headed cusps; the N. porch has a fan-tracery vault; the W. door is very curious, " a projecting panelled battlement supported by rich fan-tracery, springing from the jamb mouldings." (*P.*). The font, the Gothic screen, the roof of chancel with remains of colour, and 3 sedilia, with a painting of the Last Supper, deserve notice.

On a marble monument in memory of Mrs. Penelope Verney, first wife of Lord Willoughby de Brooke, dated Aug. 31st, 1718, the following inscription may be read:

" Under this stone doth lye,
As much virtue as could die,
Which, when alive, did vigor give
To as much beauty as could live."

(g) 2 m. S. E. of Maidsmorton, *Thornborough*, mainly Perp., with good Dec. W. door. In this parish is a large barrow, opened in 1839, when some bronze and gold relics of Roman origin were discovered.

(h) 3 m. W. of Buckingham, *Water Stratford*. The ch., E. E. and Perp., has 2 Norm. doorways, each with sculpture in the tympanum. At this place lived (1674–93) an enthusiast named John Mason, who persuaded multitudes that he was the Elias sent to proclaim the second advent of Christ. His followers continued to exist till 1740, and so firmly believed in his resurrection, that it was found necessary to open his grave and expose his body to public view.

(i) 5 m. N. E. of Buckingham is *Lillingstone Dayrell*, fine E. E., restored by *Street* in 1878, and containing some brasses.

ROUTE 16.

AYLESBURY TO BICESTER.

By Road. 16 m.

- This route is nearly in the line of the ancient Akeman Street.

3 m. *Fleet Marston*, a small Dec. and Perp. ch.

5½ m. *Waddesdon.* The ch. of St. Michael is mainly E. E., but the clerestory is Perp. It was restored in 1877-8. There is a remarkable *Brass* for Hugh Brystowe, parson, 1548, who is represented in his shroud; also the tomb of one of the Carletons, (1608). A *Church* (St. Mary, Westcott) was erected in 1867, from designs by Mr. G. E. Street, at the sole charge of the Duke of Buckingham.

Lodge Hill (built 1880) is one of the seats of Baron Ferdinand de Rothschild, who is lord of the manor. The tramway connecting Wootton with Quainton passes through this parish, and there are stations at Waddesdon Road and Westcott.

Eythorpe, in the parish of Waddesdon, was the old manor of the Dormers. The curious old house was destroyed 1810. Only some of the offices remain.

[2 m. S. is *Over* or *Upper Winchendon*, a late Norm. ch., with massive Perp. tower, having a pointed-roof turret at the S.E. angle. There is a somewhat remarkable *Brass* for John Stodely, vicar (d. 1515), who is represented in the dress of an Austin canon of St. Frideswide's, a black cassock, with white metal inlaid to represent the rochet. Over *Winchendon House* was the residence of the Marquis of Wharton (who is buried in the ch.) and his son, the

too-famous Duke, who also bore the title of Marquis of Winchendon :

> "Wharton, the scorn and wonder of our days,
> Whose ruling passion was the lust of praise;
> Born with whate'er could win it from the wise,
> Women and fools must like him, or he dies." 　　*Pope.*

The house and its splendid gardens were destroyed, 1760, by Charles, 2nd Duke of Marlborough.

2 m. S. is *Lower Winchendon.* The ch. is Dec. but with good Perp. windows inserted, and contains two 16th-centy. *Brasses*. *Winchendon Priory* (Sir T. T. Bernard,) was built by Sir John Dauncy, temp. Hen. VIII., from the materials of the monastery. It contains some old pictures; among them a very curious one of Lady Wharton and her sons. One small panelled room is inscribed with texts of Scripture.

3 m. W. is *Chilton*, the birthplace of Sir George Croke, the judge who dissented from the judgment in favour of ship-money. The ch. contains the tomb of Sir J. Croke, 1608, and his wife; his figure in plate-armour, their children kneeling in front. *Chilton House* (Augustus Campbell, Esq.) has an embattled porch, with the motto of the Crokes, "Jehovah turris mea."

Ashendon, 3 m. N. of Chilton, has a Dec. and Perp. ch. In the chancel is a cross-legged effigy in chain-mail, placed in a niche, which was probably intended for the Easter sepulchre. This place is sometimes taken to be the scene of a battle between Edmund Ironside and Canute, in which Eadnoth, the bishop of Dorchester, was slain, but this is certainly an error.

1 m. S.W. of Ashendon is *Dorton*, the ch. of which is of no interest. *Dorton House* (C. Aubrey Aubrey Esq.), a picturesque edifice, was built by Sir John Dormer, early in the 17th centy., but was partially modernized by Sir John Aubrey in 1784. The arms of the Dormers may be seen

in the pavement of a room, said once to have been the chapel. Dorton has a chalybeate spring, once of much celebrity.

2 m. W. of Dorton is *Brill*, placed on an eminence in the ancient Bernwood Forest, on the borders of Oxfordshire and Bucks, commanding fine views. Here Edward the Confessor had a hunting-lodge, and here Henry II. kept his court in 1160 (when Becket attended him as Chancellor) and 1162, John in 1205, and Henry III. in 1224.

In Nov. 1642 Charles I. placed troops here under Sir G. Gerard, who repulsed a Parliamentarian attack under John Hampden. The Earl of Essex, writing to the Speaker, April 24, 1643, says, " The King is concentrating his forces, P. Maurice is arrived, and P. Rupert hourly expected at Brill." When Reading was reduced, this garrison was withdrawn.

Brill pottery has been made from the soil of the hill even from Roman times, but the trade is no longer flourishing. The grove of trees near the village may be a relic of Bernwood Forest.

2. m. W. at the foot of the hill (and within an easy drive of Oxford) lie the picturesque remains of *Boarstall Tower*, so named from a boar which interrupted the sport of the Confessor, and was slain here by one Nigel, who received the manor as a reward on tenure of a horn, which still exists in the possession of the present owner. The Perp. gatehouse still remains, and is moated, with battlements and chimneys, and doors set with iron plates and studs; it is now a farm-house. Near it is the ch., a modern structure, built with the materials of the former edifice; it contains some monuments of the Aubreys, long lords of the manor, connected with one of whom is a melancholy story, which adds to the interest of the place.

[*Berks, &c.*]

This was an important post, during the Civil Wars, between Aylesbury and Oxford. In 1644 it was taken for the King by Colonel Gage, who battered it from the ch., when the Lady of Boarstall, Lady Denham, escaped in disguise by a secret passage.

The garrison left here did much good service, " not only in defending Oxford from mischievous incursions, but did very near support itself by the contributions it drew from Bucks, besides the prey it frequently took from the very neighbourhood of Aylesbury." — *Clarendon.* In 1645 Fairfax was beaten off in an attempt to take " this poor house, with loss, and very little to his honour." Lipscomb ('Hist. Bucks') gives the curious correspondence relative to the siege, and a picture of the house in 1695.

2 m. N. of Brill is *Wootton Underwood*, with a Dec. ch. restored and enlarged in 1873, and so completely modernised as to have little interest; it contains a 14th-centy. chapel of the Grenvilles, and a 16th-centy. *Brass* of the same family.

Wootton House (Duke of Buckingham) stands in a very extensive park ; it replaces a former mansion with a famous staircase by Sir *J. Thornhill*, burnt in 1820.

2 m. N.W. of Wootton is *Ludgershall*, where the ch. has some finely carved E. E. capitals, though the body of the building is Dec. and Perp. The *Brass* of Anne English, her daughter and granddaughter (1565), is curious. According to village tradition this was a retreat selected by Henry II. for Fair Rosamond, who is still commemorated by a lane in the woods called " Rosamond's Way."]

10 m. N. 1 m. is the village called *Grendon-under-Bernwood*, or *Grendon Underwood*, in ancient records, but commemorated in popular rhyme as

" Grendon Underwood,
The dirtiest town that ever stood."

M

Aubrey declares that Shakespeare picked up some of the humour in his 'Midsummer-Night's Dream' from the constable, when passing a night here on his way to London. The Dec. and Perp. ch. contains some monuments of the Pigott family; members of which have occupied a house in the village for several centuries. The present occupant has restored a papelled room in it, in which it is said that Shakespeare wrote the 'Midsummer - Nights Dream,' and 'Much Ado About Nothing.'

12 m. The road enters Oxfordshire, 4 m. short of Bicester (Rte. 28).

ROUTE 17.

BLETCHLEY TO BICESTER.

Bletchley Branch, L. and N.-W. Rly. 19½ m.

Leaving on N. the village of Bletchley (Rte. 18), we see at 2 m., on S., *Newton Longueville*, so called from a priory which once existed there, a cell of the Abbey of St. Faith at Longueville in Normandy. There is a statue of St. Faith on the E. end of the ch., originally E. E., but almost rebuilt by New College, Oxford, in 1442, on occasion of receiving the gift of the living from Henry VI.

On N., 1½ m. distant, is *Tattenhoe*, where a small poor ch. was built in

1540 from the materials of Snelshall Priory. Soon after its erection, it was allowed to fall into ruin, but was reconstructed and reconsecrated in 1636 by the activity of Bp. Bancroft, of Oxford. It stands in a very secluded spot, on a moated site, and is seldom visited, though worth notice. 2 m. N.W. is *Whaddon*, with a ch. originally Trans.-Norm., having Perp. windows inserted, restored in 1854, when some remarkable mural paintings were discovered, one of them representing the Martyrdom of S. Thomas à Becket. There is a *Brass* (Thos. Pygott, 1519), which affords a good illustration of the costume of the serjeants-at-law temp. Hen. VIII. The adjoining district, called *Whaddon Chase*, was part of the dower of Queen Jane Seymour. The Manorhouse was the seat of Arthur Lord Grey, who here received a visit from Queen Elizabeth. It has been replaced by *Whaddon Hall* (W. Selby Lowndes, Esq.), a stately mansion, famed for its magnificent staircase, and for the large number of deer kept in its park. Browne Willis, the antiquary, was once the possessor of this property. Whaddon was the birthplace (1499) of Richard Cox, afterwards Bp. of Ely, to whom Elizabeth addressed a discreditable letter, threatening to " unfrock him " unless he surrendered some manors of his see to one of her courtiers. In 1849 a large number of ancient British gold coins were discovered in Whaddon.

5¼ m. *Swanbourne* (Stat.) The E. E. and Perp. ch. has a *Brass*, commemorating, in verse, the fate of one Thos. Adams, yeoman and freeman of London (1626). It seems that he

" In prime of youth by bloudy theves was slaine,
In Liscombe ground his bloud y* grasse did staine."

The ch. of *Great Horwood*, 2½ m. N.W. has a Dec. chancel, of very rich work, and a good Perp. screen. A 15th-centy. *Brass* (Henry Virgine, rector) is a good example of academic costume. The ch. was restored in 1874.

7¼ m. *Winslow* (Stat.) The town was given to St. Alban's Abbey by Offa. It contains a Perp. ch. of good character. The Manor-house (belonging to the Selby Lowndes family) is a fine mansion by Sir Christopher Wren. Passing N. we reach *Addington Manor* (Rt. Hon. J. G. Hubbard), a very handsome brick edifice, with Bath stone dressings, by *Hardwick.* The Dec. and Perp. ch. has been restored.

9½ m. *Verney Junction Stat.* Here the line from Aylesbury falls in, and is continued, in a N.W. direction to Buckingham (Rte. 15) and Banbury (Rte. 24).

11½ m. *Claydon* (Stat.) There are 3 Claydons, 2 S. of the line, and 1 N. *Steeple Claydon,* the one seen from the line, stands pleasantly on a hill. The chancel of the ch. was restored in 1875, and the spire is a memorial of General Sir Harry Calvert, the well-known Adjutant-General. The *Camp Burn,* in this parish, bears an inscription which states that "around this spot the army of the Parliament, under the command of Cromwell, was encamped, March, 1644; and on the 3rd of that month advanced from hence to the attack on Hillesdon House." *East Claydon* presents nothing remarkable; but *Middle Claydon* has a good Perp. ch. restored in 1871. It stands in the park of *Claydon House*—Sir Harry Verney (formerly Calvert), Bart. M.P. —built originally temp. Henry VII., but almost entirely rebuilt by Ralph 2nd Earl of Verney, temp. George II. Part of this second house was destroyed by Lord Verney's niece, Baroness Fermanagh : but several splendid chimney-pieces and rooms covered with ornamental stucco-work still remain, with a grand staircase inlaid with ebony

and ivory, having a wrought-iron balustrade representing standing corn, which bends and rustles as you ascend. Among the pictures are some fine family portraits, especially that of Sir Edmund Verney, concerning whom there is a Buckinghamshire proverb that he was "neither born nor buried." His tomb is in the ch., with an inscription "to the ever-honoured Sir Edmund Verney, standard-bearer to Charles I. in the memorable battle of Edgehill, where he was slain, Oct. 23, 1642," in that charge when Sir E. Balfour, with a rescue of horse, broke in upon the foot belonging to the King's army. His body was never found, but there is a tradition that one of his hands was discovered among the remains of the slain on the field of battle, and indentified by a ring. There also are many other monuments of the Verneys : and the alabaster tomb of one of the Giffards, 1539 ; with the *Brasses* of Isabelle Giffard, 1523, and Roger Giffard and Mary his wife, 1542. Roger and his wife are said to have built the ch. c. 1519.

16 m. The line enters Oxfordshire ; reaching at 17¼ m. *Launton,* and at 19½ m. *Bicester.* (See Rte. 28.)

M 2

ROUTE 18.

TRING TO ROADE.

L. and N.-W. Rly.   28¼ m.

For *Tring* (Stat.) see *Handbook for Herts.* At 34½ m. from Euston Stat. the line enters Bucks.

2¼ m. W. of Tring Stat. is *Drayton Beauchamp*, where the "judicious" Hooker was rector, 1584–5, and "behaved himself so as to give no occasion of evil, but in much patience, in afflictions, in anguishes, in necessities, in poverty, and no doubt in long suffering, yet troubling no man with his discontents and wants." The *Church* is Dec. and Perp., and in its E. window are figures of the apostles in stained glass of the Tudor period. The chancel contains the large white marble monument of Lord Newhaven, 1728, and 2 fine *Brasses ;* that to William Cheyne (although it has lost the Christian name) still bears the date 1375 ; the other, assigned to Thomas Cheyne, is 1368. There is also a small headless figure of a priest, 1531. The moat of the old manor-house of the Cheynes still remains.

It was at Drayton Beauchamp that Hooker was visited by his two favourite pupils, George Cranmer and Edwin Sandys, as is so pleasantly related by Izaak Walton. They found him with a book in his hand (it was the 'Odes' of Horace), he being then tending his small allotment of sheep in a common field; "which he told his pupils he was forced to do, for that his servant was then gone home to dine, and assist his wife to do some necessary household business. When his servant returned and released him, his two pupils attended him unto his

house, where their best entertainment was quiet company, which was presently denied them; for Richard was called to rock the cradle; and the rest of their welcome was so like this, that they staid but till next morning, which was time enough to discover and pity their tutor's condition; and they having in that time rejoiced in the remembrance and then paraphrased on many of the innocent recreations of their younger days, and by other such like diversions, and thereby given him as much present pleasure as they were able, they were forced to leave him to the company of his wife Joan, and seek themselves a quieter lodging for next night. But at their parting from him, Mr. Cranmer said, ' Good tutor, I am sorry your lot is fallen in no better ground as to your parsonage; and more sorry your wife proves not a more comfortable companion, after you have wearied your thoughts in your restless studies.' To whom the good man replied, ' My dear George, if saints have usually a double share in the miseries of this life, I, that am none, ought not to repine at what my wise Creator hath appointed for me; but labour, as indeed I do daily, to submit mine to His will, and possess my soul in patience and peace.' " — (*Walton's Life of Hooker*, Oxford edit., 1824). On his return, Edwin Sandys related his tutor's "sad condition" to his father, who was then Abp. of York, and the consequence was that Hooker was, in the course of the next year, removed to London, where he became Master of the Temple.

1¼ m. W. is *Aston Clinton;* the E. E. ch. has a fine Dec. chancel, with piscina and sedilia, and has been restored. The house of Aston Clinton was the seat of Lord Lake, the captor of Delhi in 1803: it has been rebuilt in the classic style by Sir A. de Rothschild, and is famed for its collection of tapestry, china, and majolica ware. In this parish is the *Shepherd's Grave*, where the word "Faithful," cut in the turf on the hill-side, long marked the grave of a shepherd of that name, who exacted a promise from his companions that they would bury him beneath the spot where he had always sat to watch his flock when living. A Roman Amphora was found in 1871 on Vetches' Farm in this parish, near the junction of the Lower Icknield and Akeman Streets.

E. 2 m. is the wooded hill of *Ashridge Park* (Earl Brownlow), a peninsula of Bucks running into Herts, the house being in Bucks, but the stables and offices in Herts; still the place is considered a Buckinghamshire seat, and is therefore here described. The park, which abounds in deer, is wild and beautiful, and contains many fine old trees. On the opposite side it slopes abruptly to the valley, affording a fine view over the country. Box flourishes here in great abundance.

Here was the palace of Edmund Crouchback, Earl of Cornwall, who founded beside it a monastery, 1283, for the order of Bonhommes, brought by him out of the S. of France (they had only 2 other houses in England, at Bristol, and Edington, in Wilts). He secured their fortunes by presenting them with a relic of great value, a portion of the blood of Christ, with which he had previously endowed his former foundation at Hailes in Gloucestershire (see *Handbook for Gloucester*). "By the blood of Christ which is in Hailes" was long a national oath, and it proved a mine of wealth to Ashridge, being a great object of pilgrimage. This blood was publicly exhibited by Hilsey, Bp. of Rochester (formerly a Dominican friar), at Paul's Cross, Feb. 24, 1538, and proved to be only honey clarified and coloured. At Ashridge the Earl of Cornwall died, and there his bowels and heart were buried, but his body was sent to Hailes. The praises of Ashridge were sung by Skelton:—

"The Bonehommes at Asheridge beside Barcanstede,
Where the sange royal is, Christis blode so rede.
A pleasanter place than Asheridge is, harde were to finde,
As Skelton rehearseth with words few and playne,
In his distich made in verses twayne:
Fraxinus in clivo froudetque vivet sine rivo
Non est sub divo, similis sine flumine vivo."

Here Edward I. kept his Christmas 1290, and held a parliament, to the great distress of the neighbourhood, which had to furnish the provisions of the court. Here Elizabeth frequently resided as princess, having received a grant of the place in 1552; and here she was apprehended in Feb. 1554, on suspicion of being concerned in Sir T. Wyatt's conspiracy. She professed to be confined to her bed by illness, but this was disbelieved, and she was carried away in the Queen's litter, the officers saying that they "would take her either dead or alive."

The estate was given by James I. to Lord Chancellor Egerton, and it still remains in his family.

The Collegiate Ch., which contained the tombs of Chief Justice Bryan, Sir Thomas and Sir John Denham, and other notable persons, was destroyed temp. Eliz., but the Great Hall and Cloisters were entire till 1800, when the hall, which had a rich Gothic roof and painted windows, was sold piecemeal by the Duke of Bridgewater; and the cloisters, which were richly adorned with frescoes and carving, so suffered by the removal of the other buildings that it was found necessary to remove them also. Nothing now remains of the monastery but the ancient crypt. The present mansion, from designs of Wyatt, "is a varied and irregular line of towers and battlements, arched doorways, mullioned windows, corbels, and machicolations, with a massive turreted centre, fine Gothic porch, and beautifully proportioned spire, surmounting the chapel."

The *Hall* is adorned by statues of the founders and benefactors of the ancient monastery. The *Chapel* is considered the masterpiece of Wyatt; its windows are filled with fine old German stained glass. Here is the fine *Brass* of Sir John Swynstede, 1395, which belongs to the ch. of Edlesborough (*post*), of which he was rector; and from the same place comes a curious *rose brass* for John Killingworth (1412). It has the inscription, " Ecce " (in the centre), and around the edge, " quod expendi habui, quod donavi habeo, quod negari punior, quod servavi perdidi." A similar brass occurs in St. Alban's Abbey, with an English translation of the inscription.

Among the pictures are—the Death of Hippolytus, *Rubens;* Holy Family (much injured), *Luini;* Feast of the Cranes, *Snyders;* 3 Cæsars, *Titian;* the Nativity, *Giov. Bellini.* In the hall is a fine work of *Luca della Robbia.*

E. of the park are the villages of *Great* and *Little Gaddesden*, so called from the river Gade, which rises near the former (see *Handbook for Herts*).

34 m. On W. 1 m. is *Marsworth*, with a Perp. ch., chiefly remarkable for its 17th-cent. *Brass* for Edmund West, serjeant-at-law, 1681. He is represented lying in bed clad in armour, with his wife and children kneeling beside him. 1 m. N.W. is *Long Marston*, with a stat. on the branch line from Cheddington to Aylesbury. Ruth Osborne, a reputed witch, was " ducked " here, April 22, 1751. She and her husband—both of them above 70 years of age—were cross-bound and thrown into a muddy stream. The woman died from the effects of ill-usage, and Thomas Colley, a chimney-sweep, was hung for the murder.

35 m. On E. 1 m. is the fine cruciform *Church* of *Ivinghoe*, with central tower and low spire. It is of Dec. architecture, replacing an earlier edifice believed to have been built by Henry of Blois, Bp. of Winchester, and brother of King Stephen. In the chancel is an effigy in priest's robes, known by the inhabitants as " Grandfather Greybeard." It has been said to be Henry of Blois, but is more probably that of Peter de Chaseporc, Rector of Ivinghoe, 1241–54. There is a fine timber roof, a rich cinque-cento pulpit, and several *Brasses*, ranging from 1368 to 1594. According to tradition Ivinghoe was one of the three manors forfeited by an ancestor of John Hampden, for striking the Black Prince a blow with his racket, when they quarrelled.

" Tring, Wing, and Ivinghoe,
Hampden of Hampden did foregoe,
For striking of ye prynce a blow,
And glad he might escape it so."

This rhyme suggested to Sir Walter Scott the title of his novel of Ivanhoe. There is no foundation whatever for this tradition, as neither of the three manors mentioned ever belonged to the Hampdens. The village stands among the chalk hills, and there is a very agreeable walk or drive to *Edlesborough,* 3 m. N.E. The fine Perp. *Church* stands on a hill; it has a lofty tower, which was once surmounted by a spire; but that was destroyed by lightning in 1827, and has not been restored. The chancel has stalls and miserere seats; and there are still some *Brasses*, dating from 1540 to 1647; but the most remarkable have been removed to Ashridge (*ante.*)

36 m. *Cheddington Junction Stat.* Hence is a branch line to Aylesbury of 7¼ m., with stat. at Marston Gate (*ante*). (For Aylesbury see Rte. 14.) The Perp. ch. of Cheddington was restored by *Street.*

1 m. N. is *Mentmore*, with a Dec. and Perp. ch., restored 1858, which has a good open oak roof. *Mentmore Towers* (built by Baron Meyer de Rothschild, and now the property of his daughter, the Countess of Rosebery,) is a superb mansion, built, from the designs of Sir Joseph Paxton and G. A. Stokes, of Ancaster stone, and bears some resemblance to Wollaton Hall (see *Handbook for Notts*). The interior is fitted up with great magnificence, and the collection of paintings (chiefly of the French school) and Limoges enamels is very fine. In the *Hall* (48 ft. by 40) are 3 copper-gilt lanterns, surmounted by the lion of St. Mark, made in the arsenal of Venice for the use of the Bucentaur in 1470; a chimney-piece from the house of Rubens at Antwerp, said to have been designed by the painter; some fine tapestry, and marbles of the 16th centy. The *Great Dining Room* has the fittings of the carved and gilt room ordered by Louis XIV. on the marriage of the Prince de Conti. The *Library* has a splendid collection of majolica and enamels. The *Morning Room* has some good pictures, including a portrait of Michael Angelo by *Moroni*, an ebony cabinet presented to Marie de Medicis on her marriage with Henry IV., by the city of Florence, and other valuable relics.

The *Mentmore Stud Farm*, established 1853, was of great celebrity in the sporting world, during the lifetime of the Baron, and turned out many of the best horses which have appeared on the turf during the last few years.

38 m. On E. *Slapton*, with a late Dec. and Perp. ch., of which John Kemp was rector in 1407; he lived to become Bp. of London, and Abp. of both York and Canterbury, Lord Chancellor, and Cardinal (see *Handbook for Kent*). There is a curious *Brass* for Jas. *Tornay*, yeoman-at-arms to Henry VIII. (1519), his two

wives and nine children; and a small effigy for a priest (1462).

39 m. On W. 2 m. *Wing*, one of the manors traditionally said to have been surrendered by one of the Hampdens (*ante*).

Wing *Church* has been pronounced "the most remarkable in the county." It has "supposed Saxon work, a polygonal apse elevated, with a crypt beneath; the altar-slab remains in the pavement, there is a rood-loft approached by a spiral staircase in the S. wall, and a late brass ('Eccl. and Arch. Top. Bucks.') The ch. has been extensively altered; and the Saxon work remains side by side with Dec. windows, probably inserted in the 14th cent., and with Perp. work. The latest restoration was in 1850, by *Sir G. G. Scott.* There are several fine monuments for the Dormers, once lords of the manor; Sir Robert Dormer, 1552; Sir William Dormer (in gilt armour), 1575; and Robert 1st Lord Dormer, 1617. Beside *Brasses* of 15th-centy. date there is one (1648) with a rhyming inscription in praise of "honest old Thomas Cotes, sometime porter at Ascott Hall." Beneath the chancel is a very ancient crypt, which probably dates from the 7th centy. There is a plan of it in G. G. Scott's 'History of English Church Architecture.'

40¼ m. *Leighton Buzzard Junct. Stat.* On E. is a branch (7 m.) to Dunstable. The fine ch. of *Leighton Buzzard*, seen from the stat., is on the further side of the river Ouse, in Beds, and is described in the Handbook for that county.

4 m. W. is *Stewkley*, with a *Church* often pronounced equal to Iffley in the richness of its late Norm. decoration. "It has been generally called Saxon, but has nothing to distinguish it from many well-known Norm. churches."—*Rickman.* It has a short square tower between the nave and chancel, the upper part of which is surrounded by rows of small pillars and interlaced circular arches. The

roof of the chancel is groined with zigzag mouldings. The W. front is very rich; the great door, which is circular, with zigzag mouldings, has figures of dragons within the arch. The restoration of this ch. by *Street* in 1862 gave rise to a controversy, which may be read at length in *Gent.'s Mag.* for the period.

42¼ m. On W. *Soulbury*, with a Dec. and Perp. ch., restored by *Street*. In this parish is *Liscombe House* (Capt. P. C. Lovett), a large Elizabethan mansion, incorporating a chapel of the 14th centy. There are several good historical portraits in the house, but it is not usually shown.

44 m. On E., *Stoke Hammond*, a small cruciform E. E. and Perp. ch., with a fine late Norm. font, and Perp. rood-screen; there are some small remains of painted glass, and a curious poors' box, date 1610. N. and S. extend the 3 *Brickhills*, all occupying high ground, and described in the popular rhyme—

" Here stand three *Brickhills* all in a row,
　　Great Brickhill, Little Brickhill, and Brick-
　　hill of the Bow."

The ground at Bow Brickhill rises to the height of 683 ft. The *Church* of Great Brickhill is Perp.; that of Little Brickhill has a Dec. tower; that of Bow Brickhill is Perp. The two former have been well restored of late years, but the latter stands in great need of reparation, little having been done since the time of Browne Willis the antiquary (A.D. 1757).

45 m. On W. 2 m. *Newton Longueville* (see Rte. 17).

46¾ m. *Bletchley Junction Stat.* Lines W. to Oxford, &c. (Rte. 17) and E. to Bedford, Cambridge, &c.

The village of Bletchley lies to the W. The Perp. *Church*, restored in bad taste by Browne Willis in 1704, has had most of his work undone in late years, and is now a handsome edifice; the avenue of ancient yew-trees is very striking. Notice in the

interior the tomb of Richard Lord Grey de Wilton, 1442, who is buried here with his son and grandson; a curious brass tablet to Dr. Sparke, rector in 1616, and an incised slab for Rev. E. Tayler, 1693.

1 m. N. rt. 1 m. is *Fenny Stratford*, once remarkable for its inns, being on the old highway to London. The ch., dedicated to St. Martin, contains, beneath the altar, the grave of Browne Willis the antiquary, and was rebuilt (1724) by him, in memory of his grandfather, whose portrait he placed over the entrance, with some verses to his memory. Very considerable additions have been made to the original edifice.

N.E. of Fenny Stratford are some interesting churches. *Walton* (2 m.) is Dec., with a cornice composed of a hollow, with grotesque heads at intervals; there are monuments of Bartholomew Beale, 1660; Sir Thos. Pinfold, 1701, with a medallion by *Nollekens*; and Elizabeth Pixe, 1617, with the epitaph,—

" Elizabetha vale, mea lux, mea vita, quo-
　　usque,
　　Jungitur in cœlis, filia cara vale."

Milton Keynes (4 m.) has a very beautiful Dec. chancel, without the admixture of other styles; the W. front is modern. Beside a 15th-centy. brass, it has a tomb of Lewis Atterbury, rector, 1693, father of Bp. Atterbury, who was born here 1662.

51¼ m. On E. *Bradwell* (*Stat.*), with a restored E. E. and Dec. ch.; there are some remains of *Bradwell Abbey*, founded in the reign of Stephen, and now used as a farm-house. A suburb, called *New Bradwell*, is mostly occupied by the Wolverton rly. works, and a ch. and schools (by *Street*) have been erected for the population connected with them.

52¼ m. *Wolverton Junction Stat.* A branch (4 m.) runs off, on N.E., to Newport Pagnell (Rte. 18A). The village, 1 m. W., has a pseudo-Norm. ch. built in 1815, and at New Wolverton is a modern E. E. one. The population is mainly in the employ of the L. and N.-W. Rly., and there is a model lodging-house, science and art institute, &c.

2 m. W., on the Ouse, is *Stony Stratford* (Pop. 2000). It stands on the Ouse, over which a substantial bridge leads into Northamptonshire. There were formerly 2 churches here, but only the tower remains of St. Mary Magdalene, the body of the ch. having been burnt in 1742, and not rebuilt; the tower is good Perp. *St. Giles*, originally a chantry chapel, has also a good tower, built 1487, but the rest is in the style of the Georgian era (1776). The trade of the town has decayed, as Wolverton has risen, and one of the principal inns has been converted into a middle-class school. One of the Eleanor crosses stood in the town, but was destroyed in 1646. In this neighbourhood Edward IV. is traditionally said to have first met Elizabeth Woodville, and a " Queen's Oak " is still pointed out. Here also the young Edward V. was seized by Richard Duke of Gloucester, who at the same time arrested Lord Rivers, Sir Richard Grey, and other partisans of the Woodvilles.

" Last night I heard they lay at Stony Stratford."   *Richard III.*, scene iv.

3 m. S.W. is *Beachampton*, where the Bennetts long had a manor, of which the great hall still remains. The Dec. and Perp. ch., completely restored in 1874, contains the tomb of Sir Simon Bennett, a benefactor of University College, Oxford, and a curious *Brass* for William Bawdyn, blacksmith, 1600.

54½ m. *Castlethorpe*, an E. E. ch., adjoining the site of a strong fortress of the Mauduits, demolished in the time of John. 1½ m. N. is *Hanslope*, once a market town, with a fine ch., originally Norm. and E. E., but now chiefly Perp., and remarkable for its lofty spire, rebuilt in 1804, after having been destroyed

by lightning, and now 186 feet in height. The manor belonged in succession to the Mauduits and the Beauchamps, earls of Warwick, and afterwards was granted to the Duke of York who was killed at Agincourt.

59 m. The line crosses into Northamptonshire, and reaches at

60 m. *Roade* (Stat.). See *Handbook for North Hants*.

ROUTE 18 A.

WOLVERTON TO NEWPORT PAGNELL AND OLNEY.

By Rly. and Road. 9 m.

THE line to Newport Pagnell has its first stat. at *Bradwell* (Rte. 18), N. of which is *Haversham*, with a restored Dec. and Perp. ch. There is a fine alabaster altar-tomb, believed to be for Elizabeth Lady Clinton, d. 1423. She was the heiress of the De la Plaunches, one of whom had licence to crenellate his house at Haversham in 1304. There is also a *Brass* for Alice Payne, 1427 ; and another for John Maunsell, 1605, ornamented with a skeleton, and with the age of the deceased given with curious minuteness as 66 years, 4 months, and 5 days. 1 m. E. is the disused church of *Stantonbury;* it has a good Norm. chancel-arch, and an E. E. window. It has been abandoned since the building of the ch. at New Bradwell (Rte. 18).

3 m. *Linford* (Stat.). " The ch. of Great Linford seems to have been

fine early Dec., but some trouble has been taken to disfigure it as much as possible. The piers to the nave are cased up in wood, and the tracery of all the windows destroyed" (' Ecc. Top. Bucks'). There still, however, remain 3 *Brasses*, one of which (for Roger Hunt, 1473) states that he paved the ch.

4 m. *Newport Pagnell* (Stat.) The line ends here at present, but is in progress to Olney and Wellingborough (see *Handbook for North Hunts*).

Newport Pagnell (*Inns*: Anchor, Swan) stands on a gentle eminence above the Ouse, over which there is an old stone bridge, whilst a smaller stream, the Lovat, has a light iron one (Pop. 3686). The town came into the hands of Fulk Paganell soon after the conquest, whence its second name. It had a castle, which was held for the Parliament by Sir Samuel Luke, the prototype of Hudibras. The *Church* is a large edifice, with good Perp. tower; but both N. and S. porches are of early date, one with groined roof, and the other with an E. E. arcade. Notice in the churchyard the epitaph on T. A. Hamilton, 1788; it is ascribed to Cowper. Dissenters are numerous, and there is an Independent chapel of early date, in which is preserved a board, said to have formed part of John Bunyan's pulpit. On it is fastened a brass plate, with the inscription, from Cowper :—

" Revere the man, whose Pilgrim marks the road,
And guides the Progress of the soul to God."

At Green-end, a suburb of the town, Dr. Renny, a very eminent medical man of the neighbourhood, was, by his own desire, buried beside his own house, in 1805.

1 m. S.E. is *Tickford Abbey* (Mrs. Massey), occupying the site of a monastery founded by Hugh Paganell, and one of those surrendered to Wolsey for his foundations at

Oxford and Ipswich. It stands in a low situation, liable to inundations. The old cemetery has remained undesecrated, and has continued in use as a private burial-ground for the successive owners of the property.

3 m. E. is *North Crawley*, with a fine Dec. and Perp. *Church*, dedicated to St. Firmin, a French bishop, the patron of a monastery which once existed here. The rood-loft remains, and the richly-decorated Gothic screen. The latter is a Perp. specimen of open screen-work, divided into sixteen compartments, each of which contains a painted figure of Prophet, Patriarch, or Saint. The chancel was built by Peter de Guildford, rector, 1321, which is commemorated by the inscription outside :—

" Petrus cancellum tibi dat Firmine novellum,
Et cum lauderis Deo, Petri memoreris."

There is also a fine *Brass* for Dr. John Garbrand, 1589. Crawley Grange is an Elizabethan manorhouse, possessing a bedstead said to have been used by the Queen on her journey to Kenilworth in 1575.

2 m. N.W. is *Gayhurst*, or *Gothurst*, with a small ch. rebuilt in the Grecian style in 1728. The manorhouse (Lord Carington) is an Elizabethan building. It was the home of Sir Everard Digby, whose participation in the Gunpowder Plot would have caused its forfeiture, had he not taken the precaution of making his estates over in trust for his infant son. This son was the celebrated Sir Kenelm Digby, who was born at Gayhurst, 1604. Cowper, who came here from Olney, was in ecstasies at the beauty of the place. " The situation is happy, the gardens elegantly disposed, the hothouse in the most flourishing state, and the orange-trees the most captivating creatures of the kind I ever saw." A large edible snail, called *Helix pomatia*, abounds in the woods here, but is quite peculiar to the place.

It was imported from the south of France by Sir Kenelm Digby, for his wife Venetia, who was in consumption. These snails are of a whitish colour, tinged with red; they bury themselves in winter, and remain torpid till spring.

Between Newport Pagnell and Olney (5 m.) lies a flat marshy district, through which the Ouse slowly makes its way. The villages of *Lathbury, Sherrington,* and *Emberton,* are met with in the direct road; the ch. of the first has a good E. E. tower; that of the second is good Dec., with a fine Perp. W. window; and the third is Dec., with much fine work remaining, although the windows in the aisles have lost their tracery. There is a *Brass* for John Mordan (1410), formerly rector, which contains a list of books given by him to his own and other churches. To the E. of Lathbury lies *Chicheley*, a good Dec. ch. with Perp. tower, and containing some brasses of the Caves, formerly lords of the manor. *Tyringham,* on the bank of the river near Gayhurst, has a late Perp. tower, but the rest of the ch. is modern.

9 m. *Olney (Inn:* Bull), celebrated as the home of the poet Cowper. The manor was given at the Conquest to Geoffrey, Bp. of Coutance, afterwards belonged to the Earls of Chester, King-making Warwick, the Princess Mary, and Anne of Denmark. The tradition of the country is, that lacemaking was first introduced here (Pop. 2250). The ch. spire (185 ft. high) is conspicuous long before reaching the town, which is entered by a bridge of four arches crossing the Ouse, with several smaller ones over the meadow-land usually flooded in winter, alluded to by Cowper in the lines,—

" Hark ! 'tis the twanging horn o'er yonder bridge,
That, with its wearisome but needful length,
Bestrides the wintry flood."

rt. is the large ch. of SS. Peter and Paul, entirely Dec. The chancel was restored by *Scott* in 1870. The pulpit is that in which Newton and Scott the commentator preached.

" The town, the most N. in Bucks, consists of one long street, the houses built of stone, but by far the greater number thatched. At one corner of the market-place, rather taller than the surrounding houses, is *Cowper's House,* 'which wears a most desolate aspect.' It was engaged for him in 1767 by his friend Newton (then rector), and was ' so near the vicarage, that by opening a door in the garden-wall they could communicate without going into the street.' Here he was induced by Newton to join with him in the authorship of the Olney Hymns. ' Occurrences here are as rare as cucumbers at Christmas,' he wrote in one of his letters, but he entered upon what he called a decided course of Christian happiness; and it was by no means unusual to find the man of trembling sensibilities praying by the sick-bed of the poorest cottager, or guiding the devotions of some miserable being who attempted to seek God only in the departing moments of existence. The town, which Cowper describes as ' populous, and inhabited chiefly by the half-starved and ragged of the earth,' afforded him ample facilities for usefulness. Lacemaking furnished, even to unremitting diligence, so scanty a pittance that it was barely sufficient to maintain a miserable existence. When a charitable donation enabled the poet to provide six children with one pair of blankets, ' they jumped out of their straw, caught them in their arms, kissed them, blessed them, and danced for joy.' The majority of the people were brutal in their manners and heathenish in their morals. Little creatures seven years of age made the place resound every evening with curses and villanous songs; the cottages were disposed in a long dreary street, and the tottering mud walls and torn thatch of many of them were in keeping with the wretchedness of the inmates. The surrounding meadows were flooded during winter; and Cowper was often doomed to sit for months over a cellar filled with water. The air in the rainy season was impregnated with the fishy-smelling fumes of the marsh miasma; and to this he attributed the slow and spirit-oppressing fever which visited all persons who remained long in the locality. Yet none of these evils had much effect upon him during the early years of his residence. He was experiencing the truth that 'the mind is its own peace,' and the social and spiritual advantages he enjoyed made Olney a heaven to him."

Cowper's Garden is behind his house, but now belongs to a different proprietor: it is however readily shown to visitors. Here is "the gravel walk, 30 yards long, which afforded but indifferent scope to the locomotive faculty, and which yet," says Cowper, "was all we had to move on for eight months in the year." Here is the house in which he kept his tame hares, his chief amusement. "They grew up under his care, and continued to interest him for nearly twelve years, when the last survivor died quietly of mere old age. He has immortalised them in Latin and in English, in verse and in prose. They have been represented in prints and cut on seals: and his account of them, which in all editions of his poems is now appended to their epitaphs, contains more observations than had ever before been contributed to the history of this inoffensive race." In this garden also is *Cowper's Summer Parlour*, concerning which he writes, "We eat, drink, and sleep where we always did; but here we spend all the rest of our time, and find that the sound of the wind in the trees and the singing of birds are much more agreeable to our ears than the incessant barking of dogs and screaming of children."

"At Olney the Ouse changes its character; and its course becomes so winding that the distance from that place to St. Neot's, which is about 20 m. by land, is about 70 m. by the stream. This has not escaped Drayton in his description of this 'far wandering' river":—

" Ouse having Oulney past, as she were waxed mad,
From her first stayder course immediately doth gad,
And in meandering gyves doth whirl herself about,
That, this way, here and there, back, forward, in and out;
And like a wanton girl, oft doubling in her gait,
In labyrinth-like turns and twinings intricate,
Thro' those rich fields doth run."

"The walks here are beautiful," says Cowper, "but it is a walk to get at them. Weston [*Underwood*], our pleasantest retreat, is 1 m. off, and there is not in that whole mile so much shade as would cover you. Mrs. Unwin and I have for many years walked thither every day when the weather would permit; and, to speak like a poet, the limes and elms of Weston can witness for us both how often we have sighed and said, 'Oh! that our garden-door opened into this grove or into this wilderness,' for we are fatigued before we reach them, and, when we have reached them, have not time to enjoy them." The state of the road was often so bad that it gave rise to the rhyme introduced in one of his minor poems,—

" Sle, slay, slud,
Stuck in the mud,
Oh! it is pretty to wade through a flood."

Nevertheless, in Aug. 1786, Cowper and Mrs. Unwin thankfully removed to Weston, where they lived in a house still to be seen on rt. of the village. "We dwell," wrote the poet, "in a neat and comfortable abode in one of the prettiest villages in the kingdom. It affords opportunity of walking at all seasons, abounding with beautiful grass-grounds which encompass it on all sides to considerable distance. These grounds are skirted by woods of great extent." Below, in the valley, "Ouse's silent tide" flows through the green meadows. There is a good view from "*the Cliff*,"—

"Whence Ouse, slow winding through a level plain,
Conducts the eye along her sinuous course."
Task.

Mrs. Unwin's ill-health led to the poet's removal from Weston in 1795. He had a presentiment that he should never return, and wrote on the window-shutter the two sad lines which are still to be seen there :—

"Farewell, dear scenes, for ever closed to me;
Oh! for what sorrows must I now exchange ye."
'*Southey's Life of Cowper*,' *Quart. Rev.*

Not far from Olney, N., is the wild woody tract, called *Yardley Chase.* In it is a great oak, called Judith, in remembrance of the niece of the Conqueror. This tree Cowper visited, and has recorded its measurement as 28 ft. 5 in. After his death, a poem entitled 'Yardley Oak,' was found among his papers, beginning

"Time made thee what thou wast—King of the Woods!
And time hath made thee what thou art—a cave
For owls to roost in!"

1 m. E. of Olney is *Clifton Reynes*, with an early Dec. *Church.* In the N. wall of the chancel aisle, in a canopied recess, are two very remarkable oaken effigies, supposed to be Simon and Margaret de Borard, lord and lady of the manor, c. 1267. Under the arches between the chancel and its aisle are two fine altar-tombs. The lower tomb has two hollow oak effigies, supposed to represent Ralph de Reynes and his wife, Amabel Chamberlain, 1310; the upper, with stone effigies of a knight and lady and their dog Bo, is believed to be that of Sir John Reynes and his wife, Catherine Scudamore, 1428.

Clifton was the home of Lady Austen, who, after the departure of Newton, was the great friend and comforter of Cowper in his solitude at Olney, where she eventually became an inmate of the parsonage. It was she who told him the story of John Gilpin, to rouse him from the dejection into which one day she observed him sinking, and he turned it into a poem that same evening.

Newton Blossomville, 1 m. further E., has two fine Dec. windows at the E. end ; *Brayfield*, N., is a plain E. E. ch. with good porch ; and *Lavendon* has a tower, of the type formerly called Saxon.

On the W. of Olney are *Weston Underwood*, a plain E. E. ch., but with Perp. exterior, and having a fine, though mutilated, *Brass* for Lady Throckmorton and 5 daughters (1571) ; and *Ravenstone*, once a plain E. E. ch., now greatly altered, but containing the magnificent tomb of Lord Chancellor Finch, Earl of Nottingham, 1682, in his robes, under a canopy. He was remarkable for his eloquence, which gained him the appellations of the English Roscius and the English Cicero ; and he has been praised by Blackstone as a thorough master and zealous defender of the laws and constitution of his country. In the churchyard is buried the Rev. Thos. Seaton, founder of the annual prize bearing his name at Cambridge. Cowper resided at Weston Underwood from 1786 till within a few years of his death, which occurred in 1800 at East Dereham, in Norfolk.

The P:
·College

SECTION III.

OXFORDSHIRE.

INTRODUCTION.

OXFORDSHIRE is bounded on the N. and N.W. by Warwickshire, on the N.E. by Northamptonshire, on the E. by Bucks, on the S.E., S., and S.W. by Berks, and on the W. by Gloucestershire. It contains 739 sq. m., and at the census of 1871 it had 177,975 inhabitants ; which had increased in 1881 to 179,650. It, including the University of Oxford and 3 boroughs, returns 9 members to Parliament. In form it is very irregular ; its greatest length is 48 m. ; and though at its centre, near Oxford, its width is only 7 m. across, a few miles higher it is 38 m., while at no point below the city is it more than 12 m.

" Oxfordshire," says Camden, " is a fertile country and plentiful, the plains garnished with cornfields and meadows, and the hills beset with woods ; stored in every place, not only with corn and fruits, but also with all kinds of game for hound and hawk, and well watered with rivers plentiful of fish," a description which Dr. Plot (' Nat. Hist. Oxford-shire ') allows to be true in the main, except that the woods have been destroyed " in the late unhappy wars," adding that the county has now " much more cause to brag of its meadows, and abundance of pastures, wherein, as in rivers, few counties may be compared, none perhaps preferred."

Oxfordshire is divided from Berks by the Thames, often fancifully called *Isis*, which receives all the other rivers of the county in its course—viz., 1, the *Windrush*, " the nitrous Windrush," which rises in the Cotswold Hills in Gloucestershire, and passing Burford and Witney falls into the Thames at Northmoor after a course of 18 m., during which it turns many mills ; 2, the *Evenlode*, which enters from Gloucestershire, receives the Glyme, a tributary of 12 m. long, and flowing by Charlbury and Woodstock, falls in near Ensham, after a

Pavilion University
Observatory

The Parks

OXFORD

College

for Murray's Handbook.

A

University
Museum

Scale of Quarter of a Mile

Merton Cricket Gr

Pavilion

Hotels

lph. B.4
C.4

B

D

E

course within the county of 22 m.; 3, the *Cherwell*, which, rising at Charwellton in Northamptonshire, and passing Banbury and Adderbury, flows in at Oxford after a course of 30 m. in the county; 4, the *Thame*, which rises at Stewkley in Bucks, and, first touching the county at Thame, falls in at Dorchester, 15 m. lower down. The *Oxford and Warwick Canal* enters the county at its N. extremity, and, keeping near the Cherwell, joins the Thames at Oxford. The *Great Western Railway* traverses Oxfordshire from S. to N., giving off branches on W. from Oxford to Witney and to Gloucester and Worcester, and S.E. to London, through Thame. The *London and North-Western* enters on E. from Bletchley, and has branches to Oxford and to Banbury.

The *Chiltern Hills* cross the southern extremity of the county from Bucks to Berks. Their heights were formerly covered by beech-trees, which especially flourished in their chalk soil, but the hills are now used either as sheepwalks or as arable land. The highest point is Nettlebed Hill, 820 ft., near which is Nuffield Common, 757 ft. To the E. of Oxford the ground rises considerably, its highest points being Beckley and Shotover. The N. of the county is flat and uninteresting, and its stone-wall fences are dreary to look upon.

The hilly lands are bleak and exposed, the winds being little checked by the low stone boundaries of the fields. The poor chalky soil is late, but not unfavourable for agriculture. " The soils may be divided into four principal kinds, viz., the red land, 79,635 acres, partly grass, and partly fine arable land; the stonebrash, 164,023 acres, chiefly N. of Oxford and Witney, and on inferior soil; the Chiltern chalk, 64,778 acres, occupying the S. part of the county, and covered with light calcareous loam, which is very profitable; miscellaneous 166,400 acres."

" The course of crops on the lighter soils is the 4 years Norfolk rotation, usually lengthened to 6 years with pulse or oats, or with crops of equivalent character; and on the heavier soils, which have been drained, and lie on irretentive subsoils, it is the convertible system, or such as divides the whole arable land into moieties, under artificial grass, or other rotation crops, and consists usually of, 1, turnips, or other roots; 2, barley or oats; 3 or more years of clover and grass seed; next wheat, and finally beans."

" The meadows which lie along the banks of the smaller streams generally produce excellent herbage; but those on the borders of the Thames and Cherwell are subject to floods, and an interspersion of coarse aquatic plants, which not only deteriorate the herbage, but sometimes damage the cattle which feed upon them." One may look in vain for a milkmaid throughout the county, as that office is always allotted to men or boys. Brawn is made in great quantities on the large farms, and some of the Oxford college cooks are renowned for the excellent quality of what they cure."

Geology. There are many works on the rock formations of Oxfordshire, the best .known of which is the 'Geology of Oxford and the

Thames Valley,' by the late Professor J. Phillips. The oldest formation, occurring in the N.W. of the county, is the Lias, in which is
found a hard fossiliferous limestone, called Banbury marble. Belonging
to the same system we also find Marlstone and Upper Lias clays. The
Great Oolite is well represented, and many bones of the Saurians of
that period have been found in it. Forest marble, cornbrash, coral
rag, Kimmeridge clay, Portland stone, and Oxford clay, also appear in
the county. The Cretaceous system furnishes Lower Greensand, Gault,
Upper Greensand and chalk. Evidences of the Tertiary are furnished
by a few scattered remains of Eocene; there are alluvial deposits, and
remains of prehistoric man are occasionally found.

Beside Oxford, Witney, Burford, Woodstock, Chipping Norton, Banbury, Bicester, Thame, Watlington, and Henley, are the chief places
The principal manufactures are—blankets at Witney, plush and shag
at Banbury, gloves at Woodstock, woollen cloth (tweeds), girths, and
horse-cloths at Chipping Norton; lace is made in some of the villages.

Shotover Hill, near Oxford, is celebrated as supplying the best ochre
in the world. Stonesfield is renowned for the multitude of fossils found
in its calcareous slate. Burford afforded the sandstone which Wren
largely employed in his repair of Westminster Abbey.

At the time of the Roman invasion Oxfordshire was inhabited by the
Dobuni, who are said by Camden to have derived their name from
Dwfn, a British word meaning low, as they always dwelt in the plain.
The county afterwards formed part of the Roman province of Britannia
Prima, and the station of Durocornovium was founded where Dor-
chester now exists. Under the Saxons it became a part of the kingdom
of Wessex. Birinus converted Cynegils, the king, and became in 638
the first bishop of Dorchester, a huge see, comprising both Mercia and
Wessex. In 752 Cuthred of Wessex conquered Ethelbald of Mercia
on Battle Edge, near Burford; after which Oxfordshire reverted to
Wessex. In the Danish invasions Oxfordshire was greatly ravaged.
Henry I. rebuilt the palace of Alfred at Woodstock, and rendered it
"the first park in England enclosed by a wall." Here in 1163 Henry II.
received visits from Malcolm King of Scotland, and Rice Prince of
Wales; and both Woodstock and Godstow are connected with his love
of Fair Rosamond. In 1275 Edward I. held a Parliament at Woodstock; and there were born Edmund of Woodstock, second son of
Edward I., and Edward the Black Prince and Thomas of Woodstock,
sons of Edward III. In the reign of Edward II. Aylmer de Valence,
Earl of Pembroke, built the castle of Bampton. In 1387 the insurgent
nobles defeated Vere Earl of Oxford, at Radcot Bridge, on the border
of the county near Bampton. During the wars of the Roses, in 1469,
Herbert Earl of Pembroke, a Yorkist, was defeated by the rebels under
Robin of Redesdale at Danesmoor, and was taken and put to death with
his brother Sir R. Herbert and ten others. The Princess Elizabeth was
imprisoned at Woodstock by Mary.

During the Civil Wars Oxfordshire was frequently a battle-scene.
On October 23, 1642, the battle of Edgehill was fought on the borders

of the county, the King having encamped the night before on the banks of the Cherwell, between Edgecot and Cropredy. In April, 1643, a skirmish took place on Caversham Bridge; and two months later, June 18th, the Parliamentarians were repulsed by Prince Rupert on Chalgrove Field, when John Hampden received the wound of which he died six days afterwards at Thame. In 1644 was fought the battle of Cropredy Bridge, in which Sir William Waller was defeated, after which the King drew off his troops to Deddington, where he slept at the parsonage house. In 1645 the Parliamentarians gained a victory at Islip Bridge, and Bletchingdon House was forced to surrender after a long and gallant defence for the King. Oxford was long the royal head-quarters, but was yielded up to Fairfax, June 24, 1646.

Antiquities.—At Dorchester, the ancient Doricina, Roman coins and other relics have been frequently discovered. Fine tesselated Roman pavements have been found at Great Tew and Stonesfield. Between Mongewell and Nuffield is still to be seen a vallum with embankment, 2¼ m. in length, known as Grime's Dyke, or the Devil's Ditch. The Icknield Street crossed the county from N.E. to S.W., entering it at Chinnor, and leaving it at Goring on the Thames; the Akeman Street entered at Ambrosden, and passed through Chesterton, Kirtlington, Blenheim Park, and Stonesfield to Asthall, where it crossed the Evenlode into Gloucestershire.

The most remarkable object of antiquity is the circle of stones and the cromlech, near Chipping Norton, known as the Rollright stones, and considered by Bede to be the second wonder in the kingdom. Similar relics are the cromlech known as the Hoarstone at Enstone, and the scattered stones called the Devil's Quoits at Stanton Harcourt.

There are but few remains of ancient *Castles.* Of the Norman castle of Oxford there exists, beside the mound, but a single tower, a crypt, and a subterranean chamber with a well; of Banbury only the traces of the moat remain. Of the castle of Aymer de Valence at Bampton, built in the reign of Edward II., there are some fragments, with a chamber, added temp. Henry VII., decorated with the red and white roses united. At Broughton some beautiful fragments of the old castle adjoin the later building.

Oxfordshire is rich in fine specimens of later domestic architecture; among which may be mentioned the manor-houses of High Lodge, near Woodstock, Asthall, Castleton, Fritwell, Burford Priory, Wroxton Abbey, the ruins of Minster Lovell, Stanton Harcourt, with its tower and almost unique kitchen, and the old Hall of Mapledurham. Of the *Churches* the most remarkable are—Norm. *Iffley; E. E. Thame;* Dec. *Kidlington;* Perp. *Ewelme,* with its beautiful tombs ; *Minster Lovell* Mixed, Adderbury, Bloxham, Broughton, Burford, Chipping Norton, Cogges, Dorchester, Great Tew, Shiplake, Stanton Harcourt, and Witney. The *Fonts* at Dorchester (lead), Iffley, Thame, Bampton, Bloxham, and Ewelme are particularly deserving of notice. The *Brasses* are numerous, and many of them very fine ; and painted *Glass* is frequently met with, though of no especial merit.

[*Berks, &c.*]

The *Views* are not remarkable for extent or beauty. Among the best may be mentioned that of Oxford from Shotover; the course of the Thames from Shiplake; and the wooded country seen from Nettlebed, and from Stokenchurch; the latter gives a good idea of the Chilterns.

Among the *Country Seats*, Blenheim stands pre-eminent for its superb park; Blandford is little inferior; Kirtlington, Middleton Stony, Nuneham Courtenay, Shirbourne, and Thame, though fine, are not comparable with either.

The whole course of the Thames from Oxford to Henley furnishes a succession of excellent subjects for the pencil, but the rest of the county can hardly be styled picturesque. The park at Blenheim contains some fine scenery, as does that at Nuneham Courtenay, though in neither case can the buildings be commended. On the other hand, Broughton Castle, Fritwell Manor-house, Minster Lovell, Stanton Harcourt, and the market-house at Watlington, will repay the labour of the artist.

THE CITY OF OXFORD.

Fanciful antiquaries have united to make Oxford the younger brother of Troy, and of course much older than Rome. One of them, John Rous, of Warwick, who wrote in the time of Henry VII., gravely asserts that the city was built 1009 B.C. by Memphric, King of the Britons, when it was called Caer Memphric in his honour, which name was changed to Bellositum, and afterwards to Rhyd-ychin, the Celtic for a ford of oxen ; others have argued that it is mentioned under the British name of Caer-Pen-hal goit, a city on an eminence between two rivers, and adorned with woods. Others again consider it to have been a Roman city ; but the absence of Roman remains, and its position, remote from their great roads, render this very improbable.

Even the legendary history of Oxford begins only in 727, when Frideswide, daughter of Didan, governor of Oxford, embraced a religious life, with twelve maidens her companions. About this time her mother, Saffrida, died; and her father, seeking consolation from a work of piety, employed himself in the construction of a convent within the precincts of the city, of which he appointed her the abbess.

Alfred the Great is said by some writers to have resided at Oxford, and also to have had a mint there, which tradition places on the site of New Inn Hall, but the first historical reference which we have is in the Saxon Chronicle, under 912, where we read that Edward the Elder took possession of Oxford in that year, on the death of Æthered of Mercia. " A great Witenagemót was held this year (1015) at Oxford, a city whose renown as the seat of a great University belongs to later times, but which the whole course of these wars shews to have been already a place of considerable importance. Its importance, however, would seem to have been comparatively recent. The first mention of Oxford in the Chronicle counts about 100 years before this time, when it appears as one of the chief acquisitions of Edward the Elder. As a frontier town of Mercia and Wessex, we might have expected to find far earlier mention of it; but in more ancient times the now utterly insignificant Bensington (see the Chronicles in the years 571 and 777) seems to have been the chief military post of the frontier, while the now no less insignificant Dorchester was the ecclesiastical capital of a vast diocese, of which the diocese of Oxford, as it stood before recent changes, formed only a small portion. Oxford, however, was now a place of note; in the new nomenclature of Mercia it had given its name to a shire; it had been taken, retaken, and burned in the wars of Swegen; and it must have derived some further importance from the possession of the minster of the local saint Frithswyth. That minster, after an unusual number of changes in its foundation, has at last settled down into the twofold office of the cathedral church of the modern diocese and the chapel of the largest college in the University." (*E. A. Freeman,* 'The Norman Conquest.') The Danes burnt the city more than once, but it continued a royal residence, and was the scene of many important events. The Witan met at Oxford in 1013, 1015, 1018, 1022, 1026, and 1036; and here occurred the death of Harold Harefoot. After the Norman conquest, Robert d'Oiley built the castle and his nephew, also named Robert, received into it the Empress Maud, who was there besieged by Stephen. When the garrison was reduced to extremity by famine, Maud escaped on foot across the frozen river (Dec. 20, 1142), with only three attendants, and reached Wallingford in safety. Edith, the wife of the second Robert d'Oiley, founded the magnificent abbey of Osney on an island W. of the city. The palace of Beaumont was built by Henry I., 1132; Henry II. often occupied it, and his sons Richard and John were born there.

In 1190 a dreadful fire occurred, which destroyed most of the wooden houses, and led for the first time to the erection of houses of stone. In 1209 a quarrel arose between the townsmen and the students, when the summary execution of three of the latter by the citizens, in revenge for the death of a woman who was accidentally killed by one of their companions, led to the retirement of the whole University, and to the city being laid under an interdict by the Pope, who relieved the professors from their obligation of teaching in it. This was found to be so great a loss that, to induce them to return, the citizens consented, by way of penance, "to go to all the city churches, with whips in their hands, barefooted, and in their shirts, and there pray for the benefit of absolution from every parish priest, repeating the penitential psalms, and to pay a mark of silver per annum to the students of the hall peculiarly injured." In the succeeding reign of Henry III. (to which period belong the famous Provisions of Oxford), when the number of students is said to have marvellously increased, these town and gown hostilities were almost incessant; and it was long before the bitter feeling died away. Except its military occupation during the Great Rebellion, and the holding of a parliament there by Charles II. in 1681, Oxford has no modern history; the visit of the Allied Sovereigns in 1814, that of the Prince and Princess of Wales in 1863, and the controversies that have agitated the University, having little reference to the city. Its population has steadily increased, from 12,279 in 1801 to 32,477 in 1871, and 35,929 in 1881. It has a handsome Town Hall, with a free public library. The drainage, once very defective, has been greatly improved; and the city is well supplied with water by the Corporation; there are large piles of building on the newest plans for the labouring population, and rows of handsome dwellings in the suburbs, and Oxford holds, independently of the University, a high place among English cities.

THE UNIVERSITY.

Thomas Kay, or Caius as he is styled, who was Master of University College from 1561 to 1572, published a book to prove that his Alma Mater was founded by certain Greek professors who accompanied Brutus the Trojan to Britain. More moderate writers are content with Alfred as their founder, and this conclusion has been pretty generally accepted (unless by Cambridge men), although there is no authenticated history which mentions him as such. The Annals of Hyde Abbey, Winchester, speak of him at Oxford listening to the teaching of its earliest professors, St. Grymbald and St. Neot, teachers of theology, and Asser, the teacher of grammar and rhetoric; but as the earliest MS. that we possess is not older than the time of Richard II., its evidence is of doubtful value.

The earliest provisions for education in Oxford were lodging-houses for students, which took the name of Halls, and of which more than 100 are mentioned in mediæval documents. Down to the time of Henry III. the University continued to increase and prosper. In 1229 the disputes, which had always existed between the University and the town, became so violent that the students abandoned the place, and 1000 students of Paris, who had quarrelled with their own townspeople, came over at the invitation of Henry III., and settled at Oxford in their place. In 1260 the original Oxford students founded a new seminary at Northampton, from which, however, they were soon recalled by the entreaties of the people of Oxford, and the command of the King. What was till very recently the model of collegiate education both in Oxford and Cambridge, was supplied a few years after their return, by a code of statutes drawn up by Bishop Walter de Merton, originally for the college which still bears his name, but speedily adopted by the others, and by the subsequent foundations. During the reign of Edward III. conflicts between the town and University again raged with fury. Of one particularly fierce conflict, in 1354, when 62 students are said to have been killed, a recollection is maintained at the present day by the custom of Queen's and some other colleges carefully keeping their gates closed during dinner and supper, " not only to secure their plate, but chiefly to secure themselves."—*Pointer's Oxon. Acad.*

In the reign of Richard II., the University was agitated by the controversies relating to the doctrines of Wycliffe; in that of Henry VII. Erasmus came and revived the study of Greek; in the 16th century the Reformers struggled and suffered, but eventually triumphed. The University vigorously upheld the cause of Charles I., and the modern character of the bulk of the plate of the colleges still bears witness to their generosity in his behalf.* Puritan misrule succeeded ; and this was followed by the still greater trial of having to withstand the illegal proceedings of James II. Georges I. and II. made some efforts to conciliate the University, but many years elapsed ere the old attachment to the house of Stuart died out ; many of the most noted Nonjurors belonged to Oxford.

The precise dates of the foundation of the Colleges are in many cases doubtful ; it must therefore suffice to say that University, Balliol, and Merton, are of the 13th century ; Exeter, Oriel, Queen's, and New, of the 14th ; Lincoln, All Souls, and Magdalen, of the 15th ; Brasenose, Corpus Christi, Christ Church, Trinity, St. John's, and Jesus, of the 16th ; Wadham and Pembroke, of the 17th ; Worcester, of the 18th ; and Keble and Hertford, of the 19th.

The University at the present day consists of 21 Colleges, 4 Academic and 2 Private Halls, including the recently founded College in memory of Keble, having upwards of 10,000 members on their books ; and, in virtue of recent legislation, there are also "unattached students " —*i.e.*, students not belonging to any College or Hall (a recurrence to the mediæval system). Of these there are over 300. The chief difference between Colleges and Halls is, that the former are incorporated bodies, possessed of estates and rights of patronage, whilst the latter are not incorporated. The University as a whole is a corporate body, which returns two members to Parliament, and is known by the title of the Chancellor, Masters, and Scholars of the University of Oxford. Its chief officers are—*the Chancellor* (Marquis of Salisbury), chosen for life, but only appearing upon special occasions ; *the High Steward* (Earl of Carnarvon), chosen for life, who may be called upon to hear and determine capital causes according to the laws of the land and privileges of the University, and who holds the University Court-leet at the appointment of the chancellor or vice-chancellor ; *the Vice-Chancellor*, a head of a college, nominated annually, but usually holding office for four years ; *the Proctors*, two in number (distinguished by their black velvet sleeves), elected annually to attend to the discipline of the students under the degree of M.A., administrators of the discipline, and in all respects the acting magistrates. *The Visitor* of the University is supposed to be the Crown.

The constitution of the University and of the Colleges has of late

* At the meeting of the British Archæological Institute held at Oxford in June, 1850, most of the ancient plate of the colleges was exhibited. Among the more noticeable objects were :—A gold grace cup and two gold salt-cellars, 14th centy., from New College ; founder's cup, and a 14th-centy. German cup, from Wadham ; a silver-gilt chalice and paten, supposed to have belonged to St. Alban's Abbey, from Trinity College ; founder's cup, and Bp. Carpenter's gold-mounted cup, from Oriel ; founder's salt-cellar from Corpus ; a gold-mounted horn, presented by Queen Philippa, and a silver trumpet (still in use to summon to dinner), from Queen's. Of modern plate, Magdalen exhibited a gold Restoration cup, the silver-gilt cup presented by Dr. Johnson, and a gold salver, the gift of the Emperor Nicholas to its President, Dr. Routh. The rest of the modern plate does not call for remark.

undergone several important changes. From the chancellorship of Archbishop Laud (1630–41), to the year 1854, the executive government of the University was vested in a board, consisting of the Vice-Chancellor, the two Proctors, and the Heads of Houses, called the *Hebdomadal Board*, from its weekly meetings. The colleges were governed by statutes, framed at the time of their respective founders, though in some degree modified in practice to meet the changes introduced into the University by the Reformation and the lapse of time. In the year 1850 a royal *Commission* was issued to report on the best means of adapting the statutes, both of the University and of the Colleges, to the wants of the present age. On this report was founded an Act of Parliament in 1854 (17 and 18 Vict. c. 81), which, partly by its own provisions, and partly through the operation of a Commission, has effected many important changes.

For the former Board, a *Hebdomadal Council* was substituted, of very different composition—viz., 6 Heads of Houses, 6 Professors, and 6 members of Convocation, all elected by *Congregation*, with the addition of 5 ex-officio members. The Congregation is a body of ancient date, which now consists of the chief functionaries of the University, and of all resident Masters and Doctors, and has the right of discussing in English the measures proposed to it by the Hebdomadal Council. These, if adopted by Congregation, must receive their final sanction from the governing body of the whole University, which, under the name of *Convocation*, still remains comparatively unaltered. It consists of all Doctors and Masters, resident or non-resident, and has the right of discussing in Latin (unless the Chancellor, or on some occasions the Vice-Chancellor, permits the use of the English language) the measures which are brought before it, and which it then finally rejects or approves. It also has the right of electing the burgesses for the University, as well as some of the Professors. The Vice-Chancellor singly, or the Proctors jointly, have a right of veto on any measure as it passes through this body. The joint veto of the Proctors has been exercised of late years on two or three memorable occasions.

Under the same Act of Parliament the statutes of the College have also been altered to meet modern views. Thus, restrictions of kindred and locality, by which the choice to many of the fellowships and scholarships in Oxford was fettered, have been, with few exceptions, abolished; the imposition of oaths injurious to the public interest has been prohibited as illegal; and professorships have in several instances been endowed with the proceeds of college fellowships. All tests have been removed from the University except for the degrees in divinity, which are still confined to members of the Church of England.

The first *Examination* which a young man encounters is imposed, not by the University, but by the College into which he seeks admission, or by the Censors of unattached students, unless he possesses a certificate from the Oxford and Cambridge Schools Examination Board, which also passes him through "smalls." When he has passed this he is "matriculated" into the University itself. There are 4 Terms yearly, and at the end of the 6th or 8th the student goes up for his first public examination. The University examinations date in their present form from the beginning of this century, but have passed through several modifications. The first is termed " *Responsions,*" or in more popular language " *Smalls.*" The second, which consists chiefly of classical Scholarship and Mathematics, is called " *the First Public Examination,*" or in popular language " *Moderations,*" or " *Mods.*" The third, which is called " *the Second Public Examination,*" or in popular language " *Greats,*" formerly required the passing in two out of four schools, one being necessarily Classics, the other either Mathematics, Modern History and Law, or Natural Science, before a degree could be taken, but this is now modified. If a man goes in for a Pass, he must take up a language—Greek, Latin, French, German, Sanskrit, or Persian—and also any two of the following:—the above languages, ancient history, modern history, law, political economy, geometry, mechanics, chemistry, physics. If he takes up Honours, he must get a class in one of the following schools, Literæ Humaniores, Mathematics, Natural Science, Jurisprudence, Modern History, Theology. Both in the first and second public examinations honours are given. On passing the last of these examinations the *degree of B.A.* is obtained. The *degree of M.A.* is conferred, without further examination, at the end of seven years from matriculation. It is distinctive of Oxford, as contrasted with Cambridge examinations, that they are partly carried on orally: to this part the public are admitted. Beside the honours obtained in these examinations, there are many University distinctions, 20 scholarships awarded annually for proficiency in various branches of knowledge, and 17 prizes for compositions in prose and verse. No less than 42 Professors, 4 Readers, 1 Lecturer, and 7 Teachers of languages are attached to the University, but the principal instruction given to undergraduates is within their own colleges, the University merely appointing and directing the examinations necessary to the attainment of a degree.

The titles of the *Heads of Houses* are various. Christ Church is governed by the *Dean* of the Cathedral; Merton, New, All Souls, Wadham and Keble, by *Wardens*; University, Balliol and Pembroke, by *Masters*; Magdalen, Corpus, Trinity, and St. John's, by *Presidents*; Oriel, Queen's, and Worcester, by *Provosts*; Exeter and Lincoln by *Rectors*; Brasenose, Jesus, Hertford and the Halls, by *Principals.*

In former days there were many remarkable *Customs* prevailing in the University, each college having some peculiar to itself. They are enumerated in Pointer, but most of them have now passed away. Of those that remain, the chief perhaps are, the boar's head at Christmas, and the needle and thread on New Year's Day (Queen's); the singing of the mallard song is only on All Souls' Day; and the Hymn on May-morning on the top of the tower (Magdalen).

To enumerate the eminent men who have been educated at the various Colleges, would be to name the most prominent characters in all periods of English history. It may therefore suffice to remark, that from the time of William I. to the present day, princes are to be found on the roll ; the late King of Holland was educated at Christ Church, as was also the Prince of Wales and Prince Leopold ; Prince Hassan of Egypt was a member of the same College. On the list of Chancellors is found, to go no further back than the reign of Elizabeth, Dudley, Earl of Leicester, Sir Christopher Hatton, Lord Chancellor Ellesmere, Archbishop Laud, William and Philip, Earls of Pembroke, Oliver and Richard Cromwell, Lord Clarendon, James Butler, Duke of Ormond, who with his two grandsons, held the office for 90 years (1669-1759), Lords North and Grenville, the Duke of Wellington, and the late Earl of Derby.

SKELETON TOUR.

Day.
1. Rly. to Henley. Road to Dorchester. (Rte. 20.)
2. By road to Oxford. (Rte. 20.)
3, 4, 5. At Oxford. (Rte. 19.)
6, 7, 8. Excursions (see pp. 234-257.)
9. Rly. to Witney. Road to Bampton. (Rte. 25.)
10. Road to Burford and Chipping Norton. (Rtes. 25, 26.)
11. Road to Banbury by Deddington. (Rte. 24.)
12. Rly., Banbury to Oxford. (Rte. 24.)
13. Rly., Oxford to Thame. (Rte. 22.)
14. Road, by Chinnor and Stokenchurch to Wycombe. (Rte. 21.)

ROUTES.

ROUTE 19.

LONDON TO OXFORD, BY DIDCOT.

G. W. Rly. 63¼ m.

(For the journey to Didcot Junction, 53¼ m. from Paddington Station, see Rtes. 4, 11.)

The rly. leaves the main line by a sharp turn to the N., and the Sinodun hills near Dorchester soon come in view. At 55¼ m. the Thames is crossed into Oxfordshire, and on W. a range of Gothic buildings is seen in the midst of a treeless landscape. This is *Culham College* (Principal, Rev. J. Ridgway, B.D.), a training school for schoolmasters, founded by Bishop Wilberforce 1853,

and capable of containing 130 students. It consists of a chapel, hall, practising school, dormitory, and Principal's lodge. (*J. Clarke*, architect.)

56¼ m. *Culham* (Stat.) about 1 m. from the ground of Nuneham. The ch., a small cruciform building of mixed style, with Perp. tower, stands near the river, 1 m. W. On crossing the Thames into Berkshire, notice the view, E., of the fine woods of Nuneham Courtenay (Exc. *b* from Oxford), and, W., of the spire of St. Helen's, Abingdon.

57½ m. *Radley* (Stat.) whence is a *Branch Line* to Abingdon. (Rte. 8.)

1. Radley College (Rev. C. Martin).

The quaint red buildings rise behind the village and ch. (Rte. 8.) rt. *Sandford Ch.*, on a hill above its picturesque Lasher; and monument to Gaisford and Phillimore, drowned there while bathing (Exc. *b.* from Oxford.) 61 m. l. on the hill-side *Bagley Wood.* rt. *Iffley*: the Norm. ch. tower rises from the trees above an old water-mill. Near this the line to London through Thame runs off. (Rte. 22).

The towers and spires of Oxford begin to rise above the green willows on the E. bank of the river. That furthest to the rt. is the tower of Magdalen, whence the eye wanders by the dome of the Radcliffe, the spire of St. Mary's, and the towers of All Souls and of Merton, till it rests upon the great mass of Christ Ch., with its cathedral spire rising above Wolsey's hall and the dome-capped tower of Tom Gateway.

The rly. again crosses the river and re-enters Oxfordshire immediately before reaching the town. On the l. flat marshy meadows stretch away to the low hills, which are clothed with the woods of Wytham. A sheet of water, formed by accidental opening of springs in making the line, and hence styled the Railway Lake, is next passed, with the ch. of St. Thomas (*post*) on E., and we enter at

63½ m. OXFORD STATION, which, with the adjoining one belonging to the London and North-Western Rly., occupies part of the site of Rewley Abbey, founded by Edmund, Earl of Cornwall. From the G. W. stat. there are trains to London, *viâ* Thame (Rte. 22), to Worcester (Rte. 26), and to the North (Rte. 24). From the L. and N. W. Stat. to Bletchley, where the main line is joined (Rtes. 17, 28).

OXFORD.

INDEX.

(*Inns:* the Randolph, a Gothic building, at the corner of Beaumont Street (B 4), the best; the Clarendon (formerly the Star), in the Corn-market (C 4), good; the Mitre, in the High Street (C 5); the King's Arms, in Broad Street, both comfortable).

The approach from the station is through a poor suburb and narrow streets. An air of antiquity, however, prevails, and when the visitor reaches either High Street or Broad Street he finds himself amid palatial colleges, with Gothic halls and chapels, some with towers, others with spires, whose delicate pinnacles stand out brightly against the sky, while the grey masses below are broken by the brilliant green of trees or luxuriant gardens. The crumbling stone of which the majority of the edifices are built gives an appearance of age even to buildings of modern date; and the academical cos-

tume so frequently seen in the streets, imparts an additional interest and picturesqueness for the passing stranger, unaccustomed to University life. To one just hurried by train from London, the impression produced by the first sight of Oxford is most striking. " From noise, glare, and brilliancy, the traveller comes upon a very different scene—a mass of towers, pinnacles, and spires, rising in the bosom of a valley, from groves which hide all buildings but such as are consecrated to some wise and holy purpose. The same river which in the metropolis is covered with a forest of masts and ships, here gliding quietly through meadows, and scarcely a sail upon it—dark and ancient edifices clustered together in forms full of richness and beauty, yet solid as if to last for ever; such as become institutions raised not for the vanity of the builder, but for the benefit of coming ages; streets, almost avenues of edifices which elsewhere would pass for palaces, but all of them dedicated to God; thoughtfulness, repose, and gravity in the countenance and even dress of their inhabitants; and, to mark the stir and business of life, instead of the roar of carriages, the sound of hourly bells calling men together to prayer."

The late Père Lacordaire wrote: "Fancy in a plain surrounded by uplands, and bathed by two rivers, a mass of monuments Gothic and Greek; churches, colleges, quadrangles, porticoes, all distributed profusely, but most gracefully, in quiet streets terminating in trees and meadows. All these buildings, consecrated to letters and science, have their gates open. The stranger enters as he would enter his own house, because they are the asylums of the beautiful to all who are endowed with feeling. As you traverse these noiseless quadrangles, there is no crowding or din. There is nowhere such an appearance of ruin, with so much of preservation. In Italy the buildings breathe of youth. In Oxford it is time which shows itself, but time without decay, and with all its majesty. The town itself is small, but even this does not take from the grandeur of the place; the monuments serve for houses, and give it an air of vastness."

Oxford is in Domesday styled *Oxeneford*, a name commonly regarded as derived from a ford much traversed by cattle, but probably a mere corruption of Ousenford, the ford over the river Ouse, which is regarded as the ancient name of the Isis. The Pop. in 1881 was 38,289, an increase of 5,812 since 1871; the suburbs have extended considerably in every direction. The principal street, remarkable for its graceful curve, for the buildings which line it, and grand termination in the stately tower of Magdalen, is the High Street, which contains four

colleges, two noble churches, and the Botanic Gardens, as well as the best shops. It is about a mile long, running nearly E and W.; at its W. extremity it is succeeded by a greatly inferior street called Queen Street, which soon divides into two branches: Castle Street (l.), and the New Road (r.), which leads to the Stat. Broad Street runs parallel with High Street at a short distance N., and St. Aldate's and the Cornmarket run from S. to N., terminating in St. Giles's Street, with a fine avenue of elms.

The following is the order in which the hurried traveller may most easily visit the chief sights of Oxford.

Passing from the Stat. by the New Road (notice D'Oiley's Tower and the Castle Mound on r.—the Castle itself, a court-house and prison, is modern work, imitating Norman) and Queen Street, you arrive at Carfax — *quatre voies*, where 4 roads meet. After a glance E. down the High Street, turn S. down St. Aldate's Street. On rt. are the ch. of that name and Pembroke College (where Dr. Johnson was a student and Whitfield a servitor). On the opposite side of the street you pass under the Tom Gateway into Christ Church, with its quadrangles, Cathedral, Wolsey's Hall, New Buildings, and Meadows. Slightly retracing your steps, you cross the Peckwater quadrangle, and leave by Canterbury Gate, when you face, in close proximity, Corpus, Oriel, and Merton, Colleges. Oriel Street leads from Corpus into the High Street opposite St. Mary's Ch. Turning to the rt. you arrive in turn at All Souls and Queen's Colleges on l., and University and the new Examination Schools on rt. At the end of the street stands Magdalen, with its chapel, cloisters, and beautiful tower. Opposite is the Botanic Garden, and close adjoining is Magdalen Bridge, the view from which should on no account be missed.

Retracing your steps as far as Queen's Lane, and following its windings, you reach New College, whose chapel and gardens are well worthy of a visit. New College Lane brings you to Hertford College, the Old Schools, and the Bodleian Library, Brasenose College, and the classic Radcliffe Library, from the top of which the finest view of Oxford and its neighbourhood is to be obtained. Beyond the Schools are the Clarendon Building, the Sheldonian Theatre, and the Ashmolean Museum, whence a few steps will lead you to Wadham, with its pretty quadrangle and garden, beyond which you have the New Museum on rt., with Keble College opposite.

Returning to, and following the Broad Street, passing (l.) Exeter, and (rt.) Trinity, and Balliol Colleges (Lincoln and Jesus are in a street called the Turl, facing Trinity), you reach St. Mary Magdalen Ch. and the Martyrs' Memorial, near which is St. John's College, with its beautiful gardens, and memories of Charles I. and Archbishop Laud. Almost opposite are the Taylor Buildings, containing a picture gallery, statuary, and a famous collection of sketches by Raffaelle and Michael Angelo. Hence the traveller may return to the rly. by Beaumont Street (the site of the Palace), taking, if time allows, a glimpse of Worcester College, which is a good example of the contrast between ancient and modern architecture.

If content with mere outside views, the pedestrian may make the round with tolerable satisfaction in about two hours, but if he ventures on any detailed examination of any one of the colleges, with its hall, chapel, library, pictures, and gardens, the whole day will prove far too short.

"There is no place in England where Gothic architecture lingered so late as in Oxford. In other places the mixture of Gothic and classic styles first took place temp. Hen.

VII. The chief forms of Gothic were then lost. In temp. Hen. VIII. the details also became debased. In temp. Eliz. the mixture of the two styles became more complete, and though details were often incongruous, there resulted a style, which when applied to domestic buildings was highly picturesque. In the succeeding period the decline still continued, until the old style was swallowed up—the window, the most important feature of Gothic, being the last to depart.

"The following list of the late Gothic buildings in Oxford may be found useful:—

ELIZABETH.—1571. Old buildings of Jesus commenced.
1596. Library, St. John's, built.
1597. Sir T. Bodley commenced the repairs of Duke Humphrey's Library, and added the roof.
1600. Front of St. Alban's Hall built.
1602. Duke Humphrey's Library reopened after repairs.

JAMES I.—1610. First stone of the extension of Bodleian and Proscholium laid. Great quadrangle of Merton built. First stone of Wadham laid.
1612. West side of lesser quadrangle of Lincoln built.
1613. Wadham College opened.
1617. Hall of Jesus built.
1620. Hall of Trinity finished.
1621. Chapel of Jesus finished.
1624. Old Chapel of Exeter built.

CHARLES I.—1626. Library of Jesus built.
1628. Front of Bishop King's house rebuilt.
1631. First stone of garden front and lesser quadrangle of St. John's laid.
1631. Lincoln Chapel consecrated.
1634. West side of University built.
1635. West side of St. Edmund Hall opened.
1635. Front of University begun.
1637. Oriel quadrangle and Hall built.
1639. Chapel of University begun. (Finished 1665.)
1639-40. St. Mary Magdalen Chapel and Hall built.
1640. Hall, University, begun. (Finished 1657.)
1640. Staircase of Christ Church built.
1642. Oriel Chapel consecrated.
1656. Chapel, Brasenose, begun. (Finished 1666.)
1663. Library, Brasenose, opened.
1665. Chapel, University, consecrated.
1666. Chapel, Brasenose, consecrated.
1669. Library, University, opened.

Archæological Journal, vol. viii.

" Oxford was a school of great resort in the reign of Henry II., though its first charter was only granted by Henry III. It became in the 13th centy. second only to Paris in the multitude of its students and the celebrity of its scholastic disputations."—*Hallam.* (*See* University College).

" The earliest doctor of this University was the sainted Neot, whose achievements, real or imaginary, coincide with our earliest national deliverance. The long line of its colleges was parallel to the long struggle of English liberty. The first two of their founders shared in the conflicts out of which sprang the House of Commons. The charter of the last foundation was signed by the dying hand of the last sovereign of the House of Stuart. [Keble and Hertford Colleges had not been founded when this eloquent passage was written.] At every turn of the history of the University we are brought into contact with the history of the nation. The name of Balliol still lives in his father's benefaction, long after its disappearance from every other quarter. The dark shadow of the reign of the 2nd Edward rests on the college of Stapleton, Bishop of Exeter, who perished fighting in the streets of London in the cause of his unfortunate master. Masses for the soul of Hugh Despenser, the unworthy favourite of the same unhappy prince, are enjoined to be offered up in Oriel.

" From Philippa down to Charlotte the Queens of England have honoured with their favour the college which bears their name. The youth of the most illustrious of our heirs apparent, Edward the Black Prince, —Henry V., ' hostium victor et sui,' —Henry Prince of Wales, the ' Marcellus ' of the House of Stuart, —was by tradition connected with that college and Magdalen. The architect of the noblest of our royal palaces

was also the architect and founder of the most elaborate of our colleges, and the genius of Wolsey still lives in the graceful tower of Magdalen and the magnificent courts of Christ Ch. The most permanent impress of the administration of Laud was till lately to be found in the new academical constitution which sprung from his hands. All Souls is a monument of Agincourt; Queen's, of Halidon Hill; Lincoln, of the rise of Wycliffe; Corpus, of the revival of letters : the storms of the Reformation, of the Civil War, of the Revolution, swept with no ordinary vehemence round the walls of Balliol, of St. John's, and of Magdalen."— *Dean Stanley.*

Having indicated the positions of the various colleges and other chief buildings, we now proceed to describe them nearly in the same order.

I. COLLEGES, HALLS, LIBRARIES, AND MUSEUMS.

(1.) CHRIST CHURCH. (*Obs.* Tom Gateway, *Hall, *Cathedral, Library, New Buildings, Meadows and Walks.) (D 4, 5)

This noble foundation was commenced by Cardinal Wolsey in 1525, and had he been able to carry out his intention, it would have been the grandest academic institution England had ever seen ; but his disgrace prevented this, and Henry VIII. seized the funds appropriated for it. The king afterwards (1546) continued his design, but changed the original name of Cardinal's College, first into King's College, and afterwards into Christ Church. It was built on the site of a nunnery founded by St. Frideswide, who died about 740.

The principal entrance is in St. Aldate's Street, along one side of which extends the façade of the college, 400 ft. long, broken in the domed roof. This tower, added by Sir Christopher Wren in 1682, contains the *Great Bell of Oxford*, "the mighty Tom," weighing 17,000 lbs. and the clapper 342 lbs. It was brought double the weight of the great bell originally from the abbey of Osney (whose bells were the most celebrated in England); when it bore the inscription "In Thomæ laude, resono Bim Bom sine fraude," and it was recast 1680. At 9.5 every evening this bell intimates to all the colleges the usual hour for closing their gates by 101 strokes, the number of students or members of the foundation which existed at Christ Ch. before the Act of 1854 for remodelling the University. The Porter's Lodge is in the gateway, where application to view the Hall, &c., must be made.

Tom Gateway leads into the *Great Quadrangle* (which is always called "Tom Quad"), measuring 264 ft. by 261 ft. It contains the lodgings of the Dean and canons, the Hall (on rt.), and many sets of rooms occupied by senior and junior members of the college. They stand on a terrace, the earth having been excavated (1665) by Dean Fell, in order to give height to the buildings. The original design of Wolsey was to build a chapel on the N. side, and surround the whole by a cloister (of which the intended pilasters may still be seen), but this was never carried out. The Quadrangle was terribly injured during the Civil War by the intruding Dean and Canons and their supporters. The buildings were originally surmounted by an open battlement with pinnacles. I am nearly sure that the battlements have during the past 10 years been replaced by a balustrade: the incongruous balustrade, which still remains on the St. Aldate's Façade, was erected by Dr. John Fell, when he completed the court and gateway in 1660-68. In the centre is a fountain known as Mer-

centre by a noble gateway, surmounted by a six-sided tower with cury, from a paltry statue, given by Dr. Radcliffe, which formerly stood there, but has been removed to the Infirmary.

The entrance to the Hall is at the S.E. corner of the Quadrangle, where a massive tower is now built, adorned with a small statue of Wolsey and two other figures. The Hall is approached by a grand and beautiful staircase, whose delicate fan-roof, springing from a single pillar, was erected for Dean S. Fell, 1640, by one "*Smith of London*" (*Peshall*). The two open arches opposite the hall-door are of Wolsey's period, and it is considered probable, as the design of Smith's work (at a very late date for Gothic architecture) harmonizes so well with the earlier parts of the building, that the original drawings showing the intention of Wolsey's architect were preserved and made use of by him. The stairs and parapet were the work of *Wyatt*. The *Hall*, the largest and finest in Oxford (length 113 ft., width 40 ft., height 50 ft.), was finished by Wolsey himself, in the late Perp. style. The carved oak roof has very elegant pendants decorated with the arms and badges of Henry VIII. and Catherine of Aragon; the date of its completion (1529) also appears. In this hall the Sovereign is received on visiting Oxford, and on the list of royal visitors are Henry VIII., Elizabeth, James I., Charles I., George III., and George IV., who, as Prince Regent, did the honours of the University here to the Emperor of Russia, King of Prussia, and other potentates assembled in Oxford in 1814. Here Elizabeth was witnessing a play, when, "a cry of hounds having been counterfeited in the quadrangle during the performance, the students were seized with a

* Keble Hall is slightly longer, but not so high, or wide.

sudden transport, whereat her Majesty cried out ' O excellent ! these boys, in very truth, are ready to leap out of the windows to follow the hounds.' "

A play acted here in 1636 before Charles I. was remarkable for its scenes and stage machinery, which were the earliest of the kind made in England, and which are mentioned by Anthony Wood, "in order that posterity might know that what is now seen in the playhouses at London is originally due to the invention of Oxford scholars." In this hall Charles I. in Jan. 1644 assembled and addressed his fragment of a Parliament, composed of 45 Peers and 118 Commoners, his loyal adherents, in opposition to that which sat at Westminster. The subsequent meetings of the Peers were held above the Schools, and those of the Commons in the Convocation House. King Charles was lodged in this college, his queen Henrietta Maria at Merton. The portraits (about 120 in number) that line the walls, are in many cases of great interest, as Wolsey and Henry VIII., *Holbein* (copies ?); Queen Elizabeth, *Zucchero* ; Bishop Morley, *Lely* ; Lord Grenville, *Owen* ; George Canning, *Lawrence* ; Bishop King, *Jansen* ; Atterbury and Smallridge, *Kneller* ; Archbishop Robinson and Archbishop Markham, *Reynolds* ; Welbore Ellis, *Gainsborough* ; John Locke, *Kneller* ; Canon Nichol (an admirable portrait), *Reynolds* ; and Bishop Hooper, *Hogarth*. Close by the hall is the *Kitchen*, which should not be passed unnoticed, being an excellent specimen of the ancient English style; it was the first point attended to by Wolsey, and is the oldest part of his building, a circumstance which gave occasion for caustic remarks among the wits of the day. The primitive arrangements, the 3 vast fire-places, &c., can still be traced ; and Wolsey s huge gridiron is an attraction to many visitors.

At the foot of the hall staircase is the entrance to what remains of the buildings of the ancient monastery, viz., the cloisters.

THE CATHEDRAL.

The *Cathedral*, entered by a recessed portal from the Quadrangle, serves in the place of a chapel to the college, and is part of the earliest institution in Oxford, being the church of the priory of St. Frideswide, or, as she was familiarly called, St. Frid, a princess who became prioress of a nunnery founded by her father King Didan, called Didymus, circa 730. She was celebrated for a double miracle, in first striking her lover Algar blind when he attempted to pursue her, and afterwards restoring his sight. She died here Oct. 14, 740, which anniversary was long held as a gaudy, *i.e.*, commemoration day. (The gaudy day now observed is either Commemoration day, or the day after.) This was one of the 22 minor convents, of which Wolsey procured the suppression, by a bull of Pope Clement VII. in 1524, in order to endow this college and another at Ipswich with their revenues. The conversion of monasteries into colleges had been begun before this, as by Bishop Alcock at Cambridge. Wolsey commenced his operations here by shortening the nave of the ch., and altering it in various ways, designing it, as is believed, for minor services and divinity exercises, while the actual college chapel on a large and splendid scale was to have been on the N. side of the quadrangle. The existing edifice is chiefly late Norm., consecrated 1180. The tower contained 10 bells from Osney Abbey, the "bonny Christ Church bells " of Dean Aldrich, but their vibration was considered to endanger the structure, and they are now hung in the large tower, erected in 1878-9, over the staircase leading to the Hall. The spire, 144 ft. in height, is probably the earliest existing in England, but the upper part has been rebuilt.

The Cathedral Church, the restoration of which was commenced in 1856 by *Scott*, is entered from the cloisters at the S.W. corner, or from the E. side of Tom Quad. by a modern portal, and presents a mixture of different styles in which late Norm. predominates. The pier arches are double; an inner and a lower arch springing from corbels; attached to the piers beneath the main arches. Both upper and lower arches are of one date and part of the original plan. The choir was thrown open to the nave in 1856 by Dean Liddell, and further changes were made by him between 1872 and 1881. The roof of the choir, which is of the same character as that of the Divinity School (*post*), is of fan-tracery, groined, with pendants—an enrichment attributed to Wolsey. The clerestory windows are examples of the latest Norman style. Beneath the fine E. wheel window there is a very beautiful reredos of sandstone and red marble, designed by Bodley, completed in 1881, and an admirable specimen of modern workmanship. The restoration was mainly carried on between 1872 and 1875, when the seating was renewed; the choir was repaved; carved stalls and wrought-iron canopies were erected for the dean and canons; a new bay was added to the nave, and a porch opened into the great quadrangle. A fine lectern was presented at the same time, and the organ was erected at the W. end. The E. end was restored in 1871. A carved throne of Italian walnut was erected in 1876 to the memory of Bishop Wilberforce.

Attached to the choir on the N. are three aisles, the furthest of which is called the Lady or the Latin Chapel: the college Latin prayers were for-
[*Berks, &c.*]

merly read in it at the beginning of each Term, and the Regius Professor of Divinity always gives his lectures there. Notice the painted window with the legend of St. Frideswide, erected 1861. The nearer is the Dean's or St. Frideswide's Chapel, or the Dormitory, from the number of eminent persons who sleep beneath its pavement. The Latin Chapel, built by Lady Elizabeth Montacute, 1346, is of Dec. architecture, and contains stalls of Wolsey's time of good workmanship. Between the piers which separate these two chapels are 3 tombs:—1. Sir George Nowers, d. 1425, but the armour is of earlier date, so that the tomb may probably have been prepared in his lifetime; it was long supposed to be that of Sir Henry de Bath, the justiciary, d. 1261. 2. Said to be the oldest in the ch., and to represent Alexander de Sutton, Prior of St. Frideswide 1294–1316. The effigy, which has been elaborately painted, lies under a triple-arched canopy. 3. Lady Elizabeth Montacute, d. 1355, who gave Ch. Ch. meadows to the Priory: the costume and head-dress, very perfect, with broken statuettes in niches around representing her children, two of the daughters having been in succession Abbesses of Barking in Essex, and one of the sons, Simon, Bishop of Worcester, and of Ely, d. 1345. Beyond this tomb is a structure, wrongly styled the shrine of St. Frideswide (date 1480), but now supposed to have been the watching chamber of the guard or keeper of the shrine and its offerings, which were often of great value. A similar watching chamber still exists at St. Alban's, and in the ch. of North Marston, in Bucks (Rte. 15), where it guarded the shrine of Sir John Shorne. In each case the watching chamber now alone remains to testify to the wealth of the deserted shrine. Here it is of wood, ornamented with tabernacle work, and is

o

raised upon a table-tomb, from which the brasses have been removed. The shrine of St. Frideswide was frequently moved to different parts of the building, to stimulate subscriptions towards it. It was constantly visited by devout pilgrims, among whom the last of eminence was Queen Catherine of Aragon; and it was removed, but not destroyed at the Reformation. Soon after, the wife of Peter Martyr, the Protestant canon, was buried beside St. Frideswide. On the accession of Mary, the body was removed; but under Elizabeth it was brought back, and placed in the coffin of the saint, with the epitaph "Hic jacet Religio cum Superstitione." A brass plate was placed in 1880 over the spot where the shrine of St. Frideswide once stood. In the S. transept a remarkable sacristy chamber has been brought to light and restored by *Scott.*

The monuments and mural tablets are numerous. Some of them have recently been moved, and a new window (the 'Lothian window') has been put in the N. transept. Notice, in the porch, Otho Nicholson, donor of the Carfax conduit (*post*); in the ante-chapel, Dean Gaisford; at the entrance of the nave, Bishop Berkeley, with his monument against a pillar, and over his grave a stone inscribed with the single line from Pope, "To Berkeley every virtue under heav'n ;" in the N. transept, Peter Elmsley, the Greek commentator; in the Lady Chapel Bishop Fell, with a monument remarkable for being inscribed on both sides; in St. Frideswide's Chapel, Burton, the author of the 'Anatomy of Melancholy,' Democritus Junior, as he styles himself in his epitaph ; Dean Aldrich; Bishop Tanner the antiquary ; and Pococke the Orientalist. In the S. aisle is the tomb of Bishop King, the last Abbot of Osney and first Bishop of Oxford, above which is his portrait in stained glass, the background of

which is the best existing representation of Osney Abbey. This was taken down and preserved by one of the Bishop's family during the usurpation in 1648, and put up again at the Restoration. In the N. transept was formerly a beautiful statue (by *Chantrey*) of Cyril Jackson, Dean of Christ Ch. (d. 1819), who resigned his post in 1809, and retired to Felpham, where he is buried with the epitaph, "Lord, in thy sight shall no man living be justified." It has recently been removed to the library.

The E. window in the Latin Chapel has superseded one of 'Christ in the Temple,' in the grey style of the 17th cent., attributed to *Van Linge.* In the S. transept (St. Lucy's Chapel) is a window made up from fragments of ancient glass. Among these may be noticed a representation of Becket's murder, a hole marking the place where the head was knocked out at the Reformation, the destruction of all images and likenesses of Becket being especially ordained. Four divisions of the great W. window were brought thither from the Latin Chapel. Much ancient glass was destroyed when Christ Ch. was in the hands of the Puritans, among whom Henry Wilkinson, Margaret Professor of Divinity, was its great enemy, "furiously stamping upon the windows, when they were taken down, and utterly defacing them." There are four windows designed by Burne Jones, and executed by Wm. Morris, the poet and painter ; three at the E. end, and one at the N.W. corner. In St. Lucy's Chapel a new font of red-veined marble was erected in March, 1882.

Divine service is performed in the cathedral at 10 a.m. and 5 p.m.

The *Chapter-house,* in the cloister, has a fine Trans.-Norm. doorway, but the building (which cannot be visited without application to the Dean or one of the Canons) is a beautiful specimen of the E. E. style, with lancet windows and a groined vault. It was beautifully restored in 1880–81. In an adjoining chamber, panelled with oak, are placed some pictures: Mary; Elizabeth; and Peter Martyr, first Protestant canon. The portrait of Compton Bishop of London, 1675 (famous during the Revolution of 1688, when to protect the Princess Anne he resumed the buff coat and jack-boots of a trooper, having in his youth served in the royal guard) has been removed to the Deanery; John King, Bishop of London (called "King of Preachers" by James I.). On the l. wall are 2 portraits, taken at various ages, of Dean Aldrich, celebrated both as an architect, in which capacity he designed Peckwater, All Saints' Ch., and Trinity College Chapel, and for his talents as a poet and musician, shown in his various catches and songs, and still more so in his anthems. Many other portraits have been removed to the Canons' houses.

Passing down the cloister we come to the ancient Refectory of St. Frideswide, which was afterwards the "Old Library," a name it still retains, though divided into rooms for undergraduates. The S. side of the new quadrangle is occupied by the New Buildings, an ungainly Gothic pile in the style of the Museum (post), by *Deane*, which extends for a considerable distance along the side of the Broad Walk; in the centre is a gate, which gives admission to Christ Ch. meadow.

Returning and recrossing Tom Quad., notice, l., beyond the Hall, the house of the Regius Professor of Hebrew (Dr. Pusey), which possesses the oldest fig-tree in England, imported from the Levant in 1691 by Pococke the Orientalist; rt. is the house of the Regius Professor of Divinity. Dr. Bentham occupied it when Johnson visited Oxford with Boswell, and he invited them to dinner — "which Dr. Johnson told me was a high honour: 'Sir, it is a great thing to dine with the Canons of Christ Church.'" The rest of the E. side of the quadrangle is occupied by the *Deanery*, the gardens of which are very fine. It was here that Cranmer was brought, and "gently entreated," with insidious purpose. "To the intent that the doctors and divines, who busied themselves about Cranmer during his imprisonment, might win him more easily, they had him to the Dean's house of Christ Ch., where he lacked no delicate fare, played at the bowls, had his pleasure for walking, and all other things that might bring him from Christ."—*Foxe.*

The passage opposite the Hall is surmounted by a statue of Dean Fell (given by Hammond). A tower has been built here. The rooms over the gate are those that are set apart for the royal guests of the college, and they were thus occupied by the Prince and Princess of Wales in July, 1863, and later. The passage is sometimes called Kill-Canon, from the pernicious effects of its draughty situation, and forms the entrance to Peckwater, a large quadrangle of Palladian architecture, named from the inn of one Radulph Peckwether, mayor of Oxford in time of Henry III., which occupied its site. Peckwater Inn was celebrated for its grammarians; one of them was John Leland, who taught in the reigns of Henry V. and VI., of whom Wood says, that "he went beyond the learnedest of his age. It was here that William Penn, who had entered the University during the Protectorate, attacked with his associates the Christ Ch. students when they appeared for the first time after the Restoration in their white surplices, and tore the hated garments to pieces. On the S. side of Peckwater is the *Library* (1761), whose chief benefactors were Otho Nicholson, the builder of the Conduit, and Archbishop Wake, 1737.

o 2

The lower storey serves also as a picture-gallery, furnished chiefly by a bequest of Gen. Guise. This contains a few very good works, with many worthless copies. Well worthy of attention are a Virgin and Child, by *Lippi*; a Magdalen of the early Venetian school; a *Parmegiano*; the Adoration of the Shepherds: a portrait of one of the Torreani family; General Guise, by *Reynolds*; a Christ Church servant by *Riley*; a classical composition of the French School of the last century; *Ann. Caracci*, the painter and his family as butchers; *Rafaelle*, fragment of the cartoon of the Murder of the Innocents; *An. Mantegna*, Virgin and St. John, probably a fragment of a larger picture; Titian's Nativity. There are also several busts of eminent personages. A number of drawings by Leonardo da Vinci, Andrea Mantegna, and Albert Dürer, are also preserved in the Library. On the staircase is a statue of John Locke, by Rysbrach. He was a member of Christ Church, and being a friend of Shaftesbury, was expelled in 1682 for "seditious demeanour." The upper library, a noble room 142 ft. long, 30 ft. wide, and 37 ft. high, contains the libraries of Dean Aldrich, Archbishop Wake, and others. Some MSS. of interest are displayed in a case, and Wolsey's chair stands at one end of the room. The plaster work in the roof and the carved wood porch and gallery are fine of their kind.

The Canterbury Quadrangle, rebuilt 1770, mainly at the expense of Abp. Robinson, of Armagh, occupies the site of Canterbury Hall, founded by Abp. Islip, of which Wickliffe was supposed to have been Master, and where Sir Thos. More studied under Linacre. A classic gateway leads out towards Corpus, Oriel, and Merton Colleges.

The beautiful *Walks* which intersect and inclose a meadow of 50 acres, the promontory formed by the confluence of the Thames (here styled Isis) and the Cherwell, are a great and natural source of pride to Christ Ch. A famous avenue of elms, which suffered sorely from the great gales of 1881 and 1882, dating from the Restoration, stretches across the meadows, and encloses the *Broad Walk*, raised by Bishop Fell with the earth removed in excavating Tom Quad., and again by Dean Aldrich with earth removed from Peckwater. A new Walk, running at right angles to the Broad, was completed and brought into use at the Commemoration of 1871. Here on the evening of *Show Sunday*, (that immediately before Commemoration,) nearly all the members of the University, with the strangers visiting Oxford, take a promenade, and filling the walk present an animated scene. The path running parallel to this is the *Horse Path*, which was for the conveyance of food to the priory. It crossed the Cherwell by a bridge, of which the abutments still remain, and went over the meadows opposite. The walk below Merton wall, having a S. aspect, and being protected on the E. and W., is called *Dead Man's Walk*, from being much frequented by invalids.

The Christ Church walks are 1¼ m. in circuit. At the E. side the Cherwell joins the Isis. The walk by the Isis is bordered by the College barges, which are fitted up inside as writing and reading rooms. Several of these once belonged to the London Companies, and figured in the ancient processions on the Thames. During the eight-oared boat races, which take place in May, the tops of the barges are crowded by Collegians, who are ready to cheer their respective boats, and to exult in the "bumping" of the foremost by those in the rear. The grand procession of the racing-boats takes place on Monday in Commemoration Week, at which time the river banks are lined, and the barges are crowded with spectators.

(2.) CORPUS CHRISTI (D 5.) (Notice vaulted roof of Gateway, Chapel, and view from Garden.)

Founded in 1516 by Richard Fox, Bishop of Winchester. When, already in extreme and blind old age, Fox wished to devote his fortune to founding a monastic establishment at Winchester in honour of St. Swithin, but his friend Hugh Oldham, Bp. of Exeter, foreseeing the downfall of the monasteries, induced him to turn his designs to the foundation of this College. It was probably this foresight of the approaching storm that induced Fox to perpetuate a Church doctrine, in the name of Corpus Christi, which is also indicated by the chalice and paten over the gate. The College is dedicated to the patron-saints of the four Sees of which the founder was successively Bishop (Exeter, Bath, Durham, Winchester). There was formerly, besides the high altar, two altars in the chapel, dedicated respectively to the Holy Trinity and St. Cuthbert. The quadrangle remains much as it was left by the founder, and contains a remarkable cylindrical dial, with a perpetual calendar, in its centre, constructed by Robert Heggs, the mathematician, in 1605, and described by him in a MS. ("Tract. de Horologiis") in the college library. Opposite the entrance is the statue of the founder. The *Hall*, with good late Perp. roof, contains his picture. The *Chapel* has a fine altarpiece, by *Rubens*, from the collection of the Prince de Condé at Chantilly. The pastoral staff, rings, pyxes, and other valuables of Bishop Fox are in the possession of the College. The gallery connecting the chapel with the President's Lodgings contains an interesting portrait of Bp. Fox when blind, as well as portraits of the 7 bishops who were sent to the Tower.

The Library contains the founder's collection of the Aldine Classics, besides a very valuable collection of manuscripts. The rooms on the 2nd floor of the library staircase are those inhabited by the "judicious" Hooker. Cardinal Pole, Ludovicus Vivas, Bishop Jewell, and the ever-memorable Hales, were also members of this College, and in modern times Dr. Buckland, Dr. Arnold and Keble. Professorships were founded at Corpus by Fox for the then rising study of Greek, and Hebrew, as well as for Latin and Divinity, which caused Erasmus to say that "what the Colossus was to Rhodes, what the Mausoleum was to Caria, that Corpus Christi College would be to Britain," and to give it the name of "Bibliotheca trilinguis" —the library of the three learned languages. The Pelican over the gateway indicates the charitable founder, the Owl his friend Bp. Oldham. A tame fox was long kept by the College. The view from the garden in front of "Turner's Building" (called after its founder, Thomas Turner, President, 1688–1714), is very agreeable.

(3.) MERTON. (D 5.) (Notice the Chapel, Library, Hall.)

This college claims a somewhat lengthened notice, as the first fruits of the idea of a system which had no existence before the time of its founder. This was Walter de Merton, probably a native of Basingstoke, an eminent man of the time of Henry III., to whom he was twice chancellor, and who died Bishop of Rochester in 1277. He saw with regret that the parochial clergy neglected their duties to pursue the more profitable practice of law or medicine, and he purchased at Maldon and Merton in Surrey, estates, the rents of which he devoted to a kind of preparatory school there, and the support of scholars at Oxford, who should be forbidden to follow, in after-life, any other pursuit than that of parish priests. He steadily pursued his purpose for several years, and in 1264 he obtained the royal licence to found at Oxford an endowed corporation of scholars, free from vows, "qui non religiosi, religiose viverent," at once commenced his building, placing the students under a Warden, and giving them a body of statutes, which served as a pattern to future collegiate foundations. "Our founder's purpose," says Bp. Hobhouse, once Fellow of Merton, "I conceive to have been to secure to his own order in the Church, for the secular priesthood, the academical benefits which the religious orders were so largely enjoying, and to this end I think all his provisions are found to be consistently framed. He borrowed from the monastic institutions the idea of an aggregate body living by common rule, under a common head, provided with all things needful for a corporate and perpetual life, fed by its secured endowments, fenced from all external interference, except that of its lawful patron: but after borrowing thus much, he differenced his institution by giving his beneficiaries quite a distinct employment, and keeping them free from all those perpetual obligations which constituted the essence of the religious life." (*Gent.'s Mag.*, 1858–59.[*])

Walter de Merton had an especial veneration for St. John the Baptist; hence he chose the parish church of St. John for his College chapel, and hence the sculpture over the entrance gateway, which represents the founder in full pontificals, dedicating the 7-clasped Book of Knowledge to the Lamb in the wilderness, which is crowded with apes, unicorns, birds, and rabbits, the Baptist standing in the background. The *Chapel*, one of the stateliest and largest in Oxford, giving a chief feature to the city by its massive tower, consists of a choir

* ' Sketch of the Life of Walter de Merton,' a most interesting memoir, drawn up from College MSS. hitherto unpublished.

and transepts and ante-chapel. It was an enlargement of the old parish ch. by Walter, who lived to see the dedication of the high altar in 1276; the windows are of the same date, except the lower part of the E. The E. window is filled with beautiful tracery, and contains the arms of Richard, King of the Romans. The others were given by Henry de Mansfield, one of the fellows, in 1307, who is represented kneeling in each before an apostle. The castles in the border are the arms of Eleanor of Castile. The groundwork with the ivy-leaf pattern is very rare and beautiful. The nave of the parish church, which must have been small, was pulled down in 1414, and, as the beginning of a new one, the present ante-chapel and tower were built, c. 1440. The chapel has been restored, and the roof designed and painted by the Rev. J. H. Pollen, formerly a Fellow. The floor of the room originally used by the bell-ringers in the tower has been removed, and an open gallery constructed for them, by which means the 4 fine arches are shown, and the groined oak roof exposed. In the choir are 2 magnificent *Brasses*— Henry Sever (Warden 1471), in cope, with collar of SS; and of 2 bosom friends, Bloxham (Warden, 1387) and Whytton (1420), buried side by side under a beautiful Gothic cross; also a lectern of the 15th centy., inscribed, " Orate pro animâ Magistri Johannis Martok." Over the altar is a picture of the Crucifixion (Bassano, or Tintoret ?). The ante-chapel contains several monuments of members of the College — 1, Sir Thomas Bodley, founder of the Library that bears his name (*post*); 2, Antony Wood, the antiquary, who lived opposite Merton, in the little stone house where he was born, 1632; and 3, Sir Henry Savile, surrounded by the symbols of his works—1, Chrysostom; 2, Tacitus; 3, Ptolemy, with a globe; 4, Euclid, with compasses; 5, the Southern hemisphere; 6, Merton; 7, Eton. A beautifully sculptured marble bas-relief, by Woolner, was erected to the memory of Bishop Patteson in 1876.

There are two quadrangles, both picturesque. The Library Quadrangle, or "Mob Quad.," has been little altered since its erection, c. 1350. It is approached by 2 passages, with high-pointed groining of the 13th centy. Over the second of these is the exceedingly curious *Treasury*, built entirely of stone by the founder with a high-pitched ashlar roof. It contains among other curious papers the receipt of a mother for her son from the feudal lord: " Recepi filium meum." Attached to it is the Warden's tower. The *Hall* spoiled by Wyatt, but restored 1872, retains the original doorway, and the 14th-centy. oak door, with its fine ironwork. The Hall contains portraits of the founder, Bps. Jewel, Barrington, Denison, and others. The *Library*, being the earliest in Oxford, has served as a model to other colleges. It is divided into Arts, Theology, and Medicine, in which last subject it is very perfect: many of these books were left by Rede, Bp. of Chichester, d. 1415. The Library abounds in ancient Bibles. Among its curiosities are also Caxton's 1st edition of Chaucer; a MS. written by Duns Scotus; a 10th centy. MS. of Eusebius. Here also are the Globes obtained by Savile, then Warden (1621), in exchange for " the fair organs " of the chapel.

The *Inner Quadrangle*, of Jacobean style (1610), has a gateway tower in imitation of that of the Schools, with four of the Orders, the spaces between being filled with Gothic panelling. It is the work of Bentley, one of the builders of the Schools.

The north front of the College was restored by *Blore* in 1838; and in 1864 a lofty pile of buildings was added by *Butterfield*, facing the

meadow, which has obliterated the well-known Merton Grove.

The E. wall was formerly defended by a morass (where is now the nursery-garden), water being brought through a cutting from the Cherwell —that which runs under Magdalen.

The earliest Common Room in the University was fitted up at Merton in 1667. When dinner is ended here, as at Pembroke, the table is struck by the Senior Fellow 3 times with a trencher. These strokes summon the butler, who enters in his book what each Fellow has had of the buttery supplies. The gracecup is then handed round, and another stroke of the trencher summons the Bible-clerk to say grace.

Till the time of Henry VI., if not later, there existed to the W. of Merton Chapel the marble Cross, erected by the Jews as a penance for having destroyed a crucifix which was being carried in procession to the shrine of St. Frideswide on Ascension Day, 1268.

While the Court of Charles II. was at Oxford, Lady Castlemaine, afterwards Duchess of Cleveland, gave birth to a son by him at Merton. Hence " the possessor of all the virtues save one" used to go with a friend to Trinity College Chapel " half-dressed like angels," or make her entrance to the College walks with a lute playing before her.

The College possesses a small, but beautiful garden, which, however, is not accessible to the public.

Adjoining Merton is *St. Alban Hall* (D 5), built about 1230, and named after its founder, Robt. de St. Alban, a citizen of Oxford in the time of John. The Hall and Chapel are fair modern Gothic, but the small quadrangle contains a curious ancient bell-tower. This Hall was originally dependent upon the nunnery of Littlemore. Hooper the martyr, Massinger the poet, and the Speaker Lenthall, were among its members.

(4.) ORIEL. (D 5.) Founded in

1326 by Edward II., who is said to have made a vow to the Virgin, when fleeing from the field of Bannockburn, that he would found a religious house in her honour if he returned in safety. "Prompted and aided by his almoner (Adam de Brom), he decided on placing this house in the city of Alfred, and the Image which is opposite its entrance, is the token of the vow and its fulfilment to this day." The original College of Adam de Brome and Edw. II. was Tackley's Hall, so called from having belonged to the rector of that place; it stood at the back of the High Street, where its remains may still be seen in some arches and a groined crypt behind Wheeler and Day's shop. The mansion on the present site, bestowed on the College by Edward III., was called Le Oriole, and had belonged to James d'Espagne, Chaplain of St. Mary's, to whom it was granted by Eleanor, mother of Edw. II.; hence the Spanish pomegranate, which frequently appears in the decorations of the College. The word Oriole, or Oriel, was probably derived from Oratoriolum. As the small oratory was sometimes in a recess, the word was applied to projecting windows or a projecting apartment. The present buildings are all comparatively modern, having been built between 1620 and 1640; and the Library is the work of Wyatt, 1788. The Hall and Chapel, though without striking architectural merit, are extremely picturesque. The Hall contains a portrait of Edward II., and his statue, with that of Edward III., appears over the porch, beneath that of the Virgin and child. The College possesses an interesting relic, the cup of Edward II. with this inscription, "Vir racione bibas, non quod petit atra voluptas; sic caro casta datur; vis linguæ suppeditatur." The cocoa-nut cup of Bp. Carpenter, of Worcester, once provost here (d. 1476), is also curious. The chapel has some stained glass by Hardman. In the common room is a picture by Vasari containing portraits of. Dante, Petrarch, Boccaccio, and Politian. On the upper part of the porch of the Hall is an old Northern inscription in Runic characters—MADR. ER MOLDVR AVKI, "Man is but a heap of dust"—placed there by Bp. Robinson in 1719. This College, as being the first to open its fellowships to the University, was remarkable for the celebrated members it contained at one time within its walls, viz., Copleston, Davison, Whately, Keble, Arnold, Newman, Hampden, Pusey, and others. "Oriel," says Dr. Newman ('History of my Religious Opinions'), "from the time of Dr. Copleston to Dr. Hampden, had had a name far and wide for liberality of thought; it had received a formal recognition from the 'Edinburgh Review,' if my memory serves me truly, as the school of speculative philosophy in England; and on one occasion, in 1833, when I presented myself, with some of the first papers of the Movement, to a country clergyman in Northamptonshire, he paused awhile, and then, eyeing me with significance, asked whether Whately was at the bottom of them?"

Near Oriel is St. Mary Hall (C 5), an offshoot of that College, founded 1333. The Hall, with Chapel above, built about 1640, exhibits some very good tracery in the windows considering its late date. Sir Thomas More, Sir Christopher Hatton, and more recently Dr. Hampden, whose appointment to the see of Hereford occasioned so much commotion in 1848, had been members of this Hall.

For St. Mary's Church, see II.

(5.) ALL SOULS. (C 5.) (Notice the Gateway in High Street, the Chapel, the Library).

Founded in 1437 by Archbishop Chichele, as a chantry for priests to pray for the souls of all who had fallen or might fall in the French wars. With the chantry he combined a place of education on a noble scale, on the model of New College, to which he himself belonged, and this probably caused it to be spared at the Reformation, when all other chantries were swept away. There is a tradition that, in digging the foundations of this college, a large mallard issued from one of the drains, which gave rise to a mallard being the college crest, and to the song of "The Swapping Mallard" being sung by the fellows formerly on Jan. 14 each year.

Over the gate are the statues of Henry VI. and the founder, with a high relief representing the souls released from purgatory. The 1st quadrangle is in the same state in which it was erected by Chichele. The North quadrangle was designed by *Hawksmoor* in 1720, and completed in 1740. It contains the Library, Chapel, and Hall, and produces a striking effect. "The graduated stages of Hawksmoor's diminishing turret, together with other characteristics, exhibit a fantastic air of continental Gothic; but they seem to disdain all comparison, and to stand in unrivalled stateliness, challenging our admiration." The *Chapel*, restored 1872, is entered by a gateway with fan-tracery vaulting, and has the holy-water stoup still remaining, and some ancient glass in the transepts. The W. window is modern, by *Hardman*. Evelyn went "to see ye picture on the wall over ye altar at All Soules, being ye largest piece of fresco painting (or rather imitation of it, for it is in oil of turpentine) in England, not ill design'd by the hand of one Fuller. It seems too full of nakeds for a chapel." Beneath was the "Noli me tangere" of *Raphael Mengs*. During the repairs of 1872 the rich Gothic *reredos* of Chichele's time and style was discovered behind a lath and plaster screen which covered the wall beyond the altar. It was erected by Archbishop Chi-

chele in the early part of the 14 centy. and destroyed in 1549. It was beautifully restored by *Scott*, at the expense of Lord Bathurst, and is now one of the most magnificent in England. In the Library (restored 1871) is a huge statue of Sir W. Blackstone. The *Hall* is spacious, but in bad taste; it contains interesting portraits, of Jeremy Taylor and Bishop Heber, Fellows of this college, with the bust of the latter by *Chantrey*, of the founder by *Roubilliac*. The *Library*, which is a fine room built by bequest of Col. Codrington, 1716, possesses, among other interesting works, the original designs of Wren for the building of St. Paul's, &c., 300 in number. At the Commemoration in 1863, the Prince and Princess of Wales, with 600 other guests, were entertained in this Library, and in a temporary building erected in the quadrangle. In the vestibule are a tripod from Corinth, and portraits of Henry VI. and Chichele on glass, with some others. In 1867 an additional Library was erected, which is especially devoted to books on legal subjects. In the bursary is preserved a drum from Sedgmoor, and in the buttery the curious silver-gilt saltcellar of the founder, 400 yrs. old. The Warden's Lodgings contain a fine picture, by *Kneller*, of their architect, Dr. Clark, the secretary of Prince George of Denmark, writing from his master's dictation; and a portrait of Charles I., known as "the Oxford Charles," and described in the verses of Tickell.

(6.) UNIVERSITY. (C D 5.) (Notice the Gateways with statues, Chapel, the New Building.)

Founded about 1229 by William de Lanum, Archdeacon of Durham; though, according to a tradition accepted as true by the Judges of the Court of King's Bench in 1726, it owes its foundation to Alfred the Great. The earliest building purchased with the bequest of William of Durham was Drogheda Hall, opposite the gate of the present college, in 1255; and in 1263 a hall on the site of Brasenose was occupied by the society; about 1343 they removed to the present site.

The story of the foundation of Oxford by King Alfred is now proved to be a myth which had no existence until long after Alfred's time, and is due to an interpolation in Asser's Life. "The history of Oxford began in the 10th centy.; in the 11th it was a place of the first importance as a military post, and as the scene of great national gatherings. But it is not till the 12th that we get the first hint of the coming University, the first glimpses of schools, scholars, lecturers; and it is not till the 13th that we get anything like colleges in the modern sense. In that age too comes not University College, but the benefaction out of which University College grew."—Freeman.

The long front of this College, with its two tower gateways, is very imposing, and it is a great ornament to the High Street, although in the debased Gothic of the time of Charles I. The gateway leading into the W. quadrangle has on the exterior, a statue of Queen Anne, and on the interior one of James II., the gift of Dr. Obadiah Walker, Master from 1676 to the Revolution in 1688, when he was expelled. He had become a convert to Romanism, and caused the mass to be openly celebrated in a room adjoining the chapel, which James himself attended. With the exception of that in Whitehall Gardens, this is the only public statue of "the wise old gentleman who lost three kingdoms for a mass," as his friend Louis XIV. remarked. The gateway of the E. quadrangle has a statue of Queen Mary on the outside, and one of Dr. Radcliffe, its builder, inside.

The Hall, built in 1657, but remodelled in 1766 at the expense of members whose arms adorn the walls, contains portraits of Archbishops Abbot and Potter, Bishop Bancroft of Oxford, Dr. Radcliffe, Lords Eldon and Stowell, &c. The new Library, by Scott (Dec.), was built in the Fellows' Garden in 1861. It contains the statues of Lords Eldon and Stowell, designed by Watson, and executed by Nelson, intended for Westminster Abbey, but denied places on account of their colossal size.

The Chapel (dedicated to St. Cuthbert by the original founder), built 1665, had a screen by Gibbons, and some painted windows by Van Linge and Giles of York. It was remodelled in 1862 by Scott, in the Dec. style, receiving a new roof and E. window. The windows are valuable specimens of the revival of stained glass in the time of Charles I. and II. The works of the Dutch artist Van Linge, who was extensively employed in England at the latter period, "generally consist of large pictures extending over the whole or greater part of a window, irrespective of the mullions, and usually furnished with landscape backgrounds, exhibiting a great preponderance of green and blue. They are deficient in brilliancy, but are in general exceedingly rich in colour, the enamels in most cases being used rather to heighten the tint of the coloured glass, than by way of substitution for it." (Hints on Glass Painting). Gibbons' screen and cedar wainscoting, rich in carving, have been preserved. In the antechapel is a monument to Sir W. Jones, once a Fellow, by Flaxman; a fine bas-relief represents him forming his Digest of Hindoo Law, while the Brahmins are expounding to him the text of the Vedas.

The E. quadrangle is chiefly occupied with buildings formerly used as the Master's lodgings; it was built by a bequest from Dr. Radcliffe, and is open to gardens to the S. The detached New Building at the W. end is an exceedingly elegant structure by *Sir Charles Barry*, finished in 1850. A new house, for the Master was completed in 1879 (D 5).

Dr. Johnson was a frequent visitor in the Common Room here, where he used "to drink off three bottles of port without being the worse for it."—*Boswell.*

Shelley, who was expelled from this college, inhabited rooms on the first floor of the staircase to the rt. of the Hall. "In his time, books, papers, boots, philosophical instruments, clothes, pistols, linen, crockery, bags, and boxes were scattered on the floor and in every place; tables and carpets stained with large fire spots; an electric machine, air-pump, solar microscope, &c.; two piles of books supported the tongs, and then a small glass retort above an Argand lamp, which soon boiled over, added fresh stains to the table, and rose in disagreeable fumes."—*Shelley's Memoirs.*

(7.) QUEEN'S. (C 6.) (Notice the Gateway, Chapel, Hall, Library.)

Founded in 1341 by Robert de Eglesfield, confessor to Queen Philippa, from whom it took its name; and "there, according to tradition, the Prince of Wales her son, as in the next generation Henry V., was brought up. If we look at the events which followed, he could hardly have been 12 yrs. old when he became a member. . . . Queen s college is much altered in every way since the little prince went there, but they still keep an engraving of the vaulted room he is said to have occupied. . . . You may still hear the students summoned to dinner, as he was, by the sound of a trumpet; and, in the hall, you may still see, as he saw, the Fellows sitting all on one side the table, with the Head of the College in the centre, in imitation of the 'Last Supper,' as it is commonly represented in the pictures. The

very names of the Head and the 12 Fellows (the number first appointed by the founder, in likeness of our Lord and the Apostles) are known to us. He must have seen what has long since vanished away, the 13 beggars, deaf, dumb, maimed or blind, daily brought into the hall, to receive their dole of bread, beer, potage, and fish. He must have seen the 70 poor scholars, instituted after the example of the 70 disciples, and learning from their two chaplains to chant the service. He must have heard the mill within or hard by the College walls grinding the Fellows' bread. He must have seen the porter of the college going round to shave the beards and wash the heads of the Fellows."—*Stanley's Memorials of Canterbury.* The brasses of the founder, Eglesfield, of Dr. Langton, who enlarged the chapel (1518), of Bishop Robinson of Carlisle (1616), and others are preserved in the bursary, whilst in the buttery is kept a magnificent drinking-horn mounted with gold, the gift of Queen Philippa, and the curious cocoa-nut cup of Provost Bost (d. 1503) resting on four lions. The college is a modern (so-called) Grecian building, the work of Wren and his pupil Hawksmoor, the foundation stone having been laid on the 6th Feb. 1714, Queen Anne's birthday. The main entrance is surmounted by a cupola, under which is a statue of Caroline, queen of George II. The *Chapel* is a well-proportioned building, with painted windows from the history of Our Lord, and stately marble pillars. The eagle, dated 1662, bears the following inscription: — *Regina avium; avis Reginensium.* The *Hall*, designed by Wren, is a handsome, lofty room, with numerous portraits, many of royal personages, as Queens Philippa, Henrietta, Anne, Caroline, and Charlotte; Henry V., Edward IV., Charles I., and Edward the Black Prince. The *Library*, founded by Bishop Barlow (d. 1691), and since greatly added to by Dr. Mason in 1841, and well kept up by the College, now contains one of the best collections of historical works in Oxford. In the cloister underneath, which has been adapted by Cockerell, are preserved 2 windows, saved from the lodgings of Prince Henry, and his likeness on a brass plate, with the inscription :

" In perpetuam rei Memoriam.
Imperator Britanniæ,
Triumphator Galliæ,
Hostium Victor, et Sui,
Henricus Quintus, hujus Collegii
Et Cubiculi (minuti satis),
Olim magnus Incola."

Every Christmas-day a boar's head is served in the hall, after being introduced in grand procession * with a song, 'The Boar's Head;' and every New Year's day the bursar presents to the guests a needle, with thread coloured blue, red, and yellow, for the three faculties, saying, "Take this, and be thrifty;" a custom said to have its derivation from a play on the name of the founder—" aiguille," " fil."

From the corner beyond Queen's is one of the finest and most characteristic views in Oxford, and hence " the stream-like windings of the glorious street," as described by Wordsworth, are seen to the greatest advantage.

In New College Lane, opposite the E. wing of Queen's, is *St. Edmund Hall*, (C D 6), which belonged to Osney Abbey, having been founded in 1226, but was in 1557 assigned to Queen's College by one William Burnell, who had purchased it at the Dissolution. It has its name from occupying the site of a hall where the Archbishop Edmund of Abingdon used to lecture. The present buildings date from about the middle of the 17th centy.; they are of very plain character.

Nearly opposite Queen's are the

* See 'Sketch Book,' vol. ii., by Washington Irving, "The Christmas Dinner," where the words of this song are given.

new *Examination Schools* (D 6), erected by the University at a cost of nearly 90,000*l.* from designs by Mr. T. G. Jackson. They were commenced in 1876, and completed in 1882. The building occupies three sides of a quadrangle, and the N. wing which faces the High Street contains a lofty Hall with an open timber roof surmounted by a lantern, and a floor of rich marble mosaic. There are three rooms for written examinations, two of them having an area of 5000 sq. ft., and one of 3000. 25 sq. ft. of space are allotted to each man undergoing examination. These rooms are lofty and well ventilated, and the ceilings are panelled, and enriched with foliage. There are also 11 *vivâ voce* rooms. The W. staircase deserves especial notice ; it is very massive, and is constructed of carved Italian marbles, mainly red and white. The whole building, which is of the Renaissance style, is finely decorated both within and without. It is furnished with every modern convenience : there are electric bells, and electric clocks in every room ; and undoubtedly before long there will be electric lamps. It is warmed by hot water pipes, over which warm air streams into the room, while draught ventilators maintain a constant current of air.

(8.) MAGDALEN.   (D 6, 7.)   *Obs.* the Tower, West Front, Chapel, Cloisters, Hall, the Walks.)

Founded in 1457, by William Patten, Bishop of Winchester, surnamed Waynflete from his birthplace in Lincolnshire. An ancient hospital of St. John the Baptist formerly occupied this site. It was placed outside the city walls, both to guard the ferry over the river and as a hospice for the refreshment of pilgrims visiting the shrine of St. Frideswide. The " pilgrims wicket" is still distinctly traceable in the S. wall. The low embattled buildings towards the street are in part the remains of the hospital ; those round the first quadrangle, which is entered by a modern gateway (designed by Pugin in 1844), were finished shortly before the founder's death, which occurred in 1486, the Wars of the Roses having prevented his beginning to build until 1473.

This is the first college arrived at on entering Oxford by the old London road, and is distinguished at once by its graceful Perp. tower, 145 ft. high (1492-1505), rising at the side of the bridge over the Cherwell, a handsome structure, 526 ft. long.

It would be difficult to exaggerate the beauties of this college, which has enchanted every beholder, from James I., who declared that it was "the most *absolute* thing in Oxford."

Entering the quadrangle by a narrow wicket, the noble oriel over the further gate is that of the Founder's chamber, where Edward IV., Richard III., Henry VII., Prince Arthur, Henry VIII., Queen Elizabeth, and Prince Henry, have been successively entertained. This and the adjoining chambers were restored in 1857; the bed-room contains some ancient tapestry, representing the marriage of Prince Arthur and Katherine of Aragon; they are only accessible through the President's Lodgings, where Horne wrote his 'Commentary on the Psalms.' New buildings were constructed in 1882 to the W. of the President's lodging and facing the High Street. (*Bodley & Garner, archt.*) In design they are similar to the Old Quadrangle. (D 6.) In the President s garden is a picturesque fragment of the old *Magdalen Hall*. The doorway opposite leads into the chapel, and contains statues of St. John the Baptist, Edward IV., Mary Magdalen, St. Swithin, and the Founder. In the corner of the quadrangle (called St. John's from the hospital), on the rt., is a stone pulpit, where a sermon was formerly preached on St. John the Baptist's day, the court being lined with green boughs

and strewn with rushes to commemorate St. John's preaching in the wilderness.

The *Chapel*, which has a beautiful porch, was restored by Cottingham in 1833, and a series of statues has since been added to the altar screen. The altarpiece, "Christ bearing the Cross," by *Ribalta*, was brought from Vigo, 1702. The sculpture over the altar, "Christ appearing to Mary Magdalen," is by *Chantrey*. Close to the altar is a small oratory, which contains the tomb of the founder's father, Richard Patten, brought hither from the ruined ch. of Waynflete; there is a small statue of the founder himself, seated at his father's head. The choral service in this chapel is very fine: the organ is large enough for a cathedral. That which was here in the time of the Civil Wars, Cromwell liked so much, that he carried it off with him to Hampton Court. The windows are filled with painted glass, by *Hardman*. In the ante-chapel are several *Brasses*, mostly to members of the Society, but the ascription of one of them to Wm. Tibarde, the first President (d. 1480), is believed to be wrong. The chapel stands on the S. side of the *Cloisters*. This is a quadrangle of the time of the Founder, but ornamented with the rude sandstone statues erected in honour of a visit of James I. Their meaning is thus described in a MS. in the college library, styled "Œdipus Magdalenensis."

"Beginning at the S. E. corner, are the Lion and Pelican, the former the emblem of Courage and Vigilance, the latter of Parental Tenderness and Affection. Both together express the complete character of a good College governor, and, accordingly, are placed under the windows of the President's lodgings.

"On the rt., on the other side of the gateway, are 4 figures, viz., the Schoolmaster, the Lawyer, the Physician, and the Divine. These are ranged outside the library, and represent the duties and business of the students. By means of learning in general, they are to be introduced to one of the three learned professions, or else, as hinted to us by the figure with cap and bells in the corner, they must turn out Fools in the end. "On the N. of the quadrangle, the first 3 figures represent the history of David and his conquest over the Lion and Goliath, whence we are taught not to be discouraged at any difficulties which may stand in the way, as the vigour of youth will easily enable us to surmount them. The next figure is the Hippopotamus or River Horse, carrying his young upon his shoulders. This is the emblem of a good Tutor, or Fellow of a College, who is set to watch over the youth of the Society, and by whose prudence they are to be led through the dangers of their first entrance into the world. The figure immediately following represents Sobriety, or Temperance, that most necessary virtue of a collegiate life. The whole remaining train of figures are the vices we are instructed to avoid. Those next to Temperance are the opposite vices of Gluttony and Drunkenness. Then follow the Lycanthropos, the Hyæna, and Panther, representing Violence, Fraud, and Treachery; the Griffin, representing Covetousness; and the next figure, Anger or Moroseness. The Dog, the Dragon, the Deer—Flattery, Envy, and Timidity; and the last 3. the Mantichora, the Boxers, and the Lamia—Pride, Contention, and Lust."

The Hall, of which the ceiling is the work of Wyatt, c. 1790, is wainscoted with oak, carved with the linen pattern, put up in 1541; several compartments have incidents in the history of Mary Magdalen. The walls are hung with portraits of members or benefactors, including the Founder, Cardinal Wolsey, Bp. Fox, Cardinal Pole, Dean Colet,

Prince Henry, son of James I., Prince Rupert, Dr. Hammond, Addison, &c. In this hall, in 1687, sat King James's tyrannous commission, appointed to visit the President and Fellows and deprive the college of its rights.

The *Library* is a modern restoration. "Its shelves groan under the weight of the Benedictine folios, of the editions of the Fathers and the collections of the Middle Ages, which have issued from the single library of St. Germain des Prés at Paris" (*Gibbon*), but at the present day are by no means confined to them, having received many important additions.

Traversing the cloisters we reach a fine open lawn and flower garden, in which is a magnificent plane-tree planted by Bp. H. Phillpotts. Facing us are the *New Buildings*, a stately modern sash-windowed pile, behind which is the Grove, where a herd of fallow deer is kept.

On rt., *Magdalen Walks*, a meadow attached to the college, encircled by the arms of the Cherwell, and intersected by avenues of trees, along raised dykes. One of these on the N. is called Addison's Walk. Pope, a constant visitor of his friend Digby in this college, mentions—

" Maudlen's learned grove."

There is also on l. a private park, bounded by the outer wall of the college, with fine elm-trees and deer. In the meadow are found *Fritillaria Meleagris*, snakeshead, and *Arabis turrita*, tower rock-cress.

Wolsey entered this college 1485, and at 15 yrs. obtained the degree of B.A., whence his appellation of the Boy Bachelor. He was bursar of the college during the time that the tower was in progress. Of this, Dr. Ingram says, "It is in fact as a building, what Wolsey was as a man; and to him who cannot perceive and feel its beauties, it is in vain to attempt to describe them."

In accordance with an ancient custom which originated in a requiem for Henry VII., in commemoration of his visit in 1488, glees and madrigals were always sung at the top of this tower at sunrise on May morning to usher in the spring, but these have now given way to a hymn, 'Hymnus Eucharisticus,' with music by Dr. Rogers. On this occasion the bells (called by Anthony Wood the most tuneable and melodious in all these parts) are all rung, when the whole tower shakes and bends perceptibly. Those who witness this ceremony will call to mind the opening lines of 'The Scholar's Funeral' by Prof. Wilson, himself a Magdalen man:—

" Why hang the sweet bells mute in Magdalen Tower,
Still wont to usher in delightful May,
The dewy silence of the morning hour
Cheering with many a changeful roundelay?
And those pure voices, where are they,
That, hymning far up in the listening sky,
Seemed issuing softly through the gates of day,
As if a troop of sainted souls on high
Were hovering o'er the earth with angel melody?"

As the Duke of Wellington entered Oxford to be installed as Chancellor, he asked his companion, Mr. Croker, what was the building on his right hand, pointing to the long wall which connects the tower with the rest of the college. "That is the wall which James II. ran his head against," was the answer. The resistance of the Fellows of Magdalen to the arbitrary ejection of their President, John Hough, and the infringement of their chartered rights by James, formed one of the leading causes of the Revolution of 1688, and of the expulsion of the Stuarts.

"Magdalen College, founded by Wm. Waynflete, Bp. of Winchester and Lord Chancellor, is one of the most remarkable of our academical institutions. A graceful tower, on the summit of which a Latin hymn is annually chanted by choristers at the dawn of May-day, caught, far off, the eye of the traveller who came from London. As he approached, he found that this tower arose from an embattled pile, low and irregular, yet singularly venerable, which, embowered in verdure, overhung the sluggish waters of the Cherwell. He passed through a gateway overhung by a noble oriel, and found himself in a spacious cloister, adorned with emblems of virtues and vices, rudely carved in grey stone by the masons of the 15th centy. The table of the society was plentifully spread in a stately refectory, hung with painting, and rich with fantastic carving. The services of the Church were performed, morning and evening, in a chapel which had suffered much violence from the Reformers, and much from the Puritans, but which was, under every disadvantage, a building of eminent beauty, and which has in our own time been restored with rare taste and skill. The spacious gardens along the river-side were remarkable for the size of the trees, among which, towered conspicuous, one of the vegetable wonders of the island, a gigantic oak, older by a century, men said, than the oldest college in the University.

"The statutes of the Society ordained that the kings of England and princes of Wales should be lodged in their house. Edward IV. had inhabited the building while it was still unfinished. Richard III. had held his court there, had heard disputations in the hall, had feasted there royally, and had rewarded the cheer of his hosts by a present of fat bucks from his forests. Two heirs-apparent of the Crown, who had been prematurely snatched away, Arthur, the elder brother of Henry VIII., and Henry, the elder brother of Charles I., had been members of the College. Another prince of the blood, the last and best of the Roman Catholic archbishops, the gentle Reginald Pole, had studied there. In the time of the Civil Wars Magdalen had been true to the cause of the crown. There Rupert had fixed his quarters; and before some of his most daring enterprises, his trumpets had been heard sounding to horse through those quiet cloisters. Most of the Fellows were divines, and could aid the king only by their prayers and their pecuniary contributions; but one member of the body, a doctor of civil law, raised a troop of undergraduates, and fell fighting bravely at their head against the soldiers of Essex. When hostilities had terminated, and the Roundheads were masters of England, six-sevenths of the members of the Foundation refused to make any submission to usurped authority. They were consequently ejected from their dwellings, and deprived of their revenues. After the Restoration, the survivors returned to their pleasant abode. They had now been succeeded by a new generation, which inherited their opinions and their spirit."—*Macaulay's Hist.*

It was on this eminently loyal society that James II. attempted to force one Anthony Farmer as President. He was a professed Romanist, and thus statutably ineligible, even if his notorious bad character had not stood in the way. The Fellows instead chose Dr. John Hough, and though threatened by the king, refused to give way. At last a body of Visitors was sent to Oxford, who held their meetings in the College hall, and finally pronounced sentence of deprivation. Unawed by the military force that supported them, Hough utterly abjured their authority, and addressed them thus in open court: "My lords, I do hereby protest against all your proceedings, and against all that you have done, or hereafter shall do, in prejudice of me and my right, as illegal, unjust, and null; and there-

fore I appeal to my sovereign lord the king in his courts of justice."

Though this protest was disregarded, "many signs showed that the spirit of resistance had spread to the common people. The porter of the college threw down his keys; the butler refused to scratch Hough's name out of the buttery book, and was instantly dismissed. No blacksmith could be found in the whole city who would force the lock of the President's lodgings; it was necessary for the Commissioners to employ their own servants, who broke open the door with iron bars. The sermons which, on the following Sunday, were preached in the University ch., were full of reflections, such as stung Cartwright to the quick, though such as he could not discreetly resent."—*Macaulay's Hist.* Hough was restored in the following year; he died Bishop of Worcester in 1743.

At the end of the High Street, opposite Magdalen, is the *Botanic* or *Physic Garden* (on the site of the ancient Jews' burial-place), entered by a gateway, designed by Inigo Jones, and ornamented with statues of Charles I. and II., which were paid for by a fine levied on Anthony Wood for a libel on Lord Clarendon. The establishment of the garden is due to a bequest of Henry Danvers, Earl Danby, 1622, though Linacre commenced a garden at a much earlier period. It was well laid out under the energetic superintendence of the late Dr. Daubeny, the plants being arranged according to the two systems of Linnæus and Jussieu. In the Lecture-room are preserved the Herbaria of Sherard and Dillenius. There is a delightful walk by the river-side, and the small garden at the back offers a view over Merton Meadow.

A short distance W. of the college is *Magdalen College School*, mainly designed for the education of the Magdalen choristers. (D 6.) Its foundation is coeval with that of the college, but the present building is a good Perp. structure, by *Buckler*, the foundation stone of which was laid by Dr. Routh in 1849, on his 95th birthday. In *Long Wall Street*, beside the school, is a considerable portion of the old wall, which the college is bound to keep in repair. Formerly it was enlivened in summer by the bright golden flowers of the *Senecio squalidus*, or *inelegant ragwort*, the seeds of which are said to have been sent hither from the grotto of Egeria, and which is elsewhere so common that it bears the name of the " Oxford weed; " but a late restoration of the battlements has swept it away from this spot. This street leads to the picturesque group of buildings formed by *Holywell Ch.*, cemetery, school, and rectory-house, surrounded by tall elm-trees. (O 7.) The ch., of E. E. date, has been well restored. It dates probably from the 12th centy., and was restored and partially rebuilt in 1845. In the churchyard is buried Thos. Holt, the architect of the Bodleian (d. 1624). An addition to the churchyard, called the *St. Cross Cemetery*, but made before the days of burial boards, with their consecrated and unconsecrated grounds, is a beautiful spot, with handsome memorials to many members of the University, and flower-decked graves, from which the Christian symbol is, in hardly one case, absent. In the adjoining fields may be still traced some slight remains of the earthworks thrown up during the siege of Oxford by Fairfax, in 1646.

(9.) NEW COLLEGE. (O 6.) (Notice the Entrance Gate, Chapel, Hall, Gardens, and the new buildings in the Slype.) Founded by William of Wykeham, as the complement to his great school at Winchester. The first stone was laid March 5, 1380, being his 55th birthday, and the work completed

[*Berks, &c.*]

1386. Froissart says of him, " At this time reigned a priest called William of Wykeham (Bishop of Winchester and Chancellor), who was so much in favour with the King of England (Edward III.) that everything was done by him, and nothing done without him." Though the foundation is thus nearly five centuries old, "it is not without reason that it still bears the name of ' New,' since it marks a new era in University annals. Before this, the Aularian system, even in the case of Merton, had generally prevailed; but since the formation of this society, it has served as a model to nearly all founders of colleges, both here and at Cambridge."—*Ingram*.

The buildings, in the main, are the work of Wykeham, and are thus particularly interesting. We enter by a noble *Tower gateway*, with the Virgin in a niche above, to whom an angel and the founder are addressing themselves in prayer. The *Chapel*, one of the earliest Perp. buildings, has a detached bell-tower of a very massive nature. In the ante-chapel remain some of the original painted windows, and there is a large number of *Brasses*, chiefly of former wardens. Among them are Cranley, Archbishop of Dublin (d. 1417), in full pontificals, with a crozier; and Yong, Bp. of Callipolis (d. 1526), laid down by him when living, the date being left to be filled up after his death, which was never done. The bust of Antony Aylworth (rt. of the door when entering) (d. 1619) presents a minute example of costume: observe the fastening of his wristbands. In the chapel, restored 1879 at a cost of 25,000*l.*, the altarpiece is a restoration by *Wyatt*, with alto-relievos by *Westmacott*, representing the Annunciation, Nativity, Descent from the Cross, the Resurrection, and the Ascension. A reredos, which will be somewhat similar to that at All Souls', is in course of construction. In a stone recess near the altar

P

is preserved the Pastoral Staff of William of Wykeham, of silvergilt, a fine specimen of mediæval art. Beneath the crook, the bishop himself is represented on his knees. The painted glass on the S. is good, of the early part of the 17th centy., by Flemish artists ; that on the N. is by Peckett, of York. Daily choral service is performed here during Term, as well as at Magdalen (the music of high excellence). The W. door opens into the picturesque Cloisters (130 ft. by 85), remarkable for their ribbed roof, which resembles the bottom of a boat. In 1643 the cloisters were used as a depôt for the royal military stores.

The Hall, the oldest in Oxford, is entered through the muniment tower, which like the gateway has its niches still filled with statues. The screen and wainscoting are of the linen pattern, and are ascribed to Archbishop Warham ; the whole has been restored by Scott, panelled with oak, and a fine oak roof substituted for the former one. There are some portraits over the High Table. The Library, the work of Wyatt, cannot be praised. In the Audit Room are preserved the College Seals, of the age of the foundation, some records nearly of the same date, and some old pictures of saints, removed from the chapel. The collection of ancient plate and jewels is very remarkable, and includes a saltcellar and cup given by Archbishop Warham, and the remains of the Mitra Preciosa, the morse, the ring, gloves, and pax of the Founder.

Scott's building in the Slype, finished in 1878, and designed for the accommodation of thirty-six students, has been described as "the best modern example of a collegiate building."

The Warden's Lodgings contain a remarkable portrait of the Founder, supposed by Sir J. Reynolds to be an original. Till near the end of the last centy. the members of New College were called to dinner by two choristers chanting, from the Warden's lodgings to the garden gate, "Tempus est vocandi a manger tous seigneurs."

The garden court was designed by Wren. The Gardens of New College are among the most beautiful in Oxford. The mound covered with shrubs, which rises opposite the gateway, produces a pleasing illusion. The garden is enclosed on three sides by the ancient walls of the city, which, by covenant between the Founder and the corporation, the college is bound to keep in repair, and they consequently present an interesting example of old civic fortification. The iron railings and gate at the entrance of the garden were brought from Canons, the princely seat of the Duke of Chandos, near Edgeware. A door in one corner of the garden opens through what was an old postern of the town, into a strip of ground called "the Slip," or Slype, whence a picturesque view is obtained of the bastions, with the fine Perp. belltower and the chapel. In this tower Protestant members of the College were imprisoned during the reign of Henry VIII., by its warden Dr. London ; Quinby, one of the Fellows, died there of cold and starvation.

During the Great Rebellion New College was occupied as a military post, first by the Royalists and afterwards by the Parliamentarians.

At the corner of New College Lane (C 5) and facing the Bodleian, is HERTFORD COLLEGE, formerly known as Magdalen Hall. It was founded by Bishop Waynflete in 1487, removed to the present site in 1822, and reconstituted as Hertford College in 1874 by Act of Parliament. It possesses no objects of interest.

(10.) BRASENOSE COLL. (C 5.) (Notice Entrance Gateway, with

brazen nose, Quadrangle, Chapel, Hall, Library.)

Founded by Bishop Smith, of Lincoln, and Sir Richard Sutton, 1512. The name is a corruption of Brasinium, the *brasen-hus*, or brew-house of King Alfred's palace, which is supposed to have occupied its site, and to have been turned into a place of learning—a fanciful derivation! The actual name, however, is supported by a brazen nose of large dimensions, fixed over the college gate. The entrance tower is good Perp. (restored 1866), and the buildings of the quadrangle remain in their original state, except that some received an extra story in the time of James I. In the quadrangle there was formerly a statuary group of Cain and Abel, which provoked the indignation of Hearne. The place, he says, "was once a garden, which was a delightful and pleasant shade in summer-time, but was cut down by direction of the Principal and some others, purely to turn it into a grass-plot and erect some silly statue there."

The *Chapel*, built 1666, is in a mixed style. "The roof, which is a kind of hammer-beam, with fan-vaulting above, was brought from the chapel of St. Mary's College, which formerly stood in the Corn Market, founded by Henry VI., 1435" (*Arch. Journ.* vol. viii.); the windows also are Gothic, but there are Grecian columns and a Grecian altarpiece. In 1860 the windows were filled with painted glass, and the ceiling adorned in mediæval style. The *Hall* has a curious shallow porch, and contains portraits of Burton, the author of the 'Anatomy of Melancholy,' Dr. Radcliffe, and others, including King Alfred. The *Library*, built by Wren, somewhat resembles the chapel in its mixture of styles. Reginald Heber was a member of this college. He occupied rooms at the N.E. corner of the quadrangle, and a fine chestnut in

the gardens of Exeter, which overshadows them, still bears the name of "Heber's tree."

New buildings are in course of construction, which will form a quadrangle facing High Street.

The space in front, Radcliffe Square, has in its centre the Radcliffe Library, while the E. side is occupied by All Souls, the S. by St. Mary's Ch. (*post*), and the N. by the Schools (C. 5). "The assemblage of buildings in that quarter," says H. Walpole, "though no single one is beautiful, always struck me with singular pleasure, as it conveys such a vision of large edifices, unbroken by private houses, as the mind is apt to entertain of renowned cities that exist no longer."

The *Radcliffe Library* (C 5), "one of the most striking, and perhaps the most pleasing of the classical buildings in Oxford," a handsome rotunda, with a dome on an octagon base (diam. 100 ft., height 140 ft.), is the best work of Gibbs, 1749. It is named after its founder, Dr. Radcliffe, the physician of William III. and Queen Anne, a great benefactor to the University. He left 40,000*l.* for its construction, and smaller sums for a librarian, purchase of books, &c. A noble domed hall (height 46 ft. from pavement), in which the allied sovereigns dined 1814, occupies the interior, and was filled until 1861 with books on medicine and science. These, however, are now removed to the Library of the New University Museum, the Radcliffe being reserved as an adjunct to, and reading room for, the Bodleian, and appropriated to the books and periodicals of the last four years. It is open from 10 A.M. to 10 P.M. Over the door is the portrait of the founder by *Sir Godfrey Kneller*, the only original likeness extant. The *panorama* of Oxford from the roof well repays the ascent, and the small fee demanded from visitors.

A short distance N. are the Old Schools, restored and refaced externally, a quadrangular building once used for lectures in the different Faculties, but now entirely devoted to the purposes of the Bodleian Library. The entrance from Radcliffe-square is by a vaulted passage, but the central *Gate Tower* (E.) is a remarkable example of the Cinquecento style, and presents on the inside the 5 orders of architecture piled one above another. It was built (1619) by Thomas Holt, to whom Oxford was much indebted at that period. The sitting statue (formerly gilt) in the upper story represents James I. presenting his works to Fame and the University. The wooden sceptre fell from its hand on the accession of William IV. The *Public Examinations* of Candidates for Degrees were formerly held in the rooms on the ground floor. *New Schools* have been erected in High St., near University Coll. (v. p. 204).

The entire quadrangle is occupied by the *Bodleian Library* (C 5), named after its founder Sir Thomas Bodley (a retired diplomatist, b. at Exeter 1544, d. 1612), who, " with a munificence which has rendered his name more immortal than the foundation of a family would have done, bestowed on the University a library collected by him at great cost, built a magnificent room for its reception, and bequeathed large funds for its increase." The building was completed 1602, and is described by Casaubon, who visited it 1618, as " a work rather for a king than for a private man." In 1612 Bodley matured his plan for adding Public Schools for the University to his Library, but he died within the year, and was buried in Merton Chapel March 23, on the day following which the first stone of the Schools was laid. The ground plan of the older portion of the Library is in the form of the

letter H, and comprises three apartments. The centre or connecting one was built (1480), as an upper story to the Divinity Schools. The Duke of Gloucester's library was placed in it, but destroyed, together with a quantity of stained glass and sculpture, in the reign of Edward VI., when the walls were left overgrown with brambles. The Eastern or Arts end was added by Bodley, and the Western by the University in 1636 for Selden's books, with the Convocation House underneath. Among the benefactors of the library have been William, Earl of Pembroke, Archbp. Laud, Sir Kenelm Digby, John Selden, Lord Fairfax, Richard Rawlinson, Richard Gough, Edmund Malone, and Francis Douce, some of whom bequeathed also coins, medals, and drawings. The Tower and the adjoining buildings were restored -in accordance with the original design in 1882. The Library has also been augmented by purchases, and by a copy of every book entered at Stationers' Hall, which an Act of Parliament obliges the publisher to present. It is particularly rich in Oriental literature, and possesses, perhaps, the largest Hebrew collections in the world.

The Library, which now contains over 400,000 printed volumes, and 30,000 MSS., is open to all graduates of the University, and all others who present a sufficient recommendation, from 9 in the morning to 3, 4 or 5 P.M., according to the time of year; while the Radcliffe, where lights are allowed, is open from 10 .A.M. to 10 P.M.

The older printed books are in the main placed in the part of the building erected by Bodley himself; a lofty chamber, with the roof divided into square compartments bearing the arms of the University and of the founder, and walls hung with portraits. Among the curiosities of the Bodleian (some of which are placed in glass cases for the inspection of visitors) are a translation of Genesis into Anglo-Saxon by Cædmon the monk, with miniatures of the 9th centy.; Græco-Latin MS. of the Acts of the Apostles, of the 6th centy. (*Codex Laudianus*); Greek New Testament, which belonged to Ebner of Nuremberg, the binding ornamented with ivory carvings; Terence, of 12th centy., with illustrations; MS. of the Apocalypse, probably written for Henry III.;—the Hours of Mary of Burgundy;—Psalter of R. de Ormsby, monk of Norwich, beautiful miniatures, 1340;—a MS. of Wycliffe's Bible;—Latin Exercises, in the writing of Edw. VI. and Q. Eliz.; —the Confession of the Duke of Monmouth, witnessed by his signature and those of 6 bishops; the first Bible of Gutenberg, Mainz 1448, and autographs of Luther and Melanchthon; the famous long lost Mexican MS.; some curious mediæval maps and calendars. Some of the MSS. are adorned with precious miniatures by Van Eyck, Memling, or their scholars; that of Mary of Gonzaga by scholars of Raphael.

At the end of the room is some historical stained glass, representing —the Penance of Henry II. in the Chapter-house at Canterbury; Edward II., as king of Scotland, receiving the homage of the barons and abbots; the Marriage of Henry VI. with Margaret of Anjou.

Higher up on the library staircase is the *Picture Gallery*, which contains many curious historical portraits. Among them are almost all the founders of colleges. Also, Thomas Sackville Lord Buckhurst, William Herbert Earl of Pembroke, *Vandyke;* Selden, *Mytens;* Mary Queen of Scots, *Zucchero;* Lord Burleigh on his mule, in his robes as Lord High Treasurer; Handel, *Hudson;* Flora Macdonald, *Allan Ramsay*, &c. In the central division of the gallery is a bronze statue of William Herbert, Earl of Pembroke (Chancellor of the University, 1616-30), executed from a portrait of *Rubens*, by Herbert le Sœur, the modeller of the equestrian statue of Charles I. at Charing Cross. The finest picture in the gallery is a portrait of Sir Kenelm Digby, by *Vandyke*, who had been studying the colouring of Titian in Italy, and on his return found Sir Kenelm, then in mourning for his wife Venetia, a fit subject for the exercise of the art which he had learnt. Here also is the chest of Sir T. Bodley, a fine specimen of ancient iron-work; and a large number of models of classic and other buildings.

Descending to the Schools quadrangle, a vaulted vestibule leads W. to the *Divinity School.* The proper name of the vestibule is the *Proscholium*, but it commonly bears the name of the "Pig market," having, with the School to which it leads, been thus vilely misused in the time of Edward VI. It was the scene of the memorable encounter between the Vice-Chancellor (Dr. Fell) and the Parliamentary visitors, on June 4, 1647, when the latter did not appear at their appointed hour in consequence of the length of Mr. Harris' sermon at St. Mary's. The Divinity School itself is the basement story of Duke Humphrey's library, commenced in 1426, and finished, as a theological lecture-room in 1480. "Its peculiar feature is the stone roof, which consists of bold 4-centred arches, the spandrils of which are filled with tracery, and the spaces between these ribs are groined with 2 rows of pendants, finishing below in small niches, which reach much below the ribs, and form 3 arches across the span." About 1550 the fittings of the interior and the lead of the roof were carried off, but fortunately the roof itself escaped with little damage, and in the time of Mary the building was restored, sufficiently to be used for various purposes. Here Ridley and Latimer appeared before their judges: "Ridley at first stood bareheaded, but as soon as he heard the Cardinal named and the Pope's holiness, he put on his cap." In the Parliament held at Oxford in 1625 on account of the plague, the Peers occupied the Picture Gallery, and the House of Commons met in the Divinity School. It was afterwards used as a storehouse for corn, and was not restored till the beginning of the last centy. The doorway on the N., under one of the windows, was made by Wren, for the convenience of processions to the Theatre. The door at the W. end of this room admits the visitor to the *Convocation House* (1639), where the degrees are conferred and the business of the University is transacted: notice the fan-tracery of the roof, its only good feature. The Vice-Chancellor's Court is held in the ante-chamber, or Apodyterium.

(11). LINCOLN. (C 5.) (Notice the Hall and Chapel, Wesley's Rooms.)

Founded in 1427 by Richard Flemyng, Bishop of Lincoln; and augmented in 1479 by another bp. of that see, Thomas Rotherham, who afterwards became Archbp. of York and Lord Chancellor. Flemyng, the founder, had in earlier days been suspected of favouring the opinions of Wycliffe, but he built this college as a nursery for preachers against them. He, however, endowed it but meanly; and some fifty years after, when Bishop Rotherham was staying in it on a visit, the rector, Dr. Tristoppe, preached so touching a sermon on the wants of his college, from the text, "Behold, and visit this vine," &c.— Ps. lxxx. 14, 15, that the Bishop, with difficulty restraining his emotion till the discourse was ended, afterwards richly endowed it. In gratitude for this event, the vine is carefully cultivated at Lincoln to this day, and the walls of the inner quadrangle are covered with its branches.

The *Hall*, built by Dean Forest in 1436, has suffered external alteration, and the interior was remodelled in 1701 by Lord Crewe, Bishop of Durham, who also gave several pictures by Sir Peter Lely. The *Chapel*, built 1629, by Williams, Bishop of Lincoln, and wainscoted with cedar "very sweet" (*Pointer*), contains some remarkable glass of the 17th centy. brought from Italy by him; the E. window should be noticed, as giving a perfect series of types and antitypes. The seats are surmounted by ancient carved figures. In the Library are some valuable MSS.; among others, one of Wycliffe's Bible.

New buildings are in course of erection, providing accommodation for sixteen students.

The *Rector's Lodgings* were built 1465, by Bishop Beckyngton, of Bath and Wells, whose rebus several times repeated remains on the walls. The fixed meetings of this Society are still called chapters, Lincoln having been founded as a college of priests attached to the adjoining Church of All Saints.

Of this college John Wesley became a Fellow, 1726, and the pulpit from which he may have preached still remains in the ante-chapel. The society which he founded here consisted of about 15 persons, who were styled by their contemners "the Holy Club." "When first they began to meet, they read divinity on Sunday evenings only, and pursued their classical studies on other nights; but religion soon became the sole business of their meetings: they now regularly visited the prisoners and the sick, communicated once a week, and fasted on Wednesdays and Fridays, the stationary days of the ancient Church." They used to "go through a ridiculing crowd to receive the sacrament at St. Mary's," John Wesley especially attracting attention from wearing his hair remarkably long, and flowing loose over his shoulders; he did this in order to give to the poor the money he must have paid for dressing it. When remonstrated with, he replied, "I am much more sure that what leaving it thus enables me to do is according to the Scripture, than I am that the length of it is contrary." (Southey's *Life of Wesley*.)

Lincoln College has the singular distinction of having contributed a Primate to the Churches both of England and France; namely, John Potter to the Archbishopric of Canterbury, and William Giffard to the Archbishopric of Rheims. Bishop Sanderson, Sir William Davenant, and the non-jurors Kettlewell and Hicks, were also members of this College.

(12.) JESUS. (C 5.) (Notice the Chapel and Hall.)

Founded 1571 by Hugh Price, Treasurer of St. David's; but as Queen Elizabeth contributed much of the timber for the buildings, she is designated founder; and the title of "second founder" is given to Sir Leoline Jenkins, the eminent civilian and royalist, who was mainly instrumental in re-edifying it after the Restoration. Jesus was by its founder intended exclusively for Welshmen, but this has been altered by the ordinance of the University Commissioners, and more than half of the fellowships are now open to natives of any country. The *Chapel*, built 1621, and restored in 1864, noteworthy as the only one in Oxford which has a double chancel, contains the tomb of Sir Leoline Jenkins; also, the monument of Sir Eubule Thelwall, who built the Principal's House; and a fine E. window, by *Powell*. Service is conducted here in Welsh on Wednesdays and Fridays. Over the door is the appropriate motto, "Ascendat oratio, descendat gratia." The *Hall* has an elaborately carved screen in the Jacobean style, and a noble bay window. Among the portraits are those of Queen Elizabeth Charles I. and II., Sir Eubule Thel-

wall, as a child with his mother, &c. The *Library*, built by Sir Leoline Jenkins in 1667, contains many rare MSS., but its chief curiosity is "Y Llyfr Coch," or the Red Book, containing several Welsh legends, some relating to King Arthur and the round table. Both the E. and S. fronts of the college have been refaced by Buckler, with considerable improvement on the old design.

(13). EXETER. (C 5.) (Notice the Hall, Library, and Chapel.)

Founded by Walter Stapleton, Bishop of Exeter, 1314. This is one of the largest of the colleges, being, in number of members, second only to Christ Church. The greater part of the buildings are modern, and they are among the finest in Oxford. The *Hall*, which is a good specimen of a college refectory, was built in 1618 by Sir John Acland, and restored by *Nash* in 1818. Its high-pitched timber roof is very fine. The *Chapel*, was rebuilt by *Scott* in 1857-8 at a cost of 17,000l., on the site of a 15th-centy. edifice, which was removed at the same time. The present building is an imitation of the Sainte-Chapelle at Paris. The interior is highly decorated, and the painted windows by *Bell* and *Clayton*, the screen which divides the ante-chapel from the chapel, and the modern Venetian mosaics by Salviati, deserve notice. The *Library* and the Broad-street (or N.) front, also by *Scott*, are good specimens of modern Gothic; the W. front, restored by Underwood in 1832, is less striking, though its great extent makes it a notable object. The college possesses a pretty but private garden, at the corner of which is a large chestnut-tree, overhanging the adjacent street (Brasenose Street), which is called Heber's tree (*ante*).

Adjoining the Broad-street front of Exeter is the *Ashmolean Museum* (C 5), open from 11 to 4 daily, and well deserving a visit. It was entirely remodelled about 1830 by the brothers Duncan and Professor Phillips, and has now, in Mr. J. H. Parker, C.B., author of the ' Glossary of Architecture,' and other works, a Keeper well fitted to make it a most valuable museum of history and archæology. The original contents of the Ashmolean Museum were in many respects very different from its present ones. Gathered together by the two Tradescants, men of extensive knowledge in botany and natural history as then studied, they formed the contents of " Tradescant's Ark," a kind of Museum in their house at Lambeth, of which a Catalogue was published in 1656; and in 1662 it passed by bequest into the hands of " Art's great Mecænas, learned Esquire Ashmole," as his friend Lilly the astrologer terms him. He, in 1677, made an offer of it, together with his library, to the University, on condition of a suitable edifice being prepared for their reception. The offer was accepted, and the present building was erected about 1682, by a local architect named Wood, the common ascription to Sir Christopher Wren being a mistake. "The collection, with the additions of Ashmole, included birds, beasts, and fishes, especially the productions of distant countries, all that was comprised under the general name of ' Rarities.' Such was the general character of a Museum down to our own time." This miscellaneous collection has now been separated, and its parts distributed—the books and MSS. to the Bodleian, the natural history objects to the New Museum, and the portraits to the various picture galleries in Oxford. In lieu of these things, there is now to be seen a choice, though not large collection of flint implements, British, Roman, and mediæval pottery, mediæval jewellery and metal-work, besides specimens of Egyptian, Greek, and early Christian art, as well as a volume of 2000 photographs of

Roman architecture in all ages. Here is the complete collection of Anglo-Saxon remains from the Fairford graves (1852); most of those figured in Douglas' ' Nænia Britannica;' British and Saxon remains from Stanlake, with a model of the British village there (*Archæologia,* vol. xxxvii.); and most of the objects represented in the folio edition of Cook's Second Voyage; Alfred's jewel, a pear-shaped ornament of gold and enamel, probably the head of his sceptre; Henry VIII.'s sword and hawking glove, Queen Elizabeth's watch and hunting boots, Queen Mary's glove, Bradshaw's iron-lined hat, Cromwell's watch and privy seal; the Staffordshire clog almanac, the branks for punishing scolds &c. In the lower story are most of the celebrated *Arundel Marbles* (presented to the University in 1677), containing the Parian Chronicle, but some of the inscriptions remain at present built into the walls of the room that formerly contained the whole.

Immediately adjoining the Ashmolean is the *Sheldonian Theatre* (C 5), built by Wren, at the expense of Archbishop Sheldon, in 1669—a happy imitation of ancient theatres, especially that of Marcellus at Rome. " It was one of Wren's earliest, best, and most difficult works, entirely carried out under his own superintendence. Though externally it does not possess much dignity, its façade is elegant and appropriate. The roof was justly considered in that age a masterpiece of carpentry. The interior is arranged so scientifically and with such judgment, that a larger number of persons can see and hear than in any similar building in the kingdom."— *Fergusson's Mod. Arch.* The piers of the iron railing in front are surmounted by colossal heads, said to represent the Sages of Antiquity or the Cæsars, but they are really execrable copies of sportive masks, as may be seen by their ornaments. Its internal dimensions are 80 ft. by 70; its roof, an ingenious geometrical construction, is perfectly flat, and, as the classic theatres had no roof, this is designed to represent a canvas stretched over gilt cordage. It was painted by *Streater.* An octagonal cupola was added to the exterior by *Blore* in 1838, from which an excellent view of Oxford is obtained. In this building the annual "Commemoration" (when the Term has ended, usually in June) of benefactors to the University is held, prize compositions are recited from pulpits in fanciful imitation of a Roman rostrum, and honorary degrees are conferred on distinguished persons. Here in 1814 the Emperor Alexander of Russia, the King of Prussia, Blücher, the Cossack Platoff, and others received the honour, and were arrayed in the red robe of doctors. On such occasions the area below is filled with Masters of Arts and strangers; the dignitaries of the University and more distinguished visitors occupy the lower seats of the semicircle; while the galleries are crowded with undergraduates, who formerly kept up a perpetual storm of applause or hisses, not only on persons present, but on political and other noted personages, even at a distance, as their names were called out at random by any of their own body. This practice, which was an innovation of late years, has now been very much diminished by causing the upper and lower galleries to be occupied both by ladies and undergraduates.

Not many yards from the Theatre, on the E., is the *Old Clarendon Printing Office,* erected 1711, by William Townsend, and not as is commonly said by Sir John Vanbrugh, from the profits of the sale of Lord Clarendon's 'History of the Rebellion,' given exclusively and for ever to the University by the author's son. Since 1830, when the new printing office (*post*) was completed, it has been devoted to other purposes, as the Registrar's offices, a Council chamber, and the University police station. In the Clarendon, the *pall of Henry VII.* (*i.e.* the rich cloth used at the formal celebration of his obsequies by the University) was long preserved. It is now kept at the College of the Vice-Chancellor for the time being, but is not shown.

(14.) WADHAM. (B 5, 6.) Notice the Entrance-tower, Chapel, Hall, Gardens.)

Founded 1613, by Nicholas Wadham, a Somersetshire gentleman, on the site of the Austin Friars' monastery; he did not live to complete it, but his widow Dorothy fully carried out his intentions. The buildings are Gothic, of excellent character for so late a period, and were executed, it is said, by a body of Somersetshire masons specially selected for the purpose. The *Entrance-tower* is particularly handsome, and well-proportioned, and the *Chapel,* which is very striking, has a good E. window by *Van Linge.* The *Hall* has an open timber roof, " which is curious, as showing how, while the Gothic form was retained, the details were altered to suit the taste of the times," and the same may be said of the carved oak screen; " they are among the most remarkable in the University; and the great S. and oriel windows are particularly good." (*J. H. P.*) There are many portraits, as of Admiral Blake, Speaker Onslow, and others. The *Garden* is very secluded and beautiful; it contains two fine cedars. The Royal Society had its origin in the meetings of a number of learned and inquiring men, such as Dr. Wilkins, Seth Ward, Sir C. Wren, Dr. Sprat, &c., held (1650-59) in the room over the Wadham gateway.

Beyond Wadham, on the space called the *Parks* (said to be the site of the artillery park at the siege of Oxford in 1646), is the *New Museum*

(A 5, 6), built 1855–60 by *Messrs. Deane and Woodward.* It is in the style of the 13th centy., not English Gothic, but borrowed from foreign examples, and is by no means successful.

To the rt. of the Museum, on rising ground in the Parks, is the new *Observatory,* built 1874–5 and 1877–8 (A 7), containing the magnificent astronomical instruments presented to the University by Dr. Warren de la Rue. *Chursley Hall,* a private Hall, established under the statute of 1855 is on the left-hand side of the entry to the Parks.

The W. or principal front of the Museum is richly ornamented, but objection has been taken to the grand entrance being perfectly flat with the rest of the building. The E. front is left without ornament, in order that the Museum may be easily added to on that side, as occasion requires. On the N. and S. are out-lying buildings for anatomical and chemical purposes; the *Laboratory,* on the type of the Abbot's kitchen at Glastonbury, is a very conspicuous object, and a large building for the same purpose beside it was finished in 1880. At the S. E. angle is the residence of the keeper of the Museum. The Museum is open to members of the University from 10 to 4; and visitors are admitted, without fee, after 2 P.M.

The principal entrance leads to the central quadrangle, which is covered by a glass roof, supported on cast-iron columns, ornamented with coloured leafage. This court is surrounded by 2 galleries, with open arcades, which furnish, on either story, a ready means of communication to every part of the collection. "The roof and the ironwork that supports it are purposely made clumsy." — *Fergusson's Mod. Archit.* The shafts of the pillars have been selected, under the direction of Professor Phillips, as examples of the

more important rocks of the British Isles: thus those on the W. are of the granitic series; those on the E. of the metamorphic; N. calcareous rocks chiefly from Ireland; S. the English marbles. T..e capitals and bases represent various groups of plants and animals, illustrative of different climates and various epochs. Some of the capitals (by the O'Shea family), especially those of the English ferns and flora, are of a delicacy and beauty worthy of Venice. "The one really good point in the whole design is the range of pillars, with their capitals, but they are good precisely because they are not Gothic." — *Fergusson.* The corbels, in front of the piers, are occupied, or are to be occupied, by statues of those who have been famous in each of the sciences which the Museum is intended to illustrate. "As those who have laid the deepest and widest the foundations of science, Aristotle and Bacon are set up at the portal—the one given by H. M. the Queen, the other by undergraduates of Oxford. In the mathematical department are placed Euclid and Leibnitz; in the astronomical, Newton and Galileo; in the chemical, Davy and Priestly; in that of zoology and botany, Linnæus; in that of medicine, Hippocrates and Harvey; in that of applied mechanics, Watt and Stephenson" (*Acland*). A statue of the late Prince Consort, by *Woolner,* stands near the head of the great central aisle, and about 20 other statues are still wanting to complete the series. They will be provided, as the others have been, by private subscription.

The central area of the Museum * is divided into 5 compartments, or passages running parallel from W. to E.; *i.e.,* 2 N. and 2 S. of the central compartment, which faces the principal entrance. This central

* See Prof. Phillips' 'Geology of Oxford and the Valley of the Thames,'—the best companion and guide to this Museum.

compartment is devoted to birds and mammalia; the aisles N. to skeletons of vertebrata; the aisles S. to reptiles and fishes, and minerals. The N. corridor contains human crania, the E. fossils, the S. philosophical instruments, and the W. the pathological department. The *Upper Floor* has a large lecture-room, capable of containing 600 persons. Along the W. front are the Reading-rooms and Library, containing a valuable collection of books on medicine and science brought hither from the Radcliffe. The collection of marbles in the Upper Corridor was also brought from the same building. A large apartment on this floor is devoted to the entomological collection of Mr. Hope, formerly preserved in the Taylor Buildings. Probably the most special object among the fossils is the *Cetiosaurus*, an extinct creature 40 ft. long and 12 ft. high; but beside this many of the specimens here deposited have a peculiar interest as illustrating the early researches and discoveries of geologists. The most conspicuous parts of the collection are the numerous and well-selected examples of many fossil quadrupeds from the caverns of Germany, France, and the British Isles. In the investigation of these ossiferous caves no person was so distinguished as Dr. Buckland for industry and sagacity. The remarkable speculations which he advanced concerning Kirkdale and other caves have been since for the most part confirmed, and are well illustrated by the specimens preserved in the Museum.

The Local Geology of Oxfordshire has furnished some of the more conspicuous fossils. Stonesfield (Rte. 26) in particular has yielded the Megalosaurus, the flying Pterodactylus, and the small Marsupial Mammalia whose best analogues are now in Australia. Shotover Hill (Exc. *d*) has been ransacked for the bones of the Plesiosaurus, and many other interesting species. Lyme Regis, another classic land of geology, is represented by Plesiosauri and Ichthyosauri. The footprints of Cheirotherium and other reptiles are seen on the sandstones of Lochmaben, and a vast amount of Bovine and Elephantine reliquiæ, which, with bones of Rhinoceros, Hippopotamus, Megatherium, and other monsters of the earlier time, makes this the palæontological collection in some sort the monument of Dr. Buckland.

(15.) KEBLE COLL. (A 5.) Founded in 1868 by the friends of the late Rev. John Keble, author of ' The Christian Year,' and Vicar of Hursley, as a memorial to his memory. It is designed to promote a cause that he had much at heart, placing a collegiate education within the reach of many who might otherwise have difficulty in obtaining it. Those who are intended for holy orders are considered especially likely to benefit by it, but it is not confined to such students, though it is intended to train up all in the doctrine and discipline of the Church of England; " it is not to be, in any invidious sense, a 'poor man's college,' though it will be possible to live there on a smaller income than elsewhere." The sum of 45,000*l.* was first raised, and was expended on the site, some of the buildings, and the necessary outlay at starting. The buildings, by *Butterfield*, are of variegated brick; they form two sides and a half of a large quadrangle, the other half of the third side being occupied by the Chapel; the Hall and Library form the fourth side. In April, 1873, the foundation of the *Chapel*, designed by *Butterfield*, was laid by W. Gibbs, Esq., M.A., of Tyntesfield, the munificent founder, who devoted no less than 30,000*l.* to erect it. It was dedicated on St. Mark's Day, 1876. The proportions are very fine, the height from floor to roof being 70 ft., while the breadth is 35 feet, and the length 124 ft. The interior contains beautiful carving, coloured mosaics, and painted glass. In the chancel there is a large mosaic of the Crucifixion, and on the opposite side is one of the Resurrection.

The *Hall* and *Library* form the southern side of the quadrangle, and were commenced in 1876, and opened in 1879. They were erected at the cost of members of the Gibbs family. The Hall contains a few portraits, among them those of Mr. Keble and the Warden. The Library contains Keble's large collection of books, and many gifts from Cardinal Newman, Lord Beauchamp and others; also Holman Hunt's picture of the "Light of the World." A portion of a new quadrangle was commenced in 1881, and the E. wing finished 1882. There will eventually be a second and smaller quadrangle, ending in the Warden's House, opposite the Museum; and an extension of the building on the side of Keble Terrace.

The College, having been opened by the Chancellor (Marquis of Salisbury) June 22, 1870, was formally received into the University by a decree of Convocation, April 18, 1871. The Rev. E. S. Talbot is the Warden, and the number of members on Jan. 1, 1872, was 79, which in 1882 had increased to 394. In Lent Term, 1882, there were 161 students.

(16.) TRINITY. (B 5.) (Notice the Chapel—especially G. Gibbons' carvings in it—and Gardens.)

Founded in 1554 by Sir Thomas Pope, a lawyer, who had been clerk of the Star-chamber, and was then Lord Mayor of London. Upon the site stood the ruined buildings of Durham College, a foundation of the 13th centy., which once possessed the famous library of Richard de Bury, the learned Bishop of Durham (1333–1345), known as Philobiblos. Though more than half its members

were laymen, it was suppressed at the Dissolution, and it lay in ruins for many years. Sir Thomas, who had been greatly instrumental in saving St. Alban's Abbey from destruction, purchased the site, and repaired the buildings sufficiently for occupation. The present structure is all of later date than his time. The *Tower* and *Chapel* are of Grecian architecture, built by Dr. Bathurst, c. 1695, and favourable specimens of their kind. The chapel contains the fine tomb of the Founder and his wife (brought from St. Stephen, Walbrook, London), and has a most beautiful carved screen and altarpiece by Gibbons—his masterpiece, and well worth study.

In the *Library* is a chalice that belonged to St. Alban's Abbey, as also some good ancient painted glass. This was a favourite retreat of Dr. Johnson, when visiting Oxford, and a copy of Baskerville's Virgil is shown as his gift. The *Hall*, which occupies the site of the refectory of Durham College, was built in 1620, but has since undergone many alterations both internal and external; it contains portraits of the founder, Archbp. Sheldon, Thomas Warton, and others. The buildings stand back from the street, with a handsome gate and grass-plat in front, and the rather extensive *Gardens* have a trellised walk of great beauty. Dr. Bathurst, who was for 40 years President of Trinity (d. 1704), used to surprise the undergraduates, if walking in this grove at unseasonable times, with a whip in his hand,—an instrument of academic discipline, not then entirely laid aside. *See Oxoniana,* iv. 106.

At the corner of the green to the E. of Trinity stands *Kettel Hall,* (B 5.), the most picturesque specimen of domestic architecture in Oxford. It was called after its founder, Dr. Ralph Kettel, President of Trinity, as its predecessor, on the same site, Perilous Hall, was called after its founder Perles. Dr. Kettel was celebrated for his feats of bodily strength, but a story of him, which Dean Aldrich tells, cannot be reconciled to chronology, as he died in July, 1643, three years before the surrender of Oxford. The Doctor, he says, " was accustomed to attend the daily disputations in the hall of Trinity, where he sate with a black fur muff and an hour-glass before him to time the exercise. One day, when Cromwell was in possession of Oxford, a halberdier rushed in, and, breaking his hour-glass with his halberd, seized his muff and threw it in his face. The Doctor instantly seized the soldier by the collar and made him prisoner, and the halberd was carried out before him in triumph." This hall was originally intended as a lodging for students, but is now a private dwelling. Dr. Johnson resided here for 5 weeks when visiting Oxford.

(17.) BALLIOL. (B 4, 5.) (Notice the South Front, the Chapel, the North Building.)

Founded about 1263 by Sir John Balliol, of Barnard Castle, the father of John Balliol, King of Scotland. His benefaction was confirmed and added to by his widow Dervorgilla, who also founded Sweetheart Abbey (Suave Cordium) in Galloway, in order to deposit her husband's heart there. No part of the existing building is older than 1431. The south front, built by *Waterhouse* (1868), has a massive tower, of four stories in height, and is much admired for the boldness of its outline and the varied character of the detail; the free use of the shouldered arch is somewhat remarkable. The *Chapel*, which is the 4th in succession since the building of the College, was designed by *Butterfield*, and erected in 1858. It is built, in a foreign-looking Gothic style, of alternate layers of red and white

stone, and is handsome in its internal decorations, of which Derbyshire alabaster forms a conspicuous part. The windows are filled with glass from the old chapel, some of which is of the time of Henry VIII.

The *Library* is of the 15th centy. externally, but the interior was " rearranged" by *Wyatt*, about the close of the last century. The same may be said of the *Hall*, except that it has been enlarged since Wyatt's time, and which is now used as a Lecture room. The new Hall, erected by *Waterhouse*, was opened in 1877. It contains portraits of Wycliffe (once Master), Abp. Dolben, Bp. Barrington, and others. W. of the Hall extend other buildings, one of which, the North Building, by *Salvin*, 1852, has a good Gothic gate-house with oriel window.

The gridiron, carved in various parts of the college, is a memorial of its early possession (1294) of lands in the parish of St. Lawrence in London.

As Oriel was the first to open its fellowships, so this college was the first to open its scholarships, and under the auspices of a late Master, Dr. Jenkyns (d. 1854), it reached the high point of scholarship that it still maintains. Pennant says: " Within my memory majestic elms graced the street before this and the neighbouring colleges. The scene was truly academick, walks worthy of the contemplative Schools of ancient days. But alas! in the midst of numberless modern elegancies, in this single instance some demon whispered, ' Oxford have a taste,' and by the magic line every venerable tree fell prostrate."

Opposite the door of the Master's Lodging, four small stones set crosswise in the road are supposed to indicate the vicinity of the spot where Cranmer, Ridley, and Latimer suffered martyrdom, 1555, 1556. " It probably was somewhat further S., on the bank of the moat of the city wall, now covered by the houses of Broad Street, or perhaps by the footpath in front of them, where an extensive layer of wood ashes is known to remain" (*J. H. P.*). In 1850, in forming a culvert in Broad Street, an oak post burnt off at the upper end was found driven very firmly into the otherwise unmoved gravel; it is now preserved in the Ashmolean Museum, being "supposed to be a part of the stake to which one of [the bishops] was fastened."

(18.) St. John's, opposite the Taylor Museum (B 5.) (Notice the two Old Quadrangles, especially the inner one, the Chapel, and Gardens.)

Founded 1555 by Sir Thomas White, Lord Mayor of London. "White was warned in a dream that he should build a college for the education of youth in religion and learning, near a triple elm, having three trunks issuing from one root; whereupon he repairs to Oxford, and first met with something near Gloucester Hall (now Worcester College), that seemed to answer his dream, where accordingly he erected a great deal of building. But afterward, finding another elm near St. Bernard's College, supprest not long before by Henry VIII., he left off at Gloucester Hall, and built St. John Baptist College, which, with the very tree beside it, that occasioned its foundation, flourishes to this day." (*Plot,* 1677.) Two of the trunks existed in 1749, when Pointer published his 'Oxoniensis Academia;' both have perished now, but the elm in the small court opposite the President's lodging is believed to be the representative of one of them. The college has a fine terrace walk in front, shaded by a row of elms. The front and gateway tower are parts of Chichele's foundation of St. Bernard's (1437). White (the son of a clothier at Reading, and himself a

merchant in London) engrafted his foundation on this, designing it especially for the education of youths from the school of the Merchant Taylors in London, to which it was confined until the Oxford University Commissioners threw the majority of its endowments open.

In the first quadrangle is the *Hall,* once the refectory of the monks, but much modernised. The portraits that line its walls include the Founder, Abps. Laud and Juxon, Sir Walter Raleigh, Hudson the navigator, &c. The *Chapel,* built 1530, after suffering much from the Puritans, was repaired in the debased style of Charles II., but in 1843 it was restored to its original state by Blore. Sir Thomas White, the founder, and Archbishop Laud, who, from being born at Reading, entered here on the foundation of his fellow-townsman and afterwards became one of the chief benefactors of the college, are buried without monuments beneath the altar. Here also is preserved the heart of Dr. Rawlinson (buried in St. Giles's ch.), with the inscription "Ubi thesaurus ibi cor."

A vaulted passage, with rich fantracery ceiling, leads into the second quadrangle, of picturesque Palladian architecture, built by *Inigo Jones* for Archbishop Laud—a much admired example of the style. The gate-towers, adorned with classic pillars in the Cinque-cento style, are surmounted by bronze statues of Charles I. and his queen Henrietta Maria by Fanelli. Along two sides of it run cloisters, in the style of the great Hospital at Milan, resting on pillars of Bletchingdon marble. The S. and E. sides are occupied by the *Library,* partly Elizabethan, partly the work of Inigo Jones for Abp. Laud. Here is a portrait of Charles I., with the whole book of Psalms written in his hair and the lines of his face. In this apartment Charles I., his queen, the Elector

Palatine, and Prince Rupert were entertained by Laud with a superb banquet, and after it by a play or interlude, composed and acted by members of the college (1636). A portrait of the archbishop, his cap, and the walking-stick which supported him to the scaffold, are preserved here. The new buildings (B 4, 5) to the N. of the College, facing St. Giles, were erected from designs by *G. G. Scott*, in 1880–81. They contain 14 sets of rooms and a lecture room.

* St. John's Gardens, perhaps the most beautiful in the University, 5 acres in extent, were laid out by Brown and Repton. They are rich in trees, enlivened by nightingales in May, and are admirably kept up. Their beauty is much enhanced by the view of the E. front of the college, which includes the Library, with its venerable oriels and quaint stone gables.

Nearly opposite St. John's are the *Taylor Buildings* and *University Galleries* (B 4) erected in the classic style, 1845, from the designs of *C. R. Cockerell, R.A.*

This building owes its origin to two bequests—of Sir Robert Taylor (d. 1788) for a foundation to teach modern European languages, and of Dr. Randolph (d. 1796) for a building to contain the Pomfret marbles and other works of art. The E. wing facing St. John's is the Taylor Institution, and the statues surmounting it are those of France, Italy, Germany, and Spain, whose languages are here taught. It contains the leading foreign periodicals, a library of foreign books and the Finch Art Library.

The *University Galleries*, where the Oxford School of Art has its quarters, face the Randolph in Beaumont-st. (B 4.) They are open daily, except in August, 12 till 4—a good Catalogue, price 6*d.* They

* These have been admirably described by Mr. J. C. Robinson.

contain the original models of the busts and statues executed by Sir F. Chantrey, the munificent gift of his widow, Lady Chantrey, and including likenesses of most of the great men of his time: his statues of General Washington (for America), James Watt, Bishop Heber, George Canning, the 2 sleeping children of Lichfield Cathedral, Mrs. Jordan and her children, &c.; besides colossal busts of Nelson, Wellington, &c. These are the original clay models, moulded by the sculptor himself, and often more happy than the marble copies. Of the Pomfret marbles deposited here (upwards of 70 in number) the best is a statue of Cicero: "a work of happy conception, of peculiar and fine cast of drapery, and admirable workmanship."—*Waagen.* A sculpture of *Nisroch* from Nineveh was the gift of Mr. Layard.

On the first-floor the admirable collection of drawings by old masters, and paintings, are well arranged. In the ante-room of the *Picture Gallery* are 10 fine drawings by *Turner*, views for the 'Oxford Almanack,' and 40 other drawings and sketches by him, the gift of Mr. Ruskin.

The lover of art will study with delight the original drawings by Rafaelle (162) and Michael Angelo (79), a collection unequalled in the country. Among them may be recognised many of the sketches for their most celebrated pictures, of which the following are among the most remarkable:—

Rafaelle. — The Almighty surrounded with angels: a study for the ceiling picture of the Burning Bush, in the Vatican.—Study for the Disputa, executed with the silver point, on tinted paper.—Study coeval with, if not for, the Sposalizio.—Study for " the Madonna in green," in the Belvedere, Vienna.—Study for the St. George in St. Petersburg—silver point.—Study for the tapestry of the Adoration of the Kings, in the

Vatican, which proves that composition to be from Raphael's own hand.—Men in combat (pen-drawing) supposed to be for the victory of Ostia, in the Vatican.—Study for the Rape of Helen.—Study for the Phrygian Sibyl, in Sta. Maria della Pace, at Rome.—Study of Minerva, and 3 other statues, for the School of Athens.—Portrait of Raphael, at the age of 16 : a real treasure.—Entrance of Cardinal Giovanni de' Medici into Florence, probably executed by Francesco Penni.—Tobit and the Angel : study for that part of Perugino's altarpiece in the Certosa of Pavia which Raphael executed : it is now in the possession of Duke Melzi, at Milan.—Sketch for the upper part of the Disputa, in 2 rows : a most masterly pen-drawing, in bistre, 1509.—Various studies for the Entombment, 1507. —Study from nature for 2 of the figures on the steps of the School of Athens, 1510.—7 young men drinking wine at a table, 1508.—Probably St. Stephen : admirably drawn.—A sketch for the tapestry occasionally hung in the Sistine Chapel, 1515 or 1516.—Hercules Gaulois, or Eloquence.—The two undraped figures from the Borghese Entombment : very interesting.—A beautiful pen sketch of the Virgin and Child with the Baptist, for the Madonna del Cardellino, in the Tribune at Florence : instead of a bird, a book is here given and the Baptist is in a quiet position. — The Presentation, said to be by Giulio Romano.—Studies for the Heliodorus.

Michael Angelo.—The Last Judgment : admirably executed with pen and bistre.—The ceiling of the Sistine Chapel, executed by the miniature-painter, Don Giulio Clovio.—A study for one of the Sibyls in the Sistine Chapel.—A study from nature for the statue of David, Palazzo Vecchio. —Study for the Jonah of the Sistine Chapel.— Studies of horses, for the Conversion of St. Paul, in the Pau-

line Chapel.—A study for the Adam in the Sistine Chapel.—Studies for the raising of the Brazen Serpent. Sistine Chapel. — Michael Angelo and his friend Marc Antonio della Torre, occupied on anatomical studies. Study of 3 figures for the Conversion of St. Paul.—Study for the Last Judgment.—Studies for the tombs of the Medici.— *Waagen.*

These drawings formed part of the collection of Sir Thomas Lawrence, and were purchased for the University at the price of 7000*l.*, of which Lord Eldon contributed 4105*l.*

Besides these drawings the gallery contains copies of Raphael's Cartoons, and of his School of Athens ; sketches by Vandyke ; Portraits of Payne, the architect, his sons, and of Mrs. Meyrick ; of Joseph Warton, and of White the Paviour (model for the figure of Ugolino), all by *Sir Josh. Reynolds ;* sketches by Hogarth (including his Enraged Musician, Inn Yard, and Rake's Progress) ; 3 landscapes by *Wilson ;* Southampton Castle, by *Calcott ;* several Dutch pictures ; and others. There are also specimens of the early Italian school, and several fine works by Canaletti, Ostade, Teniers, Reynolds, Gainsborough, Morland and Constable. A beautiful bust of the finest period of Greek art, and a fine bronze mask of Michael Angelo are placed in this gallery.

(19.) WORCESTER. (B 3, 4.) (Notice the Chapel and Gardens.)

Founded in 1714 by Sir Thos. Cookes, Bart., of Bentley, Worcestershire, on the site of Gloucester Hall, a place of education connected with Gloucester Abbey, suppressed at the Dissolution, and given to Bishop King, of Oxford, as his palace. On his death it reverted to the Crown, and in 1559 it was purchased by Sir Thomas White, who gave it as a hall to St. John's College. Receiving an endowment in 1714 from Sir Thomas Cookes, it henceforth had the name of Worcester College. The *Chapel*, once very plain, is now gorgeously decorated with figure groups in mediæval style, on a gold ground, and in the roof by medallions and arabesques by *Burges* (1866). The *Hall* has been panelled throughout with woodwork of original and good design. In the *Library* is Inigo Jones's copy of Palladio's works, with notes and sketches by his own hand. The extensive *Gardens* are prettily laid out, and contain a large sheet of water, known as Worcester Lake. In connexion with Gloucester Hall, Dr. Woodroffe, the Principal (temp. Car. II.), built lodgings amid the ruins of Beaumont Palace for "the education of young scholars from Greece, who, after they had been here educated in the Reformed religion, were to be sent back into their own country, in order to propagate the same there. And accordingly some young Grecians were brought hither, and wore their Grecian habits; but not finding suitable encouragement, this project came to nothing."

In New Inn Hall Street, W. of the Union Society's Buildings (C 4), is *New Inn Hall*, originally Trilleck's Hall bought by William of Wykeham in 1369, and given by him to New College. This hall, about the time of Henry VIII., was mainly occupied by lawyers, and in modern times Sir William Blackstone, author of the 'Commentaries,' was its Principal (1761–66). In the Civil War, it was occupied as the royal mint, at which the plate of the different colleges, loyally contributed to furnish funds for the king's government, was converted into money. Here were struck the coins known as "Exsurgat money," from the legend on the reverse, "Exsurgat Deus, dissipentur inimici." The present buildings are modern.

Opposite New Inn Hall are the [*Berks, &c.*]

gates of *Frewen·Hall* (C 4) (on the site of St. Mary's College, where Erasmus resided, and named from Dr. Frewen, President of Magdalen, 1626–1644). It was the residence of the Prince of Wales while a student at the University, 1859–60.

(20.) PEMBROKE. (D 4.) (Notice the Entrance Tower and new Hall.)

Founded on the site of Broadgates Hall in 1624 by Thomas Tesdale, of Glympton, and the Rev. Richard Wightwick, rector of Ilsley, Berks, and named in honour of William Herbert, Earl of Pembroke, then Chancellor of the University. The scholars and Fellows were to be principally elected from the Abingdon Free-school, but this limitation has been set aside by the University Commission.

The *Entrance Gateway*, and the *Hall* (A.D. 1848) are handsome, but the rest of the buildings are very plain. George Whitefield was a servitor here, and "found the advantage of having been used to a public-house [his father kept an inn at Gloucester]. Many who could choose their servitor preferred him, because of his diligent and alert attendance; and thus, by the help of the profits of the place, and some little presents made him by a kind-hearted tutor, he was enabled to live without being beholden to his relations for more than 24l. in the course of three years. . . . At first he was rendered uncomfortable by the society into which he was thrown; he had several chamber-fellows, who would fain have made him join them in their riotous mode of life; and as he could only escape from their persecutions by sitting alone in his study, he was sometimes benumbed with cold; but when they perceived the strength as well as the simplicity of his character, they suffered him to take his own way in peace." Samuel Johnson occupied the rooms over the original gateway, from the window

Q

of which he threw in a fury the new shoes which a well-meaning friend had placed at his door, on seeing that his old ones were no longer wearable. Poverty compelled John-son to leave Pembroke before he had taken his degree. In the gate-way itself he "was generally seen lounging, with a circle of gay young students round him, whom he was entertaining with wit, and keeping them from their studies, if not spirit-ing them up to rebellion against the College discipline which, in his ma-turer years, he so much extolled." When he visited Oxford in 1754 his first call was at his old College, but his reception by the Master (Dr. Radcliffe) was so cold, that he ex-claimed, "If I come to live at Oxford, I shall take up abode at Trinity." (*Warton to Boswell.*) Some of his college exercises are preserved in the *Library.* with his bust by *Bacon,* and in the *Hall* there is an ad-mirable portrait of him by *Sir J. Reynolds.*

II. Churches.

Besides the *Cathedral* (see p. 192), the following *Churches* will be found particularly worthy of inspection.

(1.) The *Church of St. Mary the Virgin* (C 5), which is also the Uni-versity Church, in the High Street, is conspicuous by its beautiful Dec. spire (height 150 ft. , a memorial of Eleanor of Castile, as shown by the ball-flower or pomegranate ornament which lines the panels and gables of the pinnacles. The ch. was built under the superintendence of Adam de Brome, her almoner, and occupies the traditional site of a ch. founded by Alfred, and of which John of Oxford, the opponent of Becket, was dean in the reign of Henry II. The body of the ch. is good Perp., except the Italian porch on the S. side, which is a valuable historic

monument. It was erected by Mor-gan Owen, one of Archbishop Laud's chaplains, and the image of the Virgin and Child, still remaining, formed one of the articles on which the Archbishop was impeached. The present chancel (68 ft. by 24) was erected 1472 by Lyhert, Bp. of Norwich; the nave (94 ft. by 54) and aisles, 1488, under the direction of Sir Reginald Bray (the architect of Windsor and Great Malvern), whose arms, as a benefactor, formerly ornamented one of the windows. At this rebuilding, all the old chapels were swept away, except the monumental chantry of Adam de Brome on the N.   Dr. Radcliffe, the last person in Oxford who was hon-oured with a public funeral attended by the whole University. is buried at the base of the organ-loft without a monument; and at the W. door is the grave of the unhappy Amy Rob-sart, wife of Robert Dudley, Earl of Leicester, who was brought hither from Cumnor. When Dr. Babington, Lord Leicester's chaplain, preached her funeral sermon in this ch., he was so nervous that "he thrice recommended to men's memories that virtuous lady so pitifully murdered, instead of saying so pitifully slain;" at which.the people, whose minds were already predisposed, took fire, and the belief was never eradicated : Sir Walter Scott has perpetuated it in 'Kenilworth,' but later writers have questioned its truth (Rte. 9).   Near the W. end is a monumental tablet by *Flaxman* to Sir William Jones. Dr. Newman was the incumbent of this ch. from 1834 to 1843, and here were preached his "Ser-mons on Subjects of the Day," an attack on which occasioned him to write his well-known 'Apologia.' In the chancel the Mayor and Corporation, with halters round their necks, were long accustomed to do penance and pay a fine on St. Scholastica's day (Feb. 10), for an outrage committed against the Uni-

versity in 1354. Cranmer, immediately before his death, was brought
to this ch. to hear a sermon, and
to proclaim his recantation, being
placed on a platform opposite the
pulpit and surrounded by armed
men. But when the discourse was
ended, contrary to the expectation
of his enemies, he boldly repudiated
and renounced all things that he
had written "contrary to the truth"
since his degradation, adding, "As
for the Pope, I refuse him as Anti-
Christ." The auditors clamoured
against him; the preacher (Dr. Cole)
cried "Stop the heretic's mouth;"
and he was dragged to the stake.*
The ch. was restored by *Scott* in
1862.

At the N. E. end of St. Mary's is
the Old Convocation House, the only
relic of an earlier ch. on this site,
over which is a room which was—
1st, a Library founded 1320 by Cobham, Bishop of Worcester (in a measure the parent of the Bodleian, to
which the books were transferred
1840); 2nd, the Upper House of
Convocation; 3rd, a Law School.
Finally, in 1871, the lower portion
was restored, and a crypt was converted into a chapel for the unattached students of the University.

In the High Street, a short distance
W. of St. Mary's, is (2) *All Saints'*
(C 5), "built (1705-10) of the bad
Headington stone, the surface of
which constantly crumbles away, from
a design by Dean Aldrich, and exhibiting a very fair specimen of the
style of building he would inculcate
in his 'Elements of Civil Architecture.' Though altogether at variance
with our present notions of rules of
art, yet this ch. has much that is
attractive in it. The proportions of
the interior are particularly good, and
the Græco-Gothic spire and tower
perhaps the most successful attempt
of the kind existing in England"
(*J. H. P.*). In 1865 the interior was

* See Dean Hook's admirable 'Life of
Archbp. Cranmer,' 1870.

restored, and the spire was rebuilt
in 1874.

A ch. existed on this spot at a
very early date, but the fall of its
spire in 1669 reduced it almost to
ruin. Tradition tells that in its
churchyard St. Edmund of Abingdon (Archbp. of Canterbury) was
one day preaching, when a violent
storm came on. The people began
to take flight, but St. Edmund implored them to stay, and prayed
that he might be allowed to finish
his sermon without interruption;
after which, though in the neighbouring High Street torrents of rain
ran like a river, not a drop fell in
the churchyard. How St. Edmund
"preached in Alle Halowene church-
yerd," is described in an old ballad,
temp. Edward I.

(3.) *St. Peter in the East*, in New
College Lane. (C 6.) This ch. has
a Norm. crypt, really of about the
time of Stephen (A.D. 1150), but erroneously ascribed to St. Grymbald in
the 9th centy. It has two rows of
short pillars, and much resembles
the crypt of Winchester Cathedral;
Grymbald's only connection with
St. Peter's must have been with an
earlier ch. than the present one.
The chancel, also late Norm., retains
its original groined roof,—observe
the chain ornament typical of St.
Peter ad Vincula—two semicircular-
headed windows, and two E. turrets
with conical roofs. The Lady Chapel, built about 1240, by St. Edmund
of Abingdon, founder of the adjoining
hall, whose scholars used to attend
service here, contains a fine tomb
with brasses of R. Atkinson, "5
times Mayor of Oxford," d. 1574.
The Lent Sermons before the University were formerly delivered from
the stone pulpit here, which had once
two entrances, the 2nd being set
apart for the University preacher.
The nave has a rich Norm. doorway;
but the porch is Perp.

In the churchyard are the graves

Q 2

of Dillenius the botanist, and of Hearne the antiquary, who was formerly of St. Edmund's Hall. This vicarage in former times was commonly held by persons connected with royalty, the last who had it before the tithes were acquired by Wykeham, being Bogo de St. Clare, a kinsman of Edward I. Many halls congregated on this spot, which paid tithes to the incumbent, but Wykeham, by his influence with the Pope, swept them away in founding New College. Nicholas Wyking, the vicar, waited till Wykeham's death, and then took occasion of the journey of his patron Edmund de Beckyngham, Warden of Merton, as representative of the University, to the anti-papal Council of Constance, to plead his cause there. He obtained the reversal of the papal decision, but before his return Martin V. was elected, and from him the college received a confirmation of their former immunity, which they still enjoy.

(4.) *St. Giles* (A 5), in the street of that name, has a Trans.-Norm. tower, but the rest is E. E. The N. aisle has been a series of chapels, each with a separate roof and gable; the windows are good E. E., as are the S. doorway and porch. The font is temp. Henry III.

(5.) *St. Mary Magdalen* (B 4), opposite Balliol College, has a S. aisle of the time of Edward II., and a Perp. tower, in which materials from the ruins of Osney Abbey are worked up—notice in a niche on the W. side a beautiful small figure of St. Mary Magdalen; and a N. aisle, rebuilt by *Scott* in 1841, as a part of the *Martyrs' Memorial*; near its N. entrance is a relic of the Reformation in the heavy oak door brought from the prison of the bishops in Bocardo. It retains rudely carved portraits of Cranmer, Latimer and Ridley. The church was completely restored in

1875. The *Memorial* proper, built to commemorate the burning of Ridley, Latimer and Cranmer, in 1555 and 1556, stands N. of the ch., and is an imitation of the Eleanor crosses. The design was by *G. G. Scott*, and the monument was finished 1851, at a cost of 5000*l*.; it stands 73 ft. high. The statues are by *Weekes*, and are, on N. Cranmer, on E. Ridley, and S. Latimer.

(6.) *St. Michael* (B. C 4), in the Cornmarket, is remarkable for its tower, with long and short work, supposed by Rickman to be of Saxon date, and certainly little later than the Norman conquest, though a Perp. battlement has been added, c. 1500. The S. aisle is Dec., but a chapel N. of the chancel, and a S. porch are Perp. The ch. was restored by *Street* in 1855, and has a marble reredos of his gift. The E. window is modern, but some portions of ancient glass remain in others. Opposite the ch. is a Perp. house, now called St. Michael's chambers, and let as offices, which was restored in 1864 by Mr. J. H. Parker, author of the ' Glossary of Architecture,' &c.

(7.) *St. Aldate's* (D 4), fronting Christ Church. This is a fine Dec. ch., named after a British saint of the 5th centy.; it was built by Sir John de Docklington in 1336, and enlarged in 1862. The tower and spire were rebuilt in 1873. The Trinity chapel contains the tomb of John Noble, Principal of Broadgates Hall, 1522. " It was the custom for the people of the parish to eat sugar sops out of the font in this church on Holy Thursday."—*Hearne.*

(8.) *St. Thomas the Martyr* (B 2), near the Castle, occupies the site of a temporary ch. dedicated to St. Nicholas, which was built in 1142 during the siege of Oxford, when the parishioners of St. George within the

Castle (now destroyed) were excluded from their ch. The present ch. is E. E., with a good Dec. E. window, the tower Perp., and the nave partly Perp. and partly Dec., with a S. aisle in modern Dec. The ch.yard is particularly neat and well kept.

The remaining churches of Oxford call for but little remark. The most noticeable are *St. Philip and St. James*, in the Woodstock Road, an Italian Gothic structure by *Street;* *St. Barnabas*, in the poor district called Jericho, an Italian Norman basilica by *Blomfield*, remarkable for its two apses (one is the baptistery), and its style of ornament, in which colour is lavishly employed; *St. Martin Carfax* (C 4), *St. Peter-Le-Bailey* (C 4), a good Dec. structure, and *St. Frideswide* (B 1) (French Gothic) in Osney Town, opened for Divine Service in 1872.

III. Other Objects of Interest.

The remains of the *Castle* (C 3), though now reduced to a solitary tower, a high mound, and a few fragments of wall, are very interesting as a historical relic. The tower was built, probably in the reign of William Rufus, by Walter d'Oiley, a Norman follower of the Conqueror. In 1142 the Empress Maud, besieged within its walls for 3 months by Stephen, succeeded at length in escaping by sallying out (or being let down from the walls by ropes), escorted by 3 knights, and clad in white sheets, on a winter night, while snow covered the ground and the Thames was frozen over. She reached Abingdon on foot, whence she was conveyed to Wallingford. A crypt known as "*Maud's Chapel*," discovered while clearing the foundations for the new gaol, is a most interesting example of early Norm. work, and was probably the crypt under the great hall. It was found necessary to remove it, but the pillars have been replaced in

a neighbouring cellar, in the same relative position. The *Mound*, which supported the Norm. keep, is much earlier, probably of the time of the Mercian kings; in its centre is a curious octagonal vaulted chamber (temp. Hen. III.), containing a well and approached by a long flight of steps. Within the precincts of the castle was the collegiate ch. of St. George; but the parishioners not being able to get to it during the siege in 1142, the Pope permitted them to build a temporary ch. without the walls, where now stands *St. Thomas* (*ante*). *Beaumont Street*, leading from the Martyrs' Memorial to Worcester College, indicates the site of a *Palace* (*de Bello Monte*) built by Henry I. outside the town. Henry II. often resided in it, and here Richard and others of his children were born. The palace was granted by Edward II. to the Carmelite Friars in fulfilment of a vow made in the panic of Bannockburn to a friar who was with him, though it continued to be the residence of monarchs visiting Oxford. The refectory remained until the 17th centy., when the materials were used in building the Library of St. John's College. The grounds extended to the square now occupied by the city gaol, but which till so employed had been used as a bowling green.

The *City Walls*, which date from the 11th centy., and of which several of the *Gates* were standing as late as 1771, may still be traced in part of their course. Beginning from the Castle Tower and Mill in the street near which stood the West Gate, they appear to have followed the ground overlooking Paradise Square, as far as the Little Gate in St. Ebbe's; then along the terrace and S. wall of Pembroke in Brewer Street till they crossed St. Aldate Street at the South Gate between the Almshouses and Christ Church, whence passing behind the Hall and Cathedral they may be traced on the terrace between the Margaret Professor's garden and that of Corpus : thence along the S. and E. terraces of Merton, across the High Street, where stood the East Gate, in a straight line behind the houses in Long Wall ; they app'ar along the garden, hall, cha| el, and cloisters of New College, forming the E. and N. boundary of the college, the whole maintained in full preservation, and in the original state with the exception of one bastion, altered into a postern gateway leading into the "Slype," and another replaced by the lofty square belfry. At the corner of New College Lane the remains of the chapel of St. Catherine (*ante*) mark the site of a bastion, and another still standing behind the houses in Broad Street shows the direction of the walls to St. Michael's "ad Portam Borealem." so called to distinguish it from the other St. Michael's, "ad Portam Australem," which was demolished to make room for the front of Christ Church. From the North Gate (or Bocardo) which crossed behind the houses of New Inn Hall Street and George Street, the walls may be traced till they reach the Jews' Mount in Bulwarks Alley, and then complete the circuit to its narrowest extremity at the Castle-keep.

The *Monastic Remains* in Oxford are comparatively unimportant. The Franciscans and the Blackfriars both had houses in the S. part of the town, not far from the Castle, but no vestige of either remains ; though Paradise Square recalls the memory of the Franciscans' garden. Roger Bacon was a member of their house, where he died in 1292.

Osney-town, a suburb W. of the railway, occupies the site of *Osney Abbey* (C 2), founded by Edith, the wife of the builder of the Castle. According to the legend, she did this at the earnest request of the souls in purgatory, who, in the form of magpies, chattered to her as she walked

the river side, till she was induced to erect a stately priory and ch. as extensive as the buildings of Christ Ch., and, for the beauty of its architecture and arrangements, the wonder not only of Englishmen, but of foreigners, who came far and near to worship at its 24 altars, and to admire its 2 lofty campaniles, its numerous chapels, the house of its abbot, "having a hall more befitting a common society than a private man "— and its melodious chime of bells, then reputed the best in England, and now in their altered use and position in the tower of Christ Ch. almost the sole extant relics of the ancient abbey. Leland describes the tomb of the foundress Edith d'Oiley in the priory ch., with her image in stone, in the "abbite of a Vowess," holding a hart in her right hand, and the paintings on the wall over her grave, which represented "the cumming of Edith to Oseneye, and Radulph [afterwards the abbot] waiting on her, and the trees with the chattering pyes." Among the numerous pilgrims and visitors to the abbey was Henry III., who spent a Christmas here with "great revelling mirth."

There are 3 views of Osney in existence—the print by Ralph Agas in the Bodleian, that in Dugdale's 'Monasticon,' and the background of Bishop King's window in the cathedral.

The London and N. W. stat. occupies great part of the side of *Rewley Abbey* (B 2, 3), founded by Edmund, Earl of Cornwall, the nephew of Henry III. The watergate of the abbey, which stood at the N. end of the isle of Osney, existed till within the last few years ; but the neighbourhood was, and is, very squalid. Warton relates that in one of their walks together, Dr. Johnson looked on Osney and Rewley for half an hour in silence, and then said " I viewed them with indignation."—*Boswell's Johnson.*

The N. suburbs of Oxford are particularly open and pleasant. Here, on the Woodstock road, stands the *Radcliffe Infirmary*, a plain building (1770), with an ornate Gothic chapel, by *Blomfield* (1867). It was founded by the Radcliffe trustees in 1770. The Radcliffe sermon in Commemoration week is preached in aid of this institution. Adjoining this is the *Observatory*, founded, 1772, by the same trustees, and placed in an area of 10 acres of land given by the Duke of Marlborough. Mr. Manuel Johnson was long the Observer, and since 1840 the observations made here have been printed in an annual volume. The octagon building on the top of the Observatory was designed from the Temple of the Winds at Athens. In an adjoining street is the *University Press*, a classic building, by Robertson (1830). The press was first set up in 1586, under the patronage of the Earl of Leicester, then Chancellor, but it was not firmly established until 1633, when Archbishop Laud procured a patent, with very extensive powers for the University; Archbishop Sheldon was also its patron, and for a while the printing was carried on in the Theatre. In 1713 the Clarendon was built for the purpose, where the press remained until the new building was erected. It is divided into the " Learned " side (N.), where classical and miscellaneous works are produced, and the " Bible " side (S.), confined to the printing of Bibles and Prayer Books. Admission may be readily obtained on application at the gate, and the buildings are well worth inspection. *Wickliffe Hall*, on the Banbury Road, is a Theological College for preparing graduates for the ministry.

Returning to the main road, we pass *St. Giles's Church* (*ante*), and enter St. Giles's Street, which with its fine avenue of trees conducts us past the Martyrs' Memorial to the Cornmarket. On l. is the ch. of *St.*

Michael (*ante*), against the tower of which may be seen the E. abutment of the old North Gate, or *Bocardo*; the W. is hid behind the houses on the opposite side. In Bocardo, Cranmer, Ridley, and Latimer were imprisoned in the room over the gateway, which had in early times been used as a muniment room, but served as a common prison for debtors after the fortifications fell into disuse. The debtors were in the habit of letting down from one of the windows a hat, to receive charity, with the cry of " Pray remember the poor Bocardo birds." After being imprisoned here for a short time, Ridley was taken to the house of Mr. Iryah, and Latimer to that of one of the aldermen of the city, but they were all suffered to eat together in Bocardo (their food being bread, ale, cheese and pears), and Cranmer remained in that prison till his death—only being permitted to go thence to play at bowls in the Dean's garden at Christ Ch. It is said that he witnessed the burning of his fellow-bishops from the top of the neighbouring ch. tower, whence, " looking after them, and devoutly falling upon his knees, he prayed to God to strengthen their faith and patience in that their last but painful passage."—*Strype*. He suffered burning himself on the same spot 5 months after, " never stirring or crying all the while."

Somewhat lower down, on rt., approached by Frewen passage, is the *Oxford Union Society* (C 4), founded 1825, "for the maintenance of a library, reading-rooms, and writing-rooms; and the promotion of debates on any subject not involving theological questions.' The Society, under the name of the Union, first held its meetings in the college rooms of the different members in rotation; next in those of Mr. Talboys, near the Angel; next in the house of Mr. Vincent in the High Street, till in 1852 the present premises were purchased by the Society. The Library contains a good collection (about 40,000) of modern books. The old *Debating Room*, now the Library (length 62 ft.; breadth 33; height 47) was built, 1856, under *Messrs. Woodward and Deane*, and is a specimen of modern Venetian Gothic, of red brick, with stone dressings. Over the entrance is a stone carving by *Alex. Munro*, representing the Institution of the Round Table. The ceiling is richly painted, and the upper story is surrounded by frescoes of the acts of King Arthur and his knights in the following order :—1. The Education of Arthur, by Merlin, *Riviere ;* 2, Arthur's Wedding, with the incident of the White Hart and Brachet, *Riviere ;* 3, Sir Lancelot's vision of the Sangraal, *Rossetti ;* 4, Sir Pelleas and the Lady Ettarde, *Prinsep ;* 5, How King Arthur received his sword Excalibur from the Lady of the Lake. *Pollen ;* 6, King Arthur's first victory with the sword Excalibur, *Riviere ;* 7, How Sir Palomydes loved La Belle Yseult, and how she loved him not again, but rather Sir Tristram, *Morris ;* 8, Death of Merlin, *Jones ;* 9, Sir Gawaine and the three damsels at the fountain, *S. Stanhope ;* 10, The Death of Arthur, *Hughes.* The effect of these frescoes is much impaired by the 20 circular windows by which they have since been intersected, heads, arms, and legs appearing without bodies. The University debates are held in a new Debating Room, built in 1878, every Thursday evening during Term at 8 o'clock. Strangers can be taken in by members ; ladies find places in the gallery.

The fashion of modern shop-fronts has all but destroyed a fine pargeted house in the Corn-market, once the *Crown Inn,* kept by John Davenant, and where his son Sir William was born. Aubrey says that Shakespeare, who " was wont to go into Warwickshire once a year, and commonly lye at the Crowne

Taverne at Oxford, where he was exceedingly respected." Sir William Davenant was the poet's godson, and " the notion," said Pope to Spence, " of his being more than a poetical child only of Shakespeare was common in town, and Sir Wm. himself seemed fond of having it taken for truth."

Lower down, also on rt., at the crossways, called Carfax (quatre voies ?), is the *Church of St. Martin* (C 4), which was rebuilt 1822, and contains in its N. aisle a monument of John Davenant (father of Sir William), and the entry of his son's birth in its baptismal register. Attached to this ch. was Penniless Porch, a covered seat, latterly only the resort of idlers and beggars ; though Wood says that the mayor and his brethren used at one time to meet there to discuss the affairs of the city.

In front of the ch., in a spot called the Bull Ring, was the beautiful conduit of Otho Nicholson, now in Nuneham Park (Exc. *b*). The tower of St. Martin's is ancient, and was lowered in the reign of Edward III., because the scholars complained that, " in time of combat " between town and gown, the townsfolk, retreating to the top of it, as to a fortress, were wont to annoy them thence with arrows and stones. "All the licence of those violent times was shared in the fullest degree by the students of Oxford. North against south, Scotch against Irish, both against Welsh, town against gown, academics against monks, Nominalist against Realist, juniors against seniors, the whole university against the bishop of its diocese, against the archbishop of its province, against the chancellor of its own election,— were constantly in array one against another. The citizens were formed into a species of militia or burgess guard to repress the excesses of the academic mob. When the co of the nation assembled in · Oxf orders were issued to the students to absent themselves during its continuance. Carfax, the point of junction between the two hostile parties, was turned into a fortress, and thither, at the blowing of horns, the townsmen collected, either as a rendezvous for attack, or as a stronghold whence to annoy the enemy with volleys of arrows or stones. Thence too the tocsin was sounded by the town, as from St. Mary's by the university, when the two parties met in hostile array; pitched battles were fought with war standards unfurled, sometimes in the streets, sometimes in the adjacent fields;— of one of these bloody contests the memory was long preserved in 'Slaying Lane' [now Brewer Street, near Pembroke College]. One of these, in the reign of John, in which a woman was murdered by the students, led to the execution of three of the supposed culprits by the chancellor, and, in indignation at this alleged injustice, to the migration of a great body of the students to other seats of learning. In the reign of Edward III., when these riots were at their climax, there is one described in colours of which nothing in our own times can remind us, short of the wild scenes of the continental capitals in 1848—the city-gates barricaded, the chancellor interposing in person, a savage mob of 2000 countrymen bursting in, headed by black flags, and uttering wild cries of 'Slay, slay,' 'havoc, havoc'—Oxford given up to pillage for 2 days, and the cause of the students finally avenged by the demolition of the great tower of St. Michael's church, in which the insurgents had for the time intrenched themselves."—*A. P. S.* The fights between town and gown were till lately kept up, in a minor degree, on the 5th of November, and several succeeding evenings.

From Carfax, the High Street runs E., and Queen Street W. In the former, the chief edifices have been already described, but attention may be called to the handsome building by *Pearson,* for the London and County Bank (1868), on the site of Stodley's Hall, the excavation for which produced some mediæval pottery now in the Ashmolean Museum. Queen Street had, till 1870, a good pargeted house, on the S. side, but the work is now hidden by a new front. Continuing our course S. we have in St. Aldate's Street (pronounced St. Old's—"it takes its name from a bp. of Gloucester who cut Hengist king of the Saxons to pieces"—*Hearne*), on l. the *Town Hall* (C 4), on the site of an ancient institution called the "Domus Conversorum," for the reception of Jews converted to Christianity. The centre niche in the façade has a statue of Thos. Rowney, by whom it was rebuilt in 1752. A part is used as a free public library; and the *Corn Exchange,* in which a ball was given to the Prince and Princess of Wales in 1863, at which upwards of 1000 persons were present, is in the rear. Adjoining is the *Savings Bank,* by Buckeridge (1867), probably on the site of some ch., as an altar stone with 5 crosses thereon was discovered in digging the foundations. Nearly opposite to the Town Hall is the Post Office, erected in 1881; a modern Gothic edifice of Portland stone (C D 4). Lower down is the W. front of Christ Church, with St. Aldate's ch. and Pembroke College opposite. Below Pembroke are some picturesque Almshouses (D 4), begun by Cardinal Wolsey, but only finished as they now appear in 1834 by the Dean and Chapter of Christ Church. They were converted into a house by Christ Church a few years ago. In Brewer Street, adjoining, is the house in which Wolsey is said to have resided whilst his building at St. Frideswide's was going on, but apparently very inadequate to accommodate so great a man. It is now used as a house for the Christ Church Choir boys. Standing back from the street, in Rose Place, is a picturesque many-gabled house, called *Bp. King's House* (built by) Robert King, the last abbot of Osney, and first Bp. of Oxford, after the accession of Edward VI., when he was deprived of Gloucester Hall, which had before been assigned to him as a residence. The front was rebuilt in 1628. Cuddesden was not built till a centy. later, and in the interim the Bishops of Oxford had no palace. It is now divided into two dwellings, the ceilings of which are richly decorated, and in the 2nd house they bear the arms of King frequently repeated. The house was subsequently occupied by Unton Croke, a colonel in Cromwell's army, and member for Oxford. It has a handsome pargeted front, on which the date 1628 appears.

The street is closed by the *Folly* or *Grand-Pont Bridge* (E 4), which formerly consisted of above 40 stone arches, but which now is reduced to 3 (built 1825–27). In a house on this bridge the abbots of Abingdon were accustomed to keep court. Here, also, was the gate-house known as Friar Bacon's study—from Roger Bacon, the philosopher, who made it his observatory. Here tradition tells us that he made a brazen head, which was to deliver oracles, disclosing the means by which England would for ever be safe from invasion. For these oracles his friend, Friar Bungay, was appointed to watch, but he fell asleep instead, and the head, not being attended to, burst in pieces, with the exclamation, "Time is past." It was said of Bacon's study, that it would fall when a man more learned than himself passed under it, whence the line, in the 'Vanity of Human Wishes,'—

   "And Bacon's mansion trembles o'er his
      head."

It has been playfully said that it

was to avoid this risk that it was pulled down, c. 1770.

————

At the shop of Mr. Jas. Parker, in Broad St., will be found one of the largest and best collections of modern books in the kingdom. Readers of Boswell's 'Life' will remember Johnson's visit to his friend Sackville Parker, by whom the business was founded.

Beautiful *photographs* of the Oxford buildings may be obtained at Messrs. Hill and Saunders in the Corn-market, Guggenheim in High Street, at the two establishments of the Shrimptons, in Broad Street and Turl Street, at Taunt's in Broad Street, and at many other establishments.

The *print-shops* of Mr. Ryman and Mr. Wyatt in the High Street should not pass unnoticed.

The large establishment of Messrs. Spiers and Son, in the High Street, is well furnished with ornamental goods, china, guide-books, maps and stationery, and photographs : there are few shops in London better supplied. Messrs. Spiers are also able and willing to give much information to strangers visiting Oxford.

EXCURSIONS.

The following places are all within an easy walk of Oxford : where a rly. is available, it is pointed out.

(*a.*) *Iffley Church.* Cross Magdalen bridge (D E 6) and proceed along the Henley road for 1 m. Turn off on rt., and in 10 minutes you reach the village of Iffley, which, placed on a height, commands pleasant views of Oxford and the river.

" While as with rival pride their towers in-
     vade the sky,
Radcliffe and Bodley seem to vie
Which shall deserve the foremost place,—
Or Gothic strength, or Attic grace. '
                   Warton.

The name, which occurs as *Giftelei*

A.D. 945, is supposed to mean "the field of gifts." The ch. dedicated to St. Mary, built about 1170, and given to the priory of Kenilworth, is one of the best specimens' of a small Norm. Ch. in England. It has been restored. It has 3 fine Norm. doorways, of which that at the W. end has an arcade above it, surmounted by a circular window which has been filled with stained glass in memory of the author Eliot Warburton, brother of the present incumbent. The chancel is an E. E. addition; it has a good painted window by *Willement.* The arches under the tower have rich Norm. mouldings; the font is large and square, and as old as the ch. In the churchyard is a magnificent yew-tree; the churchyard cross has been restored, and groups beautifully with the old yew-tree and the Norm. tower richly coloured with yellow lichen. Close by is the old Rectory-house, a picturesque building containing some fine panelled rooms, and a very curious and unique buttery-hatch, divided by an ornamented pillar.

Charles Forbench, the vicar of Iffley, who was ejected by the Parliamentary Commissioners and was imprisoned at Woodstock for reading the Book of Common Prayer, said, on being released, "If I must not read it, I am resolved I will say it by heart in spite of all the rogues in England."

There is a pleasant walk back to Oxford, crossing the river at the old water-mill below the ch., and returning along the opposite bank as far as the barges, where there is a ferry to Christ Church Meadows.

(b.) *Sandford* and *Nuneham Courtenay.* Proceed to Iffley, as in Exc. a. 1 m. beyond is *Littlemore* (Stat.), where the ch., though modern, is interesting, as being one of the first results of the Oxford movement for the revival of Gothic architecture;

it was built under the auspices of John Henry Newman, who officiated there for some time after he had ceased to preach at St. Mary's, Oxford.

3 m. from Oxford is *Sandford*, the ch. of which was founded by Gerri de Planastre soon after the Conquest. Of this, little but the walls remain, the ch. having undergone repairs and alterations to such an extent as almost to destroy its identity. The last of these was effected in 1840, when a Norm. tower of 2 stages was added, and some of the windows remodelled. A carving in alabaster, representing the Assumption of the Virgin (15th-centy. work) is fixed against the E. wall; it was dug up in the ch.-yard, where a well-wrought Norm. capital, supposed to have belonged to the original porch, was also found a few years ago. N.W. of the ch. is a farmhouse, with a gateway bearing the date 1614, and having some fragments of sculpture built into the wall; over them is a shield displaying the cross pattée of the Templars, who had a commandery here, temp. Richard I. 1 m. E. are the remains of a nunnery, called the Minchery, founded in Saxon times, and suppressed by the Pope in 1524, in order to give its revenues to Wolsey for his new College. The seal of the establishment, a man in a gown, with flowing hair, was found here by a farmer in 1762. The river here is sometimes used as a practice-place for the Oxford boating-men, and near the *Lasher*, or weir, which has more than once been fatal to inexperienced undergraduates, is an obelisk recording the fate of Gaisford and Phillimore of Christ Church, drowned here June 22, 1843. The same fate befell Dasent, May 1872. There are 2 or 3 small islands, on one of which is a rustic *Inn*, much patronised by members of the boat clubs, who row down from Oxford.

2 m. S. of Sandford, the village

of Nuneham, transferred from the neighbourhood of the mansion by the first Lord Harcourt to the side of the old London road, attracts attention by the neat formality of its pretty thatched cottages. The ch. was erected by his grandson, the second lord, in 1764, after a design of his own, and is an extraordinary edifice. "It affords a memorable instance of the taste of that age, of which it was the misfortune that those persons who were the most liberal, and desirous to serve the Church, and who, for their private virtues, were most worthy of praise, were precisely those who did the most mischief; the fault was that of the age, not of the individual." ('Arch. Guide, Oxford.') The Harcourt Arms is an excellent country inn. Nuneham Courtenay (E. W. Harcourt, Esq.) once belonged to the De Redvers, earls of Devon. It, in the time of Charles II., was the property of Sir John Robinson, governor of the Tower, and it was purchased from his son-in-law, the Earl of Wemyss, by Simon, first Lord Harcourt. In 1830 it was bequeathed by the last Earl to his kinsman the Archbishop of York, the grandfather of the present possessor. The house is well situated on a wooded height above the river, with grounds laid out by Brown. The Park of 1200 acres abounds in fine trees; within it, on an eminence commanding a good view of the winding river, with Oxford in the distance, is the beautiful Conduit of Otho Nicholson (surrounded by his initials O. N., which formerly stood opposite Carfax ch. at Oxford, and formed one of the chief ornaments of that city, where it was erected 1610. It was removed 1787, and reconstructed here, by the second Earl. The beautiful gardens, which were partly planned by Mason the poet, are generally to be seen on Fridays on application to the gardener. Here are tablets with inscriptions by Mason and Whitehead.

The house is not shown, except as a special favour. It contains a collection of paintings, among which are—A. Caracci, Susannah and the Elders; Murillo, 2 Beggar Boys; Gent. Bellini, a Venetian Doge; Van Dyke, Henrietta Maria; Mignard, Louis XIV., Philip Duc de Vendôme; portrait of Lettice Knollys; Kneller, portrait of Pope, presented by the poet to Lord Chancellor Harcourt; Sir J. Reynolds, Lord Harcourt, the Duchess of Gloucester (Lady Waldegrave) twice, and a beautiful group of the 3 Ladies Waldegrave. Here also is a pane of glass from Pope's study at Stanton Harcourt, with an inscription written by him in 4 lines with a diamond, recording that he there completed the 5th book of Homer, 1718. "Nuneham is not superb, but so calm, riant, and comfortable, so live-at-able, one wakes in a morning on such a whole picture of beauty."—Walpole. The Park is a favourite spot for picnic parties from Oxford by water (the distance about 7 m.), and a portion of the grounds with a cottage at the water-side is liberally thrown open to visitors. The return can be made, if desired, from the Culham Stat., 1 m. W. of the park.

(c.) Dorchester. Proceed, either by road through Iffley and Nuneham Courtenay (Exc. a, b), or by rly. to Culham Stat., whence Dorchester, now a mere village but once a bishop's seat, is distant 3 m. E. On the way we pass Clifton Hampden, with a small Trans. Norm. and Dec. Church (restored by Sir G. G. Scott), most picturesquely placed on a rising ground, and containing a handsome altar-tomb for Mr. G. H. Gibbs, at whose cost the restoration was effected. The lich-gate and the taper spire, both modern, add much to the effect. A fine brick bridge erected in 1865 crosses the Thames here, from which a good view of the river in both directions may be obtained.

An episcopal see was established at Dorchester by Birinus in 634, after he had effected the conversion of Cynegils, king of Wessex. "The king," says Bede, "gave to the bishop the city called Dorcic, there to seat himself, where he built and consecrated churches, and by his labours called many to the Lord." Of these churches, no trace now remains, the present building showing nothing earlier than Trans.-Norm. work. Birinus was buried in his ch., but his body was afterwards removed to Winchester. A succession of bishops of Dorchester is traced down to the Conquest, soon after which (probably about 1078—see Hardy's 'Le Neve,' vol. ii.) the first Norm. prelate removed the see to Lincoln. Dorchester was once the largest see in England, embracing the present Dioceses of Winchester, Salisbury, Bath and Wells, Lichfield, Worcester and Hereford.

The *Dorchester Church,* ded. to *SS. Peter and Paul,* is a large, lofty, and spacious structure, of great length (300 feet) in proportion to its breadth. It was the ch. of the abbey, and being bought at the Dissolution for 140*l.* by Richard Bewforest, was by him bequeathed to the parish in 1554. The edifice is of various dates, but chiefly built between 1280 and 1300, a period of transition from the E. E. to the Dec. styles, curious mixtures of which occur. The tower is late Perp., and was almost entirely rebuilt with the old materials in the time of Charles II., and has since been repaired and partially restored. In the body of the ch. the Dec. style preponderates; but a Norm. door and window are found in the N. wall; and within the nave, which is Trans.-Norm., 1180, are 2 circular arches on square piers. The S. aisle is very large, and contains the monument of an abbot; its porch and an Early Dec. canopied buttress at the S.W. angle are both curious.

The S.E. chapel was restored in 1874 by *Scott.* A restored ch.-yard *Cross* stands beside the porch.

The most remarkable feature, however, is the *Chancel,* with its 3 fine windows. The E. window, Late Dec., is filled for nearly its whole length with tracery, and contains much good stained glass. The sculpture in the tracery of this window represents events in the life of Christ. It is of the age of Edward III. On the S. side, under a large Perp. window, dotted with fragments of armorial glass, are 3 sedilia and a double piscina richly carved, under Dec. canopies. At the back of these seats are tiny triangular windows with very beautiful mouldings, filled, at the restoration of the ch. by *Butterfield,* with glass of the 12th centy.

On the N. side is the famous *Jesse Window,* the centre mullion of which represents a genealogical tree set with figures, springing from the loins of the patriarch Jesse, who reclines below. The lateral tracery represents the branches, and on each is a statuette of one of the "House of David." The stained glass enters into the original design.

In the S. aisle are 2 monuments: (1) the effigy of a knight, cross-legged, drawing his sword; the expression of countenance remarkably fierce. "His name," says Leland, "is out of remembrance," but Mr. Addington, in his account of the ch. (published by the Oxford Arch. Society, 1845), thinks it probable that he was some follower in the train of either Richard, King of the Romans, or of Prince Edward in their crusades. (2) An effigy in legal costume, John de Stonore, chief justice of the Common Pleas, d. 1354. On the N. side is a handsome Perp. altar-tomb, with the effigy of a knight in plate-armour, known by the arms to be a Segrave; the date c. 1400. There have been many brasses, of which fragments remain, as of Sir John Drayton (1441), but the only perfect one is that of

Richard Bewforest, abbot, in a cope (c. 1510), with the inscription:

"Here lieth Sir Richard Bewfforeste, Pray Jesu geve his sowle good reste."

The very curious *Font* is a Norm. bowl of lead, moulded with 11 figures, supposed to be the apostles (without Judas), raised on a Perp. pedestal of stone.

A great deal of restoration has been effected by the present vicar, Mr. Macfarlane. An exhaustive history of Dorchester, by Mr. J. H. Parker, was published in 1882.

Near the ch. are some remains of a *Priory* of Black Canons, founded 1140 by Alexander Bp. of Lincoln, and granted at the Dissolution to Sir Edmund Ashfield, of Ewelme. They form the walls of the Grammar School and the foundations of an adjoining range of barns.

There is an old and still existing belief that no viper will live in the parish of Dorchester.

At the junction of the Thame and Isis "on the S. side of Dorchester, was a double embankment called *Dykehills*, extending in a string to the great bow of the river Isis, about ¾ m. long, 20 yds. asunder at bottom " (*Camden*), but it was nearly destroyed by agricultural operations in 1868. On the hill on the Berks side of the river is the fine camp of *Sinodun*.

(*d.*) *Shotover* and *Cuddesden*. Crossing Magdalen bridge (D E 6) you enter the suburb of *St. Clement* (E 7). The old ch.-yard occupies the angle between the Wycombe and the Henley roads, but the ch. (pseudo-Norm., built 1828) lies off to the l. near the river. Here was a holy well, said to be granted as a token of the sanctity of Edmund of Abingdon, afterwards Archbishop of Canterbury, but then a student at Oxford. "He often here, as of his extraordinary piety, conversed with God in private, particularly on a time, walking in the fields near Oxford. Jesus Christ appeared to him—whence a spring might well burst forth for joy, as St. Margaret's well at Binsey did at the entreaties of St. Frid." This pontiff was canonized.

Some of the ancient *Halls* for students were in St. Clement's. Among them, as Wood relates, were two that were the subject of small jokes. A tailor built one, and it at once got the name of Cabbage Hall. Soon after, a larger and better hall 'was built by some one else, which attracted most of the students from its predecessor. "They gave it the name of Caterpillar Hall, ' for,' as they said, ' it hath eaten up the Cabbage.' "

Halfway up the hill you turn off on rt. and ascend gradually to *Shotover Hill* (599 ft. high), whence there is a fine view of Oxford. The name is considered to be a corruption of Chateau Vert, or Chateau de Vere, a hunting lodge having existed on it from very early times. This was given up to the ranger of the day by Prince Henry, son of James I., who cut off his hand by an awkward stroke while he was holding the stag (according to custom) to be slaughtered by the royal sportsman. Hence it passed to Dr. Schutz, physician to George III., and thence to the Drurys. An ancestor of the poet Milton was ranger of Shotover; hence the family took its name from the adjoining village of Milton (Rte. 2).

Shotover is exceedingly interesting to the geologist, both from the abundance of its fossils, and from the peculiarity of its formation, which is fully described in a paper by Professor Phillips on ' The Estuary Sands of the upper part of Shotover Hill,' published in the Journal of the Geological Society, Aug. 1858. It consists of:—" 1. The Oxford Clay. 2. Calcgrit, or sands with cherty and shelly bands. 3. Coralline oolite, with shelly rag-beds. 4. Kimmeridge clay. 5. The Portland Sands, with included rock-bands and hard nodules, rich in shells. 6. Iron-sand and ochre series, to the top of the hill, 80 ft., consisting of yellow and white sands, varied with brown and even black colour, sandstones, sometimes cherty, nodular and geodic formations of oxide of iron, bands of white clay, and local accumulations of ochre."

Shotover is also interesting to the botanist. The plants found here include—*Menyanthes trifoliata*, buck-bean; *Polemonium cæruleum*, blue Jacob's-ladder; *Campanula Trachelium*, nettle-leaved bellflower; *Jasione montana*, sheep's scabious; *Camelina sativa*, gold of pleasure; *Anagallis tenella*, bog pimpernel; *Myosotis versicolor*, variegated scorpion-grass; *Lastrea Oreopteris*, mountain fern; *Blechnum Spicant*, hard fern.

"Shelley, when at University College, loved to walk in the woods, to stroll on the banks of the Thames, but especially to wander about Shotover Hill.' At a pond at the foot of the hill before ascending it, on the l. of the road, formed by the water which had filled an old quarry, he would linger in the dusk, gazing in silence on the water, repeating verses aloud, or loudly exulting in the splash of the stones he continually threw."—*New Monthly*, 1832.

Under the hill S. lies the little village of *Horsepath*, called in Domesday Horspadan. It was then in the hands of the king, but afterwards belonged to the Templars. In 1312 it was the property of John de Bloxam, a witness against them. The ch. is small, mainly E. E. but with a Perp. tower, and a chancel rebuilt in 1840. The font and stoup are curious, and of early date. Two rude figures are built into the inner wall of the tower, a man with bagpipes, and a woman; they are supposed to represent Thomas London and his wife, who built the tower.

1½ m. S.E. and nearly the same distance from Wheatley Station, we reach *Cuddesden*, which contains the *Palace of the Bishop of Oxford*. The Bishops resided originally in Oxford; first in Gloucester Hall, and afterwards in the beautiful old pargeted house in St. Aldate's, still known as "Bishop King's House." Bp. Bancroft, attracted no doubt by the fine neighbouring ch., and instigated by Laud, first built a palace here in 1635, with timber presented by Charles I. from the forest of Shotover; but this short-lived building was burnt to the ground in 1644 by Colonel Legg, the royalist governor of Oxford, for fear it should be used as a garrison by the Parliamentarians. It remained in ruins until Bp. Fell rebuilt it at his own cost in 1679. "The Palace Chapel, erected by Bp. Wilberforce in 1846, is a very good imitation of Dec. work; the windows are all filled with stained glass by the best artists of the day."—*H. P.*

The *Church* (12th centy.) is a fine cruciform edifice, with a massive tower in the centre. It was built during the transition from the Norm. to the E. E. style of architecture; it has a fine Norm. doorway at the W. end, and the pointed arches beneath the tower have beautiful zigzag mouldings. The chancel is Perp., c. 1500. The whole has been well restored. Bp. Bancroft, the founder of the original palace in 1635, is buried near the S. wall of the chancel; there are also mural monuments of Bishops Moss and Jackson, and in the churchyard the marble tomb of Maria, daughter of Bishop Lowth, on whom there is a touching epitaph.

Opposite the Palace is the *Ecclesiastical Training College*, founded by Bp. Wilberforce, of Oxford, April, 1853, and opened June 15, 1854. It is intended for the reception of theological students, members of the Universities, who have passed their final examination, and students of King's College, or graduates of Triuity College, Dublin, holding the Divinity Testimonial. The College, built from designs of *Street*, contains rooms for 21 students, a dining-hall, common-room, chapel, 8 rooms for a vice-principal, and a chapel erected as a Wilberforce memorial in 1875. The style is Dec. The roofs are of very different heights, and the upper story is lighted by large dormer windows, with hipper gables on the side of the principal roofs. An octagonal staircase turret, with pyramidal capping, makes a conspicuous and very ornamental feature on the exterior.

The return to Oxford may be made by *Wheatley*, a stat. on Oxford and Thame line (Rte. 22).

(*e.*) *Headington, Stanton St. John's, Beckley, and Elsfield.* This was an excursion much in favour with Dr. Arnold, who speaks with delight of " the wider skirmishing ground by Beckley, Stanton St. John's, and Forest Hill, which we used to expatiate over on whole holidays, and Elsfield on its green slope."

Passing through St. Clement's, the road ascends Headington Hill, the s ime by which, on June 24, 1646, the Royalists, after the surrender of Oxford, " marched out of the town, through a guard of the enemy, extending from St. Clement's to Shotover Hill, armed, with colours flying and drums beating. Prince Rupert and Prince Maurice had left with the people of quality two days before." Gibbon, in his ' Autobiography,' mentions his walks up Headington Hill whilst at Magdalen.

On the l. of turnpike road, " at the brow of the branch of the Roman way that falls down upon Marston Lane, is an elm that is commonly known by the name of Joe Pullen's tree, it having been planted by the care of the late Mr. Josiah Pullen, of Magdalen Hall, who used to walk to that place every day, sometimes twice a day, from Magdalen Hall and back again in

the space of half an hour."—*Hearne.* A stone cross formerly stood here, on the spot (then in Shotover Forest) where it is said that a student of Queen's was once attacked by a wild boar from the neighbouring forest of Shotover, when he escaped by cramming the volume of Aristotle, which he was reading, with the cry " Græcum est," down the throat of that infuriated beast. This tradition is supposed to have given rise to the Christmas ceremony of the Boar's Head at Queen's College.

King Ethelred had a palace at Headington. The *Church* has a fine Norm. chancel-arch, and a tower originally E. E. In the ch.-yard is a fine *Cross* raised on three steps. A short distance from the village is the quarry, from which much of the porous stone was taken of which so many of the Oxford edifices were built. This is an inferior kind of oolite, which is soft and easily cut in the quarry, but which hardens afterwards, unless exposed to smoke, as in the case of most of the Colleges, when it quickly crumbles away. That this is not the case when the surrounding atmosphere is clear may be seen in the garden front of Wadham, and in many of the country houses in the neighbourhood.

2 m. further, on the l., is *Stanton St. John's*, so called from the family of St. John, who possessed it from the time of Henry III. to that of Elizabeth. Here is a fine *church*, temp. Edward I., the transition from the E. E. to the Dec. style, excellently restored by a former rector, Rev. J. Murray Holland. The tower was added in the 15th centy. The chancel is of great beauty; fine E. window, also some good specimens of painted glass, 13th centy.; a few of the old seats remain, with very remarkable poppyheads, some being heads of horses, others grotesques, and others human heads in

costume of the time of Henry VIII. Milton's great-grandfather and grandmother are buried in the ch.-yard.

The road to Beckley (2 m. N.) skirts *Stow Wood*, on the borders of which is a small country inn (*Royal Oak:* clean; civil people); much resorted to by Oxford botanists. Among the plants found here are: *Scabiosa columbaria*, small scabious; *Iris fœtidissima*, stinking Iris; *Asperula Cynanchiæ*, small woodruff; *Primula elatior*, oxlip; *Turritis glabra*, smooth tower-mustard; *Aquilegia vulgaris*, columbine; *Hyoscyamus niger*, henbane.

The village of *Beckley* is situated on an eminence overhanging the S, side of Ottmoor. The British Saint Douanverdh is recorded to have been buried here. Beckley was mentioned by King Alfred in his will as his hereditary property, and here was the castellated palace of Richard, King of the Romans, of which a fragment, serving as a pigeon-house, existed in the early part of the present centy. The *Church*, Dec. and Perp., has some painted glass; the tower still retains the sanctus bell. The walls are covered with the remains of very curious fresco paintings, which chiefly represent, and with horrible minuteness, the tortures of the damned. The font has an ancient stone desk to hold the book for the officiating priest, and the pulpit retains the old hourglass-stand. In this parish is *Studley Priory* founded 1184 by Bernard de St. Valon, who was killed at the siege of Acre. At the Dissolution it was granted to John Croke, and the remains have been converted into a very picturesque Elizabethan house with a chapel added in 1639. The house is not shown; but many views of the remains of the Priory (13th and 14th cents.) are given in Sir A. Croke's 'History of the Croke Family.' *Horton* is an adjoining hamlet A church has been built on a site long known as Chapel Close.

In returning to Oxford through *Elsfield*, notice the fine view from the hill. The little ch. is a good specimen of E. E., with Dec. E. window ; the old hourglass-stand remains here also. Warton and Johnson walke l out to Elsfield in 1754 to visit Mr. Wise, the Radcliffe Librarian. "One day," says Warton, "Mr. Wise rea l to us a dissertation which he was preparing for the press, intitled, ' A History and Chronology of the Fabulous Ages.' Some old divinities of Thrace, related to the Titans, an l called the Cabiri, made a very important part of the theory of this piece : and in conversation afterwards, Mr. Wise talked much of his Cabiri. As we returned to Oxford in the evening, I outwalked Johnson, and he cried out Sufflamina,' a Latin word, which came from his mouth with peculiar grace, and was as much as to say, ' Put on your drag chain ' Before we got home, I again walked too fast for him ; and he now cried out, ' Why you walk as if you were pursued by all the Cabiri in a body.'" —*Boswell's Life of Johnson.*

(*f.*) *Forest-hill, Holton, Waterperry*, and *Waterstock*. At the 3rd mile from St. Clement's a bye-road turns off on l. to *Forest-hill*. The small Trans.-Norm. ch. is placed on the very brow of the hill, and its curious W. bell gable is visible from a considerable distance. In this ch. Milton was married to his first wife Mary, daughter of Richard Powell of this place. The house where Mr. Powell lived has been destroyed, but there still remains some ornamental plastering against the wall of two outhouses, which seems to be as old as the time of Milton, and contains allusions to the subjects of 'Paradise Lost.' This has been generally supposed to be the spot where Milton composed the 'Allegro' and ' Penseroso,' which were, however, written at his father's house at Horton in Bucks. There is no

[*Berks, &c.*]   B

record of his ever having lived here, though he may have taken many of his .ideas from this place. "The spot whence Milton undoubtedly took most of his images is on the top of the hill, from which there is a most extensive prospect on all sides .... the villages and turrets, partly shaded with trees of the finest verdure, and partly raised above the groves that surrounded them, the dark plains and meadows of a greyish colour, where the sheep were feeding at large .... The tradition of the poet's having lived there is current among the villagers. One of them showed us a ruinous wall that made part of his chamber; and I was much pleased with another, who had forgotten the name of Milton, but recollected him by the title of the Poet."—*Sir W. Jones to Lady Spencer.*

Mickle, the translator of Camoens, resided at Forest-hill, and is buried in the ch.-yard without any memorial. Several members of his wife's family (Tomkins) are also interred there, and the verses on their grave-stones are believed to be by him.*

1½ m. S. is *Holton*, with a small *Church*, Trans.-Norm. and Dec., with Perp. square tower, and a sanctus-bell turret at the E. end of the nave. In the parish register is the entry : "Henry Ireton, Commissary General to Sir Thos. Fairfax, and Bridget, daughter to Oliver Cromwell, Lieut.-Genl. of the horse to the said Sir Thos. Fairfax, were married by Mr. Dell, in the Lady Whorwood, her house, in Holton, June 15, 1646. Alban Eales, Rector." The ancient *Manor-house*, a large moated building, was pulled down in 1815. and the present house (W. E. Biscoe, Esq.) built on another site.† Milton's ancestors were till lately supposed to have lived at Holton, but

the poet is now said to have been the grandson of Richard Milton of Stanton St. John's, who is believed to have been identical with the John Milton of Holton, and ranger of Shotover, mentioned by Aubrey and Wood. In the reign of Elizabeth, Milton was a common name in the villages of the Bullington Hundred.

1 m. S.E. is *Waterperry* (Rt. Hon. J. W. Henley, M P.). In the park is the ivy-covered *Church*, mainly E.E. and Dec., but with Trans.-Norm. capital to a column in the nave. There is a Dec. *Cross* in the ch.-yard. The chancel is E.E. with Dec. E. window containing some fragments of stained glass. The W. window is Perp.; it, with most of the other windows, contains heraldic glass, some of which belongs to the Cursons, and there is a *Brass* of Walter Curson (d. 1527) and his wife Isabel, brought here from the Augustine Friars' ch. in Oxford at the Dissolution. There are also Jacobean monuments of the Cursons, and a modern one by *Chantrey* to Mrs. Greaves, daughter of the late Mr. Henley, who succeeded the Cursons in the ownership of Waterperry. 1 m. E. is *Waterstock*, modern ch. built in 1792, but with an Early Perp. tower, from the battlement of which rises a bell-cot of singular shape. The monument of Sir George Croke, the judge who voted for John Hampden on the ship-money question (d. 1641), is preserved in the chancel; the inscription is ascribed to Sir Matthew Hale. Some fragments of painted glass also remain; among them are the arms and portrait of George Neville, Archbishop of York and Chancellor of Oxford, and a younger brother of "King-making Warwick." The return to Oxford can be made from the Wheatley or Tiddington stat. on the Thame line (Rte. 22).

(*g*.) *Binsey and Godstow.* ½ m. beyond the rly. stat. on the Cheltenham road, turn to the rt., and a walk

---

* An ancient cope, of curious needlework, is preserved here.
† A cherry-tree planted by Cromwell is to be seen in the park.

of 1 m. through a bye-lane leads to the little *Church* of *Binsey*, mainly Trans.-Norm., with bell-gable and good low side window. It stands on a small island, originally called Thorney, but on a small oratory being built there by St. Frideswide, the name was changed to Binsey, which is, doubtfully, said to mean "the isle of prayer." The old oratory was built of "watlyn and rough-hewn timber," and was succeeded by the present ch. about 1132, when the manor was given to the monastery of St. Frideswide. Here was a famous image of the saint, and the pavement was worn away by the knees of the pilgrims who came to worship before it. 3 yds. on the W. is the noted well of St. Margaret, which St. Frideswide, by her prayers at the building of the chapel, caused miraculously to be opened, which was lost, but has been found and restored by the present vicar. So great was the reputation of this well, that the town of Seckworth (of which scarcely any traces remain) sprang up, and, it is said, once contained no less than 24 inns for the sake of those who came to profit by its healing powers. A short distance E. is *Medley*, another river island, mentioned by Wither:—

> " In summer-time to Medley
>   My love and I would go ;
> The boatmen there stood ready
>   My love and I to row."

In the low meadows the botanist will find *Aristolochia Clematitis*, birthwort ; *Villarsia nymphæoides*, fringed water-lily ; *Hottonia palustris*, water violet : the last a common plant in the neighbourhood of Oxford.

1 m. N.W., on the bank of the river, which has a lock here, are the ruins of *Godstow Nunnery*, founded by Edith d'Oiley, in 1138, King Stephen and his Queen Matilda laying the foundation stone. The remains are now but slight, being part of the boundary wall, and some

portion of a 15th centy. building with Perp. window of 3 lights. Wood's MS. gives an account of its former state. "The approach to the nunnery was through a large gate with lodging-rooms over it : this led into a spacious court, on the rt. or S. side of which stood the nunnery, which had a fair portion leading into it. On the l. or N. side of the court was a long range of buildings, which reached from the gatehouse almost to the end of the court. There was a little old chapel standing in the garden, and the remains of a great cloister leading from the tower of the great ch., then destroyed, to the chapel, which was called St. Leonard's Chapel, and which contained in its E. window 2 portraitures of Margaret Tewkesbury and Elizabeth Brainton, abbesses of this place. There was a second chapel, called St. Thomas's Chapel, which was used for the guests, pilgrims, and the poor who came daily." Here Fair Rosamond was educated ; here, there is every reason to believe, in spite of the story of the labyrinth, she passed the latter years of her life, and here she was buried by her parents beneath the high altar :—

> " Her body then they did entombe
>   When life was fled away,
> At Godstowe, near to Oxford towne,
>   As may be seene this daye."

Lights were ordained to be constantly kept burning at her grave, where King John is said, by Lambarde, to have erected a costly monument, with the inscription—

> " Hic jacet in Tumba, Rosa Mundi, non Rosa
>   Munda,
> Non redolet, sed olet, quæ redolere solet."

"When Hugh, Bishop of Lincoln," says Stowe (N.B. Oxford was then in the diocese of Lincoln), "came to Godstow, in 1191, and entered the church to pray, he saw there a tomb, in the middle of the quire, covered with a pall of silke and set about with lights of waxe ;

B 2

and, demanding whose tomb it was, he was answered that it was the tombe of Rosamund, sometime lemman to Henry II:, who for the love of her had done much good to that church." Then the bishop commanded that she should be taken up and buried without the church, "lest Christian religion should grow in contempt." Leland mentions Rosamund's tomb, with the inscription "Tumba Rosamundæ" upon the stone, and that " her bones were found closed in lede, and within that closed in lether (leather); when it was opened, there was a very swete smell came out of it." Among the relics shown-here till the Dissolution was the petrified trunk of a tree, which was said to have become so in answer to a prayer of Fair Rosamund, who affirmed she knew she should be saved, and that as a token of it, this tree would be turned into stone.

On the bridge at Godstow (a small part of which is ancient) was formerly a cross, inscribed—

"Qui meat huc oret, signumque salutis adoret,
Uique sibi detur veniam, Rosamunda precetur."

Opposite the ruins is a neat small *Inn,* " the Trout." well known to boating men. ¼ m. W. is *Wytham* (Berks), an exceedingly pretty village, with the *Abbey* (Earl of Abingdon) (Rte. 9). Godstow can be reached direct from Oxford by crossing the " *Port Meadow,*" a marshy level of 439 acres, mentioned in Domesday Book as a place where the burgesses of Oxford had rights of common pasturage. in the time of Edward the Confessor. It has of late been greatly improved, the roads raised, and bordered with trees. At its W. extremity is Bossom's ferry, where boats may be hired for Godstow, or the ruins may be reached by a pleasant walk along the bank of the river. The return hence to Oxford may be varied by ascending the hill and

joining the Woodstock road at *Wolvercote,* formerly Wolvescote. Here (according to a pseudo-tradition mentioned by Holinshed) in a dingle near a wood, Memphric, King of the Britons, great-grandson of Brutus, and traditional founder of Oxford, was seized and devoured by wolves. The *Church,* which was rebuilt except the Perp. tower, in 1861, contains a fine monument to Chief Baron John Walter (d. 1630) and, his 2 wives; a carved pulpit of good workmanship (t. Hen. VIII.) fell to pieces about 1868, and the ancient hourglass-stand has disappeared. The University paper mill is near the ch.

" Midway between this and Oxford was *Aristotle's Well,* where the students, especially such as studied his philosophy,. went frequently to refresh themselves."— *Hearne.* The progress of building has obliterated all traces of the fortifications thrown up in this neighbourhood during the Civil War.

(*h.*) The *Hinkseys,* 2 Berkshire villages, the most distant being 2 m. S.W. of Oxford. *North Hinksey* (often called *Ferry Hinksey,* the ferry being the shortest way, though it can also be reached by the Seven Bridges road) has a small plain ch., with E. E. tower, a good Norm. doorway, and low side window. It contains the tomb of Thomas Willis (father of Dr. Willis), who died in the royal cause during the siege of Oxford, Aug. 1643 ; and the monument of W. Finmore, Fellow of St. John's, 1646, with a curious inscription beginning " Reader, look to thy feet ; honest and loyal men are sleeping under them." In the churchyard are the remains of a Dec. Cross with a fluted shaft. In the hill-fields above the village is the *Conduit* built by Otho Nicholson of Christ Church in 1617, to supply Carfax with water.

1 m. further S., across some fields,

Archbishop of York, was born. The s,is *South Hinksey*, where John Pier Perp. ch. has a good open timber roof. Just before reaching the village is the entrance of the so-called *Happy Valley*, a pretty walk emerging on the hill near Sunningwell, one of "the little valleys that debouche on the valley of the Thames behind the Hinkseys," beloved by Dr. Arnold. From the hill between the villages Turner took his view of Oxford.

(*i.*) *Stanlake.* This neighbourhood furnishes a very good field for those interested in British remains. It is reached by crossing the Bablockhythe ferry, 4 m. W. of Oxford, and then passing westward by the village of *Northmoor*, where the ch. is worth notice. 1 m. N. is *Gaunt House*, a moated 15th-centy. building, now a farm-house; there was a brass to its builder, John Gaunt (d. 1465), in Stanlake ch. in Wood's time. During the civil war it was a garrison for the king, being the property of the loyal Dean Samuel Fell. 2 m. W. is *Stanlake*, with a cruciform ch., with octagonal tower and spire. It is mainly E. E. and Dec., but the chancel arch is Trans.-Norm.

About ¼ m. N. of the ch. is a *British village*, discovered in 1857, by Messrs. Akerman and Stone, and described in *Archæologia*, vol. xxxvii. A series of 13 "fairy rings" being then explored, it was found that they consisted of trenches very carefully made, usually about 12 ft. wide at top, sloping till their sides met at 4 or 5 ft. below the surface, and from 60 ft. to 130 ft. in diameter. The trenches were filled with dry, dull rich-looking earth, among which occurred, in some cases, fragments of rude unbaked pottery and bones of animals; in others, human bones, calcined, and in urns. The place where the bodies were burnt, a space about 15 ft. in length, was discovered

by the intense blackness of the soil. The finding a flint arrow-head in one of the trenches proved that the sepulchres belonged to a very early period, long before the effect of Roman civilisation had been felt in this island; and that the remains were those of the poor, and not of chieftains, was in the opinion of the excavators satisfactorily established: "within a portion of a circular area of 70 ft. diameter, were detected upwards of 80 interments, only two of which were accompanied by relics, and those of the simplest and most primitive description." A brass spiral finger-ring was discovered at a subsequent exploration, and is, with some of the rude urns, preserved in the Ashmolean Museum, where also a plan of the village may be seen. "That the trenched circles were not intended as inclosures for cattle seems evident from the peculiar formation observed in all of them, for their sides slope gradually from the edge to the bottom, and would therefore offer no impediment to the ingress or egress of any animal. For the same reason they are not adapted for defence against the attacks of an enemy. If the areas inclosed within them are, as may be conjectured, tabooed spots, consecrated to religious rites, further research may possibly render this apparent. The facts already elicited shed a new light on the sepulchral usages of our primitive forefathers, and they help to dissipate a very common error among antiquaries, namely, the belief that the graves of the ancient inhabitants of Britain were generally protected by tumuli, a belief founded on the description given by Tacitus of the burial of men of note among the ancient Germans (Germ. xxvii.). If read by the light which researches like these supply, we shall perceive that the words of the great historian do not imply that the tumulus was erected over the graves of the lowly and unhonoured dead; and that the interments at Stanlake rank with the latter class seems abundantly proved." —*Archæologia*, vol. xxxvii.

Three other ancient burial-places are to be found in a radius of a single mile, viz., at Cokethorpe, Yelford, and Brighthampton, but they are all of much later date. Some relics from them also are preserved in the Ashmolean Museum.

(*j.*) *Stanton Harcourt.* Leaving Oxford by the Seven Bridges road, you cross a corner of Berks, passing Botley and Cumnor, and at 4 m. reach *Bablock-hythe*, where the ferry leads into Oxfordshire again :—

" Thee at the ferry, Oxford riders blithe,
Returning home on summer nights, have met,
Crossing the stripling Thames at Bablock-hythe,
Trailing in the cool stream thy fingers wet,
As the slow punt swings round."
                                        M. Arnold.

Hence it is 2 m. to Stanton Harcourt, which has been in the Harcourt family 600 yrs., having been granted by Adeliza, Queen of Henry I., to her kinswoman Milicent de Camville, whose daughter Isabel married Richard de Harcourt. The manor-house, built in the reign of Edward IV., remained nearly entire until the end of the last century, though not inhabited by the family after the death of Sir Philip Harcourt, in 1688; some few upper rooms are now occupied by a farmer. " The buildings originally inclosed a quadrangle, with the gatehouse on one side, which remains perfect, but of later date than the rest (c. 1540); one of the corner towers, known as Pope's Tower, has the ground floor fitted up as the chapel." (*Dom. Arch.*, vol. iii. 276.) The *kitchen*, a square tower, bears a general resemblance to that at Glastonbury. It has walls 3 ft. thick, the rooms being square below and octangular above. The height is 39 ft. to the springing of

the roof, and this rises 25 ft. higher. The fires were made against the walls, and the smoke, ascending without tunnels, was stopped by the conical roof, and escaped by loopholes on every side, which were opened and shut according to the direction of the wind. The roof is surmounted by a griffin 8 ft. high.

Pope, in a letter to the Duke of Buckingham, likens the kitchen to the forge of Vulcan, the cave of Polyphemus, and the temple of Moloch. He says that " the horror of it has made such an impression upon the country people, that they believe the witches keep their sabbath here, and that once a year the Devil treats them with infernal venison, viz., a toasted tiger stuffed with tenpenny nails." He graphically describes the aged and desolate appearance of the house in his time, and concludes by affirming that " its very rats are grey, and praying that the roof may not fall upon them, as they are too infirm to seek other lodgings." He also describes one of the little rooms in the tower as walled up; " for the ghost of Lady Frances is supposed to walk there, and some prying maids of the family report that they have seen a lady in a fardingale, through the keyhole; but the matter is hushed up and the servants are forbidden to talk of it." The whole of the letter is in the same ludicrous style, and is not to be taken as anything more than a flight of fancy; an existing plan of the buildings shews that almost every one stood in some other place than the poet pleases to give it.

Pope's Tower, which stands in the garden, rises to the height of 57 ft.; it contains the *Chapel,* and 3 chambers above, each 13 ft. square. The chapel is vaulted with fan-tracery, and the ante-chapel has a flat wooden ceiling, blue, divided into squares, with gilt stones in each compartment. The upper chamber is called Pope's study. Here he spent 2 summers, and he wrote the following inscription on a pane of red glass, which was in one of the windows, but is now preserved at Nuneham Courtenay (Exc. *b*).—" In the year 1718 Alexander Pope finished here the fifth volume of Homer." While he resided here Gay was staying with the Harcourts at Cokethorpe (Rte. 25), and frequently visited him. An interesting letter of his graphically describes the death of 2 lovers who were struck here by lightning in 1718.

The *Church*, dedicated to *St. Michael*, is cruciform, and has a fine carved oak rood-screen, E. E., probably the earliest now existing in England. The nave is of the 12th, the chancel and transepts of the 13th, the tower and Harcourt Chapel of the 15th centy. On the N. of the chancel is an altar-tomb, with a beautiful Dec. canopy, said by Wood to be that of Isabel de Camville; but if so, erected long after her decease, probably temp. Edw. 1.; it is adorned with the symbols of the Passion, and is supposed to have served as an Easter Sepulchre. On the S. side is the tomb of Maud, daughter of Lord Grey of Rotherfield Greys, and wife of Sir Thomas Harcourt, in the costume of the reign of Richard II. The Harcourt Chapel contains the tombs, on the S., of Sir Robert Harcourt and his wife Margaret (1471), both (the lady being one of the only 3 known instances) decorated with the order of the Garter; on the N. that of Sir Robert, grandson of the former, and Richmond's standard-bearer at Bosworth after Sir W. Brandon was cut down; also a monument to Simon, only son of the 1st Viscount Harcourt, which has an epitaph by Pope.

Several of the Huntingdon family

are buried in this ch. Robert Huntingdon's monument has Congreve's epitaph :—

" This peaceful tomb doth now contain
Father and son, together laid,
. Whose living virtues shall remain
When they and this are quite decay'd,

" What man should be, to ripeness grown,
And finish'd worth should do or shun,
At full was in the father shown;
What youth can promise, in the son.

" But death, obdurate, both destroy'd
The perfect fruit and opening bud;
First seiz'd those sweets we had enjoy'd,
Then robb'd us of the coming good."

Here also is the monument with Pope's inscription on John Hewet and his sweetheart, killed by lightning under a tree.

The name of the village is thus fancifully accounted for by tradition. Once upon a time, a battle was fought there, when the general (name not preserved) rode up to one of his captains, named Harcourt, who was in the thick of it, and called out, " Stan' to 'un, Harcourt ! Stan' to 'un, Harcourt !" Harcourt's prowess won the battle, and the place has been called Stanton Harcourt ever since (see *Scouring of the White Horse*).

At a short distance from the village are 3 large stones known as the *Devil's Quoits*, which Warton supposes to be memorials of a battle of Bampton, fought in 614, when the Saxon princes Cynegils and Cwichelm slew more than 2000 Britons. The name refers to a popular tradition that the Devil played here with a beggar for his soul, and won by the throwing of these huge stones. If time allows, the E. E. and Dec. ch. of *Northmoor* may be taken on the way back to Bablock-hythe ferry. The Dec. windows of the nave (figured in Rickman) are very elegant; two stone coffins in the chancel, with effigies, will repay examination; and there is a picturesque Elizabethan parsonage. Or, if preferred, the return may be made by rly. from either the South Leigh or Eynsham stats. (Rte. 25.)

(k.) Islip, Oddington, and Charlton-on-Otmoor. This is a very interesting excursion of about 9 miles, keeping near the E. bank of the Cherwell; the return can be made from Islip by rly. (Rte. 28.) There is a far more interesting walk to Islip—by road about 1 m. on Bicester road; across the fields to Water Eaton, thence by the bank of the Cherwell to Islip.

Turning l. from St. Clement's, we reach at 2 m. Marston. The ch. is Trans.-Norm. and Perp. Until 1830 there was a Cross in the churchyard, and another in the village, but they were then converted into road materials—J. H. P. Marston House, now pulled down, was the seat of Unton Croke, a noted Parliamentarian, and in it the articles for the surrender of Oxford in 1646 were agreed on. At 4 m. is Wood Eaton, a very pleasant village, still preserving its green, with the fragment of a cross. The ch. is mainly E. E., with Perp. E. window and tower.

1 m. out of the direct road, and on the W. bank of the river, but well worth the detour, is the little chapel of Water Eaton, "a remarkably good specimen of the revived Gothic, of the time of James I., having at first sight the appearance of a much earlier date. It is a simple oblong chapel, with a high-pitched roof, open to the rafters, and of good plain character, without tie-beams." The style is Perp., but the windows have somewhat of a Dec. character. The Manor House to which it belonged (now a farmhouse) is exceedingly picturesque; it is a "good and perfect example of the Elizabethan style, with its courtyard, entrance gate, detached wings and chapel, all in their original state, and all

apparently built at once from the same design."—Arch. Guide, Oxford. It was the residence of Lord Lovelace during the civil war, and here his wife was seized by a party of Parliamentarians. They carried her off in her own carriage 10 miles on the road to Banbury, but then thrust her out of it, and left her at liberty to find her way back on foot. Keeping near the river, which receives the little stream of the Ray, we reach, at 7 m., Islip. The Church (restored 1861) seems to have been rebuilt in great part in the 14th centy., but portions are 2 centuries earlier. The nave is Trans.-Norm., with some Dec. additions; the aisles are Dec.; the tower Perp. On the S. wall some curious wall-paintings of the 14th centy. have been discovered. The chancel was rebuilt in 1680 by Dr. South, "the witty South," one of the most remarkable of the eminent men who have held this living. Dr. Buckland, the geologist, is buried under a granite monument in the ch.-yard; and a window has been erected to his memory.

Islip was a residence of King Ethelred and Queen Emma; and here their son Edward the Confessor was born, as appears from his own words in the Charter for the restoration of Westminster, in which he gives to that monastery the "small village wherein I was born, by name Githslepe." The chapel of the palace existed, as a barn, near the ch. till 1783; and the font in which he is said to have been baptized, though manifestly of the time of Edward I., is preserved in the rectory garden. It long remained in a barn of the Red Lion Inn at Islip, whence it was removed to ornament a garden at Kiddington, where, as Hearne records, an old lady kept her meat to cram turkeys in it, but the turkeys all died. Thence it went to Layton Farm, near Bicester, next, being presented to Lady Jersey, was placed in the ch. of Middleton Stony, but has now been restored to Islip. It bears the inscription,—

"This sacred font Saint Edward first received.
From Womb to Grace, from Grace to Glory went
His virtuous life. To this faire Isle bequeathed
Praise . . . . and to us but lent.
Let this remaine, the Trophies of his Fame,
A King baptised from hence a Saint became."

1 m. E. is *Oddington*, a small Dec. ch., with a somewhat remarkable *Brass* to a former rector, Ralph Hamsterley, Master of University College; it represents a skeleton in a shroud, and was apparently set up in his lifetime, as the date is left incomplete, "Anno 15 . . Mensis —." He died Aug. 2, 1518.

1 m. N.E. is *Charlton-on-Otmoor*, where the E.E. and Dec. *Church* contains a very beautiful *rood-screen* of richly carved oak, which retains the original painting and gilding—date c. 1500. The stone stairs to the rood-loft have been all cut away but 2; the staircase-arch, however, is left. An ancient custom is observed in this ch., a cross of evergreens and flowers being annually placed on the top of the roodloft, where it remains all the year round. Every May-day the village girls, dressed in white, bring it to the ch. in procession, when "the May-cross" is a beautiful sight.

The neighbouring churches of Merton and Ambrosden are worth a visit, but they are most readily reached from Bicester (Rte. 28).

BLENHEIM.

(*1.*) *Woodstock* and *Blenheim.* This excursion may be made by proceeding to either the Woodstock-road or the Handborough stats., but neither is very convenient, and the more usual route is by the high road.

Leaving Oxford by St. Giles' Street, *Wolvercot* is passed on W. (Exc. *g*),

and at 5 m. we reach *Begbrooke*, the small ch. of which, amid modern alterations, has preserved a good Norm. S. door, near which is a stone coffin with coped lid, supposed by Wood to be the founder's tomb. 1 m. W. is *Blaydon.* The church is a modern Gothic edifice, built 1804, and so needing no description. One of its rectors was Dr. Matthew Griffith, an eminent member of the Church Militant. He served as chaplain with the royal armies at Oxford and elsewhere, and his daughter lost her life by his side at the storming of Basing House. He continued the Church service throughout the Protectorate, at the ch. of St. Nicholas Olave, London, in spite of several imprisonments, and on the Restoration received this living, where he died in 1665.

2 m. beyond Begbrooke, the park wall of Blenheim flanks the road on the W. At length the Hensington gateway is passed, through which there is a good view of the house, and at 8 m. we enter—

Woodstock (*Inn:* Bear, tolerably good: the town in the old coaching days abounded in inns, and has now 16 public houses), a quiet sleepy town of about 1400 inhab., returning one M.P. It was once celebrated for fancy works in steel, but Birmingham and Sheffield machinery have extinguished the trade; it now produces mainly leather goods, the manufacture of which, though much reduced, still employs 1000 or 2000 persons, chiefly in the villages around. The leather is bleached in the sun, and may be seen hanging on the hedges and bushes. Gloves, waistcoats, purses, &c., may be purchased at the shops.

Woodstock was an early residence of the kings of England. Possibly Alfred here translated Boethius' 'De Consolatione,' and we know that Ethelred the Unready held a council at it. Henry I. built a palace, adding to it a vast park, where, "beside great store of deer, he appointed divers strange beasts to be kept and nourished, which were brought and sent to him from foreign countries far distant, as lions, leopards, lynxes, and porcupines."— *Holinshed.* Henry II., however, rendered the place more famous, by his love of Fair Rosamund :—

" The King therefore, for her defence
    Against the furious Queene
  At Woodstock builded such a bower,
    The like was never seen.

" Most curiously that bower was built,
    Of stone and timber strong:
  An hundred and fifty doors
    Did to this bower belong.

" And they so cunningly contrived,
    With turnings round about,
  That none but with a clue of thread
    Could enter in or out."

Nevertheless, according to the old legend, Queen Eleanor *did* enter, and poisoned Rosamund, though it is more probable that she died in Godstow nunnery. Henry III. was nearly murdered here in 1238 by a pretended priest called Ribaud, who climbed into the royal bedchamber by night through the window, but was discovered while entering, and was (according to Matthew of Westminster) torn to pieces by wild horses. Edmund of Woodstock, 2nd son of Edward I., and Thomas of Woodstock, 7th son of Edward III., took their name from this, their birthplace. Edward the Black Prince also was born here. Elizabeth was confined here in 1554–5 by her sister Mary, and narrowly escaped being burnt in her bedroom, which took fire, during her stay. Seeing a milkmaid from the palace windows, she wept through envy of her condition, and wrote on the shutter the lines—

" O Fortune, how thy restless wavering state
  Hath wrought with cares my troubled witt !
Witness this present prison whither fate
  Could bear me, and the joys I quit.
Thou caused'st the guilty to be losed
From handes wherein are innocents enclosed ;
Causing the guiltles to be straite reserved,
And freeing those that death have well deserved.

But by her malice can be nothing wroughte:
  So God send to my foes all they have
  thoughte.
" A.D. 1555.   ELIZABETH, Prisner."

The palace was seldom visited by the Stuarts ; and when the Parliamentary visitors resided in it, in 1649, for the purpose of surveying the royal property, they were terrified by the tricks of Joe Collins, "the Merry Devil of Woodstock," the prototype of "Wildrake" in Scott's novel of 'Woodstock.' At the time of their occurrence the supernatural origin of the disturbances was almost universally credited, and the Puritan clergy so described them in a diary, which was afterwards published.

Of the "ancient and renowned (royal) mansion not a stone is now to be seen, but the site is still marked in the turf of Blenheim Park by two sycamores, which grow near the stately bridge."—*Macaulay.*

" That well-built palace where the Graces
    made
  Their chief abode, where thousand Cupids
    play'd
  And couch'd their shafts, whose structure
    did delight
  E'en Nature's self, is now demolish'd quite."
                                            May.

The poet Chaucer resided at Woodstock, and is supposed to have taken much of the scenery of 'The Dream' from the neighbouring park. A so-called "Chaucer's House" is shewn, but its connexion with the poet is doubtful. It was at one time proposed to erect his statue, and Akenside prematurely furnished the following inscription :—

          " Here he dwelt
For many a cheerful day. These ancient walls
Have often heard him, while his legends blithe
He sang ; of love, or knighthood, or the wiles
Of homely life: through each estate and age
The fashions and the follies of the world
With cunning hand portraying. Though
    perchance
From Blenheim's towers, O stranger, thou art
    come
Glowing with Churchill's trophies ; yet in
    vain
Dost thou applaud them, if thy breast be cold
To him, this other hero ; who in times

Dark and untaught, began with charming verse
To tame the rudeness of his native land."

The *Church, St. Mary,* which is a chapelry of Blaydon, was partially rebuilt in 1785, on the site of a chantry founded by King John, in the very worst taste. The S. aisle is good E. E., and has a Norm. doorway, blocked up; the N. aisle and the tower are modern. On the exterior of the W. wall is a tablet to Dr. Mavor, the rector (d. 1837, aged 80), author of the Spelling-book, who is described as " the first great promoter of the catechetical method of instruction in all branches of human as well as divine knowledge." The tower contains a peal of bells, which chime a different tune each day of the week; that for Sunday is the 104th Psalm, but the rest are lively airs.

A very short distance beyond the ch. we reach the public entrance to *Blenheim Park,* the seat of the Duke of Marlborough. The house is shewn every day except Saturday and Sunday, from 11 to 1, and the gardens from 11 to 2; either can be seen separately by tickets 1s. each, obtained at the porter's lodge.* The proceeds are regularly paid over to various charitable institutions; the Radcliffe Infirmary at Oxford usually receiving the largest share.

The entrance to the park is by the Triumphal Arch erected by Sarah, Duchess of Marlborough: it is of the Corinthian order, and bears on the exterior side an inscription in Latin, with a translation on the other face, stating that it was built the year after the death of the great Duke, and referring to the column (in sight to the rt.) as " a lasting monument of his glory and her affection "—1723. Underneath is the porter's lodge, where tickets are obtained; but the park is open to the pedestrian without. No stranger may drive

* Mr. George Scharf's most instructive catalogue of the paintings may be had here.

through the park unless attended by a guide on horseback or seated on the carriage, whose fee is 2s. 6d.

Passing through the gate, a broad road conducts to the Mall, an elm avenue which leads from the Hensington gate (*ante*) to the E. front of the house. On rt. of the road is seen the Lake, beyond which rise wooded hills and the Marlborough Column; on l. the Home Lodge, with the tower of the ch. rising among the trees, and looking much better than when more closely approached.

The *Park,* containing 2700 acres, and about 12 m. in circuit, is remarkable for the variety of its surface. It abounds with old oaks and cedars, and is stocked with deer. The trees are so planted in groups as to form a plan of the battle of Blenheim, each battalion of soldiers being represented by a separate plantation. The beautiful and extensive lake (supplied by the Glyme rivulet) contains 260 acres, and was formed by "Capability Brown," who boasted that the Thames would never forgive him for what he had done here. It is crossed by a noble bridge of 3 arches, which, until the formation of the lake, bestrode a mere driblet of water, so that Walpole said of it, that, "like the beggars at the old Duchess's gate, it begged for a drop of water and was refused." Hence also it gave rise to Evans' epigram :—

" The lofty arch his high ambition shows,
The stream an emblem of his bounty flows."

Now, " the epigram is drowned."

Leaving the house on the l., and crossing this bridge, we reach on the summit of the opposite hill the *Column,* 134 ft. high, erected as a monument to the great Duke, surmounted by his colossal statue. Inscribed on the pedestal is an account of his victories like the broadside of a newspaper, by his chaplain Hare, Bp. of Chichester. " Three sides are filled with the Acts of Parliament

conferring on Marlborough his honours and domains; the 4th, facing
the house, is occupied with a panegy-
ric of his virtues drawn up by Bolingbroke, and which, while it boasts of
the justice, candour, and superior
virtue of the great Duke, forcibly
calls to mind some of those great
weaknesses which stain his character." The house appears to great
advantage from this point. At the
base of the hill, by the water-side,
near the bridge, is *Fair Rosamond's
Well*, so called from a tradition that
this rill supplied her bath during
her residence in her " Bower," which
stood in this part of the park. Sir
John Vanbrugh, much to his credit,
argued pathetically for its preservation. " It was raised," he writes,
" by one of the bravest and most
warlike of the English kings, and,
though it has not been famed as a
monument of his arms, it has been
tenderly regarded as the scene of his
affections. Nor, among the multitude of people who come daily to
view what is raising to the memory
of the great battle of Blenheim, are
there any that do not more eagerly
ask to see what ancient remains
there may be of Rosamund's Bower."
He desired to preserve the old manor
as a picturesque object, which it then
was, to be seen from the palace, but
the Duchess, perhaps imagining that
he had an eye to it as a residence
for himself, certainly to spite him
and save 200l. on its repair, gave
orders to sweep it entirely away in
1709. A little tract in the lake,
called *Queen Elizabeth's Island*, is
part of an ancient causeway leading
to the manor-house, which stood
100 yds. distant to the N. There are
no traces of the Labyrinth; indeed
its existence is now regarded by historians as fabulous.

There is a fine view from the *High
Lodge*, a curious old building, once the
residence of a celebrated ranger of
this park, Wilmot, Earl of Rochester.
He died here July 26, 1680, at the

age of 34, having, in his last illness,
been brought to repentance through
the instrumentality of Gilbert Burnet, who frequently visited him with
Dr. Fell, then Bp. of Oxford. Burnet declares that he became thoroughly convinced of the truth of
Christianity during the reading of
Isaiah liii.; " the words of which,"
he said, " had an authority which
did shoot like rays or beams in his
mind, so that he was convinced by a
power which did so effectually con-
strain him, that he did ever after as
firmly believe in his Saviour as if
he had seen him in the clouds.'

The royal manor of Woodstock
was settled upon John Churchill,
Duke of Marlborough and his heirs
(on condition of presenting a flag
with 3 fleurs-de-lis at Windsor every
2nd of August), in consideration of
his success over the allied army of
French and Bavarians, and a sum
of money was voted by parliament to
build him a palace " as a monument
of his glorious actions," but owing to
party rancour, it was not all paid.
The house received the name of
Blenheim from the little village on
the Danube (properly Blindheim),
which was the scene of his greatest
victory, August 2nd, 1704. The
building is considered the masterpiece of Vanbrugh, yet is so heavy
in its general effect that ,t gave
occasion to the epitaph on the architect—

* Lie heavy on him, Earth, for he ·
Laid many a heavy load on thee."

The building was commenced June
18, 1705, and the history of ·ts con
struction is a series of petty squabb! .,
malicious thwarting on the part of
the Duchess, and a niggardly v. h-
holding of money. Vanbrugh. it
is true was extravagant, but n(
only was he cheated of his salar).
but was even refused admittar ce t.
see his own work by an order from.
the hand of Atossa herself. In 171 '
the Duchess stopped the works, u

desired the workmen to pay no attention to the architect's orders. Already, in 1704, she had written on a contract for lime, " Is not that 7½d. per bushel a very high price, when they had the advantage of making it in the park? Besides in many things of that nature false measure has been proved." "In 1714, 220,000l. had been received from the Treasury; the debts due by the Crown amounted to 60,000l. besides; and even the shell of the building was not completed. The Duke died without ever inhabiting it. By will he left 10,000l. a year to the Duchess, according to Vanbrugh " to spoil Blenheim in her own way," and 12,000l. a year "to keep herself clean and go to law." The Duchess really did finish it in her lifetime at a total expenditure of 300,000l., of which 60,000l. was furnished by the Duke and Duchess from their own resources."

The entrance to the *Gardens* is close to the E. wing of the house; on ringing a bell the gardener will appear. The pleasure-grounds have an extent of 300 acres, and are most lovely in themselves, very varied, set off by views of the noble lakes, are remarkable for very large specimens of deodar, Portugal laurel, cedars, copper beech, and many new pines. A large part is now a full-grown grove of tall trees, whose refreshing shades, and walks of velvet turf, are particularly agreeable in summer. The walks lead to the *Temple of Health*, erected on the recovery of George III. from his illness 1789, and thence to the Aviary. Near this are some very old oaks and laurels of great size. Traversing an open grass-plot, called the Sheep Walk, a good view is obtained of the S. or garden front of the house, the centre surmounted by a trophy of one of the Duke's victories, a colossal bust of Louis XIV., which once stood above the principal gate of Tournay. Further on, in the American garden,

is the *Cascade*, "so admirably constructed of large masses of rock, brought from a great distance, that it is difficult to believe it artificial." Beyond this is the *Fountain*, copied from that in the Piazza Navona at Rome, adorned with statues of river gods by *Bernini*, presented to the great Duke by the Spanish ambassador. In the *Private Garden* is the Ionic temple of Diana, designed by Sir William Chambers. The other gardens, remarkable for their abundance of roses, include the rarest plants from all parts of the world, especially from New Holland, Norfolk Island, &c., some of them brought hither from White Knights, near Reading (formerly a seat of the Duke of Marlborough), interspersed among the venerable stems of gnarled oaks, relics of the old Forest.

The exterior of the Palace is heavy in the extreme, but imposing from its extent, its varied outline, and the skilful combination of towers, colonnades, and porticoes. "Much as Vanbrugh sinned against the principles of his art by breaking the masses and main lines, by heaviness, and overloading the ornamental parts, yet it affords at a distance very picturesque views; and the interior is very striking, from the size of the apartments, the beauty of the materials, the richness and splendour of the decorations."—*Waagen*.

The ground plan consists of a centre, throwing forward 2 wings connected with it by colonnades; each wing being a quadrangle. The entrance is by the E. or kitchen wing, which once contained the Titian Gallery, and a theatre; a conservatory has replaced the one, and the steward's office the other. Thus the mass of the building forms 3 sides of a square, enclosing a court, which is entered from the E. wing by an arch decorated with an emblematic sculpture of a lion grappling a cock.

The most remarkable apartments

are the *Hall*, extending the whole height of the building, whose ceiling is an allegorical composition by *Thornhill*, on the Battle of Blenheim; the great *Dining-room*, almost filled with pictures by Rubens and Vandyke; the *Saloon*, whose ceiling and walls are a masterpiece of *Laguerre*, representing various nations in their proper costumes, and introducing portraits of the artist and others: the *State Drawing-room*, hung with tapestry; the *Library*, 183 ft long (originally intended for a picture-gallery, and occupying the S.W. front). The collection of 17,000 volumes formed by Charles Spencer, Earl of Sunderland, was in great part sold by auction in 1881 and 1882, some of them at fabulous prices. Here is marble statue of Queen Anne, in her coronation robes of brocade and jewels, by *Rysbrach.*

The *Chapel* contains a pompous marble monument, also by *Rysbrach*, beneath which rest the conqueror of Blenheim and Ramillies, the capturer of 20 fenced cities, and his proud Duchess Sarah, with their 2 sons who died young. The Duke was buried in Westminster Abbey, but his body was brought hither on the death of his wife. The beautiful pulpit of Derbyshire spar was erected by the present Duke. The collection of china, formerly shewn at a house in the park, is now in a room in the private gardens.

The great attraction of Blenheim is its *Collection of Paintings*, which, both in extent and selectness, is one of the finest in Britain.

The enthusiastic German critic Waagen says, "If nothing were to be seen in England but Blenheim, with its park and treasures of art, there would be no reason to repent the journey to this country." The pictures by Rubens, some of them presented to the Duke by the Emperor of Germany and the great cities of the Netherlands, others purchased by himself, for he was a great admirer of Rubens, are undoubtedly genuine works of the master, almost entirely by his own hand, and chiefly of his earlier and middle periods, and form a series such as no private cabinet in Europe can boast of. There are some excellent portraits by Vandyke, and a few beautiful pictures by Italian masters. As, from frequent change in their hangings it is impossible to describe the pictures according to their rooms, a few of the best are here enumerated in alphabetical order :—*Baroccio :* Portrait of a Boy, dressed as a Knight of Santiago of Spain.—*Carlo Dolce :* 1, Madonna crowned with stars, her eyes upturned—"the expression noble, and less weak and mawkish than usual; the drawing fine, the colour uncommonly clear, the execution extremely delicate; the hand which is stretched out is justly admired for its beauty and truth to nature."—*W.* 2, Adoration of the Magi, less affected and truer in the feeling than usual.—*Claude :* Sea-view with trees. Waagen attributes it to Paul Brill.—*Clostermann :* Portrait of John, Duke of Marlborough (in the Hall), with Sarah Duchess, the Marquis of Blandford, their son, who died young, and four daughters – *Cuyp :* Alehouse Door, with Dort in the distance; a beautiful specimen of this master.—*Correggio:* Study for the Angel in the picture of the Agony in the Garden (Duke of Wellington). — *Gainsborough :* Portrait of John Duke of Bedford.—*L. Giordano :* 1, Nymphs and Satyrs. 2, Death of Seneca, highly finished for the master.—*Giorgione :* St. Jerome in meditation, a fine picture; Virgin and Child, attended by a female, and a warrior-saint.—*Guido :* Head of the Virgin.—*Holbein :* Head of a man, true to nature (about 1530); portrait of Edward VI. — *Kneller :* Sarah Duchess of Marlborough. "Far more natural, careful, and delicate than the majority of pictures of his manufacture; the ambitious, proud, violent character (of Atossa) is fully expressed in the features."— *W.* 2, The same, as Minerva. 3, John Duke of Marlborough. 4, King William III. 5, Queen Anne.—*Sir P. Lely :* portraits of Mrs. Morton and Mrs. Killigrew. "Proves by its delicate, clear colour, and elegant design, that Lely's attempt to imitate or rival Vandyke were not always unsuccessful." — *W.* — *Murillo :* two pictures, Scenes with Beggar Boys.— *Mytens :* George Villiers, Duke of Buckingham, holding a letter.—*Raffaelle :* 1, The celebrated MADONNA D'ANSIDEI, the gem of the collection, designed as an altarpiece for the chapel of the Ansidei in the church of the Serviti at Perugia, a highly important and admirable work of the master, in excellent preservation, painted after Raffaelle's first residence in Florence, and dated 1505. "A picture of surprising beauty and dignity. Besides the dreamy intensity of feeling of the school of Perugino, we perceive here the aim at a greater freedom and truth of nature, founded on thorough study." — *Kugler.* "All the parts of the picture are executed with great care and in a solid impasto. The general impression of the colours is clear, forcible and harmonious. In the flesh the shadows are grey, the local tone delicately yellowish, and the lights whitish."—*W.* The Predella of this altarpiece, "St. John preaching in the wilderness," is at Bowood. (See *Handbook of Wiltshire*). 2, portrait of Dorothea, a beautiful woman in a red robe; 3, copies of Madonna and Child, Belle Jardinière (an old copy); of Ma. del Popolo; of Ma. di Loretto.—*Rembrandt :* 1, Isaac blessing Jacob; 2, The Woman taken in Adultery, ½-length figures, size of life, "in a clear, full tone, the treatment careful, though broad; the expression of Christ very

noble."—*W.* 3, The Circumcision.— *Sir Joshua Reynolds ;* George Spencer, third Duke of Marlborough, his Duchess and 6 children : "a capital work; the arrangement, so rarely satisfactory in such pictures, is here careful and pleasing." It combines great animation in all the heads, and very careful execution of the details, with a general harmony in a full bright tone of colouring.—*W.* 2, Lady Charlotte Spencer as a gipsy girl, telling her brother his fortune; most charming from its simplicity, clear and warm; portraits of the Marquis of Tavistock; Lord Charles Spencer.—*Rubens :* 1, The Angel leading Lot and his family out of Sodom; a gift of the city of Antwerp to the Duke of Marlborough; one of Rubens' choicest works of his middle period. 2, Return of the Holy Family from Egypt; "in a cool, serene, subdued tone, which makes this one of his most remarkable and delightful productions."—*W.* 3, The Roman Daughter. "The subject is discreetly treated; the affecting expression of filial piety is happily brought forward; the execution is careful, the admirable colouring true." 4, Head of Paracelsus the alchemist, a fine landscape in the background very carefully executed. 5, Adoration of the Magi. 6, Christ blessing little children; portraits of the person for whom the picture was painted and his family in Flemish dress. They display "simple truth to nature, full of health and life, freely yet carefully modelled in a full warm tone. The head of the woman is a real masterpiece for clearness, softness, and relief. On the other hand, dignity is admirably expressed in Christ's displeasure with his 3 disciples. The colouring is of astonishing warmth and depth."—*W.* 7, The Holy Family; "of his later period, in a rather common Flemish taste; colouring brilliant." — *W.* 8, Virgin and Child on a throne,

surrounded by 6 angels, 88. Catherine, Barbara, Dominic; 3 monks,
the Archduke Albert of Austria, Ferdinand, and Archduchess Eugenia
Isabella; sketch for a larger work;
"a beautiful composition, the heads
extremely fine and animated, the
forms not exaggerated."—*W.* 9. Rubens' portrait. 10, Rape of Proser-
pine — colossal figure, "a capital
work, executed throughout with the
greatest care by his own hand; flesh
throughout of a light subdued tone.
In Diana a beauty of form seldom
met with in Rubens"—*W.* 11, a
Bacchanalian Festival. 12, Anne of
Austria, Queen of Louis XIII.—*W.*
13, his wife, Helena Forman, in the
dress of an archduchess, with her son,
or a page: "very fine, animated,
and elegant, and truly brilliant in
colouring." — *W.* 13, Andromeda
(rather heavy) chained to the rock,
Perseus in the distance. 14, Rubens,
and his 2nd wife, Helena Forman,
walking in a garden; she holds her
child in leading-strings. Presented
to the Duke of Marlborough by the
city of Brussels. A most pleasing
representation of domestic happiness, and one of the most successful
family pieces in the world. "If no
other picture of Rubens existed,
this alone would prove him to be one
of the greatest painters that ever
lived. The execution careful and
perfect, the colouring deep and full,
the whole in pleasing and perfect
harmony; in all these respects Rubens never surpassed this masterpiece."—*W.* 15, Venus and Cupid
trying to dissuade Adonis from the
Chase: presented to the first Duke
of Marlborough by the Emperor of
Germany. "Refined feeling, beautiful heads, noble forms, are here
united with brightness, warmth, and
clearness of colouring."—*W.* 16, a
Procession of Bacchanals. "In this
corpulent Silenus, in this negro, these
nymphs, the vulgarly sensual passion
of beastly drunkenness is expressed
in all its force." — *W.* 17, The Graces

—Rubens' 3 wives. 18, Lot and his
Daughters. 19, The Adoration of
the Magi.—*Bern. Strozzi:* St. Lawrence. "For force of colouring and
careful execution, a very remarkable
work of this affected master."—*W.*
—*Teniers:* numerous good pictures.
—*Titian;* 1, St. Nicholas of Bari and
St. Catherine. "A bright, clear,
carefully executed picture of the
master's early period."—*W.* 2, Portrait of Philip II. of Spain, husband
of Mary of England, admirably
drawn and warmly coloured. 3, St.
Sebastian. "Noble expression, flesh-
tone warm and clear."—*Vandyke:*
1, Lord Strafford and his Secretary.
Sir Thomas Mainwaring, ¾ length.
Strafford's head exhibits the work-
ings of earnest thought, while he
dictates an answer to the paper
(some say his death-warrant) which
he holds in his hand. "Very careful execution, tone clear and warm."
"A portrait which condenses into
one point of time, and exhibits at a
single glance, the whole history of
a disturbed and eventful life—in
which the eye seems to scrutinize us,
and the mouth to command us—in
which the brow menaces, and the
lip almost quivers with scorn—in
which every wrinkle is a comment
on some important transaction." —
Macaulay. 2, Charles I. on a cream-
coloured horse; at his side Sir
Thomas Morton, Master of the
Horse, bearing his helmet; in the
background a skirmish of cavalry.
This belonged to the Royal Collection, and was purchased by the
first Duke at Munich. "The style
of the clear, warm-toned flesh, as
well as of the landscape, reminds
one of Titian. The horse rather
clumsy."—*W.* 3, Charles I. and his
Queen. "Elegantly executed in a
clear, silvery tone."—*W.* 4, Duchess
of Buckingham, with her 3 children,
painted after the assassination of
the Duke by Felton in 1628. His
portrait hangs in the background.
5, Portrait of Charles I. in black,

half-length.   6, Henrietta Maria,
whole-length, in blue silk. 7, Marie
de Medicis, widow of Henri IV., and
mother of Henrietta Maria.   8, Catherine Wotton, Countess of Chesterfield.   9, Mary Stuart, Duchess of
Richmond, whole-length, with her
female dwarf, Mrs Gibson, the miniature painter, holding a pair of gloves
on a salver (" of the later and elegant
time of the master").   10, Madonna
and Child.   11, Time clipping the
wings of Cupid.—*Wouvermans*: 2
fine pictures, battle-pieces.

———

The preceding Excursions are all
within the compass of a day's drive,
if not walk; but it may be as well
to indicate a few others of greater
extent. Worcester, Gloucester, Malvern, Hereford, a glance at the
Forest of Dean, or the scenery of
the Wye, will each demand a long
day, but half that time will suffice
for the following; by proceeding to
the undermentioned stations :
   Banbury Stat.   Hanwell Castle,
Wroxton Abbey, and Broughton
Castle.   Or Edgehill ; or Compton
Wynyates.
   Charlbury Stat.   The scenery of
Wychwood Forest.
   Chipping Norton Stat.   The Roll-
right Stones.
   Evesham Stat.   The Abbey, and
the battle-field.
   Faringdon Stat.   Childrey, Spars-
holt, Uffington, the White Horse,
and Wayland Smith's Cave ; return-
ing from Shrivenham Stat.
   Goring Stat.   Aldworth, and the
Berkshire Downs.
   Stratford-on-Avon Stat.   The Ch.
Shakespeare's House, Anne Hath-
away's Cottage at Shottery, Charl-
cote House and Ch.
   Warwick or *Kenilworth Stat.*   War-
wick Castle, Guy's Cliff (2 m.),
Kenilworth Castle.
   Witney Stat.   Minster Lovell ; or
Bampton.

   [*Berks, &c.*]

ROUTE 20.

HENLEY TO OXFORD, BY ROTHER-
FIELD, EWELME, BENSINGTON,
AND DORCHESTER.

By Road.   23 m.

   At Twyford a *Branch line* of
4½ m. runs off on N. for Henley,
having an intermediate stat. at
Shiplake (Rte. 10, where also Henley is described).   The neighbourhood of
   Henley (*Inn* : Red Lion, excellent,
and much frequented by anglers
and oarsmen) abounds in beautiful drives and walks. By all means
walk (or row) up the river as far
as the boat-house in the grounds
of Park Place, ¾ m. by the towing-
path, above the lock and wooden
towing-bridge.   There is another,
pretty walk by the towing-path
below Henley Bridge, on the rt.
bank ; that across the fields W. of
the road to Reading, S. of Greys
Ch., commands one of the best views
of Henley, the river, and the grounds
of Park Place.   The excursion by
water from Henley to Maidenhead
(Rte. 10) is much to be recommended in fine weather.

   2 m. W. is *Rotherfield Peppard*,
with a small Norm. ch.; only a
short distance from which is *Rotherfield Greys*, so called from the noble
family of Grey, of whom John de
Grey was Baron of Rotherfield,

                                   ∎

1360–75. There is a superb brass to his memory in the chancel of the E. E. *Church*, which also contains a debased chapel, with a magnificent monument to Sir Francis Knollys, Treasurer of Queen Elizabeth's Household, and his wife, who was first cousin to the queen, and is not buried here, but in St. Edmund's chapel, Westminster Abbey. Their effigies lie under a canopy, supported by pillars of black marble. 7 sons and 6 daughters (one of whom was Lettice Knollys, the wife of Walter, Earl of Essex), with the Countess of Banbury (daughter-in-law), are kneeling beneath, while the Countess is repeated with her husband William, Earl of Banbury, in the upper part, kneeling before a desk. There is a fine brass of the last Lord Grey of Rotherfield (Robert, d. 1387) in full armour, under a canopy.

Close by is the village green, planted, as many are in this neighbourhood, with cherry-trees, of which the public are allowed to gather the fruit on one day only in the year.

1 m. distant N., in the parish of *Rotherfield Greys*, and in a picturesque little park with many old thorn-trees, is the venerable *Greys Court* (Sir John Rose). The great size of the original building may be traced by the marks in the turf. 3 towers of flint and brick still remain, one of which, now used as a pigeon-house, is of considerable size. The remains of the "large court, spayd with brick," mentioned in Camden's 'Britannia,' may also be seen. In one of the towers is a draw-well 300 ft. deep, resembling that at Carisbrook, which is worked by 2 donkeys, turning within a wheel 25 ft. in diameter. The house, in the Tudor style, has been much modernised; Carr, Earl of Somerset, and his wife, the divorced Countess of Essex, lived in it. The hall contains some stained glass and portraits of the Fanes. A curious dairy in

the grounds is filled with fine old china.

2 m. W. is *Wyfold Court*, remarkable as possessing some of the finest wych elms in England, and held by tenure of presenting a rose to the King if he happened to pass a certain road on May-day.

The road quits Henley by a stately avenue of elms, 1 m. long, called *Fair Mile*, and after an almost continuous ascent of 4 m. reaches the summit of the chalk range at Nettlebed, the views continuing to increase in extent and beauty. At 4 m. on l. is the village of *Bixgibwen*, the ch. of which has been destroyed. Nearly 2 m. from it, N., is *Bixbrand*, with a small Norm. ch., built at the cost of the Earl of Macclesfield, and opened in 1875, and, 1½ m. further, *Pishill*, which contains the fine seat of Stonor. The ch. is of much the same character as that of Bixbrand, but, especially in the Stonor chapel, has been injudiciously modernised. A barn near the ch. has remains of a doorway, of elegant form, and is probably a desecrated chapel. *Stonor Park* (Lord Camoys) stands in a thickly wooded, forest-like wild country. This place gave name to the old Roman Catholic family of Stonor, now enjoying the ancient barony of Camoys, and has for a long time been their seat. The house is a Tudor mansion of brick, containing a hall with painted windows, and it has a chapel built of flint in the reigns of Edward II. and III., one of the very few in England which have always remained in the hands of the Roman Catholic Church. The Park abounds in beautiful beechwood.

5 m. *Nettlebed*. The chalk here reaches an elevation of 820 ft. above the sea. There is an extensive view towards Wallingford. Oxford, and Windsor. The village has some

pottery works, and the ch. has been rebuilt of brick with stone dressings, in modern Dec. style, by *Hakewill.*

At 6½ m. we reach *Nuffield Heath,* 757 ft. above the sea. The small Dec. ch. has been restored by *Ferrey.* The font has an inscription in Lombardic characters:

"Fonte sacro lotum, vel mundat gracia totum, Vel non est sacramenti mundacio plena;"

and there is a small brass, to Beneit Englisa, c. 1360.

3 m. S.W. is *Ipsden,* a well-known meet for hounds. The ch., originally E. E., but much altered, has some encaustic tiles with the arms of Richard, King of the Romans, and two small palimpsest brasses for Thos. Englysche and wife (d. 1525); on the reverse is part of the effigy of a lady (c. 1420) of the Stapleton family, and a rhyming inscription.

Ipsden House (E. A. Reade, Esq.) has been long the seat of a branch of the Northumbrian family of Reade of Beedon.

In *Ipsden Wood* is a well, supposed to be of Roman origin, which obtained a notoriety in April, 1860, from the discovery in it of a living child, which had existed there without food for 2 days and nights, after being abandoned by its mother. At Stoke Row, in this parish, on nearly the highest point of the chalk, a well 368 ft. deep has been sunk, at the desire and cost of the Rajah of Benares, who whilst employing an English engineer, was by him informed of the distress of the inhabitants on account of the scarcity of water. The well is surmounted by a canopy of Oriental design, and a cottage for a warder has also been provided.

Between Nuffield and Bensington (4½ m.) the direct road offers nothing to detain the traveller; but he will meet with much of interest by turning off, rt., to *Swyncombe,* at 8 m. Here is a small Norm. ch. with apse, well

restored. The monastery of Bec had a cell here, founded by Milo Crispin, the lord of Wallingford, in 1087, the buildings of which were converted into a dwelling-house, and inhabited by Charles Brandon, Duke of Suffolk, the husband of Mary, Queen dowager of France. *Swyncombe House* (Rev. C. E. Ruck-Keene) is a handsome modern mansion, in the Elizabethan style.

2 m. N.W. is *Ewelme,* a large village which well deserves a visit on account of its fine ch. and antique almshouse or hospital. The living was down to 1871 attached to the chair of the Regius Professor of Divinity at Oxford. It is now in the gift of the Crown.

The *Church* is a remarkably fine edifice, chiefly Perp., with aisles the whole length of the building, and much resembles that at Wingfield, in Suffolk. Between the chancel and St. John's Chapel, whose walls are diapered with the letters *I. H. S.,* is the tomb of the foundress of the almshouses and church, the Duchess of Suffolk, granddaughter of Geoffrey Chaucer, and widow of William de la Pole, Duke of Suffolk, who was beheaded at sea off Dover; it is an altar-tomb bearing her effigy, and "is hardly surpassed in beauty, and certainly not in the extreme excellence of its preservation, by any monument in England. It is one of the three known examples of female effigies decorated with the order of the Garter."—*Skelton.* Beneath the tomb, which is supported on double arches and canopied, is a skeleton effigy, and round it are statues of angels curiously feathered, bearing shields, 1475. Close by is an altar-tomb, with *Brasses,* of Thomas Chaucer, her father, son of the poet, and his lady, 1435, "which from its numerous quarterings, has been an object of curiosity to the most accurate inquirers in heraldry." There are also several other brasses, ranging

s 2

from 1458 to 1585. The wood screen-work, the roof, and a rich tabernacle cover for the font deserve notice. In the churchyard lie the son and grandchildren of Sir Matthew Hale. Attached to the ch. is a very interesting *Almshouse* or *Hospital*, founded by Duchess Alice, with the name of "God's House." The buildings are of brick, enclosing a small quadrangular court, with a timber cloister, and very rich barge-boards to the dormer windows. The " palace " or manor of Ewelme was a magnificent building, and remained sufficiently in repair to be occupied by Prince Rupert in the early part of the civil war. For full particulars of the descent of the manor, called *Lawelme* in Domesday, and granted to Gilbert of Gand, nephew of Queen Matilda, reference must be made to Napier's *History of Ewelme and Swyncombe.*

11 m. *Bensington,* better known as Benson, an important posting station in the stage-coach days, but now a mere village, with its great inns converted into dwelling-houses or pulled down. It stands on the Akeman Street, which here crosses the Thames, and occupies the site of a British town captured in 571 by Cutha, the brother of Ceawlin. At the Domesday survey " Besintone " belonged to the Crown, but it was given by King John to John de Harcourt, and was afterwards possessed by Richard King of the Romans, and by Piers Gaveston. The ch., originally Late Norm., has been greatly altered, and has a modern tower, " substantially built, but a very bad imitation of Gothic " (' Arch. Guide, Oxford ').

12 m. *Shillingford,* a hamlet of Warborough, 1 m. N. It is separated from Berkshire by the Thames, which is crossed by a bridge. The *Church* of *Warborough,* originally E. E., has had its ancient features almost entirely destroyed, but it retains its

ancient leaden *Font,* "which is worthy of particular notice. The figures under the arcade round the base are repetitions of one type representing an archbishop raising the rt. hand in the attitude of blessing, and holding in the left a crosier. It is E. E. work, but the pedestal is of stone with Perp. panelling, similar to that at Dorchester " ('Arch. Guide,' where an engraving is given). On the E. bank of the Thame, 1 m. N., is *Newington,* where the Dec. ch. has a spire rising from an E. E. tower, the only one in the neighbourhood. In the S. wall of the chancel is a Dec. recess for a tomb, probably that of the restorer of the ch. in the 14th centy.

Just before reaching Dorchester, the road crosses the Thame, which, at a very short distance S., joins the far larger stream which poets style the Isis, but other people the Thames. This is the spot mentioned by Warton :—

" Whence beauteous Isis and her husband Thame
With mingled waves for ever flow the same;"

or, in the still more metaphorical language of Drayton in his ' Polyolbion,'—

" Where Isis, Cotteswold's heir, is lastly won,
And instantly does wed with Tame, old Chiltern's son."

14 m. *Dorchester.* See Exc. (c) from Oxford.

15 m. On l. is *Burcott,* a hamlet of Dorchester.

18 m. *Marsh Baldon,* a small Dec. ch., with an ivied tower. "The N. aisle has pillars and arches of wood, modern, and very bad; they appear to have been cut out of deal board." A window in this aisle contains, besides figures of the Virgin, and of 3 other saints, some heraldic glass. There are some indifferent modern monuments. *Baldon House* (Guy Thomson, Esq.) belonged to the

Pollards, who have monuments in the ch. In the grounds are some fragments from the old ch. of Nuneham Courtenay. " They consist of the jambs of a fine E. E. window, with the shafts, the section of the mouldings remarkably good ; the caps and bases of the shafts are also well moulded. By the side of this is a small plain lancet window, and adjoining to it a splendid tomb of Sir Anthony Pollard, 1577, and Philippa his wife, 1606; it is in the taste of that age, with Corinthian columns, &c., and the figures of the knight, his lady, and two children; the original colouring remains, though the whole is much mutilated." ('Arch. Guide, Oxford.')

On a hill, 1¼ m. N.E., is the small E. E. *Church* of *Toot Baldon*, often called Baldon Toot ; the prefix is supposed by Godwin to indicate its foundation by, or in the time of, Tuta, Bp. of Dorchester (A.D. 787). The N. door is Norm.; but the nave has E. E. pillars, with the stiff leaf ornament boldly sculptured. On the E. respond is a small trefoil-headed niche, supposed to have been for the holy oil used in baptism, and therefore marking the original place of the font.

20 m. *Sandford.* For this, and the remaining 3 m. of the journey, see Exc. (*b*) from Oxford.

23 m. OXFORD. (Rte. 19.) This is the most imposing entrance into Oxford, crossing Magdalen Bridge. On the l. is the Botanic Garden, on the rt. Magdalen tower, college, and gardens, while on either side " the stream-like windings of the glorious Street," the well-known High Street, exhibit a succession of colleges and churches which vie with one another in age and beauty.

ROUTE 21.

HIGH WYCOMBE TO OXFORD.

By Road. 27 m.

For *High Wycombe* and *West Wycombe*, see Rte. 12.

At 4 m. from High Wycombe the road enters Oxfordshire. We cross *Stokenham Common*, a fine open spot, commanding a good view of Bledlow ridge, and reach at 8 m. *Stokenchurch*, one of the highest points of the Chilterns. The *Church* is Dec. and Perp., but with some Trans.-Norm. and E. E. features. The Dec. chancel has been restored. There are two *Brasses*, with French inscriptions, for members of the Morley family, 1410, 1412. *Wormsley*, in this parish, is the seat of Major J. A. Fane. It belonged to Adrian Scrope, one of the regicides, who was executed in October, 1660, saying at the scaffold —" It is no reproach or shame to follow the Lord Jesus Christ, and to die in his cause, for that is it which I judge I am now going to do." Here the road sinks by a steep descent into the vale of Oxford.

The beechwoods of Stokenchurch abound with wild flowers, including *Convallaria majalis*, lily of the valley: *Monotropa hypopitys*, yellow bird's-nest: *Helleborus viridis*, green hellebore; *Orchis Herminium*, musk orchis ; *Listera Nidus-avis*, bird's-nest orchis ; *Epipactis latifolia*, broad-leaved helleborine; *Epipactis grandifolia*, large white helleborine;

Veronica montana, mountain madwort; *Lysimachia nemorum*, yellow loosestrife.

3 m. N. across the hills is *Chinnor*, a station on the Prince's Risborough and Watlington line. It is a picturesque village, from which the Whiteleaf Cross beyond Prince's Risborough (Rte. 12) is seen very clearly. The Dec. *Church* is a fine structure. In the chancel are paintings of the Apostles by *Sir J. Thornhill*, and several 14th-centy. *Brasses*; among them, a very elegant floriated cross, with head of a priest in the centre, c. 1320; and one for John Hotham, provost of Queen's College, Oxford, d. 1361. 2 m. W. is *Sydenham*, with a small plain E. E. ch. ½ m. N.E. of this is *Emington*, where the small 14th-centy. ch. occupies a singularly remote position; " there is not even a path up to the door " (*J. H. P.*), neither is there any external entrance to the tower.

10 m. On l. 1 m. *Lewknor*. The fine ch. here has a Dec. chancel, a sepulchral recess with canopies, a brass to a priest, John Alderburne, c. 1380, and an enriched Norm. font. 1 m. S. is *Shirbourne Castle* (Earl of Macclesfield). See Rte. 23.

11 m. *Aston Rowant* (Stat.). The ch. is chiefly of Dec. character, but the mullions and tracery of most of the windows have been cut out. The font is somewhat singular, E. E., with 8 detached shafts. There are some fragments of 15th-centy. brasses and the matrix of an earlier one, with cross-legged figure. The remains of a brass at the entrance to the chancel bears the following inscription in Norman French:—
" You who pass by pray for the soul of Sir Hugo le-Blount, whose body lies here. May Jesus Christ receive his soul." He is supposed to have been the founder of the church.

13½ m. *Tetsworth*, a lace-making village, with a small E. E. ch.; the S. doorway is Norm., and has some rude sculptures over it. 2 m. W. is *Great Haseley*, where the fine large E. E. and Dec. ch. has been well restored. There are 3 sepulchral recesses in the S. wall, and a cross-legged effigy. Dr. Christopher Wren, the father of the architect, was the rector, and was expelled by the Parliament. *Haseley Court*, J. P. Muirhead, Esq.

1 m. W. of Haseley is *Great Milton*, the *Church* of which is as good an example of the 14th-centy. ch. as the former is of the 13th. " The plan is complete, having the chancel, nave, N. and S. aisles, S. porch with parvise over, and a well-proportioned tower at the W. end of the nave, remaining perfect." The general features are Dec., but there are traces of an earlier structure. Over the S. porch is a small room, formerly used as a vestry, which is approached by a winding staircase, in a picturesque octagon tower. At the E. end of the nave is a slab of Purbeck marble with a cross fleurée and the Lamb, probably marking the burial place of some ecclesiastic. The E. end of the S. aisle is completely blocked by a huge monument of the Dormer family (1618), with alabaster figures of Sir Michael Dormer (who served in Germany under Sir H. Vere), his wife, and his father, with a bas-relief of a fort and encampment, and inscriptions of enormous length. The tomb of Mrs. Wilkinson, 1654, wife of the Principal of St. Mary Hall, has the strange epitaph,—

" Here lye mother and babe, both without sins.
Next birth will make her and her infant twins."

The house reputed to have belonged to the ancestors of Milton still stands with gables and mullions opposite the village well. There are some remains of the Dormers' manor-house in the adjoining hamlet of *Ascot*, but a small Dec. chapel, which stood near it, was pulled down for the sake of the materials, in 1823; its site is marked by the "Chapel Tree," an ancient elm, 21 ft. in girth.

16 m. *Tiddington*, and 19 m. *Wheatley*, have stations on the Thame and Oxford Rly., and will be found described in Rte. 22. For the remainder of the road see Exc. (*d*) from Oxford.

ROUTE 22.

THAME TO OXFORD.

Thame Branch, G. W. R. 15 m.

The line from London, through High Wycombe (Rte. 12), enters Oxfordshire about 2 m. E. of Thame; and reaches, at 48¼ m. from Paddington, *Thame Stat.*

The town of Thame (*Inn :* Eagle) consists mainly of one long, broad street. Pop. 3267. In a house, near the centre, formerly the Greyhound Inn, John Hampden died June 24, 1643, from the wound received at Chalgrove Field (Rte. 5). In Saxon times the town was a dependency of the see of Dorchester, and Oskytel, who had been its bishop, but had become

Archbishop of York, died at Thame, 970. At the Conquest, the town was given to Lincoln, and both its Abbey and its Church were founded by prelates of that see.

The *Church of St. Mary* was built in 1241 by Bp. Grosteste, and is a very fine cruciform building, E. E. and Dec., with Perp. tower. The S. porch is of great beauty, with a canopied niche and a groined ceiling. The transepts contain monuments of the Dormers and the Quatremaynes, but the principal tomb is that in the chancel, of Lord Williams of Thame, so distinguished under Queen Mary by his ardour in the burning of the bishops at Oxford, which caused him to silence the dying Cranmer when he attempted to speak from the stake, by cries of "Make short, make short." The figures of the baron and his wife are richly carved in alabaster, in the costume of the later years of Elizabeth. It is remarkable that they have their heads turned towards the E., instead of their feet. Sir John Clerke (d. 1539), who took the Duke of Longueville prisoner at the Battle of Spurs, has a *Brass*, fixed to a tomb of Tetworth marble, and there are several other brasses, for the Quatremaynes (1420, 1460), Dormers (1502), &c.

Close to the ch. is the *Grammar-School*, founded by Lord Williams, 1575. It is a picturesque gabled building, containing accommodation for 60 boarders and the same number of day boarders. John Hampden, Dean Fell, Anthony Wood, and Pococke the Orientalist, were educated at it.

A short distance from the ch. (N. W.) is the *Prebendal House* (T. J. Clifford, Esq.), a 15th-centy. dwelling, greatly modified, but containing in its grounds a beautiful little *Chapel*, built by Bp. Grosteste. "It might be taken for a part of his cathedral, and though now used for domestic purposes and divided by a floor, the E. windows of 5 lights, with the detached pillars and capitals elegantly carved with a foliage similar to that at Lincoln, make it almost certain that the bishop brought some of the same workmen to erect this little chapel."—*J. P.*

In the high street is an old house, now a small inn, called 'The Birdcage,' which has its name, according to tradition, from having been used as a cage for the temporary confinement of prisoners, among whom refractory students from Oxford were often found.

John Hampden died at Thame, June 24, 1643. He made his way thither from Chalgrove (Rte. 23) by the brook of Haseley, "where, as in his great agony and weakness it would have been impossible for him, if he had alighted, to have remounted, summoning all his remaining strength, he made his horse leap across the brook. With his head hanging down, and his hands resting upon his horse's neck, he at length arrived at the house of Ezekiel Browne, in the street of Thame. In the first moments of respite from pain he laboured to condense all his dying energies in the work of sending letters of counsel to the Parliament, and this done he devoted the last fleeting hours to his soul. His old friend, Dr. Giles, the rector of Chinnor, remained by his side and administered the last Sacrament." . . . "As he lay in that great agony he was heard to say that. 'if he had twenty lives all should go this way, rather than the gospel of our salvation should be trampled under foot.' During this time he showed a wonderful measure of patience and meekness, being full of divine sentences, speaking as if he felt no pain, saying it was nothing but what he daily expected, and that he had long prepared against that time, and he continued of perfect memory, cheerful spirit, constant in the cause, and en-

couraging others to the last. On the sixth day, having prayed aloud for his country and commended his soul to God, he departed without any pain at all, as if falling out of a sweet slumber into a deep sleep." . . . "He was a gentleman of the ancientest extraction in Buckinghamshire, Hampden of Hampden; his fortune large, his natural abilities great; and his affection to public liberty and applause in his country exposed him to many difficulties and troubles, as in the business of the shipmoney, of the loan, and now in Parliament, where he was a most active and leading member. He spake rationally and subtilly, and often proposed doubts more than he resolved. He was well beloved in his country where he had a great interest, as also in the House of Commons, and he died lamented."— *Whitelock.*

Ch.-Just. Holt was born at Thame in 1642, of whom Steele says that "He was a man of profound knowledge of the laws of his country, and as just an observer of them in his own person; he considered justice as a cardinal virtue, not as a trade for maintenance, and whenever he was judge he never forgot that he was also counsel."—*Tatler.* Here also was born Figg, so celebrated in the last century for his performances with the broadsword: the teacher of Broughton, the founder of modern boxing.

1½ m. S. is *Thame' Park* (long the seat of the late Lady Wenman, and now one of the seats of P. T. H. Wykeham, Esq.), which occupies the site of an abbey removed from Otmoor by Bp. Alexander of Lincoln in 1138. Considerable remains of the abbey are still to be seen near the mansion. The house is partly of the 15th centy., and has a good stair-turret, and a modern Gothic chapel. A richly panelled room, the work of Robert King, the last abbot and first bishop of Oxford (Rte. 19), now serves as the drawing-room; it is figured in the 3rd vol. of Parker's 'Domestic Architecture,' pp. 109, 127.

Rycote Park, 2 m. S.W., belonged to the Quatremaynes, temp. Henry VI.; they sold it to the Fowlers, and in 1539 it was purchased from them by Sir John Williams, keeper of the king's jewels, and one of the commissioners for the dissolution of the monasteries. He converted the old manor-house into domestic offices, and built a mansion which was almost a palace. In it the Princess Elizabeth was placed under his care in 1554, and Charles I. made it his residence during the session of the Parliament at Oxford in 1625. Nothing now remains of it beyond a single octagonal tower in the garden, the rest having been pulled down by the 3rd Earl of Abingdon (a descendant of Lord Norris of Rycote), and the materials employed in additions to his seat of Wytham (Rte. 9). The domestic chapel, founded by Richard Quatremayne (d. 1460), however, has been spared; it is a good Perp. edifice, with W. tower, but the interior has been fitted up in the Renaissance style, and has two large family pews; one is of two stories, and the other has a cupola surmounted by a figure of the Virgin and Child.

52 m. *Tiddington* (Stat.). Tiddington is a hamlet of *Albury*, where a modern Gothic ch., by *Rickman*, preserves the Norm. font of the former building. A Roman origin has been ascribed to the place, and popular traditions make it "the oldest place in the county." In Domesday it is styled Alwoldesberie, and it had belonged to William Fitzosbern, Earl of Hereford, but was then in the hands of the crown in consequence of the rebellion of his son Roger.

55¾ m. *Wheatley* (Stat.). Wheatley was until recently a chapelry to Cuddesden. It is now a distinct parish and a vicarage. A new church has been built with a lofty spire—seen from the station. There are doorways, windows, and chimneys, of 15th-centy. date, to some of the houses of the village; and on Castle Hill, 1 m. E., are the remains of a *Roman villa*, discovered in 1845, and described in the 'Arch. Journal,' vol. ii. It appears to have been an edifice of considerable extent, with hypocaust; and the remains have had a building erected over them for their preservation.

60 m. *Littlemore* Stat. Exc. (b.) from Oxford.

63¼ m. OXFORD (Stat.). (Rte. 19.)

ROUTE 23.

WATLINGTON TO OXFORD.

By Road. 14 m.

Watlington (Stat.) (*Inn:* Hare and Hounds, very good) is a small market town, about 10 m. S.W. of Prince's Risborough, and 6 m. N.E. of Wallingford; a line of rly. connecting it with the former was opened in 1874. The ch. is Perp.

with a few Dec. windows that belonged to an earlier edifice, built by Osney Abbey. It was restored in 1877. It contains 3 brasses, dates 1485, 1501, 1588. The *Market House*, built in 1664 by Thomas Stonor (who also built the free school), standing at the meeting of four cross-roads, is very like that of Ross on the Wye, and with its grey mullions, high pointed gables, and dark arches, is a favourite subject with artists.

Watlington Park (Mrs. Carter), is small, but very beautiful. The house, a handsome brick and stone edifice, was long the seat of the Tilson family.

1 m. N. is *Pyrton*, with a Norm. and Dec. ch. In the register is the entry, " 1619, John Hampden, of Hampden, Esq., and Mrs. Elizabeth Simeon, daughter of Mr. Edward Simeon, of Pyrton, was married the 24th June, in the 17th year of King James." Pyrton Manor-house (H. Hamersley, Esq.), an Elizabethan mansion, was the residence of Hampden's father-in-law ; when wounded at Chalgrove, he attempted to reach it, but found his way barred by the Royalists.

Almost adjoining Pyrton is *Shirbourne Castle* (Earl of Macclesfield), a moated residence, begun by Warine de Lisle in 1377, when the licence to crenellate was granted, but probably not finished till the next centy. It is nearly square, enclosing a courtyard with round towers at the angles. It is chiefly of Perp. date, is surrounded by a wide moat, approached by drawbridges, and defended by a portcullis. The interior is modernised, but contains an armoury and some very fine portraits : among these are a magnificent head of Erasmus by *Holbein ;* Archbishop Laud, *Vandyke ;* Chancellor Macclesfield ; and the celebrated picture of Queen Katherine Parr. " She is represented standing behind a highly em-

bellished vacant chair, with her hand on the back ; her dress is black, richly ornamented with precious stones : her fingers are loaded with rings, and in one hand is a handkerchief edged with deep lace. Inserted in the lower part of the frame, and covered with glass, is an interesting appendage to this portrait, a piece of hair cut from the head of Katherine Parr, in the year 1799, when her coffin was opened at Sudely Castle. The hair is auburn, and matches exactly with that described in the picture."—*Miss Strickland.*

The castle contains two valuable libraries, one of which was bequeathed by Mr. Jones, the mathematician, and father of Sir William Jones, who resided in the castle through the friendship of the 2nd Earl of Macclesfield. It is especially rich in MS. letters of mathematicians of the 17th and beginning of the 18th cents. The observatory of the 1st Earl of Macclesfield had the services of 2 remarkable men, Phelps and Bartlett, the former of whom rose from being a stable-boy, the latter from being a shepherd. The library also contains the correspondence of George Stepney, a diplomatist of the time of William III., and many unpublished autograph letters of Prior.

Shirbourne was granted to Robert d'Oiley at the time of the Conquest, who built a castle there. This castle was in 1141 surrendered to the Empress Maud, as the price of the release of William Martel an adherent of King Stephen, who had fallen into her hands. In 1321 the Barons who had entered into an association against the Despencers met at Shirbourne under Thomas, Earl of Lancaster, and when the enterprise failed, Warine de Lisle, the lord of the castle, was hanged at York. In 1377, Edward III. allowed a second Warine, the grandson of the first, to build the existing edifice. Through his female descendants it passed successively into the hands of the Beauchamps (who held it by service of 1 bow and 3 arrows without feathers), Talbots, and Quatremaynes, the last of whom, having no children, left it to the child of his servant, Richard Forster, who sold his lands, temp. Henry VIII., to the Chamberlains, a lady of which family defended the castle against the Parliamentarian forces, and surrendered to General Fairfax, 1646. Later it became for a short time the property of the Gage family, and was purchased in the beginning of the last centy. by Thomas Parker, Lord Chancellor (1721) and 1st Earl of Macclesfield, whose descendants still possess it.

There is a curious letter of Brunetto Latini, the tutor of Dante, who died in 1294, describing his journey in two days, from London to Oxford, the rough hills infested by robbers, and his sleeping at Shirbourne Castle, which he says was built by the Earl of Tancarville, one of the followers of William I.

The great earthquake of 1755 (which destroyed Lisbon and swallowed up St. Ubes) was remarkably perceptible at Shirbourne. " On Nov. 1, a little after 10 A.M., a very strange motion was perceptible in the water of the moat which surrounds the castle. There was a pretty thick fog, not a breath of air, and the surface of the water was as smooth as looking-glass, except at one corner, where it flowed in to the shore and retired again successively in a surprising manner. The flux and reflux were quite regular; every flood began gently, its velocity increasing by degrees, until at length it rushed in with great impetuosity till it had attained its full height. Having remained for a little time stationary, it then retired, ebbing gently at first, but afterwards sinking with great swiftness. At every flux the whole body of water seemed to be thrown violently against the bank; but neither during the flux nor reflux did there appear even the least ripple on the other parts of the moat.

" Lord Parker sent a man to the opposite corner of the moat, 25 yds. distant from himself, who could not perceive any motion, but another, who went to the N. E. corner, diagonally opposite, observed it equally with himself. Also, to his great surprise, he found that, when the water rose and sank at either end at the same moment, a pond just below was agitated in the same manner, but the risings and fallings did not occur at the same time as those in the moat."

A short distance W. of Watlington are 3 churches, all called Brightwell (shortened to Britwell), a name characteristic of the clear, sparkling springs which about here gush out of the chalk marls and clays. *Britwell Salome,* that nearest to Watlington, is a very small Norm. and Dec. structure, with modern E. and Perp. W. window. It contains a brass to a former rector, John Mores, d. 1492. *Britwell Prior,* ⅓ S., equally small, is Norm. and E. E., and has been restored. Near it, the late Mr. Weld of Lulworth gave a habitation for many years to a body of nuns, who left France at the time of the first Revolution. *Britwell Baldwin,* 2 m. N.W., is a handsome Dec. ch. with Perp. tower. It has some good stained glass, and some *Brasses.* One, for " Johan ye Smyth" (1371) is supposed to be the earliest with an inscription in English verse; another is for Chief Justice John Cotesmore (1439). There are also several tombs of the Carletons. Sir Dudley Carleton, the ambassador, created Viscount Dorchester by Charles I., was born here in 1573.

1 m. N.W. of Watlington is *Cuxham,*

where the *Church* demands notice from the way in which the materials of the former edifice have been used in building it, c. 1700. "The Norm. doorway is preserved, and has twisted shafts and sculptured capitals of the interlaced pattern ; the old door with the iron-work and nail heads remains ; in the jambs close to the bottom are built in two sculptured stones, which seem to have formed the lid of a stone coffin."—*Eccl. and Arch. Topog., Oxfordshire.* There is a *Brass* for John Gregory and his 2 wives (1506). 1 m. N. is the small ch. of *Ensington*, which has a good Dec. E. window, and some fragments of ancient glass.

3½ m. The *Church* of *Chalgrove* lies off the road to the W. It has Trans.-Norm. arches in the nave, but is chiefly Dec., the chancel contains several mural paintings, brought to light in 1858: also some very good windows. It has an octangular font, supported on a twisted pillar, a Jacobean imitation of Norm. work. There are *Brasses* of 2 of the family of Barentyn (1441, 1446).

Chalgrove is best known as the place where John Hampden received his death-wound. A column erected on June 18, 1843, the 200th anniversary of the event, stands near the high road, in *Chalgrove Field*, on the very spot where he had first mustered the Bucks militia, which he was then commanding. It was on June 18, 1643, that, seeing a body of royalist troops in the distant plain, he rode forward through the high standing corn to intercept them, and, according to the received account, in the first charge he received his death-wound, pierced in the shoulder by two carabine balls, while his men, overwhelmed by numbers. were either killed or put to flight. Feeling his coming death he attempted to flee towards Pyrton, which had been the home of his first wife ; but the way was cut off, and he was compelled to

turn towards Thame. (Rte. 22.) "Some had advised him not to go forth upon this party, he not being ordered to do it ; but his mettle did put him forward, and his death ensued."—*Whitelock.* An examination of his body, made in 1828, by the late Lord Nugent and others, renders it probable that his death was caused by the bursting of his own pistol, which shattered his hand in a terrible manner (Rte. 12.) The monument bears a medallion portrait, and an inscription stating that he received his death-wound on that spot while fighting in defence of the free monarch and ancient liberties of England.

6 m. *Stadhampton*, of which Dr. John Owen, Cromwell's chaplain, was a native, has a ch. of debased Perp. style, restored in 1877, and a modern tower. There is a brass for John Wylmot and wife (1508).

7 m. *Chiselhampton*, once a possession of the D'Oileys, has a modern ch., built 1763, but retains, substantially unaltered. the long bridge which was defended against Prince Rupert by the force under Hampden on the morning of Chalgrove Field, a manoeuvre for which its extreme length and narrowness peculiarly adapted it, stretching, as it does, not only over 2 branches of the river, but over a low-lying strip of meadow-land which is flooded in winter. Notice the stout angular buttresses on the N. side, to stem the force of the current.

Adjoining the ch. is *Chiselhampton House* (Rev. C. R. Powys). which has replaced the old manor-house of the D'Oileys. The two villages form but one incumbency, and their long names are commonly shortened into Stadham and Chisleton. The latter had formerly an even longer name, being styled Chevacheeshull Hampton, in the time of Henry III., according to Wood.

8 m. On l. 1 m. *Toot Baldon* (Rte. 20).

9 m. *Garsington*, on a hill a short distance N., which commands extensive views, from the Chilterns to the Wantage downs. The *Church*, which formerly belonged to Wallingford Priory, was purchased by Sir Thomas Pope, and annexed to his foundation of Trinity College. The chancel is Dec., the nave and the tower Trans. Norm. The ch. was restored in 1849 by Dr. Ingram, the President of Trinity College, when the original altar-stone, with its five crosses perfect, was found and restored to its place. There is a good brass for Thomas Radley and family (1584), and a large slab, with a cross fleurée, bears an inscription, which has been read thus:

" Isabele de Fortibus gist ici;
Deu de sa alme eyt merci."

Isabella de Fortibus, Countess of Albemarle, was the lady of the manor, temp. Edward I.. and John de la Mare, her son by her first husband, was in 1300 summoned to Parliament as Baron of Garsington.

Sir Thos. Pope built a house here as a retreat for the students of his college in case of plague, and here they took refuge in 1577; it is now occupied by the curate. Garsington was Fairfax's head-quarters in May, 1646.

12 m. *Cowley*, or Church Cowley, as it is called, to distinguish it from Temple Cowley, a short distance N. The ch., E. E. with a low Perp. tower, has been restored by *Street*, and rather freely coloured. No traces remain of the Templars' ch.. which was built on land given to them by the Empres-Maud. At the part of the parish nearest to Oxford, are the remains of *St. Bartholomew's Hospital*, consisting chiefly of a small desecrated chapel of Dec. and Perp. character, standing in a farmyard. This hospital was founded for lepers, in 1126, by Henry I. with

the overplus of the money raised for the building of Beaumont palace, and the inmates were at first fed with the broken meat from the royal table; afterwards they had several grants of land. In the time of Edward III. it was granted to Oriel College, by which society the chapel seems to have been built. During the civil war the lead was stripped from the roof for bullets, but the college restored the chapel, with rood screen and seats for the choir, all which remain tolerably perfect, with the date "1651," and the letters "O. C."—to be taken, it has been suggested, for "Oriel College." or "Oliver Cromwell," as fancy might dictate. When the building was abandoned does not appear, but in Wood's time the Fellows of New College attended a service in it every Holy Thursday, and afterwards chanted in parts round a neighbouring well called Stockwell.

14 m. OXFORD. (Rte. 19.)

ROUTE 24.

OXFORD TO CROPREDY.

Birmingham Line, G. W. R. 26¼ m.

The Great Western Railway crosses the Port Meadow, having on E.

for the first mile the Bletchley branch of the L. and N. W. Rly. (Rte. 28). The ruins of Godstow are seen on W., and at 3 m. Yarnton Junction is reached, where the Oxford, Worcester, and Wolverhampton line diverges to the N.W.

5½ m. *Woodstock Road* (Stat.). The town is 2½ m. distant, but there are omnibuses from each train, and flys for Blenheim are obtainable, at the rate of from 4s. 6d. to 8s. 6d. for the double journey, carrying from 1 to 5 persons.

For Woodstock and Blenheim see Exc. (*l*) from Oxford.

1 m. E. of Woodstock road is *Kidlington*, where the fine cruciform *Church of St. Mary* is worth visiting. It is chiefly of the 15th centy., with an E. E. tower and a handsome Perp. spire. The nave has good E. E. parts, with a Dec. window and arches: the S. porch is rich Dec., with the ball-flower mouldings, crocketed canopy and open timber roof. The chancel is chiefly Dec. and a S. chapel has a fine E. window in the same style. The stalls, which are Perp., are handsomely carved in wood. Near the ch. is an almshouse, founded by Sir William Morton in memory of his wife. The loyal John Gregory died at Kidlington, a dependant on the charity of a poor innkeeper, in 1646.

Hampton Poyle Church, of the 14th centy., restored in 1870, on the bank of the Cherwell, opposite Kidlington, has in the chancel a good late E. E. window, and in the N. aisle a good Dec. window. Here are the fine effigies of a cross-legged warrior and his lady, and a brass of John Poyle, 1434, and his wife.

Hampton Gay, 1 m. higher up the river, has a ch. of the early part of the present centy., in which some 15th.-centy. materials have been used afresh, as the battlements of the tower. An Elizabethan manor-house of stone remains nearly in its original state.

A terrible railway accident, in which 34 persons were killed and 70 injured, occurred near Hampton Gay on Dec. 24th, 1874.

Shipton, picturesquely placed on a high bank overlooking the river, has a ch. with a Dec. chancel,

7¾ m. *Kirtlington* (Stat.). Here a great Synod was held in 977, at which King Edward the Martyr and Abp. Dunstan were present. *Kirtlington Park* is the seat of Sir H. W. Dashwood, Bart.* The ch., which adjoins it, has a Norm. chancel and tower (the latter a restoration), and E. E. nave. Christopher Wren, dean of Windsor, and father of the architect, is buried in the chancel (d. 1658). His son's early life was passed here, and his first wife was Faith, daughter of Sir John Coghill of Bletchingdon.

1 m. S. is *Bletchingdon Park* (Viscount Valentia), partly rebuilt late in the last centy., on the site of a house celebrated for its magnificent staircase. It was held for the King during the Civil Wars by Colonel Windebank, who, terrified by a victory which Cromwell had just gained over Prince Rupert at Islip, surrendered the place at once on his coming thither, April 3, 1644, for which he was soon after shot by court-martial at Oxford. Plot, in his quaint Natural History (1677), declares that no snake will ever live at Bletchingdon, even if imported thither from other places.

A peculiar kind of grey marble is found here, which was used for the pillars of the cloister of St. John's College.

2 m. N. of the stat. is *Tackley*, a cruciform ch., originally E. E., with

* The hall and staircase have fine carvings by Grinling Gibbons. One of Sir Joshua Reynolds' most beautiful portraits preserved here represents Mary Helen, wife of Sir Henry Watkin Dashwood, with her infant son. She was a great friend of Queen Charlotte; and died 1796.

Perp. tower, and a Perp. altar-tomb under an E. E. recess.

11¾ m. *Heyford* (Stat.). The ch. (restored by Buckeridge), mainly Perp., has a curious painting of the Commandments, with a representation of an Elizabethan chancel. 1 m. W. is *Rousham*, seat of C. Cottrell Dormer, Esq., who represents one of the oldest families in this part of England: his great-grandfather, Sir Clem. Cottrell, inherited the estate from his cousin, General Dormer, in 1750. The grounds, which border the Cherwell, were laid out in the Italian style by *Kent,* and contain a number of statues brought from Italy, with a fine sculpture of a lion tearing a horse by *Scheemaker.* The house, built by Sir R. Dormer in the reign of James I., on the site of one visited by Elizabeth, contains a valuable collection of family portraits, among which are Sir Charles Cottrell, *Kneller;* Waller the poet, and Sir C. Cottrell, *Vandyke;* Robert Dormer, *Lely;* Lady Cottrell Dormer, *Sir J. Reynolds;* Sir Clement Cottrell Dormer, *West.* Among the members of this family were Sir Charles Cottrell, page to Villiers, Duke of Buckingham, at whose assassination he was present, and steward to Elizabeth, Queen of Bohemia, with whom he lived at Heidelberg. At the flight of the English royal family he was intrusted with the care of the little Duke of Gloucester, and in recognition of his services was presented with a magnificent chain by Charles II., which is still at Rousham, and with the office of Master of the Ceremonies, which remained in the family till the time of George III. His son Clement served as a volunteer under Lord Sandwich, and was blown up at Solebay, May 28, 1672. It is said that he called out as the boats were pulling away, "You are leaving me in good company." His faithful friend Mr. Harbord died with him, and is com-

memorated by the same tomb in Westminster Abbey. Chas. Dormer, page to William of Orange, was killed at the battle of Almanza, and died singing "Britons! strike home." Sir Julius Adelmar Cæsar, another ancestor of the family, descended from the Adelmare Counts of Genoa, who are mentioned by Dante, received a visit from Queen Elizabeth. Pope visited at Rousham, and his portrait remains at the house. There is a fine picture in the hall of Johanna Dormer, who became Duchess of Feria by marrying the Spanish Ambassador at the court of Mary; she was a favoured attendant of Isabella, queen of Philip II., and appeared as chief mourner at her funeral.

In the dining-rooms are originals of Queen Elizabeth (for which she sate for Sir J. Cæsar); James I.; Lord Falkland (*Cor. Jansen*); and on the staircase of Anne, by *Kneller.*

In the library are many valuable papers, which have been reported on by the Historical Manuscripts Commissioners. Among them are some original letters of Mary, Princess of Orange, eldest daughter of Charles I., to her brother the Duke of Gloucester, handed down by his attendant, Sir Charles Cottrell (one assuring him that as long as she possesses anything in the world he shall never want bread—in allusion to his ill-treatment by his mother Henrietta Maria); a letter of Charles II. to his aunt the Queen of Bohemia, asking her to spare her steward Sir Charles to be about his brother; other letters of Charles II. and Henry, Duke of Gloucester; of the Queen of Bohemia, many in cipher, others in invisible ink; and of Villiers, Duke of Buckingham; the 'Imitation' of Thomas à Kempis in Spanish, written by Clement Cottrell, who was blown up at Solebay; the correspondence of Mrs. Cæsar, comprising autographs of Swift, Pope, and Walpole; journals of the Cottrells, as masters of the ceremonies

1660-1779, "full of curious and amusing anecdotes and remarks," &c.

After describing his dislike of Blenheim, H. Walpole says, "The greatest pleasure we had was in seeing Sir Chas. Cottrell's house at Rowsham; it reinstated Kent with me, he has nowhere shown so much taste. The house is old, and was bad: he has improved it, stuck as close as he could to Gothic, and made a delightful library, and the whole is comfortable. The garden is Daphne in little, the sweetest little groves, streams, glades, porticoes, cascades, and river imaginable; all the scenes are perfectly classic. If I had such a house, such a library, and so pretty a wife, I think I should let King * * * * * send to Herrenhausen for a Master of the Ceremonies."

The *Church*, which is close to the house, is Trans.-Norm. and Dec.; notice the ingenious manner in which the rebuilders of the S. aisle engrafted Dec. capitals on the Norm. shafts, and divided one large arch into two. It has been restored in good taste, and contains some ancient Dormer tombs removed from Steeple Barton.

Westcott Barton Church, 2 m. N.W., is Perp. (restored by *Street* in 1856), with a good screen still retaining some of its original colouring; but the chancel arch is Trans.-Norm.

Steeple Barton, 2 m. W., is a Dec. *Church* with ivy-clad Perp. square tower. The chancel arch is boarded up, and has on it the arms of the Stuarts, with the date 1686, and the text,

" My son, feare thou the Lord and the King,
And medle not with them that are given
to change."

There are still several Elizabethan monuments, to the families of Blundel and Humfrey. The manor-house, a part of which still remains, was built by John Dormer, a merchant of the Staple, about 1524, and the

arms of that fraternity were placed by him on the walls of the court.

Barton Abbey (Hon. Mrs. Hall), occupies the site of a cell to Osney.

1 m. N. is *Steeple Aston*. The Church (restored) is mainly E. E. with Perp. tower; it has a Dec. pi⁵ᶜ¹na, and open seats with rich panelling. A remarkable altar-frontal, 14th centy., is preserved here, richly embroidered with Scripture subjects. The E. window is almost hidden by a huge monument by *Scheemaker*, to Judge Page, 1741 (Savage's Judge Page—" Hard words and hanging, if your judge be Page "), and his wife. He lived at *Middle Aston*. The house was pulled down by Sir C. Cottrell. The grounds however remain as they were, and are picturesque, with fine old cedars; the offices are turned into a farmhouse. In the churchyard a simple stone marks the grave of Thomas Mitchell, editor and translator of Aristophanes.

1 m. E. is *Heyford Warren*, where the ch. has a lofty well-proportioned Perp. tower, and a fine monument of a priest under a Dec. arch. An Elizabethan manor-house, and a tithe-barn of the 14th centy., are worth notice.

14½ m. *Somerton* (Stat.). A short distance E. the Wattlebank, or Avesditch, a British boundary, may be traced. The manor was once held by Odo of Bayeux, and afterwards by the Greys, who forfeited it as Yorkists after the battle of Bosworth, when it was granted to Jasper, Duke of Bedford. It was afterwards bestowed on William Fermor, clerk of the Crown, temp. Henry VIII., who built Tusmore (*post*). The *Church* has a Trans.-Norm. chancel arch, Dec. chancel, nave and tower, and a Perp. chantry, containing tombs and brasses of the Fermors. A very fine reredos (c. 1380) representing the Last Supper, an sculpture of the Crucifixion of same date, the 15th-cent. rood screen, and the font, which is of singular shape, deserve notice. Archbishop Juxon was rector of this living, and his arms appear on the rood screen. There are some slight remains of the manor-house of the Fermors in the meadow behind the ch.*

2 m. E. is *Fritwell*, with a small ch., Norm. and E. E. The Jacobean manor-house (Rev. S. Yorke) is a handsome building, and contains some fine wainscoted rooms. It was once the seat of Sir Baldwin Wake, who quarrelled with his brother about a lady of whom they were both enamoured, and immured him in a large lumber-room at the top of the house. This room still remains, and in it is what can only be described as a huge human dog-kennel, where the unfortunate brother was chained as a lunatic till actual madness ensued. What passes for drops of his blood are shewn, and the house, of course, is said to be haunted by a frightful apparition.

2 m. E. of Fritwell is *Bayard's Green*, which was " one of the three places appointed by King Richard I. for the first authorised tournaments which were held in England. The lion-hearted King retained to the last a predilection for his native county, and the number of cross-legged effigies connected with the Oxfordshire families prove the ardour with which they entered into his views."—*Brewer.*

A short distance N. is *Tusmore*, a handsome modern mansion, built 1770, on the site of an Elizabethan manor-house, belonging to the Fermors, an old Catholic family. This had hiding-places for priests ingeniously hidden, and the great fish-pond is said to have been dug by a

* Will Somers, the jester, lived first in the family of these Fermors: he afterwards had the courage to plead the cause of his former master with Henry VIII. (by whom he was oppressed), and carried his point with the king, who did justice to Fermor.

[*Berks, &c.*]

priest disguised as a labourer—a task that employed him and his one trusted assistant 12 years.

2 m. N. of Fritwell is *Souldern* ch. with an early Norm. tower, the walls of which are of extraordinary thickness. The S. aisle has a Dec. cornice engraved by Rickman.

1 m. N. of the stat. is *North Aston*, where the fine Dec. and Perp. *Church* was restored by *Scott* in 1866. The alabaster altar tomb is probably that of John Anne (d. 1416) and Alicia his wife; the knight is in armour, and wears the collar of SS. The Annes are a Yorkshire family, which has now assumed the name of Tasburgh. The tower is beautifully clothed with ivy, but the manor-house (W. M. Foster-Melliar, Esq.) stands so very close to it (within 3 ft.), as to interfere most materially with the view.*

2 m. W. is the Dec. and Perp. ch. of *Dunstew*, almost hidden by its covering of ivy; and 2 m. beyond it, *Sandford*, where the ch. has a remarkable window, the tracery presenting a curious mixture of the Dec. and Perp. styles. In the ch.-yd. is the huge grave of Lord Deloraine of Leudwell (a neighbouring hamlet), so arranged with openings as to shew his coffin within; it has been adopted for the burial-place of Captain Cox, who fell at Waterloo. *Sandford Park* is the residence of Dr. Guest, the archæologist, Master of Caius College, Cambridge.

16¾ m. *Aynho* (Stat.). 1 m. E. is Aynho Hall, in Northamptonshire (W. R. Cartwright, Esq.), which contains a good collection of pictures. (See *Handb. for North Hants.*)

W. 2 m, on a hill, is *Deddington*, a decayed market town, with about 2000 inhab. (*Inn: Unicorn.*) The

* On the tower is a curious hearded figure, seated, with a shield bearing three leopards.

T

Church, originally Dec., was greatly injured by the fall of the tower in 1634, and has been indifferently rebuilt with the old materials. There is still a good Dec. E. window, with sedilia and piscina of the same date. A recess in the S. wall contains a female figure of early date; and some small brasses remain, one of a civilian c. 1370 (*Haines*, 'Mon. Brasses'). Near the ch. is the Parsonage, on the site of the old Pilgrim House; it has a tall square tower, with open balustrade at top. Beneath the Plough Inn are the remains of a beautiful groined crypt. On the E. of the town are buried beneath green mounds the remains of the *Castle*, of unknown antiquity, where Piers Gaveston, the favourite of Edward II., who had surrendered to Aymer de Valence at Scarborough, on promise of his life, was seized by the earl of Warwick. Gaveston had greatly offended him years before by styling him, from his swarthy complexion, " the black dog;" and declaring that he had made no promise, he said " the witch's son should feel the black dog's teeth," which he effected by hurrying him to Warwick, and there beheading him on his own authority. Sir Thomas Pope and Chief Justice Scroggs were both natives of Deddington, and Charles I. slept at the parsonage the night after the battle of Cropredy.

2 m. N. is *Adderbury*, the Edburgberig of Domesday, a town of 1200 inhabitants. Both its Norm. castle and the house of the dukes of Buccleuch have utterly perished, but it has a fine Dec. ch. with lofty spire. The chancel was built by William of Wykeham, and the E. window contains his arms; the living still belongs to New College. The sedilia and piscina are richly ornamented, as are the canopies over the altar, which were formerly coloured. There is a good brass of a knight

and a lady, date 1460.* The vestry has a beautiful oriel window, and a muniment room over it. The old Rectory-house and the original tithe-barn remain close to the ch. A synod of bishops was held here in 1219, which sentenced to crucifixion an impostor who assumed the name and pretended to the wounds of our Saviour.

The profligate and witty Earl of Rochester lived at Adderbury green, and in the neighbouring chapel at Bodicote improvised and addressed to the clerk the lines—

" Sternhold and Hopkins had great qualms,
   When they translated David's Psalms,
      To make the heart full glad;
   But had it been poor David's fate
   To hear thee sing and them translate,
      By Jove, 'twould have drove him mad."

Pope's lines—

" With no poetic ardour fired,
   I press the bed where Wilmot lay,"—

were written in the Adderbury manor-house, when on a visit to the Duke of Argyll.

3 m. W. is *Bloxham*, which has a very handsome *Church*, restored by *Street* in 1846, mainly Dec., but with some remains of a Norm. edifice, and some Perp. windows inserted. The Dec. tower and spire are very beautiful, as is also the W. doorway, which is rich in sculpture. According to Mr. Street the church was founded in the 13th centy; the nave and aisles and N. transept were built, and the chancel rebuilt; the beautiful tower and spire are the work of the next centy. In the 15th centy. the clerestory was added, and a chapel was erected on the S. side. The porches are very handsome; and above the W. door there is a sculpture representing the Last Judgment. Traces of old frescoes remain. The respective merits of the three

* The Luke family are buried here, one of whom is said to be satirized as the hero of Butler's *Hudibras*. In a farmhouse belonging to the Risley family is preserved the portrait of Charles II., given by the king to Sir Samuel Luke when he became a royalist.

celebrated spires in this neighbourhood are thus discriminated in a popular rhyme:—

" Bloxham for length,
Adderbury for strength,
And King's Sutton for beauty."

19 m. *King's Sutton* (Stat.). (See *Handbook for Northamptonshire.*)

22½ m. *Banbury* (Stat.). Banbury (*Inn*: Red Lion), a clean and well-built town on the Cherwell, contains about 3600 inhab. and returns one M.P. " Banbury zeal, cakes, and ale," are an old proverb, and the town is still famous for its cakes and ale, and the cheese made in its neighbourhood. It is in a flourishing state, less from its manufacture of plush and horse girths, which have given way to that of agricultural implements on a large scale, than from its situation in the midst of one of the most fertile districts in England; the Oxford and Birmingham canal has greatly contributed to its prosperity. There are several good old *Houses*, with barge boards and pargeting, and dates ranging from 1570 to 1648. The ch. was pulled down in 1793, needlessly, and with so much difficulty that gunpowder was obliged to be resorted to, and many fine monuments of the Copes were destroyed. The present edifice is an ugly structure, in the Italian style, and its want of a spire, and the character the town then had for dirt, gave rise to the rhyme, how—

" Dirty Banbury's proud people
Built a church without a steeple."

The *Castle*, built by Alexander, bp. of Lincoln, in 1125, and held by his successors till the reign of Edward VI., is entirely destroyed. It was a garrison for the king during the Civil Wars, and stood two sieges, —one of 13 weeks' duration, 1644, from Colonel Fiennes, when the brave garrison was relieved after having eaten all their horses but two; the other in 1646, after which it was pulled down by Parliament, and no trace now remains, save a fragment of wall and part of the moat.

The " goodly crosse " of Banbury is well known from the nursery rhyme—

" Ride a cock-horse to Banbury Cross,
To see a fine lady get on a white horse,
Rings on her fingers, and bells on her toes,
And she shall have music wherever she goes:"

in allusion to the alleged habit of the " Old Woman of Banbury," known also as the " Witch of the White Horse." The cross was destroyed at the Reformation, but it has now a successor, by *Gibbs* of Oxford, which was erected by public subscription on occasion of the marriage of the Princess Royal in 1858 to the Crown Prince of Prussia. There were formerly several other crosses here, as the *High Cross*, the *Market Cross*, the *Bread Cross*, the *White Cross*, and the *Weeping Cross*, the last so called because the bodies of the dead, taken for burial, were set down there; the name, for the same reason, is borne by two other places, one near Stafford where the road turns off to Walsall, the other near Shrewsbury.

" He that goes out with often losse,
At length comes back by Weeping Crosse,"

is an ancient proverb. Florian (Trans. of Montaigne, bk. iii. ch. 5) says, " Few men have wedded their sweethearts, their paramours or mistresses but have come home by Weeping Cross, and ere long repented of their bargain." Before 1622 all these crosses had fallen into decay, which caused Bishop Corbet to write—

" The Crosses also, like old stumps of trees,
Or stools for horsemen that have feeble knees,
Carry no heads above ground."

The people of Banbury were noted for their Puritanic tendencies, of which our early dramatists and others make frequent mention. In Ben Jonson's ' Bartholomew Fair.' " Zeal-of-the-land-busy," the Puritan suitor to Mrs. Purecraft, is a Banbury man; and Drunken Barnaby sings—

   " In my progress travelling northward,
    Taking my farewell o' the southward,
    To Banbury came I, O profane one!
    Where I saw a puritane one,
    Hanging of his cat on Monday,
    For killing of a mouse on Sunday."

Banbury was the scene of the rendezvous of the Levellers in May, 1649, when they mustered about 5000 men, under the command of one William Thomson, a fanatic mentioned by Baxter, as disputing with him in Amersham Church. After a few days they marched southward, but were met by Cromwell, driven into Burford and obliged to surrender (Rte. 25).

A short distance from Banbury, on the Chipping-Norton road, is a supposed Roman amphitheatre, but only known in the neighbourhood by the name of the *Bear Garden.*

2½ m. S.W. of Banbury is *Broughton Castle,* the seat of Lord Saye and Sele, one of the most interesting houses in Oxfordshire, both as regards its architecture and its history. Its situation is very low, and it is still surrounded by a broad moat filled with water and defended by a gate-house. Its first appearance is that of a fine Elizabethan mansion, but a considerable portion dates from 1301 to 1307, inclusive of the hall, from which bays were thrown out in 1554, when Tudor windows were inserted instead of Gothic. The old battlements and lower part of the gatehouse and stables, along the N. side of the moat, date from 1406, when permission to crenellate was granted by Henry IV. William of Wykeham purchased the mansion and estate of the De Broughtons, and bequeathed it in 1404 to his great-nephew Sir Thomas Wykeham, whose heiress married William, Lord Saye and Sele, in the reign of Henry VI. The latest portion, including the great dining and drawing-rooms, dates from 1599.

The hall, which contains a number of interesting portraits, among others that of Nathaniel Fiennes, the "Root-and-Branch" man, (d. 1669,) opens into a state dining-room of the time of Elizabeth, with a curious internal porch added after the Restoration with the inscription, " Quod olim fuit meminisse minime juvat." This room contains a curious old picture by *Francesco di San Croce,* portraits of Charles I. and Oliver Cromwell by *Dobson,* and of Prince Maurice by *Mirevelt;* also a picture of the embarkation of Charles II. at Schevening. The ceilings of this room, and of the state drawing-room which is over it, are exceedingly beautiful. The upper room contains a very fine picture of Lady Eardley, with her daughter, afterwards Lady Saye and Sele, by *Gainsborough.* Beyond the long gallery, with its fine bay windows, is another drawing-room with a stone chimney-piece, having a sculpture of the Dance of the Dryads.

The house is well deserving of careful study, much of it being almost in its original state; and great historic interest attaching to other portions. The secret staircase may be seen, by which access was gained to a chamber where the leaders of the Parliamentary party held meetings to organise a resistance to the arbitrary measures of Charles I. and his advisers, William Fiennes, Lord Say and Sele, the then owner, being, as Clarendon says, " the oracle of the Puritans." Hallam calls him " the wise and cautious Lord Say and Sele, the acknowledged head of the Dependent sect." He became Lord Privy Seal in the first cabinet of Charles II. after his return from Schevening. The bag which belonged to the office of Privy Seal is in the possession of the present Lord.

"Lord Say," says Anthony Wood, "held meetings in his house at Broughton, where was a room and passage thereunto, which his servants were prohibited to come near; and when they were of a complete number, there would be great noises and talkings heard among them, to the admiration of those that lived in the house,: yet could they never discern their lord's companions." Popular tradition says that the entrance of the secret passage by which they gained access to the castle was in "The Giant's Cave," in an enclosure called Bretch, beyond the Broughton toll-gate. At the top of the house, among the oak timbers, is the "Old Barrack Room," where some of the Parliamentary soldiers are said to have been quartered before the battle of Edgehill, and on the roof, which opens from this room, a small house, known as the Officers' Barracks. A beautiful vaulted passage runs round the lower part of the building, and leads in one direction to the chapel, and in the other to the grand staircase. This, before the present staircases were made, must have been the only means of access to the principal apartments, while this end of the house having been the portion appropriated to the state apartments accounts for its richness of decoration. In the small dining-room is some old panelling of the earliest linen pattern. The chapel, which is small, but very lofty, and of Dec. architecture, has some old stained glass, an encaustic pavement, a stone altar, and a piscina. "The three different periods of the castle may be thus defined; the 14th centy. of the De Broughtons, the 15th of the Wykehams, and the 16th of the Fienneses."—'Dom. Arch.' vol. ii.

Close to the picturesque gatehouse is the *Church*, a good Dec. building with tower and spire. It contains a fine stone chancel-screen, and an interesting series of tombs. Among them notice John de Broughton, the founder of the castle; a coloured figure of a knight in armour reclining beneath a canopy, for the second Lord Saye, killed at Barnet, 1471, with part of his armour hanging above; and the great-nephew of William of Wykeham with his wife.

1 m. W. is *Tadmarton*, with a small Dec. ch., which has a lofty tower, and a sanctus-bell turret. On Tadmarton heath are the remains of a circular camp, and near it is a spring of pure water, called the Holy Well.

Swalcliffe, 1. m. W. of Tadmarton, has a fine ch., the exterior chiefly Dec., but with Norm. nave and Perp. tower. There is a good open timber roof, and the chancel-screen retains much of its original painting and gilding. At a spot called Blackland, in this parish, numerous Roman remains have been discovered; and a camp with a double entrenchment, supposed to be British, bears the name of *Madmarston*.

2 m. from Broughton and 3 m. N.W. of Banbury is *Wroxton Abbey*, the seat of Lt.-Colonel North, once a priory of Augustinian monks; but the remains are very slight. It passed, after the dissolution, into the hands of Sir Thomas Pope, the founder of Trinity College, Oxford, who gave it to his new foundation, of whom it was held by the Norths, Earls of Guilford. The present edifice was chiefly built in 1618, but the appearance is that of a fine Tudor manor-house. In spite of the abuse of Walpole, who says that "it is neither good nor agreeable," the interior is very interesting, and contains much beautiful carving, brought from Flanders, and many curious portraits. The Hall, a part of the earlier building, contains

the portrait of Sir T. Pope, said to be by *Holbein*, and the hawking-gloves, purse, and bag of the Great Seal, belonging to the Lord Keeper Guilford, which are also seen represented in his portrait. A drawing-room has an exquisite ceiling, and dark oak chimney-piece. In King James's room is a bed used by Charles I., and some other curious furniture of that period; and the Tapestry room contains a bed which belonged to Mary Queen of Scots, and a quilt beautifully worked by her. The chapel has a window with stained glass by *Van Linge*, and much oak carving, comprising a sacramental chest, with a statue of David upon it. In the gallery is the "North Chest," given by George III., full of plate, to his prime minister Lord North. Among the most valuable pictures are, Sir W. Pope, 1st Earl of Downe, in the robes of the Bath; a picture of Prince Henry about to kill a stag, which is held by Lord Harrington; Sir Owen Hopton, 1590; Vandyke, by himself; Elizabeth of Bohemia, *Zucchero*; Erasmus, *Holbein*; and several good portraits by *Jansen*. James I., Charles I. and his two sons, and George IV. when Prince of Wales, have been visitors here.

"Except one scene, which is indeed noble (says Walpole), I cannot much commend the without-doors. This scene consists of a beautiful lake, shut in entirely with wood; the head falls into a fine cascade, and that into a serpentine river, over which is a little Gothic seat, like a round temple, lifted up on a shaggy mount."

The Dec. ch. contains the monuments of the 1st Earl of Downe, and Lady Anne his wife, who recline under a canopy supported by black marble pillars; of Lord Keeper Guilford (who died here, 1685) and his lady; of Francis, Earl of Guilford, and his three wives; and of Lord North, the prime minister.

Here also is buried Thomas Coutts, the millionnaire.

2 m. W. of Wroxton is *Alkerton Church*, Trans.-Norm. and E. E. The E. E. tower has the cornice of the parapet sculptured with animals and figures with musical instruments. Thomas Lydiat, the mathematician and chronologer, was a native, and held the living. He d. 1646, after a life of great suffering, and is buried in the church, part of which he rebuilt.

Halfway between Banbury and Wroxton a road of 1 m. rt. leads to the remains of *Hanwell Castle*, which consist of a fine quadrangular brick tower with stone quoins. This, called by Leland "the pleasant and gallant house of Hanwell," was built by Anthony Cope, cofferer to Henry VII. (d. 1513). Here was the residence of Sir Anthony Cope, one of the early Puritan leaders, who was committed to the Tower by Elizabeth, but afterwards rose high in royal favour, and twice received James I. and his queen on a visit at Hanwell. He died in 1614, and is buried in the ch. close by. (The Cope family are now represented by the Earls of Aboyne and Delawarr.)

The fine E. E. and Dec. ch. has some curious capitals in the nave, representing grotesque figures playing upon musical instruments, and at the end of the N. aisle, where formerly was an altar, are some statues of saints under Gothic canopies.

1 m. N.W. is the ch. of *Horley*, Dec., but with a beautiful E. E. piscina. On the wall of the N. aisle a large fresco represents St. Christopher carrying Christ upon his shoulders, to whom the Saint says:

"What art thou, and art so yynge ?
Bar I never so hevy a thynge."

Christ replies :

" Yey, I be hevy, no wunther nys'
For I am the Kynge of blys."

2 m. further is the ch. of *Hornton*, Trans.-Norm. and E. E.

3 m. N. of Banbury, and very near the line on l., is the village of *Bourton Magna*, remarkable for its desecrated ch. " The nave is used as a dwelling-house, and the chancel, which is converted into a school-room [Gill's free-school] is all that remains of the original ch. at all perfect. It is Early Dec., and retains the original roof. The E. window is of two lights with good tracery, though much mutilated. The piscina and locker remain in their original positions, and there is a beautiful Dec. window in the N. wall."—*J. M. D.* in ' Eccl. and Arch. Top. of Oxfordshire.'

26¼ m. *Cropredy* (Stat.). The *Church*, restored in 1877, is a fine edifice, Dec., but with Perp. N. aisle; the tracery in the windows is very good. There remains a double pis-cina, and some Dec. screenwork, cut down and serving as a railing (figured in *Gloss. of Arch.*). Above the chancel arch there is an old painting of the Last Judgment, and the vestry contains a coffer probably of the 13th centy. The battle of Cropredy bridge where Charles I. defeated Waller (June 29, 1644), was fought not far from the ch., and many of the dead were buried in the ch.-yd. " Both parties in this fight demeaned themselves with great courage. Colonel Middleton had a particular encounter with the Lord Wilmot [father of the well-known Rochester], whom he took prisoner; but he was rescued, by the soldiers who had him in custody being wounded. Middleton routed the enemy, and pursued them near a mile, but a strong party wheeling about forced him to retreat with some loss. In the skirmish he was dismounted among the king's forces, who, taking him to be one of their commanders, mounted him again, wishing him to make haste to kill a Roundhead, by which means he escaped." — *Whitelock's Memorials.* " After the battle Waller drew up his whole army, on the high grounds which are between Cropredy and Hanwell, opposite to the king's quarters about a mile; the river of Cherwell and some low grounds being between both armies, which had a full view of each other." —*Clarendon.* Sir Edward Walker was sent to him by the king " with a gracious message," but he refused to receive it. The armies faced each other for two days, and then drew off in different directions without any further engagement.

ROUTE 25.

OXFORD TO WITNEY AND LECHLADE [BURFORD].

Witney and East Gloucestershire Branch, G. W. R., and Road 20m.

Leaving Oxford by the Worcester and Wolverhampton line, we reach at

3¼ m. *Yarnton Junction Stat.*, where the Witney branch turns off, l. Yarnton ch. is mainly E. E., but with a very late tower (1611), built by Sir Thomas Spencer, who also erected a chapel at the E. end, which contains the monuments of his family. There is some good old glass collected from various sources, and presented by Alderman Fletcher of Oxford, along with some sculptures in alabaster from the life of our Lord. The donor (d. 1826) is buried under an altar-tomb, with a brass (copied from one in St. Peter's-in-the-East, Oxford), which is one of the earliest instances of the revival of the art. In the churchyard is a mutilated E. E. cross, with figures of saints, much resembling that of Eynsham, on which abbey this ch. was formerly a dependency. Similar crosses formerly existed in all the villages dependent on the abbey of Eynsham, at which the abbot and monks performed solemn services on especial occasions. Close to the ch. is a most picturesque old manor-house.

" At Yarnton the gravel-bed has been opened very extensively to ' ballast' the neighbouring railway, and has been found richer than is usual in mammalian remains. At the bottom of the excavation, 16 or 18 ft. deep, is the ordinary bed of Oxford clay. On this rests a moist, partially coherent ferruginous mass, full of quartzose pebbles, drifted from the far-off Silurian hills near Bromsgrove; fragments of shelly oolite from the country a little to the N.; pieces of septaria, such as lie in the subjacent clay; and chips of chalk and flint from some other situation. It is not necessary to suppose that all these materials were brought by one agitation of water to their resting-place at Yarnton. On the contrary, it seems more probable that here, in the broad valley, the wide gravel-bed has been collected by secondary actions of water sweeping down from higher situations the fragments which had been scattered by previous currents of the ocean. Here were found in great abundance bones, teeth, and tusks of several

quadrupeds : viz., boar, goat, ox, horse, and elephant. As in many other cases known to geologists, teeth and tusks are the most abundant remains of the elephant. They are so numerous, and appear so perfect while in the ground, as to assure us of the existence, at no very remote period, of whole herds of these animals."—*Prof. Phillips in the* ' Oxford Essays,' 1855.

1¼ m. S.W. is *Cassington*, whose ch. was built (1159) by Geoffrey de Clinton, Chamberlain to Henry II. Part of his original foundation remains in the Norm. arch beneath the tower. This ch. has a fine Dec. spire, a chancel of the 12th centy., and contains a brass with cross fleurée for Roger Cheyne (d. 1414), and a " shroud and skeleton" brass for Thomas Nele, Hebrew Professor at Oxford (d. 1590). The people of this place were formerly buried at Cumnor. " They crossed the river with their dead at Sommerford mead, where the plank stones are still to be seen by which they passed, and came up the hill singing psalms, whence ' Songers' Lane.' "

7 m. *Eynsham* (Stat.). The large ch. is Dec. and Perp., and opposite to it is a Dec. cross. The font is Perp. and much ornamented. An important Benedictine abbey was founded here in the time of Ethelred II., but the last remnant, an elegant Dec. doorway, was removed in 1843, though the foundations may still be traced in a meadow W. of the ch. A brother of Edmund of Abingdon was a member of this monastery, and their father became one also towards the close of his life. The last abbot was Anthony Kitchen, who was made Bp. of Llandaff. Venetia Stanley, afterwards the wife of Sir Kenelm Digby, was brought up privately (left to a tenant's care) at Eynsham Abbey, " but private as that place was, her

beauty could not lie hid. She had a most lovely, sweet-turn'd face (a short ovall), delicate dark brown hair, dark browne eie-browes, above which much sweetnesse, as also in the opening of her eie-lids, the colour of her cheekes just that of the damask rose, neither too hot, nor too pale."—*Aubrey.*

9 m. *South Leigh* (Stat.). The small ch. is mostly Perp., but there is a Norm. doorway to the chancel with some singular ornaments. The church was restored in 1872. The ch. is a dependency of Stanton Harcourt, the vicar of which, John Gambold, was a friend of John Wesley, and allowed him to preach his first sermon here. "The Wesleyans of the present day make frequent visits to the spot which was the first scene of his multifarious labours."—*Arch. Guide, Oxford.*

11¾ m. *Witney* (Stat.) is a market-town on the Windrush. Pop. 3017. The name signifies "Parliament Isle" from the Saxon Witan-eye, "Island of the wise men," or "of the Parliament." There is an old proverb which says that "Witney is celebrated for 4 B.'s,—beauty, bread, beer, and blankets;" the last of these has long been a source of profit to the inhabitants, but the introduction of machinery for blanket-making in other places has considerably decreased the prosperity of the town.

The *Church of St. Mary*, conspicuous through its spire from all the country round, is a handsome cruciform structure, with a very beautiful central tower and lofty spire, large transepts, and small chancel. The tower, spire, and chancel are E. E., and the N. transept Dec. with a fine window of 7 lights; the clerestory and W. door are Perp. The whole was restored in 1867 by *Street.* On the *Brass* of R. Wenman (d. 1500) and his two wives is the inscription :—

" Man in what state that ever thow be
Timor mortis shuld truble the
For when thow leest wenyst
Venlet te
Mors superare
And so thy grave grevys
Ergo Mortis memorare. '

The old building, called the *College*, is said to have been built for the use of the Oxford students during the plague which once prevailed there. It belongs to Corpus Christi College.

Witney and its neighbourhood are thus described in uncomplimentary popular rhymes : —

" Hayley, Crawley, Curbridge, and Coggs,
Witney spinners, and Ducklington dogs,
Finstock upon the hill, Fawler down derry,
Beggarly Ramsden, and lousy Charlbury,
Woodstock for bacon, Bladon for beef,
Handborough for a scurvy knave, and Combe
for a thief."

At *Coggs*, 1 m. E., there is a remarkable *Church*, with a Dec. tower placed obliquely across the N.W. angle, a singular arrangement, of which the reason is not known. The Dec. chancel is so unusually large for the rest of the ch., that it is supposed to have been built for a large choir. On the N. side is a beautiful chantry, with a cornice composed of animals and grotesque figures. It is separated from the chancel by an arcade, under the E. arch of which is a rich 14th centy. tomb, with a female figure, supposed to be one of the Greys of Rotherfield, to whom the manor belonged temp. Edw. III. A farmhouse near the ch., believed to be a portion of the manorhouse, has two fine E. E. windows.

1½ m. S. of Witney is *Ducklington*, a fine E. E. ch., with Perp. E. window and a remarkable altarpiece carved in oak, of Italian workmanship. The N. aisle is Dec., with groups of small figures, in panels on the wall. *Yelford* and *Cokethorpe*, adjoining, are both small Perp. ch.; the first has a good rood-screen, and the second a Norm. font.

Cokethorpe Park (Mrs. Strickland, contains the picture of the family of Sir Thomas More, supposed to be by Holbein, and long in the possession of the Lenthalls, first at Besilsleigh, and afterwards at Burford. The scene is a large room, with musical instruments, books, and flowers on a table in the corner, and on the wall the family clock. On the l. is seated Sir John More in his robes as one of the justices of the King's Bench, and by him Sir Thomas in his Chancellor's robes and collar of SS., with a rose pendent before. Behind them is Anne Crisaker, who was married at 15 to John More, Sir Thomas's son. On the other side of Sir Thomas is John More, "who was little better than an idiot," which indeed he looks. In front are the three daughters—Cecilia Heron, sitting with a clasped book in her hand; Margaret Roper, with an open book in her lap; and behind them Elizabeth Dancey, standing. On the rt. 4 other figures are added in the costume of James I., which represent the descendants of Anne Crisaker, and it would seem (from the arms) that the portrait hanging in their background represents her in her old age. The hands of Sir Thomas, described by Erasmus as so clumsy and rustic, are concealed in this as in all the family pieces which Holbein painted for him. This picture much resembles that in the possession of Mr. Winn of Nostall in Yorkshire, which formerly belonged to Mrs. Roper, and which is an undoubted Holbein.

Among other pictures here is a beautiful portrait, painted by herself, of Angelica Kauffmann, struggling between the blandishments of music and painting.

2 m. S. of Yelford is the hamlet of *Shifford*, where King Alfred held one of the first English parliaments. In a manuscript in the Cottonian Library it is thus described :—
"There sate at Shifford many thanes,

many bishops, and many learned men, wise earls and awful knights; there was Earl Elfrick, very learned in the law; and Alfred, England's herdsman, England's darling; he was king of England; he taught them that could hear him how they should live."

14 m. *Bampton-in-the-Bush* (Stat.). (Pop. 1700. *Inn :* Talbot.)

The handsome cruciform *Church of St. Mary* (restored by *Christian*) is surmounted by a tall spire, at the corners of which angels mounted on columns take the place of pinnacles. "The great antiquity of this church is clearly attested by considerable portions of Norm. architecture observable in various parts of the structure. These remains are, however, so intermingled with architecture of subsequent ages, that in this building alone we have examples of almost every period, from the Conquest to the reign of Geo. III."— *Skelton.* Observe the Trans.-Norm. tower arches, the Dec. W. doorway, the Perp. Easter sepulchre, and a Dec. reredos of niches filled with our Saviour and the 12 Apostles, in the N. transept.

Aymer de Valence, earl of Pembroke, best known by his beautiful tomb in Westminster Abbey, was the builder of *Bampton Castle* (1315). The remains stand near the ch., and have been formed into two picturesque farm-houses, called Ham Court and Castle Farm. The most perfect part is an upper room, with a fine groined roof, reached by a spiral staircase, and part of a battlemented wall. Antony Wood describes the castle in the time of the Commonwealth as " a quadrangular building, moated round, with towers at each corner, and a gatehouse of tower-like character on the S. and E. sides." This gatehouse is still tolerably perfect.

Philips the poet, author of 'The Splendid Shilling' and ' Cyder,' was born at Bampton. Dr. Johnson said

of him, that "he bore narrowness
of fortune without discontent, and
tedious and painful maladies without
impatience : beloved by all who
knew him, but not ambitious to be
known."

At *Clanfield*, 2 m. S.W. from
Bampton, is a fine E. E. and Dec.
ch.; the old oak door, on the S.
side, with its original iron-work, is
worth notice.

2 m. S. is *Radcot*, a small hamlet;
its ancient *Bridge* crosses the Thames
into Berks (Rte. 5). Here De Vere,
Earl of Oxford, the minister of Richard
II., was defeated and put to flight by
the partisans of the Duke of Gloucester (Dec. 20, 1387). The bridge
is a rude structure of 3 pointed
arches, of uncertain date. 2 m. W.
is *Kelmscot*, with a small cruciform
E. E. ch., and an Elizabethan manor-
house.

2 m. N. W. from Bampton *Black
Bourton.* The *Church,* Trans.-Norm.
and E. E., has a Perp. stone pulpit. It
also contains the tomb of Sir Arthur
Hopton, ambassador of Charles I. in
Spain (d. 1649). In the Hungerford
chapel are several monuments of that
great family, once owners of the
manor, and the effigy of Eleanor
Hungerford, 1592. Here, at Hare
Hatch, in the house of Mr. Elers, her
grandfather, was born, Jan. 1, 1767,
Maria Edgeworth, the genial novelist.
She spent here her earliest years.
Within a very short distance W. are
the 4 churches of *Langford,* E. E.
and Perp., with Norm. tower—notice
the remarkable flying buttresses on
the N. side, and the sculptures of
the Crucifixion on the S. porch;
Broadwell, cruciform, Trans.-Norm.,
to Perp., restored in 1873, with a
spire almost as fine as that of Bampton; *Alvescott* (Stat.) with good
Perp. tower, and E. E. font, restored
in 1873 ; and *Kencote,* late E. E.,
but with a Norm. S. door, the tympanum of which has a sculpture of a
centaur shooting an arrow down the

throat of a monster. 2 m. N.E. from
Black Bourton is *Norton Brize,*
where the small E. E. ch. contains a
monumental effigy of John Dau-
byngne (1340): "the head and feet
are shown as if from under the stone
slab, on which the helmet and shield
are carved." ('Eccl. and Arch. Top.
Oxfordshire.') Hence to Witney is
4 m. Alvescott is the last station
on line in Oxfordshire.

Lechlade (Stat.) See *Handbook
of Gloucestershire.* The line termi-
nates at *Fairford.*

A day's drive of about 20 m. will
enable the tourist to visit many
places of interest between Witney
and Burford.

3 m. N.W. of Witney is *Minster
Lovell,* so named from a Norman
family, by which it was held at least
as early as 1107, and down to the
year 1487, when Francis, Viscount
Lovell, its owner, disappeared. He
was the son of John, Lord Lovell, a
Lancastrian, but became especially
odious to that party by taking office
under Richard III.; hence he is
mentioned with peculiar scorn in the
rhyme for which William Colling-
bourne, once sheriff of Wiltshire, was
hanged:—

" The Cat, the Rat, and *Lovell* that dog,
Rule all England under the Hog."

"The Hog is Richard himself,
alluding to the white boar which he
employed as one of the supporters of
the royal arms; the Cat is Catesby,
a lawyer, and Chancellor of the Exchequer, who was very naturally
odious, as the fines and forfeitures
were levied by him; the Rat is either
Richard or Robert Ratcliffe, both
thoroughgoing Yorkists; and Lovell
is named 'that dog' as a deserter of
the Red Rose." He was attainted
on the accession of Henry VII., but
escaped to Flanders; in 1487 he
returned, and he fought in the cause
of Lambert Simnel at the battle of
Stoke. His fate has never been
clearly ascertained : some writers

say he was slain, others that he endeavoured to escape, and was seen in the act of trying to swim his horse across the Trent. A tradition held by the inhabitants of Minster Lovell, tells us that he contrived to escape and secrete himself here, where he was sustained in a vault by the devotion of a female servant. This servant suddenly died without revealing the secret, and her lord was starved to death, together with the dog which was the associate of his captivity. "On the 6th of May, 1728, the present Duke of Rutland related in my hearing, that about 20 years then before, v.z., in 1708, upon occasion of new laying a chimney at Minster Lovell, there was discovered a large vault under ground, in which was the entire skeleton of a man as having been sitting at a table, which was b. fore him, with a book, paper, pen, &c. In another part of the room lay a cap, all much mouldered and decayed, which the family and others judged to be the Lord Lovell, whose exit has hitherto been so uncertain." Such is a memorandum, dated Aug. 7, 1737, made by William Cowper, Clerk of Parliament, the kinsman of the poet. The priory, founded by Maud Lovell in the reign of John, was a cell to the Norman abbey of Ivry, and was, like other alien priories, dissolved by Henry V. Shortly after (c. 1430) William, Lord Lovell (grandfather of the viscount), built the present *Church* and *Manor-house*. The latter, which is remarkable as being a purely domestic building, without a trace of the military aspect, is in so ruinous a state that, though the remains are considerable, it is not easy to determine the original destination of the several rooms. "Mainly for convenience of farming purposes, a road has been cut through the middle. and the stones scattered and used for repairing walls."—*J. P.*

The *Church*, dedicated to St. Kenelm, is a very fine specimen of Perp.

architecture, and its situation in a grove beside the Windrush (here crossed by a small 15th-cent. bridge) is most picturesque. "Its ground plan is very remarkable, the central tower being considerably smaller than the space left at the intersection of the cross, and the chancel narrower than the nave. The tower is mainly supported on four detached piers, with the angles chamfered off, so as to allow to the congregation, as much as possible, a view of the high altar. The arrangement resolves itself into four large hagioscopes or squints, and the appearance of the interior is singularly elegant." —*J. H. P.* The tomb of the founder, which stands in the N. transept, is much mutilated.

Minster Lovell is usually said to be the scene of Clara Reeve's story of the 'Old English Baron'; and an incident similar to that related in the novel did occur in the case of a Chetwynd, great-grandson of the last of the Lovells. It was also the scene of one of Feargus O'Connor's attempts to carry out his land scheme. Some rows of detached cottages. of uninviting aspect, were erected on an estate of nearly 300 acres, but the project was an entire failure.

17 m. from Oxford, and 5 from Witney, is *Asthall*, with a small E. E. and Dec. ch.; the N. porch has a very elegant gable cross, figured in the 'Glossary of Architecture.' A sepulchral slab, of early date, has on it a female figure, said to be that of Alice Corbett, one of the mistresses of Henry I. "In the churchyard is an ancient altar tomb, with quatrefoils and shields; it is not common to meet so good an ancient tomb out of doors."—*Rickman*. *Asthall House*, a manor of the Fettyplaces, and afterwards the residence of Sir W. Jones, Justice of the King's Bench, temp. Car. I., is now a farmhouse.

1 m. N. is *Swinbrook*, which belonged to the Fettyplaces. Rickman's description of the little ch. may be quoted: "The ch. of St. Mary has a curious small tower, open, with an arch to the W., and having a window and door in the W. wall of the ch. under this arch. There are some Norm. piers and pointed arches, and some curious windows of later date: the E. window is Perp., a good one of 5 lights [with painted glass]. There are some remains of a rood-loft and good wood screens. In this ch. are many monumental figures lying on shelves covering one side of the chancel; they seem to be subsequent to the year 1600." In the chancel are two ponderous monuments, in each of which three Fettyplaces "lie on shelves," as Rickman expresses it. The figures are all in armour, and the dates range from 1504 to 1672. There are also *Brasses* of the Fettyplaces, one dated 1510, and one for John Croston, esq., and his three wives (1470). Bp. Curwen of Oxford is buried in the ch. He gained the favour of Henry VIII. by preaching in favour of his divorce, and was made dean of Hereford in 1541. In 1555 he was appointed abp. of Dublin, and chancellor of Ireland. Becoming infirm, he resigned his offices in 1567, and was translated to Oxford, but he died the year after.

3 m. beyond Asthall and 7 m. W. from Witney is *Burford* (*Inns:* Bird in the Hand, Bird's Nest), a town once famous for its saddlery. It is mentioned by William of Malmesbury as the place where a synod was held in 705, when Aldhelm the abbot, a kinsman of King Ina of Wessex, was commissioned to write a book on the Roman observance of Easter,—a noble and royal author unknown to Walpole. Here, also, in 752, "Cuthred of the West Saxons, then tributary to the Mercians, not being able to endure any longer the cruelty and base exactions of King Ethelbald, met him in the open field with an army, and beat him, taking his standard, which was a portraiture of a golden dragon." — *Camden.* The field of battle is still called *Battle Edge*, and the people of Burford used annually to parade the streets with an artificial dragon on Midsummer-eve in memory of the event. The town was given to the Clares at the Conquest, and was afterwards possessed by Hugh Despencer, whose descendants held it until it passed to the Crown on the attainder of his grand-nephew, the Earl of Gloucester, in 1400. It is irregularly built, but contains many ancient domestic edifices, the doors of which, though plain, are of very good composition, and there are also some fine wood gables with panelling and hanging tracery. The bridge over the Windrush is old and inconvenient.

So close to the river as frequently to suffer from the floods in former days is the large *Church*, dedicated to St. John the Baptist. It has a Norm. central tower and various portions of Norm. and E. E. work adjacent, but the largest part of the ch. is Perp., of various dates, and evidently partial rebuilding, a fine Norm. door being preserved at the W. end. There are several large chapels, and a remarkably rich S. porch, Late Perp., with very beautiful fan-tracery, groining, and excellent details. The chancel and tower were restored in 1877.

There are several fine *monuments* —the principal is to Sir Lawrence Tanfelde, Chief Baron of the Exchequer, 1625, whose only daughter married Lord Falkland. In the N. aisle is the monument of Edmond Harman, his wife, 9 sons, and 7 daughters, 1569. The S.E. aisle is called Bartholomew's, and the S.W. Silvestre's, from the tombs of those families. In the S. transept is a tomb of Purbeck marble, the inscription for which is to be found on the exterior of a neighbouring window: —"Orate pro animabus patris et matris Johannis Leggare de Borford, per quem ista fenestra decoratur." The parvise over the S. porch is used as a muniment-room, and contains some ancient records. There are several piscinæ and the remains of minor altars with the squints. The vestry, which has a fine groined ceiling and was formerly a chapel, has the altar-stone still remaining. In the so-called Burghers' aisle, the place formerly occupied by an altar is perceptible, and there is a provision in the will of John Spicer (d. 1437) ordering that lights should always be kept burning there. His *brass* remains, in an imperfect state, and furnishes a very early example of the use of English for the inscription. From it we learn that he also repaired the "rood-soler." and set up a gable window. He and his wife are represented as kneeling to the Virgin, and they hold scrolls thus inscribed :—

" Mary moder mayde cler, haue m'cy on me
    Joñ Spicer."
" And on me Alys his wyff, lady for thi joyes
    fyve."

"In the nave is a stone chapel used as a seat, and another of wood, both good compositions. There is an ancient wooden pulpit, and some other good woodwork; there are also some small portions of very good ancient stained glass. The roof of the nave has been remarkably rich woodwork, but is now much mutilated and altered. The upper part of the Norm. tower has inside some arches forming a gallery round it. The spire is of Perp. date. There is a fine circular Dec. font, with niches and statues, and lined with lead; under part of the ch. is a crypt, used as a bone-house. The plan of this ch. is very irregular, but it has so many singularities and beautiful portions that it deserves minute examination." — *Rickman.* It has been restored by *Street.*

In May, 1649, the Levellers, afte holding Banbury for some days marched southward, endeavouring reach Oxford by passing over Ne Bridge. Here they were met, an driven back into Burford, whe they defended themselves for a while against Cromwell, but were almost all either killed or taken. Many of the latter were confined in the ch., a memorial of which may probably be seen in the words "Anthonye Sedley, 1649, prisner," rudely carved on the font.

The inhabitants of Burford had formerly the right of hunting for one day in the year in the royal forest of Wychwood, and till quite lately "the churchwardens, accompanied by many of the inhabitants, used to go in a kind of procession to Cape's Lodge plain, within the borders of the forest, where they chose a *lord* and *lady*, who were generally a boy and girl of Burford. These titular personages formally demanded of one or more of the keepers of the forest (who always attended for the purpose) a brace of the best bucks and a fawn, 'without fee or reward, with their horns and hoofs,' for the use of the town of Burford, to be delivered on due notice. About the first week in August the bucks were sent for, and a venison feast was provided in the town-hall for some hundreds of persons."—*Brewer.* The bucks are still claimed and consumed at a public dinner.

To "take a Burford bait" is a proverbial expression for making a greedy meal.

Dr. Heylin, and Beechey the painter, were natives of Burford, and Lord Rochester and Lord Liverpool were educated in its grammar school. A short distance S. W. of the town are St. Kitt's quarries, which yield a valuable build ng-stone. It was employed by Wren in his repairs of Westminster Abbey.

The *Priory* (Miss Youde) was granted to the Harmans at the

Dissolution, and at the time of the Civil War was the property of Lord Falkland. Being seized by the Long Parliament, it was by them granted to their Speaker, William Lenthall, and he died here, probably in the latter part of the year 1662. His will has been published by Mr. J. G. Nichols, who thinks that he "has probably received hard measure from historical writers. Two things seem established by his will: the one, that the constant assertion that he left a prodigious fortune was in all probability untrue; the other, that he was a man of an affectionate nature, and full of kindly, family feeling." He is also seen to have been grateful to persons who were willing to assist him in his "great and sore troubles" at the Restoration, naming particularly Col. W. Legg and the Earl of Norwich. The former, he says, did not perform certain conditions for which he had bound himself to pay him 200*l.*, half of which he had received, but as he, at the time of making his will (July 28, 1662), "conceived himself free from the dangers which his promise was to discharge," Legg was to have the remainder. The Priory is a very picturesque building, but is now little better than a ruin. "The front is good, and a chapel (built by the Speaker), connected by 3 arches which let the garden appear through, has a pretty effect." The famous *Holbein* of Sir Thomas More and his family, now at Cokethorpe (*ante*), was formerly here. After the Restoration the Speaker is said to have made his peace with the Government by sending his Vandykes to Lord Clarendon at Cornbury, but the above extract from his will shows that he did not trust to this alone.

1 m. E. of Burford is *Widford*, the ch. of which is worth notice. "It has a small bell-niche, and a nave and chancel; the W. door and font are Norm., the nave and chancel mostly Dec., the side windows of one

light, and E. window with 3 lights. Part of the nave, at the W. end, is of later date; the pulpit is ancient, with good wood panelling."—*Rickman*. It was closed for divine service in 1860. *Fulbrook* 2 m. N., has a Dec. ch. with Perp. tower. In the ch.-yard is a Perp. altar-tomb, and a very fine yew-tree.

ROUTE 26.

OXFORD TO CHIPPING NORTON.

Oxford, Worcester, and Wolverhampton Line, G. W. R. 25½ m.

Passing Yarnton Junction (Rte. 25) we arrive at (7¾ m.) *Handborough Stat.* The line on E. forms a junction with the London and N. W. R. near Islip. The fine Perp. *Church* has a good spire, pulpit, and part of a roodloft of the 15th centy., which retains some of its original gilding and colouring, and is enriched with carved foliage. The inner doorway is Norm., and has a sculpture of St. Peter, with a key in his hand, seated between a lion and a lamb. There is a brass to the memory of Alexander Belsyre, first President of St John's College (deprived by Elizabeth in 1559, died 1567) with a Latin inscription, accompanied by its translation :—

" That thou art now, the same was I;
And thou likewise shall suer dye;
Live so that when thou hence dost wend
Thou mayest have blysse that hath no end."

The *Brass*, which represents the deceased recumbent in his shroud, was placed by his nephew, Thomas Nele, who has himself a very similar one at Cassington (Rte. 25). This is the only brass that now remains of several mentioned by Wood. In the chancel is painted an inscription in Latin in honour of " Charles, most holy King and Martyr."

For Woodstock and Blenheim, 3 m. from Handborough Junction, see Exc. (*l*) from Oxford.

10 m. On r. *Coombe*, a good Perp. ch., the tower covered with ivy. There is a very handsome stone pulpit, a sanctus bell-turret. and an elegant cross on the E. gable of the chancel. The rectory-house is battlemented, and has bay windows with foliated heads.

11 m. l m. N. is *Stonesfield*, where a fine Roman pavement was found in 1711, measuring 35 ft. by 60, and representing Apollo bestriding a dragon, according to Hearne, or Bacchus with his panther, according to others. " No remains of this are at present to be found, unless the Roman villa in the adjoining parish of Northleigh is that intended." ('Arch. Guide, Oxford.') The village, it may be remarked, stands near the Akeman Street. The ch., restored in 1876, is E. E. and Dec., the upper part of the tower good Perp. The N. aisle of the chancel is parted off, and is used as a school-room. The village, which stands in a very bleak situation, consists mainly of a succession of fossil-shops, containing specimens obtained in the neighbourhood by the quarrymen. The sandstone is here intersected by

a thin stratum of limestone, from which, when quarried, it becomes separated by the frost.

The accumulation of organic remains in this thin slaty limestone is one of the most remarkable phenomena regarding the distribution of the fossils in the oolitic rocks.

" The fissile rock, which occurs here at the base of the Bath oolite, yields, besides zoophytes, shells, crustacea, and fishes characteristic of the oolite sea, plants, insects, reptiles, and mammalia, the spoils of some contemporary land. They were not drifted from *distant* land, by rivers bringing much and various sediment, clay, sand, and gravel in alternate layers, and mixing fresh-water shells with marine exuviæ. On the contrary, only sea-water was here, with zoantharia, echinodermata, crabs, and lobsters. mollusca of every grade —including nautili, belemnites, and ammonites—and sharks' teeth and reptilian bones in considerable quantity.

" The water was not greatly agitated; there are no pebble-beds; there is scarcely a trace of oblique lamination: the bivalve-shells were often buried with the ligaments attached;. belemnites are perfect to the point, and nautili appear in little shoals, having the attitude of flotation. Circumstances like these might occur in a shallow sea-lake, penetrated at intervals by moderate swells or gentle tides from the sea, but not exposed to oceanic storms or violent littoral fluctuation. Its constant inhabitants and periodical visitants compose a large population. Starry Zoantharia opened their coloured arms to the light ; sea-urchins threatened with their long spines, and drank in the water with their trumpet-like suckers ; Terebratulæ, dragging their anchors, lost their place in the society of the corals, and became mixed with scallops and oysters, and other rough monomyarian races. Sometimes, indeed, they were received among Trigoniæ and Pholadomyæ, those aristocrats of the oolite, or admitted to the closer coteries of the beautiful Nerinææ, Turritellæ, and Neritæ, whose coloured ornaments remain to our day. To match this variety of food we have the military orders, the Ammonite, carnivorous Belemnite. and Nautilus, allied to modern cuttles, and many predaceous shark-like fishes. Nor were turtles wanting to the feast, or giant reptiles to enjoy it—Teleosaurs, Cetiosaurs, Steneosaurs, and Megalosaurs. Some of these monsters lived in the water; others were allured from the land, and waded through the mud, as the Megalosaur; or snatched their prey from the small waves, as the Pterodactyl.

"On these waves, from time to time, floated fragments of bordering plants, whether swept down by inundations, or driven by the wind;—leaves of ferns, of zamioid plants, and evergreen coniferous bushes like cypress. The fruits of pines and cypress, and solitary nuts of other trees, are mixed with coleopterous beetles of dry land, and neuropterous insects, with wings expanded, as if in flight from their native reedy streams and pools.

"And to complete this long series of associated life, *land mammalia,* of microscopic dimensions, probably for the most part insectivorous, of *three genera,* have left us their *lower jaws.* Probably no spot in the world has yielded to the palæontologist such a harvest of suggestive phenomena. In her Museum at Stonesfield Nature has preserved specimens of her 'Mesozoic' style, under almost every aspect of adaptation, from the humblest stationary zoophyte to the most agile of quadrupeds, under circumstances which leave no doubt of their meaning.

"There has never yet been taken a complete census of the Stonesfield fossils; nor is the task an easy one, —there being nowhere a complete

[*Berks, &c.*]

collection. For many years they have been gathered by inconstant admirers, only to be dispersed; transferred by Oxford men to their country residences, to be buried under sermons, or thrown away by their children. The cabinets of the Bucklandian Museum contain many fine specimens, but not a complete series."—*Professor Phillips* in the 'Oxford Essays.' These cabinets (now part of the New Museum at Oxford) are daily receiving additions from the well-directed labours of practical geologists, and the reproach is likely to be soon wiped off. It may also be remarked that "Many of the plants at Stonesfield are noticed by Sternberg, Brongniart, and Hutton; Sowerby has figured many of the shells; the work of Agassiz may be consulted for the fishes; Dr. Buckland s 'Bridgewater Treatise,' Professor Owen's 'Report,' 1841, and other works of the same author, for the reptiles and mammalian remains."—*Penny Cyclopædia.*

1 m. S. of the line is *North Leigh,* where is an interesting *Church,* the fragment of a larger one. The low square tower has long and short work, though concealed by roughcast, and there is a good Norm. S. door, with a Perp. arch within. The Dec. chancel is spoiled by a Grecian altar-screen, painted and gilt. There are two chapels on the N. side. The E. one is very rich Late Perp., and under the arch between it and the chancel is the fine tomb of one of the Wilcotes and his wife. The other chapel is comparatively modern, in the Italian style, and has monuments of the Perrott family. A Roman pavement was discovered here in 1813. 1 m. N.W. is *Wilcote,* a small Dec. ch., with a blocked-up Norm. door. The manor formerly belonged to the Wilcotes, and afterwards to Sir William Pope, created a baronet by James I. A later holder was John Cary, the Friend.

U

13¾ m. *Charlbury* (Stat.). The town (*Inn*: Bell) once belonged to the abbey of Eynsham. The ch., restored in 1874, is supposed to have been erected in the time of Edward the Confessor; it is dedicated to St. Mary, and has some Dec. windows, with the bell-flower in the tracery; the fine and ·lofty tower is E. E., with Perp. belfry and battlements. A short distance E. of the town is *Lee Place,* (W. Gilbert Childs Esq.), a mansion built in 1640 by a branch of the Lees of Ditchley. The ceiling of the great drawing-room was designed by Gibbons.

W. of the line, and bounded by the river Evenlode, is the seat of Lord Churchill, now called indifferently *Blandford* or *Wychwood Park.* The house was built by one of the Danbys, on the site of one, called *Cornbury Hall,* where Dudley, Earl of Leicester, died in 1588 of poison, administered, it is said, by his second wife, Lettice Knollys,— "whom he suspected of love for Christopher Blount, a gentleman of his household, and intended to carry off to Kenilworth, and leave her there till her death by natural or violent meanes. But the Countess having suspicion on some secret intelligence of this treachery against her, provided artificiall meanes to prevent the erle, which was by a cordiall, which she had no fit opportunity to offer him, till he came to Cornbury Hall in Oxfordshire; wheare the erle, after his gluttonous manner, surfeting himself with much eating and drinking, fell so ill that he was forced to stay theare. Then the deadly cordiall was propounded unto him by the. Countess."—MS. quoted in *Athenæ Oxonienses,* vol. ii. pp. 75, 76.

Lord Clarendon bought the house at the Restoration, and it gave a second title to his family. Evelyn visited it in 1664, and he speaks of the house as "built in the middle of a sweete parke, walled with a dr y

wall. The house is of excellent freestone, abounding in that part, a stone that is fine, but never sweats or casts any damp; 'tis of ample dimensions, has goodly cellars, the paving of the hall admirable for its close laying. We design'd an handsom chapell that was yet wanting, as Mr. May had the stables, which indeed are very faire, having set out the walks in the park and gardens. The lodge is a pretty solitude, and the ponds very convenient; the parke well stored."

The country to the S. still bears the name of *Wychwood Forest,* but is being rapidly inclosed. What woods and coppices remain afford a variety of beautiful wild flowers, among which may be mentioned *Alchemilla vulgaris,* Lady's mantle; *Aquilegia vulgaris,* columbine; *Astragalus glycyphyllos,* wild liquorice; *Avena elatior,* tall oat-grass; *Avena pubescens,* rough oat-grass; *Carduus Acaulis,* dwarf thistle; *Convallaria maialis,* lily of the valley; *Spiræa Fillipendula,* dropwort; *Thlaspi arvense,* field penny-cress; *Daphne Mezereum,* mezereon; *Anemone Pulsatilla,* pasque flower; *Lathræa squamaria,* toothwort; *Cynoglossum sylvaticum,* green hound's-tongue; *Helleborus fœtidus,* stinking hellebore; *Helleborus viridis,* green hellebore; *Atropa Belladonna,* deadly nightshade; *Neottia Nidus-avis,* bird's-nest orchis; *Botrychium Lunaria,* moonwort, and *Polypodium calcareum,* limestone polypody.

The name *Wychwood* is said by Dr. Silver to be derived from the Wiccii, who inhabited this spot. The Forest was enlarged and enclosed with a fence by King John, and was a favourite hunting-ground with many English kings. A hunting lodge built by him at *Langley,* a hamlet on the border of the chase, seems to have been occupied even as late as the time of James I., as an entry of the burial of "a French boy from Langley, the court being there," occurs in the parish register of Shipton under Wychwood, with the date 1614. In these woods, according to local writers, Elizabeth Woodville, widow of Sir John Grey, intercepted Edward IV, while hunting, and flinging herself at his feet, entreated him to restore the confiscated inheritance of her children; when he was so captivated by her beauty that he broke off his intended match with Bona of Savoy, and made her his queen. Other historians think that it was in Whittlebury, not Wychwood Forest, that the meeting took place.

17½ m. *Ascott* (Stat.). Ascott-under-Wychwood has a *Church* with some Norm. features, but principally E. E. and Dec. The Trans.-Norm. tower has a Perp. belfry added; the original windows have Perp. labels.

18¼ m. *Shipton* (Stat.). This is the nearest stat. for Burford 4 m. N. N. E. (Rte. 25). (*Inn:* Crown.) Shipton - under - Wychwood belonged to the Laceys of Pudlicote. The large and fine *Church* (restored by *Street*) is mainly E. E., but the chancel is Perp. with an E. window (Jacobean), "curious but ugly." The tower and spire are fine E. E. work. There are several Dec. recesses for tombs, now destroyed; but a good *Brass* remains (Elizabeth Horne, 1548), with a recumbent figure in a shroud. A stained glass E. window was erected in 1874. Adjoining the ch.-yard, are some remains of Perp. buildings, of ecclesiastical character. *Shipton Court* (Sir M. G. Crofton) is a fine Elizabethan house.

21½ m. *Chipping Norton Junction* (Stat.). Here the rly. for Worcester gives off two branches: (1.) W. to Stow-on-the-Wold (see *Handbook for Gloucestershire*); (2.) N.E. to Chipping Norton.

2 m. S. is *Bruern Abbey*, a Cistercian monastery, founded 1137. The remains were burnt within the last century. The old fish-ponds still remain.

2 m. S.W. is *Fifield*, with a fine E. E. ch. The nave was rebuilt in 1840, but 2 Dec. windows were preserved. The E. window is Dec., and the tower octangular, with a lofty spire. The ch. of *Idbury*, 1 m. N., has a very rich Norm. door, and fine Dec. E. windows to both the chancel and N. aisle "An elegant bell-cot, with pinnacles, contains the old sanctus-bell, which is still used to announce the arrival of the clergyman."—*J. H. P.*

23½ m. On E. is *Sarsden*, with some remains of an ancient manor house, and a large circular earth-work. The ch. is modern. 2 m. E. is *Chadlington*, once an important place, but now only remarkable for the chimney-like tower of its E. E. and Dec. ch.

24¼ m. On E. is *Churchill*, a village remarkable as the birthplace of Warren Hastings in 1732, a fact proved by the parish register, though Daylesford, a parish in Worcestershire, is commonly named as such. That manor was held by the Hastings family for some centuries, and his grandfather had been rector there; but he fell into poverty, and his celebrated grandchild was brought up as a charity-boy in Churchill school. At the foot of the hill on which the village stands runs a brook which falls into the Evenlode and thence into the Thames. "To lie beside the margin of that stream," he wrote in later years, "was one of my favourite recreations; and there one bright summer's day, when I was scarce 7 years old, I well remember that I first formed the determination to repurchase Daylesford. I was then dependent upon those whose condition scarcely raised them above the pressure of absolute want; yet, somehow or other, the child's dream, as it did not appear unreasonable at the moment, so, in after years, never faded away."— *Fragment of an Autobiog. Memoir*

The ch. has a tower, which is a good imitation of the Magdalen tower at Oxford, on a reduced scale.

2 m. W. is *Kingham*, a Dec. ch. with Perp. tower. In the outer wall of the chancel, N., is a Dec. tomb with canopy, which is believed to be an instance of burial "neither in nor out of the ch." occasionally resorted to, and to which some wild legend is usually attached, as in the case of "Piers Shonk" at Furneaux Pelham in Herts. (See *Handbook for Herts.*)

25½ m. *Chipping Norton* (Stat.). The town (*Inn* : White Hart), which occupies a bleak eminence considerably above the Stat., consists chiefly of one broad street of stone houses on the ridge of the hill. (Pop. 4167.) It belonged to the Fitzalans, and some small remains of the castle built by them in the reign of Stephen, still exist. From them it passed to the Veres, and it was afterwards a possession of Richard Duke of Gloucester. The *Church* (rest. 1878), a large and fine building, has a Dec. chancel, but is mainly Perp. It is remarkable for having 2 N. aisles, and the S. aisle has a beautiful six-sided groined porch. There are altar-tombs of the families of Rickardes and Crofts, also some incised slabs. At the back of the modern pulpit is part of an old shrine and a 14th-centy. stone altar in a side chapel now used as the vestry. The 13th-centy. Town-hall has given place to a modern edifice, but some good carved stone-work from an adjoining building (believed to have been a religious house) has been preserved, and may be seen at the Reading-room. Chipping Norton common, a spot commanding extensive views, has been laid out as a recreation ground, near which notice the extensive factories for tweed cloths of the Messrs. Bliss.

N. of the town is the hamlet of *Over Norton*, the ch. of which has long been destroyed. About 2 m N. are the two villages of *Great* and *Little Rollright*, between which are the great antiquarian objects of the county, the *Rollright Stones*. Though much smaller than the stones at Avebury or Stonehenge, they are classed with them by Bede, and their origin is equally uncertain. They originally formed a circle 35 yds. in diameter, the centre of which is now occupied by a clump of firs, and are supposed to have been at least 60 in number, but many are now buried beneath the turf, and few rise more than 4 ft from the ground, except one at the N. point, which is 7 ft. 4 in. high. N.E. of the circle, at a distance o 84 yds. (and across the county boun dary in Warwickshire), is a weird looking stone of strange shape, abou 8 ft. high, known as the King Stone From the spot where it stands there is an extensive view over all the long ranges of neighbouring hills except towards Long Compton, whicl is hidden by an abrupt rise of the ground, the result of magic, say the tradition. The story told in the neighbourhood is, that a certain king of that part of the country desired to rule over all England and was assured that he would succeed if he once got sight of Long Compton. He had gathered an army, and was exclaiming on his march,

"If Long Compton I can see,
King of England shall I be,"

when Mother Shipton caused the ground to rise as it now appears. When the ambitious monarch arrived, the witch cried,

"Move no more! stand fast, Stone!
King of England, thou shalt be none!"

and he and his men were turned into stone on the instant. Five large stones in a field about ½ m. to the S.E. (which are supposed by Dr Stukely to have formed a kistvaen) were 5 knights attendant on his majesty, who had retired to a distance to conspire against him, and hence are still called "the Whispering Knights;" the rest were the common soldiers.   Dr. Plot, in his *Nat. Hist. Oxfordshire*, commenting on Camden's account, who makes the stones the memorial of a defeat of the Saxons under Edward the Elder at Hook Norton (*post*), inclines to the opinion that they are the remains of a place for the election of a king, and that some of the early Danish invaders may have been inaugurated there.

The churches of the two villages deserve a passing glance. That of Great Rollright has a fine Norm. S. door, and rich Dec. windows; the other is chiefly remarkable for its "ivy-mantled tower," which, though only built in 1617, has an appearance of much greater age.

2 m. N.W. of Great Rollright is *Hook Norton*, a very picturesque village, with a large Norm. ch., but with later windows inserted.   There is a Norm. font, with sculptures, and a very perfect rood loft (*J. H. P.*). The manor belonged to Ela, Countess of Salisbury, and was held by the tenure of "carving before the king, and to have the knife with which she carved."   Camden says that the inhabitants of this place were formerly such clowns, that " to be born at Hook Norton became a proverb to denote rudeness and ill-breeding." The people of the neighbouring villages now commonly call it "Hog's Norton, where the pigs play upon organs," alluding, it is said, to a native who aspired to be a musician.

1 m. E. is *Wigginton*, where the E. E. ch. has a very singular tomb, engraved by Skelton, built into the outer wall on the S. side (*J. H. P.*). The remains of a Roman villa were discovered here in 1824.

1 m. S. of Little Rollright is *Salford*, where some singular Norm.

sculptures are to be seen over the N. and S. doors; a cross within a circle, with strangely-formed animals on each side.

2 m. W. is *Chastleton*, with a Trans.-Norm. and E. E. ch.: the tower is singularly placed over the S. porch.   There are *Brasses* of the 16th and 17th cents., and many ancient tiles with heraldic devices. *Chastleton House* (Miss Whitmore Jones), near the ch., is a Jacobean house, in good preservation.   The estate is one of those that Catesby sold, to furnish means for carrying on the Gunpowder Plot, and it was bought by Walter Jones, a lawyer, who built the mansion.   In the library there is a Bible given to Bishop Juxon by Charles I. just before his execution.

2 m. beyond is the *Four Shire Stone*, 9 ft. high, at which meet the 4 shires of Oxford, Gloucester, Worcester, and Warwick, the names of which are cut on the 4 sides of the pillar.   This stone is said to stand on the spot where a battle was fought between the English and the Danes, in which the latter, under Canute, were defeated by Edmund Ironside.

ROUTE 27.

OXFORD TO CHIPPING NORTON.

By Road.   18 m.

The country between Oxford and

Woodstock has been already described—Exc. (l.) from Oxford.

At 11 m. from Oxford we reach *Glympton*, where the greater part of the ch. is modern, but some Trans. Norm. arches and a late Perp. tower remain. Here is a *Brass* for Thos. Tesdale (d. 1610), a great benefactor to Pembroke College, and a monument to his wife Maude (d. 1616), which retains some of the old painting and gilding. She is said in her epitaph to have " lovingly anointed Christ Jesus in his poor members at Glympton, Charlbury," &c

12 m. 1 m. N. is *Nether Kiddington*, the subject of Thomas Warton's History, an excellent topographical work. The *Church*, mostly Dec., has once been larger, as a Norm. chancel arch filled up with a Perp. window now forms the E. end. The present chancel arch is Dec., there is a Dec. piscina and font, both of good character, and a brass to Walter Goodere, a former rector, 1513. The arms on this brass have been almost destroyed, but the "cujus anime" still remains. " This ch." says Warton, " in common with most other parish chs., retains marks of the sordid devotion of its possessors under the dominion of Cromwell. But many of these disgraces to divine worship which Calvinism had left behind, have been lately (c. 1780) removed by a generous benefactor, with the addition of new improvements and ornaments. When a country ch. has been beautified, to use the technical phrase on this occasion, it is customary for the grateful topographer minutely to display the judicious application of some late pious legacy, and to dwell with singular satisfaction on the modern decorations of the communion table, consisting of semicircular groups of bloated cherubs. tawdry festoons, gingerbread pilasters, flaming urns, and a newly-gilded decalogue, flanked by a magnificent Moses and Aaron, in scarlet and purple, the work of some capital artist, who unites the callings of painter, plumber, and glazier in the next dirty market town. I do not regret, that the present edifice, which yet has not been without its friends, can toast none of these embellishments." In that division of the parish styled Over Kiddington, is the ruin of an old parochial cross, and a single farmhouse, called *Asterley*, about ⅛ m. S.W., is the sole representative of a parish of that name, which was incorporated with Kiddington in 1466. An adjoining field, called Chapel brake, is presumed to mark the site of the ch., as fragments of carved stone have been often dug up. The ground all about is full of inequalities caused by old foundations.

1 m. S. is *Ditchley* (Viscount Dillon), a place rendered famous by its introduction in Sir Walter Scott's novel of 'Woodstock.' The house, called by Evelyn " a low timber house with a pretty bowling-greene," is now a large stone edifice with 2 statues of Fame on the top, and is considered a masterpiece of its architect, *Gibbs*. The rooms are not large, but contain some old tapestry and fine pictures; among them, James II. as Duke of York, with Anne Hyde and the Princesses Mary and Anne, *Sir Peter Lely* ; Sir Fras. Drake, in a shirt embroidered with globes (which were his arms); Prince Henry in robes of the Bath ; Captain Lee, distinguished in the Irish wars under the Earl of Essex, 1599, full-length and almost naked ; Charles II.; the Duchess of Cleveland ; Catherine of Braganza; Mary of Modena. 2 portraits of Sir Henry Lee—one with his dog Bevis, the other at the age of 86, when the condescension of a visit from James I. at his retirement of Lee's Rest had induced him to go again to Court. The character of this Sir Henry is given by Scott to his grandson, who lived temp. Charles I. The story of

Bevis is that " a servant had formed a design to rob the house and to murder his master. But, on the night when this project was intended to be put into execution, the dog, though no favourite, nor indeed ever before taken notice of by his master, accompanied him upstairs, crept under the bed, and could not be driven away by the attendant, when at length Sir Henry ordered him to be left; in the dead of night the treacherous servant, entering the room to execute his design, was instantly seized by the dog, and, on being secured, confessed his intention."

A casket preserved at Ditchley was given to Lady Charlotte Fitzroy by her father, King Charles II. It contains a number of letters from Charles II., James II. (who addresses her as "my dear niece"), and from his brother Chevalier, and Clementina Sobieski, who corresponded with "Madame Dillon" (*née* Sheldon), wife of General Dillon, who commanded "Dillon's regiment" at the battle of Fontenoy, where one of his brothers was killed. The colours used there are now at Ditchley in the library.

2 m. W. is *Spilsbury*, which was one of the few manors of the widow of Warwick the King-maker restored to her by Henry VII. and which she left to her grandson, the unhappy earl who was beheaded in 1497. The ch., a small cruciform building, with a large Norm. tower, contains the tombs of Sir Henry Lee, of Ditchley, d. 1631, and of George Henry Lee, his descendant, 3rd Earl of Lichfield, and his Countess—" the most gallant bridegroom, and the most beautiful bride of the court of Charles II." Here also are buried the first Lord Wilmot, and his son, the profligate and witty Earl of Rochester.

A pretty memorial fountain in the village was erected to the Hon. Constantine Dillon.

14 m. 1 m. N. is *Enstone*, so called

from the Enta-stan, or Giant's Stone, a large upright stone 8 ft. high, formerly forming part of a cromlech, of which the other stones still remain near it. It is commonly known in the neighbourhood as the Hoar Stone. Similar stones have given names to other places in the neighbourhood, as at Lidstone, Taston, and Broadstone. The ch., mainly Perp., has a fine Norm. doorway, and an original solid altar at the E. end of the S. aisle; " the slab is gone, but the reredos screen is in a tolerably perfect state, filling up the space between the altar and the window over it." (' Gloss. of Arch.,' where it is figured). It is dedicated to St. Kenelm, a young son of Kenulphus, King of Mercia, murdered at the instigation of his aunt Quendreda, and secretly buried in a wood, and whose burial place, according to the legend, was made known by a white dove dropping a paper containing the information on the high altar of St. Peter's at Rome. But being written in Saxon, in letters of gold, it remained unintelligible till an angel appeared and translated it into good ecclesiastical Latin—

" In Clene sub spina jacet in convalle bovina, Vertice privatus, Kenelmus fraude necatus."

By an ancient custom christenings and weddings were always performed here in the porch, and women were churched there. A detailed history of Enstone was published by its vicar, the Rev. J. Jordan, in 1857.

At *Neat Enstone*, ¼ m. S., were some famous waterworks, established by Thomas Bushell, secretary to Lord Bacon, which were visited with much pomp by Charles I. and Henrietta Maria, when they were resident in the neighbourhood in 1636. Evelyn, in 1664, says, " I went to see the famous wells, artificial and natural grotto, and fountains called *Bushell's Wells*. It is an extraordinary solitude. There be here two mummies and a grotto, where he lay in a hammock like an Indian."

2 m. N. is Great Tew (M. P. W. Bolton, Esq.), once the seat of Lucius Cary, "the blameless Lord Falkland." His house no longer exists, and the present mansion is quite modern, but an old gateway of his time remains, and in the church Lord Falkland is buried, not only without a monument, but, owing to the haste with which his body, transferred from the fatal fight of Newbury, was interred, and the few witnesses, even the place of his grave is unknown. The entry of his burial remains in the parish register.

"He was," says Clarendon, "a person of such prodigious parts of learning and knowledge, of that inimitable sweetness and delight in conversation, of so flowing and obliging a humanity and goodness to mankind, and of that primitive simplicity and integrity of life, that, if there were no other brand upon this odious and accursed civil war than that single loss, it must be most infamous and execrable to all posterity." He fell, aged 34, "having so much despatched the true business of life that the oldest rarely attain to that immense knowledge, and the youngest enters not into the world with more innocency." (Book vii.)

"His house being within little more than 10 m. of Oxford, he contracted familiarity and friendship with the most polite and accurate men of that university (Drs. Sheldon, Morley, Hammond, Mr. Chillingworth, &c.), who found such an immenseness of wit and such a solidity of judgment in him, so infinite a fancy bound in by a most logical ratiocination, such a vast knowledge that he was not ignorant in anything, yet such an excessive humility as if he had known nothing, that they frequently resorted and dwelt with him, as in a college situated in a purer air; so

that his house was a university in a less volume, whither they came not so much for repose as for study, and to examine and refine those grosser propositions which laziness and consent made current in vulgar conversation."— Clarendon.

Great Tew Church has a very late Norm. doorway, and an E. E. porch; the nave is Dec. and Perp. "The ch. is not a large one, but in composition and execution it is superior to many about it."— Rickman. There is a magnificent brass to Sir J. Wilcotes and his wife, 1410, and another of William Bosby and his wife Agnes, 1513. Near the altar is a tablet to a daughter of Rachel, Viscountess Falkland, 1674; and in the chancel a fine monument by Sir F. Chantrey to Mrs. Boulton, 1829. The original seats remain; and there is a good Perp. front.

16 m. Heythorpe, a village with a ch. which has been almost entirely rebuilt, but preserves a good Norm. doorway, and chancel arch. and some Norm. sculptures built into the S. wall. There is also an altartomb, with brass, for John Ashfield and his wife (1521), and a painted window with their effigies. The ch. stands close to Heythorpe Park, formerly the seat of the Earl of Shrewsbury, burnt Feb. 1831. The picturesque ruins of the house, reddened and charred by the flames, remained for almost 40 years among the fine trees of the park, and a belt of dark ilex and cedars marked the site of the former garden, but the estate was sold in 1870 to Thomas Brassey, Esq., for 110,000l., and a new mansion has been built in the Italian style. (Albert Brassey, Esq.) In the park, near the house, is the modern Roman Catholic chapel.

17 m. Cold Norton. An Augustinian priory was founded here by William Fitzalan, temp. Henry II. When suppressed it was in part

pulled down, and the chapel, after various changes, became the *Chapel-House*, a well-known inn on the Worcester road, but which is now closed.

18 m. *Chipping Norton* (Rte. 26).

ROUTE 28.

OXFORD TO LAUNTON.

Bletchley Branch, L. and N. W. Rly. 14¼ m.

The line for the first mile runs side by side with the G. W. Rly., and gives views of the new Oxford churches of St. Barnabas and SS. Philip and James. At 3 m. we pass on W. the junction line leading to Yarnton, Handborough, &c., and reach at 6 m. *Islip Stat.* Islip and its neighbourhood, E., are described in Exc. (*k*) from Oxford; and the country W. in Rte. 24.

Leaving Islip, we have, on W., 3 churches, all of some degree of interest. *Weston-on-the-Green* has a good Norm. and Perp. tower, with a Grecian body added in 1743, by one of the Berties. Near the ch. stands an Elizabethan manor-house, now only tenanted by a steward,

but still containing many of the Norreys and Bertie family pictures. *Wendlebury*, rebuilt in 1762 with the old materials, has preserved its Dec. tower. *Chesterton*, probably rebuilt about 1283, when Edmund, Earl of Cornwall, gave it to his College of Bonhommes, at Ashridge (Rte. 18). It has 3 very elegant Dec. sedilia.

On E. of the line are the Dec. chs. of *Merton* and *Ambrosden*. One John Jones was vicar of Merton at the time of the Reformation, and, like the more noted Vicar of Bray, complied with all the changes of the times, dying in possession of his benefice in 1559. The manor-house, an Elizabethan building, erected by the D'Oili ys, though now a farmhouse, is of interest, many parts remaining as they were when inhabited by Sir James Harington, who is said, on doubtful authority, to have been visited here by Prince Charles Edward. *Merton Church* was restored in 1873. *Ambrosden Church* is a fine building, with a rich open parapet. This parish is the subject of an elaborate work ('Parochial Antiquities') by Bishop White Kennett, once its incumbent.

12 m. *Bicester* (Stat.). Bicester (*Inn*: King's Arms), usually called *Byster*, is styled Berencestre in Domesday. (Pop. 3306.) It had belonged to a Saxon noble, Wigod of Wallingford, but was bestowed by the Conqueror on Robert d'Oiley, the builder of the Castle of Oxford (Rte. 19). A ch. was probably built here by him, as the present edifice stands on the foundations of a Norm. cruciform structure, with central tower. It is dedicated to St. Edburg, and consists of an E. E. S. aisle, a Dec. chancel and N. aisle, with Perp. transepts and W. tower. It has lately been restored. There are some panels of sculpture let into the walls of the nave and of the S. porch, and in the N. aisle is an arch "partaking

of the supposed Saxon character."—
Arch. Guide, Oxford. There are
brasses for W. Staveley and wife
(1498) and Roger Moore (1551). In
1185 Gilbert Basset, son of Ralph
Basset, Henry I.'s justiciary, founded
an Augustinian priory here, which at
the Dissolution was granted to the
Blounts, and long continued their
residence; nothing is now left of it
beyond a mere fragment in a garden,
which is still used as a dwelling-
house.

Nearly 2 m. S., on the E. bank
of a small rivulet near Wendlebury,
is the site of a Roman station, called
by the Saxons Ealdceastre. Bishop
Kennett has treated at some length
on the subject ('Parochial Antiq.'
vol. i.).

3 m. W. of Bicester is *Middleton
Stony.* At *Middleton Park* (Earl
of Jersey) are some interesting portraits: Duchess of Buckingham and
her daughter Mary, Duchess of Richmond, with the young Lords George
and Francis Villiers,—a fine group
by *Vandyke;* George Villiers, 1st
Duke of Buckingham, whole length,
Mytens; Margaret Hughes, mistress
of Prince Rupert, *Lely;* the Bedford
family, Duke Francis as St. George;
Lord Burghersh when young, and
the Countess of Westmoreland with
a bird, *Sir J. Reynolds;* Lady Jersey
in yellow satin, Lord Jersey in robes,
whole-lengths, *Lawrence.* Middleton appears in Domesday as the
property of Earl Warren, but in the
time of Stephen it was in the hands
of a devoted adherent of his, Richard
de Camville, who is supposed to
have built the castle, of which some
traces remain close to the ch. This,
it is believed, was also built by him,
its general features being of his

time, Trans.-Norm., with an E. E.
tower, having an open arcade, subsequently added. It stands in a
very pleasant situation in the park,
and was restored in 1858.

2 m. N.E. is *Bucknell,* where the
E. E. and Perp. ch. has a very
massive Norm. central tower. *Ardley,*
1½ m. N.W., has a Dec. chancel and
tower, but the nave was rebuilt in
the last century in very bad taste,
and at the same time the bodies of
many of the Marlborough family,
whose burial-place it had long been,
were removed to Blenheim.

14¼ m. *Launton* (Stat.). The small
plain ch. has a Trans.-Norm. nave,
E. E. tower, and Perp. chancel,
with 2 sedilia and piscina. During
the civil wars, Robert Skinner, the
ejected Bishop of Oxford, was allowed to hold this living, and is
said to have continued the public
use of the Liturgy the whole time.

2 m. N. is *Caversfield,* a small ch.,
restored in 1874, Norm. and E. E.,
and having 2 so-called Saxon windows, of very rude character. The
porch has good late Norm. mouldings.
The ch. contains a very ancient bell.
1 m. E. is *Stratton Audley,* where the
Dec. and Perp. ch., dedicated to SS.
Mary and Edburga, has a fine 17th-
century monument for Sir John Bor-
lase Warren. 1¼ m. N. is *Fringford*
ch., where a very good modern
imitation of E. E. work is to be
seen; the S. doorway and 2 of the
arches of the nave are Norm. A
new tower has been added.

15½ m. The rly. crosses a branch
of the little river Ray, and leaves
the county for Bucks (Rte. 17).

INDEX.

LONDON: PRINTED BY WILLIAM CLOWES AND SONS, LIMITED, STAMFORD STREET,
AND CHARING CROSS.

HANDBOOK ADVERTISER, 1882-83.

CONTENTS.

COPENHAGEN..... Messrs. H. J. BING & SON.
CORFU .... Mr. J. W. TAYLOR.
DRESDEN .... { Messrs. SCHLOSSMANN & SCHEFFLER. Messrs. H. W. BASSENGE & Co. The Director of the Royal Porcelain Manufactory Depôt.
FLORENCE .... { Messrs. FRENCH & Co. Sig. LUIGI RAMACCI. Messrs. EMELE. FENZI & Co. Sig. TITO GAGLIARDI, Dealer in Antiquities. Messrs. MAQUAY, HOOKER, & Co. Mr. E. GOODBAN, Printseller. Mr. T. BIANCHINI, Mosaic Worker. Messrs. P. BAZZANTI & FIG. Sculptors, Lungo l'Arno.
FRANKFORT O. M. Messrs. BING, Jun., & Co. Mr. G. KREBS.
GENEVA .... MM. LEVRIER & PELISSIER.
GENOA .... { Messrs. G. & E. BARCHI BROTHERS. Mr. C. A. WILSON. Mr. H. A. MOSSA, Grande Albergo d'Italia.
GIBRALTAR ...... Messrs. JOHN PEACOCK & Co.
HAMBURG .... Messrs. J. P. JENSEN & Co. Messrs. SCHÖRMER & TENCHMANN.
HEIDELBERG ..... Mr. PH. ZIMMERMANN.
HELSINGFORS.... Messrs. LUTHER & RUDOLPH.
INTERLACKEN.... Mr. J. GROSSMANN.
JERUSALEM....... Messrs. E. F. SPITTLER & Co. Mr. M. BERGHEIM, Jun.
KISSINGEN....... Mr. DAVID KUGELMANN. Mr. H. F. KUGELMANN.
LAUSANNE ...... Mr. DUBOIS RENOU & Fils.
LEGHORN .... Messrs. ALEX. MACBEAN & Co. Messrs. MAQUAY, HOOKER, & Co.
LUCERNE .... Messrs. F. KNÖRR & Fils.
MADRAS........... Messrs. BINNY & Co.
MALAGA.......... Mr. GEORGE HODGSON.
MALTA .... { Messrs. Josh. DARMANIN & SONS, 45, Strada Levante, Mosaic Workers. Mr. FORTUNATO TESTA, 92, Strada Sta Lucia. Messrs. TURNBULL Jun. & SOMERVILLE.
MARIENBAD ..... Mr. J. T. ADLER, Glass Manufacturer.
MARSEILLES ..... Messrs. E. CAILLOL and H. SAINTPIERRE.
MENTONE......... Mr. PALMARO. Mr. JEAN ORENGO Fils.
MESSINA.......... Messrs. CAILLER, WALKER, & Co.
MILAN .... { Mr. G. B. BUFFET, Piazza di S. Sepolcro, No. 1. Messrs. FRATELLI BRAMBILLA. Messrs. ULRICH & Co. Messrs. G. BONO & Co.
MUNICH.......... Messrs. WIMMER & Co., Printsellers, Brienner Strasse.
NAPLES .... { Messrs. W. J. TURNER & Co. Mr. G. SCALA, Wine Merchant. Messrs. G. QUESTA & Co. Messrs. CERULLI & Co.
NEUCHATEL (SUISSE)........... } Messrs. BOUVIER FRÈRES, Wine Merchants.
NEW YORK .... Messrs. BALDWIN BROS. & Co.
NICE .... Madame Vᵉ ADOLPHE LACROIX & Co.
NUREMBERG..... Mr. A. PICKERT, Dealer in Antiquities.
OSTEND .... Messrs. R. ST. AMOUR & SON.
PALERMO......... Messrs. INGHAM, WHITAKER, & Co.
PARIS .... Mr. L. CHENUE, Packer, Rue Croix des Petits Champs, No. 24.
PAU .... Mr. MUSGRAVE CLAY.
PISA.............. { Messrs. HUGUET & VAN LINT, Sculptors in Alabaster and Marble Mr. G. ANDREONI, Sculptor in Alabaster.
PRAGUE.......... Mr. W. HOFMANN, Glass Manufacturer, Blauern Stern.
ROME .... { Messrs. PLOWDEN & Co. Messrs. A. MACBEAN & Co. Messrs. MAQUAY, HOOKER, & Co. Messrs. SPADA & FLAMINI. Mr. J. P. SHEA. Mr. A. TOMBINI.
ROTTERDAM...... Messrs. PRESTON & Co.
SAN REMO .... Messrs. FRATELLI ASQUASCIATI.
ST. PETERSBURG. Messrs. THOMSON, BONAR, & Co. Mr. C. KRUGER.
STOCKHOLM ...... Messrs. OLSSON & WRIGHT.
THOUNE .... Mr. JEAN KEHRLI-STERCHI.
TRIESTE .... Messrs. FILLI, CHIESA.
TURIN .... Messrs. ROCHAS, Père & Fils.
VENICE .. .... { Mr. L. BOVARDI, Ponte alle Ballotte. Messrs. S. & A. BLUMENTHAL & Co. Mr. CARLO PONTI.
VEVEY .... Mr. JULES GÉTAZ FILS.
VIENNA.. . ... { Mr. H. ULLRICH, Glass Manufacturer, 16 Kärnthner Strasse. Messrs. J. & L. LOBMEYER, Glass Manufacturers, 13, Kärnthner Strasse. Mr. PETER COMPLOJER.
ZURICH .... Mr. ORELL HESS.

CALEDONIAN RAILWAY.

TOURS IN SCOTLAND.

THE CALEDONIAN RAILWAY COMPANY have arranged a system of TOURS—about 70 in number—by Rail, Steamer, and Coach, comprehending almost every place of interest either for scenery or historical associations throughout Scotland, including—

EDINBURGH, GLASGOW, ABERDEEN, DUNDEE, INVERNESS, GREENOCK, PAISLEY, DUMFRIES, PEEBLES, STIRLING, PERTH, CRIEFF, DUNKELD, OBAN, INVERARY,

The Trosachs, Loch-Katrine, Loch-Lomond, Loch-Earn, Loch-Tay, Loch-Awe, Caledonian Canal, Glencoe, Iona, Staffa, Skye, Balmoral, Braemar, Arran, Bute, The Firth of Clyde, The Falls of Clyde, &c., &c.

☞ TOURISTS are recommended to procure a copy of the Caledonian Railway Company's "Tourist Guide," which can be had at any of the Company's Stations, and also at the chief Stations on the London and North-Western Railway, and which contains descriptive notices of the districts embraced in the Tours, Maps, Plans, Bird's-eye View, &c.

Tickets for these Tours are issued at the Company's Booking Offices at all the large Stations.
The Tourist Season generally extends from JUNE to SEPTEMBER inclusive.

The Caledonian Co. also issue Tourist Tickets to the Lake District of England, The Isle of Man, Connemara, The Lakes of Killarney, &c.

The Caledonian Railway, in conjunction with the London and North-Western Railway, forms what is known as the

WEST COAST ROUTE

BETWEEN SCOTLAND & ENGLAND.

DIRECT TRAINS RUN FROM AND TO

Glasgow, Edinburgh, Greenock, Paisley, Stirling, Oban, Perth, Dundee, Aberdeen, Inverness, and other places in Scotland.

TO AND FROM

London (Euston), Birmingham, Liverpool, Manchester, Leeds, Bradford, and other places in England.

SLEEPING & DAY SALOON CARRIAGES. THROUGH GUARDS & CONDUCTORS.

The Caledonian Company's Trains, from and to Edinburgh, Glasgow, Carlisle, &c., connect on the Clyde with the "Columbia," "Iona," "Lord of the Isles," "Ivanhoe," "Gael," and other steamers to and from Dunoon, Innellan, Rothesay, Largs, Millport, the Kyles of Bute, Arran, Campbeltown, Ardrishaig, Inverary, Loch-Goil, Loch-Long, &c., &c.

A full service of Trains is also run from and to Glasgow, to and from Edinburgh, Stirling, Oban, Perth, Dundee, Aberdeen, and the North; and from and to Edinburgh, to and from these places.
For particulars of Trains, Fares, &c., see the Caledonian Railway Company's Time Tables.

It is expected that the Caledonian Company's large and magnificent
NEW CENTRAL STATION HOTEL, GLASGOW,
will be opened during the Season of 1882, under the Company's own Management.

GENERAL MANAGER'S OFFICE,   JAMES THOMPSON,
GLASGOW, 1882.   *General Manager.*

GLASGOW AND SOUTH-WESTERN RAILWAY.

DIRECT ROUTE BETWEEN

SCOTLAND & ENGLAND.

THROUGH TRAINS ARE RUN BETWEEN

GLASGOW (St. Enoch) and LONDON (St. Pancras),

Viâ the GLASGOW & SOUTH-WESTERN and MIDLAND RAILWAYS,

Giving a Direct and Expeditious Service between

**GLASGOW, GREENOCK, PAISLEY, AYR, ARDROSSAN, KILMARNOCK,
DUMFRIES, &c., AND
LIVERPOOL, MANCHESTER, BRADFORD, LEEDS, SHEFFIELD,
BRISTOL, BATH, BIRMINGHAM, LONDON, &c.**

PULLMAN DRAWING-ROOM AND SLEEPING CARS

Are run by the Morning and Evening Express Trains between GLASGOW and LONDON.

FIRTH OF CLYDE and WEST HIGHLANDS, via GREENOCK.

EXPRESS and FAST TRAINS are run at convenient hours between

GLASGOW & GREENOCK

(St. Enoch Station)   (Lynedoch St. and Princes Pier Stations)

IN DIRECT CONNECTION WITH THE

"COLUMBA," "IONA," "LORD OF THE ISLES,"

And other Steamers sailing to and from

Kirn, Dunoon, Innellan, Rothesay, Kyles of Bute, Ardrishaig, Oban,
Inverary, Largs, Millport, Kilcreggan, Kilmun, Lochgoilhead,
Garelochhead, &c.

Through Carriages are run by certain Trains between GREENOCK (Princes Pier), and
EDINBURGH (Waverley), and by the Morning and Evening Express Trains between
GREENOCK (Princes Pier) and London (St. Pancras).

RETURN TICKETS issued to COAST TOWNS are available 'or RETURN AT ANY
TIME.

Passengers are landed at Princes Pier Station, from whence there is a Covered Way to the
Pier where the Steamers call; and Passengers' Luggage is conveyed FREE OF CHARGE
between the Stations and the Steamers.

ARRAN AND AYRSHIRE COAST.

An Express and Fast Train Service is given between GLASGOW (St. Enoch), PAISLEY,
and TROON, PRESTWICK, AYR, ARDROSSAN, FAIRLIE, &c.

From ARDROSSAN the Splendid Saloon Steamer "BRODICK CASTLE" sails daily to
and from the ISLAND OF ARRAN, in connection with the Express Train Service.

Fast Trains provided with Through Carriages are run between AYR, &c., and GLASGOW,
(St. Enoch), and EDINBURGH (Waverley).

IRELAND.

A NIGHTLY SERVICE is given by the Royal Mail Steamers viâ GREENOCK, and also
by the ARDROSSAN SHIPPING COMPANY'S Full-Powered Steamers viâ ARDROSSAN.

For Particulars as to Trains and Steamers see the Company's Time Tables.

GLASGOW, May 1882.   W. J. WAINWRIGHT, General Manager.

LONDON AND SOUTH - WESTERN RAILWAY,

LONDON STATION, WATERLOO BRIDGE.

The Cheap and Picturesque Route to Paris, Havre, Rouen, Honfleur, Trouville, and Caen, viá Southampton and Havre, every Monday, Wednesday, and Friday. The last Train from London at 9 p.m. goes into Southampton Docks alongside the Steamer. FARES throughout (London to Paris), Single Journey, First Class, 33s.; Second Class, 24s. Double Journey (available for One Month), First Class, 55s.; Second Class, 39s.

Jersey, Guernsey, Granville, and St. Malo. Daily Mail Service to Channel Isles, viá Southampton (the favourite route), every Week-day. The last Train from London goes into Southampton Docks, alongside the Steamer, leaving Waterloo each Week-day at 9 p.m. (except on Saturdays, on which day the last Train leaves at 5.20 p.m., and the Steamer goes to Jersey only). FARES throughout (London and Jersey or Guernsey), Single Journey, First Class, 33s.; Second Class, 23s.; Third Class, 20s. Double Journey (available for One Month), First Class, 48s.; Second Class, 38s.; Third Class, 30s. Direct Service, Southampton to St. Malo, every Monday, Wednesday, and Friday, according to Tide. The best Route for Dinard, Dinan, Rennes, Brest, Nantes, Laval, Le Mans, Angers, Avranches, &c.

Southampton to Cherbourg every Monday and Thursday. Last Train from the Waterloo Station, London, at 9·0 A.M. The best Route for Valognes, Carentan, St. Lo, Bayeaux, and Coutances.

Steamers run between Jersey and St. Malo, and Jersey and Granville, twice Weekly each way.

For further information apply to Mr. BENNETT, 3, Place Vendôme, Paris; Mr. LANG-STAFF, 67, Grand Quai, Havre; Mr. ENAULT, Honfleur; Mr. R. SPURRIER, Jersey; Mr. SPENCER, Guernsey; Mr. E. D. LE COUTEUR, St. Malo; Messrs. MAHIEU, Cherbourg; or to Mr. E. K. CORKE, Steam Packet Superintendent, Southampton.

GREAT EASTERN RAILWAY.

THE TOURIST'S ROUTE TO THE CONTINENT
IS viâ HARWICH.

THE Continental Express Train leaves Liverpool Street Station, London, for Rotterdam every evening (Sundays excepted), and for Antwerp on Mondays, Tuesdays, Thursdays, and Saturdays, in direct connection with the Fast and elegantly fitted up Passenger Steamers of the Company.

It is expected that a Daily Service to Antwerp will be commenced on July 1st, 1882 (Sundays excepted).

The Steamers are large powerful vessels, ranging from 800 to 1200 tons burden, with ample sleeping accommodation; and consequently Passengers suffer less from mal de mer than by any of the shorter Sea Routes.

The Provisions on Board are supplied from the Company's own Hotel at Harwich, and are unequalled in quality. Luggage can be registered through to all principal Towns on the Continent from Liverpool Street Station. Through Tickets are issued at—44, Regent Street; 48, Lime Street; and Blossom's Inn, Lawrence Lane, Cheapside, E.C.

COOK and SON's Tourist Office, Ludgate Circus, London, E.C.

GAZE and SON's Tourist Office, 142, Strand, London, E.C.

O. CAYGILL's Tourist Office, 371, Strand, London, E.C.

And the Continental Booking Office, Liverpool St. Station, London, E.C.

For further particulars and Time Books apply to the Continental Traffic Manager, Liverpool Street Station, London, E.C.

DUBLIN AND GLASGOW STEAM PACKET COMPANY.

The Company's First Class Saloon Paddle Steamers,

Duke of Argyll, Duke of Leinster, Lord Clyde, Lord Gough,
OR OTHER STEAMERS,

Are intended to Sail as per Monthly Sailing bills, unless prevented by any unforeseen occurrence, from

DUBLIN TO GLASGOW

Every MONDAY, WEDNESDAY and FRIDAY, and every alternate TUESDAY, THURSDAY and SATURDAY. From

GLASGOW TO DUBLIN

Every MONDAY, WEDNESDAY and FRIDAY, and every alternate TUESDAY, THURSDAY and SATURDAY, calling at Greenock both ways, except Saturday Boat from Dublin, which proceeds direct to Glasgow.

	£	s.	d.		£	s.	d.
Cabin Fare, (including Steward's Fees)				Return Ticket to Edinburgh (2 Months)	1	10	0
Fees)	0	15	0	Single Ticket to Edinburgh			
Return Tickets (6 Months)	1	2	6	(3rd Class and Deck)	0	8	6
Steerage	0	6	0	Return Ticket to Edinburgh			
Return Tickets (6 Months)	0	10	0	(2 Months) (3rd Class and			
Single Ticket to Edinburgh	1	0	0	Deck)	0	14	0

Passengers can travel between Greenock and Edinburgh Direct, without change of carriage, by either Caledonian or North British Railway, according to the Ticket they hold. The Caledonian Railway Stations are Cathcart Street, Greenock; and Prince's Street, Edinburgh. North British Company's—Lyndoch Street, Greenock; and Haymarket and Waverly Stations, Edinburgh.

☞ Passengers are also Booked Through between Dublin and the principal Railway Stations in Scotland.

AGENTS.—HENRY LAMONT, 93, Hope Street, Glasgow. JAMES LITTLE & Co., Excise Buildings, Greenock.

DUBLIN OFFICES.—Booking Office for Passengers—1 Eden Quay; where Berths can be secured up to 2 o'clock, p.m., on day of Sailing.

CHIEF OFFICE AND STORES.—71, NORTH WALL.

Further particulars, Monthly Bills, &c., on application to { A. TAYLOR, *Secretary*. { B. MANN, *General Manager*.

GENERAL STEAM NAVIGATION COMPANY.

From and to Irongate and St. Katherine's Wharf, near the Tower.

LONDON AND BOULOGNE.—The *Dolphin*, *Rhine*, *Cologne*, *Mosella*, or *Concordia.*—For departures see Daily Papers. FARES—London to Boulogne, 12s., or 8s. 6d.; Return 18s. 6d. or 13s.

LONDON TO PARIS direct from London, via Boulogne.—FARES—SINGLE (available for Three Days), Saloon, 1st Class Rail, 1l. 7s. 6d.; Saloon, 2nd Class Rail, 1l. 3s.; Fore Cabin, 2nd Class Rail, 19s. 6d.; 3rd Class Rail, 14s. 6d. Return (available for Fourteen Days), 2l. 12s. 6d.; 2l.; 1l. 15s.; 1l. 6s.

LONDON AND HAVRE.—*Swift* or *Swallow*—From London—Every Thursday. From Havre—Every Sunday. FARES—Chief Cabin, 13s.; Fore Cabin, 9s.; Return Tickets, 20s. 6d. and 14s.

LONDON AND OSTEND.—The *Swift* and *Swallow.*—From London—Wednesday and Sunday. From Ostend—Tuesday and Friday. FARES (Steward's Fee included). Chief Cabin, 15s.; Fore Cabin, 10s. Return, 23s. and 15s. 6d.

LONDON AND ANTWERP.—The *Hawk*, *Teal*, *Falcon*, or *Capulet*. From London—Every Tuesday and Saturday. From Antwerp—Every Tuesday and Friday. FARES, Chief Cabin, 20s.; Fore Cabin, 12s. 6d. Return, 31s. and 19s. 6d.

LONDON AND HAMBURG.—The *Libra*, *Osprey*, *Iris*, *Rainbow*, *Martin*, *Granton*, *Widgeon*, *Nautilus*, or *Alford*—From London—Every Wednesday and Saturday. From Hamburg—Three times a week. FARES, Chief Cabin, 40s.; Fore Cabin, 20s. Return Tickets, 61s. 6d. and 31s.

LONDON AND BORDEAUX.—*Kestrel*, *Bittern*, *Lapwing* and *Gannet.* From London—Every Thursday. From Bordeaux—Every Friday. FARES, Chief Cabin, 3l.; Fore Cabin, 2l. Return Tickets, Chief Cabin, 5l.; Fore Cabin, 3l. 6s. 6d.

LONDON AND EDINBURGH (GRANTON PIER).—The *Virgo* and *Stork.* From London—Every Wednesday and Saturday. From Edinburgh (Granton Pier)—Every Wednesday and Saturday. FARES, Chief Cabin, 22s.; Fore Cabin, 16s. Return, 34s. and 24s. 6d. Deck (Soldiers and Sailors only), 10s.

LONDON AND HULL.—The *Raven*, *Ostrich*, or *Hamburg.* From London—Every Wednesday and Saturday, at 8 morn. From Hull—Every Wednesday and Saturday. FARES, Saloon, 8s.; Fore Cabin, 5s. Return Tickets, 12s. 6d. and 8s.

LONDON AND YARMOUTH.—From London Bridge Wharf. During the summer there is a special passenger service. FARES, Saloon, 8s.; Fore Cabin, 6s. Return Tickets, 12s. and 9s. Steward's Fees are included in above Fares and Return Tickets by the Company's vessels are available for one month.

For further particulars apply to the Secretary, 71, Lombard Street, London, E.C.

ANTWERP.

HÔTEL DU GRAND LABOUREUR.

THIS Hotel occupies the first rank in Antwerp, and its position is most delightful. The testimonials given by Families is the best assurance of its

COMFORT AND MODERATE CHARGES.

AVIGNON.
HÔTEL D'EUROPE.

HIGHLY recommended to English Travellers on their journey to Nice, Italy, &c. First-Class and Moderate Prices. The Proprietor and his Wife having lived in England, are aware of the wants of English Travellers; and he assures them that their comforts shall be studied. Omnibus at all Trains.

AVRANCHES.	BADEN - BADEN.
Grand Hôtel de Londres.	**Grand Hôtel Belle - Vue.**
FAUVEL, *Proprietor.*	First-class and large establishment, most delightful
The best in the Town. Spacious Garden. English spoken, and English Newspapers.	situation of all, in the Alli-Lichtenthal in the centre of a fine park. Really well-kept. Arrangements for a séjour.
	RIOTTE, Proprietor.

BADEN - BADEN.

VICTORIA HOTEL.

Proprietor, Mr. FRANZ GROSHOLZ.

THIS is one of the finest-built and best-furnished First-class Hotels, situated on the new Promenade, near the Kursaal and Theatre; it commands the most charming views in Baden. It is reputed to be one of the best Hotels in Germany. The Table and Wines are excellent, with prompt attendance and great civility. Prices very moderate. English and other Journals.

BADEN - BADEN.

HÔTEL DE HOLLANDE and Dependance.

AU BEAU SÉJOUR.—A. ROESSLER, Proprietor. This favourite and first-class Hotel, situated near the Kursaal, Promenade, and Theatre, commands one of the most charming views in Baden. The Hotel and Dependance consist of One Hundred and Sixty Sleeping Apartments, elegant Sitting-rooms, and a Garden for the use of visitors. Extensive and airy Dining-room, and a comfortable Public Sitting-room, with Piano and Library. It is conducted under the immediate superintendence of the Proprietor, who endeavours, by the most strict attention and exceedingly Moderate Prices, to merit the continued patronage of English and American visitors. English and American Newspapers. The Table d'Hôte and Wines of this Hotel are reputed of the best quality in Baden. Fixed moderate charges for everything. Rooms from 2s. and upwards.

PENSION Prices for a longer stay.

c

CORFU.
HÔTEL ST. GEORGE.

THIS FIRST-CLASS HOTEL, very well situated on the best side of the Esplanade, close to the Royal Palace, is fitted up after the English style, affording first-rate accommodation for Families and Single Gentlemen. Excellent Pension, and prices very moderate. A large addition to the Hotel just now finished makes it one of the most comfortable of the Continent, with splendid Apartments, Conversation Saloon, Reading Saloon and Library, Smoking and Billiard Rooms, and Bath Room. Magnificent Carriages and Horses, the whole new, neat, and elegant. All Languages spoken. Ladies travelling alone will find here the greatest comfort and best attendance. The Hotel is under the patronage of King George I., the Emperor of Austria, and the Grand Duke of Mecklenburgh.

Madame Vve S. P. MAZZUCHY & FILS, Proprietors.

COWES, Isle of Wight.
DROVER'S MARINE HOTEL.
PARADE, ISLE OF WIGHT.
FIRST-CLASS FAMILY HOTEL.

The Comfort of Visitors carefully studied. Board on Low Terms during the Winter Months.

CREUZNACH.
HÔTEL DE HOLLANDE.

THIS FIRST-CLASS HOTEL offers superior accommodation at very Moderate Charges to Families and Single Gentlemen. It is situated in the finest and healthiest part of the town, and is surrounded by a beautiful Garden. It is fitted up after the English and American style. Splendid large Dining Rooms, and newly fitted-up Conversation Saloon. Comfortable and well-furnished Apartments (with many Balconies). Good Baths. Excellent Board. Arrangements can be made for a protracted stay. Pension in Winter.

FOLDTYNSKI & WODG, Proprietors.

CREUZNACH (BAD).
PRIVATE HOTEL BAUM.

FIRST-CLASS Family Hotel, best situated. Great cleanliness. Comfortable Baths. Beautiful Garden. Excellent Cooking, Choice Wines. Pension moderate charges. Recommended.

JEAN BAPTISTE BAUM, Proprietor.

CREUZNACH (BAD).
HÔTEL KAUTZENBERG.

THIS First-Class Hotel is beautifully situated, close to the Kurhaus, adjoining the Promenade. Large Garden. Baths in the Hotel. The Table d'Hôte and Wines of this Hotel are reputed the best in Creuznach. Moderate Charges.

F. EISENREICH, Proprietor.

DIJON.
GRAND HÔTEL DE BOURGOGNE. Near the Station. Well situated in an open Square. Enlarged in 1880. Apartments for Families. Table d'Hôte. Carriages. English Newspapers. Omnibuses to meet all Trains.

Wines Exported by the Proprietor.

2 vols., royal 4to. 42s. each.

ETCHINGS FROM THE LOIRE AND THE MOSEL.

A Series of Forty Plates, with Descriptive Letterpress.

By ERNEST GEORGE.

JOHN MURRAY, ALBEMARLE STREET.

D

KILLARNEY.

LAKES OF KILLARNEY.
By Her Most Gracious Majesty's Special Permission.

THE ROYAL VICTORIA HOTEL,

Pa'ronized by H.R.H. THE PRINCE OF WALES; by H.R.H. PRINCE ARTHUR, and by the Royal Families of France and Belgium, &c.

THIS HOTEL is situated on the Lower Lake, close to the water's edge, within ten minutes' drive of the Railway Station, and a short distance from the far-famed Gap of Dunloe. It is lighted with gas made on the premises; and is the Largest Hotel in the district. A magnificent Coffee-room, a public Drawing-room for Ladies and Families, Billiard and Smoking-rooms, and several suites of Private Apartments facing the Lake, have been recently added.

TABLE D'HÔTE DURING THE SEASON.

Cars, Carriages, Boats, Ponies, and Guides at fixed moderate charges.

Drivers, Boatmen, and Guides are paid by the Proprietor, and are not allowed to solicit gratuities. The HOTEL OMNIBUS and Porters attend the Trains.

THERE IS A POSTAL TELEGRAPH OFFICE IN THE HOUSE.

Boarding Terms from October to June, inclusive.

It is necessary to inform Tourists that the Railway Company, Proprietors of the Railway Hotel in the Town, send upon the platform, *as Touters for their Hotel,* the Porters, Car-drivers, Boatmen, and Guides in their employment, and exclude the servants of the Hotels on the Lake, who will, however, be found in waiting at the Station-door.

JOHN O'LEARY, Proprietor.

LAUSANNE - OUCHY.

HÔTEL BEAU RIVAGE.

DIRECTOR, A. MARTIN-RUFENACHT.

THIS splendid Establishment, constructed on a grand scale, is situated on one of the most beautiful spots on the shore of the Lake of Geneva, surrounded by an English Park and Garden. It is near the Steamboat Landing and the English Church.

WINTER PENSION
FROM OCTOBER UNTIL MARCH, AT VERY MODERATE PRICES.

Constant communication with the City and Railway Station by Omnibus.

Baths, Telegraph, and Post Office in the Hotel.

E 2

FIRST - CLASS HOTEL.

PARIS.

HÔTEL MEURICE.

RUE DE RIVOLI.

PAU.

A WINTER RESORT, renowned for the numerous cures which a residence has effected, particularly in cases of Affections of the Chest, Heart, Larynx, and Throat.

PAU possesses a mild and salubrious climate, lying in the midst of scenery of great grandeur; on three days in each week Fox-hunting and Polo Matches take place, and during the winter and spring there are Horse Races twice every month.

In addition to these attractions, there are Good Clubs, a Theatre, Opera, two Casinos, Balls, Pigeon Shooting Matches, Cricket Matches, Skating Rinks, &c., &c.

FIRST-CLASS HOTEL AND GOOD BOARDING HOUSES.

Villas, Houses, and Furnished Apartments to Let,
AT VARIOUS PRICES.

All particulars sent gratuitously, address Mr. FREDERIC DANIEL, *Directeur Gérant de l'Union Syndicale, 7, Rue des Cordeliers, Pau.*

PENZANCE.
QUEEN'S HOTEL. (*On the Esplanade.*)
Patronised by Her Majesty the Queen of Holland.

THIS magnificent Hotel has a frontage of over 170 feet, all the Rooms of which overlook the Sea. It is the only Hotel that commands a full and uninterrupted view of Mount's Bay. Apartments *en suite.* Penzance stands unrivalled for the variety and quiet beauty of its scenery, whilst the mildness of its climate is admirably adapted to invalids. *Ladies' Coffee and Drawing Rooms. Billiard Room. Hot and Cold Baths.* Table d'Hôte at 7 o'clock. An Omnibus meets every Train. Posting in all its Branches. Yachts, &c.

A. H. HORA, Proprietor.

ROME.

HÔTEL MINERVA.

THIS large Establishment, whose direction has lately been taken up again by the Proprietor, M. Joseph Sauve, has been considerably ameliorated both as regards the perfect service and the most elaborate comfort. Large Apartments as well as small, and Rooms for Parties with more modest tastes, both very carefully furnished, are to be found here.

Its position is one of the most advantageous. It is situated in the very centre of the Town, and close to the most remarkable Monuments, the Post and Telegraph Offices, the House of Parliament, and the Senate.

The Ladies' Drawing Room, the Smoking Room, and Reading Rooms, where the principal Newspapers of every country are to be found, and the Bathing Rooms, are always carefully warmed.

TWO OMNIBUSES BELONGING TO THE HOTEL MEET EVERY TRAIN.

THE WAITERS AND CHAMBERMAIDS SPEAK ALL THE PRINCIPAL LANGUAGES.

VERY MODERATE TERMS.

ROME.

CONTINENTAL HÔTEL.

ONE OF THE LARGEST AND MOST COMFORTABLE HOTELS IN ITALY.

Facing the Railw.y Station, in the most elevated part of the Town, and the nearest to all the Antiquities and Attractions.

PROPRIETOR OF THE WELL-KNOWN HÔTEL D'ALLEMAGNE.

SITUATED IN THE CENTRE OF THE CITY OF ROME.

HEATED WITH HOT-AIR STOVES.

ELEVATOR WITH SAFETY BRAKE.

P. L. LUGANI. Proprietor.

ROME.

GRAND HÔTEL DE RUSSIE, ET DES ILES BRITANNIQUES. This First-Class Establishment possesses the advantage of a beautiful Garden, and is situated near the English and American Churches; the principal Apartments face the South, the entire Hotel being warmed by two calorifères, and the whole arrangements and moderate prices give universal satisfaction.

MAZZERI, Proprietor.

ROME.

HÔTEL ANGLO-AMERICAIN, Vià Frattino, 128. Between the Corso and Piazza d'Spagna. The nearest Hotel to the Post and Telegraph Offices. Situated full South, in the most *healthy part* of the Town. Large and small Apartments. Table d'Hôte. Restaurant. Salon. Reading Room, with Newspapers in four languages. Smoking and Billiard Room. Bath Room. Pension, and arrangements for Families. Moderate Charges. Omnibus at the Station to meet every Train. The principal languages are spoken.

VISCIOTTI & MERLI, *Proprietors.*

ROTTERDAM.

H. A. KRAMERS & SON,

IMPORTERS OF FOREIGN BOOKS.

Mr. MURRAY's 'Handbooks for Travellers,' BRADSHAW's 'Monthly Railway Guides, BAEDEKER's 'Reisehandbücher,' and HENDSCHEL's 'Telegraph,' always in Stock. Books in all Languages imported every day, and a great variety of New Books kept in Store.

26, GELDERSCHE KADE, 26.

ROUEN.

GRAND HÔTEL DE FRANCE, 97-99, Rue des Carmes. Entirely and carefully reorganised by the new Proprietor. This First-Class Hotel is now a curiosity more in the Town, and situated in central position near the Public Buildings and Theatres, specially recommended to Families visiting the Normandy Coasts. Large Courtyard and Garden, where Breakfast, Luncheons, and Dinners are served in the Summer. Ladies' Room, Smoking Room, Table d'hôte at 6 o'clock. First-Class Restaurant.

E. BARBIER, *Proprietor.*

ROUEN.

GRAND HÔTEL DE PARIS.

FIRST-CLASS HÔTEL.

SPLENDIDLY SITUATED ON

THE QUAI DE PARIS,

COMMANDING PICTURESQUE

VIEWS OF THE SEINE AND MOUNTAINS.

SPECIALLY RECOMMENDED TO

FAMILIES AND SINGLE TRAVELLERS.

Conversation Saloon.   Smoking Room.

MODERATE PRICES.

TABLE D'HÔTE.   SERVICE À LA CARTE.

INTERPRETER.   *RECOMMENDED.*

GUÉNARD BATAILLARD, *Proprietor.*

ZURICH is the Central Point of Eastern Switzerland for Traffic. Commerce, Industry, and for its Social Life.
Most beautifully situated on the Lake and the River Limmat, with extended Panorama of the Alps from the Uetliberg Railway, the Zurichberg and the "Waid." Celebrated Town Library. Scientific Collections in the Polytechnic.
University, Observatory. Well-known Reading-Room in the Museum. Summer Theatre. Daily Concerts in the Concert Hall.

HÔTELS.

On the Lake and in the Vicinity.	*Central Part of Town.*	*Near the Railway Station.*
Baur au Lac, TH. BAUR.	Baur en Ville,	National, MICHEL.
Bellevue au Lac, POHL.	Faës BREKFER.	
Du Lac, MOOSER.	—	St. Gotthard, ZOLLIKER.
Zürcherhof, LANG.	Schweizerhof, MEUTER.	Wanner's Garni, WANNER.
Falken, WEBER.		
Hecht, WALDMEIER-BOLLER.	Schwanen, BRÜGGER.	Limmathof, PÜTZER.
	Rothhaus, BRUNNER.	
Kreuz, Seefeld, MEYER.	Schiff, SCHÄTTI.	Sieberz, SIEBERZ.

Boarding Houses and Curative Establishments:—

HOTEL and PENSION "UETLIBERG," on the Uetliberg.
J. BOLLER and Sons.

HOTEL and PENSION SCHWANEN, on the Muhlebach,
J. BOLLER and Sons.

PENSION NEPTUN, Seefeld. VVE. METTLER.

Gastwirth-Verein—Societé des Hôteliers – United Hotel-keeper's Society.